THE HISTORIANS' HISTORY
OF THE UNITED STATES

The Historians' History
of the United States

Edited by

ANDREW S. BERKY

and

JAMES P. SHENTON

VOLUME II

G. P. Putnam's Sons   New York

© 1966 BY ANDREW S. BERKY AND JAMES P. SHENTON

*All rights reserved. This book, or parts thereof, must not be repro-
duced in any form without permission. Published simultaneously in
the Dominion of Canada by Longmans Canada Limited, Toronto.*

Library of Congress Catalog
Card Number: 66-20295

PRINTED IN THE UNITED STATES OF AMERICA

Contents

VI

Expanding Horizons

THE *Civil War ended and in its aftermath came an explosion of energy that catapulted the United States into the front rank of industrial powers. In the three decades and a half remaining of the nineteenth century, fortunes without parallel were piled up; the values of a simpler agrarian age crumbled; the frontier disappeared as transcontinental railroads spanned the once seemingly endless reaches of the West. The Indian and the cowboy had their brief day, faded into legend, and regained life in the spangled world of Hollywood. The titans of industry had their complements in the masters of the political machine. It was an age of soaring optimism and plummeting dreams; it spoke a language of hyperbole; it surrounded itself with an architecture of gingerbread and gilt. Its spokesmen preached the gospel of free enterprise while in the halls of Congress and state legislature they bought favors. Change governed the day so completely that Henry Adams, returning to New York after almost a decade of absence, wrote: "Had they [his family] been Tyrian traders of the year B.C. 1000, landing from a galley fresh from Gibraltar, they could hardly have been stranger on the shore of a world, so changed from what it had been ten years before." Concealed within its gaudy color and hushed within its strident tone were the dislocations of a too swift industrialism, the hidden tragedies of cities that outstripped even their rudimentary facilities, and the failure of the bountiful agriculture to secure for most people anything but a bare existence. Mark Twain called it the Gilded Age.*

The old Jeffersonian ethos of an agrarian paradise perished, and the historian of the age, lamenting the vanished promise, salvaged the killer of the dream. Charles A. Beard defined its new masters as an "onrushing plutocracy" governed by "the cash nexus pure and simple." His predecessor, Henry Adams, beheld only an onrushing chaos in which materialism reigned supreme. Walt Whitman foresaw a new Rome, vast in body, but soulless. Nonetheless, of all its traducers, none did a more thorough job than Vernon L. Parrington (1871-1929), a professor of English, who in his monumental Main Currents in American Thought *related American literature to the whole of the national civilization. Agitated by an acute Progressive social consciousness, he indicted the last decades of the nineteenth century as a time "with no social conscience, no concern for civilization, no heed for the future of democracy it talked so much about. . . ." In his vivid language, the Gilded Age emerged as "the Great Barbecue," a time of corrupt politics, bad taste, economic exploitation, and the vulgarization of human values. And so the image remains, one that needs badly a new look, an era which needs a historian who can look beneath both its own and its previous historian's*

flights of rhetoric. For beneath the agitating words is the beginning of the
industrial-urban America that in the twentieth century has prevailed.

THE BEGINNINGS OF CRITICAL
REALISM IN AMERICA

by Vernon Louis Parrington

The pot was boiling briskly in America in the tumultuous post-war years.
The country had definitely entered upon its freedom and was settling its
disordered household to suit its democratic taste. Everywhere new ways
were feverishly at work transforming the countryside. In the South another
order was rising uncertainly on the ruins of the plantation system; in the
East an expanding factory economy was weaving a different pattern of industrial life; in the Middle Border a recrudescent agriculture was arising
from the application of the machine to the rich prairie soil. All over the
land a spider web of iron rails was being spun that was to draw the remotest
outposts into the common whole and bind the nation together with steel
bands. Nevertheless two diverse worlds lay on the map of continental
America. Facing in opposite directions and holding different faiths, they
would not travel together easily or take comfort from the yoke that joined
them. Agricultural America, behind which lay two and a half centuries of
experience, was a decentralized world, democratic, individualistic, suspicious;
industrial America, behind which lay only half a dozen decades of bustling
experiment, was a centralizing world, capitalistic, feudal, ambitious. The one
was a decaying order, the other a rising, and between them would be friction
till one or the other had become master.

Continental America was still half frontier and half settled country. A
thin line of homesteads had been thrust westward till the outposts reached
well into the Middle Border—an uncertain thread running through eastern
Minnesota, Nebraska, Kansas, overleaping the Indian Territory and then
running west into Texas—approximately halfway between the Atlantic and
the Pacific. Behind these outposts was still much unoccupied land, and beyond stretched the unfenced prairies till they merged in the sagebrush
plains, gray and waste, that stretched to the foothills of the Rocky Mountains.
Beyond the mountains were other stretches of plains and deserts, vast and
forbidding in their alkali blight, to the wooded coast ranges and the Pacific
Ocean. In all this immense territory were only scattered settlements—at
Denver, Salt Lake City, Sacramento, San Francisco, Portland, Seattle, and
elsewhere—tiny outposts in the wilderness, with scattered hamlets, mining
camps, and isolated homesteads lost in the great expanse. On the prairies
from Mexico to Canada—across which rumbled great herds of buffalo—
roved powerful tribes of hostile Indians who fretted against the forward
thrust of settlement and disputed the right of possession. The urgent business

of the times was the subduing of this wild region, wresting it from Indians and buffalo and wilderness; and the forty years that lay between the California Gold Rush of '49 and the Oklahoma Land Rush of '89 saw the greatest wave of pioneer expansion—the swiftest and most reckless—in all our pioneer experience. Expansion on so vast a scale necessitated building, and the seventies became the railway age, bonding the future to break down present barriers of isolation, and opening new territories for later exploitation. The reflux of the great movement swept back upon the Atlantic coast and gave to life there a fresh note of spontaneous vigor, of which the Gilded Age was the inevitable expression.

It was this energetic East, with its accumulations of liquid capital awaiting investment and its factories turning out the materials needed to push the settlements westward, that profited most from the conquest of the far West. The impulsion from the frontier did much to drive forward the industrial revolution. The war that brought devastation to the South had been more friendly to northern interests. In gathering the scattered rills of capital into central reservoirs at Philadelphia and New York, and in expanding the factory system to supply the needs of the armies, it had opened to capitalism its first clear view of the Promised Land. The bankers had come into control of the liquid wealth of the nation, and the industrialists had learned to use the machine for production; the time was ripe for exploitation on a scale undreamed-of a generation before. Up till then the potential resources of the continent had not even been surveyed. Earlier pioneers had only scratched the surface—felling trees, making crops, building pygmy watermills, smelting a little iron. Mineral wealth had been scarcely touched. Tools had been lacking to develop it, capital had been lacking, transportation lacking, technical methods lacking, markets lacking.

In the years following the war, exploitation for the first time was provided with adequate resources and a competent technique, and busy prospectors were daily uncovering new sources of wealth. The coal and oil of Pennsylvania and Ohio, the copper and iron ore of upper Michigan, the gold and silver, lumber and fisheries, of the Pacific Coast, provided limitless raw materials for the rising industrialism. The Bessemer process quickly turned an age of iron into an age of steel and created the great rolling mills of Pittsburgh from which issued the rails for expanding railways. The reaper and binder, the sulky plow and the threshing machine, created a large-scale agriculture on the fertile prairies. Wild grass-lands provided grazing for immense herds of cattle and sheep; the development of the corn-belt enormously increased the supply of hogs; and with railways at hand the Middle Border poured into Omaha and Kansas City and Chicago an endless stream of produce. As the line of the frontier pushed westward new towns were built, thousands of homesteads were filed on, and the speculator and promoter hovered over the prairies like buzzards seeking their carrion. With rising land-values money was to be made out of unearned increment, and the creation of booms was a profitable industry. The times were stirring and it was a shiftless fellow who did not make his pile. If he had been too late to file on desirable acres he had only to find a careless homesteader who had failed in some legal technicality and "jump his claim." Good bottom land could be had even by latecomers if they were sharp at the game.

This bustling America of 1870 accounted itself a democratic world. A free people had put away all aristocratic privileges and conscious of its power went forth to possess the last frontier. Its social philosophy, which it found adequate to its needs, was summed up in three words—preemption, exploitation, progress. Its immediate and pressing business was to dispossess the government of its rich holdings. Lands in the possession of the government were so much idle waste, untaxed and profitless; in private hands they would be developed. They would provide work, pay taxes, support schools, enrich the community. Preemption meant exploitation and exploitation meant progress. It was a simple philosophy and it suited the simple individualism of the times. The Gilded Age knew nothing of the Enlightenment; it recognized only the acquisitive instinct. That much at least the frontier had taught the great American democracy; and in applying to the resources of a continent the lesson it had been so well taught the Gilded Age wrote a profoundly characteristic chapter of American history.

In a moment of special irritation Edwin Lawrence Godkin called the civilization of the seventies a chromo civilization. Mark Twain, with his slack western standards, was equally severe. As he contemplated the slovenly reality beneath the gaudy exterior he dubbed it the Gilded Age. Other critics with a gift for pungent phrase have flung their gibes at the ways of a picturesque and uncouth generation. There is reason in plenty for such caustic comment. Heedless, irreverent, unlovely, cultivating huge beards, shod in polished top-boots—the last refinement of the farmer's cowhides— wearing linen dickeys over hickory shirts, moving through pools of tobacco juice, erupting in shoddy and grotesque architecture, cluttering its homes with ungainly walnut chairs and marble-topped tables and heavy lambre- quins, the decade of the seventies was only too plainly mired and floundering in a bog of bad taste. A world of triumphant and unabashed vulgarity with- out its like in our history, it was not aware of its plight, but accounted its manners genteel and boasted of ways that were a parody on sober good sense.

Yet just as such comments are, they do not reach quite to the heart of the age. They emphasize rather the excrescences, the casual lapses, of a genera- tion that underneath its crudities and vulgarities was boldly adventurous and creative—a generation in which the democratic freedoms of America, as those freedoms had taken shape during a drab frontier experience, came at last to spontaneous and vivid expression. If its cultural wealth was less than it thought, if in its exuberance it was engaged somewhat too boisterously in stamping its own plebeian image on the work of its hands, it was only natural to a society that for the first time found its opportunities equal to its desires, a youthful society that accounted the world its oyster and wanted no restrictions laid on its will. It was the ripe fruit of Jacksonian leveling, and if it ran to a grotesque individualism—if in its self-confidence it was heedless of the smiles of older societies—it was nevertheless by reason of its un- couthness the most picturesque generation in our history; and for those who love to watch human nature disporting itself with naïve abandon, running amuck through all the conventions, no other age provides so fascinating a spectacle.

When the cannon at last had ceased their destruction it was a strange new America that looked out confidently on the scene. Something had been released by the upheavals of half a century, something strong and assertive that was prepared to take possession of the continent. It did not issue from the loins of war. Its origins must be sought elsewhere, further back in time. It had been cradled in the vast changes that since 1815 had been reshaping America: in the break-up of the old domestic economy that kept life mean and drab, in the noisy enthusiasms of the new coonskin democracy, in the romanticisms of the California gold rush, in the boisterous freedoms discovered by the forties and fifties. It had come to manhood in the battles of a tremendous war, and as it now surveyed the continent, discovering potential wealth before unknown, it demanded only freedom and opportunity —a fair race and no favors. Everywhere was a welling-up of primitive pagan desires after long repressions—to grow rich, to grasp power, to be strong and masterful and lay the world at its feet. It was a violent reaction from the narrow poverty of frontier life and the narrow inhibitions of backwoods religion. It had had enough of skimpy, meager ways, of scrubbing along hoping for something to turn up. It would go out and turn it up. It was consumed with a great hunger for abundance, for the good things of life, for wealth. It was frankly materialistic and if material goods could be wrested from society it would lay its hands heartily to the work. Freedom and opportunity, to acquire, to possess, to enjoy—for that it would sell its soul.

Society of a sudden was become fluid. With the sweeping-away of the last aristocratic restraints the potentialities of the common man found release for self-assertion. Strange figures, sprung from obscure origins, thrust themselves everywhere upon the scene. In the reaction from the mean and skimpy, a passionate will to power was issuing from unexpected sources, undisciplined, confused in ethical values, but endowed with immense vitality. Individualism was being simplified to the acquisitive instinct. These new Americans were primitive souls, ruthless, predatory, capable; singleminded men; rogues and rascals often, but never feeble, never hindered by petty scruple, never given to puling or whining—the raw materials of a race of capitalistic buccaneers. Out of the drab mass of common plebeian life had come this vital energy that erupted in amazing abundance and in strange forms. The new freedoms meant diverse things to different men and each like Jurgen followed after his own wishes and his own desires. Pirate and priest issued from the common source and played their parts with the same picturesqueness. The romantic age of Captain Kidd was come again, and the black flag and the gospel banner were both in lockers to be flown as the needs of the cruise determined. With all coercive restrictions put away the democratic genius of America was setting out on the road of manifest destiny.

Analyze the most talked-of men of the age and one is likely to find a splendid audacity coupled with an immense wastefulness. A note of tough-mindedness marks them. They had stout nippers. They fought their way encased in rhinoceros hides. There was the Wall Street crowd—Daniel Drew, Commodore Vanderbilt, Jim Fisk, Jay Gould, Russell Sage—blackguards for the most part, railway wreckers, cheaters and swindlers, but picturesque in their rascality. There was the numerous tribe of politicians—Boss Tweed, Fernando Wood, G. Oakey Hall, Senator Pomeroy, Senator Cameron, Roscoe Conkling, James G. Blaine—blackguards also for the most part, looting city treasuries, buying and selling legislative votes like railway stock, but picturesque in their audacity. There were the professional keepers of the public morals—Anthony Comstock, John B. Gough, Dwight L. Moody, Henry Ward Beecher, T. De Witt Talmage—ardent proselytizers, unintellectual, men of one idea, but fiery in zeal and eloquent in description of the particular heaven each wanted to people with his fellow Americans. And springing up like mushrooms after a rain was the goodly company of cranks —Victoria Woodhull and Tennessee Claflin, "Citizen" George Francis Train, Henry Bergh, Ben Butler, Ignatius Donnelly, Bob Ingersoll, Henry George—picturesque figures with a flair for publicity who tilled their special fields with splendid gestures. And finally there was Barnum the Showman, growing rich on the profession of humbuggery, a vulgar greasy genius, pure brass without any gilding, yet in picturesque and capable effrontery the very embodiment of the age. A marvelous company, vital with the untamed energy of a new land. In the presence of such men one begins to understand what Walt Whitman meant by his talk of the elemental.

Created by a primitive world that knew not the machine, they were marked by the rough homeliness of their origins. Whether wizened or fat they were never insignificant or commonplace. On the whole one prefers them fat, and for solid bulk what generation has outdone them? There was Revivalist Moody, bearded and neckless, with his two hundred and eighty pounds of Adam's flesh, every ounce of which "belonged to God." There was the lyric Sankey, afflicted with two hundred and twenty-five pounds of human frailty, yet looking as smug as a banker and singing "There were ninety and nine" divinely through mutton-chop whiskers. There was Boss Tweed, phlegmatic and mighty, overawing rebellious gangsters at the City Hall with his two hundred and forty pounds of pugnacious rascality. There was John Fiske, a philosophic hippopotamus, warming the chill waters of Spencerian science with his prodigious bulk. There was Ben Butler, oily and puffy and wheezy, like Falstaff larding the lean earth as he walked along, who yearly added more flesh to the scant ninety-seven pounds he carried away from Waterville College. And there was Jim Fisk, dressed like a bartender, huge in nerve as in bulk, driving with the dashing Josie Mansfield down Broadway—prince of vulgarians, who jovially proclaimed, "I worship in the Synagogue of the Libertines," and who on the failure of the Erie coup announced cheerfully, "Nothing is lost save honor!"

Impressive as are the fat kine of Egypt, the lean kine scarcely suffer by contrast. There were giants of puny physique in those days. There was Uncle Dan'l Drew, thin as a dried herring, yet a builder of churches and founder of Drew Theological Seminary, who pilfered and cheated his way to wealth with tobacco juice drooling from his mouth. There was Jay Gould, a lone-hand gambler, a dynamo in a tubercular body, who openly invested in the devil's tenements as likely to pay better dividends, and went home to potter lovingly amongst his exotic flowers. And there was Oakey Hall, clubman and playwright, small, elegant, and unscrupulous; and Victoria Woodhull who stirred up the Beecher case, a wisp of a woman who enraged all the frumpy blue-stockings by the smartness of her toilet and the perfection of her manners; and little Libby Tilton with her tiny wistful face and great eyes that looked out wonderingly at the world—eyes that were to go blind with weeping before the candle of her life went out. It was such men and women, individual and colorful, that Whitman and Mark Twain mingled with, and that Herman Melville—colossal and dynamic beyond them all—looked out upon sardonically from his tomb in the Custom House where he was consuming his own heart.

They were thrown up as it were casually out of the huge caldron of energy that was America. All over the land were thousands like them, self-made men quick to lay hands on opportunity if it knocked at the door, ready to seek it out if it were slow in knocking, recognizing no limitations to their powers, discouraged by no shortcomings in their training. When Moody set out to bring the world to his Protestant God he was an illiterate shoe salesman who stumbled over the hard words of his King James Bible. Anthony Comstock, the roundsman of the Lord, was a salesman in a dry-goods shop, and as careless of his spelling as he was careful of his neighbors' morals. Commodore Vanderbilt, who built up the greatest fortune of the time, was a Brooklyn ferryman, hard-fisted and tough as a burr-oak, who in a lifetime of over eighty years read only one book, "Pilgrim's Progress," and that after he was seventy. Daniel Drew was a shyster cattle-drover, whose arid emotions found outlet in periodic conversions and backslidings, and who got on in this vale of tears by salting his cattle and increasing his—and the Lord's—wealth with every pound of water in their bellies—from which cleverness is said to have come the Wall Street phrase, "stock-watering." Jim Fisk was the son of a Yankee peddler, who, disdaining the unambitious ways of his father, set up for himself in a cart gilded like a circus-wagon and drove about the countryside with jingling bells. After he had made his pile in Wall Street he set up his own opera house and proposed to rival the Medici as a patron of the arts—and especially of the artists if they were of the right sex. A surprising number of them—Moody, Beecher, Barnum, Fisk, Comstock, Ben Butler—came from New England; Jay Gould was of Connecticut ancestry; but Oakey Hall was a southern gentleman; Fernando Wood, with the face of an Apollo and the wit of an Irishman, was the son of a Philadelphia cigar-maker and much of his early income was drawn from sailors' groggeries along the waterfront; Tweed was a stolid New Yorker, and Drew was a York State country boy.

What was happening in New York was symptomatic of the nation. If the temple of Plutus was building in Wall Street, his devotees were everywhere. In Chicago, rising higgledy-piggledy from the ashes of the great fire, Phil Armour and Nelson Morris were laying out stockyards and drawing the cattle and sheep and hogs from remote prairie farms to their slaughter-houses.

In Cleveland, Mark Hanna was erecting his smelters and turning the iron ore of Michigan into dollars, while John D. Rockefeller was squeezing the small fry out of the petroleum business and creating the Standard Oil monopoly. In Pittsburgh, Andrew Carnegie was applying the Bessemer process to steel-making and laying the foundations of the later steel trust. In Minneapolis, C. C. Washburn and Charles A. Pillsbury were applying new methods to milling and turning the northern wheat into flour to ship to the ends of the earth. In San Francisco, Leland Stanford and Collis P. Huntington were amassing huge fortunes out of the Southern Pacific Railway and bringing the commonwealth of California to their feet. Everywhere were boom-town and real-estate promoters, the lust of speculation, the hankering after quick and easy wealth.

In the great spaces from Kansas City to Sacramento the frontier spirit was in the gaudiest bloom. The experiences of three centuries of expansion were being crowded into as many decades. In the fifties the highway of the frontier had run up and down the Mississippi River and the golden age of steamboating had brought a motley life to Saint Louis; in the seventies the frontier had passed far beyond and was pushing through the Rocky Mountains, repeating as it went the old frontier story of swagger and slovenliness, of boundless hope and heroic endurance—a story deeply marked with violence and crime and heart-breaking failure. Thousands of veterans from the disbanded armies, northern and southern alike, flocked to the West to seek their fortunes, and daily life there soon took on a drab note from the alkali of the plains; yet through the drabness ran a boisterous humor that exalted lying to a fine art—a humor that goes back to Davy Crockett and the Ohio flatboatmen. Mark Twain's "Roughing It" is the epic of this frontier of the Pony Express, as "Life on the Mississippi" is the epic of the preceding generation.

The huge wastefulness of the frontier was everywhere, East and West. The Gilded Age heeded somewhat too literally the Biblical injunction to take no thought for the morrow, but was busily intent on squandering the resources of the continent. All things were held cheap, and human life cheapest of all. Wild Bill Hickok with forty notches on his gun and a row of graves to his credit in Boot Hill Cemetery, and Jesse James, most picturesque of desperadoes, levying toll with his six-shooter on the bankers who were desecrating the free spirit of the plains with their two per cent a month, are familiar heroes in Wild West tales; but the real plainsman of the Gilded Age, the picturesque embodiment of the last frontier, was Captain Carver, the faultless horseman and faultless shot, engaged in his celebrated buffalo hunt for the championship of the prairies. Wagering that he could kill more buffalo in a day than any rival hero of the chase, he rode forth with his Indian marker and dropping the miles behind him he left an endless trail of dead beasts properly tagged, winning handsomely when his rival's horse fell dead from exhaustion. It was magnificent. Davy Crockett's hundred and five bears in a season was but 'prentice work compared with Captain Carver's professional skill. It is small wonder that he became a hero of the day and his rifle, turned now to the circus business of breaking glass balls thrown from his running horse, achieved a fame far greater than Davy's Betsy. With his bold mustaches, his long black hair flying in the wind, his sombrero and chaps and top-boots, he was a figure matched only by Buffalo Bill, the last of the great plainsmen.

Captain Carver was picturesque, but what shall be said of the thousands of lesser Carvers engaged in the same slaughter, market-hunters who discovered a new industry in buffalo-killing? At the close of the Civil War the number of the western plains was estimated at fifteen millions. With the building of the Union Pacific Railroad they were cut asunder into two vast herds, and upon these herds fell the hunters with the breech-loading rifles, shooting for the hide market that paid sixty-five cents for a bull's hide and a dollar and fifteen cents for a cow's. During the four years from 1871 to 1874 nearly a million head a year were slain from the southern herd alone, their skins ripped off and the carcasses left for the coyotes and buzzards. By the end of the hunting-season of 1875 the vast southern herd had been wiped out, and with the building of the Northern Pacific in 1880 the smaller northern herd soon suffered the same fate. The buffalo were gone with the hostile Indians—Sioux and Blackfeet and Cheyennes and a dozen other tribes. It was the last dramatic episode of the American frontier, and it wrote a fitting climax to three centuries of wasteful conquest. But the prairies were tamed, and Wild Bill Hickok and Captain Carver and Buffalo Bill Cody had become romantic figures to enthrall the imagination of later generations.

It was an abundant harvest of those freedoms that America had long been struggling to achieve, and it was making ready the ground for later harvests that would be less to its liking. Freedom had become individualism, and individualism had become the inalienable right to preempt, to exploit, to squander. Gone were the old ideals along with the old restraints. The idealism of the forties, the romanticism of the fifties—all the heritage of Jeffersonianism and the French Enlightenment—were put thoughtlessly away, and with no social conscience, no concern for civilization, no heed for the future of the democracy it talked so much about, the Gilded Age threw itself into the business of money-getting. From the sober restraints of aristocracy, the old inhibitions of Puritanism, the niggardliness of an exacting domestic economy, it swung far back in reaction, and with the discovery of limitless opportunities for exploitation it allowed itself to get drunk. Figures of earth, they followed after their own dreams. Some were builders with grandiose plans in their pockets; others were wreckers with no plans at all. It was an anarchistic world of strong, capable men, selfish, unenlightened, amoral—an excellent example of what human nature will do with undisciplined freedom. In the Gilded Age freedom was the freedom of buccaneers preying on the argosies of Spain.

Certainly the Gilded Age would have resented such an interpretation of its brisk activities. In the welter of change that resulted from the application of the machine to the raw materials of a continent, it chose rather to see the spirit of progress to which the temper of the American people was so responsive. Freedom, it was convinced, was justifying itself by its works. The eighteenth century had been static, the nineteenth century was progressive.

It was adaptable, quick to change its ways and its tools, ready to accept what-ever proved advantageous—pragmatic, opportunist. It was not stifled by the dead hand of custom but was free to adapt means to ends. It accepted progress as it accepted democracy, without questioning the sufficiency of either. The conception accorded naturally with a frontier psychology. Complete opportunism is possible only amongst a people that is shallow-rooted, that lives in a fluid society, scantily institutionalized, with few vested interests. In a young society it is easy, in a maturing society it becomes in-creasingly difficult.

Dazzled by the results of the new technique of exploitation applied on a grand scale to unpreempted opportunities, it is no wonder the Gilded Age thought well of its labors and confused the pattern of life it was weaving with the pattern of a rational civilization. It had drunk in the idea of progress with its mother's milk. It was an inevitable frontier interpretation of the swift changes resulting from a fluid economics and a fluid society in process of settling into static ways. It served conveniently to describe the changes from the simplicities of social beginnings to the complexities of a later order. It was made use of following the War of 1812 to explain the stir resulting from the westward expansion and the great increase in immigration; but it was given vastly greater significance by the social unsettlements that came with the industrial revolution. With the realization of the dramatic changes in manner of living—the added conveniences of life, release from the laborious round of the domestic economy, ease of transportation—that re-sulted from the machine order, it was inevitable that the idea of progress should have been on every man's tongue. The increase of wealth visible to all was in itself a sufficient sign of progress, and as the novelty of the industrial change wore off and the economy of America was more completely in-dustrialized, it was this augmenting wealth that symbolized it.

In such fashion the excellent ideal of progress that issued from the social enthusiasms of the Enlightenment was taken in charge by the Gilded Age and transformed into a handmaid of capitalism. Its duties were narrowed to the single end of serving profits and its accomplishments came to be exactly measured by bank clearings. It was unfortunate but inevitable. The idea was too seductive to the American mentality not to be seized upon and made to serve a rising order. Exploitation was the business of the times and how better could exploitation throw about its activities the sanction of idealism than by wedding them to progress? It is a misfortune that America has never subjected the abstract idea of progress to critical examination. Content with the frontier and capitalistic interpretations it has confused change with betterment, and when a great idealist of the Gilded Age demonstrated to America that it was misled and pointed out that the path of progress it was following was the highway to poverty, he was hooted from the market-place.

Having thus thrown the mantle of progress about the Gold Dust twins, the Gilded Age was ready to bring the political forces of America into harmony with the program of preemption and exploitation. The situation could hardly have been more to its liking. Post-war America was wholly lacking in political philosophies, wholly opportunist. The old party cleavage between agriculture and industry had been obscured and the logic of party alignment destroyed by the struggle over slavery. Democrat and Whig no longer faced each other conscious of the different ends they sought. The great party of Jefferson and Jackson was prostrate, borne down by the odium of slavery and secession. In the North elements of both had been drawn into a motley war party, momentarily fused by the bitterness of conflict, but lacking any common program, certain indeed to split on fundamental economic issues. The Whig Republican was still Hamiltonian paternalistic, and the Democrat Republican was still Jeffersonian "laissez faire," and until it was determined which wing should control the party councils there would be only confusion. The politicians were fertile in compromises, but in nominating Lincoln and Johnson the party ventured to get astride two horses that would not run together. To attempt to make yoke-fellows of democratic leveling and capitalistic paternalism was prophetic of rifts and schisms that only the passions of Reconstruction days could hold in check.

In 1865 the Republican party was no other than a war machine that had accomplished its purpose. It was a political mongrel, without logical cohesion, and it seemed doomed to break up as the Whig party had broken up and the Federalist party had broken up. But fate was now on the side of the Whigs as it had not been earlier. The democratic forces had lost strength from the war, and democratic principles were in ill repute. The drift to centralization, the enormous development of capitalism, the spirit of exploitation, were prophetic of a changing temper that was preparing to exalt the doctrine of manifest destiny which the Whig party stood sponsor for. The middle class was in the saddle and it was time to bring the political state under its control. The practical problem of the moment was to transform the mongrel Republican party into a strong cohesive instrument, and to accomplish that it was necessary to hold the loyalty of its Democratic voters amongst the farmers and working-classes whilst putting into effect its Whig program.

Under normal conditions the thing would have been impossible, but the times were wrought up and blindly passionate and the politicians skillful. The revolt of Andrew Johnson came near to bringing the party on the rocks; but the undisciplined Jacksonians were overthrown by the appeal to the Bloody Flag and put to flight by the nomination of General Grant for the presidency. The rebellion of the Independent Republicans under Horace Greeley in 1872 was brought to nothing by the skillful use of Grant's military prestige, and the party passed definitely under the control of capitalism, and became such an instrument for exploitation as Henry Clay dreamed of but could not perfect. Under the nominal leadership of the easy-going Grant a loose rein was given to Whiggish ambitions and the Republican party became a political instrument worthy of the Gilded Age.

The triumph of Whiggery was possible because the spirit of the Gilded Age was Whiggish. The picturesque embodiment of the multitude of voters who hurrahed for Grant and the Grand Old Party was a figure who had grown his first beard in the ebullient days before Secession. Colonel Beriah Sellers, with his genial optimism and easy political ethics, was an epitome of the political hopes of the Gilded Age. With a Micawber-like faith in his country and his government, eager to realize on his expansive dreams and looking to the national treasury to scatter its fructifying millions in the neighborhood of his speculative holdings, he was no other than Uncle Sam in the boisterous days following Appomattox. The hopes that floated up out of his dreams were the hopes of millions who cast their votes for Republican Congressmen who in return were expected to cast their votes for huge governmental appropriations that would insure prosperity's reaching certain post-office addresses. Citizens had saved the government in the trying days that were past; it was only fair in return that government should aid the patriotic citizen in the necessary work of developing national resources. It was paternalism as understood by speculators and subsidy-hunters, but was it not a part of the great American System that was to make the country rich and self-sufficient? The American System had been talked of for forty years; it had slowly got on its feet in pre-war days despite the stubborn planter opposition; now at last it had fairly come into its own. The time was ripe for the Republican party to become a fairy godmother to the millions of Beriah Sellerses throughout the North and West.

It is plain as a pikestaff why the spirit of Whiggery should have taken riotous possession of the Gilded Age. With its booming industrial cities America in 1870 was fast becoming capitalistic, and in every capitalistic society Whiggery springs up as naturally as pigweed in a garden. However attractive the disguises it may assume, it is in essence the logical creed of the profit philosophy. It is the expression in politics of the acquisitive instinct and it assumes as the greatest good the shaping of public policy to promote private interests. It asserts that it is a duty of the state to help its citizens to make money, and it conceives of the political state as a useful instrument for effective exploitation. How otherwise? The public good cannot be served apart from business interests, for business interests are the public good and in serving business the state is serving society. Everybody's eggs are in the basket and they must not be broken. For a capitalistic society Whiggery is the only rational politics, for it exalts the profit-motive as the sole object of parliamentary concern. Government has only to wave its wand and fairy gifts descend upon business like the golden sands of Pactolus. It graciously bestows its tariffs and subsidies, and streams of wealth flow into private wells.

But unhappily there is a fly in the Whiggish honey. In a competitive order, government is forced to make its choices. It cannot serve both Peter and Paul. If it gives with one hand it must take away with the other. And so the persuasive ideal of paternalism in the common interest degenerates in practice into legalized favoritism. Governmental gifts go to the largest investments. Lesser interests are sacrificed to greater interests and Whiggery comes finally to serve the lords of the earth without whose good will the wheels of business will not turn. To him that hath shall be given. If the few do not prosper the many will starve, and if the many have bread who would begrudge the few their abundance? In Whiggery is the fulfillment of the Scriptures.

Henry Clay had been a prophetic figure pointing the way America was to travel; but he came a generation too soon. A son of the Gilded Age, he was doomed to live in a world of Jacksonian democracy. But the spirit of Henry Clay survived his death and his followers were everywhere in the land. The plain citizen who wanted a slice of the rich prairie land of Iowa or Kansas, with a railway convenient to his homestead, had learned to look to the government for a gift, and if he got his quarter-section and his transportation he was careless about what the other fellow got. A little more or less could make no difference to a country inexhaustible in resources. America belonged to the American people and not to the government, and resources in private hands paid taxes and increased the national wealth. In his favorite newspaper, the "New York Tribune," he read daily appeals for the adoption of a patriotic national economy, by means of which an infant industrialism, made prosperous by a protective tariff, would provide a home market for the produce of the farmer and render the country self-sufficient. Money would thus be put in everybody's pocket. Protection was not robbing Peter to pay Paul, but paying both Peter and Paul out of the augmented wealth of the whole.

The seductive arguments that Horace Greeley disseminated amongst the plain people, Henry Carey purveyed to more intelligent ears. The most distinguished American economist of the time, Carey had abandoned his earlier "laissez-faire" position, and having convinced himself that only through a close-knit national economy could the country develop a well-rounded economic program, he had become the most ardent of protectionists. During the fifties and later he was tireless in popularizing the doctrine of a natural harmony of interests between agriculture and manufacturing, and to a generation expanding rapidly in both fields his able presentation made great appeal. It was but a step from protectionism to governmental subsidies. Beriah Sellers and Henry Clay had come to be justified by the political economists. (Note that amongst Carey's converts were such different idealists as Wendell Phillips and Peter Cooper.)

*   *   *   *   *

Perhaps one cannot penetrate more directly to the heart of the Gilded Age than in taking account of certain of its heroes, figures of earth whom it accounted great in its generation, and to whom its admiration flowed out in unstinted measure. It is our own secret desires we attribute to our gods, and if from the muck of the times a queer lot of heroes was singled out, if an undisciplined generation rioting in its new freedoms chose to honor men who had scrambled upward in uncouth ways, it only suggests that such figures were a composite picture of the secret desires of an age vastly concerned with getting on. From a host of striking personalities two must suffice to suggest the spirit of the times, authentic folk-heroes of the Gilded Age, fashioned out of the commonest stuff and realizing such greatness as multitudes of Americans were then dreaming of; and over against them a third figure, a mordant intellectual, who sardonically swam with the stream of tendency and in serving all the gods of the Gilded Age gained for himself a brilliant career.

Greatest of all the heroes of the age was the victor of Appomattox. His fame was in all men's mouths, and his reputation was substantial enough to withstand the attacks of enemies and the gross shortcomings of his own character. It was not for any singular or remarkable qualities of mind or personality that General Grant was taken to the heart of his generation, but rather because he was so completely a product of the times, so strikingly an embodiment of its virtues and weaknesses. In his spectacular career were the sharp contrasts that appealed to a plebeian people wanting in fine and discriminating standards of appraisal. He had come up from the people and the marks of his origins—the slovenly manners and uncritical force of frontier folk-ways—were stamped on him as indelibly as they were stamped on his fellow soldiers who proclaimed his greatness. To a later generation he seems an odd and unaccountable figure for the high role of national hero, yet he was as native and homespun as Lincoln, like him sprung from the common stock and learning his lessons from harsh experience, a figure blown to huge dimensions by the passions of civil war. A generation that discovered something praiseworthy in the "smartness" of Jim Fisk, in the burly acquisitiveness of Commodore Vanderbilt, or in the clever humbuggery of Barnum the Showman, certainly would judge with no very critical eyes the claims to greatness of a grim leader of armies who succeeded where so many before had failed.

General Grant was no conventional military hero. It was not the gold stars on his epaulets that dazzled his generation. The people of the North had seen too many gold stars rise and set on the military horizon, they had been stricken too sorely by the bitter struggle, to be caught by military popinjays. They had gone through the fire and any hero of theirs must himself have passed through the fire. It was something veracious in the man, something solid and unyielding in the soldier, something plain as an old shoe in the field marshal of bloody battles, that caught the imagination of the North and made Grant a hero—this together with a certain gift of pungent phrase, befitting the leader of democratic hosts, that served to spread his fame amongst the common people. Vicksburg did much for his reputation, but the demand for "unconditional surrender," sent to a Confederate leader, did far more. The words fixed his character in the popular mind. Here at last was a fighting man who instead of planning how to fall back, as other generals did, thought only of going ahead; so the popular judgment shut its eyes to his dull plebeian character and set a wreath on his brows. It rested there somewhat grotesquely. In spite of a deep unconscious integrity and a stubborn will that drove him forward along whatever path his feet were set on, he was the least imposing of military heroes. Short, stooped, lumpish in mind and body, unintellectual and unimaginative, devoid of ideas and with no tongue to express the incoherent emotions that surged dully in his heart, he was a commonplace fellow that no gold braid could set off. He hated war and disliked soldiering, yet accepting life with a stolid fatalism he fought his bloody way to ultimate victory.

Graduated from West Point after four sterile years of drill, quite uneducated and unread even in his profession, he served for a time at different army posts, went through the Mexican War—which he looked upon as a stupid imperialistic debauch—as quartermaster without gaining distinction, and eventually, oppressed by the eventless routine of garrison life, he fell into the habit of solitary drinking and was dismissed from the service. Misfortune that it seemed, it was his making. Only as a volunteer could he have risen so quickly to high command; as a captain or major in the regular army he would have been detailed as drill-master to the raw troops and have had no chance. Nevertheless hard times came with his dismissal. Indolent by nature and inclined to drift, he was as incompetent a man in practical affairs as one could find in a frontier township. But with a wife and children to support he must turn his hand to something, so he tried his luck at farming, selling real estate, and various odd jobs, yet all the time growing poorer and seedier, till the war came and picking him up flung him to mountain heights of popularity and reputation. Thereafter till his death he was accounted the greatest American of his generation. No accumulating evidence of his well-meaning but witless incapacity in civic and political affairs could pluck from his brows the wreath that had been thrust upon him.

In his spectacular career Grant was an embodiment of the dreams of all the Beriah Sellerses of the Gilded Age. He was a materialistic hero of a materialistic generation. He was dazzled by wealth and power, and after years of bitter poverty he sat down in the lap of luxury with huge content. He took what the gods sent, and if houses and fast horses and wines and cigars were showered upon him he accepted them as a child would accept gifts from a fairy godmother. He had had enough of skimping meanness; with his generation he wanted to slough off the drabness of the frontier; he wanted the good things of life that had so long been denied him, and he was not scrupulous about looking a gift horse in the mouth. He sought out the company of rich men. He was never happier than when enjoying the luxury of Jay Cooke's mansion in Philadelphia or riding with A. T. Stewart in Central Park. As he grew fat and stodgy the vulgar side of his plebeian nature was thrown into sharper relief. He accepted gifts with both hands, and he seems never to have suspected the price that would be exacted of the President for the presents to the General. He never realized how great a bill was sent to the American people for the wine he drank or the cigars he smoked with his wealthy hosts; yet if the wine had been molten gold and the cigars platinum they would have been far cheaper. In return for a few boxes of choice Havanas, Jay Cooke laid his hands on millions of western lands for the Northern Pacific Railway. It was the way of the Gilded Age, and Grant was only doing what all his friends and associates were doing. If he accepted a fifty-thousand-dollar house in Philadelphia, his comrade General Sherman accepted a hundred-thousand-dollar house at Washington. Such gifts were not bribes; they were open and aboveboard; it was the free and easy way of the times. What the age was careless about is the fact that it is hard to refuse a reasonable request from one's fairy godmother, and what the General never understood is that if one is President such a godmother is certain to be a very dangerous member of the family.

There was far too much of that sort of thing all about him for Grant to serve as President with credit to himself or profit to the country. Honest himself, he was the source of more dishonesty in others than any other American President. His eight years in the White House marked the lowest depths—in domestic affairs at least—to which any American administration has fallen. They were little better than a national disgrace. All the festering evils of post-war times came to a head and pock-marked the body politic from head to foot. Scandal and corruption whispered all about him, the hands of his closest advisers were dirty; yet he stubbornly refused to hear the whispers or see the dirt. In judging men and policies he was no more than a child. He could never distinguish between an honest man and a rascal. He was loyal to his friends and open-handedness he regarded as a mark of friendship. In the end it turned out that like the thieves of Jericho his blatant followers despoiled him of pretty nearly everything.

In what must pass for his political views Grant was as naïvely uninformed as a Wyoming cowboy. Utterly wanting in knowledge of political principles, he was a fit leader for the organized mob that called itself the Republican party, whose chief objective was the raiding of the treasure-box of which it was the responsible guardian. He had been nominally a Democrat and the first vote he cast for President he cast for Buchanan. After Lincoln's death he turned naturally to President Johnson and was one of his supporters till the wily Radical group got his ear and carried him over to the rival camp. They wanted his reputation to hide under, and they took possession of it with no great credit to the General's reputation. Thereafter he was a Republican of the Whig wing. It was where he belonged. He was swayed politically by his emotional reactions and it was natural for him to drift into the opulent camp of money and power. His frontier democracy sloughed away and with his generation he went over easily to a buccaneer capitalism. No social conscience obtruded itself to give him trouble. His millionaire friends were Whig Republicans and with his respect for rich men, his admiration for material success, he found himself in congenial company amongst the Whig group. About the only political policy he ever interested himself in was the policy of a protective tariff, and his Whig associates took care that his interest did not wane. Yet so completely did the naïve General reflect the spirit of the Gilded Age that his noisy followers, conspiring to confuse in the public mind southern reconstruction and capitalistic expansion, and hiding a precious set of rascals in the folds of the bloody flag, came near to making him President for a third term. The General was bitterly disappointed at their failure, and the General's wife, who liked to live in the White House, was even more disappointed. To millions of Americans Grant was an authentic hero, to Mark Twain he was a very great man, and to Jay Cooke he was a pawn to be used in the noble strategy of fortune-seeking. What a comedy it all seems now— yet one that leaves an unpleasant taste in the mouth.

Yet to dismiss the stolid General thus is scarcely to do justice to the substantial core of the man. There remains the work written in pain during his last days, the two volumes of "Memoirs" that in their plain directness—as uninspired, says a late biographer, as "a bale of hay"—laid bare his honest simplicity and rugged meagerness. No blackguard and no charlatan could have written such pages. If General Grant was not the great man so many thought, he was a native growth from American soil, endowed like his age with a dogged will and a plodding energy, and he gave his country what he had. Though the branches of the tree were ungainly and offered too hospitable shelter to unseemly birds of the night, the gnarly trunk was sound at the heart.

THE accumulation of wealth has always commanded American admiration; the emphasis, therefore, in the Gilded Age on wealth was not a departure from the norm. The difference was simply in the amount of wealth a single person could accumulate. The Protestant ethic traditionally emphasized that wealth underscored the possession of grace freely given by God. The moguls of the Gilded Age did not doubt their possession of grace, but they preferred to think that they had helped wrench it loose from the divine grasp. The system of values by which they operated emphasized an unadorned self-made laisser-faire. The function of government had been fulfilled when it protected property against the marauding attacks of the lesser orders.

Wealth has rarely been content to hide its light under plain cloth. The emphasis in the declining decades of the nineteenth century among the surging bourgeoisie was often a combination of gaudy ostentation and self-serving apologias. Once the gospel was preached according to Matthew, John, Mark, and Luke; Andrew Carnegie subsidized the gospel according to wealth. But the privileged orders found their expectations and presumptions did not go unchallenged. The workingmen, left to the vagaries of an uninhibited capitalism, confined to the festering slums, increasingly doubted the virtue of their betters, and subscribed to one workingman's journal's comment on Cornelius Vanderbilt's $105,000,000 fortune: "What an amount of robbery those figures represent!" Intellectuals shared the despair of Whitman, who wrote, "Society, in these States, is canker'd, crude, superstitious, and rotten."

The praise and condemnation existed side by side. Vulgarity and philanthropy provided a bar sinister for more than one contrived bourgeois gentilhomme escutcheon. A best-selling novel of 1868, Sunshine and Shadow in New York, used as its frontispiece a contrast between the $2 million marble mansion of A. T. Stewart and the moldering ruin of a slum. The depth of these contrasts and their contradictions which riddled the Gilded Age is neatly suggested by Merle Curti (1897-). One of the most influential

of living American historians, he pioneered the development of both intel-
lectual and social history. Ideas move men to act, and thus are worthy of
investigation and analysis. Perhaps the most significant contribution of
Curti was to emphasize that men and ideas are one; to divorce the one from
the other is to reduce both to meaningless detail.

THE GROWTH OF AMERICAN THOUGHT

by Merle Curti

Of the forces creating a new nation in the years between the Compromise
of 1850 and the last decades of the century, the rapid advance of the business class was unquestionably one of the most important for American
intellectual life. The advance of business was, to be sure, inextricably associated with the more basic transition from a society mainly rural and
decentralized to one largely urbanized, mechanized, and centralized. The
men of big business, the organizers of the new integrated economy, did not
effect this transition, but in the sphere of intellectual history they were
dramatic symbols of it. Even before the Civil War business itself or its
spokesmen had begun to develop a rationale or justification for capitalistic
enterprise, but intellectual leadership in the country had lain with professional men, with cultured representatives of old and established mercantile
families, and with educated interpreters of the agricultural way of life. This
leadership and the values associated with it were now challenged by the
great economic and political power that a new type of entrepreneur came
to wield in the third quarter of the century. The triumph of business enterprise created new and challenging issues in American intellectual life.

Perhaps the first in importance was the fate of what James Truslow
Adams has called the American dream. This dream, it will be recalled, was
born of the Enlightenment and of Christian humanitarianism and was nourished by the ample opportunities afforded by a new country thinly peopled
but rich in natural resources. Especially after 1870 did the rapidly increasing power of large-scale business rest on and give focus to materialistic
and acquisitive values that differed appreciably from those that had been
characteristic of the older America. In earlier times materialistic acquisition
had in general been looked on not as an end in itself, not as something for
the few, but as the means by which everyone in every walk of life might
achieve comfort, security, education, the enrichment of personality—in
short, the good life. Now the ruthlessness of the few great titans of industry
and finance who piled up huge fortunes through manufacturing or land
and railway manipulation threatened to block the progress of the plain
people in their quest for the means to secure comforts and to fulfill modest
cultural aspirations. In addition, the new order of business monopoly or
near-monopoly seemed to emphasize the acquisition of material fortunes as
ends in themselves rather than as a means to security, comfort, and personal

development. The morning promises were no longer so bright and fresh as in the "golden day" when everyone took for granted an open road to moderate success.

A second leading issue posed by the rapid growth in importance of the business element was its attitude toward esthetic and intellectual values and achievements. Conceivably the great figures in railway and land promotion and speculation and in industrial and banking enterprise might ignore or deprecate the values of scholarship, the creative arts, the humane tradition generally. Or they might consciously or unconsciously put so high a premium on the type of training and skills useful in an age of business enterprise that the older humane values would be overshadowed. Or they might become patrons of the arts and of education, influencing the whole current of intellectual and artistic life.

The third leading issue raised by the triumph of business enterprise was the reaction of scholars, journalists, men of letters, the clergy, and related groups that had enjoyed intellectual leadership. Would spokesmen of the intellectual life identify themselves with the new order of monopoly and enterprise, of get-rich-in-any-way-you-can, singing its praises, lending their pens to an elaboration and popularization of the business rationale that had already been formulated in broad outline? Or would the professional classes challenge the new order of acquisitive materialism directed by the few great leaders and reassert and reinterpret the older American dream of democratic opportunities for everyone, opportunities designed to promote universal well-being, to provide rounded and rich personalities in every walk of life and an esthetic and intellectual culture shared by all? Might the new dominance of business and the accompanying tendency toward the integration of society blight the creative esthetic life and the intellectual endeavors of scholars?

MASTERS OF CAPITAL AND INTELLECTUAL LIFE

In the defense of commerce and industry which writers had begun to elaborate in the pre-Civil War decades an effort was made to broaden the concept of culture to include business. Freeman Hunt, editor of the leading business periodical, did his best to convince business men and the general public that business is both a science and an art. He wrote in *Wealth and Worth* (1856) that trade had already penetrated the world and given the keynote to civilization. Before long, he continued, someone would construct a rationale of business management which might be studied by the merchant's clerk just as students of law and medicine equipped themselves for their profession by becoming familiar not only with the techniques but with the underlying as well as the auxiliary disciplines.

The argument was also heard in the 'fifties that the merchant and industrialist was showing an inclination to elevate his mind by familiarizing himself with the classics, the modern poets, the philosophers and scientists, the authorities on public affairs. Addresses at the mercantile societies and the books listed in mercantile libraries suggest that in addition to the practical or utilitarian motive for self-culture, merchants felt that a familiarity with humanistic culture might elevate their rank in the eyes of society, enable them to pursue wealth with a higher and nobler purpose, and fortify themselves against possible misfortunes through the acquisition of values and interests unconnected with their main concern. Spokesmen of business reminded the American public that the acquisition of wealth had always been the chief index of civilization and that without it no cultural refinement, no great intellectual achievement, had ever been or ever could be realized.

Other considerations, however, are important in explaining the culture and knowledge of certain business leaders and their sons. Sheer love of art and zeal for collecting account for James Jackson Jarves of Boston, who spent a fortune in acquiring Italian masterpieces that rivaled the great Bryan collection which had come to America in 1853. J. Pierpont Morgan, who had acquired a passion for rare books and pictures during his student days at Göttingen, believed that the love of finer things was of practical utility in leavening life's trials. Henry Lee Higginson, the Boston financier, was governed by a less purely personal consideration. When he founded the Boston Symphony Orchestra in 1881 he was carrying out a youthful dream of his Viennese student days, a dream of enriching American life by enabling his fellow countrymen to enjoy permanently the symphonies of the great masters. It is also true that Higginson was not without class interest in the attitude he took toward philanthropy on occasion. In urging a wealthy kinsman to endow Harvard liberally, he bluntly declared that democracy had got fast hold of the world and that we must educate "to save ourselves and our families and our money from the mobs!"

The rise of obscure and uncultivated men to great wealth was even more significant for the intellectual character of the period than the role of the cultured rich. It had been common to emphasize the narrow social outlook of the titans who through shrewdness and strength made immense fortunes. No one can well deny that their social philosophy often crudely identified exploitation of natural resources with progress, that it was frequently marked by a kind of law of the jungle, and that from a social standpoint it was irresponsible. Of lust for speculation and preemption, of huge wastefulness of natural wealth, of bustling materialism, of splendid audacity, there was indeed much in the attitudes and behavior of the new business class. Nor is it easy to overemphasize their identification of private gaingetting with public good. In Parrington's picturesque words, this expressed itself in a grand paternalistic barbecue in which booms and land promotion and land stealing went hand in hand with a free and easy way of giving and taking bribes and with even more sensational scandals which hardly marred the crude and greedy enjoyment of the feast. It has been equally common to emphasize the Gargantuan vulgarity of the new business class. Its tawdry and grandiose buildings, its conspicuous waste and display, its generally meretricious splendor have more than once been celebrated in song and story.

From such a group not much could be expected in the way of individual pursuit of intellectual culture. The titans were self-made men, and in general self-culture was not a part of the self-making. In commenting on the proper steps to a business career, Henry Clews, the successful Wall Street broker, advised an early practical training, "even to the partial neglect of school and college." Practical business, he continued, was the best school and college from which young men could possibly graduate. The well-informed publisher, George Haven Putnam, had the products of such a training in mind when he regretted that the new wealthy class was too little interested in literature to buy and read books. "I didn't get very much schooling—somehow never took to it," remarked Daniel Drew. "I always got spelled down the very first time around. But I never minded that very much." Men of action did not mind being spelled down and were not ashamed of their lack of formal schooling. But even if they had yearned for book knowledge they were for the most part too busy on the exchange, too immersed in building gaudy palaces and buying swift race horses and cutting a figure. Nor were their women folk inclined to cultivate their minds.

Nevertheless, some did confess to a yearning for book knowledge. "I'd give a million dollars today, Doctor," declared Commodore Vanderbilt to a clergyman, "if I had your education. Folks may say that I don't care about education; but it ain't true; I do. I've been to England, and seen them lords, and other fellows, and knew that I had twice as much brains as they had maybe, and yet I had to keep still, and couldn't say anything through fear of exposing myself." Andrew Carnegie, with an income of fifty thousand a year and only on the threshold of his career as a great steel-maker, turned over in his mind the appeal of a three-year sojourn at Oxford "to get a thorough education" and "to make the acquaintance of literary men." He at least brought Matthew Arnold to America as his guest and began to cultivate such scholars as Lord Bryce, John Morley, and Frederic Harrison. He did more; he avidly read Herbert Spencer, "the man to whom I owe most," as he put it. But business men were seldom scholars themselves. A woolen manufacturer, Rowland Gibson Hazard of Rhode Island, stands out because both before and after his retirement in 1866 he wrote on philosophical, political, and economic questions. He corresponded and even conversed with John Stuart Mill, who wrote that Hazard's *Letters on Causation and Freedom in Willing* (1869), like his previous books, did honor to American thought. Indeed, Mill quite naturally approved Hazard's thesis that the moral government of human beings rested on either their expectation of consequences from their acts or on their feelings of desire and aversion toward those consequences. The great English philosophher wrote that he wished Hazard "had nothing to do but philosophize . . . for I see in everything that you write a well-marked natural capacity for philosophy."

Only a few of the self-made "robber barons" went in for the cultivation of literary men or for writing, but many patronized the other arts. It is true that when thirst for praise led newly rich men to dig into their pockets for the rising Metropolitan Museum in New York, they were cold-shouldered by the older aristocracy on the ground that they were not gentlemen. Nevertheless, it became increasingly customary for promoters of such ventures to enlist the support of the new business titans and for these in turn to shower gifts on established institutions or preferably to endow new ones bearing their names.

The conception of art as a relic of past grandeur and as something to be acquired as an evidence of success and "culture" dominated the thought of the new men of wealth. William H. Vanderbilt became a great collector of the art of the past. Silliman, a New York banker, went in for Rembrandts and Titians, with which he embellished his house. William A Clark filled the art gallery in his palatial New York residence with Titians, Rembrandts, Van Dycks, Hals, with Reynolds and Gainsboroughs, and with Gobelin and Beauvais tapestries. William Corcoran, who had begun to collect art in 1859, opened his gallery in Washington in 1872. Baker collected jades. Gates collected Corots. By the early eighteen-eighties James J. Hill, railway promoter and empire builder, was collecting French paintings. On the Pacific coast Adolph Sutro, mining engineer and tunnel-maker, built up a rich collection of incunabula by ransacking European repositories; the portion saved from destruction in the San Francisco fire in 1905 found its way into the public library of that city. Frick, the great steel magnate, was later remembered as sitting on a Renaissance throne under a baldacchino holding a copy of the *Saturday Evening Post!*

A few of the new men of wealth did have some faint notion that art is a living thing, but they were the exceptions. William Ralston, whose huge fortune rested on railroads, steamship lines, and factories, patronized the drama and other arts in San Francisco. Harriman insisted that nothing except American art decorate his estate, Arden. The great rich sometimes made personal an interest in the finer things by throwing open their palaces to creative artists. Thus at the Fifth Avenue mansion of Alexander T. Stewart, the fabulously wealthy retail and wholesale merchant, struggling musicians and artists mixed with diplomats and millionaires. By and large, however, the men who had made gigantic fortunes and who had no background in taste thought of art as consisting of relics of older times rather than as a living means of enlarging the realm of beauty.

Sometimes magnates spent part of their surplus accumulations in endowing existing universities or founding new ones. George Peabody, who accumulated an immense fortune through marketing American securities in London, not only generously endowed public education in the South but founded great museums of natural history at the oldest American colleges. Cyrus McCormick of reaper fame gave liberally to Presbyterian seminaries and colleges. The University of Wisconsin owed its observatory to the great milling magnate of the Twin Cities, Cadwalader Washburn; the University of California owed its great telescope, the most powerful in the world, to James Lick, who had made his fortune largely in real estate speculation. Armour Institute in Chicago trained young men for the technical world and perpetuated the name of the great meat-packing family. Jonas Clark, a successful New England industrialist, had decided by 1880 to establish some sort of technical school at Worcester, Massachusetts. The million dollars he gave for the purpose enabled G. Stanley Hall to build a remarkable center for graduate study. In Baltimore the Quaker bachelor, Johns Hopkins, whose mercantile and financial pursuits won him a sizable fortune, handsomely endowed a university which became an even greater center of research. Under Daniel Coit Gilman the new Johns Hopkins University, the first truly graduate school in America, lived up to the hope of its founder in avoiding ecclesiasticism and partisanship and in widening many fields of knowledge. Ezra Cornell, carpenter and mechanic, having piled up a fortune in the telegraph business and public lands, was persuaded by Andrew D. White to enlarge his original idea for advancing agricultural education. The institution bearing the founder's name became a living tribute to his conviction that the "industrial and productive classes" deserved the best facilities for mental culture and practical knowledge. While Cornell became an institution where any person whatever could find instruction in any study, Vassar, Wellesley, and Smith, similarly founded by the newly rich, concentrated on establishing opportunities for women to achieve the highest standards in collegiate education. From the fortune which Leland Stanford harvested in railroading emerged the university which he and his wife lovingly built in memory of their son.

The most important of the newly established universities was that which John D. Rockefeller endowed at Chicago. In 1896 the fabulously wealthy oil "king" could declare that the great secular university he had founded was the best investment he had ever made in all his life. "The good Lord gave me the money, and how could I withhold it from Chicago?" he asked. The philanthropies which he increasingly supported not only greatly advanced the cause of original research but gradually tended to lessen popular hostility against the man who had driven so many little fellows to the wall in building his great oil empire.

It remained for Andrew Carnegie to develop the best-articulated philosophy of philanthropy. In 1889 there appeared in the *North American Review* an article entitled "The Gospel of Wealth." It bore the name of the steel magnate and was introduced with the highest praise of the editor. In this essay Carnegie, after justifying the free enterprise system on the ground that it accorded with natural law, democracy, and human nature, went on to speak of the obligation of men of wealth to pour large parts of their means into socially useful causes. By so doing, Carnegie concluded, profits were socialized with the least possible harm to the free enterprise system, and any shortcomings in the workings of that system were compensated for with interest. The Scottish immigrant who had so miraculously succeeded at Pittsburgh had already established a public library. On the score that libraries were the most democratic form of educational enterprise he began on a grand scale to encourage that type of philanthropy. By insisting that provision be made for the upkeep of the libraries he built, Carnegie gave more than an initial impulse to the movement. In 1896 he founded the Carnegie Institute at Pittsburgh—the first of twenty-two Carnegie foundations devoted to scientific and historical research, the advancement of the teaching profession on the university level, and education for international peace.

Education and the life of the mind in general were affected by the expanding forces of business through the leadership of educators as well as under the aegis of business men themselves. With the inauguration of Charles W. Eliot as president of Harvard in 1869, a new type of college administrator appeared. Eliot was primarily neither a teacher nor a research scholar. He had not come from a business family, nor were his associations in his formative years principally with business men; but he was above all else an administrator, and with the skill and foresight and persistence of a man in business he guided the transformation of Harvard from a small undergraduate institution with a few loosely affiliated schools into a great modern university. What Eliot did with such notable success was likewise done by William R. Harper at Chicago, by James B. Angell at Michigan, and by Andrew D. White at Cornell. At the same time business men came increasingly to dominate boards of trustees and regents, and almost imperceptibly and unconsciously university administration took on many of the attributes of business organizations.

The needs of an expanding industrial and business civilization were reflected in the discussions of educational objectives. Long before the Civil War, of course, the issue of practical versus classical offerings in the college curriculum had been debated. Radical innovations in the direction of scientific and non-classical subjects generally fell by the board, but gradually the so-called modern disciplines made their way into the curriculum. The new demands for professional training, for technical pursuits, and for business became increasingly acute in the Civil War decade. The old debate was resumed with great intensity. In some respects this debate, which gave no sign of ending, reflected a parallel one in England arising from similar problems. Herbert Spencer and Thomas Huxley were arguing that education must serve the needs of an industrial and democratic order. In his famous essay, *What Knowledge Is of Most Worth* (1859), Spencer held that science must be accorded a much larger place in education inasmuch as it was more valuable than the classics for the chief functions of living; these, according to Spencer, included self-preservation, health, earning a livelihood, parenthood and citizenship, and the enjoyment of art and leisure. On the other hand Matthew Arnold upheld the primary value of the classical languages and literature in forming mind, character, and taste, in acquainting man with the best that had been said and thought throughout the ages. In the United States the arguments advanced by Spencer and Huxley were received with applause by such champions of scientific education as Edward L. Youmans, who spread the word through lectures, manuals, and the *Popular Scientific Monthly*. The exponents of the classical tradition received the arguments of Matthew Arnold with enthusiasm.

Step by step concessions were made to the modernists who spoke principally for the needs of an expanding civilization in which the natural and social sciences were foundation stones. The first great step was the elective system which President Eliot inaugurated at Harvard. It is true that this reflected not only the needs of the new industrial civilization but the good old Emersonian doctrine that the individual knows what is best for him and can be trusted to rely on himself. In any case the elective system dealt a blow to the classics and opened the way to collegiate training more directly suited to the needs of a business and technical civilization.

In 1871 the authorities of Yale published a brochure entitled *The Needs of the University*. This was very different in spirit from the famous Yale report of 1828, which had upheld the classical curriculum without concession to anything else. The Yale authorities still emphasized the value of mental discipline and liberal education, but they conceded that the study of the laws and forces of material nature by so-called laboratory or object lessons was of great importance. The claims of the Sheffield Scientific School were not overlooked. The appointment of Josiah Willard Gibbs to a new chair of mathematical physics at Yale in 1871 was, it is true, hardly a recognition of the needs of a new class of industrial capitalists concerned with steam and machines. But in time industry would handsomely profit from Gibbs' labors in thermodynamics.

In the ever more unrestrained acquisitive order the individual's desire to acquire money and property seemed to necessitate some educational reorganization. On every side demands were heard that education must become more practical, that it must train more specifically for industrial and business pursuits. In 1867 Professor Jacob Bigelow of Harvard put the argument on high ground. It was the duty of educational institutions, he insisted, to "adapt themselves to the wants of the place and time in which they exist. It needs no uncommon penetration to see that we are now living in a great transition period." The dead languages, Professor Bigelow went on, were dead, but modern sciences and studies were full of vitality, expansion, progress. Nor were the utilitarian subjects without their beauty. What was more beautiful than a railroad train shooting by with a swiftness that made its occupants invisible—sinuously winding through forests, cleaving hills and mountains asunder, steady, smooth, unerring, like a migratory bird!

The pioneer champion of technology was not without support in some esthetic quarters. James Jackson Jarves, author of a whole series of books on the Italian masters and collector without peer, praised fire engines, locomotives, and other machines for their equilibrium of lines, proportions, masses. "Their success [that of machines] in producing broad general effects out of a few simple elements," he observed, "and of admirable adaptations of means to ends, as nature evolves beauty out of the common and practical, covers these things with a certain atmosphere of poetry." Such a generous view of the industrial machine, however, was far from typical in academic circles.

The requirements of a technical and business world were too great for traditional institutions to meet, in spite of their concessions. The land-grant colleges and private technical and business schools arose in answer to the needs. The Civil War decade alone witnessed the foundation of twenty-five scientific institutions designed, like the new Massachusetts Institute of Technology, to train engineers and technicians for the new age of business enterprise. These technical schools provided industry with new secrets for utilizing materials formerly wasted and thus added appreciable sums to the budgets of corporations. On the level of business itself the Wharton School of Finance broke precedents when in 1884 it decided to give men the new degree of Bachelor of Finance as proof of special competence in this field.

Even the public schools felt the new impulses. The great international exhibitions brought home to American industrialists the importance of drawing and design in certain types of competitive production. By 1870 Massachusetts, the leading textile state, required instruction in drawing in the schools of the larger towns and cities, and in the same year Walter Smith was brought from South Kensington Art School in England to become state supervisor of drawing and art. Three years later the Massachusetts Normal Art School was opened. Although other factors entered into the picture, the need of industry was a major consideration in all this development. Powerful impetus was given to a similar movement when William T. Harris, the outstanding superintendent of the St. Louis schools, pioneered in introducing scientific instruction into the curriculum. This he justified in part on the ground that an industrial civilization requires skills and training in the sciences.

But these were by no means the only influences of business on schools. In the appeals for enlarged support of secondary public education much was made of the training that high schools would give to future clerical workers. Even more was said of the value of a high school education in giving the voters of tomorrow sound economic knowledge and fortifying them against the lure of false panaceas.

THE INTELLECTUALS AND THE TRIUMPH OF BUSINESS

The aid that school men consciously or unconsciously gave the new industrialism was paralleled in other intellectual circles. A leading historian of the period has maintained that journalism degraded itself in the post-Civil War years in an unprecedented degree. Never before, according to Oberholtzer, "had newspaper owners been such creatures of the corporation financier and the politicians who were being fed from the rich man's hands." That a similar generalization could be made concerning a considerable segment of the legal profession is beyond reasonable doubt. In the eyes of some of his colleagues David Dudley Field, a leading New York lawyer, was guilty of chicanery in promoting the interests of such "criminals" as Fisk and Gould. Field came uncomfortably close to being expelled from the bar association. Other lawyers found fortune if not fame in devising legal formulas by which monopolists rode to power and escaped the penalty of statutes.

Literary men, educators, and publicists also lent support to the man of new fortunes in the post-Appomattox decades. Older arguments for the sanctity of property rights were applied as well as they could be to the activities of the new type of entrepreneur, manipulator, and monopolist. Mark Hopkins, president of Williams College, declared in his *Lectures on Moral Science* (1862) that men with a strong desire for property had done the most for public institutions. "As men now are," he observed, "it is far better that they should be employed in accumulating property honestly, to be spent reasonably, if not nobly, than that there should be encouraged any sentimentalism about the worthlessness of property, or any tendency to a merely contemplative and quietistic life, which has so often been either the result or the cause of inefficiency or idleness." On one occasion J. G. Holland, popular novelist, moralist, and journalist, wrote that wealth, being "a legitimate spur to endeavor," is a natural good. "There always will be rich men and there always ought to be rich men," he concluded. According to the Reverend Jonathan Harrison, the superficial character of the culture of the more fortunate classes should be the main concern of intellectuals. "It will not do to confine our interest or efforts to the lower strata." In a somewhat similar vein the Reverend Samuel Henry Lee, an influential figure in the Congregational Church, declared that education could provide the means for the increase and the stability of property; "the way to get a market that shall be stable is to promote the higher civilization of the people." Nor was it less important, Lee declared, to keep in mind that business might become "sanctified and transfigured" through "a hearty alliance with learning."

Property-conscious intellectuals did not stop with assertions of the real value of acquisition and philanthropy, and the possibility of elevating the men of great wealth. Critics of the new industrial order and advocates of the rights of labor or of some control of business or of outright socialism were roundly denounced. Oliver Wendell Holmes used his bright wit to excoriate labor leaders as blindly selfish; Thomas Bailey Aldrich in *The Stillwater Tragedy* (1880) described the walking delegate as "a ghoul that lives upon subscriptions and sucks the senses out of innocent human beings"; and John Hay, in *The Breadwinners* (1884), pictured labor as violent, lawless, and overambitious. President Theodore Woolsey of Yale summoned much erudition to attack socialism and communism and to defend the rights of property. In brief, the main arguments outlined in the pre-Civil War defense of commerce and industry were asserted and applied, with some qualifications and hesitancy, to the rising business titans and the consolidation of corporate wealth under their auspices. Only after big business became the object of drastic and far-reaching criticism in the late 'eighties and early 'nineties was the conservative defense thoroughly elaborated and widely publicized.

But this is only a small part of the story of the reaction of intellectuals to the triumph of business enterprise in the third quarter of the century. Many, perhaps a majority, refused to have any more traffic than necessary with the giants of industry, and some did not hesitate to express disdain for them. "I have known, and known tolerably well," remarked Charles Francis

Adams, "a good many 'successful' men—'big' financially—men famous during the last half-century; and a less interesting crowd I do not care to encounter. Not one that I have ever known would I care to meet again, either in this world or the next; nor is one of them associated in my mind with the ideas of humor, thought or refinement." His brother, Henry Adams, was no less severe. "America contained scores of men worth five millions or upwards, whose lives were no more worth living than those of their cooks," he observed. The Adamses spared neither their scholarship nor their spleen in damning "caesarism in business." Their withering indictment of the Fisks, Goulds, Drews, and Vanderbilts remains a classic in the literature of railroad high finance.

The Adamses were not alone. In certain circles in Boston wealth counted for little unless it was accompanied by some degree of intellectual distinction. This at least was the fond belief of such wealthy and cultured Bostonians as Henry Cabot Lodge. Charles Eliot Norton bemoaned the fact that art and letters "led a difficult existence in the midst of the barbaric wealth of the richest millions of people in the world." Bayard Taylor similarly regretted that money and leisure were in the power of a people who had little or no intellectual training. The heartlessness of trade, its unjustice, and its antipathy to the immaterial values of chivalric love, the beauties of nature, the satisfactions of art, and the kindliness of Christianity formed the theme of Sidney Lanier's novel *Tiger-Lilies* (1867) and his poem, "The Symphony." Even Walt Whitman's ebullient faith in the power of his beloved states to create a great and distinctive culture suffered some strain as he contemplated the ruthlessness, the injustice, the inhumanity, the crass materialistic barbarism displayed by titans of wealth.

Intellectuals thus disillusioned with the new business class and the cheap and dishonest temper of the times could follow one of several paths. The easiest, and the one that was largely taken in Boston, was the revival of the old colonial feeling toward Europe—the old feeling of deference. As Van Wyck Brooks has observed, intellectuals of the older families that had not adjusted themselves to the new order found themselves rootless, adrift in a world beyond their ability to understand. Commerce and business, absorbing as they did the lion's share of prestige, left those of taste and ideas doubtful about the country of their birth, the country that in an earlier time of cultural nationalism had aroused their proud enthusiasm. Thus they turned to Europe. If they could not live there, they could at least bring as much of Europe as possible into their midst. "Boston is very well up in all things European," wrote Henry Adams in 1873, "but it is no place for American news." Indeed, the intellectuals in the "hub of the universe" for the most part turned their backs on the traditional reform causes and went in for esthetics in a big way. Arnold, Ruskin, Browning, and Tennyson were on everyone's lips; Siennese architecture and Roman inscriptions and primitive paintings were the order of the day. Henry Cabot Lodge wrote of the dominance of English habits among his class in the post-Appomattox years: "Our literary standards, our standards of statesmanship, our modes of thought . . . were as English as the trivial customs of the dinner table and the ballroom."

Henry James is, of course, the classic example of escapism. In 1870 he wrote to his friend Charles Eliot Norton: "It behooves me, as a luckless American, diabolically tempted of the shallow and the superficial, really to catch the flavour of an old civilization (it hardly matters which) and to strive to raise myself, for one brief moment at least, in the attitude of observation." In somewhat the same vein the future novelist of the cosmopolitan American and the American who tried unsuccessfully to be cosmopolitan wrote complainingly of the vulgar, ignorant, crude self-complacency of his bad-speaking and bad-mannered countrymen. It was therefore appropriate for James to take as his main theme the plight of Americans in the sophisticated society of Europe. *Roderick Hudson* (1876) portrayed the collapse of the integrity of a New England sculptor when he abandoned Puritan discipline for the rich culture of the Old World. In *The American* (1877) a retired gentleman who could neither cast off his Americanism nor understand the subtle ways of the French family into which he married came to grief. Similarly *Daisy Miller* (1879) was the tragedy of an American girl whose American manners gave a Europeanized fellow countryman an erroneous impression of her true character.

Henry James set an example. In varying degrees others sought the same escape from what they regarded as a culture devoid of beauty, antiquity, and interest. They did not need to be told by Matthew Arnold, who visited the United States in the eighteen-eighties, that their country was without an interesting civilization because it lacked roots, the discipline of awe and respect—everything, in short, that made for distinction. In Europe it was easier for them to close their eyes to the self-made business men, many of whom shared with their American fellows crude materialistic values. It is true that Mark Twain, in his witty and satirical *The Innocents Abroad* (1869), refused to look with awe on the "museum of magnificence and misery" he saw in Italy, and refrained from adulation of overrated landscapes, dingy ruins, desolation, and decay. William Dean Howells could appreciate the charms of the Old World, but he was a leader of those who chose to write about common actualities in his own country. Nevertheless, a large number of American men of letters, artists, and other intellectuals preferred with Henry James and F. Marion Crawford to become virtual expatriates or to live and think, so far as it was possible, like Europeans.

The escape from an acquisitive, materialistic society in which the new rich set the tone and dominated the stage was not the only answer made by men and women of thought and feeling. Far from turning their backs on the American scene, an impressive number of gifted American writers responded to the new currents of the machine, industrialism, and big business by depicting in literary form the impact of these forces on American life. By and large, these writers vigorously criticized the new business order and reasserted the older values of a democratic society in which everyone might seek a moderate well-being with reasonable expectation of success.

Some sixty novels dealing with the American businessman were written before the end of the century, and of these at least fifty were critical of the activities and values of this group.

The most outstanding writers dealing with this medium—Mark Twain, Hamlin Garland, William Dean Howells, and Edward Bellamy, all agreed in presenting a generally critical picture of big business. Mark Twain, in collaboration with Charles Dudley Warner, depicted in *The Gilded Age* (1871) the itch for speculation that had captured the country and portrayed vividly many of the corrupt political figures of the day together with land promoters, lobbyists, and others of that ilk. Far from having thwarted Twain's natural genius, industrial capitalism seems to have stimulated him both to criticism and satire on the one hand and to the proclamation of humane, democratic values on the other. If, in focusing attention on the spoils-loving West as the source of political corruption, Twain failed, as Parrington thought, to do justice to the rapacious capitalists of the East and to the relations between the desire for profits and corruption, the authors of *The Gilded Age*, by implication at least, excoriated economic exploitation. *The Connecticut Yankee*, a defense of industry and the machine and a satire on romantic feudalism, did not fail to reveal the withering blight that an exaggerated property-consciousness cast over civilization. Hamlin Garland's stories portraying the evil effects of monopoly on rural and especially mid-western America expressed the older faith in economic equalitarianism. Howells' *Annie Kilburn*, *A Hazard of New Fortunes*, and *A Traveler from Altruria* displayed the sterility of the lives of many of the new rich, the corrupting effect of materialistic acquisitiveness on mind and heart, and the social and human injustice of an economics of exploitation. All this he depicted with the new technique of literary realism.

These major writers did not stand alone. Henry F. Keenan's *The Money-Makers* delineated the character of a pitiable tool of unscrupulous capitalists and revealed the blighting effect of the thirst for big money on law, morals, and all decent human values. Joaquin Miller, fresh from California, asked Jay Gould at a New York dinner party for a "tip" on the market. The man who "knew" stated the exact opposite of the truth, namely, that he was buying Vandalia Railroad and selling Western Union. Joaquin Miller, taking the "tip," had his fingers burned; in fact, by following Gould's tricky lead, he lost most of his fortune. *The Destruction of Gotham* was Miller's reply. In this novel the poet of the Sierras excoriated the iniquities of the stock exchange and the class identified with it. Such examples could be multiplied.

While many writers spent their talents in ridiculing and condemning the moneyed class, in emphasizing the withering effects of unrestrained competition for gold, others took the part of the laborers. The *Atlantic Monthly* published Rebecca Harding Davis's "Life in the Iron Mills," an early portrait, fierce and stark, of the lot of the industrial worker. Seven years later the same periodical brought to the public a story in which the brutalizing insecurity of labor was dramatically depicted when a factory collapsed, with its inevitable havoc to lives already twisted by deprivation and toil. The author, Elizabeth Stuart Phelps, again pleaded for Christian justice to the mill worker in a subsequent piece of fiction, *The Silent Partner* (1871). Less unctuous than this Puritan idyll was Edward Bellamy's *The Duke of Stockbridge* (1879). Far from flawless as a piece of literature, this historical novel of Shays' rebellion revealed fairly acute understanding of exploitation, injustice, and revolt. These evidences of humane sympathy for the underdog and of sharp criticisms of the ways of the rich were merely the beginnings of a crop of novels, stories, and essays which in the eighteen-eighties and -nineties testified to the sympathies of a great company of American writers.

If some intellectuals contented themselves with literary onslaughts against the new business class and with sympathetic portraits of industrial workers, others went further. In 1871 a journalist in California who had known the sting of poverty in that land of fabulous wealth published a little tract that contained the germ of the single-tax idea and of the movement subsequently launched in its behalf. About the same time the veteran abolitionist, Wendell Phillips, was striking out boldly on new paths. Refusing to share the contentment displayed by most of his fellow workers in the antislavery crusade, Phillips continued to excoriate intellectuals for their indifference toward new social evils. He himself bestowed sympathy on the movement for the eight-hour day, spoke and labored for a cooperative system of production, and demanded heavy taxation of a profit economy. For the most part, however, intellectuals who ventured into the sphere of action shrank from anything that betokened genuine struggle over class relationships.

THE CALL FOR CIVIC RESPONSIBILITY

E. L. Godkin, a brilliant emigrant from Protestant Ireland, a journalist of great talent, and a disciple of Mill and the English Utilitarians, was a leader in emphasizing the idea that American intellectuals should assume a greater measure of civic responsibility. This, rather than government control of industry, seemed to Godkin the most promising way of combating corrupt political machines, public dishonesty, and the undue influence of the shoddy aristocracy and the venal henchmen. Through *The Nation* he contended for civil service reform and for honesty, decency, and competency in political life.

In reply to the contention that a cultivated man had no chance for a political career this vigorous champion of the duty of intellectuals to cleanse the Augean stables cited the work of Edward Everett, George Bancroft, Andrew D. White, George W. Curtis, Dorman Eaton, and James Russell Lowell. If the man of culture would but drop his own sense of superiority over the people, Godkin argued, he had, other things being equal, a great advantage in the competition for public office over a man devoid of polish and education. But Godkin failed to understand why the standard of honesty in public life was so flagrantly violated by the captains of industry under the banner of the very economic individualism upheld by the high-minded intellectual himself.

The growing civic consciousness on the part of intellectuals and educated citizens generally was greatly deepened and broadened by the interest aroused by James Bryce's *The American Commonwealth* (1888). Bryce admired much in America and went so far as to write that the United States had reached "the highest level, not only of material well-being, but of intelligence and happiness which the race has yet attained." Hence this friendly visitor, so well and favorably known as a distinguished British scholar, man of letters, barrister, and parliamentarian, could make far-reaching criticisms the effect of which was to challenge rather than antagonize Americans. His reports were furthermore largely based on what Americans themselves told him. His great book was a fairly accurate picture of the corruption and timidity of legislators before business pressure, of the boss and the spoils system, of the contempt that most cultured Americans felt toward politics. *The American Commonwealth* did much to prepare the ground for the growing interest in reform.

The protests and actions of the intellectuals who refused to apologize for and serve the new business giants or to escape into the culture of the Old World merely heralded the more drastic and wide-spread criticism of the last decade of the nineteenth century and the first years of the twentieth. Meantime other currents of thought were dividing both the leaders of intellectual life and ultimately the plain people themselves.

THE West has exercised a fascination on the American mind from the beginning. Here the lost hopes of the old establishments could be reclaimed: past failures forgotten; and a new Genesis written. The West also provided an endless series of challenges to the American, for here, time and again, the unforeseen happened. The West and the new were interchangeable in the American mind. And it provided a setting within which man and nature met to resolve elemental conflicts. So long as the unconquered West remained, Americans had at their disposal a world commensurate to man's capacity for wonder.

When the guns fell silent in 1865, Americans stood at the verge of the Great Plains and the looming mountains beyond. A previous generation had been arrested by the ominous sound of the description given the area— the Great American Desert. As a stream of westward migrants had learned, it was a dubious appellation. Yet, no voyager through the endless fields of grass, surrounded by a horizon as limitless as that of the sea, could ignore the vagaries of the region. The blistering heat of summer and the icy fingers of winter, the seasons of drought and the deluges of rain, the spring tornado and the summer zephyr added up into an exhausting challenge. It was as if sky and land were a lurking beast ready to pounce upon the unthinking wayfarer.

It also gave a final home to the retreating Indian. Beyond the Plains and

Mountains, for him there was nowhere further to go. The three vast herds of buffalo, numbering more than 10 million in 1865, gave the aborigine food, shelter, clothing, warmth, and weapons. So long as the white man had not settled upon the land, the nomadic Indian was free to wander. But the coming first of the miner, then the cattleman and sheepherder, and finally the farmer brought the final confrontation between the two races. The Indian wars that have been woven into the legendary cowboy-Indian tales lasted a bare decade and a half. When they were over in 1880, the Indian had capitulated to the American apartheid: the reservation. By 1890, the Sioux, a hopeless people in a land of limitless hope, dreamed of a Messiah, and danced the Ghost Dance, singing: "My Father, have pity on me! I have nothing to eat, I am dying of thirst—Everything is gone!" The once bounteous buffalo were reduced to a straggling few thousand. All that remained were the ghosts and the legend.

The remarkable history of the Great Plains and the human ingenuity used to conquer it was given its definitive writing by Walter P. Webb (1888-1963). Texas born and largely self-educated, he paralleled many of the conclusions of Frederick Jackson Turner. But he had been careful to avoid reading the great frontier historian. His findings underscored those of his predecessor, and his accounting of the Last Frontier recalled the color, the dreams, the ghosts, and the agony of a land that still preys upon the unwary.

THE GREAT PLAINS

by Walter Prescott Webb

THE SPREAD OF THE KINGDOM

We have no statistics as to the number of cattle in Texas in 1865. The census for 1860 . . . gives 3,535,768, which a later estimate raised to 4,785,400. The census of 1870 gives the number on farms at 3,990,158, whereas the actual figures probably ran a million more, making approximately 5,000,000 head. We know that at that time these cattle must have been confined to the eastern settlements and the old region of the Nueces in southwest Texas. We are quite certain that practically no cattle were at that time west of the ninety-ninth meridian. Even in the census of 1880, after the kingdom had spread, we find that out of a total of 4,894,698 cattle in Texas, only 731,827 head were to the west of the hundredth meridian, whereas 4,162,871 were east of that meridian, and of that number 221,597 were in the small area south of the Nueces.

The price situation in 1865 was as follows: cattle in Texas could be bought for $3 and $4 per head, on the average; but even so, there were no buyers. The same cattle in the Northern markets would have brought $30 or $40, "and mature Texas beeves which cost in Texas $5 each by the herd were worth $50 each in other sections of the United States." It was easy for a Texan with a pencil and a piece of paper to "figure up" a fortune. If he could buy five million cattle at $4 and sell them in the North at $40 each, his gross profit would amount to the sum of $180,000,000 on an investment of $20,000,000 plus the cost of transportation! This exercise in high finance is, of course, fanciful, but it does show what men did on a small scale. Five million cattle? No. Three thousand? Yes. Profit, $108,000. How the Texans needed the money in those hard days! They took vigorous measures to connect the four-dollar cow with a forty-dollar market. As a matter of fact they did within fifteen years actually deliver to the North the five million head of cattle, and more, though the actual profits fell short of the paper figures. At the same time the number of cattle remaining on the breeding ground in Texas was greater than before by more than eight hundred thousand head.

When the Texans started their rangy longhorns northward—and they were fortunate in having such tough customers for such a perilous journey —they had no intention of setting up a new economic kingdom: they were merely carrying their herds to market. The fact that the market happened to be twelve or fifteen hundred miles away was no fault of theirs. And if we follow the history of their drives for five years, we see that they were groping, experimenting, trying this and that, until by the familiar system of trial and error, which has characterized all progress in the Plains country, they came at length, and after great sacrifice, upon success. They beat out the trail, learned to avoid the timber and the farmer, to whip the Indian, to cross the quicksanded rivers; they reached the railroad, found buyers and a steady market, and heard once more the music made by real money rattling in the pocket. And the North had meat, sometimes tough and unsavory, but the worst of it good enough for factory workers and the pick-and-shovel men of the railroads and too good for the Indians of the reservation under the corrupt regime of Grant Republicans.

As has been stated, the purpose of the Texans in making the first drives to the north was to find a market for their cattle. Their immediate objective was a railhead from which the cattle could be shipped East. An examination of the railroad maps of 1866 will show that several railroads had nosed their way across the Mississippi and followed population to the edge of the Great Plains. Among these roads was the Missouri Pacific, which had reached Sedalia, Missouri.

It is estimated that two hundred and sixty thousand head of Texas cattle crossed Red River for the northern markets in 1866. The objective of most of these herds was Sedalia, Missouri, which offered rail facilities to St. Louis and other cities. But disaster awaited the Texans and their herds in southeastern Kansas, southern Missouri, and northern Arkansas, where armed mobs met the herds with all possible violence. The pretext for this opposition was that the cattle would bring the Texas fever among Northern cattle, but in some cases, at least, robbery and theft were the real motives.

The southwestern Missouri roads leading to Sedalia were the scenes of the worst of the work of these outlaws. . . . When outright murder was not resorted to as the readiest means of getting possession of a herd of cattle, drovers were flogged until they had promised to abandon their stock, mount their horses, and get out of the country as quick as they could. A favorite scheme of the milder-mannered of these scoundrels to plunder the cattle-men was that of stampeding a herd at night. This was easily done, and having been done the rogues next morning would collect as many of the scattered cattle as they could, secrete them in an out-of-the-way place,— much of the country being hilly and timbered—and then hunt up the owner and offer to help him, for an acceptable money consideration per head, in recovering his lost property. If the drover agreed to pay a price high enough to satisfy the pirates, they next day would return with many, if not all, of the missing cattle; but if not, the hold-ups would keep them, and later take them to the market and pocket the entire proceeds.

The Texas drovers soon learned to avoid this region. Some turned to the east and others to the west, away from the bandit-infested country around Baxter Springs. Those who turned east did so in the northeastern part of the Indian Territory, driving along the Missouri-Arkansas boundary and laying their course toward St. Louis or some rail point east of Sedalia. This route had few attractions. The country was timbered and broken, and the cattle reached the market in poor condition. Other drovers turned west along the southern boundary of Kansas for one hundred and fifty miles, until they were beyond the settlements and well out on the grassy plains. When far enough north they turned eastward, most of them reaching the railroad at St. Joseph, Missouri, and shipping direct to Chicago. Other cattle found their way to feeding pens in Iowa and Illinois. To the west some cattle went as far north as Wyoming.

On the whole the season of 1866 was disastrous to the Texans. It was a year of groping experiment, trial, and error. But one clear fact emerges from the welter of uncertainty of that year, and that is that the cattle trail of the future would lie to the west. Ferocious Plains Indians were there on horseback, but they were to be preferred to the Missourians. Why the Texans who had raised their cattle on the prairies, or, at least, gathered them there, did not immediately realize that it would be best to drive on the prairie may seem strange; yet what they had done was perfectly natural, namely, to seek the most direct route to market. In spite of the losses which most of them experienced, the drovers saw that they had an unlimited market for their cattle if they could only find a way of getting them safely through. They met buyers as well as thieves. Their future problem was to establish permanent relations with the buyers and avoid— or, better, kill, as they sometimes did—the thieves.

The man who first saw the desirability of establishing a permanent and fairly safe point of contact between the Eastern buyer and the Texan drover was J. G. McCoy, who, with his two brothers, was engaged in a large live-stock shipping business in Illinois. McCoy, a dreamer with a practical bent, conceived the notion that there must be a strategic point where the cattle trail from Texas would cut the railroads then pushing west. At this point of intersection Texas cattle drovers would be met by

Northern and Eastern buyers, and all would prosper together. "The plan," says McCoy, "was to establish at some accessible point a depot or market to which a Texan drover could bring his stock unmolested, and there, failing to find a buyer, he could go upon the public highways to any market in the country he wished. In short, it was to establish a market whereat the Southern drover and the Northern buyer would meet upon an equal footing, and both be undisturbed by mobs or swindling thieves." In other words, McCoy proposed to establish, and did establish, the first cow town of the West—Abilene, Kansas. This act constituted the third step in the founding of the cattle kingdom.

At first McCoy was uncertain where this town should be, and he spent much time studying maps, trying to decide whether it should be on the Western prairies or on some Southern river. At this stage of his meditation a business trip took him to Kansas City, where he met some men who were interested in a herd of cattle reported to be coming up from Texas, destination unknown. McCoy became more interested. He went to Junction City and proposed to purchase land there for a stockyard, but found the price too high. He next made the rounds of the railroad offices. The president of the Kansas Pacific promised aid, but showed only mild enthusiasm for the plan, which he thought impractical. The president of the Missouri Pacific ordered McCoy out of his office, declaring that McCoy had no cattle, had never had any, and probably never would have any. A few hours later McCoy had signed a contract with the general freight agent of the Hannibal and St. Joe Railroad granting favorable rates from the Missouri River to Chicago. McCoy thought that this incident—the action of the official of the Missouri Pacific—turned the cattle business permanently from St. Louis to Chicago.

McCoy now had rail connection on the Kansas Pacific to the Missouri River, and thence on the Hannibal and St. Joe to Chicago and other markets farther east. He now hurried back to Kansas to select the site of his town on the Kansas Pacific. Neither Salina nor Solomon City was hospitable to the idea of being a cow town, and McCoy finally selected Abilene, the county seat of Dickinson County. In McCoy's words,

> Abilene in 1867 was a very small, dead place, consisting of about one dozen log huts, low, small, rude affairs, four fifths of which were covered with dirt for roofing; indeed, but one shingle roof could be seen in the whole city. The business of the burg was conducted in two small rooms, mere log huts, and of course the inevitable saloon, also in a log hut, was to be found.

Just how poor the town must have been is indicated by the fact that the saloon-keeper supplemented his income and provided himself amusement by tending a colony of prairie dogs and selling them to Eastern tourists as curiosities. The time was near when the saloon-keepers of Abilene would have too much business to stoop to prairie-dog culture. However, the presence of the prairie-dog town tells us significantly that Abilene was across the line, a town of the West. Says McCoy:

Abilene was selected because the country was entirely unsettled, well watered, excellent grass, and nearly the entire area of country was adapted to holding cattle. And it was the [farthest] point east at which a good depot for cattle business could have been made.

McCoy labored with energy, zeal, and intelligence. Pine lumber was brought from Hannibal, Missouri, and hard wood from Lenape, Kansas. The work of building stockyards, pens, and loading chutes went forward rapidly, and within sixty days Abilene had facilities to accommodate three thousand head of cattle; but as yet it was a cow town without any cows.

McCoy had not overlooked the cows, however. As soon as he chose Abilene he sent to Kansas and the Indian Territory a man well versed in the geography of the country and "accustomed to life on the prairie," "with instructions to hunt up every straggling drove possible—and every drove was straggling, for they had nowhere to go—and tell the drovers of Abilene, and what was being done there toward making a market and outlet for Texan cattle." This man rode almost two hundred miles into the Indian Territory, cut the fresh trail of cattle going north, followed it, overtook the herd, and informed the owner that a good, safe place with adequate shipping facilities awaited him at Abilene.

This was joyous news to the drover, for the fear of trouble and violence hung like an incubus over his waking thoughts alike with his sleeping moments. It was almost too good to be believed; could it be possible that someone was about to afford a Texan drover any other reception than outrage and robbery? They were very suspicious that some trap was set, to be sprung on them; they were not ready to credit the proposition that the day of fair dealing had dawned for Texan drovers, and the era of mobs, brutal murder, and arbitrary proscription ended forever.

Yet they turned their herds toward the point designated, and slowly and cautiously moved on northward, their minds constantly agitated with hope and fear alternately.

The first herd to reach Abilene was driven from Texas by a man named Thompson, but was sold to some Northern men in the Indian Territory and by them driven to Abilene. Another herd owned by Wilson, Wheeler, and Hicks, and en route for the Pacific states, stopped to graze near Abilene and was finally sold there. On the fifth of September the first cattle were shipped from Abilene to Chicago. A great celebration was held that night, attended by many stock-raisers and buyers brought by excursion from Springfield, Illinois, and other points. Southern men from Texas and Northern men from Lincoln's home town sat down to "feast, wine, and song," heralding the initiation of the cattle kingdom, which was to rise immediately after the fall of the cotton kingdom. Who can say that Abilene was less significant than Appomattox?

Abilene! Abilene may be defined. It was the point where the north-and-south cattle trail intersected the east-and-west railroad. Abilene was more than a point. It is a symbol. It stands for all that happened when two civilizations met for conflict, for disorder, for the clashing of great currents which carry on their crest the turbulent and disorderly elements of both civilizations—in this case the rough characters of the plain and of the forest. On the surface Abilene was corruption personified. Life was hectic, raw, lurid, awful. But the dance hall, the saloon, and the red light, the dissonance of immoral revelry punctuated by pistol shots, were but the superficialities which hid from view the deeper forces that were working themselves out round the new town. If Abilene excelled all later cow towns in wickedness, it also excelled them in service,—the service of bartering the beef of the South for the money of the North.

Through Abilene passed a good part of the meat supply of a nation. That part of the story belongs to the East, and we are not concerned with it here. But Abilene's service was no less to the West. From Abilene and other like towns Texas cattle, blended with American cattle, swarmed out to the West and covered the Great Plains—the empire of grass—from the California mountains to the Illinois prairies. Not all the cattle that reached Abilene were fit for market, and at times there was no market. In such cases the surplus cattle were "held on the prairie" or established on permanent ranches to be fattened.

In this way the cattle kingdom spread from Texas and utilized the Plains area, which would otherwise have lain idle and useless. Abilene offered the market; the market offered inducement to Northern money; Texas furnished the base stock, the original supply, and a method of handling cattle on horseback; the Plains offered free grass. From these conditions and from these elements emerged the range and ranch cattle industry, perhaps the most unique and distinctive institution that America has produced. This spread of the range cattle industry over the Great Plains is the final step in the creation of the cattle kingdom.

The first step was made when the Spaniards and Mexicans established their ranches in the Nueces country of southern Texas, where natural conditions produced a hardy breed of cattle that could grow wild; the second step occurred when the Texans took over these herds and learned to handle them in the only way they could have been handled—on horseback; the third step was taken when the cattle were driven northward to market; the fourth came when a permanent depot was set up at Abilene which enabled trail-driving to become standardized; the fifth took place when the overflow from the trail went west to the free grass of the Great Plains.

Thus far we have followed the cattle from the plains of southwest Texas along the trail to Abilene, Kansas, and have noted that from 1866 to 1880 nearly five million head went north. In addition to the five million head sent to the Kansas market and the ranges north and west, many herds were turned directly west to the ranges of New Mexico, Arizona, and Colorado; others went to Montana, Wyoming, and the Dakotas, and some into Canada. Despite this migration of cattle, the number remaining on the home range of Texas was greater than before. If we visualize the process by which the Great Plains ranges were stocked, we see an unending stream of cattle coming up from the south, many of them going east from Abilene or its successors, but as many more were going north and west, to supply the herds for the numerous ranches that were being opened up.

The spread of the range and ranch cattle industry over the Great Plains in the space of fifteen years—the movement was fairly complete in ten or twelve—is perhaps one of the outstanding phenomena in American history. The fur-hunters did not move faster, and since they destroyed that which supported them they had no claim to permanency; but the cattlemen spread the institution of ranching over the empire of grass, the Great American Desert, within a period of fifteen years. During that period and for ten years after, men, cattle, and horses held almost undisputed possession of the region.

Our interest is not primarily in cattle, however; it is rather in the process by which man in relation to his environment evolved around cattle the institution of ranching. In this evolution the Plains worked their will, and man conformed. The Plains put men on horseback and taught them to work in that way. The southern Plains offered the natural conditions in which cattle could breed and multiply without care. Men struck out for markets— first by the forest roads, only to meet disaster and failure. The remorseless conditions pushed them out of the timber lands onto the open highway of the Plains, where cattle could travel and live in a suitable environment until they reached the railroad which carried them to the Eastern market. And the surplus cattle, if we may personify them, saw the rolling grassy plains stretching from their trail to the western mountains and recognized them as their natural home. They went west to the recesses of the Rockies and north to the snows of Canada, carrying with them ranchman and cowboy with lariat, six-shooter, and horse. In the end the cattle kingdom occupied practically the whole Great Plains environment; it was the most natural economic and social order that the white men had yet developed in his experiment with the Great Plains.

But, with all this, we must not ignore the fact that, after all, the West (even including Texas) did not produce many cattle. In 1880 the whole United States had 39,675,533 head. Of this number the sixteen Western states and territories, including both Dakotas, had only 12,612,089 head, or only about 34 per cent. If we exclude the Pacific states, then the true Plains area, including Texas, produced 11,000,846 head, or 27.7 per cent of the total. If we exclude Texas and the Pacific states, then the other Plains states rounded up but 6,106,223 head, or about 15.4 per cent of the total.

If the West produced comparatively so few cattle, then why is it that we think of the West, of the Plains, as the center of the cattle industry? Why do we call it the cattle kingdom? The answer is found in the method and not in the results. The thing that has identified the West in the popular mind with cattle is not the number raised, but the method of handling them. A thousand farms in the East will each have six or seven cows, with as many more calves and yearlings—ten thousand head. But they attract no attention. They are incidents of agriculture. In the West a ranch will cover the same area as the thousand farms, and will have perhaps ten thousand head, round-ups, rodeos, men on horseback, and all that goes with ranching. Hot days in the branding pen with bawling calves and the smell of burned hair and flesh on the wind! Men in boots and big hats, with the accompaniment of jingling spurs and frisky horses. Camp cook and horse wrangler! Profanity and huge appetites! The cattle industry in the East and that in the West were two worlds as different from each other as the East is different from the West. And the ninety-eighth meridian lies between. The East did a large business on a small scale; the West did a small business magnificently.

THE EVOLUTION OF THE RANGE AND RANCH CATTLE INDUSTRY, 1866-1928

In the preceding pages an effort was made to show that the cattle industry, as carried on in the Plains country, rose in a natural manner and spread with amazing rapidity over the whole area to which it was adapted. Enough has been said to show that the industry was new, without counterpart or analogy among the institutions of the humid country of the East. In short, it was an industry remarkably adapted to the country that it appropriated. When approached in this manner, the ways of life in this region appear logical, reasonable, almost inevitable.

It should be stated, however, that no sooner had the cattle kingdom been set up as a natural institution adapted to its environment than the forces of the Industrial Revolution began to modify and destroy it. Up from the South came the natural institution, something new, something without antecedents, something willing to conform to all the laws of necessity; but from the East came the old institutions, seeking, through the forces of the Industrial Revolution, to utilize the land after the manner of men in the humid timber lands. . . .

Though the civilization of the cattle kingdom was as complete within itself as was that of the Old South, it was not independent, but subject to the general conditions of the nation. It was affected by economic conditions in the East, such as the panics of 1873 and 1893, the boom of 1885, and the condition of the world market in general; it was affected by the railroad extension, the invention of barbed wire, and the adaptation of the windmill—things which altered the whole nature and economy of range practice; finally, it was affected by the immigration of the small farmer, granger or nester, into the West.

The area of the cattle kingdom has already been indicated. The unit of production in this area was the ranch, which term is used to include the houses and all the range of the cattle, whether fenced or unfenced. The practice of raising cattle on a large scale is ranching, and the owner of a ranch is a ranchman or cattleman. The cowboy is an employee whose business it is to handle the cattle. In the beginning of ranching in the West the country was wide open and free, and grass was without limit throughout the whole region. The cattle were of Texas origin, low-grade and hardy.

In selecting a ranch site the ranchman's main considerations were grass and water. In the beginning there was no thought of securing water from wells or of impounding it in large dirt ponds, called "tanks" in the West. The ranchman who was seeking a location usually established his head-quarters camp, which later became a ranch house, along some stream, oc-cupying either bank or both banks. At first he had no neighbors, and his range covered about all the country that the cattle wanted to roam over; but after a time another ranchman would establish himself, either above or below the first, and appropriate a water front on the same stream. Across the divide was another stream, and there also ranches would be established. Thus it came about in a few years that the original ranchman had neighbors all around him, not in sight, but within fifteen or twenty or fifty miles—close enough, in the opinion of the ranchman. The result of this was that the range (the term applied to the whole open and unfenced country) was divided. As yet no ranchman owned any land or grass; he merely owned the cattle and the camps. He did possess what was recognized by his neighbors (but not by law) as range rights. This meant a right to the water which he had ap-propriated and to the surrounding range. Where water was scarce the con-trol of it in any region gave control of all the land around it, for water was the sine qua non of the cattle country. For example, if the first ranchman occupied both sides of the stream, then his recognized range extended back-ward on both sides to all the land drained by the stream within the limits of his frontage; if he held but one side, then his range (for thus it was called) extended back only on that side. In the range country "divides" became of much importance, marking the boundary between the ranchmen of one stream-valley and those of another. Up and down the same stream the problem was not quite so simple, but the ranchmen were careful to recognize that possession of water gave a man rights on the range. Moreover, it was not good form to try to crowd too much.

Under such conditions it was impossible to keep the cattle of one ranch from mingling with those of another. In fact, there was little effort at first to do so; the range was theoretically free to all, and the cattle, generally speaking, came and went at will, identified by their brands just as automobiles are today identified by number plates. In many cases, however, it was the practice of the cowboys to throw the neighboring cattle across the divide, or to "drift" them back toward their own ranges. This was a neighborly act, advantageous to everybody, and was not resented so long as there was plenty of room.

The cattle were rounded up twice a year, in the spring and in the fall. Since the range was what it was, the round-up had to be a community enterprise in which all ranchmen of the vast and undefined territory par-ticipated. In both round-ups all unbranded animals were put to the iron. If a drive was to be made, as in the early days of the range, the herd was started in the spring; but if the cattle were shipped, this might better be done in the fall, when they were fat from the summer grass. Under the open-range system it was almost impossible to improve the blood of the herds. The aggressive native bulls on the range, together with the naturally hard conditions of survival, made the process of improvement by breeding slow and uncertain; therefore the cattle remained of low grade, rangy, and able-bodied.

The range situation as outlined here may be said to have obtained in the Great Plains country from 1867 to 1876 or 1880, though, of course, practices varied from place to place. In some ways range life was idyllic. The land had no value, the grass was free, the water belonged to the first comer, and about all a man needed to "set him up" in the business was a "bunch" of cattle and enough common sense to handle them and enough courage to protect them without aid of the law. But farsighted men must have seen that things could not go on as they were. Single outfits claimed "range rights" over territory as large as Massachusetts and Delaware combined. It could not last.

In 1862 the Federal Homestead Law was passed; in 1874 the first piece of barbed wire was sold in the United States. These two facts combined to break the even tenor of the cattleman's way.

Until 1873 the establishment of cattle ranches in the West proceeded without interruption. Until 1870 the herds sent to Abilene and other rail-heads sold on a steady or rising market. Prices were particularly good in 1870, with the result that the drive from Texas in 1871 was the greatest in history—seven hundred thousand head going to Kansas alone. Besides the Texas cattle, the other Western states were beginning to contribute to the beef supply and to reap the benefits of the high prices. But in 1871 the market conditions had changed, and the drovers found almost a complete reversal of the situation of the year before. There were few buyers, and they were reluctant rather than eager purchasers. Business conditions were slackening, the currency issue was agitating the country, and the railroads had put an end to a rate war which hitherto had benefitted the cattlemen. Half the cattle brought from Texas remained unsold and had to be wintered at a loss on the prairies of Kansas. The drive from Texas in 1872, therefore, was only about half what it had been in 1871. The market had revived somewhat by then, but the demand was for a better grade of beef; consequently cattle from the Northern ranges did better than Southern, or Texas, cattle. In the same year a heavy corn crop was made in the corn belt, and there was considerable demand for cattle as feeders. This condition marked an important change in the Western cattle industry. Henceforth cattle were raised in Texas and transferred North to be fattened for market. Before 1872 the surplus cattle had gone to stock the Northern ranges; but these ranges were now fairly well supplied, so that the Texans had to look elsewhere for an outlet. "This," as a writer declared in 1904, "marked the beginning of the great business of transferring Texas cattle to Northern ranges and there rounding them out for market—a business that is still going on." In Texas the situation in 1873 was bad. The corn crop promised but a poor yield, the Northern ranges needed no more stock cattle, and the market demand was weak. The climax was reached on September 18, 1873, when the New York banking firm of Jay Cooke & Company closed its doors, precipitating the first panic known to the range cattleman. A single firm of shippers lost $180,000 in three weeks. One stockman took his cattle to Chicago and did not get enough money for them to pay the shipping expenses. Out of this disaster the Southern cattlemen learned two things: that they could no longer hope to market scrub stock for the range in the North, and that they must either deliver good beef or good animals which could be fattened for beef. Another effect of the disaster of 1873 was that it led to an effort to organize the Live Stockmen's National Association. The organization was launched at Kansas City about the middle of September, with J. G. McCoy as secretary. The panic broke about three days later, and the organization disappeared in the general debacle.

After the panic of 1873 the range cattle industry began to struggle upward once more, though the drives from Texas were less frequent owing to the approaching saturation of the range and the fact that the railroads were extending into the West and diverting the cattle from the trails. Many herds were now sent from Texas to Arizona, to New Mexico, and some to the Indian Territory and to Colorado. Whereas the drive for 1873 had been 400,000, for 1874 it fell to 165,000 and for 1875 to 150,000, consisting largely of beeves and feeders. Agricultural immigrants were gnawing with plows on the eastern margin of the Plains from Texas to Canada, and cattle were going farther west, into the more arid country. In the meantime the Industrial Revolution was raising packing plants at St. Louis, Kansas City, and Chicago,—all on or near the margin of the Plains,—and people were learning to eat canned and cured meat, while refrigeration enabled fresh carcasses to be delivered anywhere in the United States or in Europe. The result was that cattle production fell off in the East, and people came more and more to depend on the Plains for meat.

By 1876 the cattle industry was recovering from the panic of three years before, and there was a steady demand for cattle, with a rising market—premonitory symptom of the cattle boom of the eighties. During the last four years of the seventies (1876-1880) the cattle business expanded on a steady or rising market. In the last year two million head were marketed. A well-matured Northwestern ranger would bring about $60 in the Northern markets, and a Texan steer about $50. Grass was still free, the range was open, and the farmer was far away. Again, it could not last.

✦ ✦ ✦

THE *obituaries published after the Civil War frequently described the deceased as "a statesman of the old school" or "an editor of the old school." Americans of the postwar period knew that war had wrought profound changes and, not infrequently, they were not certain they enjoyed the result. To a large extent, the historian, shaped in his judgment by the evidence, most likely drawn from the uneasy and the disenchanted observer, drew a portrait that had many of the characteristics of a caricature. It presented the judgment of the critic without attempting to assess it through the eyes of those who concluded it had real and meaningful benefits. But since the contented are likely to accept life without comment, much which was constructive in the Gilded Age passed unnoticed.*

But as Walt W. Rostow noted, America on the eve of its Civil War had reached the "take-off stage" of economic growth. And though historians disagree sharply on the effects of the Civil War on economic growth, no one doubts that the three decades following Appomattox saw the United States emerge as the world's greatest industrial power. Within a single generation, the American mastered his last frontier, accelerated the movement from farm to the city, and launched a technological revolution that allows contemporary man to reach for the moon and the stars. The economic system that shaped this result is called capitalism; it granted to its masters a huge reward but also a monumental incentive to succeed. And though few reaped the ultimate benefits, it spread the benefits wide enough to create what is undoubtedly the largest middle class the world has ever known. Out of the abundance of the American land was made a people of plenty.

Allan Nevins (1890-　), two-time Pulitzer Prize winner, one of America's most prolific historians, came to history by way of journalism. His colorful vignettes and his command of sources provide an historical narrative underwritten by revealing detail. He has also challenged the traditional image of the industrial giants of the Gilded Age as marauding thieves. He has emphasized instead their constructive role in building vast industries that survived their lives. Beyond their vast rewards was a more meaningful result, the creation of the means with which modern man is able to satisfy every conceivable need. The technology upon which they built has emancipated Americans, in good part, from the drudgery of labor. Whether the capitalist system they used might better have been replaced by another system begs the historical question. It is why did this system prove so successful? And in a world where other routes to economic growth have been followed, who can question Nevins' conclusion that, despite all the injustice and suffering that colored the final decades of the nineteenth century, American capitalism was perhaps the least harsh of the economic systems used to propel a people from an economy of scarcity to one of abundance.

THE EMERGENCE OF MODERN AMERICA, 1865-1875

by Allan Nevins

The victorious end of the war and the return of labor from the armies gave increased buoyancy to enterprise in every field. A leading Northern manufacturer, testifying under oath, said that his rate of profit in 1865 had been "painfully large"; and the special commissioner of revenue reported at the end of the following year that the returns of business had been almost unprecedentedly high. Scarcely a record in industry escaped being broken during the next five years. More cotton spindles were set revolving, more iron furnaces were lighted, more steel was made, more coal and copper were mined, more lumber was sawed and hewed, more houses and shops were constructed and more manufactories of different kinds were established, than during any equal term in our earlier history. Moreover, the improvements in the quality of manufactures equaled the increase in quantity.

The high prices which war-time demands and the issue of greenbacks had brought about continued in nearly all markets. The elation of Northern victory, the feeling of recuperative power, the sense of enormous Western wealth waiting only to be unlocked, were reflected in industry. "The truth is," John Sherman wrote his brother in the fall of 1865, "the close of the war with our resources unimpaired gives an elevation, a scope to the ideas of leading capitalists, far higher than anything ever undertaken in this country before. They talk of millions as confidently as formerly of thousands." Sherman himself thought of leaving politics to engage in railroading, banking or manufacturing in Ohio. The home market was steadily expanding, partly through the inflow of immigrants from Europe, partly through the rapid settlement of the Western prairies. The war had tended to break down the previous economic dependence upon Europe, and behind a high tariff wall a host of new manufactories were making articles formerly shipped from abroad. In 1859 there had been one hundred and forty thousand manufacturing establishments; in 1869 there were two hundred and fifty-two thousand with a commensurate increase in the number of employees. A succession of foreign wars, beginning with the Austro-Prussian War of 1865-1866 and the coalition of Brazil, Argentina and Uruguay against Paraguay, also benefited American trade.

Although the modern steel age was born in 1856, when Henry Bessemer in England invented his process, it did not gain a real foothold in America for a decade. Till after the Civil War steel was rare and costly, used chiefly in cutlery and fine tools. The demands of the conflict gave manufacturers no taste or time for experimenting, so that not until 1864 was the Bessemer process first used, at a short-lived plant in Wyandotte, Michigan, and even in 1867 only two thousand six hundred tons of steel ingots were produced. Then, steel making expanded with striking speed. The new process excited the wonder of all who witnessed it: the pouring of the molten iron into a great converter, the dazzling shower of sparks as the air was forced through the incandescent mass and the drawing off of the flaming metal as white-hot steel. The first steel king arose in the person of Captain Eber S. Ward of Detroit, who at the close of the war began making and selling steel under the American patents of William Kelly. He soon found his chief rival in Alexander M. Holley of Troy, New York, who had bought the Bessemer rights. Since neither could make steel satisfactorily without infringing upon the legal prerogatives of the other, Ward, who was growing old, surrendered his patents to Holley, a dashing young industrialist still in his early thirties, in return for a thirty-per-cent share in the consolidation. Holley thus for a time stepped forth as the leading steel-and-iron maker of America.

Steel speedily became as cheap as cast iron and its cheapness created such a keen demand that by 1875 a dozen important Bessemer works had been established. Before the war the iron business of the nation had been widely diffused, with bloomeries and furnaces scattered from the Adirondacks and Berkshires to Virginia and Tennessee. Now the greatest steel works, including the Cambria Works, which Daniel J. Morrell established in Johnstown (1871), the Bethlehem Works (1873) and the J. Edgar Thomson Steel Works (1875, as Carnegie called his establishment near Pittsburgh, rose in Pennsylvania alone. When the first proposal came to Carnegie to use the Bessemer process, the young ironmaster demurred, saying that "Pioneering doesn't pay a new concern: we must wait until the process develops." But he soon afterwards saw it demonstrated in England, and hurried home to organize the firm of Carnegie, McCandless & Co., to develop the new methods with a capital of seven hundred thousand dollars. Meanwhile smaller works were flourishing in Cleveland, Chicago and St. Louis. The American production of steel rose steadily to three hundred and seventy-five thousand tons in 1875 and nine hundred and twenty-nine thousand in 1879, even the Panic of 1873 producing little visible check. Hard on the heels of the Bessemer process came that of the open hearth, but its progress was slow, for it required more time and the more careful instruction of the steel workers. A Siemens regenerative furnace was installed by John Fritz at the Bethlehem plant in 1872, and about nine thousand tons of open-hearth steel were being made two years later. Thousands of men found work and high wages in the steel plants, producing a commensurate development of the Michigan iron mines. But the social importance of steel production lay beyond all comparison in its contribution to the improvement of transportation, engineering and building construction. The greater part of the steel went into rails, the output of which exceeded two hundred and ninety thousand tons in 1875 and nine hundred and fifty thousand tons in 1880. Their durability as compared with iron rails was an indispensable quality. The huge crops of the Middle West and the growing volume of manufactured goods from the Mississippi Valley could never have been carried without them.

The years 1865-1873 also witnessed the emergence of the four factors whose combination made possible the development of the American meat-packing business upon an international scale. These were the tidal overflow of the plains by the cattle ranchers, the ramification of railways throughout the cattle country, the invention of refrigeration and the appearance of men astute enough to organize the distribution of livestock and meats in an efficient way. In the first year of peace the railway reached Kansas City, a cattle market and shipping point was established at Abilene, and some thirty-five thousand cattle were sent East from this terminus. It was clear to far-sighted men that the West would shortly become one vast livestock range, crying for a market.

Already in Milwaukee and Chicago two of the great packers of the future, Philip D. Armour and Nelson Morris, had established themselves in readiness for this rich opportunity. Armour, an adventurous New Yorker, had risen during the war to be partner in Jacob Plankinton's packing house in

Milwaukee, then the fourth largest of its kind in America. The business, thanks to large war contracts and to Armour's careful watch upon price fluctuations, expanded rapidly, throwing out branches in Chicago and Kansas City; and he determined to head a firm of his own. A flood of cattle and hogs had poured in war times into the Chicago slaughterhouses, becoming so unmanageable that the Illinois legislature was compelled in 1865 to incorporate the Union Stockyards, which on Christmas day of that year opened its new facilities—three hundred and forty-five rather swampy acres just south of the city limits—to the livestock shippers. Two years later Armour and Company, an enterprise in which Philip Armour was assisted by several able brothers, began meat packing in Chicago, and it was not long before the Armour brand was known in all parts of the world. Nelson Morris, a young Bavarian Jew, had been even earlier in entering the Chicago field. He went into meat packing at twenty-two, in the first days of the Civil War, and had no difficulty in securing large army contracts. When the conflict ended his business was flourishing. By 1870 Armour and Nelson Morris in Chicago and Jacob Plankinton in Milwaukee had emerged as the foremost Western packers, and were already taking the leadership from the older Eastern houses, like those of Jacob Dold in Buffalo and the Cordukes in Cincinnati.

One Eastern packer possessed a driving energy equal to their own— Gustavus F. Swift. A Cape Cod Yankee, Swift had risen so rapidly from the position of a local butcher that by the middle seventies he was conducting one of the largest dressed-beef businesses in New England. He knew that his natural sphere was the West and the year 1875 found him cautiously looking about for a site for a plant. In a very short time he had a large slaughterhouse in Chicago and was packing meats in competition with Armour and Morris. It was he who saw that beef might be fully dressed in Chicago and sent East, perfectly fresh, in refrigerator cars; and in initiating this fresh dressed-beef business on a large scale, he revolutionized the packing industry. The industry now concentrated itself in a few great cities to an extent previously impossible, with large resulting gains in the cheapness and quality of the meat served on American tables. The local butcher, especially in the East, was thrust to the wall, and even large Eastern slaughterhouses faced a competition from the Mississippi Valley which they had difficulty in meeting. Kansas City, with her packing houses still closer than Chicago to the range, sent two carloads of refrigerated meats to New York and one to Boston in the fall of 1875, thus opening a business which increased steadily. By the end of the seventies a general effort was being made by Western packers, and with success, to develop an Eastern market for all the beef and pork they could dress.

As the control of the meat-packing business passed to Chicago and Kansas City, simultaneously the seats of the milling-industry were transferred to Minneapolis and in lesser degree to St. Louis and Chicago, with direct benefits both to wheat growers and customers. Its Western development heralded the ultimate extinction of the small gristmills scattered by thousands over the nation and it made possible the rapid settlement of Minnesota wheatlands

and the overflow of farmers into the Dakota valleys. Here, too, we meet
picturesque and aggressive figures in the persons of three Minneapolis
millers: Cadwallader C. Washburn, Charles A. Pillsbury and George M.
Christian. The two former were New Englanders by birth, Washburn being
one of a group of Maine brothers who achieved a singularly varied
eminence, while Pillsbury had worked his way through Dartmouth College
in the class of 1863. Christian was an Alabamian who came North after the
war in search of opportunities lacking at home, and in 1869 was made a
partner in Washburn's establishment. With wheat fields, railways and water
power all at hand in Minneapolis, these men were further aided by the introduction of new mechanical processes. They adopted the "gradual reduction" method brought to them in 1870 by a Minnesotan named Edward
La Croix, which preserved much of the gluten previously lost with the bran.
This process was of cardinal importance to the Northern wheat belt, for
whereas previously winter wheat had made the best flour, now the hard
spring wheat furnished as good a product. But men like Pillsbury were
still not satisfied. Early in the seventies he and other Northwesterners went
to Europe to investigate the milling processes of various nations, but particularly of Hungary, where for decades wheat had been reduced to flour by
slowly passing it through a series of chilled iron rollers. In 1874 the Hungarian system was adopted, with modifications, in the Washburn and Pillsbury
establishments and gradually extended to other American mills. The result
was a fine flour which attracted every buyer by its snowy whiteness and
made better bread than Americans had ever before eaten.

Even more Aladdin-like was the development of the Pennsylvania oil
fields. Petroleum was destined to be the foundation for a host of new industries, and though few of its uses were discovered between 1865 and 1878,
these few were important in themselves and still more important for the
vistas they opened up. At the beginning of our period only six years had
elapsed since Colonel E. L. Drake sank the first oil well near the village of
Titusville in western Pennsylvania. In 1864 it was a district of more than four
hundred square miles dotted over with derricks and producing during the
twelve months more than two million one hundred thousand barrels. Already
some of the uses of the new product, which a half-dozen years earlier had
been a quack Indian medicine, were known through half the world. It
lubricated machinery in Manchester and Lyons; Swiss peasants and English
noblemen illuminated their abodes with its mellow rays; it was used to light
mariners in the wild Indian Ocean and along the South American coasts.
Many New Bedford mariners, reading the fate of their trade, had abandoned
whale fishing to see the oil fields. There was no lack of a market, and the
rapidity with which oil lamps sold in homes, rich and poor alike, assured it
of a steady expansion.

The hold which petroleum had gained upon the popular imagination in
the East was illustrated by the speculative mania of 1865, precipitated by
the sudden opening in January of a new basin on Pithole Creek. Within six
weeks an almost untouched sylvan district became the site of Pithole City
and its ten thousand inhabitants, which steadily increased until it held five

thousand more. The typical evolution of the mining or oil town was crowded into a few months: tents and shanties gave way to good frame residences, to long streets of restaurants, saloons, land offices and stores. For a time Pithole City, which not many years later reverted to an open wheat field, had a postal business outrivaling all cities in the state except Philadelphia. Stimulated by the new discovery, a fever of speculation seized the large Eastern centers. The capital of the oil companies of public record, which had been computed early that year at three hundred and twenty-six million dollars, rose by midsummer to at least five hundred million dollars, with new companies springing into life every hour. The rush of population lifted numerous hamlets almost overnight into small cities; the almost continuous loss of life due to carelessness and lawlessness proved no deterrent.

The chief initial difficulty of the industry, which despite constant vicissitudes and disappointments kept on growing, was to store and transport the oil. The expedients of the early days were picturesquely crude. Oil Creek had been navigable to the Allegheny in freshets and the desperate producers resorted for a time to artificial floods. That is, they repaired the old mill dams, collected water behind them and loosed it at prearranged hours, sweeping a crowded flotilla of oil boats—sometimes six hundred—down to the river. More commonly they relied upon teamsters who were as rough and undependable as the muddy roads. Naturally it was not long before inventive men hit upon the remedy, and in 1865 the first extensive pipe line, carrying eighty barrels of oil every hour over a stretch of seven miles, was placed in operation despite the teamsters' protests. It was followed by others, and the price of delivering oil to the Allegheny River boats was reduced from two dollars and fifty cents or three dollars a barrel to one dollar or even fifty cents. At the same time the tank car, invented by Charles P. Hatch, began to take the place of ordinary cars loaded with barrels. Before 1870 long lines of wooden tank cars became familiar in Pennsylvania and Ohio, and soon afterwards these leaky and inflammable carriers were replaced by tubular iron cars.

As the oil fields developed, a great new refining industry sprang up, offering work to thousands. By 1865 there were a number of large refineries, producing benzine, gasoline, coal oil, paraffin and tar. Very shortly the refineries began to mass themselves at two points, Cleveland and Pittsburgh. The former city in 1865 had thirty such businesses and at the end of the following year sixty. For some time the two centers ran neck and neck, but at the beginning of the seventies the superior position of Cleveland became evident, for having the Great Lakes and Erie Canal as well as the New York Central, it lay upon competitive transportation lines, while Pittsburgh was completely dependent upon the Pennsylvania Railroad. A centralization of the refining business was inevitable. The keen competition in refining methods, which were susceptible of great improvement, alone sufficed to drive many small manufactories from the arena.

It was at this moment that there appeared upon the scene the decisive factor in the sweep toward unification: a leader sufficiently astute, aggressive and merciless to drive it to its logical conclusion, the erection of a monopoly.

In 1865 John D. Rockefeller, a young Cleveland commission dealer of twenty-six, launched into the oil trade under the firm name of Rockefeller & Andrews. The Civil War had given him, as it did Armour and others, the capital needed for commercial undertakings on a large scale. Rockefeller saw that the necessary economies in refining were beyond the reach of any firm which had less than a half million in capital, and that the larger the unit the greater would be its efficiency. He pursued a policy of steady expansion. A second refinery was established. H. M. Flagler was accepted as partner, a New York office was opened, and one rival manufactory after another was absorbed. In June, 1870, there appeared the Standard Oil Company of Ohio, with a capital of a million dollars and a position of towering strength in the industry. It was the largest company in the largest refining center of the country, with a daily output of one thousand five hundred barrels, or about one seventh of the whole production of Cleveland. Rockefeller's ambition, however, was far from satisfied.

Thus the oil industry stood at a crucial point in 1870. Petroleum was being pumped from a large district of northwestern Pennsylvania, and wells were being sunk from West Virginia to Missouri in the hope of finding new fields. A business of which nobody had dreamed ten years earlier was giving the world more than five million barrels of oil annually, of which one hundred and fifty million gallons were going abroad, together with millions of gallons of gasoline, naphtha and benzine. Hardly less than two hundred million dollars was invested in the business. The refineries had to keep pace with the oil harvest: Pittsburgh was now refining almost six thousand barrels a day, New York City more than nine thousand, the oil fields about nine thousand and Cleveland about twelve thousand. The leading railways reaching the oil region, the Pennsylvania, New York Central and Erie, were keenly aware of the rich prize at stake and were bending every effort to gain the central stream of the traffic. It was under these circumstances that Rockefeller, who had already for two or three years insisted that the Erie and New York Central systems grant him secret freight rebates, planned a new coup. This was nothing less than the formation of a great pool of refiners which, by using the weapon of discriminatory freight rates, should take control of the oil market. The story of this attempt, its temporary failure and eventual success, must be left to a later time.

Meanwhile industries which could not be called new were exhibiting a large-scale standardization, involving also a concentration of capital, which gave them an appearance of entire novelty. In this roster the manufacture of men's clothing and of boots and shoes stood preeminent. During the Civil War a farsighted Scotchman, Gordon McKay, built up a huge business in supplying the army with machine-made shoes. Manufacturers East and West adopted the new machinery, which was rapidly improved, until it was hardly a fiction to say that leather was put in at one end and came out finished footwear at the other. Not only were shoes cheapened by the new process, but they were made more attractive and comfortable than the product of the ordinary artisan at the bench. A single workman was able to turn out three hundred pairs in one day, and a single factory in Massachusetts was soon producing as many shoes as thirty thousand Paris bootmakers.

The manufacture of ready-made clothes had as striking a growth just after the Civil War. The first thought of the discharged soldier was to obtain good civilian clothes and this demand was sustained by the development of the West and the heavy immigration. Since it was difficult for garment cutters to keep pace with the sewing machines, inventors brought out mechanical cloth cutters, the first of which was made on Staten Island in 1872. Few sights struck foreign travelers so forcibly as the enormous piles of ready-made suits exposed in shop windows at surprisingly low prices.

But this consolidation of industrial enterprises was evident in almost every field of business. Not until the Civil War did any cotton mill have a hundred thousand spindles, or any iron furnace produce more than three hundred tons a week. The success of the Waltham enterprise in making watches by factory methods instead of slowly and expensively by hand led to the establishment of the American Watch Factory at Elgin, Illinois, in 1865. The sewing-machine factory, the farm-implement factory, the piano and organ factory, all improved their processes, their subdivision of labor and their capacity for quantity production in these flush years. Many small businesses sprang into a hothouse life, for money was abundant, but all the while the principal manufactories—those at the top—grew astonishingly. Less and less did the American people consume goods made in small and simple establishments managed by individual proprietors; more and more did they use goods from large factories managed by corporate boards.

A pronounced westward thrust of industry became evident quite apart from the birth of the meat-packing and flour-milling undertakings of the Northwest. Besides the Elgin watch factory and the Union Stock Yards in Chicago, the first year of peace saw large pottery works started at Peoria, woolen mills at Atchison, a farm-implement factory at Moline, and an important stove foundry at Quincy, Illinois. Two years later George Pullman founded the Pullman Palace Car Company in Chicago. William H. Seward remarked of McCormick's reaper that through its use "the line of civilization moves westward thirty miles each year," and it was natural that the makers of agricultural machinery should move west too. McCormick's own factory stood on the north bank of the Chicago River. In Akron and Canton, Ohio, during 1865 about ten thousand mowing machines were made, though the price averaged one hundred and twenty-five dollars each. Two of the heritages of the war were a beet-sugar industry in Illinois and Wisconsin, and a flourishing tobacco industry in the latter state. Particularly interesting was the progress of the brewing business in St. Louis and Milwaukee, with their large German population, for the nation was beginning to appreciate the fact that beer was less harmful than ale or spirits, while the excise tax placed upon it was comparatively small. In 1865 Milwaukee, where the Schlitz and Pabst companies were active, was producing fifty-five thousand barrels of beer, while in 1873 the sale had risen to two hundred and sixty thousand.

This westward march of manufacturing was plainly indicated by the census of 1870. It showed that in the nation as a whole the number of establishments had increased in the decade almost eighty per cent. But in Indiana they had more than doubled, in Illinois they had trebled, and in Missouri they had more than trebled. Before the war the great states along the upper Mississippi had been almost wholly agricultural and their cities had depended upon the trade of the farms; now the smoke of factory chimneys showed that they were definitely passing out of the pioneer state. In the East, the agglutination of industry in strategically placed centers interested every observer. Bridgeport, Connecticut, for example, was just rising to a place of prominence as the seat of the Wheeler & Wilson Sewing-Machine Company; the Simpson Waterproof Cloth Company, which had made trainloads of raincoats for the soldiers; the Hotchkiss Company, which had turned from shells to general hardware; and the newly established Mallory Hat Company.

Financial institutions responded to the buoyant expansion of the time like vegetation to a tropical sun. The inflation of credit made banking a business which tyros could enter with success. The federal government having established a great new national banking system, between the fall of 1864 and the fall of 1865 the number of such banks rose from five hundred and eighty-four to 1,566. But even more remarkable was the multiplication of savings banks. The workmen were enjoying what seemed high pay, and needed repositories for it. In Massachusetts there were ninety-three savings banks in 1862, and one hundred and eighty in 1875; in New York State in the same period the number increased from seventy-four to one hundred and fifty-eight. Costly offices were hired and fitted up, high rates of interest were promised and extravagant salaries were granted. Insurance companies, many of them speculative ventures with insufficient capital, incompetent management and a shocking inattention to sound actuarial principles, rose on every hand. Until these years trust companies had been almost unknown in the United States, but now there sprang up a sudden realization of their usefulness and opportunities, and between 1864 and 1875 no fewer than forty came into existence. Many observers became alarmed by the disturbance of the former balance between production and consumption, pointing to the huge growth of all businesses of exchange—trade agencies, commission houses, brokerage, banking, retailing—as not wholly legitimate but in large part the forced fruit of inflation. When the census of 1870 was taken, it was found that while the population had been increasing twenty-two and one-half per cent, the trading classes, including those engaged in transportation, had increased forty per cent. Francis A. Walker computed that the nation was maintaining a useless array of middlemen and retailers equivalent to the standing armies of the British Empire and with a greater number of dependents.

In answer to the heavy demands of industry upon the labor market, and to the alluring spectacle of prosperity, comfort and opportunity presented by American life, the stream of European immigration rose rapidly to a torrent. The Fenian movement and land troubles in Ireland, the panic of 1866 in England and the Austro-Prussian conflict gave tens of thousands of

Europeans a special incentive to emigrate to the United States. For the first time American manufacturers combined in considerable numbers to send agents to Europe to stimulate emigration, and their efforts advertised the opportunities open to active men. The increasing speed and cheapness of transatlantic travel was also a factor of importance. In 1856 a mere handful of European newcomers, some five thousand in a total of one hundred and thirty-one thousand, had arrived in steamships, the others using sailing vessels; but in 1865 the great majority were transported by steam. Not quite a quarter of a million immigrants were admitted in 1865, and thereafter the number rose year by year until in 1873 it reached the then amazing total of four hundred and sixty thousand.

∾§ §∾

THE history of humanity has witnessed many great migrations and with them attending upheavals. The centuries of Pax Romana ended in the West with the barbarians surging over the imperial borders. We forget that these events of migration continue into the present century. For what sets apart an American is that we are all, with the solitary exception of the Indian, descendants of, if we are not ourselves, immigrants. It is the bond of union which makes us all one.

The dimensions of this experience can hardly be overstated. Between 1840 and 1924, no less than 37 million immigrants flocked to American shores. They came from the anguish and misery of the potato blight that racked Ireland between 1846 and 1850, killing by hunger and disease no less than a million souls, and sending into panicked flight 3 million more. Out of the social dislocations that shook Germany and Scandinavia between 1850 and 1880, as the industrialization and the political unification of the former, and the internal disunity which racked the united kingdom of Sweden and Norway undermined old expectations, millions more joined the procession westward. The Irish, German, Scandinavian, and the Britisher added nearly 10 million to the American population between 1840 and 1880. These were called the "old immigration," supposedly because they were more readily integrated into the "native" population.

The stream from northwestern Europe slackened to a rivulet after 1880 but grew to flood proportions as the Jew fled the Russian pogrom, the Italian peasant forsook a land that one recent author wrote "even Christ forgot," and the Slav abandoned Tsar, Emperor, Sultan, and roboti: the system of labor that bound him to the land to work for those who possessed the land. The exotic touch was added as the Greek abandoned his sun-baked acre and the Oriental turned east toward the lure of the Pacific coast.

By the end of the nineteenth century, the United States, unknowingly, had become the first multi-ethnic, multi-racial, and multi-creed society of the world. Its cities were crowded with inhabitants drawn from the world metropolises and many of its farms knew the touch of a peasantry rooted to the land even as the crops they grew. Out of the sweat of their labor the wealth of a virgin continent was made. In the babel of a thousand tongues, God was invoked to make the new land a better land. The first American had turned his back upon Europe only to have the European join him. The century-long isolation of America from European political upheaval was only half the story, for America in accepting the immigrant never strayed far from the latest wind of doctrine that swept European society. Nor did she in granting refuge lose sight of her revolutionary tradition; instead, she saw the newcomer as proof that she led the vanguard of humanity.

Oscar Handlin (1915-), a 1952 Pulitzer Prize winner, has probably done more than any living historian to capture the drama of the immigrant migration. As the time recedes from when America welcomed all, the United States reaps the full richness of these millions of voyagers. Out of the multiplicity of American origins, the nation forges a pluralistic democracy that will make of her variety a legacy of richness and the talisman of a new society.

THE UPROOTED

by Oscar Handlin

Settlement in America had snipped the continuity of the immigrants' work and ideas, of their religious life. It would also impose a new relationship to the world of space about them. In the Old Country setting, the physical scene had been integral with the existence of the men in it. Changes would have explosive repercussions.

In the United States, the newcomers pushed their roots into many different soils. Along the city's unyielding asphalt streets, beside the rutted roads of mill or mining towns, amidst the exciting prairie acres, they established the homes of the New World. But wherever the immigrants went, there was one common experience they shared: nowhere could they transplant the European village. Whatever the variations among environments in America, none was familiar. The pressure of that strangeness exerted a deep influence upon the character of resettlement, upon the usual forms of behavior, and upon the modes of communal action that emerged as the immigrants became Americans.

The old conditions of living could not survive in the new conditions of space. Ways long taken for granted in the village adjusted slowly and painfully to density of population in the cities, to disorder in the towns, and to distance on the farms. That adjustment was the means of creating the new communities within which these people would live.

Although the great mass of immigrants spent out their days in the great cities, there was always an unorganized quality to settlement in such places that left a permanent impress upon every fresh arrival. Chance was so large an element in the course of migration, it left little room for planning. The place of landing was less often the outcome of an intention held at the outset of the journey than of blind drift along the routes of trade or of a sudden halt due to the accidents of the voyage. Consequently the earliest concentrations of the foreign-born were in the chain of Atlantic seaports: Boston, Philadelphia, Baltimore, New Orleans, and most of all New York, the unrivaled mart of Europe's commerce with America. For the same reasons, later concentrations appeared at the inland termini, the points of exchange between rail and river or lake traffic—Cleveland, Chicago, Cincinnati, Pittsburgh, and St. Louis.

In all such places the newcomers pitched themselves in the midst of communities that were already growing rapidly and that were therefore already crowded. Between 1840 and 1870, for instance, the population of New York City mounted by fully 50 per cent every ten years; for every two people at the start of a decade, there were three at its end. (In all, the 312,000 residents of 1840 had become 3,437,000 in 1900.) Chicago's rise was even more precipitate; the 4000 inhabitants there in 1840 numbered 1,700,000 in 1900. Every ten-year interval saw two people struggling for the space formerly occupied by one.

These largest cities were representative of the rest. The natural increase through the excess of births over deaths, with the additional increase through the shift of native-born population from rural to urban areas, and with the further increase through overseas immigration, all contributed to the enormous growth of American municipalities. To house all the new city dwellers was a problem of staggering proportions. Facilities simply did not keep pace with the demand.

To house the immigrants was more difficult still. For these people had not the mobility to choose where they should live or the means to choose how. Existing on the tenuous income supplied by unskilled labor, they could not buy homes; nor could they lay out much in payment of rent. Their first thought in finding accommodations was that the cost be as little as possible. The result was they got as little as possible.

The willingness to accept a minimum of comfort and convenience did not, however, mean that such quarters would always be available. Under the first impact of immigration, the unprepared cities had not ready the housing immigrants could afford. The newcomers were driven to accept hand-me-downs, vacated places that could be converted to their service at a profit.

The immigrants find their first homes in quarters the old occupants no longer desire. As business grows, the commercial center of each city begins to blight the neighboring residential districts. The well-to-do are no longer willing to live in close proximity to the bustle of warehouses and offices; yet that same proximity sets a high value on real estate. To spend money on the repair or upkeep of houses in such areas is only wasteful; for they will soon be torn down to make way for commercial buildings. The simplest, most profitable use is to divide the old mansions into tiny lodgings.

The rent on each unit will be low; but the aggregate of those sums will, without substantial investment or risk, return larger dividends than any other present use of the property.

Such accommodations have additional attractions for the immigrants. They are close to the familiar region of the docks and they are within walking distance of the places where labor is hired; precious carfare will be saved by living here. In every American city some such district of first settlement receives the newcomers.

Not that much is done to welcome them. The carpenters hammer shut connecting doors and build rude partitions up across the halls; middle-class homes thus become laborers'—only not one to a family, but shared among many. What's more, behind the original structures are grassy yards where children once had run about at play. There is to be no room for games now. Sheds and shanties, hurriedly thrown up, provide living space; and if a stable is there, so much the better: that too can be turned to account. In 1850 already in New York some seven thousand households are finding shelter in such rear buildings. By this time too ingenuity has uncovered still other resources: fifteen hundred cellars also do service as homes.

If these conversions are effected without much regard for the convenience of the ultimate occupants, they nevertheless have substantial advantages. The carpenter aims to do the job as expeditiously as possible; he has not the time to contrive the most thorough use of space; and waste square feet leave luxurious corners. There are limits to the potentialities for crowding in such quarters.

There were no such limits when enterprising contractors set to work devising edifices more suitable for the reception of these residents. As the population continued to grow, and the demand with it, perspicacious owners of real estate saw profit in the demolition of the old houses and the construction, between narrow alleys, of compact barracks that made complete use of every inch of earth.

Where once had been Mayor Delavall's orchard, Cherry Street in New York ran its few blocks to the East River shipyards. At Number 36, in 1853, stood Gotham Court, one of the better barrack buildings. Five stories in height, it stretched back one hundred and fifty feet from the street, between two tight alleys (one nine, the other seven feet wide). Onto the more spacious alley opened twelve doors through each of which passed the ten families that lived within, two to each floor in identical two-room apartments (one room, 9 x 14; one bedroom, 9- x -6). Here without interior plumbing or heat were the homes of five hundred people. Ten years later, there were some improvements: for the service of the community, a row of privies in the basement, flushed occasionally by Croton water. But by then there were more than eight hundred dwellers in the structure, which indeed continued in use till the very end of the century.

That these conditions were not then reckoned outlandish was shown in the model workmen's home put up by philanthropic New Yorkers at Elizabeth and Mott Street. Each suite in this six-story structure had three rooms; but the rooms were smaller (4 x 11, 8 x 7, and 8 x 7). There were gas lights in the halls; but the water closets were in sheds in the alleys. And well over half the rooms had no windows at all.

At the middle of the nineteenth century, these developments were still chaotic, dependent upon the fancy of the individual builder. But the pressure of rising demand and the pattern of property holding gradually shaped a common form for the tenement house. The older barracks still left waste space in alleys, halls, and stair wells; and they did not conform to the uniform city real-estate plot, twenty or twenty-five feet wide and one hundred feet deep. As the cost of land went up, builders were increasingly constrained to confine themselves to those rectangular blocks while pushing their edifices upward and eliminating the interstitial alleys.

Ultimately, the dumbbell tenement lined street after street, a most efficient structure that consumed almost the entire area of the real-estate plot. Attached to its neighbors on either side, it left vacant only a strip, perhaps ten feet deep, in the rear. On a floor space of approximately twenty by ninety feet, it was possible, within this pattern, to get four four-room apartments.

The feat was accomplished by narrowing the building at its middle so that it took on the shape of a dumbbell. The indentation was only two-and-a-half feet wide and varied in length from five to fifty feet; but, added to the similar indentations of the adjoining houses, it created on each side an air-shaft five feet wide. In each apartment three of the rooms could present their windows to the shaft, draw from it air and light as well; only one chamber in each suite need face upon the street or rear yard. The stairs, halls, and common water closets were cramped into the narrow center of the building so that almost the whole of its surface was available for living quarters.

These structures were at least six stories in height, sometimes eight. At the most moderate reckoning, twenty-four to thirty-two families could be housed on this tiny space, or more realistically, anywhere from one hundred and fifty to two hundred human beings. It was not a long block that held ten such tenements on either side of the street, not an unusual block that was home for some four thousand people.

There were drastic social consequences to living under these dense conditions. The immigrants had left villages which counted their populations in scores. In the Old World a man's whole circle of acquaintances had not taken in as many individuals as lived along a single street here. By a tortuous course of adjustments, the newcomers worked out new modes of living in response to their environment. But the cost of those adjustments was paid out of the human energies of the residents and through the physical deterioration of the districts in which they lived.

The tenement flourished most extensively in New York, the greatest point of immigration concentration. But it was also known in Boston and in the other Atlantic ports. In the interior cities it was less common; there land values were not so rigid and commercial installations not such barriers to the centrifugal spread of population. From the barracklike buildings of the area of first settlement, the immigrants could move out to smaller units where at least the problems of density were less oppressive. Little two-story

cottages that held six families were characteristic of places like Buffalo. Elsewhere were wooden three- or four-floor structures that contained a dozen
households. Even single homes were to be found, dilapidated shanties or
jerry-built boxes low in rent. Yet internally these accommodations were
not superior to those of the tenement. In one form or another, the available
housing gave the districts to which the immigrants went the character of
slums.

Well, they were not ones to choose, who had lived in the thatched peasant
huts of home. Nor was it unbearably offensive to reside in the least pleasant
parts of the city, in Chicago over against the slaughterhouses, in Boston
hemmed in by the docks and markets of the North End, in New York
against the murky river traffic of the East Side. Such disadvantages they
could survive. The hardship came in more subtle adjustments demanded of
them.

Certainly the flats were small and overcrowded. In no room of the dumbbell tenement could you pace off more than eleven feet; and the reforming
architects of 1900 still thought of chambers no larger than those of Gotham
Court. In addition, the apartments shrank still further when shared by more
than one family or when they sheltered lodgers, as did more than half those
in New York at the end of the century. But that was not the worst of it.

Here is a woman. In the Old Country she had lived much of her life, done
most of her work, outdoors. In America, the flat confines her. She divides up
her domain by calico sheets hung on ropes, tries to make a place for her
people and possessions. But there is no place and she has not room to turn
about. It is true, everything is in poor repair, the rain comes through the
ceilings, the wind blows dirt through the cracks in the wall. But she does not
even know how to go about restoring order, establishing cleanliness. She
breaks her back to exterminate the proliferating vermin. What does she get?
A dozen lice behind the collar.

The very simplest tasks become complex and disorganizing. Every day
there is a family to feed. Assume she knows how to shop, and can manage
the unfamiliar coal stove or gas range. But what does one do with rubbish
who has never known the meaning of waste? It is not really so important to
walk down the long flight of narrow stairs each time there are some scraps
to be disposed of. The windows offer an easier alternative. After all, the
obnoxious wooden garbage boxes that adorn the littered fronts of the houses
expose their contents unashamed through split sides and, rarely emptied,
themselves become the nests of boldly foraging rodents.

The filthy streets are seldom cleaned; the municipality is not particularly
solicitous of these, the poorest quarters of the city. The alleys are altogether
passed by and the larger thoroughfares receive only occasionally the services
of the scavenger. The inaccessible alleys and rear yards are never touched
and, to be sure, are redolent of the fact. In the hot summer months the
stench of rotting things will mark these places and the stained snow of winter
will not conceal what lies beneath. Here and there an unwitting newcomer
tries the disastrous experiment of keeping a goat, adds thereby to the
distinctive flavor of his neighborhood.

It was the same in every other encounter with the new life. Conveniences not missed in the villages became sore necessities in the city; although often the immigrants did not know their lack till dear experience taught them. Of what value were sunlight and fresh air on the farm? But how measure their worth for those who lived in the three hundred and fifty thousand dark interior rooms of New York in 1900!

There was the rude matter of what Americans called sanitation. Some of the earliest buildings had had no privies at all; the residents had been expected to accommodate themselves elsewhere as best they could. Tenements from mid-century onward had generally water closets in the yards and alleys, no great comfort to the occupants of the fifth and sixth floors. The newest structures had two toilets to each floor; but these were open to the custom of all comers, charged to the care of none, and left to the neglect of all. If in winter the pipes froze in unheated hallways and the clogged contents overflowed, weeks would go by before some dilatory repairman set matters right. Months thereafter a telling odor hung along the narrow hallways.

What of it? The filth was inescapable. In these districts where the need was greatest, the sewerage systems were primitive and ineffectual. Open drains were long common; in Boston one such, for years, tumbled down the slope of Jacob's Ladder in the South Cove; and in Chicago the jocosely named Bubbly Creek wended its noisome way aboveground until well into the twentieth century.

With the water supply there had always been trouble at home too: poor wells, shallow, and inconveniently situated. The inconvenience here was not unexpected. Still it was a burden to carry full tubs and jugs from the taps in the alley up the steep stairs. Not till late was city water directly connected with the toilets; it was later still to reach the kitchen sink; and bathrooms had not yet put in an appearance in these quarters. Then, too, the consequences were more painful: city dirt was harder to scrub away, and there was no nearby creek. It could well be, as they came to say, that a man got a good bath only twice in his life: from midwife and undertaker.

All might yet be tolerable were not the confining dimensions of the flat so oppressive. The available space simply would not yield to all the demands made upon it. Where were the children to play if the fields were gone? Where were things to be stored or clothes to be hung? Beds or bedding consumed the bedroom; there was only one living room, and sink and stove left little free of that. The man in the evening, come home from work, found not a niche for rest; the tiny intervals of leisure were wasted for want of a place to spend them. Privacy now was more often sought for than in the Old Country where every person and every thing had its accustomed spot. Yet privacy now was difficult to achieve; there was no simple way of dividing space too small to share. Under pressure of the want, the constricted beings bowed to a sense of strain.

Disorganization affects particularly the life of the home. In these tiny rooms that now are all they call their home, many traditional activities wither and disappear. Not here will the friends be welcomed, festivals commemorated, children taught, and the family unite to share in the warmth of its security. Emptied of the meaning of these occurrences and often crowded with strange lodgers, home is just the feeding and sleeping place. All else moves to the outside.

The street becomes the great artery of life for the people of these districts. Sometimes, the boys and girls play in back in the narrow yards, looking up at the lines of drying clothes that spiderweb the sky above them. More often the crowded street itself is the more attractive playground. They run in games through the moving traffic, find fun in the appearance of some hopeful street musician, or regard with dejected envy the wares of the itinerant vendors of seasonal delicacies, the sweet shaved ice of summer, the steaming potatoes and chestnuts of fall and winter.

The adults too drift out, sit on the steps, flow over onto the sidewalks. The women bring their work outdoors, the men at evening hang about, now and then talk. They begin to be neighborly, learn to be sensitive to each other. That is the good of it.

There is also the bad. The street in its strangeness is the evidence of the old home's disintegration. Why, the very aspect is forbidding: the dear sun never shines brightly, the still air between the high buildings is so saturated with stench it would take a dragon to hold out. These are all signs of the harshness of the physical environment, of the difficulties of living in these quarters, of the disintegration here of old ways. Those children in earnest play at the corner—who controls them, to what discipline are they subject? They do not do the things that children ought. No one does the things he ought. The place prevents it.

Almost resignedly, the immigrants witnessed in themselves a deterioration. All relationships became less binding, all behavior more dependent on individual whim. The result was a marked personal decline and a noticeable wavering of standards.

Some of the reactions to the new conditions of living were immediate, direct, and overt. The low level of health and the high incidence of disease were certain products of overcrowding. Residents of the tenements did not need the spotted maps of later students to tell them where tuberculosis hit, a terror of an illness that spread from victim to victim in the stifling rooms. If the cholera came, or smallpox, or diphtheria—and all did in their time—it was impossible to limit their decimating course. Little else by now remained communal; but contagion and infection these people could not help but share with each other.

The mortality rate was an indication of their helplessness against disease. The immigrants were men and women in the prime of life, yet they died more rapidly than the generality of Americans. Everywhere their life expectancy was lower; and, as might be anticipated, it was particularly infants who suffered. In one Chicago precinct at the end of the nineteenth century, three babies of every five born died before they reached their first birthday.

That, they might say, was sad, but in the nature of things. No act of will, no deed of commission or omission could stay the coming of death.

The grim reaper, an old familiar fellow, had simply emigrated with them. But other consequences of living in these quarters confronted the new-comers with a choice or at least with the appearance of a choice. Under the disorganizing pressure of the present environment, men found it diffi-cult, on the basis of past habits, to determine what their own roles should be. They could question neither the validity of the old values nor the exigencies of the new necessities. Having inherited the conceptions of their proper roles, they had been projected into a situation where every ele-ment conspired to force them into deviations. They yielded at the points of least resistance; not every one of them, but many, at one point or another. And those who withstood the pressure did so at the expense of continuous, exhausting strain.

What if a man were to think then (as some did) and say to himself: *Why shall I forever beat my head against this unyielding wall? There will be no end to my toil, and my labor gains me nothing. For what a life do I work. And did not the time in any case come of idleness, when not a crust was in the house and I must go cap in hand for help?* His whole being would at first have revolted at the indignity of the thought; in the peasant world the person who did not earn his own bread was not fully a man, lost thereby status and esteem in the eyes of the community. But what status had the laborer in America to lose, what esteem? Was it then such a reprehensible thing to get by without work?

They recalled as they thought of it that at home also there were some who had habitually lived at the expense of others. That had itself been not so terrible; and indeed the beggars had even a magical or religious quality. The humiliation had come from the circumstance that forced a man into alms seeking: from his improvidence, or lack of foresight, or dissolute char-acter, or spendthrift habits. But in America, pauperism was not sought out; it came of itself to good and wicked alike. No blame could attach here to him who could not always earn a livelihood, who came to depend for his sustenance on the gifts of charity.

In what they had there was precious little to keep those weary of the effort from following the persuasive logic of this line of thought. Almost without self-pity and altogether without reproach, they surrendered to the institutions that maintained the dependent, or they abandoned their families, or they became not quite permanent clients of the relief agencies. If they were aged and infirm the choice was quicker made; if they were victims of accident or illness, quicker still; and if they were left widowed or father-less, then the doubt hardly existed.

Suppose a man found the surrender to pauperism no solution, was unwill-ing to throw up the burden of his own maintenance; but thought about it and struggled with it. Every morning he would wake to face it, see through the big eyes of fear the oppressive problems of the day ahead. He could look through the narrow airshaft out at the blank wall of his own exist-ence, regard despondently the symbols of a hopeless future. Loaded down with unbearable obligations; many sighed with him who admitted, *Were it not for my soul for which I am anxious, lest I lose it in eternity, I should have drowned myself.* Some, in that last extremity, found the charge of their own souls too heavy a responsibility.

Others yielded in a different way. They closed their eyes; and as the lids of delusion fell and blotted out the brass ugliness of the bed's footboard, they perceived in the sudden perceptions of madness visions of the utmost delight. The darkening walls fell away, revealed an undefined brightness through which they, yes they themselves, ran lightly and effortless, wrapped up in the enjoyment of some unimaginable pleasure.

Or, as on any other morning, you might come down in the chill pre-dawn, half awake on the stairs, counting the creak of your own treads, and turn, in hope of something today, onto the street that led to market or shop. Only there would be something peculiar this now in the shape of the shadows as you hurried from island to island around the flickering pillars of light. As your thoughts wandered their habitual way over yesterday's disappointments and the fears of tomorrow, you began to pick out the fall of following footsteps; round a corner and still they came; again; till, trotting heavily, you outdistanced them—that time. What if they should lie in secret wait, however; and what if among the jostling strangers who swept around you as you hastened onto the avenue were those already on to you? Who would hear your cry, or care? They eyed you with their hostile stares, condemning, pressed in upon you in seeming random movements. When you stopped against the tall board fence to take the dreadful blow, you knew at once that this was he, and struck and struck, till they pinned you down; and that was all, while the foreign tongues murmured on above you.

The woman too found relief; so many dangers worried her. Today they would not survive, the man and the young ones perilously outside. He would lose the job or not bring home the pay. There would be not enough to eat and, sickening, no money for the doctor. She could no longer swallow her anxiety and rubbed the harder on the board, over and over, for the gray spots kept reappearing as she endlessly washed them out.

Psychopathic disorders and neuroses, they were all one to the admitting officers who kept the count of the insane. On their rolls the immigrants were disproportionately prominent.

There were other means of release, temporary of duration and therefore more subject to control. It was thus possible, for a time, to dissolve in alcohol the least soluble of problems. After a day's effort to hammer happiness out of the unyielding American environment it was good, now and then, to go not to the narrow realities of home but to the convivial places where the glass played the main part. The setting could take a variety of forms: basement shops, combination kitchen-and-bars, little cafés, the Irish grocery of 1850, the German Bierstube of 1870, the Italian speak-easy of 1900 to which prohibition would later bring another clientele. But the end was the same, a temporary relaxation of tension. And the end was so clear that some could achieve it alone, in the fastness of their own rooms, with the solitary company of a bottle.

There were immigrants who came to America with the inclination to drunkenness already well established. In Ireland, whisky went farther than bread as a relief from hunger; in Norway, eighteen quarts of alcohol were consumed for every person in the country each year; and elsewhere through Europe the habit of imbibing was well known. There were other new-comers who learned to know the consolations of a dram in the course of the crossing. A bit of grog was the regular prescription for sea-sickness; if it effected no cure, it dulled the misery.

It was that relief a man needed as much as the eyes in his head. Some-times he drank away without thought what he had bathed in sweat to earn; but he gained in return an interval free of recollection or anticipation. In the good company, as his burdens lightened, he discovered in himself alto-gether unexpected but exhilarating powers acquired daring and self-confi-dence beyond any sober hope. Well, and sometimes it would lead to a brawl, and the falling clubs of policemen, and the cold awakening of a cell; or, if not that, simply to the next day's throbbing reckoning of costs: what things the money might have bought! But there was none to point the finger of blame; and temptation came again and again. Not a few succumbed in every group of immigrants, though more in some groups than in others.

There was still another way of entering immediately into a realm of hope that shone in bright contrast to the visible dreariness about them. In that realm the evil dame, Chance, was transfigured into a luminous goddess; no longer as in real life did she strike down the lowly, but elevated them. Chance, here, ceased to deal out disaster; instead, conjured up the most heartwarming dreams.

Sometimes the men gambled among themselves, drew cards or lots for little stakes. There was a finger game Italians played, and among eastern Europeans a liking for pinochle. But these were sociable as much as gam-bling occasions, and had unpleasant disadvantages. The sum of little for-tunes around the table hardly made a total worth the winning. One man's gain was another's loss; the joy of one, another's sorrow. Chance had not free rein; skill was as well involved, and the strain of calculation. Most of all, there was not the solitude in which the mind could drift away from time and place and rock itself in the comfort of hope.

Much preferable was some form of the lottery: the stakes were small, the rewards enormous; one might win, but none lost much; and chance was absolute. Lottery took many guises from the informal picks and chances of bar and shop to the highly organized enterprises city-wide in extension. Beneath was the attractiveness of an identical dream.

He can sit with a card, one of scores, in a club or saloon, check the squares, wait the call. Over and over and over again the little cage spins and no one knows when the little cage stops and a little ball hops and the number comes forth for the fortunate man. There's no telling—who knows? This may be when. The word's on his lips; let but chance give the sign and he will rise, *keno, lotto, bingo;* and all will be his.

She buys the slip from a policy man, who may be the corner grocer, the mailman, or anyone who in a daily round encounters a constant circle of people. Her number costs what she can spare, a dime, a nickel, just a penny. She chooses by what signs chance may give, a dream, an omen, a sudden intuition; and all day carries hope in her apron.

Did they really think to win who could not afford to lose? Yes, in a way they did, although they knew what odds were against them. But *why not* they? They would grant you that thousands lost for one who won, but could they surrender that one hope too? His hand that holds the card is soft and white, a hand that signs checks and gestures commands, the hand of a man who will drive to the comfort of a decent home. Her slip rests in the pocket of a gown, a gown that rustles leisurely as she walks with shining children up the steps. Indeed they have so often spent the money, and had the pleasure of dreaming it, it hardly mattered that they lost. At the price they paid, such dreams were cheap enough.

It was significant of such deviations—pauperism, insanity, intemperance, gambling—that they represented a yielding to the disorganizing pressure of the environment. These men did not step out of their roles as sober, industrious, thrifty breadwinners as a means of defying society, as a pure act of will. They deviated out of compulsion.

Where willful defiance of law was involved, the immigrants drew back. The rate of crime among the foreign-born was lower than among natives. There were frequent arrests for drunkenness; but those involved neither will nor, generally, crimes. And occasional petty thefts represented mostly a lack of clarity about property distinctions that had not applied at home. The peasant had recognized certain kinds of taking that were not robbery, by one member of a family from another, for instance, or of raw materials not the product of human labor, such as wood or game. The attempt to do the same in the United States led to trouble.

But the crime willfully planned and executed for gain rarely involved the immigrant. The lawbreakers often congregated in the districts in which the newcomers lived and sometimes recruited the American-born children, but not the immigrants themselves.

It was not hard to know what was going on, for after 1870 certainly these quarters were plunged into a regime of violence from which no one could escape. Organized gangs in alliance with the police terrorized whole territories. It was in the North End in Boston or down near the East Side in New York that their enterprises could most conveniently be planted: dance halls, saloons, gambling places, houses of prostitution, out of sight of the respectable citizens. The guardians of the law were unconcerned, beyond the need of recouping the investments paid out for their jobs. Already by 1900 Al Adams, the New York policy king, had a wide-spread network; and increasingly crime was removed from the area of free enterprise.

The sharpers and thugs found in the poor their readiest victims. Sometimes the boys at the corner would beat up a passer-by not so much for the handful of change they shook out of his pockets, but simply because his looks offended them, or for no reason at all. There'd be no thought of complaints; no one would listen and he who bore tales to the authorities would find the gangsters swift and merciless in retaliation. Death was never far from the door, why hasten its visit? In the New World, the immigrants feared to have recourse to the traditional peasant crimes of revenge, arson, and homicide. Here was too much risk, too great an exercise of the will.

The inability to use force was the crowning irony of the immigrants' disorganization; the fact that they were law-abiding was less the product of their own choice than of fear to make a choice. As in so many other ways, the constricting environment forced them into deviations from their proper roles. If only a small number actually plunged into pauperism, or insanity, or drunkenness, many more lived long on the verge. And more still lived under the tension of avoiding the plunge; you could tell it by their new habits, endless smoking and the intrusion of profane swearing into their conversation.

Without a doubt they wished also to escape from the physical environment itself. As the years went by they got to know that the city held also pleasant tree-shaded streets where yards and little gardens set the houses off from each other. To these green spaces the most daring hearts aspired.

After 1850, cheaper rapid-transit systems brought the suburbs closer to the heart of the city. On the street railway the trolley took the horse's place and was joined by subway and elevated lines. Through these channels, the laboring masses spilled out from the district of first settlement to the surrounding regions. Naturally, this was a selective process; those who had a modicum of well-being, who could afford the higher rents and transportation charges, moved most freely. The poorest were immobilized by their poverty.

Those who went gained by going, but not by any means all they hoped for. Somehow, what they touched turned to dross. The fine house they saw in their mind's vision across the bridge or over the ferry turned out in actuality to have been converted into narrow flats for several families. In the empty spaces, little cottages rose; and long rows of two- and three-story attached buildings shut off the sight of the trees. The trouble was, so many moved that these newer places began to repeat the experience of the area of first settlement.

Never mind, for a time at least it was better. There was room to keep a goat, a few chickens; the men could sit at ease in their own front rooms facing the friendly street, while the women visited through the sociable low windows. This was a home to which attachments could grow, a place where deviations were less likely to appear.

And if in time the pressure of mounting population brought here too the tenement, and the spreading slum engulfed this first refuge, then those who could launched upon a second remove. Then a third. Till at last the city was a patchwork of separated districts, the outlines of which were shaped by the transit facilities, by the quality of available housing, and by the prior occupancy of various groups of immigrants. Always in this winnowing process the poorest were left in the older sections; the ability to move outward went with prosperity. Unfortunately it was the outer regions that were the thinnest settled. Least capable of organizing their lives to the new environment, the great mass long clustered at the center.

On the farms, space was too ample, not too little. Emptiness, not over-crowding, was the disorganizing element; and for those whose habits of life were developed in the peasant village, the emptiness of the prairie farm was in its own way as troublesome as the crowding of the city slum.

Here they called them neighbors who lived two or three miles off. Here one could stand on the highest rise of land and see nowhere but in the one farmstead any sign of man's tenancy. Such distances were too great to per-mit easy adjustment by the newcomers.

The peculiar characteristics of the prairie where the distances were great-est tested the immigrants to the utmost. In the midst of the open places they came by wagon and confronted the problem of shelter. They would live in what they could themselves build, for there was no community to help them; and certainly nothing was ready, awaiting their arrival. If they were fortunate, they found a nearby wood where the stove could rest and they could camp while the men chopped the logs for the cabin.

The cabin, no doubt, had its defects as a residence. It was small, perhaps twelve by fourteen feet in all; and above and below and about was mud, for the floor was as they found it and the spaces in the roof and walls were chinked with clay to keep the weather out.

But the people who settled into such quarters had only to compare situa-tions with those who found no wood nearby, to count their own blessings. The cost of bringing timber in was at first prohibitive. If there were none on the spot, home would be of another material. Some would burrow dug-outs into the slopes, return unknowingly to the life of the caves. Many cut the sun-baked surface of the earth, piled the sod in a double wall with dirt between, and in these huts spent a long period of trial.

Often years went by before such farmers advanced to the dignity of a frame house, with separate plastered rooms. There were first a barn and all the appurtenances of agriculture to be acquired. Meanwhile they got on in narrow quarters, felt the wind of winter through the cracks, heard the sides settle in the spring thaw, saw surprised snakes or gophers penetrate the floor.

Under such circumstances, there was an additional depth to their help-lessness. No trees shielded them against the blast of winds. They were parched in the dry heat and they perished in the merciless blizzards. Hail and drought came and the clouds of grasshoppers that ate up their crops. On a limited monotonous diet the immigrants sickened, from the sudden shifts in climate the ague got them, from the prevalence of dirt, the itch. No doctors were near and home remedies or self-prescribed cures from bottles put a sad but decisive end to their misery. Alone in these distances they could expect no help.

That was the worst of it. The isolation which all immigrants sensed to some degree, on the farm was absolute; and not only on the prairie but everywhere. In the older Midwestern states, where the newcomers were not the first to settle, they found homes built and clearings made at their arrival; and soil and climate were not so hostile. Still, even there, they were detached, cut off from the company of other men. Each family was thrown in upon itself; every day the same faces round the same table and never the sight of outsiders. To have no familiar of one's own age and sex was a hard deprivation.

They would think sometimes of the friendly village ways, of the common tasks lightened for being done in common; they would remember the cheering inn, and the road on which some reassuring known figure could always be seen. At such times, alone in the distance, helpless in their isolation, a vague and disturbing melancholia fell over them. It was easier for them when they added acres and when stocked barns and heavy wagon-loads gave a sense of substance and achievement to their lives. Still, even then would come regrets for the disorganization wrought in their existence by the place. Insanity appeared among some; others sought solace in alcohol; and most continued to work, under strain, eager for relief.

They would probably have said that it was the mill town made the least demand upon them. This was not so large as a single city ward and here space was not at a premium; yet neither was there here the complete isolation of the farm. The immigrants' round of activities here fell into a unit the size of which they could comprehend.

What pressure there was came from the situation of such communities. Often a single company or at most a single industry supplied the employment for all the residents. Any man who came to work in the mine or factory was altogether dependent upon the sole hirer. He was not free to choose among jobs or to argue long about terms; he could only acquiesce or leave. In that sense, it was a condition of his membership in this community that he cut himself off from the world outside the town.

Confined within the immediate locality, the laborers discovered that there was plenty of space, but not plenty of housing. Despite the low density of population, the available quarters were so restricted there was serious overcrowding. As the workers arrived they found at first only the farm or village buildings, quickly converted to their use. The single men were likely to live in makeshift boarding-houses; those with families in cut-up portions of the old houses. Shortly either the company or individual investors threw up additional facilities. Into the surrounding farm land, narrow alleys were pushed, lined with three-story frame tenements or with tiny two-room cottages. The company which controlled all was hardly interested in increasing the supply of housing to an unprofitable excess over demand; nor was it anxious to go to the expense of providing gas, water, and sewerage. The results matched those of the city slums.

Still, the open fields were not far off, and there was not the same total lack of space. The disorganizing effects of the environment were therefore probably less harsh, the deviations less pronounced. What strain there was, was the product of confinement in the town and of constricted housing.

To some degree, these factory town immigrants, like those who went to the cities and those who settled on farms, found the physical conditions of life in America hostile. Nowhere could they recapture the terms of village life; everywhere a difficult adjustment began with the disorganization of the individual, now grown uncertain as to his own proper role. Reorganization would involve first the creation of new means of social action within which the man alone could locate himself.

From the physical as from the religious experience with the New World, the immigrants had gained a deep consciousness of their separateness. It seemed sometimes as if there were only one street in the world, and only a single house on it, and nothing more—only walls and very few people, so that *I am in America and I do not even know whether it is America.* This street was apart as if a ghetto wall defined it. On other streets were other men, deeply different because they had not the burden of this adjustment to bear. This street and those did not run into each other; nor this farm into those. If the immigrants were to achieve the adjustment to their new environment, it had to be within the confines of the ghettos the environment created.

◄§ ѯ►

FREE *enterprise is a tenet of American capitalism, but it has hardly existed in large areas of the American economy since the late nineteenth century. In the twilight years of the nineties and the first of the twentieth century, corporations dominating whole segments of the economy had been formed. Termed trusts, they precluded competition. The small entrepreneur's imagination boggled as he read that between 1898 and 1904, no less than 234 trusts, capitalized at more than $6 billion, had been organized. Whether Americans liked it or not, the figures indicated that in a nation of Davids a breed of Goliaths had sprung up. And it was painfully obvious that there were not enough slings to go about.*

No single corporation excited more anger than the brain child of John D. Rockefeller: The Standard Oil Corporation. The result of unrestrained competition, it had been formed by a group of Cleveland oil refiners under the inspiration of Rockefeller to reduce the threat of feast or famine that plagued the early industry. Its intention was to regulate the flow of oil to conform to demand by the simple technique of confronting the oil producers with a single consumer. Its volume of production permitted it not only to regulate production but also to dictate prices to the railroads that carried the oil to market. Standard Oil eliminated the marginal producer, but it also thought in terms of a mass market. And as Rockefeller understood, the key to volume was price, and the key to lower prices was efficiency. To cut costs, to increase consumption, were the passions of Standard Oil.

The success of the Standard Oil technique assured its masters enormous profits from which it could finance its own expansion and extend its activities into other areas of production. It obliterated competition and disproved every cardinal rule of classical economics. It established the elementary rule that in the absence of government control an efficient producer could create an unassailable monopoly. And the very size of its wealth suggested the emergence of a state within a state, one answerable to no one but its owners. It is hardly surprising that contemporary journals commented upon the development of corporate autonomy. The old Jacksonian fear of monster corporations was engrained in the American character. So it was that Henry Demarest Lloyd (1847-1903), a reporter for the Chicago Tribune, aroused by increasing evidences of industrial injustice during the last two decades of the nineteenth century, wrote his indictment of Standard Oil. It proved a forerunner of muckraking journalism. It did not attempt to come to grips with the economic implications of corporate growth; it settled, instead, for a scathing indictment, and asked an unnerving question: Could democracy survive the existence of such monoliths of economic power? It was a question that would give the Progressive movement much of its impetus.

WEALTH AGAINST COMMONWEALTH

by Henry Demarest Lloyd

It was an American idea to "strike oil." Those who knew it as the "slime" of Genesis, or used it to stick together the bricks of the Tower of Babel, or knelt to it in the fire temples, were content to take it as it rose, the easy gift of nature, oozing forth on brook or spring. But the American struck it.

The world, going into partial eclipse on account of the failing supply of whale oil, had its lamps all ready for the new light, and industries beyond number needed only an expansion of the supply.

DeWitt Clinton, with the same genius that gave us the Erie Canal, suggested as early as 1814 the use of petroleum for light. Reichenbach, the great German chemist, predicted in 1830 that petroleum would yield an illuminating oil equal to the finest. Inventors and money-makers kept up close with scientific investigators in France, Great Britain, and America.

As early as 1845 the manufacture of coal-oil, both for light and other purposes, had become important in France. Selligue had made himself master of the secrets of petroleum. His name, says one of his chroniclers, "must forever remain inseparably connected with that of the manufacture of light from oil, and to his researches few have been able to add."

The name of this genius and benefactor of humanity has remained almost unknown, except within a small scientific world. He was a member of the French Academy, and almost every year between 1834 and 1848 he came to it with some new discovery. On one occasion he reminds his associates that he holds a patent, granted in 1832, for making illuminating oil from coal, and declares that the business can be developed to any extent which commerce or the arts may require. By 1845 he had unlocked nearly every one of the hidden places in which this extraordinary product has stored its wonders. He found out how to make illuminating oil, illuminating gas, lubrication oil, colors, paraffine for candles, fertilizers, solvents for resin for painters, healing washes, chemicals. He had three refineries in operation in the Department Saône-et-Loire, as described in the report of a committee of the French Academy in 1840. He exhibited his oils in the London Exhibition of 1851, and twelve years before, in the Parisian Industrial Exhibition of 1839, he had crude and refined oils and paraffine to show. "Among the most important objects of the exhibition," said its German historian, Von Hermann, "if they can be prepared economically." This Selligue accomplished. Between 1837 and 1843 he refined more than 4,000,000 pounds of oil, and 50 per cent of his product was good illuminating oil.

Before 1850, the Scotch had succeeded in getting petroleum, called shale oil, out of bituminous coal, had found how to refine it, and had perfected lamps in which it would burn. Joshua Merrill, the pioneer of oil refining in this country, with his partners, successfully refined petroleum at Waltham, Mass., where they established themselves in 1853. The American manufacturers were making kerosene as early as 1856 from Scotch coal, imported at a cost of $20 to $25 a ton, and getting experts like Silliman to analyze petroleum, in the hope that somehow a supply of it might be got. By 1860 there were sixty-four of these manufactories in the United States. "A crowd of obscure inventors," says Felix Foucon, in the *Revue des Deux Mondes*, "with unremitting labors perfected the lamp—when it was premature to dream that illumination by mineral oil should become universal." All was ready, as the eminent English geologist, Binney, said, "for the start of the vast American petroleum trade." It was not a lack of knowledge, but a lack of petroleum, that hampered the American manufacturer before 1860. The market, the capital, the consumer, the skilled labor, the inventions, and science were all waiting for "Colonel" Drake.

With Drake's success in "striking oil" came to an end the period, lasting thousands of years, of fire temples, sweep and bucket, Seneca oil; and came to an end, also, the Arcadian simplicity of the old times—old though so recent—in which Professor Silliman could say, "It is not monopolized by any one, but is carried away freely by all who care to collect it."

The oil age begins characteristically. As soon as Drake's well had made known its precious contents, horses began running, and telegrams flying, and money passing to get possession of the oil lands for the few who knew from those who did not know. The primitive days when "it was not monopolized by any one" were over. Thousands of derricks rose all over the territory, and oil scouts pushed with their compasses through the forests of the wilderness in all directions. Wells were bored all over Europe, as well as America, wherever traces of oil showed themselves, sometimes so close together that when one was pumped it would suck air from the other.

As soon as the petroleum began to flow out of the ground, refineries started up at every available place. They were built near the wells, as at Titusville and Oil City, and near the centres of transportation, such as Pittsburg and Buffalo, and near the points of export, as Philadelphia, Baltimore, New York. Numbers of little establishments appeared on the Jersey flats opposite New York.

There was plenty of oil for every one; at one time in 1862 it was only ten cents a barrel. The means of refining it had long before been found by science and were open to all; and even poor men building little stills could year by year add on to their works, increase their capital, and acquire the self-confidence and independence of successful men. The business was one of the most attractive possible to capital. "There is no handsomer business than this is," said one of the great merchants of New York. "You can buy the [crude] oil one week, and sell it the next week refined, and you can imagine the quantity of business that can be done." Men who understood the business, he said, "if they had not the capital could get all of the money they wanted."

Whatever new processes and contrivances were needed the fertile American mind set about supplying. To carry the oil in bulk on the railroads tubs on flat cars were first used; but it was not long before the tub was made of iron instead of wood, and, laid on its side instead of bottom, became the tank of the cylinder car now so familiar.

The fluid which lubricates so many other things on their way through the world is easily made to slip itself along to market. General S. D. Karns was the author, in 1860, of the first suggestion of a pipe line. He planned only for oil to run downhill. Then Hutchinson, the inventor of the Hutchinson rotary pump, saw that oil could be forced through by pressure, and the idea of the pipe line was complete. The first successful pipe line, put down by Samuel Van Syckel, of Titusville, in 1865, from Pithole to Miller's Farm, four miles, has grown into a net-work of thousands of miles, running through the streets of towns, across fields and dooryards, under and over and beside roads, with trunk lines which extend from the oil regions to Pittsburg, Cleveland, Buffalo, Baltimore, New York, Williamsport, Chicago, and the Ohio River.

There was a free market for the oil as it came out of the wells and out of the refineries, and free competition between buyers and sellers, producers and consumers, manufacturers and traders. Industries auxiliary to the main ones flourished. Everywhere the scene was of expanding prosperity, with, of course, the inevitable percentage of ill-luck and miscalculation; but with the balance, on the whole, of such happy growth as freedom and the bounty of nature have always yielded when in partnership. The valleys of Pennsylvania changed into busy towns and oil fields. The highways were crowded, labor was well employed at good wages, new industries were starting up on all sides, and everything betokened the permanent creation of a new prosperity for the whole community, like that which came to California and the world with the discovery of gold.

But shadows of sunset began to creep over the field in its morning time, and the strange spectacle came of widespread ruin in an industry prospering by great leaps. Wherever men moved to discover oil lands, to dig wells, to build refineries or pipe lines, to buy and sell the oil, or to move it to market, a blight fell upon them.

The oil age began in 1860. As early as 1865 strange perturbations were felt, showing that some undiscovered body was pulling the others out of their regular orbits.

Before the panic of 1873—days of buoyant general prosperity, with no commercial revulsion for a cause—the citizens of this industry began to suffer a wholesale loss of property and business among the refineries in New York, Pittsburg, Cleveland, and elsewhere, the wells of the oil valleys, and the markets at home and abroad.

To the building of refineries succeeded the spectacle—a strange one for so new a business—of the abandonment and dismantling of refineries by the score. The market for oil, crude and refined, which had been a natural one, began to move erratically, by incalculable influences. It went down when it should have gone up according to all the known facts of the situation, and went up when it should have gone down. This sort of experience, defying ordinary calculations and virtues, made business men gamblers.

"We began speculating in the hope that there would be a change some time or other for the better," testified one who had gone into the business among the first, and with ample capital and expert skill.

The fright among the people was proportionate to the work they had done and the value of what they were losing. Since the first well was sunk the wilderness had become a busy region, teeming with activity and endowed with wealth. In ten years the business had sprung up from nothing to a net product of 6,000,000 barrels of oil a year, using a capital of $200,000,000 and supporting a population of 60,000 people. The people were drilling one hundred new wells per month, at an average cost of $6000 each. They had devised the forms, and provided the financial institutions needed in a new business. They invented many new and ingenious mechanical contrivances. They had built up towns and cities, with schools, churches, lyceums, theatres, libraries, boards of trade. There were nine daily and eighteen weekly newspapers published in the region and supported by it. All this had been created in ten years, at a cost of untold millions in experiments and failures, and the more precious cost of sacrifice, suffering, toil, and life.

The ripe fruit of all this wonderful development the men of the oil country saw being snatched away from them.

More than once during these lean years, as more than once later, the public alarm went to the verge of violent outbreak. This ruinous prosperity brought stolid Pennsylvania within sight of civil war in 1872, which was the principal subject before the Pennsylvania Legislature of that year, and forced Congress to make an official investigation.

The New York Legislature followed Congress and the Pennsylvania Legislature with an investigation in 1873.

"There was great popular excitement. . . . It raged like a violent fever," was the description it heard of the state of things in Pennsylvania.

There was panic in oil speculation, bank failures, defalcations. Many committed suicide. Hundreds were driven into bankruptcy and insane asylums.

Where every one else failed, out of this havoc and social disorder one little group of half a dozen men were rising to the power and wealth which have become the marvel of the world. The first of them came tardily into the field about 1862. He started a little refinery in Cleveland, hundreds of miles from the oil wells. The sixty and more manufacturers who had been able to plant themselves before 1860, when they had to distil coal into petroleum before they could refine petroleum into kerosene, had been multiplied into hundreds by the arrival of petroleum ready made from below. Some of the richest and most successful business men of the country had preceded him and were flourishing. He had been a bookkeeper, and then a partner, in a very small country-produce store in Cleveland. As described by his counsel some years later, he was a "man of brains and energy without money." With him were his brother and an English mechanic. The mechanic was bought out later, as all the expert skill needed could be got for wages, which were cheaper than dividends. Two or three years later another partner was added, who began life as "a clerk in a country store," and had been in salt and lumber in the West. A young man, who had been in the oil region only eleven years, and for two of the eleven had been errand-boy and bookkeeper in a mixed oil and merchandise business, a lawyer, a railroad man, a cotton broker, a farm laborer who had become refiner, were admitted at various times into the ruling coterie.

The revolution which revolved all the freemen of this industry down a vortex had no sooner begun than the public began to show its agitation through every organ. The spectacle of a few men at the centre of things, in offices rich with plate glass and velvet plush, singing a siren song which drew all their competitors to bankruptcy or insanity or other forms of "co-operation," did not progress, as it might have done a hundred years ago, unnoticed save by those who were the immediate sufferers. The new democracy began questioning the new wealth. Town meetings, organizations of trades and special interests, grand juries, committees of State legislatures and of the United States Senate and House of Representatives, the civil and criminal courts, have been in almost constant action and inquiry since and because.

It was before the Committee of Commerce of the National House of Representatives in 1872 that the first authentic evidence was obtained of the cause of the singular ruin which was overwhelming so fair a field. This investigation in 1872 was suppressed after it had gone a little way. Congress said, Investigate. Another power said, Don't investigate. But it was not stopped until the people had found out that they and the production, refining, and transportation of their oil—the whole oil industry, not alone of the valleys where the petroleum was found, but of the districts where it was manufactured, and the markets where it was bought and sold, and the ports from which it was shipped abroad—had been made the subject of a secret "contract" between certain citizens. The high contracting parties to this treaty for the disposal of an industrial province were, on one side, all the great railroad companies, without whose services the oil, crude or refined, could not be moved to refineries, markets, or ports of shipment on river, lake, or ocean. On the other side was a body of thirteen men, "not one of whom lived in the oil regions, or was an owner of oil wells or oil lands," who had associated themselves for the control of the oil business under the winning name of the South Improvement Company.

By this contract the railroads had agreed with this company of citizens as follows:

1. To double freight rates.
2. Not to charge them the increase.
3. To give them the increase collected from all competitors.
4. To make any other changes of rates necessary to guarantee their success in business.
5. To destroy their competitors by high freight rates.
6. To spy out the details of their competitors' business.

The increase in rates in some cases was to be more than double. These higher rates were to be ostensibly charged to all shippers, including the thirteen members of the South Improvement Company; but that fraternity only did not have to pay them really. All, or nearly all, the increase it paid was to be paid back again—a "rebate." The increase paid by every one else—"on all transported by other parties"—was not paid back. It was to be kept, but not by the railroads. These were to hand that, too, over to the South Improvement Company.

This secret arrangement made the actual rate of the South Improvement Company much lower—sometimes half, sometimes less than half, what all others paid. The railroad officials were not to collect these enhanced freight rates from the unsuspecting subjects of this "contract" to turn them into the treasury of the railroads. They were to give them over to the gentlemen who called themselves "South Improvement Company." The "principle" was that the railroad was not to get the benefit of the additional charge it made to the people. No matter how high the railroads put the rates to the community, not the railroads, but the Improvement Company, was to get the gain. The railroads bound themselves to charge every one else the highest nominal rates mentioned. "They shall not be less," was the stipulation. They might be more up to any point; but less they must not be.

The rate for carrying petroleum to Cleveland to be refined was to be advanced, for instance, to 80 cents a barrel. When paid by the South Improvement Company, 40 cents of the 80 were to be refunded to it; when paid by any one else, the 40 cents were not merely not to be refunded, but to be paid over to his competitor, this aspiring self-improvement company. The charge on refined oil to Boston was increased to $3.07; and, in the same way, the South Improvement Company was to get back a rebate of $1.32 on every barrel it sent to Boston, and on every barrel any one else sent. The South Improvement Company was to receive sums ranging from 40 cents to $1.32, and averaging a dollar a barrel on all shipments, whether made by itself or by others. This would give the company an income of a dollar a day on every one of the 18,000 barrels then being produced daily, whether its members drilled for it, or piped it, or stored it, or refined it, or not.

To pay money to the railroads for them to pay back was seen to be a waste of time, and it was agreed that the South Improvement Company for its members should deduct from the ostensible rate the amount to be refunded, and pay the railroads only the difference. Simplification could not go further. The South Improvement Company was not even to be put to the inconvenience of waiting for the railroads to collect and render to it the tribute exacted for its benefit from all the other shippers. It was given the right to figure out for its members what the tribute would amount to, and pay it to them out of the money they owed the railroads for freight, and then pay the railroad what was left, if there was any left. The railroads agreed to supply them with all the information needed for thus figuring out the amount of this tribute, and to spy out for them besides other important details of their competitors' business. They agreed to make reports every day to the South Improvement Company of all the shipments by other persons, with full particulars as to how much was shipped, who shipped, and to whom, and so on.

The detective agency thus established by the railroads to spy out the business of a whole trade was to send its reports "daily to the principal office" of the thirteen gentlemen. If the railroads, forgetting their obligations to the thirteen disciples, made any reduction in any manner to anybody else, the company, as soon as it was found out, could deduct the same amount from its secret rate. If the open rate to the public went down, the secret rate was to go down as much. For the looks of things, it was stipulated that any one else who could furnish an equal amount of transportation should have the same rates, but the possibility that any one should ever be able to furnish an equal amount of transportation was fully taken care of in another section clinching it all.

The railway managers, made kings of the road by the grant to them of the sovereign powers of the State, covenanted, in order to make their friends kings of light, that they would "maintain the business" of the South Improvement Company "against loss or injury by competition," so that it should be "a remunerative" and "a full and regular business," and pledged themselves to put the rates of freight up or down, as might be "necessary to overcome such competition." Contracts to this effect, giving the South Improvement Company the sole right for five years to do business between the oil wells and the rest of the world, were made with it by the Erie, the New York Central, the Lake Shore and Michigan Southern, the Pennsylvania, the Atlantic and Great Western, and their connections, thus controlling the industry north, south, east, west, and abroad. The contracts in every case bound all the roads owned or leased by the railroads concerned. The contracts were duly signed, sealed, and delivered. On the oil business of that year, as one of the members of the committee of Congress figured out from the testimony, the railroad managers could collect an increase of $7,500,000 in freights, of which they were to hand over to the South Improvement Company $6,000,000, and pay into the treasury of their employers—the railways—only $1,500,000.

The contract was signed for the New York Central and Hudson River

Railroad by its vice-president, but this agreement to kill off a whole trade was too little or too usual to make any impression on his mind. When publicly interrogated about it he could not remember having seen or signed it.

"The effect of this contract," the vice-president of the Erie Railway Company was asked, "would have been a complete monopoly in the oil-carrying trade?"

"Yes, sir; a complete monopoly."

Of the thirteen members of the South Improvement Company which was to be given this "complete monopoly," ten were found later to be active members of the oil trust. They were then seeking that control of the light of the world which it has obtained. Among these ten were the president, vice-president, treasurer, secretary, and a majority of the directors of the oil trust into which the improvement company afterwards passed by transmigration. Any closer connection there could not be. One was the other.

The ablest and most painstaking investigation which has ever been had in this country into the management of the railroads found and officially reported to the same effect: "The controlling spirits of both organizations being the same."

The freight rates were raised as agreed and without notice. Rumors had been heard of what was coming. The public would not believe anything so incredible. But the oil regions were electrified by the news, February 26, that telegrams had been sent from railroad headquarters to their freight agents advising them of new rates, to take effect immediately, making the cost of shipping oil as much again as it had been. The popular excitement which broke out on the same day and "raged like a violent fever" became a national sensation. The Titusville *Morning Herald* of March 20, 1872, announces that "the railroads to the oil regions have already put up their New York freight from $1.25 to $2.84, an advance of over one hundred per cent." Asked what reason the railroads gave for increasing their rates, a shipper said, "They gave no reason; they telegraphed the local roads to put up the rates immediately." This advance, the superintendents of the railroads told complaining shippers, had been made under the direction of the South Improvement Company, and they had been instructed to make their monthly collections of oil freights from that concern.

The evidence even seems to show that the South Improvement Company was so anxious for the dance of death to begin that it got the freight agents by personal influence to order the increased rates before the time agreed upon with the higher officials. Strenuous efforts were made to have the public believe that the contracts, though sealed, signed, delivered, and put into effect, as the advance in rates most practically demonstrated, had really not been put into effect. The quibbles with which the president of the South Improvement Company sought to give that impossible color to the affair before the committee of Congress drew upon him more than one stinging rebuke from the chairman of the committee.

"During your whole examination there has not been a direct answer given to a question." "I wish to say to you," said the chairman, "that such equivocation is unworthy of you."

The plea needs no answer, but if it did, the language of the railroad men themselves supplies one that cannot be bettered. To the representatives of the people, who had telegraphed them for information "at once, as the excitement is intense, and we fear violence and destruction of property," General McClellan, of the Atlantic and Great Western, replied that the contract was "cancelled"; President Clark, of the Lake Shore, that it was "formally abrogated and cancelled"; Chairman Homer Ramsdell, of the Erie, that it was "abrogated"; Vice-President Thomas Scott, of the Pennsylvania Railroad, that it was "terminated officially"; Vice-President Vanderbilt, of the New York Central and Hudson River Railroad, that it was "cancelled with all the railroads."

Contracts that were not complete and in force would not need to be "cancelled" and "abrogated" and "terminated." These announcements were backed up by a telegram from the future head of the oil trust then incubating, in which he said of his company: "This company holds no contracts with the railroad companies." But in 1879 its secretary, called upon by the Ohio Legislature to produce the contracts the company had with the railroads, showed, among others, one covering the very date of this denial in 1872.

Before Congress the South Improvement Company sought to shelter themselves behind the plea that "their calculation was to get all the refineries in the country into the company. There was no difference made, as far as we were concerned, in favor of or against any refinery; they were all to come in alike."

How they "were all to be taken in" the contract itself showed. It bound the South Improvement Company "to expend large sums of money in the purchase of works for refining," and one of the reasons given by the railroads for making the contract was "to encourage the outlay." Upon what footing buyer and seller would meet in these purchases when the buyer had a secret arrangement like this with the owners of the sole way to and from wells, refineries, and markets, one does not need to be "a business man" to see. The would-be owners had a power to pry the property of the real owners out of their hands.

One of the Cleveland manufacturers who had sold was asked why he did so by the New York Legislature. They had been very prosperous, he said; their profits had been $30,000 to $45,000 a year; but their prosperity had come to a sudden stop.

"From the time that it was well understood in the trade that the South Improvement Company had . . . grappled the entire transportation of oil from the West to the seaboard . . . we were all kind of paralyzed, perfectly paralyzed; we could not operate. . . . The South Improvement Company, or some one representing them, had a drawback of a dollar, sometimes seventy cents, sometimes more, sometimes less, and we were working against that difference."

It was a difference, he said, which destroyed their business.

He went to the officials of the Erie and of the New York Central to try to get freight rates that would permit him to continue in business. "I got no satisfaction at all," he said; "I am too good a friend of yours," said the representative of the New York Central, "to advise you to have anything further to do with this oil trade."

"Do you pretend that you won't carry for me at as cheap a rate as you will carry for anybody else?"

"I am but human," the freight agent replied.

He saw the man who was then busily organizing the South Improvement Company. He was non-committal. "I got no satisfaction, except 'You better sell, you better get clear.' Kind of *sub rosa*; 'Better sell out, no help for it.' "

His firm was outside the charmed circle, and had to choose between selling and dying. Last of all, he had an interview with the president of the all-conquering oil company, in relation to the purchase of their works. "He was the only party that would buy. He offered me fifty cents on the dollar, on the construction account, and we sold out. . . . He made this expression, I remember: 'I have ways of making money that you know nothing of.' "

For the works, which were producing $30,000 to $45,000 a year profit, and which they considered worth $150,000, they received $65,000.

"Did you ascertain in the trade," he was asked, "what was the average rate that was paid for refineries?"

"That was about the figure. . . . Fifty cents on the dollar."

"It was that or nothing, was it not?"

"That or nothing."

The freight rates had been raised in February. This sale followed in three weeks.

"I would not have sold out," he told the Legislature, "if I could have got a fair show with the railways. My business, instead of being an enterprise to buy and sell, became degraded into running after the railways and getting an equal chance with others."

"The only party that would buy" gave his explanation a few years later of the centralization of this business.

"Some time in the year 1872," he swore, "when the refining business of the city of Cleveland was in the hands of a number of small refiners, and was unproductive of profit, it was deemed advisable by many of the persons engaged therein, for the sake of economy, to concentrate the business, and associate their joint capital therein. The state of the business was such at that time that it could not be retained profitably at the city of Cleveland, by reason of the fact that points nearer the oil regions were enjoying privileges not shared by refiners at Cleveland, and could produce refined oil at a much less rate than could be done at this point. It was a well-understood fact at that time among refiners that some arrangement would have to be made to economize and concentrate the business, or ruinous losses would not only occur to the refiners themselves, but ultimately Cleveland, as a point of refining oil, would have to be abandoned. At that time those most prominently engaged in the business here consulted together, and as a result thereof several of the refiners conveyed" to his company, then as always the centre of the centralization, "their refineries, and had the option, in pay therefor, to take stock" in this company, "at par, or to take cash." This company, he continued, "had no agency in creating this state of things which made that change in the refining business necessary at that time, but the same was the natural result of the trade, nor did it in the negotiations which followed use any undue or unfair means, but in all cases, to the general satisfaction of those whose refineries were acquired, the full value thereof, either in stock or cash, was paid as the parties preferred."

The producers were not to fare any better than the refiners. The president of the South Improvement Company said to a representative of the oil regions substantially: "We want you producers to make out a correct statement of the average production of each well, and the exact cost per barrel to produce the oil. Then we propose to allow you a fair price for the oil."

Within forty-eight hours after the freight rates were raised, according to programme, "the entire business of the oil regions," the Titusville *Herald*, March 20, 1872, reported, "became paralyzed. Oil went down to a point seventy cents below the cost of production. The boring of new wells was suspended, existing wells were shut down. The business in Cleveland stopped almost altogether. Thousands of men were thrown out of work."

The people rose. Their uprising and its justification were described to the Pennsylvania Constitutional Convention of 1873 by a brilliant "anti-monopolist," "a rising lawyer" of Franklin, Venango Co. The principal subject to which he called the attention of his fellow-members was the South Improvement Company, and the light it threw on the problems of livelihood and liberty. Quoting the decision of the Pennsylvania Supreme Court in the Sanford case, he said:

"That is the law in Pennsylvania today. But in spite of this decision, and in spite of the law, we well know that almost every railroad in this State has been in the habit, and is today in the habit, of granting special privileges to individuals, to companies in which the directors of such railroads are interested, to particular business, and to particular localities. We well know that it is their habit to break down certain localities, and build up others, to break down certain men in business and to build up others, to monopolize certain business themselves by means of the numerous corporations which they own and control, and all this in spite of the law, in defiance of the law.

"The South Improvement Company's scheme would give that corporation the monopoly of the entire oil business of this State, amounting to $20,000,000 a year. That corporation was created by the Pennsylvania Legislature along with at least twenty others, under the name of improvement companies, within a few years past, all of which corporations contain the names as original corporators of men who may be found in and about the office of the Pennsylvania Railroad Company, in Philadelphia, when not lobbying at Harrisburg. The railroads took but one of those charters which they got from the Legislature, and by means of that struck a deadly blow at one of the greatest interests of the State. Their scheme was contrary to law, but before the legal remedy could have been applied, the oil business would have lain prostrate at their feet, had it not been prevented by an uprising of the people, by the threatenings of a mob, if you please, by threatening to destroy property, and by actually commencing to destroy the property of the railroad company, and had the companies not cancelled the contract which Scott and Vanderbilt and others had entered into, I venture to say there would not have been one mile of railroad track left in the County of Venango—the people had come to that pitch of desperation. . . . Unless we can give the people a remedy for this evil of discriminations in freight, they will sooner or later take the remedy into their own hands."

Soon after this attorney for the people was promoted from the poor pay of patriotism to a salary equal to that of the President of the United States, and to the place of counsel for the principal members of the combination, whose inwardness he had descried with such hawk-eye powers of vision. Later, as their counsel, he drafted the famous trust agreement of 1882.

The South Improvement Company was formed January 2d. The agreement with the railroads was evidently already worked out in its principal details, for the complicated contracts were formally signed, sealed, and delivered January 18th. The agreed increase of freights went into effect February 26th. The pacific insurrection of the people began with an impromptu mass-meeting at Titusville the next day, February 27th. Influential delegations, or committees, on transportation, legislation, conference with press, pipe lines, arresting of drilling, etc., were set to work by the organization thus spontaneously formed by the people. A complete embargo was placed on sales of oil at any price to the men who had made the hateful bargain with the railroads. The oil country was divided into sixteen districts, in each of which the producers elected a local committee, and over all these was an executive committee composed of representatives from the local committees—one from each. No oil was sold to be used within any district except to those buyers whom the local committee recommended; no oil was sold to be exported or refined outside the district, except to such buyers as the executive committee permitted. One cent a barrel was paid by each producer into a general fund for the expenses of the organization.

Steps were taken to form a company with a capital of $1,000,000 subscribed by the producers, to advance money, on the security of their oil, to those producers who did not want to sell.

Able lawyers were employed and sent with the committees to all the important capitals—Harrisburg, Washington, the offices of the railway companies. The flow of oil was checked, the activities of the oil world brought near a stop.

Monday, March 15th, by the influence of the Washington committee, a resolution was introduced into the House of Representatives by Representative Scofield, ordering an investigation of the South Improvement Company. Immediately upon this the frightened participants cancelled the contracts. By the 26th of March the representatives of the people had secured a pledge in writing from the five great railroads concerned of "perfect equality," and "no rebates, drawbacks, or other arrangements," in favor of any one thereafter. March 30th, Congress began the investigation which brought to light the evidence of the contracts, and meanwhile the committees on legislation and pipe lines were securing from the Pennsylvania Legislature the repeal of the South Improvement Company charter, and the passage of a "so-called" Free Pipe Line law, discovered afterwards to be worthless on account of amendments shrewdly inserted by the enemy.

It was an uprising of the people, passionate but intelligent and irresistible, if the virtue of the members held good. Until April 9th the non-intercourse policy was stiffly and successfully maintained. But by that time one man had been found among the people who was willing to betray the movement. This man, in consideration of an extra price, violating his producer's pledge, sold to some of those concerned in the South Improvement Company a large quantity of oil, as they at once took pains to let the people know. The seller hoped to ship it quietly, but, of course, the object in buying and paying this additional price was to have it shipped openly, and the members of the South Improvement Company insisted that it should be done so.

This treachery had the effect planned. Every one became suspicious that his neighbor would be the next deserter, and would get the price he would like to have for himself. To prevent a stampede, the leaders called a mass-meeting. Reports were made to it of what had been done in Congress, the Legislature, and the other railway offices: the telegrams already referred to were read affirming the cancellation of the contracts. Amid manifestations of tumultuous approbation and delight the embargo on the sale of oil was declared raised.

"We do what we must," says Emerson, "and call it by the best name possible." The people, as every day since has shown, grasped the shell of victory to find within the kernel of defeat.

The committee of Congress noticed when the contracts were afterwards shown to it, that though they had been so widely declared to be "cancelled," they had not been cancelled, but were as fresh—seals, stamps, signatures and all—as the day they were made. This little circumstance is descriptive of the whole proceeding. Both parties to this scheme to give the use of the highways as a privilege to a few, and through this privilege to make the pursuit of livelihood a privilege, theirs exclusively—the railroad officials on one side, and their beneficiaries of the South Improvement Company on the other—were resolute in their determination to carry out their purpose. All that follows of this story is but the recital of the sleuth-like tenacity with which this trail of fabulous wealth has been followed.

The chorus of cancellation from the railroads came from those who had meant never to cancel, really. In their negotiations with the representatives of the people they had contested to the last the abandonment of the scheme. "Their friendliness" to it "was so apparent," the Committee of the Producers reported, "that we could expect little consideration at their hands," and the committee became satisfied that the railroads had made a new contract among themselves like that of the South Improvement Company, and to take its place. Its head frankly avowed before the Investigating Committee of Congress their intention of going ahead with the plan. "They are all convinced that, sooner or later, it will be necessary to organize upon the basis on which the South Improvement Company was organized, including both producers and refiners."

This conviction has been faithfully lived up to. Under the name of the South Improvement Company the arrangement was ostentatiously abandoned, because to persist in it meant civil war in the oil country as the rising young anti-monopolist lawyer pointed out in the Constitutional Convention. Mark Twain, in describing the labors of the missionaries in the Sandwich Islands, says they were so successful that the vices of the natives no longer exist in name—only in reality. As every page will show, this contract no longer exists in name—only in reality. In the oil world, and in every other important department of our industrial life—in food, fuel, shelter, clothing, transportation, this contract, in its various new shapes, has been kept steadily at work gerrymandering the livelihoods of the people.

The men who had organized the South Improvement Company paid the public revolt the deference of denial, though not of desistance. The company had got a charter, organized under it, collected twenty per cent of the subscription for stock, made contracts with the railroads, held meetings of the directors, who approved of the contracts and had received the benefits of the increase of freights made in pursuance of the agreement. This was shown by the testimony of its own officers.

But "the company never did a dollar's worth of business," the Secretary of the Light of the World told Congress, and "there was never the slightest connection between the South Improvement Company and the Standard Oil Company," the president of the latter and the principal member of both said in an interview in the New York *World*, of March 29, 1890. "The South Improvement Company died in embryo. It was never completely organized, and never did any business. It was partly born, died, and was buried in 1872," etc.

Still later, before a committee of the Legislature of New York, in 1888, he was asked about "the Southern Improvement Company."

"There was such a company?"

"I have heard of such a company."

"Were you not in it?"

"I was not."

So help me God!

At almost the moment of this denial in New York, an associate in this and all his other kindred enterprises, asked before Congress who made up the South Improvement Company, named as among them the principal members of the great oil company, and most conspicuous of them all was the name of this denier.

The efficiency with which this "partly born" innocent lived his little hour, "not doing a dollar's worth of business," was told in a summary phrase by one of the managers of the Pennsylvania Railroad, describing the condition of the oil business in 1873:

"All other of our largest customers had failed."

When the people of the oil regions made peace after their uprising it was, as they say, with "full assurance from the Washington committee that the throwing off the restrictions from trade will not embarrass their investigation [by Congress], but that the Sub-Committee of Commerce will, nevertheless, continue, as the principle involved, and not this particular case alone, is the object of the investigation."

The Committee of Commerce did not "continue." The principal witness, who had negotiated the contracts by which the railroads gave over the business of the oil regions to a few, refused in effect, beyond producing copies of the contract, to be a witness. Permission was given by the Committee of Congress during its first zeal to the Committee of Producers from Pennsylvania to copy the testimony as it was taken, but no official record of its discoveries exists. This transcript was published by the producers, and copies are possessed by a few fortunate collectors. The Committee did not report, and in the archives of the national Capitol no scrap of the evidence taken is to be found. All has vanished into the bottomless darkness in which the monopoly of light loves to dwell.

***

"I NEVER *met in America with any citizen so poor as not to cast a glance of hope and envy on the enjoyments of the rich,*" Alexis de Tocqueville wrote in 1840, "*or whose imagination did not possess itself by anticipation of those good things which fate still obstinately withheld from him.*" *The self-made millionaire has always had an allure for the American. His existence is accepted as one of the touchstones that supports the national belief that the United States is the land of opportunity. In addition, as Calvinist theology taught, wealth is a mark of grace, one that before the Civil War, as Tocqueville noted, led not to an excess of gratification but to an indulgence in quiet pleasures. "To build enormous palaces, to conquer or to mimic Nature, to ransack the world in order to gratify the passions of a man, is not thought of: but to add a few roods of land to your field, to plant an orchard, to enlarge a dwelling, to be always making life more comfortable and convenient, to avoid trouble, and to satisfy the smallest wants without effort and almost without cost." The sign of antebellum wealth was genteel restraint.*

But once the war had ended, the explosive marshaling of the industrial resources of the nation, already in the take-off stage of development at war's beginning, set in motion an accumulation of wealth for the fortunate few without parallel in history. Whereas before the war the number of millionaires ranged in the low hundreds, by 1892 the number was some-

*where between 3,045 and 4,047, and in 1900 no fewer than twenty-five of
their number had found their way into the Senate. The single fortune of
John D. Rockefeller, on the eve of the depression of 1892, was reputed to be
$815,647,796.89, while Andrew Carnegie, in 1900 alone, garnered a profit
from his steel enterprise of $40,000,000. Gentility had been superseded by
opulence, and, as many critics complained, an arrogant, unbridled power.
The corporations which managed whole segments of the American economy
loomed up as states within a state; their captains resembled increasingly the
nobles of old, answerable to none but their imprecise consciences.*

*The historical treatment of the rise of the great fortunes has, until the
recent past, emphasized two conflicting themes. The first is that of the self-
made man who is viewed as typical of entrepreneurial success. Henry Steele
Commager and Samuel Eliot Morison neatly state the case when they write:
"The most typical figure of the industrial age was undoubtedly Andrew
Carnegie. A poor immigrant boy from Scotland, he followed and helped
to perpetuate the American tradition of rising from poverty to riches, and
his success he ascribed entirely to the political and economic democracy
which obtained in this country." Simultaneously, the same group are deemed
to have succeeded because they were "unhindered by moral scruples." Not
infrequently, they have been labeled "pirates," "buccaneers," "freebooters,"
who, operating "in more or less accordance with the forms of law," systematically corrupt both legislature and judicial chamber to increase their
gains. The latter image has been most starkly rendered by Matthew Josephson (1899-   ), who, Marxist-oriented, emphasized an uninhibited power
of the few systematically looting the many.*

*Within the past three decades, a number of historians have challenged the
usual view of these men of wealth. Allan Nevins argued in his biography of
John D. Rockefeller that he ought better be viewed as an industrial statesman who brought rational order to a segment of the American economy, and
as a consequence well-being to a vast consumer population. Thomas C.
Cochran (1902-   ) has questioned the "pathological" preoccupation of
historians with the exceptional "robber barons," who serve as a neat antith-
esis of the bad, grasping, and unscrupulous capitalist marauding on the
"good" public. He called instead for "entrepreneurial historians" interested
in understanding the business process in society rather than in delivering
moralistic warnings against "robber baron" activity. William Miller (1912-
) has posed in a series of essays published as* Men in Business *(revised
1962) a large challenge to the image of the self-made American businessman.
In an extensive statistical analysis of the origins of the American business
elite, he concluded that the historian's emphasis upon the "typically lower-
class, foreign, or farm origins" of the business elite flew in the face of the
facts. They were but a bare three percent of the sample. The bulk were
men born into an environment "in which business and a relatively high social
standing were intimately associated with his family life."*

THE ROBBER BARONS

The Great American Capitalists, 1861-1901

by Matthew Josephson

By 1866 Commodore Vanderbilt in pursuance of his plans of consolidation had bought enough stock in the Erie Railroad to announce confidently that he intended to add this line to his growing system.

The group of railroads thrown together as the Vanderbilt system complemented each other nicely: the Harlem gave a terminus and franchise in New York; the Hudson River Railroad continued from its juncture with the Harlem tracks up the east shore of the river to Albany; and thence the New York Central ran up the Mohawk Valley to Buffalo, and connected with the Lake Shore (in which the Commodore had also invested) as far as Toledo. His eye was fixed upon the Michigan Southern and its Chicago terminal, when he perceived that the Erie Railroad was moving in the same direction. In apprehension, he made overtures of friendship to Uncle Daniel Drew, purchased about 20,000 shares of Erie stock and had himself elected a director of the road. He now owned a prominent share of its capital, had the secret collaboration of Drew as he believed, and might subdue the Erie's opposition to his triumphant westward march.

But soon sufficient signs appeared that all was not well. There was no trusting the deep Uncle Daniel; for shares of Erie stock were pressed steadily upon a declining market, as if flowing from a concealed underground stream, while Vanderbilt continued buying. In 1866 Drew had loaned his railroad, of which he was treasurer and chief stockholder, $3,480,000 on the security of 28,000 unissued shares of its stock, and $3,000,000 of its convertible bonds. Now Drew bought and sold Erie stock in Wall Street, using the collateral he possessed—whether lawfully or unlawfully it is not known—to cover his operations. This was one source of supply; but there were more.

In the same year, at the proposal of Jay Gould, who roamed about trading in little railroads, Drew together with his agents Fisk and Gould had bought a small company, the Buffalo, Bradford & Pittsburgh Railroad, as a private transaction of their own, for $250,000. Against this sum of assets the new owners had with splendid imagination issued $2,000,000 in bonds. They then proceeded to lease their road to the expanding Erie system for 499 years, the ransom being assumption of the smaller company's bonded indebtedness by the larger one. Thus $2,000,000 of Erie convertible bonds (convertible into shares of capital stock) passed into the hands of the three confederates in exchange for their Buffalo, Bradford & Pittsburgh, which had cost them one-eighth of the sum. Through the right of bond conversion

Drew, Gould and Fisk now had a large reserve supply of Erie stock, which they continued to sell steadily through 1866, as far as they dared, while agents of the great "bull" Vanderbilt purchased them almost as soon as they were offered.

"Buy Erie," Vanderbilt ordered his brokers. "Buy it at the lowest figure you can, but buy it!" His holdings increased visibly, and knowing nothing of the secret acquisitions of the Erie ring he assumed that the market would soon be bare of offerings. He possessed more shares than were known to exist. Erie's stock climbed to 95. The shorts, he told himself gloatingly, would be soon trapped as in the famous Harlem corner. But suddenly a wave of crisp, newly printed Erie shares struck Wall Street, 50,000 of them, and smashed the market, so that the price broke to 50 a share, and Vanderbilt in the calamitous process was loser by some millions of dollars to the party headed by Daniel Drew.

The rage and mortification of the Commodore now passed all bounds. Determined upon defeating his treacherous adversary, and also seizing control of the opposing railroad in order finally to form a combination or pool for fixing traffic and freight rates, he now took elaborate measures to assure himself of ownership. A group of Boston financiers headed by John S. Eldridge, in charge of the small Boston, Hartford & Erie Railroad, had been building westward—largely under Massachusetts subsidy—and had planned to connect with the Erie to bring Erie coal to Boston. This railroad too had been overladen with debt by its builders, and was without funds for further construction. Its directors had previously purchased a sizable block of Erie shares as a means of bringing about a consolidation. The Boston financiers were a new factor in the control of Erie, and courting Vanderbilt's favor they now entered into a secret agreement with him to vote their shares at the approaching election of directors so that Drew would be ousted. In return, Vanderbilt would have the Erie absorb their New England railroad, by advancing them four millions in bonds, thus furnishing them with funds for the construction they so loved to carry on.

Daniel Drew was now given notice that his days at the head of the Erie were numbered; moreover an injunction issued at the Commodore's complaint overhung him, and restrained him from voting his illegally obtained stock.

Hat in hand, and with tears flowing from his old eyes, Drew came to beg his ancient rival for mercy. Was it by a whim, a moment of sentimental weakness that Vanderbilt forgave the old drover—something that he was rarely known to do? More likely Drew had convinced his adversary that in happy accord, they, as two mercenary captains, might win many fruitful victories at the cost of common enemies, the "outsiders." Thus a successful pool formed with the purpose of advancing Erie stock might easily erase Vanderbilt's recent losses, and Vanderbilt had to admit that no one knew better how to manage such forays nimbly than did the Speculative Director of Erie. Finally, Vanderbilt undoubtedly admired the wily old man and was the last one to be shocked by his ruthless proceedings.

The bargain was struck. It was agreed that in response to the clamor of the outside public Drew was to be officially ousted, and a "dummy" director put in his place, while he remained in actual charge of their mutual affairs. This was done at the stockholders' meeting of October 18, 1867, and the new interests, including the Boston financiers, elected their directors. The two young, almost unknown, allies of Drew, James Fisk, Jr., and Jay Gould, who appeared to have intruded themselves in the Boston faction, were among the new members of the executive board of a great railroad for the first time in their lives, with the approval of Vanderbilt. Then, soon afterward, to Wall Street's surprise, Drew reassumed his former position. Peace, and subservience to Vanderbilt control, was the order of the day; and Erie's mercurial stock rose rapidly under the bidding of the new pool which Vanderbilt interests backed.

But soon all did not appear well to the Commodore; he found mysterious selling of Erie in the market, readily offered shares. When he called a meeting of the New York Central and Erie directors together to pool traffic and equalize rates, he found to his surprise that Drew, Gould and even his recent allies from Boston had grown disaffected and were ranged against him. And to his great anxiety, he learned that the Erie Railroad proposed to make large new issues of bonds for purposes of construction and expansion. Its rails were six feet apart; and it was now planned to spend many millions to lay a third rail, inside, at the standard gauge, so that trains from the Michigan railroads could connect with its lines. And, with unsurpassed boldness, in defiance of Vanderbilt, the Executive Committee of Drew, Fisk and Gould, the "Erie ring," now secretly authorized the issuance of a mass of new convertible bonds, ten millions more!

Once more the impetuous Vanderbilt saw that he had been outwitted and deceived; that he must at once buy an absolute majority of the much augmented supply of Erie's stock in the open market if he would control the situation. And with a great oath he ordered his brokers again to "buy every damn share that's offered."

But what if the Erie ring simply printed infinite quantities of stock, issued unlawfully against "convertible" bonds which had not even been publicly sold, against which no funds had been paid to the railroad? How could he shore up the flood of paper pouring from their printing presses? He must have the law upon the conspirators.

Early in 1868, the highly obliging Judge George C. Barnard of the New York State Supreme Court (and of the Tweed ring) enjoined the Erie directors from further issues of securities, and ordered them to return to the treasury one-fourth of the shares recently issued, as well as the $3,000,000 of convertible bonds dated 1866. Jove-like, Judge Barnard fired injunctions like bolts of lightning, while the cohorts of Vanderbilt took heart, and Erie's stock rose 30 points to 84. Vanderbilt and his party had some 200,000 shares accumulated; and it looked as if the Erie bears, thanks to the majestic intrusion of the Law, were badly cornered at last.

Out of their midst, however, Jay Gould now emerged as the effective leader, displaying craftiness, promptitude and boldness in action which showed him a worthy foe of the craggy Vanderbilt. Hurrying to the town of Binghamton, New York, he uncovered a judge of the state's Supreme Court who heeded fully his own substantial reasoning, and sent forth counter-injunctions. But better still, before the hour of Judge Barnard's injunctions, Drew, Gould and Fisk, with forethought of what was coming, had taken the whole $10,000,000 of recently issued bonds, and assigning them to a broker unaffected by the court orders, had them converted into 100,000 shares of stock. Then, always pretending to obey the court's orders, a messenger boy was ordered to carry the stock-book containing these new and forbidden shares to a place of deposit assigned by the court. But by prearrangement the burly Fisk, lurking outside the door, intercepted the boy, wrenched the stock-book from his hands, and disappeared!

In the financial markets there spread the most terrible uncertainty as to what was coming, not only for the contestants but for business in general, as a consequence of so much deviltry. Drew and Fisk suddenly flung a great mass of the disputed Erie shares (whose fate none had known) upon the market, causing a riot in Wall Street, "as though a mine had been exploded." Upon the stock exchange trading was suspended in Erie; brokers poured out into the street shouting and gesticulating like madmen; and above their tumult sounded the mad roars of the Cyclopean Vanderbilt who, it appears, had been cheated once more out of an enormous sum of money reckoned at between five millions and seven millions of dollars.

Again and again the Commodore had grasped hungrily for the Erie Railroad and each time by a deft move his opponents had wrested the prize from his reaching arms. The more shares he bought with his good money the more they printed, in order to reduce his portion of the ownership. Jim Fisk had said publicly: "If this printing press don't break down, I'll be damned if I don't give the old hog all he wants of Erie!"

There was no more time for temporizing. Calling upon Judge Barnard again, Vanderbilt had him order the arrest of Drew, Gould and Fisk for contempt of court. Then for the unhappy railroad a receiver friendly to Vanderbilt was appointed.

But once more the rulers of Erie had been forewarned of the enemy's strokes. At the railroad headquarters on West Street, amid great excitement, they gathered quickly all the funds received from their stock-market transactions, all cash in banks or in the company's treasury, all securities, documents and incriminating evidence, and made ready to flee.

Notices, warrants and writs were known to be on their way at ten o'clock of the morning of March 11, 1868, when Daniel Drew, Jim Fisk and Jay Gould, after emptying the safes in West Street, and cramming a great bundle of six millions in greenbacks into a valise, threw themselves into a hack and rode at top speed toward the Hudson River. At the Jersey City ferry, a formidable bodyguard of Erie porters and detectives already waited to escort them on their westward journey into the free and open spaces of New Jersey. It was a close call; the deputies, hard on their heels, had managed to arrest two directors and clap them into Ludlow Street Jail. Some others had escaped in rowboats across the river.

Arrived in Jersey City the men of Erie established their main offices in the hotel known as Taylor's Castle, hard by the Erie depot. They threw armed guards about the place and renamed it "Fort Taylor." To the newspapers which followed the *cause célèbre* day by day, the breezy and irrepressible Fisk made the following statement:

> The Commodore owns New York, the Stock Exchange, the streets, the railroads and most of the steamships there belong to him. As ambitious young men, we saw there was no chance for us there to expand, and so we came over here to grow up with the country. . . . Yes, tell Mr. Greeley from us that we're sorry now that we didn't take his advice sooner—about going West.

To the huge entertainment of the general public, the War of Erie continued to rage all through the year 1868, with mounting effects of the burlesque and the sinister. Daniel Drew now seemed the much subdued prisoner of Gould and Fisk, who held him bound to them in a manner that showed their complete grip over his darkest affairs. Intensely aroused by the prize of millions of greenbacks in their grasp, the two young men surpassed themselves in brilliant stratagems directed against the Vanderbilt party. On the one hand they undertook a famous division of spoils with the local statesmen and judges, which the parsimonious Commodore, though goaded to extremities, felt too poor to attempt on such a scale. In the next breath, before the press and the people, in raillery or in earnestness, they denounced their famous enemy as one who lusted for monopoly at all costs, "of all the railroads that tie up with the West," and presented themselves to popular opinion as friends of the masses. And to lend color to such claims, Jay Gould reduced passenger rates to Buffalo from seven dollars to five, a strong blow at the hard-pressed Vanderbilt. Finally, having high respect for the Commodore's prowess, and not trusting the foregoing measures, they also had recourse to arms. Jersey City's Chief of Police furnished at their request a squad of police to augment the force of railroad detectives who patrolled the streets and wharves near "Fort Taylor"; three twelve-pound cannon were mounted on the piers; and Jim Fisk, at the head of a squad of four dozen men, equipped with Springfield rifles and lifeboats, strutted about, bursting with pride: he was now "Admiral" Jim Fisk.

In the financial center of New York, a period of stringency followed the flight of the Erie ring. The removal of between six and seven millions in currency, at a time when Vanderbilt and the bankers who financed him were reported to be embarrassed, caused a decline in securities, and even a fall in the dollar. But with iron nerve the Commodore held on, no one knew how. He had a mass of Erie shares, upon which the banks refused to lend him further sums of money, as a fraudulent security; they would accept only his New York Central stocks as collateral.

"Very well, gentlemen," his broker said, as if by authority, "if you don't lend the Commodore half a million on Erie at 50, and do it at once, he will put Central on the market tomorrow and break half the houses on the street! You know whether you will be among them."

Vanderbilt was ready to bring the whole financial structure down in his ruin. With pistol pointed at their head, the bankers and the disheartened speculators continued to follow their leader, willy-nilly, in his dark hours.

As exiles in Jersey City, the rulers of Erie—with the exception of Drew who shut himself up in a room and prayed most of the day—had arranged their lives tolerably well among the unfamiliar scenes. The undersized, almost effeminate Jay Gould showed at this juncture his heroic qualities. The management of the great railroad system was in his hands and all its departments were brought together in the Jersey City hotel. Silent, humorless, and under a habitual nervous tension, the little man with piercing black eyes labored tirelessly or calculated all the day upon their involved affairs. Even Drew, grown senile, could no longer fathom the limitless ambitions of this deep young man, who spoke little, stroked his black beard continually, or nervously tore up pieces of paper into thousands of little bits for hours at a time, at his desk.

Jim Fisk, though he got on famously with his strange confederate, offered a remarkable contrast to him. Where Gould was abstemious, Fisk was openhanded and spent his money freely; where Gould, who kept his mouth shut and his money hidden, was cautious or diffident, Fisk was loud and self-confident. Yet his braggadocio concealed his real shrewdness, and with his verve, his ready jests, his strewings of charity—like a Robin Hood—he diverted attention from his monumental unscrupulousness. And though Gould's life was a torment, showing too plainly the cross of his overweening money-lust, Fisk rejoiced, brangled and drank while engaged with unequaled zest in the multitudinous details of his office. At the railroad headquarters of Taylor's Castle, he installed his buxom mistress, Josie Mansfield, whose dazzling white skin, whose thick black hair and gray eyes enthralled him so long and fatally, for whom he had forsaken his lawful spouse, and upon whom he lavished vast sums of money in his mad infatuation. Though Gould was himself puritanical in his private life, and disapproved of his partner's lavish style, he would say nothing. Though his was the directing brain, he knew how much he owed his success at the outset to the brimming energies, the audacity, and the unfailing good spirits of Fisk, whose cunning cynicism he understood better than anyone else.

Cut off from the financial capital, their situation was by no means comfortable, and the aging Drew complained bitterly. They held Erie, but the enemy held New York. It was rumored that Vanderbilt had offered a prize of twenty-five thousand dollars for the kidnaping of the trio; and one day a band of forty evil-looking New York toughs had crossed the river, and laid siege to the Erie offices. They retired to the Empire State only upon the appearance of superior forces.

After but a few weeks of enforced exile, Jay Gould suddenly departed for Albany upon a secret mission of tremendous importance. He bore with him a big valise containing $500,000 in greenbacks. At the state capitol, as Charles F. Adams explains, "he assiduously cultivated a thorough understanding between himself and the legislature," an understanding which later figured in the books of Erie as "legal expenses," eventually costing $1,000,000.

Gould, convinced that he had not heeded the letter of the law sufficiently, lobbied for a measure which would legalize the new issues of Erie convertible bonds for the sake of "construction and improvements." On behalf of Vanderbilt a formidable body of legal counselors, headed by the young, silver-tongued Chauncey Depew, descended upon Albany to advocate the condemnation of the Erie ring and all its lawless proceedings. Faced with such moneyed contestants, the excitement of the tribunes of the people passed all bounds. Never had such bounties been offered for good-will of state Senators. Riotous scenes were succeeded by more secret and muffled ones behind closed doors in hotel rooms or in saloons with the agents of both forces. On the whole, led by the astute Senator William Tweed, the statesmen conducted themselves with remarkable poise, and led the Erie and the New York Central men to bid against each other until the maximum levies were gathered from both.

Gould, arrested by order of the Supreme Court, remained in the custody of a sheriff's deputy, but continued his elaborate negotiations from his hotel suite. He admitted afterward having overpaid one man "in whom he did not take much stock" by $5,000. What did he pay then to those in whom he did take stock? Others were said to have received as much as $100,000, while, according to Charles F. Adams's account, still others received $70,000. Above all Senator Mattoon, chairman of the committee reporting the Erie Bill, appears to have been marvelously enriched after confidential interviews with both sides, and aroused the bitterest envy among his colleagues.

> Fabulous stories were told of the amounts which the contending parties were willing to expend [reports Adams]; never before had the market quotations of votes and influence stood so high.

An "investigation" ordered by the Senate thereafter (April 10, 1873) showed that more than a million dollars had been expended by Drew, Gould and their associates in the one year 1868 "for extra and legal services." But in the final stage Gould's extravagant generosity—perhaps owing to inexperience—was justified when the tide of battle swung to him. It had become known that Vanderbilt, with whom Tweed pretended to side because of an earlier pledge, would pay no more to have the bill defeated. In a rage the legislature had turned against him and passed the measure substantially as Gould desired it, and Governor Fenton, also believed to have been "assiduously cultivated," signed the bill. The indefatigable, unsleeping Gould in his first great political campaign, moving soft-footed everywhere, pressing money upon each lawgiver or menacing him through many quarters with defeat in his home district, triumphed at last by bold, hard work. His actions were made legal; his rule of the 800-mile trunk line was unchallenged —save in the city of New York, where a trivial charge of contempt of court overhung him.

In the following year his enemies made a serious effort to have the act of 1868 repealed, but Gould, testifying before the New York Senate Railroad Commission, spoke with impassioned eloquence in his own behalf. These continual hearings and investigations by the representatives of the people were the great public comedies of the times. His judges included members such as Mattoon, to whom he had previously justified his great designs behind the closed doors of hotel rooms or saloons by proofs valued as high as $20,000 at a time. And now before the same judges, turned sanctimonious and impartial, he must appear to justify in the eyes of the world what he had already proved in private. This shadow-play was part of the period's moral customs and social traditions, and Gould showed himself equal to his part. Though his heart might be full of contempt for the vultures who preyed upon his business, he would proceed to justify his ways to God and man, by pleading pathetically or impetuously in his own defense, and by playing upon their fears.

It was he, Jay Gould, who had saved the Erie Railroad:

> And as long as that law [of convertible bonds] is unrepealed, I should do what I did again; I should save the road. . . . If that was re-pealed, I think Mr. Vanderbilt would have the road, but as long as it is not repealed it is held *in terrorem* over him.

Gould invoked, perhaps for the first time—here is immortal comedy—the specter of the arch-monopolist of railroads devouring the common people. The only way by which Mr. Vanderbilt's New York Central could continue to make exorbitant profits upon its watered stock would be through the control of the Erie and the end of its competition:

> They would then control clear through to the Pacific shore; they could make the price of flour every day in New York or New England a dollar less or five dollars more; they could make the price all winter long. . . .

He, Jay Gould, was for "competition," first, last and always. Warning, cajoling and appealing, Gould won his case and continued on his triumphant way.

The public, on the whole, seemed tolerably satisfied that the omnipotent Vanderbilt had been dislodged by new elements. Gould moreover had shown the highest abilities. He had shown himself equal to Vanderbilt in direct combat; he won acclaim through having seized a great railroad system in the teeth of the most ruthless adversary, who possessed the largest fortune in the country. He had shown himself master of Drew in both cunning and imagination, manipulating the markets with surpassing brilliance and working the printing press with even more reckless abandon. When the going was roughest, when the plot lay thickest, Gould had seemed only more dispassionate, his voice softer, only his eyes glowing more black. And from the whole campaign which so enriched him, he also absorbed rich lessons in statesmanship which he was never to forget.

In a statement made under oath before an investigating committee of the New York State Legislature, in 1873, he explained the principles of his successful political tactics, saying:

In a Republican district, I was a Republican; in a Democratic district I was a Democrat; in a doubtful district I was doubtful; but I was always for Erie!

He had learned, moreover, that it was not enough to conquer a whole legislature; but one must buy the judges as well. In this direction his jovial and florid comrade, Fisk, operated with great sagacity after the spring of 1868; he made overtures to Tammany Hall and was soon well regarded there. As a means to ensure undisturbed rule over Erie's domain, William Tweed and his colleague, Peter Sweeney, had both been elected to the board of directors of the Erie Railroad. And though officially pledged to Vanderbilt, their secret influence, it was widely believed, had been thrown to the side of Gould.

Finally it was still necessary to make peace with Vanderbilt, a mighty power who must somehow be mollified. In the summer of 1868 overtures were made by both sides. Vanderbilt himself had written to Uncle Daniel a secret message.

Drew: I'm sick of the whole damned business. Come and see me.
                                            Van Derbilt.

When the two met at Vanderbilt's house, the Commodore is believed to have said with his usual forthrightness: "This Erie war has taught me that it never pays to kick a skunk." He proposed terms which were severe, but appealed to the exiles more than perpetual isolation and attack from such powerful quarters. Drew, Gould and Fisk were to make restitution, repaying the Commodore $2,500,000 in ready money, another $1,000,000 subsidy in return for an option on fifty thousand shares of his stock, and $1,250,000 in bonds—in all a total of some $4,550,000 which he asserted had been stolen from him by way of the printing press. Drew accepted the terms meekly; and at further conference early one morning in September, 1868, at which Gould and Fisk appeared in the Washington Place residence, a lasting accord was established, which brought immunity on old charges against them. It would appear that the Erie men assented to Vanderbilt's hard terms, somewhat reluctantly according to Fisk's account:

> The Commodore was sitting on the side of the bed with one shoe off and one shoe on. He got up, and I saw him putting on the other shoe. I remember that shoe from its peculiarity: it had four buckles on it. I had never seen shoes with buckles in that manner before, and I thought if these sort of men always wear that sort of shoe I might want a pair.
> He said I must take my position as I found it; that there I was, and he would keep his bloodhounds (the lawyers) on our track; that he would be damned if he didn't keep them after us if we didn't take the stock off his hands. I told him that if I had my way I'd be damned if I would take a share of it; that he brought the punishment on himself and he deserved it. This mellowed him down. . . . I told him that he

was a robber. He said the suits would never be withdrawn until he was settled with. I said (after settling with him) that it was an almighty robbery; that we had sold ourselves to the devil, and that Gould felt just the same as I did.

Vanderbilt had lost in any case about a million and a half in his jousts with Gould, and gave the new rulers of Erie a wide berth after this. He swore that he would "never have nothing more to do with them blowers," and he never did. But the transactions which brought peace were probably unique, as Fisk judged, in all the annals of "high" capitalism.

* * * * *

But all through the summer of 1869, the unfathomable Jay, moving about with soft tread and grave mien, was in pursuit of far greater game than a small Eastern coal road. It was the mark of his genius that nearly every defeat he suffered was turned into a victory: in the Albany & Susquehanna affair, after long litigation he was to end by liquidating his hard-won shares at a large profit in the final settlement. And with each fresh conquest he hastened without rest to undertakings more hazardous and difficult, and of a greater magnitude. He had a true gift for large affairs, and a kind of virile power to conduct many of them at the same time. His decisive conquest of Vanderbilt had stamped him as a master of railroad "operations." Though in its physical character as a machine of transportation, as a part of the American social-economic order, the Erie steadily augmented its ill-fame; although, as the historian Gustavus Myers had estimated, Gould may have added not a locomotive, a train or a station while increasing its fixed capital by about sixty-five millions in the few years of his reign, he might have explained if he wished that such criticisms touched matters of little consequence. The grand objectives from which his eyes never wavered lay in a totally different direction from any conceivable form of social duty, which in any case no authority was so senseless as to urge upon the great freebooters of his age.

The reservoir of money which lay in the Erie treasury under the nervous hands of Gould was in itself an engine useful for mighty "operations." Through its alliance with "Boss" Tweed the Erie ring also had some voice in the management of the New York City funds, amounting to between six and ten millions of dollars, deposited in New York banks. During seasons when markets were cheerful and money was "easy," the wizard of Erie could manipulate some twenty millions in currency, in conjunction with the Tammany men. Now as Gould's far-flung plans matured he applied with masterly skill the technique of stock speculation which he had learned from Uncle Daniel Drew.

After having sold Erie short at a good moment, Gould would cause his associates to make sudden large withdrawals of cash from the banks under their control, so that money became "tight," loan rates shot upward (sometimes to over 100 per cent per annum), while stocks and grains and cotton collapsed in time with the planned raids, which were executed from season to season, without warning and with unfailing success. It was widely known that on certain occasions Henry N. Smith of the brokerage firm of Smith, Gould and Martin, together with Tweed, "drove up to the Tenth National Bank, the Black Friday institution, in a cab, and drew their balances out, Smith alone taking $4,000,000 with him, which he kept several days at home under lock and key."

Emboldened by his success in corralling a great part of New York's supply of ready money, Gould's mind was soon possessed by a scheme which envisaged nothing less than cornering the whole nation's currency. With the resources at his command, he could easily manage the floating supply of gold traded in every day in the Gold Room of the New York Stock Exchange. It remained only to take care of the federal Treasury's holdings of some seventy-five to eighty millions in some manner. If he could but lay his hands on this hoard, or *neutralize* it, the price of gold, metal basis for the national currency, could be manipulated at will and driven up to a tremendously inflated figure.

At the very time of the Erie wars on various fronts, Gould had begun to encircle government officials at Washington. In May, 1869, Abel R. Corbin, lawyer, speculator and lobbyist, wedded to President Grant's sister and considered very close to the White House, was tactfully approached by the Mephistopheles of Wall Street, and persuaded to contract for the purchase of $1,500,000 of gold at 133, though without payment on his part. Corbin, an old man, was very excited at the prospects which Gould unfolded for him, and apparently showed a lively sense of gratitude for the favors extended to him. To him and to other politicians high in the President's confidence, Gould also stressed the noble political motives underlying his campaign: the cheapening of greenbacks, renewed inflation, would cause the Western grain crops to move rapidly, and to be sold in Europe, stimulating all trade, and incidentally enriching the railroads. For never had farmers and merchants prospered so much as when it had taken, during the war, some $2.80 to buy a dollar's worth of gold, he argued. The dollar was too close nowadays to its gold parity; gold must be raised again; the dollar must fall.

In the gold market, where brokers traded every day against the legitimate currency needs of importers and commercial houses, rumors were stealthily introduced of Gould's coming campaigns, and in view of the general respect entertained for him as a free-roving economic power, created a vigorous following movement. But opposed to the bulls in gold were massive vested interests; the great banking houses, such as Jay Cooke & Co., which had bought and sold over two thousand millions in government bonds and "legal tender" and reinvested and multiplied their profits in inflated money. Now they exhorted the government to complete the process of deflation and make all obligations redeemable once more in "hard money" valued at the traditional gold standard. Upon a rising trend, the tide swayed backward and forward, in response to the masterly touches of Mephistopheles' golden baton.

In June President Grant, passing through New York on his way to a great

Peace Jubilee in Boston, stopped at Corbin's. There the confederates besieged him with their entreaties; and on board the *Providence*, the following
day, luxurious floating "palace" of the Narragansett Line, belonging to Fisk,
Grant had become the guest of the Prince of Erie himself, who paraded in
the uniform of an admiral after his own fancy among the glittering mirrors,
the carved gilt furniture and the stirring airs of a brass band. While Fisk,
bursting with vanity and flashing with all his sparklers, blocked the view
of the assembled journalists and the brilliant crowd, Gould always hovering
at the President's ear pressed his views upon him anew, but got no reply
from the stolid little man, who puffed at his black cigar without uttering a
word of his opinions. Disappointment at the President's evasiveness or uncertainty leaked out; gold dropped several points toward 125.

Unresting worker, Gould tried at least to keep himself intimately informed of the government's immediate fiscal policy. Through his and Corbin's direct influence, General Daniel Butterfield, prominent Union League
politician and a friend to the Goldbugs (as they were popularly called),
was appointed federal subtreasurer at New York. Propaganda for inflation
was now actively disseminated in the press; hired lobbyists besieged all the
doors of the statesmen.

In New York, for effect, a great banquet was given to Secretary of the
Treasury Boutwell, at which the Erie ring played their part; and Boutwell,
"with a superficial parade of purity and superior virtue, as well as genius,"
according to the *New York Herald*, "declared that he would not heed the
gold gamblers, and that what was done in Wall Street was 'none of his
business.' " Gold resumed its rise, and was quoted at 133.

The President's brother-in-law, Corbin, was then paid a check for
$25,000 against his part of the profits, perhaps to show him how it felt, or
to inspire him further. When next the President passed through New York
on September 2, 1869, and visited Gould's accomplice, Corbin seemed to
have exerted himself in earnest. Word went forth like wild fire that Grant
had given orders to Secretary Boutwell not to sell any of the government's
gold, advising him to continue "without change until the present struggle
between bulls and bears is over." In a swift flurry, gold was marked up to
137.

The pool, which had been proceeding cautiously up to now, began its
drive in earnest. A purchase of $1,500,000 in gold was opened in the name
of subtreasurer Butterfield, without payment on his part; an attempt to confer a similar service was apparently made for General Horace Porter, private
secretary to the President. And then Gould, the inscrutable, toward September 15 disclosed his plans to Jim Fisk (who had by his own relation known
them only vaguely and remained skeptical), telling him in a guarded manner
probably that Mrs. Grant and thereby her heroic spouse as well were involved in their net. Fisk now entered the affair with his combined gusto
and slyness. In the marketplace he spread the amazing rumors by queer
winks and nods; while Gould brought to bear his heaviest artillery with the
mathematical precision he was noted for in such engagements. During the
general buying-wave which drove the price of gold above 141, the Tenth

National Bank, Tammany-controlled, placed all its resources at the service of the ring. Its certified checks were issued in unlimited amounts against purchases of gold which were used as collateral. Up to the night of Thursday, September 23, when gold closed at 144¼, Gould and his confederates were believed to have accumulated forty millions in gold, or twice the available floating supply, thanks to the boundless credits opened by his banks. The man who in youth had busied himself inventing mousetraps was at the end of September, 1869, in a strategic position to engineer a gigantic "squeeze" in the national money market—unless the government entered the situation in determined fashion.

But here, at this fruitful stage, the alarm was suddenly given. That perennial friend and watchdog for the people, Horace Greeley, began thundering against the Goldbugs in the *Tribune,* after September 15, denouncing a vast gold conspiracy and calling upon the Treasury to sell gold and purchase bonds so as to relieve the growing currency tension. In Washington the Tycoon himself, Jay Cooke, made urgent representations to Boutwell and Grant, while the volatile Wall Street mob with rising excitement swung back and forth from one side to the other.

In their extremity the Goldbugs now applied the screws to the old simonist Corbin, who upon the spot wrote an importunate letter to President Grant, confessing his predicament and beseeching him not to ruin his own kin by unloading the government's gold. The slow-moving or wavering military hero, now thoroughly apprized of the situation, was deeply agitated and determined at last to move upon them with the force he usually showed when aroused. At his order a letter was written by his wife to Mrs. Corbin, urging that Mr. Corbin should sell his gold at once, and stating that the President disavowed all connection with him. Corbin, paralyzed with fear, must have communicated this alarming turn of affairs to Jay Gould in the night of September 23, or early the following morning. It needed but little more to convince Mephisto that the game was up.

What Jay Gould's final dispositions were for the business day that followed will always remain an obscure page of our history. Fisk always vowed that he was misled, the innocent tool of that "singular man" Gould. It was strange if no one smiled or coughed at Fisk's assertions. He was neither impoverished by his misadventures, nor were his intimate ties with Gould weakened in the least thereafter. . . .

Friday, September 24, 1869, was plainly marked to be the climax of the gold ring's campaign. Jim Fisk in person was to unloose an avalanche of buying orders, which would close the great trap, tightening the gold corner unbearably, so that the price might soar toward 200! But his buying was to be done in the name and at the sole responsibility of his brokers, Belden and Speyer, according to signed agreements made ready for that fateful day. The buying drive was to be continued unremittingly with rising pressure until word came by telegraph from Washington during the day that the federal government was in motion.

The market of "Black Friday" opened in pandemonium, after successive days of increasing tension. Above the uproar could be heard always the bellowing of the stout Fisk to his brokers to bid for all the gold that was offered; while reports were circulated publicly that Gould had prepared a list of names of 200 firms which had sold him gold futures, and would demand settlement without mercy. Starting from 150 gold climbed spectacularly amid frenzied trading to 160 and 165, while concerns of all sorts hysterically directed their agents to buy gold at any price. The riotous scenes that developed in exchanges all over the country were like to engulf the whole nation in ruins. During the mad gyrations of the day, from Boston to San Francisco banks and brokerage houses closed their doors, while the streets of the financial centers were thronged by a milling mob. In Philadelphia, the clocklike indicator of the gold market could no longer keep up with the lightning fluctuations, and finally a black flag with a skull and crossbones was thrown over its face by some distracted humorist, and trading continued under the funereal emblem. But in the temple of the New York money-changers the scene, almost surpassing all powers of description, has been painted by Gustavus Myers in a purple passage of his "History of the Great American Fortunes":

> Here could be seen many of the money masters shrieking and roaring, anon rushing about with whitened faces, indescribably contorted, and again bellowing forth this order or that curse with savage energy and wildest gesture. . . . The little fountain in the Gold Room serenely spouted and bubbled as usual, its cadence lost in the awful uproar; over to it rushed man after man, splashing its cooling water on his throbbing head. Over all rose a sickening exhalation, the dripping, malodorous sweat of an assemblage worked up to the very limit of endurance.

What deepened the calamity was not merely the rise, but the catastrophic fall of gold which began with dramatic suddenness at midday as the government swung into action, when Boutwell ordered millions flung upon the market "as publicly as possible." Within fifteen minutes the whole structure toppled and the price broke at once to 138. While brokers swooned in the crush and stampede, "the agony depicted on the faces of men who crowded the streets," as the newspaper accounts affirm, "made one feel as if Gettysburg had been lost and the rebels were marching down Broadway." In the morning men who had been unable to buy gold announced themselves ruined with wild laments; and after the noon hour, great numbers who had paid too much in turn announced themselves insolvent with equally unrestrained expressions of grief, and menaces of death to the crazed brokers of the gold ring.

At the height of the frenzy, two of Fisk's "queens," by common report, had driven merrily through the financial section to witness their hilarious patron's triumph. But they had seen to their horror only a mob of ruined speculators besieging the offices Fisk and Gould were wont to frequent, crying for the heads of the conspirators. Fisk, perhaps feigning not to have heard of last-minute developments, made his way to the house of the abject Corbin to abuse him for a treacherous scoundrel; while Gould had fled from the lynchers by a back door.

Like an inspired fiend, Jay Gould had ridden out the storm to safety. He, "the guilty plotter of all these criminal proceedings," as the Congressional Committee of 1870 held, "determined to betray his own associates, and silent and imperturbable by nods and whispers directed all." He had miraculously saved himself in the face of disaster on the morning of September 24, selling all the gold he possessed upon the crest of the buying wave evoked by his agents. The cyclone of calamity had given favoring winds to his escape. Opinion differed afterward as to whether he had gained nothing, lost all he possessed, or garnered eleven millions of dollars at one coup.

In the aftermath, Jay Gould obtained twelve sweeping injunctions and court orders from his complaisant judges, prohibiting the Stock Exchange and the Gold Board from enforcing contracts or rules of settlement which he broke. The Erie ring's brokers, Belden and Speyer—the latter of whom had gone temporarily insane—defaulted completely and none of the bids they made were ever honored. Their bankruptcy did not affect Fisk in any way, since all the buying they had done to drive up the market was "in their own name and at their sole risk" according to signed documents found in his possession. Everything had been foreseen! No written order signed by Fisk was ever found. It was said that he and Gould had agreed to settle a large annuity for life upon each of the bankrupt brokers, and that Fisk's payment was through a perfectly satisfactory division of the prize with Gould.

President Grant was compromised by "indiscreet acceptance of courtesies," for the trail of the investigation, as Garfield wrote confidentially, "led into the parlor of the President." Though it did not touch him, it touched a member of his family; and so the conventional hearings by legislators ordered in 1870, and directed by men who held stock in the notorious Crédit Mobilier, took evidence which, as Henry Adams has said, "it dared not probe and refused to analyze." Executives, judiciary, banks, professions and people were all smirched, Adams concluded, "in one dirty cesspool of vulgar corruption."

How could Gould as a private individual have been punished for his perfectly legal whim to buy whatever quantities of gold he could obtain? There was not a law in the country that struck at the actions of the prodigious "self-made man" and no one understood this better than the unhappy "Railway Congressmen," Garfield and Blaine. Moreover, his motives, as he insisted at the ensuing investigation without once losing his self-possession, were blameless; he labored only in the interests of the people and especially the Western farmers. But Fisk had proved to be a bull in the china shop. He had turned the solemn hearings into low farce.

In a vein of injured innocence he dwelt on the "treachery" of the President's brother-in-law Corbin. With his own hands he had tried to punish the old man for his "infamy." Then, beside himself with more or less feigned excitement, Fisk called Heaven to witness that he had been wronged. He desired only to make a clean breast of everything. Let Mrs. Corbin, and finally Mrs. Grant, he clamored, be brought to the bar of justice. Alternately frightened and amused, the tribunes in Washington chose to pay him off with immunity, as a respectable merchant placates a loud-mouthed fishwife so that she may leave his respectable premises the sooner.

"Let everyone carry out his own corpse!" Fisk bellowed. And his inquisitors of the Congressional committee, understanding him perfectly, asked no further questions. They reported only what everyone knew: that "for many weeks the business of the whole country was paralyzed" and that the "foundations of business morality were rudely shaken."

ᒃᔆᒃ ᔆᔆ

Corruption permeated every aspect of American life in the Gilded Age. Nowhere was this more obvious than in the urban centers. And no single person demonstrated the affluence awaiting seizure in the city more flamboyantly than William Marcy Tweed, Tammany Boss, who in the late 1860's looted the New York City treasury of somewhere between $75 million and $200 million. The excesses reached such proportions that in 1872, after The New York Times had published a searing exposé, a Democratic committee chaired by Samuel J. Tilden, a wealthy railroad lawyer, ousted Tweed, set in motion prosecution of his ring, and brought about reform of the city's government. He was swept into the New York governorship in 1874 as a reform candidate and promptly set to work reinforcing his image as a reformer. The Democratic party in 1876 nominated him as their candidate. The intention was obvious, to exploit the reform issue on the federal level, where the Grant administration produced scandal as other administrations produced legislation. The Republicans met the challenge by nominating Rutherford B. Hayes, widely known as the reform governor of Ohio.

On November 7, 1876, Tilden carried a popular margin of 250,000 votes, but the Republicans challenged the results in Florida, Louisiana, and South Carolina. Without the electoral vote of one of these states, Tilden was one vote shy of the 185 electoral votes needed. Republican election boards in the three Southern states threw out enough Tilden votes to give Hayes their vote. In an atmosphere of threatening violence, with two sets of electors from each of the disputed states, Congress convened in December. The Constitution provides that "The President of the Senate shall, in the presence of the Senate and the House of Representatives, open all certificates and the votes shall then be counted." The question was whether the Republican Senate or Democratic House would do the actual counting. The nation still recuperating from the mutilating effects of the Civil War found itself confronted with the threat of renewed civil upheaval. Congress dodged the issue by creating an Electoral Commission to determine the allotment of the disputed votes. On March 2, 1877, the Commission found in favor of Hayes, and by an electoral vote of 185-184 he edged out Tilden. Historians have generally agreed that Tilden probably carried at least one of the disputed states and should have become the President. But until recently, although most historians believed that considerable behind-the-scenes bargaining had gone on, no one knew precisely what had happened.

Edward Stanwood (1841-1923) gave a graphic narrative account of the disputed election, but he did not attempt to go to the root of the bargain that sealed Hayes' election. C. Vann Woodward (1908-   ), one of the most gifted of living historians, in Reunion and Reaction (1951) elucidated the bargain in a detailed account that resembled a detective story. The price the Southern Democrats exacted from the Republicans for their acceptance of the Electoral Commission's findings was the final withdrawal of federal troops from the South, the appointment of a Southerner to the Cabinet, federal appropriations for Southern internal improvements, and the return of Southern whites to control of racial relations. It meant the end of Reconstruction and was for all practical purposes the treaty of peace that terminated the Civil War. It was also a commentary on the long journey the South had made since, when in the winter of 1860-61, it rebelled against a constitutionally elected President, and in the winter of 1876-77, it traded away a constitutionally elected President.

A HISTORY OF THE PRESIDENCY
FROM 1788 TO 1897

by Edward Stanwood

It began to be rumored in 1875 that General Grant would be a candidate for a third term. Since the time of Washington it had been an unwritten law that eight years should be the limit of any man's service at the head of the government. The idea that the rule established by the Father of his Country was to be broken was highly displeasing to a large body of Republicans, and still more so to all Democrats. There was much public and private discussion on the subject. The President himself allowed it to be understood that he was not disposed to refuse a third term if it should be offered him. In a letter addressed to General Harry White, of Pennsylvania, he expressed himself in terms that could not be misunderstood. The Republican state convention, over which General White presided, had passed a resolution of unalterable "opposition to the election to the presidency of any person for a third term." This drew from General Grant the letter referred to, in which he said: "Now for the third term. I do not want it any more than I did the first"; but he also remarked that the people were not restricted to two terms by the Constitution; that the time might come when it would be unfortunate to make a change at the end of eight years; and that he "would not accept a nomination if it were tendered, unless it should come under such circumstances as to make it an imperative duty,—circumstances not likely to arise." The universal interpretation of these phrases was that General Grant's friends were at liberty to make it appear the imperative duty of the Republicans to nominate him again, and of the President to accept the nomination. But the idea made little headway except among the officials of the government and the most devoted adherents of the President. There was, nevertheless, much apprehension that the close organization of the official class would make it possible to manipulate the primary meetings and secure his nomination. A death-blow to the movement was dealt soon after the opening of Congress, in December, 1875. A Democratic member from Illinois offered a resolution, "that, in the opinion of this House, the precedent established by Washington and other Presidents of the United States, in retiring from the presidential office after their second term, has become, by universal concurrence, a part of our republican system of government, and that any departure from this time-honored custom would be unwise, unpatriotic, and fraught with peril to our free institutions." This resolution was passed by the immense majority of 234 to 18. Not only did all the Democrats present support it, but 70 out of the 88 Republicans voting were also found in the affirmative.

Nothing more was heard that year of the third term, and the Republicans who had been willing to entertain the idea turned their attention to other candidates, while the Republican leaders who had been special friends of the administration felt themselves at liberty to become candidates for the Republican nomination. There were many candidates. The favor of the administration was believed to have gone chiefly to Senator Conkling, of New York, when General Grant himself was put out of the running; but there was no hostility to Senator Morton, of Indiana, who ultimately secured most of the southern delegations. Both of these gentlemen had been ardent defenders of the President whenever he had been attacked, and trustworthy supporters of all administration measures.

The strongest movement, outside of the official circles, was in favor of Mr. James G. Blaine, of Maine. Mr. Blaine had been six years Speaker of the House of Representatives, and had gained extraordinary popularity among members of Congress. At the beginning of the Forty-fourth Congress, in 1875, the control of the House having passed into the hands of the Democrats, he had become the natural leader of the minority on the floor, and had drawn the attention of the country by some brilliant parliamentary victories. Many Republicans, however, regretted that in so doing he had revived memories of the war which they were entirely willing should be forgotten. When the movement to make him the Republican candidate became formidable some of them felt constrained to oppose him. Soon afterward whispers were heard that his public career was not free from acts which, if not corrupt, involved corrupt motives and desires; and these insinuations took a form which led to an investigation into Mr. Blaine's connection with the Little Rock and Fort Smith Railroad

Company and the Union Pacific Railroad Company. In brief, Mr. Blaine had, as Speaker, given a decision which facilitated the passage of a bill authorizing the State of Arkansas to aid in the construction of the Fort Smith road. Afterward he had become interested in the securities of the company; and it was asserted that he had traded upon the service he had rendered to the company to obtain specially favorable terms from those who had the disposal of the securities. Mr. Blaine's prominence in public affairs, and the strong position he occupied as a candidate for the Republican nomination, caused the scandal to attract general attention. The letters he had written upon the subject were in hostile hands. Mr. Blaine obtained possession of them, and in a memorably dramatic scene read them, with his own explanation, to the House of Representatives. The effect was precisely what might have been expected: those who were previously convinced of his guilt saw in them proof of the charges against him; his ardent admirers, of whom there was a host in all parts of the country, accepted them as a complete exoneration. The present writer, who enjoyed a lifelong personal friendship, and for many years was on terms of intimacy, with Mr. Blaine, always believed in his innocence not only of the charges here referred to, but of others which his political opponents made against him. The unpleasant chapter in his history is recorded here because it had an important bearing upon his aspirations to the presidency, but with keen regret that a perpetuation of it is necessary.

A strong movement was organized in the party in favor of Mr. Benjamin H. Bristow, the Secretary of the Treasury. Mr. Bristow had won the high opinion of the country by his vigorous proceedings against the western "whiskey rings." The heavy tax upon distilled spirits was a great temptation to fraud in its manufacture. Evidence was obtained that many western distilleries were enabled by collusion with government officers to manufacture vast amounts of whiskey upon which no tax was paid. They secured a great profit, which profit was divided between those who committed the frauds and those who permitted them. Certain persons near the administration were implicated, or at least open to serious suspicion. The President directed that the prosecutions should be pressed with all vigor; but Mr. Bristow received most of the credit for the unrelenting vigor with which the prosecutions were carried to a successful issue. Accordingly he became the favorite candidate of those who were most opposed to what it was the fashion to call "Caesarism" and "Grantism."

Ohio presented her governor, Rutherford B. Hayes, a general in the Union army during the war, formerly a member of Congress, and in 1876, for the third time, governor of Ohio. Governor John F. Hartranft, of Pennsylvania, and Mr. Marshall Jewell, who had been governor of Connecticut, minister to Russia, and Postmaster-general were also candidates.

The leading candidate on the Democratic side was Governor Samuel J. Tilden, of New York, but his supremacy was not undisputed. Mr. Hendricks, of Indiana, who had received most of the votes of Democratic electors in 1872, after the death of Mr. Greeley, had strong western support. General Hancock was a favorite of the soldiers, as he had been in

1868. Ohio was in the field with ex-Governor William Allen, who had carried the State in 1873. But as the state and district conventions made Mr. Blaine the leading candidate on the Republican side, so those of the Democrats placed Mr. Tilden far in advance of all competitors. Mr. Tilden had gained a high reputation by his warfare against the "Tweed ring" in New York city some years before, and had added to it by his career as governor of the State of New York. But he was opposed most warmly by the Tammany organization in his own city, and this was deemed by many a sufficient reason why he should not be nominated. Such was the situation when the season of national conventions began, in May, 1876.

*   *   *   *   *

The Republican convention met at Cincinnati on June 14. As the day approached, the public interest in the meeting became very great. The delegates elected in most of the States were pledged to one or another of the candidates. Each of the three largest States had a candidate of its own. New York, with 70 delegates, was substantially unanimous for Mr. Conkling; Pennsylvania, with 58 delegates, was instructed to vote for General Hartranft; Ohio, whose delegates numbered 44, was united in support of Governor Hayes. These three candidates thus held 172 votes out of the 756 to which all the States and Territories were entitled. Mr. Morton had, in addition to the 30 votes of his own Indiana delegation, nearly 100 more pledged to him, every one of which was from the Southern States. The Bristow strength was unknown, but was believed to be about 100 votes. It was evident from the beginning that, if the forces of these five candidates could be united, the defeat of Mr. Blaine, whose delegates were more than twice as numerous as those of any other candidate, was assured. The party was roughly divided into two wings, one of which was warmly in favor of the Grant administration, while the other desired "reform within the party." The prevailing sentiment was decidedly hostile to a perpetuation of the Grant administration under a new head. The administration strength was represented, accurately enough, by the Conkling and Morton contingents. The rest of the delegates were, for the most part, opposed to any one who might seem to be the political heir of the President. Many of the adherents of Mr. Bristow were as strongly opposed to Mr. Blaine as they were to what they called "the Grant Dynasty." The charges brought against Mr. Blaine were in process of investigation almost up to the very day that the convention met. Many delegates believed the charges to be true; and although a large majority of the delegates probably disbelieved them, some of them deemed it bad policy to nominate a man who was so seriously assailed. On the Sunday morning before the convention, Mr. Blaine suffered a sunstroke, and was, for a day or two, believed to be dangerously ill. This also was unfortunate for him, and probably cost him some votes.

Theodore M. Pomeroy, of New York, was temporary chairman of the convention, and Edward McPherson, of Pennsylvania, was the permanent president. On the second day the adoption of the rules drafted by the committee on rules introduced some important reforms in national convention work. It was decided that the report of the committee on credentials should be disposed of first, the platform next, and only then should the nomination of candidates be in order. Another rule put an end to the practice of "stampeding," by providing that the roll-call should in no case be dispensed with; and that after the vote of a State for candidates was announced it should not be changed on that ballot.

There were several contested elections, but the only important case was that of Alabama, where one delegation, headed by Senator Spencer, was in favor of Mr. Morton, the other, headed by Mr. Haralson, a colored member of Congress, was divided between Mr. Blaine and Mr. Bristow. The Spencer delegation was refused admittance by a vote of 375 to 354, and the Haralson delegation was admitted.

*   *   *   *   *

On the third day the nominations were made. On the first vote Mr. Blaine received 285; Mr. Morton 125; Mr. Bristow 113; Mr. Conkling 99; Mr. Hayes 61; Mr. Hartranft 58; Mr. Jewell 11; and Mr. William A. Wheeler, of New York, 3. Mr. Blaine's strength was made up of 77 votes from the South, and of 208 from Northern States, including some votes from almost every State except those which presented candidates of their own. Mr. Morton had 30 votes from Indiana, and 95 from Southern States. Mr. Bristow's votes were given by seventeen States and one Territory, and were strictly scattering, except the votes of Kentucky, his own State, 17 from Massachusetts, and 10 from Tennessee. Mr. Conkling's 99 were made up of 69 from New York and a few scattering votes from nine other States; the South contributing 25 of the 30. Mr. Hayes had 17 votes from other States than Ohio. The other candidates received no votes except from their respective States. Seven trials were necessary to effect a choice. They resulted as follows:—

	1st	2nd	3rd	4th	5th	6th	7th
Blaine	285	296	293	292	286	308	351
Morton	125	120	113	108	95	85	—
Bristow	113	114	121	126	114	111	21
Conkling	99	93	90	84	82	81	—
Hayes	61	64	67	68	104	113	384
Hartranft	58	63	68	71	69	50	—
Jewell	11	—	—	—	—	—	—
Scattering	3	4	3	5	5	5	—
Whole Number	754	754	755	754	755	755	756
Necessary	378	378	378	378	378	378	379 [sic]

The nomination of Mr. Hayes was made unanimous. It seemed to be inevitable when the fifth ballot was announced. Mr. Hayes was the only candidate who had made a gain on every vote; and as he was entirely unobjectionable to the friends of all other candidates, it was less difficult to concentrate votes upon him than upon any other person in the list. Mr. Blaine, who was informed by telegraph at his house in Washington of the progress of the voting, wrote a dispatch congratulating Mr. Hayes immediately on receiving the result of the fifth vote.

During the progress of the voting a stormy scene took place upon the demand of four Pennsylvania delegates to have their votes separately recorded. The delegation had been instructed to vote "as a unit," and these delegates claimed the right to vote for themselves. Mr. McPherson, the president of the convention, sustained their demand, and, on an appeal, his decision was affirmed, 395 to 354. Thus was broken the famous "unit rule," which, after one more contest at Chicago, four years later, was abandoned by the Republicans, no doubt forever.

Several candidates were presented for the nomination for Vice-President, but, as the voting proceeded, nearly all the votes were for William A. Wheeler, of New York. The other candidates were thereupon withdrawn, and Mr. Wheeler was unanimously nominated. The convention soon afterward adjourned, with cheers for the ticket.

The Democrats met at St. Louis two weeks later. The convention was deprived of much of its interest by the fact that Mr. Tilden's lead for the nomination was so great. He was known to have more than four hundred delegates out of the whole convention of 744, and, while his candidacy was opposed, the opposition came from States which nevertheless sent delegations unanimously in his favor. The delegates who were not for him were not against him. His nomination was therefore universally expected, except by the more sanguine friends of other candidates.

Mr. Henry Watterson, of Kentucky, was the temporary chairman, and General John A. McClernand, of Illinois, the permanent president.

*   *   *   *   *

The convention then proceeded to the work of nominating a candidate for President. After the formal presentation of names, two votes were taken amid great excitement, with the following result:—

	First	Second
Samuel J. Tilden, New York	417½	534
Thomas A. Hendricks, Indiana	140½	60
Winfield S. Hancock, Pennsylvania	75	59
William Allen, Ohio	54	54
Thomas F. Bayard, Delaware	33	11
Joel Parker, New Jersey	18	18
Allen G. Thurman, Ohio	—	2

The whole number of votes on the second ballot being 738, the number necessary to a choice was 492,—the two-thirds rule having been adopted.

Mr. Tilden was accordingly nominated, and the choice was enthusiastically made unanimous. On the next day Thomas A. Hendricks was nominated for Vice-President by a unanimous vote, though the Indiana delegation protested that they did not know if he would accept the second place on the ticket, and the convention shortly afterward adjourned.

The canvass which followed was comparatively spiritless. Mr. Hayes was not sufficiently well known to arouse enthusiasm, and Mr. Tilden, though commanding respect for his ability, was not a candidate to draw to himself strong personal supporters. The Republicans were on the defensive; but this fact served to make the political discussion of the time more strictly a debate about measures and policies than it had been for many years. The Democrats denounced the record of the Republicans; the Republicans derided the reform professions of their opponents as insincere. Great efforts were made by the Republicans to cast discredit upon Mr. Tilden for his connection with certain railroad enterprises; and a suit was brought against him for income tax alleged to be due by him to the government. The Democrats sneered at Mr. Hayes as an unknown man, and roundly denounced the political assessments which were levied mercilessly upon the office-holders for funds to carry the elections. The Republicans made much of the opposition of the Democrats to the resumption policy, though it was well known that Mr. Tilden was a "hard-money man." But on the whole there was less than the usual amount of excitement during the canvass, and less of the usual fireworks of presidential campaigns. Not many Republicans were confident of success, and the result of the early elections, particularly that of Indiana in October, indicated that the Democrats would have enough Northern votes, together with the "solid South," to give them a victory.

Thirty-eight States participated in the election. Colorado had been admitted to the Union in August, 1876, and, in order to save an additional election, the choice of electors for that occasion was conferred upon the legislature. All the other States appointed them by popular vote. The polls had hardly closed on the day of election, the 7th of November, when the Democrats began to claim the presidency. The returns came in so unfavorably for the Republicans that there was hardly a newspaper organ of the party which did not, on the following morning, concede the election of Mr. Tilden. He was believed to have carried every Southern State, as well as New York, Indiana, New Jersey, and Connecticut. The whole number of electoral votes was 369. If the above estimate were correct, the Democratic candidates would have 203 votes, and the Republican candidates 166 votes. But word was sent out on the same day from Republican headquarters at Washington that Hayes and Wheeler were elected by one majority; that the States of South Carolina, Florida, and Louisiana had chosen Republican electors.

Then began the most extraordinary contest that ever took place in the country. The only hope of the Republicans was in the perfect defense of their position. The loss of a single vote would be fatal. An adequate history of the four months between the popular election and the inauguration of Mr. Hayes would fill volumes. Space can be given here for a bare reference only to some of the most important events. Neither party was over-scrupulous, and no doubt the acts of some members of each party were grossly illegal and corrupt. Attempts were even made to find a Republican elector who would vote for Mr. Tilden in consideration of a large sum of money as a bribe. The funds were provided, and mysterious correspondence by telegraph was held between men who were connected with Democratic political committees and those in the several States who were seeking for a venal elector. The whole scandal came to light afterward when the key to the famous "cipher dispatches" was discovered.

In four States, South Carolina, Florida, Louisiana, and Oregon, there were double returns. In South Carolina there were loud complaints that detachments of the army, stationed near the polls, had prevented a fair and free election. Although the board of state canvassers certified to the choice of the Hayes electors, who were chosen on the face of the returns, the Democratic candidates for electors met on the day fixed for the meeting of electors and cast ballots for Tilden and Hendricks. In Florida there were allegations of fraud on both sides. The canvassing board and the governor certified to the election of the Hayes electors, but, fortified by a court decision in their favor, the Democratic electors also met and voted. In Louisiana there was anarchy. There were two governors, two returning boards, two sets of returns showing different results, and two electoral colleges. In Oregon the Democratic governor adjudged one of the Republican electors ineligible, and gave a certificate to the highest candidate on the Democratic list. The Republican electors, having no certificate from the governor, met and voted for Hayes and Wheeler. The Democratic elector, whose appointment was certified to by the governor, appointed two others to fill the vacancies, since the two Republican electors would not meet with him, and the three voted for Tilden and Hendricks. All of these cases were extremely complicated in their incidents, and a brief account which should convey an intelligible idea of what occurred is impossible. For the first and only time in the history of the country, the election ended in such a way as to leave the result in doubt; and in two States the number of legal votes given for the electors was in dispute. In these States the returns were also open to the suspicion of having been manipulated by each party to bring about a desired result.

As soon as the electoral votes had been cast it became a question of the greatest importance how they were to be counted. Congress was divided, politically. The Senate and its President *pro tempore*, Mr. Ferry, of Michigan, were Republican; the House of Representatives was Democratic. It was evident that the Senate would refuse to be governed by the twenty-second joint rule,—in fact the Senate voted to rescind the rule,—and it was further evident that if the count were to take place in accordance with that rule it would result in throwing out electoral votes on both sides on the most frivolous pretexts. It was asserted by the Republicans that, under the

Constitution, the President of the Senate alone had the right to count, in spite of the fact that the joint rule, the work of their party, had assumed the power for the two Houses of Congress. On the other hand, the Democrats, who had always denounced that rule as unconstitutional, now maintained that the right to count was conferred upon Congress. A compromise became necessary, and the moderate men on both sides determined to effect the establishment of a tribunal, as evenly divided politically as might be, which should decide all disputed questions so far as the Constitution gave authority to Congress to decide them. The outcome of their efforts was the Electoral Commission law of 1877, which was passed as originally reported.

*   *   *   *   *

In neither House was the bill treated as a partisan measure. In the House of Representatives 191 members voted in favor of it, of whom there were 158 Democrats and 33 Republicans; 86 members—68 Republicans and 18 Democrats—voted in the negative. In the Senate an attempt was made to forbid the commission to "go behind the returns," but the amendment was rejected, yeas 18, all Republicans; nays 47, of whom 27 were Democrats and 20 Republicans. The bill was passed by the Senate, yeas 47,—26 Democrats and 21 Republicans; nays 17,—16 Republicans and 1 Democrat. The bill became a law, by the approval of the President, on the 29th of January. On the next day each House proceeded to choose five members of the commission. The Senate made choice of Senators George F. Edmunds, Oliver P. Morton, and Frederick T. Frelinghuysen, Republicans, and Allen G. Thurman and Thomas F. Bayard, Democrats. The House of Representatives chose Messrs. Henry B. Payne, Eppa Hunton, and Josiah G. Abbott, Democrats, and James A. Garfield and George F. Hoar, Republicans. The four justices of the Supreme Court designated by the act were Justices Nathan Clifford, William Strong, Samuel F. Miller, and Stephen J. Field, of whom Messrs. Clifford and Field were Democrats in national politics; and they selected Justice Joseph P. Bradley as the fifth member of the commission on the part of the Supreme Court. Mr. Bradley was a Republican. The natural choice of the justices would have been their associate, David Davis; but he had been elected five days before as a senator from Illinois, and it was regarded by him and by others as improper that he should serve. Thus the commission consisted of eight Republicans and seven Democrats. If Judge Davis had been selected, the majority would have been reversed, and the ultimate result might have been different.

When the count began, on the 1st of February, 1877, each party was confident of victory. The Democrats relied upon a great variety of objections which had been prepared, the sustaining of any one of which would be sufficient to give the election to Mr. Tilden. The Republican hope was in a refusal of the commission to "go behind the returns." Senator Thomas W. Ferry, of Michigan, President *pro tempore* of the Senate, was the presiding officer, Vice-President Wilson having died in 1875. The count proceeded, under the law, in the alphabetical order of the States. When the vote of Florida was reached, the certificates of the Hayes and also those of the Tilden electors were read. Objections were made to each. The Democrats asserted that the Hayes electors were not duly chosen; that the certificate of the governor to their election was the result of a conspiracy; that its validity, if any had been annulled by a subsequent certificate by the governor, to the effect that the Tilden electors were chosen; that a court decision made certain the election of the Democratic electors; and that one of the Republican electors was a shipping commissioner under appointment from the government of the United States at the time of his election, and was therefore disqualified. The Republican objection to the Tilden votes was that the returns were not duly authenticated by any person holding at the time an office under the State of Florida. It was only on the 7th of February that the commission, after long arguments by eminent counsel selected to appear for the two parties, decided the case of Florida. The decision was that it was not competent for the commission "to go into evidence *aliunde* the papers opened by the President of the Senate, to prove that other persons than those regularly certified to by the governor" were appointed. With reference to the case of the elector alleged to have been disqualified, it was decided that the evidence did not show that he held an office on the day of his appointment. The several votes were passed by eight to seven,—all the Republicans being on one side, and all the Democrats on the other. The formal decision, which was submitted to the two Houses, was that the four Hayes electors, naming them, were duly appointed electors, and that their votes were the constitutional votes. The Houses met on February 10, and received this decision. Formal objection was then made to the decision of the Electoral Commission, and the Houses separated to consider it. The Senate, by a strict party vote, decided that the votes should be counted. The House of Representatives, by a vote which was on party lines, except that one Democrat voted with the Republicans, voted that the electoral votes given by the Tilden electors should be counted. The two Houses not having agreed in rejecting the decision of the commission, it stood, and the joint session was resumed.

The votes of Florida having been recorded, the count proceeded until Louisiana was reached. The Republican objections to the Tilden votes from Louisiana were, like those to the votes of Florida, brief and formal. The government, of which W. P. Kellogg was the head, had been recognized by every department of the government of the United States as the true government of Louisiana, and the certificates of the Hayes electors certified by him were in due form. The Democrats made a great variety of objections to the Hayes votes. They asserted that John McEnery was the lawful governor of the State; that the certificates asserting the appointment of the Hayes electors were false; and that the canvass of votes by the returning board was without jurisdiction and void. Special objection was made to three of the electors: to two of them as being disqualified, under the Constitution; and to the third, Governor Kellogg, because he certified to his own election. Several days were consumed in argument before the commission. On the 16th of February the commission voted, once more by eight to seven, that the evidence offered to prove that the Tilden electors were chosen be not received, and that the certificates of the Hayes electors were the true votes of Louisiana. The decision having been communicated to the two Houses, the count was resumed on the 19th. Objection was made to the decision of the commission, and the two Houses separated again to act upon them. The Senate voted, by 41 to 28, that the decision of the commission should stand. The House voted that the electoral votes cast by the Hayes electors for Louisiana ought not to be counted,—173 to 99. In each case this was a party vote except that two Republicans in the House voted with the Democrats.

The Houses then met again on the 20th, and resumed the count, which proceeded without dispute as far as the State of Michigan, when objection was made from the Democratic side to one vote from that State, on the ground that one of the persons chosen by the people held a Federal office at the time of his appointment, and that the act of the other electors in filling the alleged vacancy caused by his failure to act was not justified. This not being a case of double returns, the two Houses separated to decide it for themselves. The objection was overruled by each House. A somewhat similar case of an elector for Nevada was the next stumbling-block in the count, and it too was decided in favor of the elector objected to. Oregon was reached in the count on the 21st. An outline sketch of the extremely complicated situation of affairs in Oregon has been given already. There were objections from both sides to the votes, and the papers were referred to the Electoral Commission, by whom further argument was heard. The commission unanimously rejected the made-up vote of the Tilden board of electors, but decided, eight to seven, that the full board of Hayes electors were the legal electors for the State. The decision was objected to, when communicated to the two Houses. Once more they separated, and each decided, substantially by a party vote, as before,—the Senate for accepting the decision, and the House of Representatives for rejecting it. They then met again, and resumed the count. In the vote of Pennsylvania another case was encountered of an elector alleged to have been ineligible by reason of his having been a centennial commissioner. The other electors treated the place as vacant, and chose another person to act in it. The Senate agreed, without a division, to a resolution that the vote be counted. The House rejected it, 135 to 119, the affirmative consisting entirely of Democrats, and the negative containing only 15 of that party. The full vote of Pennsylvania was accordingly counted under the law, the two Houses not having agreed to reject. Rhode Island furnished a case not very different, but the two Houses this time concurred unanimously in deciding that the disputed vote should be counted.

To the Hayes votes in South Carolina the Democrats next objected that there was no legal election in the State, that there was not, in South Carolina, during the year 1876, a republican form of government, and that the army and the United States deputy marshals stationed at and near the polls prevented the free exercise of the right of suffrage. The Republicans asserted that the Tilden board was not duly appointed, and that the certificates were wholly defective in form and lacking the necessary official certification. The papers having been referred to the Electoral Commission, that body met again on the 26th. Senator Thurman was obliged to retire from service upon the commission, on account of illness, and Senator Francis Kernan took his place. After a day devoted to arguments, the commission voted unanimously that the Tilden electors were not the true electors of South Carolina, and, by the old majority of eight to seven, that the Hayes electors were the constitutional electors duly appointed. The two Houses separated upon renewed objections to the decision of the commission, and as before the Senate sustained the finding; the House voted to reject it.

There were two further objections, the first to a vote cast by an elector for Vermont, substituted for an ineligible person who had been chosen by the people, on which the result was the same as in the other similar cases; the other was a case of the same kind in Wisconsin, which was decided in like manner. The Vermont case was complicated by the presentation, by Mr. Hewitt, of New York, of a packet purporting to contain a return of electoral votes given in Vermont. The President of the Senate having received no such vote, nor any vote different from that of the regularly chosen Hayes electors, refused to receive it.

The count had begun on the first day of February, and the final vote upon Wisconsin was not reached until the early morning of March 2. As question after question was decided uniformly in favor of the Republicans, it became evident to the Democrats that their case was lost. They charged gross partisanship upon the Republican members of the Electoral Commission, in determining every point involved in the dual returns for their own party, though as a matter of fact there does not seem to have been much room for choice between the two parties on the score of partisanship. Each member of the commission favored by his vote that view which would result in adding to the electoral vote of his own party. But as the result of the count became more and more certainly a Republican triumph, the anger of the Democrats rose. Some of them were for discontinuing the count; and the symptoms of a disposition to filibuster so that there should be no declaration of the result gave reason for public disquietude. But the conservative members of the party were too patriotic to allow the failure of a law which they had been instrumental in passing to lead to anarchy or revolution, and they sternly discountenanced all attempts to defeat the conclusion of the count. The summing up of the votes was read by Mr. Allison, of Iowa, one of the tellers on the part of the Senate, at a little after four o'clock, on the morning of the 2d of March, amid great excitement. That result, as declared, was as follows:—

STATES	HAYES and WHEELER	TILDEN and HENDRICKS	STATES	HAYES and WHEELER	TILDEN and HENDRICKS
Alabama	—	10	Missouri	—	15
Arkansas	—	6	Nebraska	3	—
California	6	—	Nevada	3	—
Colorado	3	—	New Hampshire	5	—
Connecticut	—	6	New Jersey	—	9
Delaware	—	3	New York	—	35
Florida	4	—	North Carolina	—	10
Georgia	—	11	Ohio	22	—
Illinois	21	—	Oregon	3	—
Indiana	—	15	Pennsylvania	29	—
Iowa	11	—	Rhode Island	4	—
Kansas	5	—	South Carolina	7	—
Kentucky	—	12	Tennessee	—	12
Louisiana	8	—	Texas	—	8
Maine	7	—	Vermont	5	—
Maryland	—	8	Virginia	—	11
Massachusetts	13	—	West Virginia	—	—
Michigan	11	—	Wisconsin	10	5
Minnesota	5	—			
Mississippi	—	8	Total	185	184

Mr. Ferry thereupon declared Rutherford B. Hayes elected President, and William A. Wheeler Vice-President, of the United States. The decision was acquiesced in peaceably by the whole country, and by men of every party. But the Democrats have never ceased to denounce the whole affair as a fraud, and some newspapers have steadily refused to speak of Mr. Hayes as having ever been rightfully in possession of the presidential office. Their anger at the time was very great, and it was excusable, since they honestly believed that Mr. Tilden was fairly elected. It is to be hoped that the patriotism of the American people and their love of peace may never again be put to so severe a test as was that to which they were subjected in 1876 and 1877.

VII

The Republic Marks Time

THE *succession of Presidents between Lincoln and Theodore Roosevelt produced no towering figure. Far from it, they generally seemed content to preside in the White House, accepting the proposition that their office was one of limited powers. Effective power was vested in the Congress where between 1874 and 1896 the Democrats generally controlled the House of Representatives and the Republicans as invariably controlled the Senate. The sentiment seemed to be against the Executive reclaiming the large role defined for it by Jackson and employed by Lincoln. Woodrow Wilson's influential* Congressional Government *(1885) concluded, "Congress is fast becoming the governing body of the nation," and added, "Our latter-day Presidents live by proxy; they are the executive in theory." It was not until 1898, when Henry Jones Ford published his* The Rise and Growth of American Politics, *that a dissenting view of the Presidency was postulated: "The truth is that in the presidential office, as it has been constituted since Jackson's time, American democracy has revived the oldest political institution of the race, the elective kingship."*

Nonetheless, the very lack of dominating Presidents during the era of the politicos, one that struck contemporaries and historians, has tended to conceal the constructive efforts of President and Congress during the concluding decades of the nineteenth century. It has also obscured the acts of the Executive that extended presidential power. The most significant of these efforts was the institution of civil service reform. The long-prevalent view set forth by Matthew Josephson (1899-   ) was that it was part of a "Comedy of Reform." When national revulsion against the assassination of Garfield by a disappointed office seeker culminated in the Civil Service Act of 1883, one biographer of Chester A. Arthur explained his support of the measure with ". . . Arthur had no 'faith in reform' but was simply yielding to popular sentiment." What was not mentioned was that civil service reform, no matter how limited, reduced legislative pressure on the Executive to provide patronage with which to reward their supporters. As Rutherford B. Hayes had understood during a bitter struggle "to break down congressional patronage," the intent was to establish executive appointment autonomy. Success would obviously mean an increase in presidential power and Hayes and his successors understood this would be the result. The institution of Civil Service put the spoils system on the road to extinction; it also acknowledged that an expanding republic needed a trained elite to meet the administrative needs of government. The result was not only an increase of executive power but as Henry Cabot Lodge

noted it freed Congress from the impediment of having to divide offices and
allowed it to do its intended job: legislation.

Harry T. Peck (1856-1914) was a trained classical philologist and a
dabbler in literary criticism. He taught classics at Columbia from 1884
onward. Over the years he maintained an amateur interest in politics which
resulted in Twenty Years of the Republic *(1906). It is a gossipy chronicle*
that gives something of the flavor of the final decades of the nineteenth
century. It was long on detail and opinion but short on interpretation. As
many other works of its genre, it has become a source to which historians
in search of colorful anecdote turn, and might better be called a source
from which history is written than a work of history.

TWENTY YEARS OF THE REPUBLIC, 1885-1905

by Harry Thurston Peck

On the fourth day of March, 1885, Grover Cleveland of New York took
the oath prescribed by the Constitution and became, in doing so, the twenty-
second President of the United States. As he paused for a moment, after
pronouncing the solemn words, and looked out over the multitude which
filled the vast expanse before the Capitol, he must have felt, unimaginative
though he was, a thrill of irrepressible emotion. Three years before, his
name had been unknown beyond the limits of the provincial city where
he lived. Now, the tumultuous cheers that drowned even the thunder of
saluting cannon, acclaimed him as the elected ruler of the mightiest republic
upon earth. He had accomplished the impossible. He had succeeded where
men of large experience and wide renown had ignominiously failed. He
had led to victory a political party which seemed to have incurred the fate
of perpetual banishment from power. And, in achieving this, he, a country
lawyer with no especial knowledge of statecraft or of national policies,
had defeated the most brilliant, the most resourceful, and the most passionately loved of all American party leaders.

Washington had never before seen so great a concourse assembled to
witness the inauguration of a President. More than half a million people
had poured into the city during the preceding week. They came from every
State and Territory of the Union, eager to share in celebrating the return of
the Democratic party, at last again triumphant. The military display was in
itself a splendid spectacle. Not since the great reviews which marked the
end of the Civil War had so many marching regiments swung down the
noble boulevard which leads from the White House to the Capitol. Every
arm of the regular establishment was represented,—cavalry, infantry,
artillery, and engineers,—with detachments of blue-jackets and marines. A
whole division of the National Guard of Pennsylvania was in line. A body
of Southern soldiers, headed by General Fitzhugh Lee, and with the famous
Fifth Maryland in the van, was there. Contingents from New York and

Rhode Island in the East, and from Missouri in the West, marched close behind the regulars. There was also a battalion of coloured troops, whose fine appearance called forth hearty and prolonged applause. The civic organisations were still more numerous; and political clubs, with picturesque regalia and often in striking costume, completed the long line which later passed in review before the President to the music of a hundred military bands. The day was redolent of spring; and as the stream of bayonets flashed in the sunshine and the flags unfurled their folds in the soft west wind, the sight was inspiring in its animation and movement and vivid colour.

Yet the throng which lined the avenue was no less interesting in the variety of types which it exhibited. It was a different gathering from that which Washington had been wont to see at the inauguration of Republican presidents. The men of the South were far more numerous, and there were many present who had long been strangers to the capital city. For them it was the dawning of a new era; and their mingled faith and triumph were almost touching to behold. There were, besides, not a few gaunt figures of an old-time quaintness, intense and half fanatical partisans from remote localities, displaying with a sort of pride the long white beards which, years before, they had vowed never to shave until a Democratic president should be inaugurated. A feeling of eager expectancy, of pleasurable excitement and frank exultation swayed the entire multitude; and even those who owed allegiance to the defeated party could not wholly resist the spell. It was, for the moment, an apotheosis of the Democracy.

When the new President entered the carriage which was to convey him to his official home, few gave any thought to a gentleman who had stood quietly beside him throughout the simple ceremonial, and who presently took friendly leave of him with a cordial clasp of the hand and a word or two of congratulation and good will. It was the familiar little scene that has been so frequently enacted in our country—when one who, for a few short years, has been the ruler of a nation and the peer of monarchs, goes back, at the stroke of the clock, into the obscurity of private citizenship, unheeded and unheralded amid the strident din that welcomes his successor. There is always something half pathetic in this sudden transformation, yet it is impressive too; for it symbolises American reverence for law. Ex-President Arthur, though unnoticed at the moment when he quietly slipped away from Washington, carried with him into private life the respect and confidence of all his countrymen, for he had governed well and wisely. Yet no President had ever entered into office under circumstances of such perplexity and personal embarrassment. Mr. Arthur had been nominated for the Vice-Presidency on the ticket with General Garfield, in the hasty, almost reckless, fashion of our national conventions. He was chosen not because he was thought to be peculiarly fitted for the honour, but simply, as the politicians' slang expresses it, to "placate" the Stalwart or Conkling wing of the Republican Party, which had fought bitterly to secure the selection of General Grant, and which resented fiercely the nomination of General Garfield.

At that time the country knew very little of Mr. Arthur, and what it did know was not wholly favourable. He was regarded as a typical New York politician, an active member of the so-called "Custom-House gang," which parcelled out the local Federal appointments and dickered for the petty spoils of office. This estimate was not entirely unjust. Mr. Arthur had been by no means too fastidious in his political associations. He had kept some rather dubious company while acting as the lieutenant of the aggressive Conkling, whose intimate friend he was. But Mr. Arthur had another side of which the country was not then aware. He was one who drew a very sharp line between his public and his private life. Personally he was a gentleman of cultivated tastes, a university graduate, familiar with the usages of polite society, and having an easy adaptability which made him equally at home in a lady's drawing-room, in the *fumoir* of a club, or in the noisome atmosphere of a riotous ward primary. Intellectually he was well trained and disciplined. In the years preceding the Civil War he had attained to eminence in the practice of law. He conducted to a successful issue a case which affected the validity of the Fugitive Slave Law, and he secured a decision which is still a classic in American politico-legal history. Nor was he without experience of administrative responsibility. During the war he had at different times been Inspector-General and Quartermaster-General of the State of New York, and had won high commendation for his efficiency in organising and equipping the six hundred thousand troops with which that State met the requisitions of President Lincoln. Later, he had been Collector of the Port of New York under President Grant. But when he became Vice-President in 1881, the country at large knew him only as a local politician of no very high repute. He sided with Senator Conkling when that arrogant leader soon after declared open war on President Garfield for refusing to let the New York Senator dictate the Federal appointments in his State; and Mr. Arthur was loyal to Conkling throughout the bitter strife that followed. Then in the midst of it, the President was shot down by a crazed fanatic, Charles Guiteau, and lay for months fighting against death with splendid courage.

With the first shock of grief and horror which stirred the nation when Garfield fell, there was mingled a feeling of deep resentment. It was held that indirectly the President was a victim of the Conkling faction, whose denunciations of him had worked upon the morbid mind of his assassin. Some, in their excess of feeling, went further still. Strange rumours flew about, and sinister accusations were made in private talk. Men even cherished a wild belief that a conspiracy had planned the murder of the President. In the first excited hours it was hinted that, either with or without his knowledge, a plot had been formed to place Mr. Arthur in the presidency, and in this way to deliver the administration into "Stalwart" hands. Few, even then, were willing to listen to so wild a charge; yet the feeling against Mr. Arthur for a time was very bitter. The newspapers, especially in the Eastern States, spoke of him in terms of rancour. They deplored the possibility that "this pot-house politician," as they called him, might take the place of Garfield, whom popular sympathy had already idealized as a martyr. Throughout these trying months, when the country hung upon the daily bulletins from Elberon, Mr. Arthur made no sign. Just what he suffered no man knew. But his dignified reserve was never broken; and when it was hinted that he might act as President during the period of Mr. Garfield's incapacity, he repelled the suggestion with indignant sternness. At last came the death of Garfield in September, 1881. Mr. Arthur assumed the office which thus came to him under circumstances so distressing. Before long the country learned to know the man as he really was. From the very outset he was the President of no faction, of no party, but of the entire people. Firm, wise, and vigilant, his administration was one of the very best in all our history. To his former political allies he showed no undue favour. To his former enemies he manifested no unfairness, but stood between them and the anger of Conkling, whose vindictive spirit led him in consequence to break off all relations with the President. Garfield's appointees were retained in office. Even the request of General Grant could not secure the displacement of the Secretary of the Navy and the substitution of a Stalwart.

Many of those whom Mr. Arthur thus protected repaid his generosity with the blackest ingratitude. All through his administration, they and other friends of Garfield carried on an underhanded warfare against him, a warfare of pinpricks rather than of blows delivered in the open. Calling themselves "the Garfield Avengers," they tried in every way to belittle Mr. Arthur's public acts and even to discredit his private life. In this manner, between the frank reproaches of his former friends and the treacherous enmity of his former foes, President Arthur's term of office afforded him no very pleasurable experience. Yet, at least, he never gave his ill-wishers the satisfaction of seeing that he winced. He was not one who wore his heart upon his sleeve, but he went on his way with an outward serenity that did honour to his strength of character. His political courage was shown in some very striking acts. Although there is no doubt that he desired a second term of office, he never flinched from what he held to be his duty, however unpopular the discharge of it might be. Thus, he vetoed the Chinese Exclusion Bill of 1882 in the face of the unanimous and excited demands of the Far Western States for its enactment into law. In the same year he vetoed a foolishly extravagant River and Harbour Bill appropriating some $19,000,000. Again, although in former years he had himself been emphatically a spoilsman, as President he advocated and secured the passage in 1883 of an act reforming the Civil Service, and establishing an effective Civil Service Commission. He did all that was possible to secure the prosecution and conviction of those corrupt officials who had systematically robbed the Government through the notorious "Star-Route" contracts in the postal service. But his most enduring claim to honourable remembrance is found in his energetic efforts to build up an efficient navy in place of the grotesque collection of antiquated hulks on which the Grant administration had spent sums sufficient to have given the United States a modern fighting fleet. President Arthur was, in fact, the true creator of the new American navy, of which the first vessels —the *Chicago*, the *Atlanta*, the *Boston*, and the *Dolphin*—were laid down while he was President.

Upon its personal and social side his presidency was one to be long remembered. The honours of the White House were done with a graceful dignity, such as had never yet been known there. The President had lost his wife some years before; but his sister, Mrs. McElroy, an accomplished woman of great social charm, frequently presided at official functions. The diplomatic dinners were rescued from the smothered ridicule with which the foreign envoys had always viewed them; and the pungent epigram of Mr. Evarts, à propos of one of President Hayes's entertainments, suddenly lost its point. As for the President himself, he must be regarded as the only man of the world, in the best sense of that term, who has ever occupied the White House. Jefferson might, perhaps, have been cited as another instance, were it not that, during his first term, he cultivated an ostentatious boorishness such as would have been impossible in a thoroughbred. President Arthur, however, was an ideal host both to his public and his private guests. Of a fine presence, courteous, witty, tactful, and possessing infinite *savoir vivre*, he was a living refutation of the taunt which Europeans sometimes level at us, to the effect that eminence in American politics is unattainable by one who is a gentleman at heart. Mr. Arthur kept the domestic side of his *ménage* a thing entirely apart from his official life. Coarse-minded, peeping correspondents, male and female, found scant material here for vulgar paragraphs of kitchen gossip. There were published no foolish, nauseating chronicles of the "daily doings" of the White House. The President's children were not photographed and paragraphed and made the subject of a thousand flat and fatuous stories. Beyond the veil of self-respecting privacy, which was drawn before the President's personal affairs, few ever penetrated. The only tale that reached the public was one that made even the Paul Prys of the press ashamed of their own curiosity. It became known that in one of the President's private apartments there was hung the portrait of a woman, before which every morning, by Mr. Arthur's personal order, great masses of cut flowers were heaped. Here was a rarely promising hint for the greedy journalist, eager to give his next despatch from Washington a touch of *sauce piquante*. With vast ingenuity and by bringing the resources of the press to bear, the secret was ferreted out at last, and the portrait was found to be that of the President's dead wife. It was very characteristic of the man who, to the world at large, was always the master of practical affairs with just a suggestion of the *viveur* about him, that he should in private have cherished this delicate sentiment which did him so much honour.

Perhaps it was precisely President Arthur's dignity and perfect taste that shut him out from the broader popularity which some other Presidents have enjoyed. Democracies prefer their idols to have feet of clay. Their ruler must not be too far above those whom he rules, and he must not show too markedly those finer traits which instinctively arouse the furtive suspicion and half dislike of the ignorant and unenlightened. The many-headed monster fawns only at the feet of those who flatter it by imitation, or who unconsciously partake of its uncouthness. The Orsons and Calibans of politics have an innate antipathy to a gentleman. It is not likely that even so great a man as Lincoln could have kept his powerful hold upon the masses had he not possessed some qualities which many of his truest friends deplored. His ultimate success was due, no doubt, before all else, to his sagacity, his perfect knowledge of human nature, and his infinite patience; yet much of it must surely be ascribed to the awkwardness of his appearance and the unconventionality of his manners. The Hoosiers and Suckers of the still untutored West could not rightly understand the consummate statecraft of which he was a master—his inborn genius for the task of government; but when they heard that he slapped his visitors upon the back and told indecent stories and received the ministers of foreign powers while sprawling in a wooden rocking chair, shoeless, and with his huge feet covered with blue yarn socks—then they felt that he was one of themselves, not President Lincoln, but "Good Old Abe." That which repelled a Sumner or an Adams gripped and held fast the hearts of the men of Sangamon. But Mr. Arthur had not been bred in such a school. His type was one that neither likes nor courts the familiarity of a mob's approval. He had no eccentricities, no traits that were either crude or whimsical, no suggestion of self-consciousness or pose. He was simply a dignified and courteous gentleman—*flos regum Arthurus*, as one of his admirers quoted of him. And looking back upon his brave and honourable bearing under the strain of incessant vexation and temptation, the American people have reason to be proud because the roll of their chief magistrates contains the name of Chester Alan Arthur.

At the time when Mr. Cleveland was inaugurated there had been no Democratic President for a full quarter of a century. A whole generation had been born and had grown to manhood and to womanhood without ever having lived under any but Republican rule. This long continuance in power of a single party had led many citizens to identify the interests of that party with the interests of the nation. The Democrats had been so invariably beaten at the polls as to make Republicans believe that the defeated party had no decent reason for existence, and that it was composed only of wilful obstructionists or of persons destitute of patriotism. On the other hand, the Republican party, identified as it was with success and with so much creditable achievement, was held by them to monopolise all the political virtues of the American people. To criticise its leaders or to attack its policies seemed to many almost treasonable. To it were ascribed not only the successful conduct of a great war, the extinction of slavery, and the triumph of nationalism over the particularistic spirit of secession, but also the maintenance of the country's commercial credit and of its financial honour. Few remembered that without the support of loyal Democrats at the North, the Government must have yielded to the Confederacy. Few took the trouble to recall the fact that of the great Union commanders, Sherman, Sheridan, McClellan and Meade were Democrats, while Grant himself, though a resident of Lincoln's own State, had never voted for a Republican until after the war ended. Nor was it kept in mind that Stanton, the remarkable military administrator, and Chase, the great finance minister, had been Democrats; that Lincoln's second nomination to the presidency came to him not from the Republican party, but from a Union Convention composed of Republicans and Democrats alike. These things had been long forgotten.

Partisan Republicans had come to look upon the existence of the Democratic party as a rather sorry joke, in the face of its long record of disaster and defeat. That it could ever return to power appeared to them not only an improbable, but even a ludicrous, assumption.

Among the ablest of the Republican leaders, however, a much saner view prevailed. These men were acutely conscious of certain facts of which their followers were ignorant. No political phenomenon, indeed, is more remarkable than the almost even balance between the two great parties from 1860 down to 1884. The large majorities which the Republican candidates had received in the Electoral College were utterly misleading as an indication of the comparative strength of the two parties throughout the country. A glance at the popular vote in each presidential election revealed a very interesting state of things, and showed that it was the distribution of the voters, rather than their numbers, which had given to the Republicans success. For example, in the election of 1860, as is well known, Mr. Lincoln, who had a clear majority of 57 electoral votes, was only a minority candidate in the popular vote; for had both wings of the Democracy been united, the ballots which they cast would have outnumbered those given to Mr. Lincoln by more than a quarter of a million. In the election of 1864, which took place at one of the most critical periods of the war, Mr. Lincoln had an electoral majority over General McClellan of 191 votes, and a popular majority of 407,000 votes; but in this election the eleven Southern States, being then outside the Union, took no part. At the election of 1868, out of a popular vote of nearly 6,000,000, General Grant, then at the very climax of his fame, received a popular majority of 305,000 votes, or almost one-quarter less than had been cast for Lincoln, while three Southern States were still unrepresented in the count.

In 1872, Grant's first administration had caused such widespread discontent that the Liberal Republican schism took place, headed by such well-known leaders as Senator Sumner, Carl Schurz, Charles Francis Adams, Horace Greeley, and Whitelaw Reid. Had the Democrats at this time made good use of the opportunity afforded them, they might have gained a signal victory. A candidate such as Charles Francis Adams, of high character and proved ability, could probably have won. But the nomination of Horace Greeley led to the lamentable fiasco which continued President Grant in office by a popular majority of 762,000 votes. This proved, however, in the end to be a Pyrrhic victory. The very fulness of their triumph removed all feeling of restraint from the Republican leaders, and there followed four years of government tainted by public scandal of every description. The Secretary of War resigned to avoid impeachment for bribery. The Navy Department was honeycombed with jobbery. The revelations in connection with the Whiskey Ring startled and disgusted honest men throughout the country. The President's own relatives and intimate friends were proved to have traded on their influence with him. Mr. Colfax, the Republican Speaker of the House and afterward Vice-President, several Senators and a number of Representatives, were smirched by their connection with the Crédit Mobilier. Moreover, the use of Federal troops in sustaining the iniquities of "carpet-bag" government in the South had become more and more distasteful to the people of the North. The dissatisfaction of the country over such a state of things was shown at the election of 1876, when on the fact of the returns the Democratic candidate, Mr. Tilden, had a clear majority of the electoral vote. This result was disputed, and the Electoral Commission created by Congress canvassed the returns in such a way as to give the Presidency to Mr. Hayes by a majority of one vote,—185 to 184,—Mr. Tilden having a popular majority of 250,000 votes. This election seemed to the more astute Republican leaders like the handwriting on the wall, presaging an end of Republican supremacy. The administration of President Hayes, however, considerably strengthened the party to which he belonged. A man of very moderate ability, he was, nevertheless, precisely the President that the country needed at the time. Henry Ward Beecher once described his administration as "a bread poultice"; and the description, though not wholly complimentary, was fairly just. Party feuds were healed. Governmental scandals came to an end. Federal troops were withdrawn from the South. Under the able management of Secretary Sherman, the Treasury resumed specie payments. Hence, at the next election—that of 1880—the Republicans were again successful, and General Garfield had an electoral majority of 59 votes. Yet the record of the popular vote was exceedingly significant. Nearly 9,000,000 ballots had been cast, and out of these 9,000,000 ballots Garfield's majority over Hancock was only 815. The numerical difference, therefore, between the Republican and Democratic parties at this time was equal only to the population of an insignificant village. So extraordinarily close a division had never before been known. It was obvious that Republican success at the next election hung, as it were, by a very slender thread.

It was while the political scales were in this state of almost perfect equipoise that the Republican Convention met in Chicago on June 3d, 1884, to nominate its candidates for President and Vice-President respectively. President Arthur hoped for a nomination, and on the first ballot he received 278 votes; but even at the outset he was outstripped by James G. Blaine of Maine, who led with 334½ votes. This lead was steadily maintained in spite of the opposition of many distinguished Republican leaders; and on the fifth ballot Mr. Blaine received 541 votes, and was declared the nominee amid a scene of tumultuous enthusiasm. General John A. Logan of Illinois was nominated for the Vice-Presidency. The Democratic Convention, meeting in St. Louis on July 8th, took but two ballots. In the first of these, Grover Cleveland of New York led with 392 votes as against 170, cast for Mr. Bayard of Delaware; and on the second ballot he secured the nomination by 683 votes to 145½ cast for Mr. Thomas A. Hendricks of Indiana. As soon as Mr. Cleveland had been nominated as the Democratic candidate for the Presidency, Mr. Hendricks was unanimously named for the office of Vice-President.

*   *   *   *   *

Then came the day of the election on November 4th. Early on the following morning it was known that Cleveland had carried all the Southern States, besides New Jersey, Connecticut and Indiana. New York was still in doubt, but it seemed to have gone Democratic. The New York *Sun*, which had supported the farcical Greenback candidacy of General B. F. Butler, and which was bitterly opposed to Cleveland, conceded his election. The *Tribune*, on the other hand, kept its flag still flying, and declared that Blaine had won. It was evident that the result depended upon a few hundred votes in the outlying counties of New York. A very ugly feeling was manifested among the Democrats. They suspected that a plot was on foot to cheat them of their rights and to repeat the discreditable history of 1876. This suspicion was intensified when the Republican National Committee issued the following bulletin:

"There is no ground for doubt that the honest vote of this State has been given to the Republican candidate; and though the defeated candidate for the presidency is at the head of the election machinery in this State, the Democratic party, which has notoriously been the party of frauds in elections for years, will not be permitted to overthrow the will of the people."

Mobs filled the streets in the vicinity of the newspaper offices, watching intently every bulletin that was posted, and from time to time breaking out into savage cheers or groans. Violence was attempted in several cities, and bodies of men marched up and down as they had done at the outbreak of the Civil War. The excitement was most intense in the city of New York, where it was believed that Jay Gould, who controlled the Western Union Telegraph Company, was leagued with the more unscrupulous of the Republican managers to tamper with the delayed returns. Gould was one of the most sinister figures that have ever flitted, bat-like, across the vision of the American people. Merciless, cold-blooded, secretive, apparently without one redeeming trait, this man for many years had been the incarnation of unscrupulous greed. A railway-wrecker, a corrupter of the judiciary, a partner of the notorious Fisk, the author of the dreadful panic of Black Friday in 1873, when he drove hundreds of victims to ruin, to self-murder or to shame, Jay Gould, even at the present day, typifies so vividly all that is base and foul, as to cause even the mention of his name to induce the shudderings of moral nausea. No sooner was his repulsive personality associated with the belief that the election returns were being altered, than popular indignation broke loose from all restraint. An angry mob marched to the Western Union Building with shouts of "Hang Jay Gould!" Gould added to his other despicable traits the quality of cowardice. Fearing for his life, he besought police protection; and then from some inner hiding place he despatched a telegram to Mr. Cleveland, conceding his election and effusively congratulating him upon it.

On the evening of the 18th of November, the official count was ended; and then the country knew that a plurality of 1149 votes in the State of New York had given the presidency to Mr. Cleveland. On that same night, Mr. Blaine appeared at the door of his house in Augusta, Maine, and said to a sombre, sullen crowd which had assembled there: "Friends and neighbours, the national contest is over, and by the narrowest of margins we have lost."

The election of Mr. Cleveland marks an epoch in our national history, the importance of which can only now be fully understood. It meant that, with the exception of the Negro question, the issues springing from the Civil War had been definitely settled. It meant the beginning of a true re-union of all States and sections. It meant that the nation had turned its back upon the past, and was about to move forward with confidence and courage to a future of material prosperity, and to a greatness of which no one at that time could form an adequate conception. And it meant, although none then surmised it, that, as a result of new conditions, there was ultimately to be effected a momentous change in the whole social and political structure of the American Republic.

President Cleveland, from the very outset of his administration, was destined to confound the predictions of his political adversaries. The misrepresentations concerning him with which the country had been flooded during the campaign of 1884 had found lodgment in the minds of millions. Now that he was actually in office, a shiver of nervous apprehension ran through those Republicans who honestly believed that a Democratic administration meant ruin and disaster. They had been told that Mr. Cleveland was a man of limited intelligence, of low tastes, and of disreputable associations. Partisan newspapers had prophesied that his Cabinet would be made up of bar-room politicians and old-time party hacks. It was said, for instance, that John Kelly would be appointed Secretary of the Treasury in return for the support which Tammany Hall had reluctantly given to Mr. Cleveland. Editorial writers let their imaginations run riot in suggesting other like appointments as not only possible but probable. At the North there were many who feared lest the results of the Civil War should be undone and lest the government of the United States should be given into the hands of "rebels." The Negroes in the South were told that a Democratic President might seek to re-enslave them. Not a few timorous souls all over the country looked for immediate commercial panic and financial ruin.

In this respect, history was only repeating itself. Just as the Federalists in 1801 had raised the cry that President Jefferson was an atheist, a satyr, a Jacobin, and an enemy to law and to the rights of property, and just as the Whigs, in 1829, had thought to alarm the country by describing President Jackson as a gambler, murderer, and border ruffian, so Mr. Cleveland's accession to the presidency was declared to be the beginning of a political saturnalia. His brief inaugural address, however, surprised those persons who had thought of him as dull and as capable of nothing more than platitude. Not only was it dignified and wholly worthy of the occasion, but it contained more than one passage of grave and almost stately eloquence. The following sentences embody a spirit which will be found to have animated Mr. Cleveland's whole career of public service. It expresses the ideal principle of true democracy:

"But he who takes the oath today to preserve, protect, and defend the Constitution of the United States only assumes the solemn obligation which every patriotic citizen—on the farm, in the workshop, in the marts of trade, and everywhere—should share with him. The Constitution which prescribes his oath, my countrymen, is yours; the Government you have chosen him to administer for a time is yours; the suffrage which executes the will of free-men is yours; the laws and the entire scheme of our civil rule, from the town-meeting to the State capitals and the national capital, are yours. Your every voter, as surely as your Chief Magistrate, under the same high sanction, though in a different sphere, exercises a public trust. Nor is this all. Every citizen owes to the country a vigilant watch and close scrutiny of its public servants and a fair and reasonable estimate of their fidelity and usefulness. Thus is the people's will impressed upon the whole frame-work of our civil polity—municipal, State, and Federal; and this is the price of our liberty and the inspiration of our faith in the Republic."

At the close of the inaugural ceremonies, President Cleveland transmitted to the Senate the names of the men whom he had chosen to constitute his Cabinet. For Secretary of State he had selected Senator Thomas Francis Bayard of Delaware, a portly gentleman, who bore a name justly famous in American political history, since for five generations some member of the Bayard family had represented the State of Delaware in the national Senate, of which body Mr. Bayard himself had been temporary President in 1881. The new Secretary of War was Mr. William Crowninshield Endicott of Massachusetts, a very Brahmin of the Brahmins, being a descendant of John Endicott, who was one of the six gentlemen to whom the first royal patent for the Massachusetts Bay territory had been granted in 1628; and who was Colonial Governor in 1630 and 1664, and President of the United Colonies of New England in 1658. Mr. Endicott was a Harvard graduate, a lawyer of ability, and had served for ten years as a Justice of the Supreme Court of Massachusetts. He had taken an active part in political life and was an earnest advocate of reform in the Civil Service. For Secretary of the Navy, the President nominated Mr. William C. Whitney of New York. Mr. Whitney was sprung from old New England stock. Educated at Yale and Harvard, he had engaged in the practice of the law, and in 1871 had done effective work in destroying the Tweed Ring. Mr. Whitney was a man of wealth, an enthusiastic sportsman, possessed of a winning personality, generous, popular, and widely known. He was also a most astute politician and had conducted Mr. Cleveland's campaign in New York with consummate skill.

Mr. Daniel Manning, of New York, received the Treasury portfolio, although usage was against giving two Cabinet offices to citizens of the same State. Mr. Manning had been better known as an active party manager than as a financier. He had been Mr. Tilden's trusted lieutenant, and had shown himself to be adroit and full of resource. He was the head of an important bank in Albany, and was soon to prove himself no less able in dealing with large financial problems than he had been fertile in political strategy. For Secretary of the Interior, the President named Senator L. Q. C. Lamar of Mississippi. Senator Lamar had drafted the ordinance of secession at the Mississippi Convention of 1861, and had served in the Confederate army for two years, and as Judge Advocate for a few months. He had, however, accepted the results of the war with frankness and sincerity, and was known to be as liberal-minded and patriotic as he was liked and respected. Senator Lamar had the tastes of a scholar. He was fond of books and of philosophical researches, and was an admirable type of the cultivated Southern gentleman. The new Attorney-General was Senator Augustus H. Garland of Arkansas, who had opposed secession in 1861, though subsequently he had been a member of the Confederate Congress, and later, after the war ended, Governor of Arkansas. President Cleveland chose for the office of Postmaster-General, Colonel William F. Vilas of Wisconsin, a Union soldier who had fought under Grant at Vicksburg. During the campaign he had served as chairman of the Democratic National Committee.

Altogether, the new Cabinet was one against which no reasonable criticism could be brought. More than that, it was a very remarkable body of administrators. For personal distinction it had had few, if any, superiors in the whole history of the Government. For ability it had not been equalled since the days of President Lincoln. Those deluded partisans who expected the new President to surround himself with a group of henchmen, unknown or only too well known, were put to silence. Those who had looked for a government of ex-Confederates had naught to say. There was even some significance in the fact that President Cleveland's first official act after making his Cabinet nominations, was to sign the commission of Ulysses S. Grant, restoring that illustrious but now impoverished soldier to the retired list of the army with the rank and pay of General.

Fortune soon gave the President a chance to show that in dealing with the foreign relations of the United States he could act with admirable energy and decision. Only a few days after his inauguration, a revolt broke out upon the Isthmus of Panama, headed by a local incendiary named Pedro Prestan. Prestan raised a motley force, proclaimed a revolutionary government, took the City of Aspinwall (now Colon), levied contributions on the merchants, both native and foreign, and threatened to take possession of the Isthmian railway. Growing bolder, he seized an American steamship, the *Colon*, and imprisoned her officers. The United States Consul, who protested, was thrown into a dungeon (March 31). President Cleveland took instant action. Five vessels of war were ordered to the Isthmus. A strong body of marines, with Gatling guns and a battery of light artillery, were landed; and the armed forces of the United States soon held the whole line of the Panama railway. The *Colon* was taken from Prestan under the guns of the cruiser *Galena*, and his prisoners were rescued. The revolt collapsed. Colombian troops retook the city of Aspinwall, and Prestan himself was promptly hanged as a common malefactor. Not long after the South American republic of Ecuador received a needed lesson. The government of that country had imprisoned one Julio Santos, an American citizen, and had refused either to release him or to bring him to trial. President Arthur's Secretary of State had again and again protested, but in vain. President Cleveland took up the case with a sharp decisiveness which gave the Ecuadorians a shock. A man-of-war, the *Iroquois*, appeared at Guayaquil. A peremptory demand was made; and Mr. Santos was promptly set at liberty.

The country viewed with interest still another proof of the administration's capacity for action. In 1882, Congress had passed the so-called Edmunds Anti-Polygamy Bill, aimed against the plural marriages of

Mormonism. The enforcement of this law had greatly irritated the leaders of the Mormon Church, who had always secretly regarded Utah as outside the jurisdiction of the nation's laws. Perhaps they now accepted the Republican estimate of President Cleveland, and fancied that he would prove to be a second Buchanan, nerveless and irresolute. At any rate, the Mormons in Salt Lake City began to show a spirit of insolence and insubordination. Armed companies of them were formed and drilled by night. On the Fourth of July, the national flag was half-masted in derision by a Mormon officer. Threats were made that all Gentiles were to be forcibly expelled from Salt Lake City in defiance of the national Government. If such a *coup* had actually been planned, it was speedily made impossible. By orders from Washington, two batteries of United States artillery and a regiment of infantry were stationed at Fort Douglas, which dominated the city; and in the Military Department which included Utah, two thousand regular troops were held in readiness for instant service. Whatever plans for a Mormon outbreak had existed were crushed before they reached a head.

All these circumstances attending the early days of Mr. Cleveland's administration gave the country at large an entirely new conception of the President and of his capacity for government. Moderate Republicans recognised the fact that he well deserved the full measure of their respect. Partisans who hoped that he would justify the unfavourable pictures which they had diligently painted, were compelled to wait in sullen silence for some future opportunity of censure. The governmental departments were most efficiently conducted. The country remained as prosperous as ever. The awful panic which had been predicted proved to be only another fiction of the campaign orators. Moreover, Republicans who had occasion to make the new President's acquaintance came away with nothing but pleasant words for his easy, unaffected and good-humoured ways. It was not many weeks, indeed, before Mr. Blaine himself appeared at the White House, to make a friendly call upon his late opponent. He was received with the greatest courtesy, and the two men chatted pleasantly together in the President's library. One of the unwritten laws of American public life permits a defeated candidate for the presidency to ask a political favour of his successful competitor, and Mr. Blaine desired to avail himself of this gracious little privilege. He requested the President not to remove from office Mr. Joseph H. Manley, who was postmaster at Augusta, Mr. Blaine's home city. Mr. Manley was an old friend and earnest supporter of Mr. Blaine, and the President very cordially granted the request, after which the interview terminated with every evidence of personal good feeling. Some time after, a visiting delegation at the White House was found to include among its members the redoubtable Dr. Burchard himself; and a smothered cheer went up, with not a little laughter, when the alliterative clergyman shook the President's hand and expressed his pleasure at finding him in such good health. Altogether, these days afforded as near an approach to an era of good feeling as Mr. Cleveland ever enjoyed throughout his years of public office. They represented the lull in political warfare that always follows an election in which passion has for the time exhausted itself and kindly feeling has resumed its normal sway. Americans are proverbially the best-natured people in the world; and in the case of a new President, they always feel disposed to let him orient himself before the din of party strife begins again.

⤳ ⤶

A FAIR *description of the election of 1884 would emphasize that it allowed a choice between "Tweedledee" and "Tweedledum." The Republican James G. Blaine had a long career in Congress behind him and with it frequent lapses into questionable behavior. Some felt he had used his office as a mart in which to sell favors. When his nomination was made known in Republican Boston, the staid Massachusetts Reform Club rebelled, for as Richard Henry Dana recollected: "All was excitement, and everybody was on fire. Not a man in the room wished to support Blaine." The disaffection within Republican ranks enhanced Democratic chances and they responded by nominating blunt, honest, massive, but dull Grover Cleveland whose governorship of New York was a model of rectitude. To the business community he gave assurances that "No harm shall come to the business interests as the result of administration policy so long as I am President." But no one thought Blaine would do less; the difference would at most be that Cleveland would give to business what Blaine would have tendered at a price.*

In the campaign that followed, the Mugwump reformers defected to Cleveland; their intention neatly put by James Russell Lowell was to "emancipate the respectable white man." And though Cleveland was revealed to have fathered a bastard son, his manful acknowledgment of the fact reinforced the wide respect felt for his forthrightness. Once in the White House, after having eked out a narrow victory, Grover Cleveland revealed what Allan Nevins has called "courage" in following the dictates of his conscience. His roots in Jacksonian Democracy were revealed as he insisted upon confining the role of government to the necessary task rather than as an agent of innovation. Grimly adhering to principle, he accepted the lesson "that though the people support the Government the Government should not support the people." It was as if the old Jacksonian banner proclaiming "The world is too much governed" were once again being unfurled. But as heir of Jackson, Cleveland had inherited a tradition of a vigorous use of executive power, but only within the confines of a strict division of powers. "I believe the most important benefit that I can confer on the country by my Presidency," he declared in early 1886, "is to insist upon the entire independence of the Executive and Legislative branches of the government, and to compel the members of the legislative branch to see that they have responsibilities of their own."

It is, therefore, not surprising to learn that he left it to Congress to advance the Interstate Commerce Act in 1886, and that he signed it with misgivings both about its constitutionality or workability. But his democratic colors showed when in his annual message of 1887 he swung into a denuncia-

tion of "the vicious, inequitable and illogical" tariff system, particularly since it threatened to advance the "grasping centralization" of federal power. He would reduce the tariff rates and confine government. Reform for Cleveland was justified proportional to its fulfillment of the immutable laws of laisser-faire, and he applied himself with vigor to gain that goal.

Robert McElroy (1872-1959), long a Princeton professor, had far-ranging interests. His work included biographies of Jefferson Davis, Levi P. Morton, as well as that on Cleveland. He also devoted considerable attention to the history of the Far West and to his native Kentucky. His biography of Cleveland made sensible use of the large Cleveland manuscript collection, but his treatment was eulogistic, a result which might have been foreseen since it had been authorized by the late President's family. It was not until the publication of Allan Nevins' Grover Cleveland: A Study in Courage (1934) that both an admiring and an objective analysis of the 22nd and 24th President appeared which would stand the test of time.

GROVER CLEVELAND
THE MAN AND THE STATESMAN

by Robert McElroy

Mr. Cleveland planned to be, not a civil service reformer with Democratic tendencies, but a President of the United States, believing in civil service principles. "Those who have complained," he once declared, "have entertained a very different understanding of what is meant by civil service reform from that which the law required me to observe and that it was practicable to carry out. The President is clothed with many and various responsibilities. He is expected, primarily, to do all in his power to secure good government. That imposes upon him the exercise of discretion in making many appointments. It is admitted that in filling many places the importance of securing persons in sympathy with the political views of the dominant party is properly to be considered. My civil service friends have sometimes seemed to think that the Government was to be conducted merely for the purpose of promoting civil service reform. To me the importance of general administrative reform has appeared to be superior to the incidental matter of civil service reform. Good government is the main thing to be aimed at. Civil Service Reform is but a means to that end."

A few days after his inauguration he received a long letter from Carl Schurz reminding him, in specific terms, of what the reformers expected, and ardently pleading for the retention of the Republican Postmaster of New York: "The reappointment of Mr. Pearson," the letter declared, "is . . . regarded as a test of your policy." By failing to keep him in his position, you "would disappoint the hopes of those of your supporters who have the success of your endeavors to reform abuses and to purify the political atmosphere, most earnestly at heart. They cordially appreciate the noble resistance you have offered to the pressure of the spoils politicians, and they would be much pained at seeing that record blurred. . . . Owing . . . to the fact that your performances have always gone beyond your formal promises, public expectation is now higher than it has ever been before. . . . If now, in spite of your own inclination . . . considerations of a partisan character . . . maintain their ascendancy, keeping the field open for a future revival of spoils politics, the disappointment would indeed be great." Doubtless Mr. Cleveland was better able than even Mr. Schurz to estimate the effect of such a policy, as he had cautiously presented the problem to the public, through inspired leaders in the press, and had watched the reaction, a practice quite common with him.

The effect on the spoilsmen had been immediate and violent. One wrote to Lamont: "You are aware of the President's civil reform declarations and the amount of capital the Republican papers and members of the party are making out of it. . . . Not less than twenty of our best workers here, come right out and say, if Mr. Cleveland proposes to retain the Republicans that are in office, throughout his administration, they will go back on the party forever. I have no doubt but what this same feeling exists throughout the state. . . . Should Mr. Pearson be reappointed Postmaster in N. Y. City, it would make the greatest commotion, and would cause the loss of not less than 10,000 votes in this state."

A few days after this letter was written, the wily Tammany leader, John Kelly, wrote to Charles P. Britton: "I am under the impression that President Cleveland will be successful in administering the Government of the United States, as he undoubtedly was in discharge of the duties of the office of Governor of this State. He is calm, dignified, thoughtful, and acts after mature deliberation. Besides, he possesses the qualification of listening, and saying but very little, although he is very agreeable, social and is fond of interchanging views and opinions as any person can be holding the dignified and important position of President of the United States. Of course it is a great gift to be able to listen and analyze and draw conclusions from what may be said of him by the various persons who appeal to him, from time to time, for place or favor of some kind."

Evidently Mr. Kelly felt that Tammany must adopt a course different from that pursued in the case of Senator Grady, if they were to get their part of the spoils of victory. At the end of the letter, clearly designed for transfer to the President's own hand, Kelly added this sentence, eloquent when taken in connection with the idea of Mr. Pearson's reappointment as Postmaster of New York: "Besides, his [the President's] ambition is not so great as to inaugurate measures that would cause great discussion and violent opposition. I wish him every success in life, and hope that he may succeed in discharging the duties of the Presidency of this country to the entire satisfaction of the people."

In view of the threat that by persisting in Mr. Pearson's reappointment the President would lose "not less than 10,000 votes" in New York, Mr. Kelly's plan was adroit; and, as the Tammany leader had doubtless expected, Mr.

Britton promptly sent Kelly's neat words of praise to Lamont, with the following suggestive comment, bearing date, March 22, 1885: "I note by the papers that Mr. Kelly is in Washington today . . . and I presume he will call at the White House. . . . I trust that both you yourself and the President will receive him with great cordiality, for I assure you from positive knowledge that *personally* he *desires it*, and he is just the man (and I presume in just the state of mind) to *appreciate* magnanimity on the part of President Cleveland, and this too without a thought as regards patronage for his henchmen. For them, individually or collectively, I care nothing; but for him, personally, I have great respect. I *know* what he did for us during the campaign against an opposition that would have crushed an ordinary man. . . . *It is of the utmost importance to us, in our future work, that the entente cordiale be established at once between the President and Mr. Kelly.*"

But neither the consideration of 10,000 votes in New York, nor the sweet reasonableness of John Kelly could save the New York post-office for the Democrats. Pearson's name went to the Senate, and to the press went the following inspired leader, the manuscript of which is in Mr. Cleveland's own hand:

"A gentleman very near the President and undoubtedly speaking from actual knowledge, reports that the reappointment of Mr. Pearson was made after a most patient examination of all the facts connected with the charges against him and his answer to the same, which was yesterday submitted and read by the President. The appointment therefore may be considered a complete vindication of the postmaster.

"It is further stated that the reappointment of Mr. Pearson will constitute a notable exception to the course which the President may be expected to pursue. The New York post-office is the largest and most important in the country and of interest to all the people and especially to the vast business enterprises centered in the metropolis. It is today a complete illustration of the successful application of civil service reform principles to an immense governmental establishment. This condition has been brought about very largely by the intelligent effort of Mr. Pearson, and he is thus identified in the closest manner with this example of the success of the reform. To retain him insures faith and confidence in the movement, which would receive a shock from his removal. His retention was earnestly requested by a large number of business men of the city, both Democrats and Republicans, and very generally by the Independent Republicans who did such good service in support of the Democratic candidates in the last campaign.

"This act of the President must not be regarded as indicating that in other cases those opposed to the party of the President will either be appointed or retained after the expiration of their terms of office.

"In answer to the suggestion that the reappointment of Mr. Pearson might cause great dissatisfaction in the ranks of his party, the President is represented as saying: 'The Democratic party is neither hypocritical, unpatriotic or ungrateful—they will understand the whole matter and be satisfied.'"

At each new venture along the line of reform, to which not he alone but his party, was committed, similar protests poured in upon him; but they failed to dominate him. Some old political supporter would find his application for a minor Federal appointment denied on the ground that it was covered by the civil service law. This he could endure; but when he saw an active secretary of a Blaine and Logan club, whose name happened to stand high on the eligible list, awarded the coveted post by the President whom he had helped to elect, his submission was turned to rage, which rage was not lessened by the Republican taunt, "You got your President, but you can't get your Postmaster." Nor was the fact that the taunt was true calculated to make disappointed Democrats love the grim figure in the White House, who was heroically facing the task which they had assigned him.

The more radical reformers, headed by Schurz, continued to urge him to "aim straight at the non-partisan service," but, in so urging, asked more than could have been reasonably expected. Mr. Cleveland believed that the chief object of civil service reform is not to prevent removals from office, but to supply a body of competent persons, tested by examinations, from whom appointments can be made. He believed that if the incompetent should be weeded out there would be ample opportunity to gratify the natural desires of the Democrats for recognition, without dropping any, of whatever party, who had shown special fitness for their places. This was a perfectly fair standard, and one which could be adhered to without complete disregard of party obligations. Chosen by a party which had known, not seven lean years, but more than two lean decades, Mr. Cleveland knew that a purely non-partisan plan for the distribution of patronage would mean suicide in office and a fruitless administration.

At times he made serious mistakes, or was led into error, but in the light of new evidence he did not hesitate to reverse his decisions, offend whom it might.

*　　*　　*　　*　　*

He was painfully conscientious in searching for the best candidates for office and painfully alert to avoid misrepresentations. "I have fallen into the habit lately of wrestling very hard with this cursed office-filling in my dreams," he wrote to Charles W. Goodyear, on June 16th. And, a month later, he describes himself as "pitching about half asleep and half awake, trying to make postmasters." But despite his caution, he was occasionally misled, at times deliberately, by men who wished either to accommodate friends, or to shift the burden of refusal to the President's shoulders. To one such, who had ventured to express surprise at the appointment of a candidate whom he had himself thus recommended, the President wrote, in unmeasured condemnation:

Executive Mansion, Washington,
August 1, 1885.

Dear Sir:

I have read your letter of the 24th ult. with amazement and indignation. There is but one mitigation to the perfidy which your letter discloses, and that is found in the fact that you confess your share in it. I don't know whether you are a Democrat or not; but if you are the crime which you confess is the more unpardonable. The idea that this administration, pledged to give the people better government and better officers, and engaged in a hand-to-hand fight with the bad elements of both parties, should be betrayed by those who ought to be worthy of implicit trust, is atrocious; and such treason to the people and to the party ought to be punished by imprisonment.

Your confession comes too late to be of immediate use to the public service, and I can only say that while this is not the first time I have been deceived and misled by lying and treacherous representatives, you are the first one that has so frankly owned his grievous fault. If any comfort is to be extracted from this assurance you are welcome to it.

Yours truly,
GROVER CLEVELAND

The pressure for office coming from his Buffalo friends was hardest to bear, and their complaints caused him keen distress, but they did not cause him to swerve from the rigid standards of public duty which he had set himself.

* * * * *

It was his physical salvation, during the trying years of conflict that followed, to be able, when the strain grew unbearable, to take down his beloved rod, or sling over his shoulder his shotgun—modestly named "Death and Destruction"—and seek the restoring balm of God's glorious solitude. They might slander him, as they did; they might trick him with cunning, deceive him with lies, torture him with reproaches of ingratitude and of unfriendliness to friends; but no one could rob him of his duck marshes, or prevent the shy trout and agile bluefish from turning his mind away, for a time, from all worries. God made him a sportsman, and the instinct served him as the protective coloring serves the wild things in the great, free world of outdoors.

Early in September he returned to the White House, conscious that the clamor for office had not diminished nor would for many weary months. His heart had been lightened, however, by the discovery, made during the summer, that he was mistaken in his judgment concerning his Buffalo intimates of whose unfriendliness he had so bitterly complained to Goodyear. As soon as he reached his desk he wrote acknowledging that misjudgment and, incidentally, recorded his general distaste for the life of a President:

"I feel that I am in the treadmill again and look forward to the time when another respite shall be due to me and all that must take place between now and then with the gravest concern. If it were not for the full faith I have in the Higher Power that aids honest, faithful endeavor, I should be frightened by all I see before me. But I have not a particle of real fear, though I confess to anxiety, because so much depends upon me. It's a curious state of mind to be in, when all the value of life is measured by its relation to other persons and other things, and when the natural desire to live for the sake of living and enjoying life is nearly gone."

In his absence, King Leopold of Belgium had sent him a formal announcement that the mandatory of the Congo, which the Powers had recently conferred upon Belgium, "will hereafter form the independent state of the Congo," and that he had "taken . . . the title of Sovereign" of that new state. Mr. Cleveland's reply was a formal recognition of conditions in the creation of which he had had no part, and for the cruel and unforeseen outcome of which, "the horrors of the Congo," he can be held in no degree responsible.

ESTEEMED AND GREAT FRIEND:

I have had much pleasure in receiving your Majesty's letter of the 1st of August last, announcing that the possessions of the International Association of the Congo will hereafter form the Independent State of the Congo, and that your Majesty, under the authorization of the Belgian Legislative Chambers, and in accord with the association, has assumed the title of Sovereign of the Independent State of the Congo. I observe your Majesty's further statement that the convention between Belgium and the new State is exclusively personal. This government at the outset testified its lively interest in the well being and future progress of the vast region now committed to your Majesty's wise care, being the first among the Powers to recognize the flag of the International Association of the Congo as that of a friendly State; and now that the progress of events has brought with it the general recognition of the jurisdiction of the association and opened the way for its incorporation as an independent and sovereign State, I have great satisfaction in congratulating your Majesty on being called to the Chief Magistracy of the newly formed government.

The Government and people of the United States, whose only concern lies in watching with benevolent expectation the growth of prosperity and peace among the communities to whom they are joined by ties of friendship, cannot doubt that under your Majesty's good government the peoples of the Congo region will advance in the paths of civilization and deserve the good-will of all those States and peoples who may be brought into contact with them.

I am, my esteemed and great friend, your faithful friend.

GROVER CLEVELAND

Done at Washington, this 11th day of September, 1885, by the President.

T. F. BAYARD,
Secretary of State.

Once more in harness, the President again faced the political bread-line. The Pendleton Law already covered some thirteen thousand five hundred offices, but there remained subject to Mr. Cleveland's appointment forty-nine thousand fourth-class postmasters, and five thousand miscellaneous posts mostly packed with Republicans. For each there were at hand many expectant Democratic officials, backed by not less expectant Democratic politicians hunting votes. These were they who had ranted on the stump, organized gigantic torchlight parades, "gathered the coin," or fed the columns of a party press during the late campaign. They could see no excuse for a President who would not fill vacancies with the faithful, or make vacancies where none existed, and shrieked traitor at each non-partisan appointment, however excellent.

On the other hand, Republicans who had fed the fires of personal slander, had cheered themselves hoarse at the mention of the name of James G. Blaine, and had ransacked the political garbage cans for new filth to hurl at the then Governor of New York, loudly cried hypocrite at each removal, however necessary, while despite his honest and persistent fight for reform against an increasingly powerful faction in his own party, many even among civil service reformers looked upon the President as a betrayer of their confidence, a wolf in sheep's clothing, a champion spoilsman camouflaged. This was his penalty for leadership of a party not yet regenerate. Over and over again his friends broke party pledges in the belief that the President would never know. They made partisan removals in such numbers as to justify the complaint that the Democrats were no more attached to reform than the Republicans had been, and the reckless manner in which Congressmen, Senators, and others high in office lent their names to undesirable candidates caused the President to wonder whether any recommendation could be considered of value. "The Vice-President, and at least half the Democratic Senators, and nearly all the Democrats of the House," commented the *Commercial Gazette*, "[have] banded themselves together to break down the President and his Cabinet, and force him to do their bidding. . . . The first surprise of the President was as nothing compared with his amazement over the later features of the office-seekers' raid."

Yet the more judicial reformers knew that he was reforming, slowly, cautiously, practically, but really; working as one who knows the limitations of executive power must work if permanent results are to be attained. "Since the spoils system was first generally introduced into our national administration," wrote George William Curtis, after watching the New President for only five months, "no President has given such conclusive evidence both of his reform convictions and of his courage in enforcing his convictions as Grover Cleveland." And, during the same summer, Gladstone remarked to Theodore L. Cuyler, who was visiting England: "Cleveland is the noblest man that has filled the Presidential chair since Lincoln."

The President's frank and uncompromising methods made for him relentless enemies who, in various sections of the country, poured vitriol into a personally conducted press, causing it to produce many stories more interesting than authentic. In turn, he generalized too freely, and his sweeping denunciations appealed to the *esprit de corps* of editors, disposed, and not unjustly, to resent blanket indictments of their order. They busied themselves making and printing collections, built on the line of modern three-foot shelf libraries, to show the public "how the people's President slanders the people's press." The newspaper clippers, who in those days were employed to make presidential scrapbooks, filled volumes with their gleanings, letters many of which the President had written for private, not public eyes.

*   *   *   *   *

Under such conditions it is not remarkable that the public was for a time deceived concerning the real nature of the man whom they had chosen President, and that the slanders of the campaign of 1884 were kept alive in the minds of the people. His critics, for the most part, either failed to understand what he had promised, were misinformed as to his actions, or intentionally misrepresented him. By refusing to go to one extreme with the reformers, he lost their confidence; by refusing to go to the other extreme with the spoilsmen, he lost theirs. But he yielded to neither, considering that his duty lay between, in which position he became the target of both.

The months, as they passed, brought no cessation of the conflict. "All this time, like a nightmare," he wrote to Charles Goodyear, "this dreadful, damnable office-seeking hangs over me and surrounds me," and to Bissell he used even stronger language: "The d--d everlasting clatter for office continues . . . and makes me feel like resigning and hell is to pay generally."

*   *   *   *   *

Political prophets, with minds set upon approaching presidential elections, are always deeply interested in congressional elections in local political sentiment. These are the straws which show the direction of political winds. Early in July, 1886, Texas held her first congressional convention and renominated Crane of the seventh district. Incidentally, the convention resolved: "That we recognize in Grover Cleveland a Democrat and patriot, who, under the heavy cares of his great office, has displayed masterly ability, unimpeachable integrity, and heroic courage; and that we commend the fidelity with which he has fulfilled his pledges to the people in the face of great pressure to violate them."

The Galveston *News*, the leading Democratic paper of the state, stamped this resolution as representative, not of the seventh Texas district alone, not of Texas alone, but of the entire South, declaring that nine Democrats out of ten in that part of the country and exclusive of office-seekers, were perfectly satisfied with Cleveland's administration, and that, if the convention were held immediately, the South would be solid for his renomination. But the fact that the South stood ready to renominate the only Democrat who had occupied the White House since the Civil War was, after all, not very significant, especially as great metropolitan journals like the New York *Sun* and the New York *World* longed to see the President's political scalp drying in the sun, before Tammany Hall, or any other long house. Their attacks were incessant and very bitter.

"Not long ago," said *Public Opinion*, on March 5, 1887, "the New York *Sun* advocated the passage of the interstate commerce bill, but no sooner was it passed and approved by the President than that journal found numerous objections to it, and actually condemned the President for not vetoing it. The same paper contained column after column of editorial matter exposing the job known as the dependent pension bill, and called on the President to veto it. The President did veto it, and the *Sun* at once makes the veto an occasion for another stab at its author. The New York *World* took the same position in regard to the pension bill, and called on

the President to veto it, but no sooner did he do so than the *World* makes
the remarkable discovery that public sentiment is not as it represented it to
be, but that among the G. A. R. there is a 'practically unanimous call from
New York and other states for Congress to override the veto.' The *Courier-
Journal* advocated the civil-service bill, indorsed a plank in the Democratic
platform demanding the enforcement of the civil-service system, applauded
the President's pledge that he would enforce it, and then turned suddenly
to denounce bitterly both the law and the President for respecting it. It
is highly complimentary to the President that these ingenious and pestiferous
critics can find no other ground to justify their abuse of him than his
adherence to his pledges and his enforcement of the law. After all their
enterprise and busy zeal, they are left without a pretext for their hostility,
except what is found in the fact that the President has simply done what,
at one time or another, they demanded of him. It is the old story over again
of the lamb who muddies the water below the wolf, except that the President is somewhat of a wolf himself when he has a mind to be."

But despite such attacks President Cleveland continued to follow his own
judgment, demonstrating more and more every day that he was as ready
to act without party support as with it, when convinced that his course lay
in the line of duty. Such an attitude bred increased resentment on the part
of Democratic politicians, although optimistic Democratic sheets labored
hard to prove that gossip in the Republican press about differences between
the President and the leaders of the party was the sheerest folly.

More and more definitely, as the months passed, was the rift apparent.
The Democratic politicians did not like Grover Cleveland: he could not be
counted upon to "play the game." If there were dreams of a second term,
it was not they who dreamed them, and in their narrow abuse they utterly
failed to appreciate the impression which his honesty and fidelity in the discharge of duty had made upon the masses of the people. The Democratic
politicians were against the President, but the Democratic people were for
him.

"I have seen," declared ex-Senator Thurman of Ohio, "a good many
Presidents in my long life. I have known several of them personally, and
I have read the history of the administration of them all. I have seen and
I know—and I think I know him full well—Grover Cleveland, our President
of the United States; and on my honor as a man who is bound to tell you
the truth, if ever a man was bound to tell the truth to his fellow-man, I
don't believe that a more honest, braver, truer man ever filled the Presidential
chair of the United States." This opinion the people shared.

How much they were for him appeared in his tour of glory of that
autumn, his swing round the circle. He visited a dozen or more of the chief
cities in the Middle West and South, and everywhere was greeted with
the applause of expectant throngs. He won his audiences, not by the discussion of public issues, for he rarely discussed them, but by the personal
and friendly manner of his approach to his fellow citizens in each city that
he visited. In St. Paul, for example, where Mrs. Cleveland had once been
for a short time in school, he wrote into his address this telling paragraph:

"My visit to you being a social one, and trusting that we have a sort of friendly feeling for each other, I want to suggest to you a reason why I am particularly and personally interested in St. Paul and its people. Some years ago, I won't say how many, a young girl dwelt among you and went to school. She has grown up and is my wife. If anyone thinks a President ought not to mention things of this sort in public, I hope he or she does not live in St. Paul, for I don't want to shock anybody when I thank the good people of this city because they neither married nor spoiled my wife; and when I tell them that I had much rather have her than the Presidency."

In October he returned to his executive duties, conscious that in the South and Middle West at least he was a President with prospects. The country was prosperous, and understood how false had been the dire prophecies of those who had hailed the return of Democracy as the beginning of a long calamity.

With a presidential year almost in sight, it was the part of the wise politician to say nothing definite, arouse no new animosities, and so drift again into power. But Cleveland's masterful conscience was driving him onward toward quite another course. By degrees he had become convinced of the iniquities of the existing tariff laws and of his duty to open an uncompromising attack upon them. This conviction had come slowly, but with a controlling definiteness.

When first chosen President he had considered himself unequipped to form an opinion upon the tariff question. Having had no responsibility for the tariff, save that which falls to the lot of every citizen, he had not felt called upon to study the subject as he always studied every subject which came within the range of his official duty. And being devoid of pretense and of the pride of erudition, he frankly confessed to his friends his need of help, following unconsciously but literally the advice which Charles Dickens once gave a group of students: "Admit ignorance of many things and thus avoid the more terrible alternative of being ignorant of all things."

Carl Schurz has left this account of a conversation which he had with Mr. Cleveland shortly after the latter's first election:

"With characteristic directness [he] asked me what big questions I thought he ought to take up when he got into the White House. I told him I thought he ought to take up the tariff. I shall never forget what then happened. The man bent forward and buried his face in his hands on the table before him. After two or three minutes he straightened up and, with the same directness, said to me: 'I am ashamed to say it, but the truth is I know nothing about the tariff. . . . Will you tell me how to go about it to learn?'

"Of course I said I would. So I gave him a list of books to read. Did he read them? Indeed he did, and came back for more. Nobody ever worked harder to master a new subject than the determined Cleveland worked to master the tariff."

Realizing the strength of the arguments upon each side of the problem, the President at first halted between two opinions; but by slow degrees he grew to feel that a protective tariff, in the sense in which that term had been interpreted since the Civil War, was iniquitous, involving favoritism for the few at the expense of the many. At times, during the two decades since Lee's surrender, Congress had shown signs of similar views, and had moved in the direction of reducing the war tariffs; but the perseverance of the saints had been denied them, and the tariffs had one by one reappeared. Even when President Arthur's tariff commission, which consisted entirely of protectionists, had drawn up a bill aiming at a twenty per cent reduction, Congress had stilled its conscience, or its political forebodings, by cutting down this reduction to three or four per cent. Thus, despite many professions, the tariffs remained practically undisturbed until President Cleveland's day, not for the sake of revenue, as the treasury surplus was a great embarrassment; not for protection merely, as such rates were far in excess of those required to equalize the difference in wages between the United States and other manufacturing countries, but, as Mr. Cleveland's study convinced him, in order that the manufacturer should enjoy a rich subsidy at the expense of the consumer.

In his first annual message Mr. Cleveland ventured upon the general suggestion that, as the revenues were greatly in excess of the actual needs of an economical administration, they ought to be reduced in such a way as not to injure or destroy "interests which have been encouraged by such laws" and with a view to the protection of American labor. During the year following he sought the advice of many men learned in tariff history— cabinet members, Congressmen, Senators, and unofficial experts. As a consequence, the tone of his second annual message was more definite and more aggressive regarding the maintenance of war tariffs in time of peace. He pointed out the fact that the income of the government was greatly in excess of public necessities, receipts having increased by about fourteen million dollars, of which almost twelve million came from customs, and declared that "When more of the people's substance is exacted through the form of taxation than is necessary to meet the just obligations of the Government and the expense of its economical administration . . . such exaction becomes ruthless extortion and a violation of the fundamental principles of a free government."

It was not tariff to which he objected, but tariff in excess of the needs of the Government. He was no idealist thinking free trade thoughts in a world of nations devoted to protection, but a practical, honest trustee insisting upon administration in the interest of the people. His increasingly bitter denunciations of the robber aspect of the tariff, as then administered, recall the picture of the Moorish pirate, Taric, Tarik, or Tariff, hovering about the entrance of the pillars of Hercules, forcing merchant vessels to share their cargoes with him. Historically, the word tariff means, in the language of frank piracy, the share of imported goods or money equivalent, which a government exacts as the price of admission. To Grover Cleveland, in that autumn of 1887, existing American tariff laws conjured up the vision of the grim Tarik plundering his helpless victims.

As he watched the mounting surplus, bringing with it the inevitable evils of extravagance and inefficiency, he conceived the idea of bringing the facts to the notice of the public by devoting his entire message to this one topic.

This, being an absolutely new departure, would in itself focus the attention of the country and cause comment and discussion of the issue which he was so urgently recommending. The facts, if once understood, would constitute sufficient argument in favor of reform.

The average rate of tariff paid upon imports during the year 1887 had been exceeded only thirteen times in the history of the United States, and the amount so collected during the fiscal year was over fifty-five million dollars above the requirements of current expenses, while the estimated surplus for the succeeding year was vastly larger. Congress had refused to revise the tariff. The President would bring the pressure of public opinion to bear upon Congress.

His political advisers for the most part opposed the plan. To them it seemed sheer political suicide to force such an issue in the face of a presidential campaign. But the outcome of that campaign was to the President a small matter compared with the duty which he saw before him. When one alarmed political prophet warned him that his defeat lurked in a too bold deliverance upon this subject, he replied: "I would stultify myself if I failed to let the message go forward from any fear that it might affect my election." To another he answered: "What is the use of being elected or re-elected, unless you stand for something?" And so, in defiance of warning, and in the face of friendly dissuasion, he prepared the now famous tariff message, which sacrificed his immediate political future, and made of the tariff a living issue.

On December 6, 1887, the message went to Congress, carrying consternation among his followers and jubilation into the camp of the enemy. It was not a radical document and not a free-trade document. "Our progress toward a wise conclusion," it declared, "will not be improved by dwelling upon the theories of protection and free trade. This savors too much of bandying epithets. It is a condition which confronts us—not a theory."

With the precise language of a definite mind, he called attention to the fact that "while comparatively few use imported articles, millions . . . purchase and use things of the same kind made in this country, and pay therefor nearly or quite the same enhanced price which the duty adds to the imported articles. Those who buy imports pay the duty charged thereon into the public treasury, but the great majority of our citizens, who buy domestic articles of the same class, pay a sum at least approximately equal to this duty to the home manufacturer."

At once blessings and curses descended upon his head. Henry George sent a cordial letter of congratulation; and the anti-protection journals were ecstatic in praise. The *Nation* pronounced it "the most courageous document that has been sent from the Executive Mansion since the close of the Civil War," laying down "a platform for the next national campaign as clean cut as any high-tariff politician could possibly desire." The *Post* declared: "This message . . . makes the revenue question the paramount and controlling one in American politics." The protectionist journals, on the other hand, were bitter and at times indecently insulting. "Free-trade, cant, and humbug," commented the headlines in the Chicago *Journal*.

"Ignoramus, dolt, simpleton, idiot—firebug in public finance," were the epithets employed by the *Commercial Gazette*.

James G. Blaine, then in France, cabled an interview designating the message as "Free trade," and intimating that it was in the interest of Great Britain, which cable the New York *Tribune* interpreted in the phrase: "Mr. Blaine in Europe speaks as an American. Mr. Cleveland in America speaks as a British manufacturer, anxious to be admitted without any charge to a share of the best and largest market in the world." And some of the London papers, by their enthusiastic praise of the message, made easier the task of those seeking to convict the President of unholy British sympathy. The London *Morning Post* of December 12th, after praising "that remarkable state document," and the wisdom and high courage of the man who had dared to deliver it, ventured upon the prediction that "sooner or later this Congress will recognize the wisdom of the President's advice and resolve to reduce the Federal revenues." But no such flash of wisdom followed. There followed instead cries of indignation from thousands of Irish voters, susceptible to the faintest suspicion of pro-British sympathy on the part of an American public man; and thus the chief aim of the distortion was secured.

In Congress an abortive attempt was made, under the leadership of Roger Q. Mills, to push through a bill providing for a reduction of tariff revenues by about $53,000,000, with other reductions amounting to a quarter of a million. The measure was conceived in a partisan spirit, and did not fairly represent the reform for which the President had pleaded.

Round this Mills Bill raged the great tariff debate of 1888, Mills and Carlisle crossing swords with McKinley and Reed. The opponents of the President, including ex-Speaker Randall, rang the changes upon Blaine's suggestion that the Democrats were playing into the hands of the British merchant. Reed of Maine interpreted the policy of the administration in the following words: "A nice little dog . . . trotted along happy as the day, for he had in his mouth a nice shoulder of succulent mutton. By and by he came to a stream bridged by a plank. He trotted along, and, looking over the side of the plank, he saw the markets of the world and dived for them." He emerged, said Mr. Reed, "the most muttonless dog that ever swam ashore." The Democrats, however, had a safe majority in the House, and on July 21st, they passed the Mills Bill, by a vote of 162 to 149, fourteen not voting.

The Republican Senate, under the leadership of Allison and Aldrich, promptly produced a substitute as narrow and partisan as the Mills Bill itself. In the conflict which ensued both bills were blocked, and the tariff question, still unsettled, remained the dominant issue for the elections of 1888. Thus Mr. Cleveland's message forced the two great parties to adopt definite positions upon the tariff, and to those positions they have in general adhered since that day. It also accomplished what Mr. Cleveland's friends had predicted, disaster to all dreams of his re-election in 1888.

Indeed, many Democrats high in party councils, and a few with well-defined ambitions for the succession, hoped that the tariff message had made impossible even the renomination of President Cleveland. Others sought to add to this longed-for disqualification the unquestioned fact that in his letter of acceptance of 1884, he had said: "We recognize in the eligibility of the President for reelection a most serious danger to that calm, deliberate, and intelligent political action which must characterize a government by the people." They believed, or professed to believe, that that statement bound Grover Cleveland to a single term. Such was not, however, a fair interpretation. Mr. Cleveland had merely suggested the idea that Presidents should be rendered ineligible for second terms. But no such law had been passed, no such action taken, either by Congress or by the people. Had the public responded to his suggestion, it would have found him ready to co-operate. Having failed to do so, it left him free to seek a second term, should he so desire.

⚜ ⚜

No *single aspect of American history is more puzzling than the long neglect of urban history. And this despite the fact that the one overwhelming social trend since mid-nineteenth century has been the movement from a rural to an urban environment. It is as if Americans have secretly agreed that the city is the skeleton in the closet to be acknowledged in silence and spoken of only in furtive whispers. For the affection with which Walt Whitman spoke of New York City, there are dozens who decried it as the epitomization of the city wilderness. And if given the choice of wildernesses, the American would settle for that made by God rather than man. The pronouncement of Ralph Waldo Emerson, "Whilst we want cities as the centers where the best things are to be found, cities degrade us by magnifying trifles," set the tone for the nineteenth-century judgment of the city. In the city, no matter where, innocence was enveloped by "dreary," "melancholy," "foul," "wicked" corruption. Americans unconsciously juxtaposed the city to a lost Eden, and "Gomorrah" sprang easily to their lips when they contemplated the city.*

The psychological bias against the city obtained support from the urban realities that prevailed at the end of the nineteenth century. The speed with which cities grew brought acute dislocations. Services which a modern urban dweller takes for granted such as police, fire department, welfare, health, and proper drainage were primitive or unknown. Streets were often seas of mud and often cluttered with mountains of debris and carcasses of dead animals. Tenement life required a Hogarth to depict it; as late as 1894, only 306 persons of a total of 255,033 living in New York slums had bathing facilities in their hovels. To accentuate the brutality of urban conditions, reformers found it possible to compare unfavorably conditions in New York with those of Bombay. As the great Danish-born reformer Jacob A. Riis sorrowed, the urban slums were filled with the "cry of the soul that is perishing."

The obvious agent to alleviate the worst excesses of urban life was munici-
pal government, but as one observer noted in 1890, "with very few excep-
tions, the city governments of the United States are the worst in Christendom
—the most expensive, the most inefficient, and the most corrupt." The native
middle-class, long since displaced by the Irish politician in city hall, accepted
without question the proposition that American cities were governed by
"insurrections of decent folk!" But governed as the middle class was by a
general commitment to laissez-faire *government, they failed to come to grips*
with the human element, one that the reform mayor of New York Seth Low
realized consisted of "strangely different component parts." The immigrant
masses huddled in American slums were not concerned with temperance or
woman's rights, but with help when he found himself in trouble. It was
their recognition of this elemental need that secured the alliance of the many
poor with the urban machine. For in the absence of institutional arrange-
ments, the local boss took up the function of providing welfare, and a goodly
portion of the graft he exacted went to meet that need.

Arthur Schlesinger, Sr. (1888-1965) was one of those rare historians of
whom it could be said, he was a historian's historian. From the time he pub-
lished his Colonial Merchants and the American Revolution *(1918), his repu-*
tation was made. It was his New Viewpoints in American History *(1922),*
however, emphasizing as it did the unexplored fields in American history,
that assured him his unique position. A whole generation of young historians
would take their inspiration from his suggestions and launch research which
radically altered accepted concepts. His own The Rise of the City, 1878-
1898 *is, in retrospect, one of the first landmarks of urban history. It helped*
remind historians that in the neglected cities was where the action is.

THE RISE OF THE CITY, 1878-1898

by Arthur Meier Schlesinger

In the Middle West and the North Atlantic states rural America, like a
stag at bay, was making its last stand. The clash between the two cultures—
one static, individualistic, agricultural, the other dynamic, collectivistic, urban—was most clearly exhibited in the former section, for the march of
events had already decided the outcome in the East. Agriculturally the
Middle West, unlike the Great West, was beyond its period of growing
pains. Farming was no longer pioneering and speculative; save in some of
the newer districts the tendency everywhere was toward stabilization and
a settled routine. Though the corn belt cut a wide swath through the lower
tier of states and wheat predominated in the colder climes, the individual
farmer was apt to supplement his main product with hay, orchard fruits
and vegetables and to raise horses, cattle and hogs as well as crops, meantime
guarding his soil resources through systematic rotation and the use of fertilizers.

The maturity of agriculture was mirrored in the physical appearance of the farms, particularly in the older regions. Neat frame dwellings housed the owners. Barns of increasing size and solidity, built of trimmed painted boards and perhaps protected below the ground line by stonework, sheltered the livestock and crops in place of the pioneer's slender framework of poles covered with straw. Instead of the old-time zigzag fences of split logs now appeared orderly rail fences or the new-fashioned wire variety. One observant Old World visitor formed a distinctly favorable impression of Middle America as it flashed by his car window. "The tall corn pleased the eye," he wrote afterwards, "the trees were graceful in themselves, and framed the plain into long, aërial vistas; and the clean, bright gardened townships spoke of country fare and pleasant summer evenings on the stoop." That this "flat paradise" was "not unfrequented by the devil" was suggested to him only by the billboards along the car tracks advertising cures for the ague.

Economic stabilization bred political caution. Though the Granger agitation and the Greenback propaganda of earlier years had centered largely in the Middle West, the agrarian unrest which shook the trans-Missouri country and the South in the 1880's won little response. Already in the preceding decade the growth of a prosperous dairying interest in Wisconsin and Iowa had caused opposition to the demands of the wheat growers for greenback inflation. Even more notable results appeared in the eighties as mixed farming became the rule and agricultural products found a ready market in near-by cities. Urban sentiment, always hostile to agrarian panaceas, also colored the farmers' thinking in countless imperceptible ways and helped confirm their new-found conservatism. In 1893 the states from Ohio to Iowa and Minnesota would vote more than seven to one in both houses of Congress for Cleveland's proposal to repeal the silver-purchase act, while the Solid South and the Great West would plump heavily in the other direction.

It should further be noted that the migration of many sons of the Middle West into the trans-Missouri farming country and into the cities did much to relieve the pressure on the means of rural livelihood. As we have seen, the Far West, like another Eve, was formed out of a rib taken from the side of Middle America. By 1890 a million native Mid-Westerners lived in Kansas, Nebraska and the Dakotas and six hundred thousand more in the region beyond. Still others were trying their luck in the newer parts of Texas and Arkansas. This great exodus drew off many restless and adventurous souls whose staying might have given the politics of the home states a distinctly radical cast. Professor Turner has pointed out that the agrarian leadership in the new Western commonwealth came chiefly from the ranks of natives of the Middle West.

While great numbers of immigrant farmers settled in the section, they generally shunned the older agricultural regions, flocking rather into Minnesota, Michigan and other of the less developed parts. Though the promise of an easier living beckoned them further westward, they preferred to consort with fellow countrymen who had already firmly established themselves and were well satisfied with the returns of their toil. State immigration boards in Minnesota, Wisconsin, Michigan and Missouri exerted themselves to attract alien newcomers, but with diminishing energy as the decade advanced. In 1884 Iowa frankly discontinued all official efforts, no longer desiring people "merely to count up in the census."

Norwegians, Swedes and Danes, following the well-worn tracks of their countrymen in earlier years, came in such numbers as to make of Minnesota and Wisconsin a New Scandinavia. Industrious, thrifty, law-abiding, highly literate, these descendants of the Vikings contributed materially to the prosperity and civic advancement of their adopted states. The whole family—ten children were common, twenty not unknown—toiled in the fields, at least until comparison with Yankee ways planted seeds of revolt in the daughters' breasts. There were two hundred and sixty-five thousand more Scandinavians in the Middle West in 1890 than a decade before. Most of them became agriculturists, a third settling in the single state of Minnesota.

Like the Scandinavians, a majority of the four hundred thousand Germans who came in the 1880's turned farmer. But they were less imbued with the true pioneer spirit and generally bought the partly worked farms of Americans who were itching to be up and doing elsewhere. As thrifty and hard working as the Scandinavians, they were also deeply interested in education and quite as easily assimilated. They were not, however, such stern Protestants, many indeed being Catholics, and they brought to rural life a *Gemütlichkeit*, a sociability, which set them apart from all other racial elements. On local political issues the two north European peoples were often divided, particularly when the Teutonic bias in regard to "blue laws" and the liquor traffic entered as a factor. By 1890 more than half the Germans and Scandinavians resided in the Middle West, about the same proportion of the Swiss and Poles and nearly two thirds of the Dutch and Bohemians.

A traveler familiar with the great stretches of country toward the Pacific and the Gulf would have been immediately aware that in the Middle West the traditional rural culture of America was rapidly dissolving and a new form rising in its stead. Though occasional cities, some of them populous and wealthy, were to be found in the Great West and the South, their existence merely accented the general rural character of the civilization which encompassed them. But in the great triangular central region, extending from Ohio to Missouri and Minnesota and containing nearly one third of all the people of the nation, the migration from the country districts had attained a momentum that was fast giving the city a dominant position in the social organism. In 1880 one out of every five Middle Westerners lived in urban communities of four thousand or more inhabitants, ten years later one out of every three. In the single decade the number dwelling in such centers doubled, attaining a total of six and a quarter million. Illinois and Ohio boasted nearly one hundred and twenty towns and cities, including some of the largest in the land, while even in Minnesota and Missouri three out of every ten persons in 1890 were townsfolk.

The drawbacks of life on the farm had, of course, been felt by earlier generations, but never before with such compelling force. At least since the adoption of a national land policy in 1785, isolation and loneliness had been the almost inescapable conditions of country existence, for by the ordinance of that year the government rejected the New England system of farmer communities and provided for large, scattered, individual holdings. These tendencies were confirmed and strengthened by the homestead law of 1862. Thus in the less developed parts of the Middle West such as Minnesota and Wisconsin, or in the near-by territory of Dakota, country neighbors dwelt too far apart for friendly intercourse, being but four to the square mile when land was held in quarter sections and even farther away if the homesteads were larger or tracts remained unoccupied. Even in the older farming districts families generally lived out of sight of other habitations; they had no mail deliveries; and the balm of a telephone was denied to all but a tiny minority.

As urban communities increased in number and importance, the farmer's feeling of isolation was deepened by a knowledge of the pleasant town life not many miles away. The craving for solitudes is not as natural as the craving for multitudes; and the companionable sense of rubbing elbows, even if anonymously, with one's fellows compensates for many of life's repulses and frustrations. If the chief historian of the Scandinavian Americans is correct, the cheerlessness and hardships of farm life accounted for the uncommonly high proportion of insanity among the Norwegians and Swedes in the Middle West. Certainly where families of different nationalities occupied the same neighborhood social intercourse was at a minimum, though a homogeneous immigrant community sometimes succeeded for a time in keeping alive the friendly social customs of the home land.

Despite such drawbacks many farmers valued the free open country life above all else and would not willingly have exchanged it for any other type of existence. Rural life, too, had its occasional cherished diversions for both young and old: its picnics and its gatherings at the swimming hole in summer, its nutting and hunting expeditions in the fall, its annual county fair and horse races, its family reunions at Thanksgiving, its bob-sled parties of merrymakers in winter, its country dances in all seasons of the year. Even its religious revivals might be so regarded. Funerals, too, were as much social events as solemn obsequies, attracting people from miles around and affording a treasured opportunity for brushing shoulders and exchanging gossip on the doorstep of the church or under the horse sheds. For those with eyes to see, nature itself in its vagrant moods and infinite variety was a never ending source of pleasure. A field of growing wheat—"deep as the breast of man, wide as a sea, heavy-headed, supple-stalked, many-voiced, full of multitudinous, secretive, whispered colloquies"—was to the aesthetic "a meeting-place of winds and of magic."

But such pastimes and diversions paled before the bright attractions of the city, for, after the manner of human nature, the country dweller was apt to compare the worst features of his own lot with the best aspects of urban life. Nor, in the thinking of many, especially the younger fold, did these occasional pleasures repay for the drudgery and monotony which attended much of the daily toil, only to yield in the end a modest living. Farm work in former days had been spiced with greater variety. Now the advent of railroads and the lowered cost of manufactures led the farmer to buy over the store counter or through the mail-order catalogue multifarious articles which he had once made for himself. With no apparent reduction in the amount of labor, the kinds of tasks were fewer and often less appealing to his special interests and aptitudes. In contrast the city offered both better business openings and a greater chance for congenial work.

*   *   *   *   *

The extraordinary growth of its bigger cities was one of the marvels of Middle Western life in the eighties. Chicago, which best represented the will power and titanic energy of the section, leaped from a half million in 1880 to more than a million ten years later, establishing its place as the second city of the nation. The Twin Cities trebled in size; places like Detroit, Milwaukee, Columbus and Cleveland increased by from sixty to eighty per cent. Of the fifty principal American cities in 1890 twelve were in the Middle West.

The rapid urbanization was, of course, accelerated by the swarm of foreigners into the section. During the eighties the immigrant population of Middle America increased nearly nine hundred thousand, reaching a total at the close of the decade of three and a half million. Every fifth or sixth person in 1890 was of alien birth. Though the Scandinavians, as we have seen, generally preferred the farm to the city, seventy thousand of them were working in Chicago in 1890, the men as mechanics or factory hands, the daughters usually as domestic servants. Fifty thousand more dwelt in the Twin Cities. The Germans also divided their allegiance. James Bryce heard German commonly spoken on the streets of Milwaukee; the Teutonic element in Chicago, while thrice as numerous, was less conspicuous because of the babel of other tongues. As skilled workers the newcomers from the *Vaterland* were generally found in such trades as photography, tailoring, baking, locksmithing and lithography. The nationalities which most thoroughly identified themselves with city life, however, were the Irish and particularly the increasing stream of Russian and Polish Jews and Italians who constituted the "new immigration."

So great was the influx of all races into Chicago that its foreign-born inhabitants in 1890 numbered nearly as many as its entire population in 1880. A writer in the nineties, analyzing its school census, pointed out that "only two cities in the German Empire, Berlin and Hamburg, have a greater German population than Chicago; only two in Sweden, Stockholm and Gotenborg, have more Swedes; and only two in Norway, Christiania and Bergen, more Norwegians." If the "seacoast of Bohemia" was a figment of the poet's imagination, the third largest city of Bohemians in the world could at least boast an extended lake front.

*   *   *   *   *

In so far as the swiftly growing urban localities drew population away from the countryside, the effects were severe enough to threaten many rural districts with paralysis. A map of the Middle West, shading the counties which suffered the chief losses between 1880 and 1890, would have been blackest across central Missouri and in the eastern half of Iowa, northern and western Illinois, central and southeastern Indiana, southern Michigan and central and southern Ohio. Though some of the depletion, particularly in Iowa and western Illinois, was connected with the building up of the agricultural country to the west, much of it was due to the cityward flight. In Ohio 755 townships out of 1316 declined in population; in Illinois 800 out of 1424. Yet during the same decade every Middle Western state gained substantially in total number of inhabitants—Ohio about one seventh and Illinois nearly a quarter—an advance only in part to be accounted for by immigrant additions and the natural increase of population.

Such indications of rural decay, however, were mild as compared with conditions in the North Atlantic states. In this great seaboard section stretching from the Potomac to the St. Croix the city had completed its conquest. Already in 1880 about half the people—seven and a half million—lived in towns and cities of four thousand or more inhabitants; within a decade the proportion grew to nearly three fifths or eleven million. In 1890 about two out of every three persons in New York and Connecticut were townsfolk, four out of every five in Massachusetts and nine out of every ten in Rhode Island. Only the states of northern New England preserved their essentially rural character. In the East, too, most of the nation's great cities were to be found. New York City, with already more than a million people in 1880, reached a million and a half in 1890 without the help of Brooklyn which contained eight hundred thousand more. Philadelphia attained a million in 1890, though since the previous census Chicago had supplanted her as the second city of the United States. Boston, Baltimore and Washington had about half a million each, Buffalo and Pittsburgh a quarter million each. Countless smaller places spotted the landscape and gave to the entire region a strongly urban cast.

In striking contrast were the rural backwaters. "Sloven farms alternate with vast areas of territory, half forest, half pasturage," an observant foreign traveler wrote of Pennsylvania and New England, "farm buildings, partly in ruins, testify at once to the former collapse." Then, "all at once, on rounding a hill, one comes upon a busy valley, its slopes dotted with charming cottages, while at the further end rise the immense blocks of buildings and chimneys that tell of the factory."

The census of 1890 first revealed the extent of the rural exodus. Two fifths of Pennsylvania, a good quarter of New Jersey, nearly five sixths of New York state and much of New England had fallen off in population during the decade. The eclipse of the Eastern countryside had, of course, been long in process, indeed ever since the old farming districts of the Atlantic states first felt the competition of the virgin lands of the interior. After the Civil War the pressure became even greater, for the opening of new railway lines enabled the prairie farmers, with the aid of favoring freight rates, to undersell Eastern farmers in their own natural markets. The normal drain on the older agricultural districts was intensified by the drift of country boys and girls to the towns and cities as industry boomed and the lure of the near-by metropolis captured their imaginations. Far removed from the free lands of the Great West, the rural youth was not less inclined to ask "Where is the fittest farm?" than "Where is the fitter vocation?"

New England was hardest hit of all, especially those parts in which agricultural retrogression was not offset by corresponding urban development. Three fifths of Connecticut, three fourths of Vermont and nearly two thirds of New Hampshire and Maine declined in population. Out of 1502 townships in all New England 932 had fewer people in 1890 than at the start of the decade. Cellar holes choked with lilac and woodbine, tumble-down buildings, scrubby orchards, pastures bristling with new forest growths, perhaps a lone rosebush—these mute, pathetic memorials of once busy farming communities attested the reversal of a familiar historic process, with civilization retreating before the advancing wilderness.

Official inquiries at the end of the eighties revealed more than a thousand farms in Vermont abandoned for agricultural purposes, over thirteen hundred in New Hampshire, nearly fifteen hundred in Massachusetts and more than thirty-three hundred in Maine. Vermont farms with good buildings went begging at five dollars or less an acre. Nor did the upland villages escape the general debacle. "The proportion of abandoned wagonshops, shoe-shops, saw-mills and other mechanical businesses has far outstripped the abandonment of farms," wrote one contemporary. Judge Nott of Washington, D.C., happening upon a stricken village in southern Vermont, found that

> the church was abandoned, the academy dismantled, the village deserted. The farmer who owned the farm on the north of the village lived on one side of the broad street, and he who owned the farm on the South lived on the other, and they were the only inhabitants.

All others had fled—"to the manufacturing villages, to the great cities, to the West." Where once had dwelt "industry, education, religion, comfort, and contentment," there remained "only a drear solitude of forsaken homes."

Generally the people of push and initiative migrated while the less enterprising stayed at home. Thus Yankee energy, though continuing to contribute vitally to the upbuilding of America, did so at a terrible cost to the stock it left behind. Ministers and humanitarian workers in the country districts were appalled by the extent of inbreeding, the prevalence of drunkenness, bastardy and idiocy, the lack of wholesome amusements and the almost universal poverty. In nearly the same words two Congregational preachers reported, "My people are degenerates; the people all through my district are degenerates." It may well be believed that such characterizations applied to the most neglected communities rather than to typical ones. Yet everywhere the process of folk depletion was going on at an alarming rate, lending color to the assertion that New England's woods and templed hills were breeding their own race of poor whites.

Dismayed by the trend of the times, the close of the eighties saw the several state governments engaged in frantic efforts to promote a back-to-the-country movement. Few literate Americans were allowed to remain ignorant of the bargains in land and farm buildings that might be found in

New England's rustic parts. Vermont even tried the expedient of colonizing three small groups of Swedish immigrants on deserted tracts. The situation, however, had to grow worse before it could become better. Once the nation-wide agricultural sickness of the early nineties had run its course, rural New England would discover sources of new wealth in dairying, truck garden-ing, the expansion of wood-working industries based on second forest growths and, last but not least, the rapid development of the summer-boarder business.

Despite the decline of rural population in New England and other parts of the East the attractions of city life were so great that from 1880 to 1890 the section in general gained twenty per cent in number of inhabitants. By the latter year nineteen million, or somewhat less than a third of all the na-tion, lived there. Urban growth, even more than in Middle America, was nourished by foreign immigration. A larger proportion of the alien arrivals settled in the East and fewer of them took up farming as a livelihood. The census of 1890 disclosed a million more immigrants than a decade earlier. In the section as a whole one out of every five persons was foreign-born.

Nor could one assume, as ten years before, that any immigrant he met was likely to belong to the older racial strains that had fused into the historic American stock. The Eastern commonwealths with their great ports and thriving industries were the first to feel the impact of the new human tide that was setting in from southern and eastern Europe. While in 1890 they contained more Irish and Britons than did any other section—a total of two and a third million—and with nine hundred thousand Germans ranked in that respect next to the Middle West, they also embraced more Italians, Russians and Hungarians than any other section, to the number of a quarter million.

A fourth of the people of Philadelphia and a third of the Bostonians were in 1890 of alien birth. New York-Brooklyn was the greatest center of immi-grants in the world, having half as many Italians as Naples, as many Germans as Hamburg, twice as many Irish as Dublin and two and a half times as many Jews as Warsaw. Four out of every five residents of Greater New York were foreigners or of foreign parentage. Different from Boston and Philadelphia, the newer type of immigrant had become a considerable element in the city's population though the Germans and Irish still greatly predominated.

These latest arrivals, ignorant, clannish, inured to wretched living condi-tions, gravitated naturally to the poorest quarters of the city toward the tip of Manhattan and gradually pushed the older occupants into the better sec-tions to the north. Lower New York was like a human palimpsest, the writ-ings of earlier peoples being dimmed, though not entirely effaced, by the heavier print of the newest comers. Through the eighties the Italians crowded into the old Irish neighborhoods west of Broadway, while the Russian and Polish Jews took possession of the German districts to the east with the tenth ward as their center. The Hungarians settled thickly east of Avenue B, about Houston Street, and the Bohemians near the river on the upper East Side from about Fiftieth to Seventy-sixth Street. Smaller groups like the

Greeks and Syrians also had their special precincts where picturesque Old World customs and trades prevailed; and in the heart of the lower East Side grew up a small replica of San Francisco's Chinatown.

Quite as strange to Americans as the south Europeans were the French Canadians who began their mass invasion of New England shortly after 1878. For over two centuries these descendants of the pioneers of New France had tilled the soil of the province of Quebec where, intensely race-conscious and devoted to Catholicism, they had stubbornly maintained their identity and language apart from the conquering English. Harried, however, by hard times from the 1860's on and tempted by better opportunities elsewhere, many of them sought escape in migration. Some moved westward to set up farm colonies in Ontario and Manitoba. Others, feeling the pull of the busy mill towns across the international border, succumbed to *le mal des États-Unis*. Presently the trickle of population into New England became a flooding stream. About fourteen thousand had removed to Rhode Island by 1875, sixty-four thousand to Massachusetts ten years later. Northern New England made less appeal though occasional settlements of farmers and lumberjacks were to be found. By 1890 the French Canadians, then numbering two hundred thousand, formed approximately a sixth of the entire immigrant population of New England. Nearly half of them were in Massachusetts.

Living in the manufacturing towns, they were eagerly welcomed by employers who found them not only hard workers but also slow to give trouble even when conditions were galling. The opprobrium of being the "Chinese of the Eastern states," however, they scarcely deserved, although their ready acceptance of low living standards naturally roused the ire of organized labor. Religiously, too, they were viewed askance by the older elements. Added to the already large Irish Catholic contingent, their presence seemed to threaten the traditional Puritan and Protestant character of the section. "Protestant New England will soon have within itself, a Roman Catholic New France, as large as, if not larger than itself," cried one alarmist. As a matter of fact, the language barrier and the desire of the newcomers to import their own priests caused more friction than friendship between them and the resident Irish-American clergy. It was said that French-Canadian support of the Republican party at the polls was due to no reason so good as that the Irish preferred the Democrats.

A race so resistant could hardly be expected to adopt new ways of life overnight. Yet, scattered in a hundred different communities and obliged constantly to rub elbows with people unlike themselves, the chemistry of Americanization worked as quickly with them as with most other alien groups. Intermarriage, while not common, took place most readily with Anglo-Canadians. Less adept politically than the Irish, they nevertheless gradually found their way into local offices and by 1890 thirteen French Canadians were members of New England legislatures. Different from other immigrant peoples, however, they massed themselves in New England, few of them going into the Middle West or even into other parts of the East.

As a lodestone for both immigrant and native-born the city had decisively placed the East under thrall. Its hand already lay heavily upon the Middle West. Even in the farther West and the South its power and distant allure were strongly felt though society as yet lingered in an agricultural state. Through the nation in general every third American in 1890 was an urban dweller, living in a town of four thousand or more inhabitants. Cities of from twelve to twenty thousand people had since 1880 increased in number from 76 to 107; cities of from twenty to forty thousand from 55 to 91; larger places up to seventy-five thousand inhabitants from 21 to 35; cities of yet greater size from 23 to 39.

Moreover, the concentration of population had been attended by a significant concentration of wealth. This latter circumstance furnished ample basis for the agrarian contention that the rural districts were not sharing proportionately in the advancing national wealth. In 1890 the value of farms was returned as thirteen billion while other real estate—mostly urban—was listed at twenty-six billion. Nor did the people on the farms and in the rural hamlets of the East fare better than those of the West and South. On the contrary, the farms in the Eastern states declined in absolute value during the decade.

If personalty were included, the contrast between city and country became even sharper, particularly since the tangible personalty on the farms was in considerable degree offset by mortgages held in the towns and cities. The most careful contemporary student of the subject estimated that in 1890 the average wealth of families in the rural districts did not exceed $3250 while the average wealth of city families was over $9000. The wider implications of urban growth, however, reached far beyond exigent considerations of wealth and income. These, as they affected the character of American civilization for good or ill, remain yet to be examined.

THE *city and town were logical outgrowths of expanding industry. The expansion of urban settlement is almost a graph of a rapidly burgeoning industry: the two were interdependent. It is often forgotten that American industrialization had on the eve of the Civil War only reached, in the words of Walt Whitman Rostow, "the take-off stage." And historians, no longer as easily prepared to accept the Civil War as a confrontation of an industrial North and an agrarian South as once they were, disagree on whether the Civil War impeded or accelerated industrialization. It is true, however, that in the aftermath of civil war, the once decentralized provincial-oriented market of the United States was changed in little more than three decades into a vast national market. The process of this change has fascinated economic historians and still commands their attention as they seek to understand the processes of economic growth.*

It is obvious that the construction of a national railway system that united both coasts provided a necessary keystone. Not only did it provide swift movement of goods and people over continental distances, but it also set into motion the first great corporate consolidations. In the years immediately after the war, the names of Vanderbilt and the New York Central, Scott and the Pennsylvania, Garrett and the Baltimore and Ohio, Gould and the Union Pacific became synonymous. The vast fortunes that resulted created a new class which sought to justify its possession by appeals to Social Darwinism: as the Puritans had seen in their wealth proof of election, so the new wealth saw in theirs proof of fitness. But the concentration of ownership brought with it social unease as Americans grew to wonder whether wealth or commonwealth would dominate future society. Nothing less than the future of democracy seemed at stake.

As the industrial economy grew, it left its searing mark on the land. Whole forests were leveled; once-green valleys were hidden in smog; and the ugly sprawl of the city gave sharp point to Hawthorne's harsh suggestion: "All towns should be made capable of purification by fire, or of decay, within each half-century." Before the century had closed, one reform-minded agitator concluded the nation had been reduced to two classes, "millionaires and tramps." The evidence of social dislocation was everywhere, and the price of industrialization obviously came high, but it was also obvious that the creation of a national market had released an energy without parallel. The wealth of a continent once tapped promised an affluence undreamed of in the life of mankind. The dislocations, heavy and disabling though they were, proved the price that the generation at the end of the nineteenth century paid to insure their heirs unfailing abundance. There is some small consolation in knowing that slowly, often imperceptibly, even this generation knew improvement in their lives.

Ida Tarbell (1857-1944) earned considerable notoriety as a muckraker at the turn of the century for McClure's *and* American Magazine. *Her* History of Standard Oil Company *(1904), originally published in* McClure's, *set in motion the litigation that resulted in the breakup of the combination. Her painstaking care with facts and her use of personal interviews gave her work particular pertinence. It also suggested the narrow line that separates top-flight journalism and history. Her indictment of Standard Oil as guilty of "contemptuous indifference to fair play," and its officers as governed by "greed and unscrupulousness," led to the final charge that its "huge bulk, blackened by commercial sin" loomed as a challenge to democracy. She had written scrupulously factual history, and embued it with her sense of moral outrage. But she did not oppose business simply because it was business; quite the reverse, she admired the businessmen's efficiency, and when they exercised their power responsibly, she approved them heartily, as her biographies of* Elbert H. Gary *(1925) and* Owen D. Young *(1932) demonstrate. Ida Tarbell was more than a historian; she revealed the underlying assumptions of much of the Progressive Era, particularly its fear of unrestrained power, and, as a consequence, she made history even as she wrote it.*

THE NATIONALIZING OF BUSINESS, 1878-1898

by Ida M. Tarbell

The trend toward combination was quite as strong in manufacturing as in the electrical industry or in the field of communication. It was forced mainly by what was called overproduction, but which might more correctly be called underconsumption. Through the use of machinery the manufacturer had learned how to double, treble or even more greatly multiply his output. He had been taking full advantage of every new labor-saving device with little or no regard to its effect on either markets or labor. Where the efficient broom maker had formerly kept seventeen men busy making five hundred dozen brooms in a week, he now had nine men turning out twelve hundred dozen. Carpet manufacturers were using one man where thirty years before they had used from ten to twenty. Where once a first-class journeyman made from six hundred to a thousand two-pound cans by hand, now with a machine he turned out from two thousand to twenty-five hundred. A fifty-per-cent displacement of labor was not unusual.

This output was thrown on the market before the labor displaced had been absorbed. This meant, for a time at least, cutting off the purchasing power of those who had lost their jobs. In general, there was little scientific attempt to measure demand. Production outstripped consumption alarmingly in some instances. As a case in point, the output of the iron industry in five states doubled between 1885 and 1888. This was the result of improved processes, for the number of furnace stacks declined. Under the pressure of a wanton production the weaker producer went to the wall, thus still further curtailing purchasing power.

Behind the manufacturer, pushing him to build or enlarge plants regardless of existing capacity, were men who, having idle capital to invest, were willing to go into iron or glass or wire or textiles or any other line that promised big profits. What they were seeking was not active business but, in the words of David A. Wells, to convert their wealth "into the form of negotiable securities paying dividends or interest with regularity, and on the recipiency of which the owner can live without personal exertion or risk of the principal." Frequently, though perhaps less often than was popularly supposed, the marketing of such securities was a pure speculation on the part of those who had formed the company or corporation. They organized to sell stock, not to mine iron or run a railroad; stock promoters and speculators fed on the avidity with which many people seized a new issue without scrutinizing what was behind it. Without a greedy and gullible public they could not have lived.

Overproduction sooner or later forced prices too low for profits, causing bankruptcy of the weak, temporary losses for the strong, short or long periods of unemployment and general business instability. In every considerable industry attempts were made to correct this instability. The favorite form was the pool. In essence, this was a voluntary secret agreement of all or of a majority of the units of an industry to produce and handle their product according to a fixed set of rules. The agreement and its regulation differed in almost every case; so also did the results.

The most substantial pool in 1878 was that of the salt producers of Michigan, known as the Michigan Salt Association. The industry had gone up and down since it was started in 1859, largely according to its degree of success in curbing overproduction. Public opinion agreed that the combinations had improved the grade of salt by the system of inspection they had established and, as long as they lasted, had brought "order and stability" into the business. Also, the public had paid a little higher for its salt. But no association had long endured. When it was seen that the producers were making money, capital pushed in, price-cutting followed, and there was a gradual return to unchecked competition. As an observer characterized one such disastrous period, "It was a Donnybrook Fair in the salt market. When you saw a head, you hit it." The plight of the individual Michigan manufacturer was the worse because the great salt districts of New York and Ohio were well organized.

As an escape from this unprofitable warfare, and also as a treaty-making power with the Ohio and New York districts, the leaders of the industry in 1876 formed the Michigan Salt Association. It was a stock company in which the amount of stock held by any concern was limited to one share for each barrel of its average daily capacity. The association's business was the manufacturing and marketing of salt. Each member was obliged to make an annual contract to turn over to it his full product or to lease his plant to the association. A seven-per-cent dividend, together with the losses and expenses of handling, was deducted from the proceeds of sales before a division of profits was made. The agreement was limited to five years. When at the end of that time the association expired, it was continued for a second five-year period; again, in 1886, it was reorganized for a third five-year period.

The association was fortunate in securing an efficient management, one experienced enough to detect weaknesses or raids, and flexible and shrewd enough to take care of them. Controlling about eighty-five per cent of the output, it did not hesitate, when challenged, to squeeze out a troublesome competitor. The public interest in cheaper salt was, on the whole, satisfied. Among other things, the association prevented a practice which under full competition had regularly raised prices to consumers and cut them for producers, the practice whereby large dealers bought great quantities of salt in the summer when it was cheap and plentiful and stored it until winter when it became scarce. They could demand a high price from which they alone profited. Under the new arrangement they received a small commission for each barrel sold.

A looser and much less enduring form of pool was that of the makers of cordage, binding twine, rope of all kinds. Cordage was an inviting industry since it required little capital and fed a constantly growing market. Since

1860, pools had been formed from time to time to limit the overproduction which the inrush of fresh capital and consequent cutting of prices below the profit mark caused. They rarely lasted over three years. "Breaking up, fighting and getting together again" was their story. The plan customarily followed was later explained to the Industrial Commission by J. M. Waterbury, a member of the pool existing in 1880:

> Well, all manufacturers would meet and agree to divide the business of the country upon certain percentages, and when they had agreed on the percentages the rule was that each manufacturer should make his returns monthly to a supervisor, and if his business ran beyond his percentage he paid in to the supervisor so much per pound on the excess beyond his percentage; and then those that went below that percentage drew out from the supervisor an amount as much per pound as they went below their percentage. The supervisor acted as a clearing house for the manufacturers.

The member which profited most by this agreement was the long-established Plymouth Cordage Company in Massachusetts, which in 1936 remained an independent concern after one hundred and twelve years of continuous operation. It was its policy to exceed its allotment and cheerfully pay the fixed amount on this surplus, which was distributed to those who fell short of their quota. The result was that at each renewal of the arrangement its percentage grew greater while that of some of its less enterprising competitors dwindled. By 1885 the Plymouth Company's allotment, originally ten per cent, had risen to twenty.

Not all the minor pools formed around 1880 were as loose in construction as the cordage pool. The American Wall Paper Manufacturers' Association, which included practically every factory in the country, fixed prices and maintained them at a high point. The administration was in the hands of a commissioner. Each company furnished security for its performance of the agreement; those which failed to live up to the terms were fined. An interesting feature of the wall-paper pool was the attempt to drop the middlemen and deal directly with customers. This had the unexpected effect of causing many middlemen to go into the business for themselves. The pool broke down because certain manufacturers secretly sold goods at less than the scheduled prices.

Pools proved an unsatisfactory instrument for establishing order and stability in a business because they suffered from two basic defects. In the first place, they violated underlying principles of both common and statute law, and hence could not be enforced in the courts. The only guarantee of good faith came from the creation of deposits, the imposition of fines and other more or less cumbersome devices. The second difficulty lay in the fact that, under the circumstances, pools could be but temporary expedients. They could afford no certainty for stability of prices or of industrial policy over any extended period.

Industry, however, had not been depending solely on the pool as an instrument of stability. As a means of avoiding the shortcomings of that device, business magnates often obtained control of some element essential to the life of an industry. The railroads, the telegraph, the telephone had such a whip hand in their exclusive franchises. Control of raw materials would accomplish the same end, but usually nature had scattered raw materials so widely and so prodigally as to make it exceedingly difficult for any man or group of men to monopolize the supply. An exclusive patent afforded an advantage which might temporarily give a monopoly; but here nature interfered in another way, endowing many men with inventive capacity. A patent which created a monopoly was usually followed quickly by other inventions which performed the same function, sometimes more efficiently. An advantage much sought by industry was a privileged relation to transportation. If a manufacturer could ship his raw material and his product at a lower rate than his competitor, he could undersell him and finally bring him to terms. Though public opinion was strongly opposed to such discriminations, not until the mid-eighties did the opposition crystallize in a federal statute defining and forbidding them.

The most brilliant illustration of the supremacy possible through a control of shipping rates was the practical monopoly of the petroleum industry which since 1872 had been developed by an oil-refining and marketing concern of Cleveland, Ohio, known as the Standard Oil Company. Yet considering the remarkable abilities of John D. Rockefeller, who headed the Standard, it may well be asked whether the company had needed to resort to unfair methods of competition in order to gain preeminence in the field. Rockefeller was a man who gave himself entirely to his business, saw it as a whole, its tiniest detail as well as its largest possible ramification. He knew how to select and handle his associates, knew what to tell them and what to conceal. He took deep satisfaction in economies, hated waste whether in small or great things. Combined with these qualities was a genius for organization which it would be difficult to parallel in the history of American industry. With such an equipment nothing could have prevented him from becoming one of the leaders, probably the greatest, in the oil business.

But Rockefeller detested and feared free competition and the disorder and uncertainties which attended it. It interfered with stable prices and profits; it glutted the crude and refined markets; it was wasteful. He had seen no way to bring order and stability into the industry but for him and those with him to take over the entire oil-refining and marketing business of the country. By this means it could be run economically, efficiently and profitably for those in the combination. This could be done most expeditiously by getting special rates from the railroads. It was fair to ask them, he held, because the Standard would be the biggest and the most regular shipper. Aided by these special advantages over competitors, the Rockefeller group had acquired, through stock purchase or through direct or indirect property purchase, some seventy-four refining concerns, including many of the most successful in their districts. Contracts limiting the quantity of oil to be refined had also been made with certain firms strong enough to refuse to sell. In 1878 the Standard Oil Company was manufacturing over ninety per cent of the output of the country.

In securing mastery of the refining industry the Standard had been aided by its success in carrying out one of the most farsighted policies in its history, that of controlling the pipe lines which carried oil from the wells to the railway shipping points as well as to the tanks in which surplus was stored. So great had become its power over transportation facilities that in 1879, on representation of the Petroleum Producers' Union, the state of Pennsylvania, which produced the bulk of the world's oil, brought suit in equity against the Pennsylvania Railroad and the several pipe lines which the Standard owned or controlled. The upshot was an indictment in April of John D. Rockefeller and seven of his associates. The indictment charged a conspiracy to secure a monopoly of the oil business through the control of transportation.

This indictment, together with the demonstration of the methods employed by the Standard, naturally attracted public attention. It was an object lesson in success, also in evasion, for the men were never brought to trial. There were repeated postponements, sought by the defendants "on advice of counsel." An investigation in New York state at the same time interfered. Moreover, so the producers believed, the railroads brought such pressure to bear on the state authorities to drop the prosecution that they were glad to seize any pretext for delay. The independents finally tired of the struggle and in 1880 a settlement was arranged. With it the Petroleum Producers' Union came to an end.

Meanwhile the Rockefeller group took steps to consolidate their control of the various companies they had acquired in order to obviate competition. To overcome the objections inherent in the pool, they devised a novel form of industrial organization: the trust. It was an old legal device fitted to new conditions. Adopted in 1879 and revised in 1882, the plan provided for a board of nine trustees to which all the capital stock of the constituent companies was assigned, the original shareholders accepting "trust certificates" in lieu of their former evidences of ownership. The trust was an improvement upon the pool both as regards effectiveness and stability. Its success soon prompted other industries to adopt a similar form of organization. As the sequel was to show, however, trusts were vulnerable legally because the agreements upon which they were based were matters of record. Hence they could be moved against by the courts under the common law.

Efforts by competing companies to escape the effects of the transportation monopoly which the Standard had established continued. The most ambitious scheme was to build a pipe line to the seaboard by which an independent producer could ship crude oil directly from the wells without favor of the railroads. An attempt to lay such a line from the oil regions to Baltimore had been made in 1876 by the Pennsylvania Transportation Company, the chief engineer being General Herman Haupt, the Civil War bridge builder. The project attracted great attention, but failed through a combination of railroad opposition and bad financial management. The idea continued to be cherished, however, and in the fall of 1878 the Tidewater Pipe Company was organized to lay a conduit from the Bradford (Pennsylvania) oil field, by this time the center of production, over the Allegheny

Mountains to a point where it would connect with the Reading Railroad. That road, which heretofore had carried no oil, was glad to get the freight until the line could be finished.

The right of way was quickly obtained, but as soon as work began the railroads and the Standard interests manifested strong opposition. This took the form of ridicule, of assertions that oil could not be pumped over the mountains, of rumors of financial weakness and of guerrilla-like efforts to break the right of way. But it did not prevent the completion of the project. In late May, 1879, the time arrived to test the question whether or no nature could be flouted and oil be forced over the mountain barrier. It was an exciting occasion. The westernmost pump was started on the twenty-eighth. The oil flowed up and on about as fast as a man could walk, being attended on its way by both believers and doubters. In seven days it covered the distance of a hundred and nine miles and reached the junction point with the Reading.

There was no question thereafter in the minds of either the Tidewater Pipe Company or the Standard that pipes rather than rails would carry the oil of the future. Bitterly the railroads fought the interloper. Rates were lowered on the oil-carrying roads until they were far below cost. The pipe line, completing its way to the seaboard after its successful demonstration, encountered the same guerrilla tactics that it had fought on its first lap. Not until 1886 did the Tidewater pipe line reach New York City. But by that time the company was no longer a free agent. It had attempted to protect its business by acquiring refineries of its own and developing its own markets. The Standard Oil Company had so vigorously opposed it that in 1883 a division of interests was effected which gave the Standard eighty-eight and a half per cent of the business and the Tidewater the rest.

This "gentlemen's agreement" between the Tidewater and the Standard did not end the struggle of the independent companies. A fringe of irreconcilable producers, refiners and local pipe-line men persisted in efforts to do business in an industry which was being swamped by an ever greater production of oil. As a form of mutual help they organized the Producers' Protective Association in 1887. Late in the year a shutdown was tried for a few months, but, like all such efforts at artificial control, it benefited in the end only the stronger concerns. In 1888 and 1889 cooperative oil companies were organized to furnish pipe lines and storage tanks to take care of the independent producers' output, accommodations which the Standard alone was then giving. The Standard thwarted this effort by buying control of the companies. This marked a new departure, for up to 1887 the Standard had not been an oil producer. Now, however, the difficulty of controlling the industry to its liking forced it into production. The last step was taken to complete integration.

Enough producers remained, however, to keep up the fight. To achieve a closer-knit organization, they formed in 1891 the Producers' Oil Company with a capital of six hundred thousand dollars. Over a thousand producers subscribed to the stock, also the few independent refiners left in the oil region. The two interests joined in building a pipe line from the wells to the refineries; but the problem remained of getting the refined product to the seaboard, for the railroads declined shipments at reasonable rates. Again necessity forced a solution. Under the leadership of Lewis Emery, Jr., of Bradford, one of the most aggressive and resourceful of the independents, they undertook the laying of double pipes to the seaboard, one line for crude oil and one for refined. They encountered all the difficulties, even to physical violence, which had beset the first seaboard line, but in 1893 they attained their object. The eventual outcome of this struggle was an entirely independent company, the Pure Oil Company, a ten-million-dollar concern into which in 1900 the three interests which had united their resources, the producers, the refiners and the pipe-line owners, were consolidated. It was an aggregation as completely integrated as the Standard Oil Company itself, owning and controlling its crude oil, its refining, its transportation on land and sea and its marketing facilities at home and abroad.

Next to petroleum, the trend toward combination evidenced itself most strikingly in iron and steel. It was the industry upon which all others directly or indirectly depended. For the fifty million people of the United States it was of vital importance that iron and steel be produced as cheaply and efficiently as possible. The price of these products affected the cost of practically everything the people bought—tools of all sorts, wagons and plows, the stoves on which the women cooked—as well as freight rates on the shipments of farmers, merchants and manufacturers. In 1878 the leading iron-producing region was Michigan. The value of the yield was something over six million a year. Next came Pennsylvania with a little over four million, followed closely by New York state.

But while these were the most productive centers, other fields were about to undergo rapid development. There was the immensely rich Vermilion Range in Minnesota, discovered in 1868, but so inaccessible that not until 1875 could a capitalist be induced to build the sixty-mile railroad necessary to carry the ore to a shipping point on Lake Superior. He was Charlemagne Tower, a Pennsylvania millionaire, who sank some four million dollars in the project before the first cargo was shipped in 1884. In the same year a second Minnesota district, the Gogebic, began to send ore to market. Coal, a necessary ingredient in the making of steel, lay plentifully at hand, for already in 1880 the near-by bituminous fields of Illinois were yielding over six million tons a year. The old Northwest, however, was no longer the farthest outpost of the industry. Several Western states were making iron and steel products by 1880, including California, Kansas, Missouri, Texas and Wyoming. The year 1881 saw the opening of the first furnace of the Colorado Coal and Iron Company at Pueblo.

At the same time a rich area was being developed in the South, around Birmingham in Alabama. Within a radius of a few miles there existed large deposits of iron ore, of coal, of dolomite, of lime—all the elements needed for the industry. The Confederacy had made steel and iron in this district during the Civil War. Despite various attempts to develop the industry in the years following, little success was attained until the 1880's. Then the Alabama Coal Company began operation on a large scale. Eight new concerns—rolling mills, furnaces, mining companies—opened in the Birmingham district between 1880 and 1884. The demand for the pig iron they turned out was greater than the mills could supply. Abram S. Hewitt, an authority on iron and steel matters, said in 1883 that the Birmingham district was "the only place on the American continent where it is possible to make iron in competition with the cheap iron of England." He added, "I think this will be a region of coke-made iron on a grander scale than has ever been witnessed on the habitable globe."

Not only had the American iron and steel industry the advantage of these well-distributed and apparently inexhaustible supplies of ore and coal, but it seized and adapted to its purposes the many revolutionary technological advances which came from English and German experimenters. In 1881 Captain William R. Jones, general superintendent of Andrew Carnegie's first steel plant, the Edgar Thomson, at Braddock, Pennsylvania, which had amazed American and English competitors by its output, told the British Iron and Steel Institute why in his judgment his works could produce five hundred and fifty-five tons to a Britisher's four hundred and twenty. One reason was that, "while your metallurgists, as well as those of France and Germany, have been devoting their time and talents to the discovery of new processes, we have swallowed the information so generously tendered through the printed reports of the Institute, and have selfishly devoted ourselves to beating you in output." The other reasons were the employment of young ambitious men, a strong but pleasant rivalry between plants, a working force of mixed nationalities, the eight-hour day, and the use of the most up-to-date machinery.

The demands on the industry for increased production, particularly of steel, grew annually. Thus, in 1870 less than 30,500 tons of Bessemer steel rails had been made in the United States. Ten years later the output was over 850,000 tons, in 1890 nearly 1,900,000. In 1880 about fifty per cent of the rails used were iron, but by 1890 less than one per cent. Just as steel was taking the place of iron in rails, so it was supplanting iron in bridge building. It had first been used structurally in the Eads Bridge across the Mississippi at St. Louis, completed in 1874. Four years later a bridge entirely of steel was opened across the Missouri River at Glasgow. By 1890 it was generally accepted as the material from which a bridge should be made, replacing iron as iron had in its turn replaced wood. Another new use appeared in the form of structural steel for the modern style of office buildings known as skyscrapers. The transformation of the American navy from wood to steel provided a fresh source of demand. In 1887 the Bethlehem Iron Company signed a contract for the first American-made armor plate —6700 tons at $536 a ton. The next year the Bethlehem Iron Company began the first steel shaft for propellers of United States warships.

A stalwart set of ironmasters, with highly developed and well-placed plants, many of them dating from before the Civil War, led the industry. In the East were the Cooper Hewitt Works at Phillipsburg, New Jersey, an outgrowth of Peter Cooper's ironworks, established at Trenton in the thirties; the Pencroyd Iron Works, near Philadelphia, founded in 1852 by Percival

Roberts, a man as deeply interested in the art of iron making as in his tonnage; the Cambria Iron Works of Johnstown, Pennsylvania, and those of Jones & Laughlin in Pittsburgh, two concerns in successful operation since 1853. The Cambria had provided at least two men of unique value to the industry: Captain "Bill" Jones whom Carnegie in 1871 had placed in charge of his first steel mill, and John Fritz who since 1860 had headed the Bethlehem Iron Company. In the West the most important single concern was the Illinois Steel Company, the outgrowth of a mill built in 1857. There were great numbers of smaller plants; the census of 1880 gave the number as 1005. In the South the Tennessee Coal, Iron and Railway Company was organized in 1881.

The stronger concerns, forced into a struggle for materials and markets, faced a necessity for quickly adopting new processes and of taking on new lines of production. All this required money in sums which the business itself rarely could supply. As a result, they found themselves obliged to employ not only new operations but also new financial methods. A furious contest ensued which ended in the swallowing up of many of the 1005 smaller plants. The most significant man in this bitter warfare was Andrew Carnegie, easily by 1878 the dominating figure in the iron and steel business. He was less an ironmaster than a master promoter and money-maker, a type which was to render the old-fashioned ironmaster secondary in the industry. His success was due in part to his ability to pick men. He once suggested as his epitaph: "Here lies the man who was able to surround himself with men far cleverer than himself." Along with this astuteness went his foresight in safeguarding supplies of essential raw materials.

Carnegie exercised both talents in 1882 when he made certain of the permanency of his coke supply by buying out and taking into his business Henry C. Frick. Frick had gained control of most of the coke ovens of the Connellsville district in Pennsylvania by taking advantage of the bargains in coal lands which the depression of the seventies had thrown on the market. By 1882 he controlled four fifths of the output of coke. Carnegie acquired a large share of the H. C. Frick Company, but allowed Frick to remain master of it.

The two men made a remarkable team. Carnegie was the inspiring leader, imaginative and warmly human. Frick was the cold, hard-headed man of affairs. He filled Pittsburgh with hordes of laborers brought from every obscure village of eastern and southern Europe, and was a determined foe of trade unionism. Under the leadership of these men and their associates the Carnegie company made rapid strides. In 1892 the Carnegie Steel Company, Limited, was formed with a capitalization of $25,000,000. In the quarter-century from 1875 to 1900 the Carnegie interests paid profits aggregating $133,000,000; in the single year 1900 the profits amounted to $40,000,000, of which Carnegie's personal share was $25,000,000.

Other companies made similar progress. The Illinois Steel Company benefited greatly from its enterprise in early acquiring ownership of exclusive supplies of ore. The Colorado Fuel and Iron Company enlarged its capitalization in 1892 to thirteen million dollars. By that time the Tennessee Coal,

Iron and Railway Company had attained gigantic proportions, being the biggest single possessor of coal and ore lands and iron furnaces in the country. By the close of the century the United States led the world as a steel producer, its output almost doubling that of Great Britain.

In other fields of economic life similar processes of combination and integration were at work. For many years the whisky distillers had been perplexed by over-production and price-cutting competition. Agreements to restrict production had been tried without success. A temporary wave of prosperity struck the industry from 1879 to 1881 because crop failures abroad caused a heavy demand and higher prices for American whisky. But at the same time new capital rushed into the field, the number of distilleries increased, and, with the falling off of the European demand, the producers found themselves in greater distress than before. The upshot was the formation in 1881 of a pool, the Western Export Association, which was intended to limit the output.

This and later similar attempts failed to stabilize the industry; and in the spring of 1887 the leading distillers, taking a leaf from the experience of the Standard Oil Company, formed a trust. The organization was called the Distillers' and Cattle Feeders' Trust. The new plan enabled those in authority to reduce production at the source instead of exporting the surplus at a loss, as had been done under the old pools. The trust put prices high enough to pay good dividends to the members and to accumulate a financial war chest to wage battle with independent distillers. But the scheme of the allied distillers was soon disturbed. Higher prices brought new people into the industry. Distilleries, big and little, multiplied, vastly complicating the price-cutting campaigns on which the trust depended to clean up all outsiders. Nevertheless the combination maintained its predominant position.

In the same year that the whisky trust was formed, the National Cordage Company was organized under the leadership of what was called the Cordage Big Four. These four concerns in and near New York City, the largest of them Waterbury & Company, controlled over forty per cent of the industry. The device by which they expected to whip the other sixty per cent into their amalgamation was control of the world's supply of manila hemp, the raw material of rope making. This supply was handled by four or five firms in the Philippines, and with these firms the National Cordage Company contracted for practically their entire stock. Armed with these contracts, it gave its competitors the choice of entering the combination and enjoying its advantages or of staying out and paying a higher price for raw material. Soon nearly seventy per cent of the industry had joined the combination.

The only important concern which refused was the Plymouth Cordage Company. A bitter fight followed. The National attempted to secure stock control of the Plymouth by running up prices, but the majority of the stockholders thwarted this maneuver by forming themselves into a voting trust. Its next attack was on the company's supply of raw materials. On one occasion the National held up in New York Harbor a cargo of hemp ordered by the Plymouth. When the latter sought to take it by a writ of replevin, the National anchored it at sea beyond the three-mile limit, and hence out-side the jursidiction of the court. Only threats of immediate criminal pro-ceedings brought the hemp to Plymouth. By such determined resistance the Plymouth was able to retain its independent existence and, at the same time, share in the high prices which the rope trust succeeded in maintaining.

Both the preferred and common stock of the National Cordage Company were on the exchange. J. M. Waterbury, the president, later testified before the Industrial Commission that his first application to the stock-exchange committee had been to list only the preferred stock, but the committee, after questioning him, asked him "to list the whole thing." "So," continued Water-bury, "the common stock was listed at the request of the Stock Exchange committee at that time, because they thought we had a pretty sound scheme of consolidation." From the first, National Cordage stock was a favorite, and the speculation in it ran high. Purchasers, of course, did not know that the enhanced prices which the rope combination was exacting were having much the same result as in the case of the whisky trust. They were investing capital to build a fresh crop of competition and were putting money into the coffers of existing plants for enlargement and for defense funds.

The centripetal trend which we have been following aimed at the control of an entire industry, that is, a monopoly, or at a complete integration of essential parts in order to insure safety against attack by ruthless com-petitors. The success attained inspired outsiders with the notion that, if an industry did not consolidate itself, they should shoulder the task. The greatest of these promoters in the closing decades of the century was "Judge" W. H. Moore, head of the Chicago legal firm of the Moore Brothers, which had long specialized in corporation law.

Their first important venture was the reorganization of the Diamond Match Company, involving an increase of the capitalization for $3,000,000 to $7,500,000 and later to $11,000,000. Into this organization went practically all the saw mills and factories on which the trade depended. But matches require boxes, and the Moores followed their first promotion with a second, the merger of the leading manufacturers of strawboard into a seven-million-dollar corporation. In 1890 they brought several Eastern cracker manu-facturers together into the New York Biscuit Company with a capitalization of $9,000,000. Eight years later followed the National Biscuit Company which, with a capital of $55,000,000, commanded a monopoly control of ninety per cent of the cracker-biscuit companies of the country. By this time they were being besieged with requests to organize companies "from the marshes of Maine to the Pacific Coast." The Moores insisted on economy, efficiency and centralized management in the mergers they effected, and possessed a knowledge of the intricacies of corporation law which generally enabled their clients to steer clear of the courts.

A less spectacular promoter, but one so active that he became known as the "Father of Trusts," was Charles R. Flint, Jr. Unlike "Judge" Moore, Flint was a merchant and banker, but, like him, he believed that combina-tion was a necessary and inevitable step in industrial evolution. The trust he defined as "an alliance of work, brains and money," of "labour, intelligence and capital." In his mind it had nothing in common with "corners" or the creation of a monopoly. If he is to be believed, he always advised against consolidation when there were no advantages of importance to be secured. He was critical of overcapitalization, of bankers who indorsed securities without knowing whether they were sound, of a public which bought recklessly for speculation, not investment. Combinations meant to him better business, better service to the people. No promoter of the time made out a better case for consolidation or warned more frankly of possible abuses. He organized or helped organize combinations in starch, rubber and other commodities.

By 1890 at least fifteen great trusts and combinations had been formed in addition to those with which the period began. Among the more important of those which have not been discussed were the American Cottonseed Oil Trust in 1884, the National Linseed Oil Trust in 1885, and the National Lead Trust and the Sugar Refineries Company, both in 1887. "In an incredible number of the necessaries and luxuries of life, from meat to tombstones," declared one contemporary,

> some of the inner circle of the "fittest" has sought, and very often obtained, the sweet power which Judge Barrett found the sugar trust had: It "can close every refinery at will, close some and open others . . . artificially limit the production of refined sugar, enhance the price to enrich themselves and their associates at the public expense, and depress the price when necessary to crush out and impoverish a foolhardy rival."

To this despondent observer it seemed that the letters, U. S. A., were rapidly coming to signify the "United Syndicates of America." It looked as though nothing could stop the movement.

🙚 🙘

THE *men and women who made Progressivism were taught to accept the proposition that the function of government was not to make men happy, but rather it was the duty of every man to achieve happiness in his own way. The state served to provide security of rights and a neutral politics in which each person would begin with an equal chance. No one defined more succinctly the prevalent view at the end of the nineteenth century of the proper role of society than the political scientist William Graham Sumner (1840-1910). He argued: "An immoral political system is created whenever there are privileged classes—that is classes who have arrogated to themselves rights while throwing duties upon others. . . . But the real danger of democracy is, that the classes which have the power under it will assume all the rights and reject all the duties—that is, that they will use the political power to plunder those-who-have. Democracy, in order to be true to itself, and to develop into a sound working system, must oppose the same cold resistance to any claims for favor on the ground of poverty, as on the ground of birth and rank."*

With such beliefs, it is hardly surprising that Americans were dismayed to learn in the 1890's that a bare 200,000 out of 63,000,000 citizens controlled 70 percent of the national patrimony, or that 88 percent of all families possessed barely 12 percent of the national income. In a country where the annual income averaged less than $500, the knowledge that Andrew Carnegie had an annual tax-free income of $24,000,000 not infrequently led to the conclusion that such concentrations of wealth seriously endangered the structure of democracy. The size and scope of corporations, many of which possessed extensive operations scattered through the states, and many of which commanded resources and employed manpower that threw states into the shade, precluded effective state regulation. Progressives not surprisingly concluded: "The subject [of regulation] is national, and the federal government with its national outlook can by organized investigation and accumulated experience best acquire the skill and knowledge necessary for its just and efficient regulation."

Unable to reconcile the values with which they had been bred with the realities surrounding them, the Progressive moved to invoke federal power to regulate the huge economic concentrations. It was his support of legislation to regulate trusts that gave Theodore Roosevelt his reputation as a trust-buster. He flatly argued, "A combination should not be tolerated if it abuses the power acquired by combination to the public detriment." But he also made it obvious that he did not oppose combinations simply because they had combined. If anything, he felt the development of economic consolidation was inescapable. Both Roosevelt and Wilson accepted it as inevitable that all aspects of life would be "sustained, or at least supplemented, at every point by governmental activity." They diverged over how to control economic concentration, with Roosevelt demanding political regulation and Wilson seeking to restore through legislation the precepts of laisser-faire.

The progressive concern over the implications of economic concentration, balanced as it was by their no less concern lest government grow too big, was best stated by Vernon L. Parrington when he wrote: "We must have a poltical state powerful enough to deal with corporate wealth, but how are we going to keep that state with its augmenting power from being captured by the force we want it to control?" It was the formulation of a problem originally spelled out by John Moody (1868-1958) at the turn of the century in his muckraking The Truth About the Trusts *(1904). He had a long career as a financial analyst and as editor of several investment journals. His most significant contribution to contemporary understanding of corporate growth was a description of the process which described it as "a perfectly natural evolution." From the result he drew the significant conclusion: "The old economic axiom has been reversed in the past twenty-five years. Competition has not been the life of trade; it has been the death of industry in the United States. Monopoly has been built up on its ruins, and it is built to stay." This pessimistic conclusion shifted the debate over how to bust trusts to the question of how to shift effective power from the non-elected titans of Wall Street to the elected agents of democracy.*

THE MASTERS OF CAPITAL

A Chronicle of Wall Street

by John Moody

In this story of fabulous wealth and phenomenal prosperity we have almost lost sight of the disastrous panic of 1893, from which most of the large industrial enterprises of the United States emerged in a dilapidated condition. In the long depression which followed, manufacturers everywhere were forced into bankruptcy. Capital was scarce, the demand for goods was small, and thousands of plants remained in total or partial idleness for several years. This was particularly true of the steel and iron industry. Most of the steel plants, always excepting the Carnegie Works, were dormant or moribund. Dividends were discontinued; foreclosures were the order of the day; investors had lost their capital.

The tariff changes of 1894 had been a hard blow to many industries which had grown up and fattened in a quiet way during the long period of high protection from the close of the Civil War to the second Cleveland administration. Then, too, the Sherman Act of 1890, aimed particularly at combinations in restraint of trade, had frightened investors away from such "industrial trusts" as the Standard Oil Trust, the Cordage Trust, the Sugar Trust, and the Whiskey Trust which in the eighties had thrived, unmolested by the law. While they were all finally reorganized in such a way as to avoid the penalties of the law, banking and investment prejudice was strongly against them.

But when the Republican party returned to power in 1897 and immediately enacted a new tariff law, with high protective duties, and when at the same time certain court decisions were handed down which seemed to limit the scope of the Sherman Act, a wave of reviving prosperity swept over the country, and capital turned with new confidence to the industial field. Several of the earlier trusts besides Standard Oil had survived the panic and had been reorganized to conform to the law, notably, the American Sugar Refining Company and the American Tobacco Company. The new industrial combinations were modeled after these. Instead of placing the control of acquired plants in the hands of "trustees," holding companies were formed, which acquired all or a majority of stocks in certain competing plants and merged these plants under one control, often by exchanging the stock of the holding company for the stock of the plant.

The industrial consolidation movement was aggressively under way by 1899, when the time for it was ripe. Money was cheap, credit was everywhere available, and prosperity was rising throughout the country. All the important railroad reorganizations, as we have seen, had been carried through, and the great bankers, whose coffers swelled with huge underwriting commissions, were looking for new business. When the promoters of the new type of industrial combination sought banking support in Wall Street, they met with little difficulty. Wall Street was not slow to perceive great possibilities in the financing of big industrial enterprises. A conspicuous example was the American Tobacco Company, which had been created in 1890 as a combination of Allen and Ginter of Richmond, W. Duke, Sons and Company of Durham, North Carolina, and a number of other well-known manufacturers. Its original capital had been ten millions of preferred stock, representing the cost of the properties, and fifteen millions of common stock, representing good will or "water." But the business had forged ahead so rapidly that by 1898 the "capital" was multiplied fivefold, creating a new group of millionaires.

Then arose the great Amalgamated Copper Company, under the direction of Henry H. Rogers, and speculation in "industrials" became more and more the order of the day on the Stock Exchange. In quick succession a long string of new combinations followed; notably the American Smelting and Refining Company, with more than one hundred millions of capital and embracing over one hundred plants; the American Woolen Company, consolidating a large number of New England woolen mills under a fifty million dollar capitalization; the American Car and Foundry Company, merging the large car-building plants; the American Hide and Leather Company, consolidating over twenty large manufacturers of upper leathers; the International Paper Company, a fifty million dollar combination of paper manufacturers; and a large number of other similar mergers in various lines of industry.

But the biggest of all the industrial trusts was the merger of the steel and iron interests of the country, which began with the incorporation of the Federal Steel Company in September, 1898, as a holding company to acquire the stocks of the Illinois Steel Company, the Minnesota Iron Company, the Lorain Steel Company, and the Elgin, Joliet and Eastern Railway, a belt line operating about the city of Chicago. The authorized capital of this new concern was two hundred million dollars, of which about one-half was issued at the start. It was a powerful combination and was in the hands of strong and able financiers. The firm of J. P. Morgan and Company took a leading part in financing the enterprise. The general counsel of the Illinois Steel Company, Judge Elbert H. Gary, a leading corporation lawyer of Chicago, thus came into close touch with "Jupiter" Morgan and was chosen as the first president of the new company. The wisdom of the choice was well demonstrated by subsequent experience.

Following came the American Steel and Wire Company, with ninety millions of capital, fathered by the well-known John W. Gates. This was a combination of big western plants, many of them specializing in barbed wire, nails, and wire fencing, but including many other industries and encroaching more or less closely on the field preempted by the Federal Steel Company. Gates had originally been a barbed wire salesman and was a notorious speculator. There followed still other companies: the American Tin Plate Company, with fifty millions of capital, the American Steel Hoop Company, the National Steel Company, and two Morgan consolidations, the National Tube Company and the American Bridge Company.

Carnegie and his associates were watching the situation closely. The great revival in steel and iron had naturally favored them, and their power was steadily growing. But Carnegie and his two chief partners, Frick and Phipps, viewed the empire of business from different angles. For a decade or more Carnegie had been genuinely anxious to retire. He had made his millions, he was getting on in life, and he had no desire to become a great banker with multitudinous outside interests, like Morgan, William Rockefeller, or Stillman. Henry C. Frick, on the other hand, was a natural master of capital; he foresaw the trend of the times. To his mind the days of one-man power were over; great enterprises in the future would be dominated and controlled by groups of capitalists of diverse interests; and even complete industries, if they hoped to live, would of necessity become allied with others. He believed that combination must take the place of competition and that he and his associates must sooner or later become a part of the consolidation movement. Carnegie saw in the movement only an opportunity to sell out at his own price. Naturally Carnegie and Frick quarreled. Frick was becoming more and more interested in matters outside of the steel business. He had been connected with William Rockefeller and Henry H. Rogers in various enterprises and was even then one of the largest stockholders in the Pennsylvania Railroad, a director in many corporations, and a conspicuous figure in Wall Street. These activities displeased Carnegie. His other partner, Henry Phipps, sided with Frick and so also estranged himself from Carnegie.

Meanwhile a group of Chicago speculators and promoters had come to the front. William H. Moore, a daring promoter, had organized the Diamond Match Company, the National Biscuit Company, and the American Tin Plate Company. He and his associates had made several millions out of the organization of the American Steel Hoop Company and the National Steel Company. Flushed with success and with big cash balances, Moore now approached Carnegie and offered him a million dollars for a ninety-day option on his stock in the Carnegie Steel Company, the price being $157,950,000 of which over a third was to be in cash. Carnegie agreed, provided Moore would take Frick and Phipps with him. Carnegie guessed that while Moore single handed might not be able to raise the money, Frick, Phipps, and Moore together surely would. But it was not all plain sailing. Morgan had not yet become convinced of the soundness of the industrial movement; the Rockefellers could not be made to see the possibilities of such a gigantic scheme as this, though John D. Rockefeller had personally taken some interest in the Federal Steel Company. And just then a temporary panic occurred in Wall Street, as a result of the sudden death of Roswell P.

Flower, who had been the conspicuous operator in the inflated bull market. This incident hampered the efforts of Frick and Moore and before they could raise the necessary money the ninety-day option had expired. Carnegie refused to extend it a single day and quietly pocketed the million dollars which had been given him for the option.

As the steel business continued to flourish and the country enjoyed great prosperity, Carnegie decided that his first offer had been entirely too cheap, and a little later, when John D. Rockefeller tried to buy him out, he placed his price at $250,000,000. It was Rockefeller's desire to solidify his interests in the ore lands and ore railway in Minnesota, as well as the capital invested in his fleet of ore-carrying vessels on the Great Lakes. But Carnegie's price was too high for Rockefeller, and nothing came of the proposal.

When Andrew Carnegie was laying the foundations of his steel and iron business, he built a small summer bungalow at Cresson Springs, Pennsylvania. Here there was a livery stable run by a man named Schwab, from whom Carnegie was in the habit of hiring horses. Schwab had a son called Charlie who used to hang around the livery stable, a merry, good-natured youngster whom every one liked. The boy had a good voice and interested Carnegie, who was very fond of music. "When that boy of yours is ready for a job, send him to me," said Carnegie to the father one day.

And so, by good luck, in 1880, at the age of eighteen, Charles M. Schwab entered the employment of Carnegie in the Edgar Thomson Steel Works. The young fellow made good and became chief engineer and assistant manager. When Carnegie bought out an important competitor at Homestead, Schwab was selected as superintendent of the plant and showed his mettle by promptly making the Homestead Steel Works the most profitable of all the Carnegie properties. In 1889 he was brought back to Braddock and placed in charge of the Edgar Thomson Steel Works and three years later was made general superintendent of both plants.

Some time afterward Carnegie told Schwab that he had decided to make him a vice-president, to which Schwab replied:

"No, Mr. Carnegie, I am no good carrying out other men's orders, and I should have to do that as a vice-president. As superintendent I am boss of the plants I manage."

Later again Carnegie approached him. "Well," he said, "if you won't be vice-president, I suppose we'll have to make you president." And they did. In 1897 Charles M. Schwab became president of the Carnegie Steel Company.

Schwab naturally adopted Carnegie's ideas and business policy. He was long opposed to Frick's theory that the future of successful business lay in combination and interdependence. "A big business enterprise," he said, "is invariably built up around one man." But this was simply an echo of the philosophy of Carnegie, and when the "community of interest" movement began to dominate American industry Schwab gradually changed his view. He was but thirty-eight years old, and his life was still before him. Carnegie at sixty-five was naturally wedded to the theories of the old school. Besides, Carnegie wanted to retire from business, while Schwab felt that he was just getting into business. At a banquet given to him at the University Club in New York, the younger man came out strongly in favor of combination among corporations and deprecated cutthroat competition and the rule-or-ruin policy.

After the failure of the negotiations with Moore and Rockefeller for the sale of his business, Carnegie quietly bided his time until the Morgan interests had plunged so deeply into the steel business in connection with the Federal Steel Company, the National Tube Company, and the American Bridge Company, that they could not possibly back out. Then he set on foot a series of operations designed to create havoc among all the steel corporations of the country. To fight Morgan, he announced that he would go into the tube business in direct competition with the National Tube Company, and he actually acquired five thousand acres of land at Conneaut on Lake Erie and let contracts for the construction of a twelve million dollar tube plant. To fight John W. Gates and his American Steel and Wire Company, he announced that a gigantic rod-mill would be erected at Pittsburgh. To fight Rockefeller, he ordered the construction of a large fleet of ore-carrying steamships to operate on the Great Lakes. To fight the Pennsylvania Railroad, he set a corps of surveyors laying out a railroad route from Pittsburgh to the Atlantic Ocean. He also planned the immediate construction of an ore-carrying railroad of vast capacity from Lake Erie to the Pittsburgh district.

Such threats as these were taken seriously, for everybody recognized that Carnegie had the power to carry them through. Already he had the whip hand in the steel world. The profits of his corporation in 1900 had been over forty million dollars; he was already making over one-fourth of the Bessemer steel produced in the country and half of the structural steel and armor plate. His costs were lower than those of any of his competitors, and he had no debts. The entire steel trade of the country was thrown into confusion. There was an actual panic among the millionaires of Wall Street. "We must get rid of Carnegie," they all shouted. "He will wreck both himself and us; he is a business pirate." And the frightened financiers, whose millions were tied up in Federal Steel, American Steel and Wire, and the other great companies, rushed to Morgan for help. The Standard Oil bankers were appealed to; but the undertaking called for such a gigantic outlay and was fraught with such uncertainties, that even these bold financiers hesitated, evidently preferring that Morgan should bear the brunt of the responsibility.

Just at this time, Charles M. Schwab and John W. Gates put their heads together and agreed to interview Morgan. Whether Schwab's overtures were directed by Carnegie or not may never be known, but Schwab by this time saw as clearly as any one that interdependence in the steel business was absolutely essential to its future prosperity. As for Gates, his motives were clear enough: he was one of the panic-stricken millionaires who were threatened with disaster. Schwab and Gates spent eight hours trying to convince Morgan of the necessity of buying Carnegie out. Schwab set forth the strong features of the Carnegie business and the glittering possibilities of industrial peace by means of a combination. Tradition says that he spoke with much eloquence; at any rate he made the sale; Morgan agreed to pay Carnegie his price. This price was much higher than that stated to Frick and Moore only eighteen months before, higher even than the price named to John D. Rockefeller the previous year. Frick and Moore could have bought the entire Carnegie business for about $157,000,000; it was offered to Rockefeller for $250,000,000; but the amount Morgan paid in January, 1901, was equivalent to a cash price of over $447,000,000. This was represented by giving Carnegie and his associates $303,450,000 in bonds and nearly two hundred million dollars' worth of stock which immediately had a market value of about $144,000,000. It was the greatest sale in the history of the world.

Carnegie was now definitely shelved, so far as the steel business was concerned; his tube plant scheme at Conneaut, his plans for a railroad from Pittsburgh to the sea, and his big rod-mill project at Pittsburgh were all abandoned. But Morgan found his hands full when he came to deal with the other big steel interests. The Federal Steel directors, aside from Judge Gary, had opposed the idea of allowing Carnegie to sandbag them; Gates now felt that Morgan should pay him a bigger price for American Steel and Wire than he had first named; Rockefeller, with his rich Lake Superior ore beds, also wanted large concessions if he was to become a party to the combination. In short, all the companies which it was planned to put into the merger suddenly discovered that their properties were worth millions more, now that the menace of Carnegie had been removed.

It was indeed a difficult task that confronted Pierpont Morgan. The various smaller steel "trusts" that had been formed during the two previous years were overcapitalized and had issued reams of "watered" stocks. For when the mania for consolidation was under full swing during the period which began with the close of the war with Spain in 1898, discretion had been thrown to the winds, and industrial plants of every type had been bought up by promoters regardless of price. An incident is told which—whether true or not—will illustrate the tendency. When one of the smaller "trusts" was being formed, a party of steel men were on their way to Chicago one night after a buying tour. The men had been drinking and were in a convivial mood. Said one, "There's a steel mill at the next station; let's get out and buy it." "Agreed!"

It was past midnight when they reached the station, but they pulled the plant owner out of bed and demanded that he sell his plant.

"My plant is worth two hundred thousand dollars, but it is not for sale," was the reply.

"Never mind about the price," answered the hilarious purchasers, "we will give you three hundred thousand—five hundred thousand."

The story is not improbable, for most of the constituent plants had been bought at prices far above their true values. Consequently, the corporation to be formed must have a fabulous capitalization; and stocks and bonds must be issued many times in excess of what the properties would have brought at forced sales in normal times. But Pierpont Morgan was equal to the emergency. He first called in his big lieutenants, one of whom was his young partner, George W. Perkins—a man destined to influence profoundly the policy and fortunes of the corporation about to be born—and the magnates of the independent companies, including Elbert H. Gary, Marshall Field, Norman B. Ream, Henry C. Frick, and H. H. Rogers. It was Morgan's plan at first to include in the combination only those steel companies with which his firm had already become identified, but it was soon seen that it would be dangerous to exclude the others. If the Gates interests were left out, they might become a menace to the peace of the new concern, for John W. Gates would surely attempt to sandbag Morgan as Carnegie had done. If the Moore brothers were left to shift for themselves, they might get together with others and do the same thing. The chief danger was, however, from the Standard Oil. To allow John D. Rockefeller to remain independent, with his big Lake Superior deposits and his fleet of ore-carrying vessels on the Lake, might easily lead to disaster. A second monster steel business might easily be built up under Standard Oil control. Therefore it must be a case of all or none. The steel industry must be completely merged into one, and all companies of strong financial connections or large resources must be included.

Judge Gary was appointed to open up negotiations with the independents. Daniel G. Reid, of the American Steel Hoop Company, was brought in, and he induced the Moore brothers to join the combination. The Gates group received what they demanded, and then Henry C. Frick was sent to see what he could do with John D. Rockefeller. Frick's position at this time was somewhat unique. Since his break with Carnegie a couple of years before he had become more of a Wall Street speculator than a mere steel man. He had not definitely allied himself with either Morgan or Rockefeller but was on friendly terms with both. He had close associations with Henry H. Rogers and James Stillman; he had gone into Federal Steel; he was a powerful factor in the affairs of the Pennsylvania Railroad; altogether, he was looked upon as one of the leading protagonists of the "community of interest" idea which had been so strongly championed by Cassatt of the Pennsylvania Railroad, Harriman of the Union Pacific, and Hill of the Great Northern.

Frick succeeded without much trouble in bagging Rockefeller, although the price he paid looked high at the time. Rockefeller received eighty millions in the stock of the new corporation, of which half was preferred stock, besides eight and one-half million dollars in cash for his ore-carrying fleet. These were huge concessions, but the control of the Lake Superior iron mines was absolutely essential, for these deposits represented two-thirds of the new corporation's ore supply.

Having thus gathered together all the important steel interests of the country, Morgan launched the United States Steel Corporation. The stock capitalization was in excess of a billion dollars, with a bonded debt of more than three hundred millions, and both the big banking groups of Wall Street were firmly tied to the enterprise. The great merger dominated by Morgan drew into its orbit even the Standard Oil "Money Power." Among the big names included in the syndicate, aside from Morgan and his partners, were H. H. Rogers and Daniel O'Day of Standard Oil; Marshall Field, William H. Moore, James H. Moore, Elbert H. Gary, John W. Gates, H. H. Porter, and Norman B. Ream, of Chicago; Samuel Mather of Cleveland; Nathaniel Thayer of Boston; and Daniel G. Reid, Henry C. Frick, Charles M. Schwab, and D. O. Mills, of New York. So under the control of a single corporation passed seventy per cent of the American iron and steel industry. That industry, instead of being operated on the old plan of individual control or independent corporate control, was now linked with scores of banks of great power, with railroads, and with numerous other corporate undertakings.

Edward H. Harriman was the son of a poor and unsuccessful Episcopal clergyman who spent the latter days of his life as a bookkeeper in the old Bank of Commerce in New York. Born in 1848, young Harriman was just fourteen years old when his father obtained a job for him as office boy with DeWitt C. Hays, a Wall Street stockbroker. This was just about the time when Pierpont Morgan was preparing to get into business in America; when Andrew Carnegie was accumulating his first money in speculative oil and railroad ventures under the tutelage of Scott and was scanning the horizon of the new Bessemer steel business; when John D. Rockefeller was laying the foundations of Standard Oil; and when Henry C. Frick—one year younger than Harriman—was doing duty as an errand boy in Mount Pleasant.

From the very first, young Harriman displayed unusual ability. He also had that trait of audacity which had shown so conspicuously in the characters of Frick, Carnegie, and Morgan. Almost immediately he began to make a little money in stocks. And he widened his acquaintance rapidly. He became intimate with Lewis Livingston, a member of one of the oldest New York families, who had a son named James. When in 1870, after having worked himself up to the position of bookkeeper of the Hays firm, young Harriman bought a seat in the New York Stock Exchange at a cost of about three thousand dollars, he induced James Livingston to go into the stock brokerage business with him and supply capital through his father. Harriman was successful at once—so successful that within a few months he dissolved partnership with Livingston and formed a new firm with himself at the head and his brother William as a partner. He cultivated the friendship of people of means and social standing and in a few years became prominent among the younger "aristocrats" of New York. In this environment he ultimately came into close touch with the people associated with the Illinois Central Railroad, which had been built during the years prior to the Civil War and had proved wonderfully successful from the start. Running north and south, it caught broadside the westbound tide of migration; its government grant of rich Mississippi Valley lands was sold early at a good price; soon after it was built the Civil War gave it a big business, and it escaped the ruinous competition which so long devastated the trunk lines running east and west.

A group of old New York merchants had built this road. Though they sold five-sixths of its stock in England and Holland, it became a favorite solid investment for many of the old families of New York. The Astors and the Goelets and the Cuttings were large holders of its stock in the seventies and eighties. The Illinois Central, indeed, was quite the "society railroad" of New York. During the long period from 1857 to 1883 the property had remained under the direct control and operation of William Henry Osborne, an old Manila merchant who had returned from the Philippines in the fifties with a fortune and who had operated the Illinois Central all these years as he would have operated his own warehouse. Osborne had a summer home at Garrison, New York, where he was a neighbor of the old and rich Fish family, a younger member of which was Stuyvesant Fish. The latter became Osborne's secretary in 1872 and a few years later was made a director of the railroad. In 1883 when Osborne died, he practically bequeathed the management of the railroad to his secretary, although Fish did not actually become president until some years later.

Harriman and Fish had known each other for many years, and as young men had traveled about town a great deal together. In 1880 they were both directors in the Ogdensburg and Lake Champlain Railroad, a property of which Harriman had hoped to acquire the control, for by this time Harriman had made very substantial progress in business, having accumulated several hundred thousand dollars through shrewd trading in securities. He was now beginning to turn away from mere brokerage to railroad management and finance.

The Illinois Central had acquired control of an extensive system of lines south of St. Louis, known as the Chicago, St. Louis and New Orleans, and Stuyvesant Fish had sought Harriman's assistance in placing the bonds. In this work Harriman was notably successful. Meanwhile he had himself acquired a large block of Illinois Central stock and had become more and more the confidential adviser of Fish. At that time there was a large Dutch stockholding interest in the road, whose votes were cast collectively by the firm that had originally placed the stock in Holland, Boissevain Brothers. One member of this firm came on a visit to America. Harriman met him, gained his confidence, and then arranged to hold his proxies in the Illinois Central meetings. Soon afterwards Harriman was elected a director and became the close associate of Stuyvesant Fish in the actual operation and control of the road.

No two men could have been more dissimilar in personality and bearing than these two. Harriman was small, quiet, restless, and secretive; Fish was a big, open-faced, easy-mannered young man, whose blond hair and great stature had earned for him in the financial district the name of "White Elephant." For a time, however, the two men worked together in harmony. They bought a portion of the old Wabash, St. Louis and Pacific after its failure in 1884; in 1887 they bought the Dubuque and Sioux City Railroad; in the early nineties they bought (much against the will of Collis P. Huntington) the chain of roads with which Huntington had planned to hitch his Southern Pacific system to the Atlantic seaboard; they bought an important section of the St. Louis, Alton and Terre Haute, which George Foster Peabody had been developing in southern Illinois, thus securing an entry of their own into St. Louis; and they purchased a great number of small roads, until, from the two thousand miles they had in 1883, they owned and controlled in 1897 a system of over five thousand miles.

This policy of expansion did not bring disaster, as had been the case with so many other lines. All through this period the road's credit remained high, and even in the early eighties it was able to sell three and one-half per cent bonds while other roads of good credit were raising money at five or six per cent. This high credit of the Illinois Central was very largely due to the rigid policies which Harriman introduced and developed. Harriman was more than a mere banker or broker; he was a practical railroad operating man. He had made a thorough study of railroading and had early adopted the theory that the first duty of railroad management was to maintain the character of the physical property and to consider mere current profits as secondary. Thus, in the management of the Illinois Central, he never "skinned" the road to pay dividends; he never allowed the roadbed or equipment to become inefficient. Another sound idea he adopted was always to provide ample funds and reserves for contingencies; never to allow his property to take financial chances in times of dullness or depression. Even when he was raising large amounts of new capital for extensions or purchases, he always provided far more cash assets than were currently needed.

Harriman had very soon grown powerful enough to cross the path of Pierpont Morgan. In 1887, Morgan held the proxies of the stockholders in the Dubuque and Sioux City Railroad, which Harriman wished to buy for the Illinois Central. Harriman fought his plan through and defeated Morgan. This coup was regarded as a ten days' wonder in Wall Street. From that time on Morgan disliked Harriman. Again, in 1894, Harriman and Morgan crossed swords. Harriman owned a few hundred thousand dollars worth of underlying bonds about the time that Morgan announced his plan of reorganization for the Erie Railroad. Harriman objected to the proposed treatment of his securities, brought suit to prevent the drastic reorganization, and in the end forced Morgan to make concessions.

Harriman was as yet little known outside of Wall Street. Although chairman of the finance committee of the Illinois Central and the power behind the throne, he was eclipsed by the figure of Fish. But in 1895 Harriman stepped to the front. The Union Pacific Railroad security holders were looking in vain for some strong banking interests to finance their property. The road was a frightful wreck with a tangled mass of subsidiary companies, and the United States Government was aggressively insisting on the payment of the huge debt representing the original government loans, with the interest that had accumulated since its building thirty years before. Morgan had rejected the suggestion that he reorganize it, as he was too fully occupied with the rejuvenation of many other railroad systems. Harriman then saw his chance. He decided to reorganize the Union Pacific himself, to make it a subsidiary of the Illinois Central, and to utilize the credit of the latter company for the gigantic financing which would be necessary. But before he had progressed very far in this plan he met with opposition from Kuhn, Loeb and Company, who had become bankers for the Chicago, Milwaukee and St. Paul, the Great Northern Railway, and other properties, and now also were bent upon reorganizing the Union Pacific.

A keen contest for mastery followed. At first Jacob H. Schiff, the head of Kuhn, Loeb and Company, persistently ignored Harriman, feeling confident that no interest in New York could successfully reorganize the property except Morgan or himself; but Harriman soon forced him to change his mind. The two were brought together, and, in Wall Street parlance, laid their respective cards on the table. It was an interesting and convincing show-down. Schiff could raise the much needed hundred millions of new capital at five or six per cent through his strong German connections; but Harriman showed how he could raise this sum, and more, on the Illinois Central credit, at from three and one-half to four per cent. Schiff capitulated, and finally reached an agreement with this new master of capital. The road was reorganized by Kuhn, Loeb and Company, and Edward H. Harriman was made the first chairman of its board of directors and later its president.

Harriman had now leaped at a bound into public notice. And, coincidently, as we have already seen—an event of great significance—the powerful Standard Oil capitalists interested themselves in Wall Street affairs.

Too much credit cannot be given to the men who carried out this reorganization of the Union Pacific Railroad. In the first place, they paid to the Federal Government over forty-five million dollars in cash on a bankrupt railroad—all the principal and full interest at six per cent on the Union Pacific debt, which had accrued for thirty years. Then they put the bonds and preferred stock of the reorganized road on a straight four per cent basis; and finally after these prudential measures, they began to spend money by the tens and hundreds of millions upon this ramshackle property running across the "Great American Desert."

In all these operations Harriman was the masterful leader. Fortune played into his hands. For the first time in years the arid farming sections of the West had copious rains and fine crops. The Spanish-American War resulted in American occupation of the Philippines; and the Union Pacific got a great business from these new possessions. Harriman not only spent money but he spent it quickly, accomplishing in two years' work what had been estimated to take five. And he was reaping the fruit of his enterprise. In three years, under his direction, the system expanded from less than two thousand miles to over fifteen thousand.

⋙ ⋘

THE Constitution provides in Article 3, section 1 that "The judicial power of the United States is to be vested in one Supreme Court, and in such inferior courts as the Congress may, from time to time, ordain and establish."

From the institution of the federal judiciary, it was assumed that it would constitute a concurrent branch of government and that "the supposed danger of judiciary encroachments on the legislative authority . . . is in reality a phantom." The masterful achievement of John Marshall and his courts was that they established the broad scope of power vested in the Supreme Court, but then they left it as a foundation upon which later courts could build. Although the Marbury v. Madison *decision in 1803 had determined the right of the court to pass upon the constitutionality of federal legislation, only once before the Civil War, and that in the* Dred Scott *decision of 1857, did the court assert its power.*

In the aftermath of the Civil War, the Court, responding to the swift pace of industrialization, steadily extended the role of the federal government in regulating the economy. The Court's position when defining the federal role responded to an elementary fact: a national market required national regulation. The power of Congress to establish a national currency, either in paper or coin, redeemable for all obligations, was upheld in Juilliard v. Greenman (1884). *Significantly, the Court added a definition of that power which subordinated the property rights of the individual to the well-being of the whole. "If, upon a just and fair interpretation of the whole Constitution, a particular power or authority appears to be vested in Congress," Justice Gray argued, "it is no constitutional objection to its existence or to its exercise that the property or the contracts of individuals may be incidentally affected."*

But it was in the cases affecting the railroads after the Civil War that the scope of regulation of "business affected with a public interest" was enlarged. Such property was defined in Munn v. Illinois (1877), *a case dealing with regulation of grain elevator rates, as that "when used in a manner to make it of public consequence, and affect the community at large." The subsequent* Wabash *decision (1886) denied the right of a state to regulate a company operating in interstate commerce, but it provoked a storm of protest and compelled Congress, albeit reluctantly, to pass the Interstate Commerce Act (1887). Responsibility for regulating interstate commerce was subsequently firmly established as a federal task. The same tendency manifested itself in the growing demand that the federal power be used to restrain the trusts. Even as conservative a President as Cleveland warned: "Corporations, which should be the carefully restrained creatures of the law and the servants of the people, are fast becoming the people's masters." Under the guidance of Senator John Sherman of Ohio, who contended, "The power of Congress is the only power that can deal with these corporations [and] that can regulate the internal commerce of this country," Congress passed the Sherman Anti-Trust Act in 1890.*

The Court vigorously enforced the act but largely in a laissez-faire *spirit. They seemed more intent on maintaining free enterprise than on making enterprise socially responsible. But the drift of judicial decision as well as of regulatory legislation spelled out a future expansion of federal power. Rear-guard defenders of states' rights saw the handwriting on the wall and* could only lament the coming centralization of power in the Washington government.

Charles Warren (*1868-1954*), a Massachusetts born lawyer, who had a distinguished career both in private and public practice, long maintained an interest in legal and judicial history. His Pulitzer Prize-winning The Supreme Court in American History (*1923*) broke away from the traditional emphasis upon legal analysis of cases and made a successful effort to restore the cases to the "very vital social, political and economic contests" that they reflected in their time. As Oliver W. Holmes had struggled to reclaim the legal profession from the realm of revealed and finished truth, so Warren worked to remind his readers that "A word is not a crystal, transparent and unchanged, it is the skin of a living thought and may vary greatly in color and content according to the circumstances and the time in which it is used." In his hands, the Supreme Court became, as it always has been, a vital agency of government, whose decisions have shaped, still do shape, and will continue to shape the future of the republic.

THE SUPREME COURT IN UNITED STATES HISTORY

by Charles Warren

In 1885, the Court rendered a decision which marked a new era in the development of the domain of National power and which restricted in a large measure the sovereignty of the States. Since the case of *Osborn* v. *Bank of the United States* in 1824, there had been practically no instance in which the Courts of the United States had sustained an action against a State official for administering an unconstitutional law. On the contrary, attempts to sue such officials had been discountenanced and defeated in many cases, on the ground that they were in violation of the Eleventh Amendment prohibiting suits against a State. Between 1875 and 1885, however, conditions had arisen in many States in this country which made of the Eleventh Amendment simply a shield for State dishonesty. Owing to the devastation due to the Civil War, the corruption of their "carpet-bag" Legislatures and the financial depression after the panic of 1873, many Southern States had attempted to default in the payment of bonds issued or guaranteed by them. The extent of this repudiation had become a National scandal. "Today more than $100,000,000 and, if we include interest, more than $200,000,000 are due to creditors from repudiating States. . . . The whole country is in disgrace by reason of this horrid spectacle," said the *Independent*, in 1883. "Public morality has suffered from the foul contagion. Municipal corporations have caught the disease. . . . Repudiation is simply the highwayman's morality. When practiced by States, it is power against right. As an exhibit of sovereignty, it is the sovereignty of rascality.

State repudiation in this country is a criminality that has behind it millions of offenders. The people are the State and control its action." The Court, nevertheless, in almost every attempt made to enforce compliance by a State with its obligations, was confronted with the Eleventh Amendment. Though determined to uphold principles of honesty in business and to enforce rigidly the Impairment of Obligation of Contract Clause of the Constitution in suits involving private individuals, it had thus far met with an insuperable obstacle in suits involving State officials. The situation was well illustrated by three cases decided in 1883. In *Louisiana* v. *Jumel*, 107 U.S. 711, the Court upheld the right of the State and its officers to be exempt from a mandamus suit requiring officials to apply funds in the State Treasury to payment of State bonds. Judges Field and Harlan vigorously dissented, stating that they would continue to do so, "until the prohibition inserted in the Constitution, as a barrier against the agrarian and despoiling spirit which both precedes and follows a breach of public faith, is restored to its original vigor"; otherwise, they said, "public faith will be the synonym of public dishonesty." In *Cunningham* v. *Macon & Brunswick R.R.*, 109 U.S. 446, the Court held that a bill in equity by mortgage bondholders to foreclose on a railroad whose bonds had been endorsed by the State of Georgia, which had been taken possession of by that State, could not be maintained, since the State was an indispensable party and could not be sued. In *New Hampshire* v. *Louisiana*, 108 U.S. 76, the Court refused to sanction an attempted evasion of the Eleventh Amendment by creditors who had assigned their bonds to a State which accepted them simply for the purpose of bringing suit.

While these decisions were undoubtedly wise and in full conformity with the Constitution, they profoundly disturbed the conservative element of the community, which saw in them only encouragement for future municipal and State defaulters; and they even evoked a demand for the abolition of the Eleventh Amendment. "We do not believe in the wisdom or justice of this Amendment at all," said the *Independent*. "It ought to be amended out of the Constitution. . . . The repudiation of State debts under the cloak of this Amendment has become the shame and disgrace of our country, and the proper remedy to arrest this enormous evil is to give to the Federal Courts the power which the Eleventh Amendment took away, and authorize Congress by appropriate legislation to carry that power into full and complete effect." "The Supreme Court should be able to compel a State to pay its debts. With this power lodged in the Supreme Court and lodged in Congress, the system of State repudiation would come to an end, greatly in the interests of justice." A resolve was actually introduced in the House for the repeal of the Eleventh Amendment and for the grant to Congress of the power to provide by appropriate legislation for enforcement of the obligation of contracts entered into by any of the States of the Union. Fortunately, no such radical move was found necessary; for the Court, in 1885, finally enounced a doctrine as to suits against State officials which, to a certain extent, relieved the situation, and marked a new era in the relations of the National Judiciary and the States. The case in which this momentous decision was made was one of a long series from 1881 to 1887, involving the notorious Mahone-Riddleberger legislation in Virginia, by which that State had practically repudiated $11,000,000 out of a refunded debt of $30,000,000, had cut in half the interest on its outstanding bonds, and had repealed the provisions of law which made coupons on its bonds receivable in payment of taxes. This violation of the State's express agreement with its bond and coupon holders had been held by the Court, in 1881, in *Hartman* v. *Greenhow*, 102 U.S. 672, to be invalid as an impairment of obligation of contract; and in an answer to the argument that legislation as to receipt of taxes, binding future Legislatures, might result in crippling the power and resources of the State in time of war or other great calamity, Judge Field had said, quoting the Virginia Court of Appeals: "At such a time, however, the honored name and high credit secured to a State by unbroken faith, even in adversity, will, apart from all other considerations, be worth more to her in dollars—incalculably more—than the comparatively insignificant amount of interest on a portion of the public debt enjoyed by breach of contract. The Court thus expressed a great truth, which all just men appreciate, that there is no wealth or power equal to that which ultimately comes to a State when in all her engagements she keeps her faith unbroken." In an effort to avoid the force of this decision, Virginia had proceeded to pass legislation imposing such restrictions upon bondholders as practically to destroy the commercial value of the bonds and coupons; and when bondholders declined to comply with these new restrictions, the State officers attempted to distrain their property in payment of taxes. It was at this point that the Court, in 1885, proclaimed a doctrine which relieved the situation, and which made the provisions of the Eleventh Amendment far less onerous than they had been hitherto supposed to be. In *Poindexter* v. *Greenhow*, 114 U.S. 270, it pointed out that there was a clear distinction between a suit against a State or a State official to compel it or him to perform an obligation of the State, and a suit against a State official to recover damages for an act performed in carrying out an unconstitutional State law; and that no official could claim exemption from personal responsibility for acts committed under such an invalid law. Accordingly, it sustained a suit in detinue against a city treasurer, and held that the treasurer could not justify, under an unconstitutional State statute, his action in seizing property after the taxpayer had made a valid tender of coupons in payment of his tax. There is an important distinction between the government of a State and the State itself, and governing officials within the sphere of their agency are the State, but outside of their agency are lawless usurpers, individual trespassers, said Judge Matthews, in substance. "This distinction between the government of a State and the State itself is important. To deny it or blot it out obliterates the line of demarcation that separates constitutional government from absolutism, free self-government based on the sovereignty of the people, from that despotism, whether of the one or the many, which enables the agent of the State to declare and decree that he is the State, to say '*L'Etat, c'est Moi*' . . . How else can these principles of individual liberty and right be maintained, if, when violated, the judicial tribunals are forbidden to visit penalties upon individual offenders, who are the instruments of wrong, whenever they interpose the shield of the State? The doctrine is not to be tolerated. The whole frame and scheme of the political institutions of the country, State and Federal, protest against it. Their continued existence is not compatible with it. It is the doctrine of absolutism, pure, simple and naked; and of communism, which is its twin; the double progeny of the same evil birth." Judges Bradley, Miller, Gray and the Chief Justice dissented, saying that: "A State can only act by and through its constituted authorities and it is represented by them in all the ordinary exhibitions of sovereign power. It may act wrongly; it may act unconstitutionally; but to say that it is not the State that acts is to make a misuse of terms, and tends to confound all just distinctions. It also tends, in our judgment, to inculcate the dangerous doctrine that the Government may be treated and resisted as a usurpation whenever the citizen, in the exercise of his private judgment, deems its acts to be unconstitutional." They asserted that against unconstitutional oppression by the State or its officers, the citizen had sufficient redress by habeas corpus, by defense to prosecutions, by injunction or by mandamus; but this right, they said, is "a very different thing from the right to coerce the State into a fulfillment of its contracts." That these suits were attempts to coerce the State, they held to be plain. "It is useless to deceive ourselves by an adroit use of words, or by a train of metaphysical reasoning. . . . This is the first time, we believe, since the Eleventh Amendment was adopted, in which a State has been coerced by Judicial proceedings at the suit of individuals in the Federal Courts."

With this decision and similar decisions in the next year, 1886, there began a new epoch in the relation of the Federal and State powers. "It marks another revolution in constitutional construction, which will be regarded by some as a virtual change of the Constitution itself, and by others as an adaptation of conflicting parts to the broad requirements of justice," said the *Nation;* and it added, with considerable grounds for the statement: "Since the State can act only through its agents, of whom the tax collector is one, the point (made by the Court) seems to be forced, and although in accord with principles of justice, yet practically a change of the Constitution and one of exceeding gravity." A few weeks later, the *Nation* pointed out how largely the partisan line had broken down in the Court, in the consideration of the broad issue. "The question of State-Rights in its more extreme form was directly involved in this matter, and it might have been expected that the strong Republican bias of our highest Bench would have produced a close approach to unanimity against the traditional Democratic side of that issue. It certainly might have been supposed that the one representative of the Democratic party in the Court would plant himself firmly upon the Eleventh Amendment. . . . In point of fact, Judge Field took the contrary ground, while it was from the lips of a Republican Judge, speaking for three party associates, as well as himself, that there issued a rather heated protest against the attempt of the Court to treat the Eleventh Amendment as a mere jingle of words, to be slurred over by cunning subtleties and artificial methods of interpretation, so as to give it a little compliance, without regarding its substantial meaning." Still later, the *Nation* pointed out with great force, "the great triumph of honesty over fraud," and the immense importance of these cases in bringing constitutional law into conformity with morals. "If they are accepted without resistance, they will make the first victory of the Supreme Court over a really recalcitrant and angry State. . . . Until the present time, the United States has never been victorious in its Judiciary department over a State determined to defy it. . . . There have been many other cases before the Supreme Court in which acts of State Legislatures have been declared unconstitutional and void, but never, when the State has used all its civil power, its intellect and obstinacy, backed finally by a united public opinion, to frustrate the constitutional demands of hated creditors. These decisions are, then, the first absolutely peaceable triumph of the Constitution and its honest principles over the narrowness, bitterness and often dishonesty of local popular will, and as such they form an epoch in constitutional history. It is a triumph of the regular power of the National Government over the irregular power of the State."

While there were, in subsequent years, some vacillations and inconsistencies in the decisions of the Court involving State officials, the principles laid down in the various *Virginia Coupon Cases* have been, in general, the foundation for an extension of National power over the states which has had a profound effect on the course of American law.

In this connection, it should be noted that, in spite of its tendency to uphold the authority of the Nation in the exercise of political power, the Court showed itself as determined to defend the rights of an individual, when trespassed upon by an officer of the National Government, as when injured by the action of a State officer; and in a memorable opinion in 1882, it had applied to the National Government itself the same principles of distinction between the right to sue a Government officer for his personal illegal acts and the right to sue the Government itself, which it later applied to the State. In *United States* v. *Lee*, 106 U.S. 196, the son of Gen. Robert E. Lee sued to recover possession of eleven hundred acres known as the Arlington estate, which was formerly the property of Mrs. Lee as heir of her grandfather, George Washington Custis Lee. This estate had been bid in by the United States Government at a tax sale during the Civil War, and later used as a National Cemetery, being in the possession and under the control of the defendants in this case, who were military officers placed in charge by the President. In the lower Court, the Attorney-General of the United States, Charles Devens, had, without making the United States a party to the suit, filed a motion to dismiss, on the ground that the property belonged to the Government and was in actual possession of its officers, and that therefore the Court was without jurisdiction to entertain the suit. The Court, in a notable opinion rendered by Judge Miller, considered with great fullness the doctrine of immunity of the Government from suits without its consent, and held that this immunity did not apply when suit was brought against Government officials in unlawful possession of property.

"No man in this country is so high that he is above the law. No officer of the law may set that law at defiance, with impunity. All the officers of the Government, from the highest to the lowest, are creatures of the law and are bound to obey it." "Shall it be said," he asked, "that the Courts cannot give a remedy when the citizen has been deprived of his property by force, his estate seized and converted to the use of the government without lawful authority, without any process of law and without compensation, because the President has ordered it and his officers are in possession?" To sanction this would be to sanction tyranny. "The evils supposed to grow out of the possible interference of judicial action with the exercise of powers of the Government essential to some of its important operations, will be seen to be small indeed compared to this evil." Moreover, said Judge Miller, answering the arguments of the Attorney-General: "Hypothetical cases of great evils may be suggested by a particularly fruitful imagination in regard to almost every law upon which depend the rights of the individual or of the Government, and if the existence of laws is to depend upon their capacity to withstand such criticism, the whole fabric of the law must fail." And he concluded with a striking characterization of the Judiciary, as inherently the weakest of the three branches of the Government: "Dependent as its Courts are for the enforcement of their judgements, upon officers appointed by the Executive and removable at his pleasure, with no patronage and no control of purse or sword, their power and influence rest solely upon the public sense of the necessity for the existence of a tribunal to which all may appeal for the assertion and protection of rights guaranteed by the Constitution and by the laws of the land, and on the confidence reposed in the soundness of their decisions and the purity of their motives. From such a tribunal no well-founded fear can be entertained of injustice to the Government, or purpose to obstruct or diminish its just authority." In accordance with its opinion, the Court, finding the tax sale illegal, gave judgement for the Lee heirs and ousted the Government from possession. An elaborate dissenting opinion, concurred in by Chief Justice Waite and Judges Bradley and Woods, was given by the new Judge, Gray, in which it was contended that the suit was simply an action, "To invade the possession of the sovereign and to disregard the fundamental maxim that the sovereign cannot be sued."

Though the decision is now regarded as one of the glories of American law, there were varied views taken of it at the time of its rendition. The greater part of the Bar, however, shared in the feelings which were very strikingly expressed in the New York World that: "All self-respecting Americans will rejoice to learn that the Supreme Court has restored to the heirs of General Robert E. Lee the Arlington estate, which for twenty years past has been lawlessly and violently held by the Government without a penny of compensation to the owners. . . . The decision is of especial interest and importance at this time, as reaffirming conspicuously the supreme sovereignty of the Law, 'the State's collected will,' above all the heats and fluctuations of popular and sectional passion. The highest tribunal of the Union by its decision, in short, has recognized the wisdom and solidity of a response made by Judge Shipman to one member of the Court, during the proceedings—a response which will, let us hope, become proverbial in American thought and speech. 'Do I understand your position to be,' said one of the Supreme Court Judges to Judge Shipman, 'that if the title to a piece of land on which the Government has set up a lighthouse should be disputed, the claimant might bring an action of ejectment, and if successful, remove the lighthouse?' 'Certainly,' replied the intrepid lawyer. 'That is my position. Far better extinguish all the lighthouses in the land than put out the light of the Law.' "

The decision appealed also to independent journals like the *Springfield Republican*, as being "very sensible law"; and while it "greatly modifies the doctrine that the Government cannot be sued by the private citizen, it correspondingly strengthens the safeguards of private right in property. . . . It was in one of the most despotic of those monarchies in the last century that the stubborn miller, whose windmill adjoined, and still adjoins, the palace of Frederick the Great, replied to the covetous efforts of his Majesty to get possession, 'There are still Courts in Berlin, sire,' and he relied on the Courts to protect him, as they did." On the other hand, a writer in the *American Law Review* expressed the view that the decision was an infringement on the sovereignty of the United States, and that the rule that the Government cannot be sued has had "its vitality almost wholly emasculated, by the further ruling that the principle cannot be invoked by any officer of the Government against whom, in the discharge of his duty, an action is brought. The reasoning of the majority is certainly forcible, even plausible; but that of the minority through Mr. Justice Gray is invincible. . . . The majority opinion goes so far that a recoil will be the natural result." And a paper of extreme views on the subject of the war bitterly attacked the decision, which, it said, "will strike the man who fought to preserve that very Court, and the bones of whose comrades lie whitening on these plains, with something like a feeling of disgust, if not amazement. . . . The argument used by the Court in granting possession was, in brief, that public officers, acting under the power of sovereign prerogative while the Government was repelling treason, were answerable, after that treason had been crushed, to judicial authority. That authority now revoked the action of the Government done under peculiar and, we think, justifiable circumstances. The future action of this Government's officers will be watched with interest."

Concomitant with the policy of the Court in setting its face against State repudiation of its bonded obligations was its firm condemnation of all attempts by States to avoid compliance with their solemn legislative contracts in corporate charters containing exemptions from State taxation. While holding that such charters must be construed with utmost strictness against the corporations, and that no exemption from taxation was to be established by implication or other than by the most express phraseology, it continued to adhere to its doctrine, first enounced in 1854, that it was competent for a State Legislature to grant to a corporation an irrevocable tax exemption and that such a grant could not be impaired by a subsequent Legislature.

This doctrine had always met with powerful resistance from State officials, and had been the subject of constant and numerous dissents by members of the Court itself. Nevertheless, in 1878, it had been reaffirmed in an eloquent opinion rendered by Judge Swayne in *Farrington* v. *Tennessee*, 95 U.S. 679. "Contracts," he said, "mark the progress of communities in civilization and prosperity. They guard, as far as possible, against the fluctuations of human affairs. They seek to give stability to the present and certainty to the future. They gauge the confidence of man in the truthfulness and integrity of his fellow-man. They are springs of business, trade and commerce. Without them, Society could not go on. Spotless faith in their fulfillment honors alike communities and individuals. Where this is wanting in the body politic, the process of descent has begun, and a lower plane will be speedily reached. To the extent to which the defect exists among individuals, there is decay and degeneracy. . . . A Republican government can have no foundation other than the virtue of its citizens. When that is largely impaired, all is in peril. It is needless to lift the veil and contemplate the future of such a people. History but repeats itself. The trite old aphorism that 'honesty is the best policy' is true alike of individuals and communities. It is vital to the highest welfare." But while still refusing to invalidate these tax exemptions, the Court plainly showed, in the trend of its decisions, a reflection of the public sentiment which was being aroused by the arbitrary, corrupt and monopolistic activities of many of the corporations of the day, For as in the *Granger Cases* and in the *Sinking Fund Case* it evidenced its intention to strengthen the control of both State and National Governments over such corporations, so now it displayed an equally marked tendency to restrict the scope of corporate tax exemptions and to uphold the State's denial of their legal existence, wherever possible. As Judge Brown said, later: "Exemptions from taxation are not favored by law. . . . It is not too much to say that Courts are astute to seize upon evidence tending to show that they have become inoperative by changes in the original constitution of the companies." Here, as elsewhere throughout the law, the Court was responsive to the spirit of the times and to the new and constantly increasing demand for the subordination of private rights and privileges to the interests of the public welfare.

Another form of repudiation continued to be sternly discountenanced by the Court, in a long series of opinions in which it declined to modify its doctrine, announced as early as 1863, with reference to municipal bonds, valid when issued but subsequently held illegal by State Courts. During Chief Justice Waite's term of service, nearly two hundred cases involving such bonds were decided by the Court, and in very few instances were the efforts of the municipalities to escape payment successful. Attempts to avoid payment of bonds, by the creation of a new municipal corporation in place of the corporation issuing the bonds, were dealt with by the Court in *Barkley* v. *Levee Commissioners* and *Broughton* v. *Pensacola*, 93 U.S. 258, 266, in 1876; and an attempt by the city of Mobile to escape payment of its debts, by dissolution of the municipal corporations and legislative creation of a new corporation containing less territory but substantially the same population and property, was defeated in *Mobile* v. *Watson,* 116 U.S. 289, in 1886. In *Louisiana* v. *Pilsbury,* 105 U.S. 278, the contract contained in bonds issued by the city of New Orleans was held to be impaired by extraordinary legislation which provided for bonds the time of whose payment both as to principal and interest was to be determined by chance in a lottery.

One result of this firm policy of the Court in requiring cities and counties to pay their debts was to awaken in parts of the country—notably in Missouri, Iowa, Kansas, Wisconsin, Michigan and the Southern States—a considerable feeling of hostility, which led to the introduction of a bill in Congress, in 1878, providing that no municipal or public corporation should be sued in the United States Courts. Such jurisdiction, it was said, "leads to centralization" and "deprives a State of a free and right exercise of its sovereignty." Congress took no action; and the general public agreed with the *Nation* in saying that: "Instead of interfering to make repudiation easy for these bodies, it is the plain duty of Congress to arm the National Courts with whatever additional powers are necessary to be used in bringing them to a sense of their legal obligations." The antagonism to these Courts, on account of their decisions in the municipal bond cases committing county officials to jail for refusal to levy taxes to pay bonds, remained active in several States for many years; and as late as 1893 the Governor of Missouri sent a message to the State Legislature, reviewing the situation with respect to such imprisoned officials, and recommending that action should be taken by the State "to assert the outraged dignity of the State against usurpation of power by the Federal Judiciary."

While the Court, between 1878 and 1889, was thus steadily strengthening the political and governmental powers of the Nation and its control over the industrial and economic interests of the country, these powers and this control were being further enhanced by the immense increase in litigation which came within the jurisdiction of the inferior Courts of the United States—an increase caused, not merely by the growth of subjects of litigation, but also by the extension of National jurisdiction through Congressional action. Mention has already been made of the volume of cases in these Courts which arose out of municipal bond repudiation, out of the Reconstruction Laws, out of the enlargement of the scope of admiralty, out of State railroad regulation, out of railroad receiverships, and out of the insistence by litigants on testing the validity of State statutes under the Fourteenth Amendment. Notwithstanding all this increased burden upon the United States Courts, Congressional legislation, between 1867 and 1885, had opened still further fields of jurisdiction.

An early attempt by Congress to enlarge the jurisdiction of the Supreme Court itself had been defeated by a decision of vast importance rendered by the Court, in 1875 in *Murdock* v. *Memphis,* 20 Wall. 590, a case which involved a question whose decision seemed destined to affect profoundly the whole subsequent legal history of the country and which arose as follows. By the Act of February 5, 1867, Congress in amending the original Judiciary Act of 1789, had enacted (among other changes) a new section in place of the famous Twenty-Fifth Section relative to writs of error to State Courts.

It had omitted the last clause of the old Act which had in express terms limited the power of the Supreme Court, in reversing the judgment of a State Court, to a consideration of errors on the face of the record and of errors respecting Federal questions only. The issue presented was, whether Congress, by this omission, intended that the Court should, on future writs of error, examine into *all* errors in the record, whether respecting Federal questions or otherwise. If the Court should decide that this was the intention, not only would its work be enormously increased, but the class of matters coming within its jurisdiction and presented for decision would be revolutionized. Such was the importance of the case that, after it had been first argued, January 21, 1873, by W. J. Scott and J. B. Heiskell against W. T. Otto, B. M. Ester, J. M. Carlisle and J. D. McPherson, it was re-argued at the request of the Court on April 2, 3, 1873, by the same counsel and by Philip Phillips and Benjamin R. Curtis, who "in response to the invitation of this Court," appeared as *amici curiae*. The contention was made by counsel that the new statute was passed just after the overt acts of rebellion had been suppressed by the force of Federal arms, but while it was uncertain how far the spirit of opposition, though covert, yet remained both alive and active, and that the new statute showed an apprehension that Federal justice would be obstructed by local and State animosities and revenges, and that the record in State Courts might artfully suppress the fact that Federal questions had been actually adjudicated. It was pointed out that other Congressional legislation about the same time, providing for extension of the right of habeas corpus and for removal into the United States Courts in case of the existence of local State prejudice, showed a general intention on the part of Congress to enlarge the jurisdiction of those Courts. That these contentions were correct, and that it was the real intention of Congress to provide, by this amendment, that every question passed on by the State Court should be open for reconsideration in the Supreme Court, is highly probable. Undoubtedly, the whole trend of the legislation of the period sustained this view. The Court, nevertheless, in an opinion by Judge Miller rendered on January 11, 1875, over one and a half years after the argument, held that Congress, by dropping the clause from the old Judiciary Act, had not intended to change the law as it had existed for eighty years; and that, if it had actually intended such a change, it would have legislated in express and affirmative terms. In reaching this conclusion, it is evident that the Court was largely influenced by a consideration of the alarming results which would have followed from the opposite interpretation of the statute. For it stated that if a party could bring here, for decision on all matters involved, any case from a State Court, by merely raising a Federal question, and if the Court, on examination in conference, finding the Federal question clearly untenable, were obliged to examine the rest of the record and decide all points involved, it would follow that there would be "no conceivable case so insignificant in amount or unimportant in principle that a perverse and obstinate man may not bring it to this Court by the aid of a sagacious lawyer raising a Federal question in the record— a point which he may be wholly unable to support by the facts, or which he may well know will be decided against him, the moment it is stated." Hence, it said, it would require "a very bold reach of thought, and a readiness to impute to Congress a radical and hazardous change of a policy vital in its essential nature to the independence of the State Courts, to believe that that body contemplated or intended" such a result. Judge Bradley in dissenting, believed that Congress did intend exactly this "radical" change, however unwise it might be, and that the omission of the original clause from the Judiciary "meant something and effected something."

While this decision restricted the jurisdiction of the United States Courts, the legislative policy which Congress had adopted during the war, and which it now continued to pursue, led to extension of such jurisdiction in many directions. By the Acts of March 3, 1863, and of April 9, May 11, and July 27, 1866, Congress had authorized the removal into these Courts of any prosecution in a State Court based on acts committed under National authority in suppressing the Rebellion; and these statutes had been vigorously upheld in *Mayor of Nashville* v. *Cooper*, 6 Wall. 247, in 1868, the Court saying: "It is the right and the duty of the National Government to have its Constitution and laws interpreted and applied by its own judicial tribunals. . . . The decisions of the Courts of the United States, within their sphere of action, are as conclusive as the laws of Congress made in pursuance of the Constitution. This is essential to the peace of the Nation, and to the vigor and efficiency of the government." By the Act of March 2, 1867, Congress gave to plaintiffs the right to remove a case from the State Courts under certain conditions, that right having theretofore been confined to the defendants; and the Court held, in *Chicago & Northwestern Railway Co.* v. *Whitton*, 13 Wall. 270, in 1872, that such a right of removal was not properly an exercise of appellate jurisdiction, "but rather an indirect mode by which the Federal Court acquires original jurisdiction of the case"; and that there was no constitutional objection to such a provision, "where a plaintiff discovers, after suit brought in a State Court, that the prejudice and local influence, against which the Constitution intended to guard, are such as are likely to prevent him from obtaining justice."

By the Act of March 3, 1875, passed two months after the decision in *Murdock* v. *Memphis*, Congress still further enlarged the powers of the Circuit Courts by granting to them for the first time jurisdiction in all suits arising under the Constitution and laws of the United States. This statute greatly increased the classes of cases removable from the State into the National Courts; and since, in cases taken on writ of error or appeal from the Circuit Court to the Supreme Court, all questions whether Federal or State, presented on the record were passed upon by the latter Court, Congress thus practically enabled that Court to review matters, which the decision in *Murdock* v. *Memphis* had tended to eliminate from its consideration. Naturally, the United States Courts soon became overwhelmed with litigation. Examples of two classes of cases which were thus brought within the National control, were illustrated by decisions in the following important cases, in 1884 and 1885. In *Ames* v. *Kansas*, 111 U.S. 449, which was an action brought by the State of Kansas to invalidate the consolidation of one of its corporations, the Kansas Pacific Company, with the Union Pacific Railway Company, the Court held that a suit brought by a State in a State Court was removable into the Circuit Court; and that the fact that the Supreme Court had original Federal jurisdiction of suits by a State did not exclude Congress from granting similar jurisdiction to inferior Federal Courts. "It rests with the Legislative department of the government to say to what extent such grants shall be made," said Chief Justice Waite, "and it may safely be assumed that nothing will ever be done to encroach upon the high privileges of those for whose protection the constitutional provision was intended." In the *Pacific Railroad Removal Cases*, 115 U.S. 1, the Court held that a suit against a railroad chartered by the United States arose "under the laws of the United States," and was therefore removable into the Circuit Court. The decision had important results in the Western States, as it transferred the trial of tort cases to a large extent from the State to the United States Courts.

The enhancement of the National power through these Removal Acts and the ensuing decisions of the Court aroused a considerable sentiment of jealous opposition in the States, and their resentment at the extent to which litigants, especially corporations, took advantage of the right to remove suits into the United States Courts led to the enactment in many States of statutes providing that no corporation should be permitted to do business within the State, without first filing an agreement not to remove any case from a State Court. The constitutional validity of these State laws was tested as early as 1874, and in *Home Insurance Co.* v. *Morse*, 20 Wall. 445, such an act of Wisconsin relative to fire insurance companies was held invalid, the Court deciding that both individuals and corporations had a right to appeal to the Courts of the United States, which right was protected by the Constitution, and in 1887, this doctrine was reaffirmed in *Barron* v. *Burnside*, 121 U.S. 186, in which the Court held invalid a statute of Iowa relative to removal of suits by foreign corporations. The decision was attacked by many writers as hostile to the interests of the Western States, which had "particularly suffered from foreign corporations, especially railroad and insurance."

Another enlargement of the powers of the National Judiciary was made by Congress by the Act of March 3, 1885, in which it restored the right of appeal to the Supreme Court in cases of habeas corpus arising out of the restraint of any person in violation of the Constitution or laws of the United States. This right of appeal had been in abeyance for seventeen years, ever since the Act of February 5, 1867, granting such an appeal had been repealed in 1868, at the time of the *McCardle Case*. The effect of this repeal, enacted in the passionate era of Reconstruction, had been disastrous in many ways, and most especially since it left final action in habeas corpus cases with the District Supreme Court. These inferior Court Judges, particularly in the Southern and Western States, had gone to so great length, in the issue of writs on behalf of persons restrained by State authority, that their assumption of power had greatly alarmed those who believed in the necessity of preserving intact the respective lines of National and State authority. The Federal Judges have asserted power "to annul the criminal judgments of the State Courts, and to pass finally and conclusively upon the validity of the criminal codes, the police regulations, and even the Constitutions of the States," wrote a noted jurist in 1884. Consequently, Congress was called upon for action, and a bill was reported restoring the right of appeal to the Supreme Court, the House Committee on the Judiciary stating in its report that: "The jurisdiction assumed by Federal Judges, if allowed to continue, and continue unrestrained and unquestioned, cannot fail to bring the two judicial systems into serious and powerful conflict unless the State Courts shall tamely submit to be shorn of the jurisdiction they have exclusively exercised since the Government existed. . . . With this right of appeal restored, the true extent of the Act of 1867 and the true limits of the Federal Courts and Judges under it will become defined, and it can then be seen whether further legislation is necessary."

During the entire fifteen years of Waite's term of office, the Court's growing hesitation to limit the powers of the National Legislature was further illustrated by the fact that in only eight cases did it exercise its function of declaring Acts of Congress unconstitutional. Three of these cases related to Reconstruction legislation, already noted. Of the other five, only one—the *Trade Mark Cases*, 100 U.S. 82, decided in 1879—had an important effect upon the history or development of the country; in this case the Act of Congress providing for registration of trademarks was held invalid, on the ground that its scope was not confined to the only subject on which Congress had power to legislate, namely, commerce between the States and with foreign nations; and the Court again expressed its regret at being obliged to take this action, saying that: "A due respect for a coordinate branch of the government requires that we shall decide that it has transcended its power, only when that is so plain that we cannot avoid the duty." Nevertheless, though the Court's action in this respect was highly circumspect, it gave rise, at this period, to a more careful and scholarly examination into the legal and historical basis for the exercise of the power of the Court to pass upon the validity of an Act of Congress, than had hitherto been made. As will be recalled, the existence of this power had been attacked by the Democrats (the Republicans of those days) in 1802 and again in 1819, and by the Republicans in 1857 and 1867, but on all these occasions the attack had been made by politicians and had been based on political prejudices. In 1885, the basis of the power became subject to investigation and consideration by jurists of distinction; and a number of valuable articles were written presenting each side of this controversy—the beginning of a long line of publications which has lasted to the present day.

ONE *of the less pleasant aspects of American history has been that dealing with labor. Until the middle 1930's, the laws governing labor organization*

are best described as hostile. No result of the Sherman Anti-Trust Act proved more unexpected than its wholesale use against labor unions. When an 1892 strike tied up a good part of the economic life of New Orleans, the then Attorney-General William H. H. Miller directed a suit against the unions under the act. The court called upon to issue an injunction did so and concluded that the intent of anti-trust legislation included "combinations of labor, as well as of capital; in fact, all combinations in restraint of commerce, without reference to the character of the persons who entered into them." The implications of this approach were made painfully obvious when a sweeping federal injunction broke in 1893 the back of the Pullman strike. It was not until the passage of the Clayton Anti-Trust Act in 1914 and the Norris-La Guardia Anti-Injunction Act of 1932 that the sweeping consequences of these interpretations were turned aside.

The growth of the city had been complemented by the expansion of industry. Whereas in 1860 there were only nine cities with over 100,000 population, twenty years later the figure was twenty, and the 2,500,000 urban dwellers in cities of this size in 1860 had increased to over 6,000,000 by 1880. The slightly less than 1,300,000 workers laboring in 140,000 manufacturing establishments in 1859 had increased to 4,000,000 laboring in 355,000 such establishments thirty years later. The value of their products had risen in that period from below $2 billion in 1859 to more than $9 billion in 1889.

The booming condition of industry brought with it dismal consequences for the worker. His housing conditions were characterized by "filth, overcrowding, lack of privacy and domesticity, lack of ventilation and lighting, and absence of supervision and of sanitary regulation." Streets were often cluttered with debris, not infrequently with dead animals. The factory fitted its environment well. The worker's ears were assaulted by a constant din, and, as one worker recalled, an iron factory was filled with "half-naked, soot-smeared fellows, . . . their scowling faces . . . lit with fire." Outside of thousands of factories, as the evening whistle blew ending a ten-hour day, crowds "of tired, pallid, and languid looking children," worn by a long day of work, usually undernourished, poured homeward to their warrens to sleep and prepare for another day's work.

Given the conditions that existed, it is remarkable that there did not occur greater violence. As industry shifted from a provincial base to one of national dimension, skilled workers organized national craft unions, and by 1870, no less than 30 existed with a membership of about 300,000; a bare six years later, after three years of disabling depression, fewer than 50,000 workers remained in unions. Probably one out of every four workers was unemployed, and thousands wandered helplessly scraping a living from dump refuse or begging local police to jail them as vagrants. Profits before wages governed the behavior of employers, and their usual response to depression conditions was to cut wages. In 1877, when conditions reached unbearable levels, railroad workers, and then other workers, went out on strike. A wave of violence followed which saw the torch put to large areas of Pittsburgh and Baltimore. By midsummer, the nation seemed on the edge of revolution, and newspapers wondered whether "war between labor and capital has begun in earnest." Recent memories of the communards that had turned Paris into a bloodbath sent the chilling thought among the privileged classes that "after all our brag about modern civilization, it is capable of decomposing at any moment into anarchy, barbarism, and diabolism."

In the end, after the use of federal troops and state militias, the strike was contained. The slow return of prosperity lessened the tensions, but among middle-class spokesmen, the feeling spread that "the ballot must be restricted," and as Walter Gresham significantly added, "I suppose that can be done only through blood." Again in Chicago in 1886, during the bitter McCormick Harvesting Machine Company strike, violence would erupt and culminate in the Haymarket Affair, as it would in the Homestead strike of 1892 and the Pullman strike of 1894. Efforts to achieve a mass industrial union through the Knights of Labor in the 1880's would fail, and only the American Federation of Labor organized in 1886 on the craft union principle would survive in the essentially hostile atmosphere of the late nineteenth and early twentieth centuries.

Samuel Yellen (1906-   ), writing when labor was finally obtaining recognition under the New Deal, emphasized the bitter class divisions that lay thinly concealed during the pre-New Deal decades. No doubt they existed, but the remarkable fact is that they were contained and did not erupt to overturn the political system. The explanation for this not happening is traceable to the flexibility of the American system, one which prided itself in providing opportunity to all. The emphasis of Samuel Gompers, long head of the A.F. of L., on "bread and butter" unionism succeeded because the abundance of the American economy allowed for a steady and observable improvement. The hordes of immigrants who manned American industry, divided as they were by language and history, had often fled a more oppressive society, and found, no matter how compromised, in America hope. Perhaps the explanation for the absence of final upheaval was best stated in the newspaper editorial published during the Great Strike of 1877: "Put not thy unhallowed touch upon the pinnacles of the holy temple which God, not we, have reared in the new world—new for a new people and a better; new for a new age and a higher; new for a new religion and a purer; and new for a new Jerusalem, which is from God out of heaven." So long as Americans continued to believe that their society was a unique experiment, and that in it there was a way out for everyone, then discontent could be and was channeled.

AMERICAN LABOR STRUGGLES

by Samuel Yellen

Just as the panic of 1873 marked the birth of a national and self-conscious labor movement, it also marked the birth of a practical and realistic socialism, to replace the remote Utopian wishes of the earlier Socialists, contented with lofty intellectual conversations and romantic essays. From this time the Socialists, rather than hope idealistically for the morrow, began to act in the today by organizing hunger parades, unemployed demonstrations, strikes, mass meetings, and political tickets. At first they operated as the Workingmen's Party of the United States, which was formed in 1876, and which played a considerable part in the railroad strikes of 1877, especially in Chicago and St. Louis. After the failure of the railroad strikes the Workingmen's Party was reorganized as the Socialist Labor Party, with political action as its principal function, although friendly relations with trade-unions were to be maintained. When this change was made, the National Executive Committee of the Socialist Labor Party ordered the holding of mass meetings to present to legislative bodies resolutions for an eight-hour law, for the abolition of all conspiracy acts directed against labor, and for the purchase of railway and telegraph lines by the federal government.

But the socialist movement in America reflected the schism that had taken place in the First International, and split into two factions over questions of tactics and method. The Internationalists held for secret arming and direct preparation for the social revolution, with trade-unionism and politics as auxiliary activities to be strictly watched lest they led into the treacherous waters of opportunism. The Lassalleans, on the other hand, sought the gradual achievement of a new society through education, political organization, and parliamentary procedure. For a few years the Lassalleans controlled the policies of the party, and even Chicago, the stronghold of the trade-union and the revolutionary elements, dedicated itself to the ballot. A controversy soon arose, however, over the workingmen's military organizations. The largest of these, the "Lehr und Wehr Verein," had been formed by the German Socialists in Chicago during 1875 as a protection against the physical intimidation of the older political parties at the polls; the need for its protection had further been shown during a strike of cabinet-makers in July, 1877, when the police raided peaceful meetings and attacked those present with outrageous brutality. A repudiation, therefore, of all such military organizations by the National Executive Committee of the Socialist Labor Party antagonized still more the Chicago revolutionary element. This hostility grew acute in 1880 after the discouraging slump of the Socialist vote in the elections; and the revolutionaries denounced the moderates for a compromise made that year with the Greenback Party. Moreover, the single Socialist alderman reelected in Chicago was barred from taking his seat, through tricky manipulation by the Democratic city council; and the revolutionaries pointed out the futility of attempting to win a new society through the ballot-box. A great influx of refugees from the German anti-Socialist decree of 1878 augmented the revolutionary groups, and led finally to a convention of them in October, 1881, at Chicago.

Not until the arrival of Johann Most in America did the revolutionary groups precipitate into an active movement. The appearance of Most—disciple of Bakounin and Nechayeff, and founder of the anarchistic International Working People's Association, known then as the Black International—swept aside the parliamentary Socialists. In theory Most was not a pure anarchist; nevertheless, in practice he advocated the anarchist tactics of terroristic action against Church and State by the individual on his own initiative, so that the entire movement might not be endangered if the actor in any single deed were captured. Arms alone, he believed, secured for the worker some sort of equality with the police and troops. He issued a pamphlet: "Science of Revolutionary Warfare. Manual for instruction in the use and preparation of nitro-glycerine and dynamite, gun cotton, fulminating mercury, bombs, fuse, poisons, etc., etc." He urged the formation of rifle corps and the extermination of the "miserable brood," the "reptile brood," the "race of parasites." In another pamphlet, "Beast of Property," he declared that with existing society there could be no compromise, only relentless war until the beast of property "has been pursued to its last lurking place and totally destroyed."

Spurred on by the agitational energy of Most, representatives from revolutionary anti-parliamentary groups in 26 cities convened in Pittsburgh on October 14, 1883, to reorganize the International Working People's Association. Here again there were two distinct elements, united only by their opposition to political action. The delegates from New York and the eastern cities, led by Most, favored the individualistic tactics of anarchism; but those from Chicago and the western cities, under the guidance of Albert Parsons and August Spies, held for a mixture of anarchism and syndicalism that came to be known as the "Chicago idea." This modification actually approached syndicalism closer than it did anarchism, inasmuch as it recognized the trade-union as the "embryonic group" of the future society and as the fighting unit against capitalism. However, the trade-union was not to contend for the superficial and opportunistic benefits of high wages and short hours; it was to be satisfied with nothing less than the complete extinction of capitalism and the formation of a free society. In the struggle with capitalism it was not to resort to political action, was to distrust all central authority, and was to guard against betrayals by its leadership. All its faith was to rest in the direct action of the rank and file. Only two principles were lacking to make the "Chicago idea" conform with modern syndicalism: the general strike and sabotage, neither at that time theoretically developed.

Since the western faction was by far the larger, the convention confirmed the importance of the trade-union. And direct action—force, violence—was the core of the tactics to be employed. The platform of the International, published in the "Alarm," a Chicago paper edited by Parsons, read in part:

> The present order of society is based upon the spoliation of the non-property by the property owners, the capitalists buy the labor of the poor for wages, at the mere cost of living, taking all the surplus of labor. . . . Thus while the poor are increasingly deprived the opportunities of advancement, the rich grow richer through increasing robbery. . . . This system is unjust, insane, and murderous. Therefore those who suffer under it, and do not wish to be responsible for its continuance, ought to strive for its destruction by all means and with their utmost energy. . . . The laborers can look for aid from no outside

source in their fight against the existing system, but must achieve deliverance through their own exertions. Hitherto, no privileged class have relinquished tyranny, nor will the capitalists of today forego their privilege and authority without compulsion. . . . It is therefore self-evident that the fight of proletarianism against the bourgeoisie must have a violent revolutionary character; that wage conflicts cannot lead to the goal. . . . Under all these circumstances, there is only one remedy left—force. . . . Agitation to organize, organizations for the purpose of rebellion, this is the course if the workingmen would rid themselves of their chains.

Here was a program advocating without camouflage the annihilation of the existing economic and political order, a program that could not be ignored.

In Chicago, thanks to the long history of police atrocities, many workers joined the International, so that this city alone had more than one-third of the 5,000 to 6,000 members. Moreover, the most able and intelligent leaders were here—men like Parsons, Spies, Samuel Fielden, and Michael Schwab. In fact, the Internationalists in Chicago published five papers: the "Alarm" in English, with an edition of 2,000 twice a month; in German, the daily "Chicagoer Arbeiter-Zeitung," edited by Spies, with an edition of 3,600, the "Fackel," and the "Vorbote"; and in Bohemian, the "Budoucnost." This revolutionary nucleus quickly penetrated the trade-union movement. Under its influence the local Progressive Cigar Makers' Union in June, 1884, called upon all the unions in the city to secede from the conservative Amalgamated Trades and Labor Assembly and to organize a new Central Labor Union with a militant policy. Four German unions answered the call— the metal workers, butchers, carpenters and joiners, and cabinetmakers— and a declaration of principles was adopted: that all land is a social heritage, that all wealth is created by labor, that between labor and capital there can be no harmony, and that every worker ought to cut loose from the capitalist political parties and devote himself to the trade-union. From its inception the Central Labor Union was in communication with the Internationalist group. The Socialist Labor Party, on the other hand, remained with the Amalgamated Trades and Labor Assembly.

For a year the growth of the new Central Labor Union was slow; nevertheless, by the end of 1885 it had 13 unions, whereas the Amalgamated Assembly had 19. Within a few months, however, by April, 1886, the Central Labor Union outstripped its rival and consisted of 22 unions, among which were the 11 largest in the city. It retained its contact with the International and united with it in processions and mass meetings. It began strong agitation for the eight-hour day, although its motives were different from those of the conservative Amalgamated Assembly and the Knights of Labor, since it regarded as paramount, not the attainment of the shorter working day, but the common labor front and the class struggle. It adopted the following resolution, introduced by Spies in October, 1885:

Be it Resolved, That we urgently call upon the wage-earning class to arm itself in order to be able to put forth against their exploiters such an argument which alone can be effective: Violence, and further be it Resolved, that notwithstanding that we expect very little from the introduction of the eight-hour day, we firmly promise to assist our more backward brethren in this class struggle with all means and power at our disposal, so long as they will continue to show an open and resolute front to our common oppressors, the aristocratic vagabonds and the exploiters. Our war-cry is "Death to the foes of the human race."

The initiative in the eight-hour movement in Chicago was left in the hands of an Eight-Hour Association, composed of the Amalgamated Assembly, the Socialist Labor Party, and the Knights of Labor, but the Central Labor Union cooperated energetically. On the Sunday preceding May 1 it organized a huge eight-hour demonstration, in which 25,000 took part, and at which Parsons, Spies, Fielden, and Schwab spoke. When the day of the struggle arrived, the main portion of the eight-hour movement in Chicago acted under the banner of the Central Labor Union and the International.

The strike opened in Chicago with a display of great strength and much promise of success. Nearly 40,000 workers walked out on May 1 as prearranged, and the number jumped to 65,000 within three or four days. Nor was this the full strength of the movement in the city: more than 45,000 were granted a shorter working day without striking, the bulk of them— 35,000—workers in the packing-houses. In addition, there were already several thousand men on strike at the Lake Shore, the Wabash, the Chicago, Milwaukee and St. Paul, and other freight yards in protest against the hiring of non-union labor. With such a mass movement on foot, Chief of Police Ebersold apprehended difficulties and called upon the entire detective and police force to be on duty Saturday, May 1; and his force was augmented by Pinkerton detectives previously engaged by the railroads, and by special deputies, many of whom were selected from the Grand Army of the Potomac. In spite of these martial preparations, Saturday passed peacefully. The city, with hundreds of factories idle and thousands of strikers and their families promenading the streets, had a holiday appearance. There were processions and mass meetings, addressed in Bohemian, Polish, German, and English.

Faced with a strike of unexpected power and solidarity, the leading business men and manufacturers united to crush it. On April 27 the Western Boot and Shoe Manufacturers Association, with 60 firms represented in person and 160 by letter, was formed in Chicago for combined action. The chief iron and steel foundries, as also the copper and brass, declared that they would reject the eight-hour demand. A session of the principal planing mills was held on the morning of May 1 at the office of Felix Lang to determine procedure against the strikers. In the evening these were joined at the Sherman Hotel by all the lumber yards and box factories, and the lumber industry in concert decided to grant no concessions to the workmen. Nevertheless, by Monday, May 3, the spread of the strike was alarming. Lumber-laden craft blocked the river near the Lumber Exchange, and 300 more vessels with cargoes of lumber were expected to join the idle fleet. The building interests, then enjoying a boom, were suddenly paralyzed. The great metal foundries and the vast freight yards were tied up. To break the strike aggressive action was needed. On Monday police clubs began to scatter processions and meetings.

That afternoon serious trouble arose at the McCormick Harvester Works. The soreness here was old. It had begun in the middle of February, when Cyrus McCormick locked out his 1,400 employees in reply to a demand by the men that the company quit its discrimination against certain of their fellows who had taken part in a former strike at the plant. In the following two months strike-breakers, Pinkertons, and police had attacked the locked-out men with wanton savagery. Bogart and Thompson say of this period:

> The police force of Chicago reflected the hostility of the employing class, regarding strikes per se as evidence that the men had placed themselves in opposition to law and order. During these months of unrest it became a pastime for a squad of mounted police, or a detachment in close formation, to disperse with the billy any gathering of workingmen. The billy was an impartial instrument: men, women, children, and shop-keeping bystanders alike composed its harvest. It was the police, aided by the "Pinkertons," who added the great leaven of bitterness to the contest. To the workingmen they furnished concrete and hateful examples of the autocracy against which they protested.

But a greater police provocation was reserved for Monday afternoon, May 3. At this time 6,000 striking lumber-shovers met near Black Road, about a quarter of a mile north of the McCormick works, to appoint a committee to be sent to the lumber-yard owners. While August Spies was addressing the meeting, a group of some 200 detached itself spontaneously from the crowd of strikers, marched to McCormick's, and heckled and attacked the scabs, who were just then leaving for their homes. Within 10 or 15 minutes there were more than 200 policemen on the spot. Meanwhile Spies, who was still speaking, and the strikers at the meeting, seeing patrol wagons and hearing gunfire, started toward McCormick's, but were met by the police. The clubs and guns broke up the crowd; the police fired deliberately into the running strikers, so that at least four were killed and many wounded.

Spies, indignant at this fresh outrage, hurried to the printing shop of the "Arbeiter-Zeitung" and issued a circular in both English and German:

> REVENGE!
> WORKINGMEN, TO ARMS!!!
>
> The masters sent out their bloodhounds—the police; they killed six of your brothers at McCormicks this afternoon. They killed the poor wretches because they, like you, had the courage to disobey the supreme will of your bosses. They killed them because they dared ask for the shortening of the hours of toil. They killed them to show you, "Free American Citizens" that you must be satisfied and contented with whatever your bosses condescend to allow you, or you will get killed!
>
> You have for years endured the most abject humiliations; you have for years suffered unmeasurable iniquities; you have worked yourself

to death; you have endured the pangs of want and hunger; your Children you have sacrificed to the factory lord—in short: you have been miserable and obedient slave(s) all these years: Why? To satisfy the insatiable greed, to fill the coffers of your lazy thieving master? When you ask them now to lessen your burdens, he sends his bloodhounds out to shoot you, kill you!

If you are men, if you are the sons of your grand sires, who have shed their blood to free you, then you will rise in your might, Hercules, and destroy the hideous monster that seeks to destroy you. To arms we call you, to arms!

YOUR BROTHERS.

A second circular called for a protest mass meeting the following evening in the old Haymarket on Randolph Street.

The morning of Tuesday, May 4, saw a police attack upon a column of 3,000 strikers near Thirty-fifth Street. Attacks upon gatherings of strikers continued during the afternoon, in particular one at Eighteenth and Morgan in the southwest part of the city. Mayor Carter H. Harrison, however, gave permission for the mass meeting that evening, and at 7:30 people began to assemble in Haymarket Square, the center of the lumber-yard and packing-house district. Between eight and nine o'clock about 3,000 persons were present, among them Mayor Harrison, who attended as a spectator to see that order was maintained. Only half a block distant was the Desplaines Street police station, where a good-sized detail of police was in readiness. The meeting was very quiet. Spies addressed the crowd from a wagon in front of the Crane Bros. factory. Then Parsons spoke, confining himself to the eight-hour demand; he was followed by Fielden. Toward 10 o'clock a threatening rainstorm began to disperse the gathering; by that time Spies and Parsons had left. Only Fielden remained to speak to the few hundred who had not yet gone. Mayor Harrison, having found the meeting peaceful and believing that all was over, left shortly after 10 o'clock, called in at the Desplaines Street station to report that there had been no trouble, and went home to bed.

A few minutes after the mayor left, however, Inspector John Bonfield, hated throughout the city for his record of extreme brutality, led a detachment of 180 policemen to break up what remained of the meeting. There was no excuse for this expedition, except Bonfield's desire for another head-clubbing party, according to Governor Altgeld, who declared ". . . that Capt. Bonfield is the man who is really responsible for the death of the police officers." The police halted a short distance from the speakers' wagon, and Captain Ward commanded the gathering to disperse. Fielden cried out that it was a peaceable meeting. As Captain Ward turned to give an order to his men, a bomb was thrown from a point on the sidewalk a little south of the wagon. It exploded in the midst of the policemen and wounded 66, of whom seven later died. The police immediately opened fire hysterically and shot round after round into the crowd, killing several and wounding 200. The neighborhood was thrown into terror. Doctors were telephoned. Drug stores were crowded with the wounded.

Who threw the bomb is still undetermined. There are three possibilities. (1) Governor Altgeld, in his pardon message of 1893, contended that the bomb was thrown by someone as reprisal for all the atrocities committed by Bonfield and the police:

> . . . it is shown here that the bomb was, in all probability, thrown by someone seeking personal revenge; that a course had been pursued by the authorities which would naturally cause this; that for a number of years prior to the Haymarket affair there had been labor troubles, and in several cases a number of laboring people, guilty of no offense, had been shot down in cold blood by Pinkerton men, and none of the murderers were brought to justice. The evidence taken at coroners' inquests and presented here, shows that in at least two cases men were fired on and killed when they were running away, and there was consequently no occasion to shoot, yet nobody was punished; that in Chicago there had been a number of strikes in which some of the police not only took sides against the men, but without any authority of law invaded and broke up peaceable meetings, and in scores of cases brutally clubbed people who were guilty of no offense whatever.

(2) The possibility of an "agent provocateur" must not be dismissed offhand. The police officials in Chicago were at this time quite equal to such a scheme. On the morning after the bombing, Inspector Bonfield declared:

> We will take active measures to catch the leaders in this business. The action of last night will show that their bombshell and dynamite talk has not been empty vaporings. . . . *The attack on us was brutal and cowardly.* . . . (Italics mine.)

The emphasized sentence indicates perhaps an antecedent wish to prove that the "dynamite talk" was not "empty vaporings."

(3) There is a strong possibility that Rudolph Schnaubelt, an anarchist and brother-in-law to Michael Schwab, was guilty. The circumstance that he was twice arrested and both times released, at a period when the police were arresting and holding all the anarchists and sympathizers they could lay their hands on, arouses the suspicion, almost the certainty, that the police wanted him out of the way, in order that they might be able to condemn the eight more important revolutionary leaders. In this connection Bogart and Thompson report:

> In a statement now on record in the Illinois Historical Survey, made by Mr. Wallace Rice, June 25, 1919, and concurred in by Mr. Clarence S. Darrow and Mr. George A. Schilling, all of whom were in a position to know the inside history of the case, Mr. Rice says: "It was the impression of all the newspaper men informed in the premises that the fatal bomb was made by Louis Lingg and thrown by Rudolph Schnaubelt. Many of them believed further that this fact was also known to the police and that Schnaubelt was allowed to go after they had taken him into custody because he could not be connected in any way with

the other men afterward condemned, with the possible exception of Lingg and of Michael Schwab, who was husband to Schnaubelt's sister. Lingg, however, was thought to be the only one of the defendants who had guilty knowledge of the bomb and its throwing. Schnaubelt, after his release by the police, went as far and as fast from the scene of the crime as he could, and when an indictment was found against him at last, was believed to be in southern California near the Mexican line, whence he could easily escape to another country. . . .

Judge Gary, when reviewing the case seven years after the trial, admitted the strong likelihood of Schnaubelt's guilt, and the release twice by the police of the man who was the chief actual suspect. Gary added: "But whether Schnaubelt or some other person threw the bomb, is not an important question."

The newspapers, not only in Chicago, but everywhere, assumed an attitude of panic. They demanded the instantaneous execution of all subversive persons. Within a few days the police arrested the chief anarchists and revolutionaries in the city—Spies, Fielden, Schwab, Adolph Fischer, George Engel, Louis Lingg, Oscar Neebe; and many others, including the 25 printers in the "Arbeiter-Zeitung" shop, were taken into custody. The only one missing was Parsons, whom the police were unable to capture, notwithstanding a rigorous hunt. When the death of police officer Mathias J. Degan was announced, the press cried for speedy indictments by the grand jury. It kept fanning for weeks the feeling of terror aroused in the public. Its headlines screamed: Bloody Brutes, Red Ruffians, Red Ragsters, Bomb Makers, Red Flagsters, Dynamarchists, Bloody Monsters, Bomb Slingers, Bomb Throwers. The "Chicago Tribune" wrote, May 6: "These serpents have been warmed and nourished in the sunshine of toleration until at last they have been emboldened to strike at society, law, order, and government." The "Chicago Herald," May 6: "The rabble whom Spies and Fielden stimulated to murder are not Americans. They are offscourings of Europe who have sought these shores to abuse the hospitality and defy the authority of the country." The "Chicago Inter-Ocean," May 6: "For months and years these pestiferous fellows have uttered their seditious and dangerous doctrines." The "Chicago Journal," May 7: "Justice should be prompt in dealing with the arrested anarchists. The law regarding accessories to crime in this State is so plain that their trials will be short."

Stimulation of public hysteria became the main activity of the police. Inspector Bonfield and Captain Schaack, in particular, wanted to sustain the ferment of dread and hatred after the bomb-throwing, in order to keep the citizenry excited. Three years later, in an interview, Chief of Police Ebersold confessed: "It was my policy to quiet matters down as soon as possible after the 4th of May [1886]. The general unsettled state of things was an injury to Chicago. On the other hand, Capt. Schaack wanted to keep things stirring. He wanted bombs to be found here, there, all around, everywhere. . . . After we got the anarchist societies broken up, Schaack wanted to send out men to again organize new societies right away." The police seized the subscription lists of the "Arbeiter-Zeitung" and instituted a long series of raids. Meeting halls, printing offices, and private homes were broken into and searched; everyone suspected of the remotest connection with the radical movement was held. The police saw to it that the raids were fertile. Each day there were discovered ammunition, rifles, swords, muskets, pistols, bayonets, billies, anarchist literature, red flags, incendiary banners, cartridges, dirks, bullets, bulk lead, materials for manufacturing torpedoes, bullet molds, dynamite, bombs, shells, percussion caps, infernal engines, secret trap-doors, underground rifle ranges. Each find announced by the police was well played up by the press. A rumor was spread that Herr Most was coming from New York, evidently to take charge of further assassinations; and the police even produced a show of detectives at the railroad station. A crowd gathered to await the dangerous arrival, but Herr Most did not appear. The proper atmosphere for the trial was being carefully prepared.

When the grand jury met in the middle of May, it quickly indicted August Spies, Michael Schwab, Samuel Fielden, Albert R. Parsons, Adolph Fischer, George Engel, Louis Lingg, and Oscar Neebe, all prominent in the International, for the murder of Mathias J. Degan on May 4. The trial was set for June 21 at the criminal court of Cook County, with Joseph E. Gary as judge. State's Attorney Julius S. Grinnell took command of the prosecution. The accused men were represented by William P. Black, William A. Foster, Sigmund Zeisler, and Moses Salomon. While the police were making their alarming finds, while the newspapers poured forth stories of anarchist plots for wholesale murder and the public clamored for the immediate execution of the indicted men, the trial opened. Just as the preliminary examination of talesmen commenced, the missing Parsons, who had baffled a police search for six weeks, walked into court and surrendered himself for trial, joining his comrades on the defendants' bench.

At the outset two circumstances prevented any approximation to a fair trial. First, Judge Gary forced all eight defendants to stand trial together, increasing the danger that all sorts of evidence would be admitted. Second, through an extraordinary device the jury was packed: the candidates for the jury were not chosen in the customary manner by drawing names from a box; instead, a special bailiff, nominated by the State's Attorney, was appointed by the court to select the candidates. A Chicago business man, Otis S. Favor, made affidavit that this bailiff had said to him in the presence of witnesses: "I am managing this case, and know what I am about. These fellows are going to be hanged as certain as death. I am calling such men as the defendants will have to challenge peremptorily and waste their time and challenges. Then they will have to take such men as the prosecution wants." By the adroit questioning of the judge, many who openly admitted their prejudice against the defendants were pronounced fit for jury service and had to be peremptorily challenged by the defense. It took 21 days to select the jury: 981 talesmen were examined. Ultimately the defense exhausted all its peremptory challenges and the final 12 men were picked, among them a relative of one of the victims of the bomb.

The introductory speech by State's Attorney Grinnell, after the presentation of evidence began on July 14, assured the jury that the man who had thrown the bomb would be produced. This, of course, the prosectuion was unable to do. It did at first, however, attempt to fabricate, by means of the testimony of two alleged anarchists who had turned State's evidence, a terroristic plot for the dynamiting of all police stations when the word "Ruhe" appeared in the "Arbeiter-Zeitung." Under cross-examination the testimony of these two witnesses was largely impaired. When this failed, other strange evidence was disclosed. One witness named Gilmer, shown by cross-examination to be a professional liar who had in all likelihood been paid for testifying, swore that he saw an object resembling a bomb pass between Spies, Schwab, and Schnaubelt, and that he saw the latter throw the bomb among the police. Also several policemen tried to prove that Fielden had fired upon them from behind the speakers' wagon, but their assertions were contradictory. Regarding the witnesses and testimony produced by the State, Governor Altgeld said in his pardon message:

> It is further shown here that much of the evidence given at the trial was a pure fabrication; that some of the prominent police officials, in their zeal, not only terrorized ignorant men by throwing them into prison and threatening them with torture if they refused to swear to anything desired, but that they offered money and employment to those who would consent to do this. Further, that they deliberately planned to have fictitious conspiracies formed in order that they might get the glory of discovering them. In addition to the evidence in the record of some witnesses who swore that they had been paid small sums of money, etc., several documents are here referred to.

In spite of the generation of an emotional fog, the State, as Altgeld remarks, never discovered who threw the bomb. Nor was it able to show any specific conspiracy entered into by the accused men.

It soon developed that the eight men were on trial for their ideas, even though the defense was not permitted to introduce testimony concerning the theory of anarchism. On the grounds that the general principles of the anarchists urged the destruction of all capitalists, Judge Gary allowed the prosecution to establish a resultant specific conspiracy. The jury was deluged with readings from inciting articles in the "Alarm" and the "Arbeiter-Zeitung." Furthermore, the police exhibited on a table before the jury-box all fashions of dynamite and bombs, with all their infernal mechanism, although these destructive engines were found often miles from the scene of the bombing and weeks afterward and had no association with the defendants. The display produced the desired effect: it aroused terror. Time and again the defense objected to the presentation of irrelevant evidence whose purpose was the evocation of emotionalism, but it was overruled by the court. In other ways too, as Altgeld later pointed out, Judge Gary revealed his bias. While he confined the defense in its cross-examination to the specific points touched on by the State, he permitted the State to wander to matters entirely foreign to those the witnesses were examined in. Besides, he made insinuating remarks in the hearing of the jury that proved much more damaging than anything the prosecution could have produced. Foster, of the defense counsel, pleaded that there existed no proof of the influence on the bomb-thrower of any spoken or written word by the defendants, nor of the instigation of the deed by the defendants. He persisted in conducting the case as one of homicide, since that was the charge; he confined himself to plain facts and law; and he wanted even to admit some criminal folly in the utterances of the defendants, but this they refused to permit.

The summing up before the jury began on August 11. It was concluded by State's Attorney Grinnell, whose final words were: "Law is upon trial. Anarchy is on trial. These men have been selected, picked out by the grand jury and indicted because they were leaders. They are no more guilty than the thousands who follow them. Gentlemen of the jury; convict these men, make examples of them, hang them and you save our institutions, our society." As was foreseen, the jury brought in on August 20 a verdict of guilty and fixed the penalty at hanging for seven of the defendants, the exception, Oscar Neebe, being given 15 years' imprisonment. A motion by the defense in September for a new trial was denied by Judge Gary, and the convicted men were called upon to speak before sentence was pronounced. They delivered eloquent speeches lasting three days, addressed beyond the court to workers everywhere. After a long summary of his beliefs, Spies said:

> Now, these are my ideas. They constitute a part of myself. I cannot divest myself of them, nor would I, if I could. And if you think that you can crush out these ideas that are gaining ground more and more every day, if you think you can crush them out by sending us to the gallows—if you would once more have people to suffer the penalty of death because they have dared to tell the truth—and I defy you to show us where we have told a lie—I say, if death is the penalty for proclaiming the truth, then I will proudly and defiantly pay the costly price! Call your hangman.

George Engel said:

> I hate and combat, not the individual capitalist, but the system that gives him those privileges. My greatest wish is that workingmen may recognize who are their friends and who are their enemies.

And with the defiance he had displayed throughout the trial, the twenty-one-year-old Lingg said:

> I repeat that I am the enemy of the "order" of today, and I repeat that, with all my powers, so long as breath remains in me, I shall combat it. . . . I despise you. I despise your order; your laws, your force-propped authority. Hang me for it!

On October 9 sentence, as decreed by the jury, was pronounced by Judge Gary.

Execution of the sentences was postponed while the case was carried before the Supreme Court of Illinois. After several months of consideration, the Supreme Court, although it admitted that the trial had not been free of legal error, affirmed in September, 1887, the verdict of the lower court. An attempt to appeal to the Supreme Court of the United States failed when that body decided that it had no jurisdiction. Labor organizations everywhere asked for mercy for the condemned men; the American Federation of Labor adopted such a resolution, while the Noble Order of the Knights of Labor was prevented from doing likewise only through the personal intervention of Powderly, who hated the anarchists and wanted to clear his Order of any association with them. During the last days Fielden and Schwab petitioned for executive clemency and asked for commutation of their sentence. The others demanded liberty or death. Governor Oglesby commuted the sentence of Fielden and Schwab to life imprisonment, and they joined Neebe in the State Penitentiary at Joliet. Lingg escaped the scaffold the day preceding the execution by exploding a dynamite tube in his mouth. The remaining four were hanged on November 11, 1887.

> The nooses were quickly adjusted, the caps pulled down, and a hasty movement made for the traps. Then from beneath the hoods came these words:
> Spies: "There will be a time when our silence will be more powerful than the voices you strangle today."
> Fischer: "Hurrah for anarchy—"
> Engel: "Hurrah for anarchy!"
> Fischer: "This is the happiest moment of my life!"
> Parsons: "Will I be allowed to speak, O men of America? Let me speak, Sheriff Matson! Let the voice of the people be heard! O—"

At the funeral 25,000 working people marched. William P. Black, who had been of the defense counsel, spoke over the graves:

> . . . I loved these men. I knew them not until I came to know them in the time of their sore travail and anguish. As months went by and I found in the lives of those with whom I talked the witness of their love for the people, of their patience, gentleness, and courage, my heart was taken captive in their cause. . . . I say that whatever of fault may have been in them, these, the people whom they loved and in whose cause they died, may well close the volume, and seal up the record, and give our lips to the praise of their heroic deeds, and their sublime self-sacrifice.

᯽

As *early as 1846, the then Secretary of the Treasury noted in his annual report that American agriculture had reached a crisis of overproduction, and that unless new foreign markets were found, the American farmer would be ruined. It proved to be a crisis that steadily worsened during the nineteenth century as the farm surpluses grew to flood proportions. It had a particularly piquant note since the farmer had fallen victim to abundance; his success had proven his undoing. The obvious solution, as the farmer thought, was to meet declining prices by increasing the volume of his production. But the result of their effort was to glut further their markets and to reduce prices to the bone. Burdened with heavy fixed costs and large interest charges, farmers were increasingly forced to leave the land or to sell out their land and then to work it as tenants. The Jeffersonian image of a self-reliant yeomanry proved increasingly blurred as the nineteenth century drew to its close.*

The rapid expansion westward, with its exploitation of virgin lands, compounded the woes of the farmers. Once the vast grain production of the Great Plains poured eastward, their eastern competitors had little choice other than abandoning the land or switching to specialty production geared to supply the exploding cities. Otherwise the land disgorged their displaced farmers into the expanding industries. The grain farmers of the New West destroyed their competition, but they too faced difficult problems. As numerous critics of Turner's "safety-valve theory" of the frontier have argued, it took a considerable capital investment to succeed in farming new land. A fortunate few farmers had sufficient capital but most were dependent upon bank credit. Invariably the demand for credit exceeded the supply, and the result was a large interest rate. In addition, the markets supplied by staple crop farmers were distant, and the fixed costs of rail transportation as well as of elevator storage added to their burdens. Not insignificant were the natural disasters inflicted by weather and insects upon their crops. A single hailstorm could destroy a ripening field of wheat; a plague of grasshoppers could devour everything green in a matter of minutes.

Susceptible as the farmer was to a market mechanism beyond his control, it is hardly surprising that when he failed to reap expected profits, he often struck out at the hidden source of his discomfort. And he labeled it as a form of organization, one which usually conveyed the idea of capitalistic exploitation. The size and power of the assumed enemy persuaded the farmer that only organized protest would meet his enemy with an effective challenge. On December 4, 1867, the Patrons of Husbandry, better known as the Grangers, a secret farm organization, was organized. Its major target was all chartered monopolies and it particularly emphasized the need to regulate railroad rates. Education and organization, particularly political, were its major answers to the farmer's problems. By the middle of the 1870's, several Middle-Western states had legislated controls on railroad, warehouse, and elevator rates. The so-called Granger Laws were upheld by the Supreme Court in 1877, only to be reversed in 1886. But pressure from the Grangers and the newer Farm Alliances produced a violent protest, one which Congress could not ignore.

The rise of organized agrarian protest found its historian in Solon J. Buck (1884-1962). After receiving his education at the University of Wisconsin and Harvard, he taught at several Middle-Western state universities. The unique focus of his original research was the Granger Movement which then broadened to include the later Alliances and Populists. The undercurrent of farm protest complemented the sporadic labor upheavals. It reinforces the conclusion that the final decades of the nineteenth century were a time of incipient violence. In retrospect, the observer can only comment half in wonder that the political system absorbed the protest and directed it into peaceful channels.

THE AGRARIAN CRUSADE

by Solon J. Buck

Alliances, wheels, leagues—all the agrarian organizations which multiplied during the eighties—gave tangible form to the underlying unrest created by the economic conditions of that superficially prosperous decade. Only slowly, however, did there develop a feeling that a new political party was necessary in order to apply the remedies which, it was believed, would cure some if not all the ills of the agricultural class. Old party ties were still strong. Only with reluctance could the Republican or Democrat of long standing bring himself to depart from the familiar fold. Then, too, the recent ignominious failures of the Greenback party might well cool the ardor of all but the most sanguine advocates of a third party movement. Among the leaders of the agrarian organizations were many, moreover, who foresaw that to become involved in partisan politics could mean nothing less than the defeat of all their original purposes.

One disappointment after another, however, made it apparent that little was to be expected from the Republican or the Democratic party. Trust in individual politicians proved equally vain, since promises easily made during a hot campaign were as easily forgotten after the battle was over. One speaker before a state convention of the Northwest Alliance put into words what many were thinking: "There may be some contingencies when you may have to act politically. If other parties will not nominate men friendly to your interest, then your influence will have to be felt in some way or you may as well disband. If all parties nominate your enemies, then put some of your own friends into the race and then stand by them as a Christian stands by his religion." In other words, if nothing was to be gained by scattering votes among the candidates of the old parties, independent action remained the only course. Hence it was that the late eighties saw the beginnings of another party of protest, dominated by the farmers and so formidable as to cause the machine politicians to realize that a new force was abroad in the land.

After the Greenback party lost the place it had for a fleeting moment obtained, labor once more essayed the role of a third party. In 1886, for instance, the Knights of Labor and the trades unions, for once coöperating harmoniously, joined forces locally with the moribund Greenbackers and with farmers' organizations and won notable successes at the polls in various parts of the Union, particularly in the Middle Atlantic and Western States.

Emboldened by such victories, the discontented farmers were induced to cast in their lot with labor; and for the next few years, the nation saw the manifestoes of a party which combined the demands of labor and agriculture in platforms constructed not unlike a crazy-quilt, with Henry George, James Buchanan, and Alson J. Streeter presiding at the sewing-bee and attempting to fit into the patchwork the diverse and frequently clashing shades of opinion represented in the party. In 1888, Streeter, ex-president of the Northwestern Alliance, was nominated for President on the Union Labor ticket and received 146,935 votes in 27 of the 38 States. Despite its name and some support from the Eastern workers, the new party was predominantly Western; more than half of its total vote was polled in Kansas, Texas, Missouri, and Arkansas. In the local elections of 1889 and 1890 the party still appeared but was obviously passing off the stage to make way for a greater attraction.

The meager vote for Streeter in 1888 demonstrated that the organized farmers were yet far from accepting the idea of separate political action. President Macune of the Southern Alliance probably voiced the sentiments of most of that order when he said in his address to the delegates at Shreveport in 1887: "Let the Alliance be a business organization for business purposes, and as such, necessarily secret, and as secret, necessarily non-political." Even the Northwestern Alliance had given no sign of official approval to the political party in which so many of its own members played a conspicuous part.

But after the election of 1888, those who had continued to put their trust in non-political organizations gradually awoke to the fact that neither fulminations against transportation abuses, monopolies, and the protective tariff, nor the lobbying of the Southern Alliance in Washington had produced reforms. Even Macune was moved to say at the St. Louis session in December, 1889: "We have reached a period in the history of our Government when confidence in our political leaders and great political organizations is almost destroyed, and estrangement between them and the people is becoming more manifest every day." Yet the formation of a new party under the auspices of the Alliance was probably not contemplated at this time, except possibly as a last resort, for the Alliance agreed to "support for office only such men as can be depended upon to enact these principles into statute laws, uninfluenced by party caucus." Although the demands framed at this St. Louis convention read like a party platform and, indeed, became the basis of the platform of the People's Party in 1892, they were little more than a restatement of earlier programs put forth by the Alliance and the Wheel. They called for the substitution of greenbacks for national bank notes, laws to "prevent the dealing in futures of all agricultural and mechanical productions," free and unlimited coinage of silver, prohibition of alien ownership of land, reclamation from the railroads of lands held by them in excess of actual needs, reduction and equalization of taxation, the issue of fractional paper currency for use in the mails, and, finally, government ownership and operation of the means of communication and transportation.

The real contribution which this meeting made to the agrarian movement was contained in the report of the committee on the monetary system, of which C. W. Macune was chairman. This was the famous sub-treasury scheme, soon to become the paramount issue with the Alliance and the Populists in the South and in some parts of the West. The committee proposed "that the system of using certain banks as United States depositories be abolished, and in place of said system, establish in every county in each of the States that offers for sale during the one year $500,000 worth of farm products—including wheat, corn, oats, barley, rye, rice, tobacco, cotton, wool, and sugar, all together—a sub-treasury office." In connection with this office there were to be warehouses or elevators in which the farmers might deposit their crops, receiving a certificate of the deposit showing the amount and quality, and a loan of United States legal tender paper equal to eighty per cent of the local current value of the products deposited. The interest on this loan was to be at the rate of one per cent per annum; and the farmer, or the person to whom he might sell his certificate, was to be allowed one year in which to redeem the property; otherwise it would be sold at public auction for the satisfaction of the debt. This project was expected to benefit the farmers in two ways: it would increase and make flexible the volume of currency in circulation; and it would enable them to hold their crops in anticipation of a rise in price.

The Northwestern Alliance also hesitated to play the role of a third party, but it adopted a program which was virtually a party platform. In place of the sub-treasury scheme as a means of increasing the volume of currency in circulation and at the same time enabling the farmer to borrow money at low rates of interest, this organization favored the establishment of a land loan bureau operated by the Government. Legal tender currency to the amount of $100,000,000 or more if necessary, was to be placed at the disposal of this bureau for loans upon the security of agricultural land in amounts not to exceed one-half the value of the land and at an interest rate of two per cent per annum. These loans might run for twenty years but were to be payable at any time at the option of the borrower.

With two strong organizations assuming all the functions of political parties, except the nomination of candidates, the stage was set in 1890 for a drama of unusual interest. One scene was laid in Washington, where in the House and Senate and in the lobbies the sub-treasury scheme was aired and argued. Lending their strength to the men from the mining States, the Alliance men aided the passage of the Silver Purchase Act, the nearest approach to free silver which Congress could be induced to make. By the familiar practice of "log-rolling," the silverites prevented the passage of the McKinley tariff bill until the manufacturers of the East were willing to yield in part their objections to silver legislation. But both the tariff and the silver bill seemed to the angry farmers of the West mere bones thrown to the dog under the table. They had demanded *free* silver and had secured a mere increase in the amount to be purchased; they had called for a downward revision of the duties upon manufactured products and had been given more or less meaningless "protection" of their farm produce;

they had insisted upon adequate control of the trusts and had been presented with the Sherman Act, a law which might or might not curb the monopolies under which they believed themselves crushed. All the unrest which had been gathering during the previous decade, all the venom which had been distilled by fourteen cent corn and ten per cent interest, all the blind striving to frustrate the industrial consolidation which the farmer did not understand but feared and hated, found expression in the political campaign of 1890.

The Alliance suited its political activities to local necessities. In many of the Southern States, notably Florida, Georgia, and the Carolinas, Alliance men took possession of the Democratic conventions and forced both the incorporation of their demands into the platforms and the nomination of candidates who agreed to support those demands. The result was the control of the legislatures of five Southern States by members or supporters of the order and the election of three governors, one United States Senator, and forty-four Congressmen who championed the principles of the Alliance. In the West the Alliance worked by itself and, instead of dominating an old party, created a new one. It is true that the order did not formally become a political party; but its officers took the lead in organizing People's, Independent, or Industrial parties in the different States, the membership of which was nearly identical with that of the Alliance. Nor was the farmer alone in his efforts. Throughout the whole country the prices of manufactured articles had suddenly risen, and popular opinion, fastening upon the McKinley tariff as the cause, manifested itself in a widespread desire to punish the Republican party.

The events of 1890 constituted not only a political revolt but a social upheaval in the West. Nowhere was the overturn more complete than in Kansas. If the West in general was uneasy, Kansas was in the throes of a mighty convulsion; it was swept as by the combination of a tornado and a prairie fire. As a sympathetic commentator of later days put it, "It was a religious revival, a crusade, a pentecost of politics in which a tongue of flame sat upon every man, and each spake as the spirit gave him utterance." All over the State, meetings were held in schoolhouses, churches, and public halls. Alliance picnics were all-day expositions of the doctrines of the People's Party. Up and down the State, and from Kansas City to Sharon Springs, Mary Elizabeth Lease, "Sockless" Jerry Simpson, Anna L. Diggs, William A. Peffer, Cyrus Corning, and twice a score more, were in constant demand for lectures, while lesser lights illumined the dark places when the stars of the first magnitude were scintillating elsewhere.

Mrs. Lease, who is reported to have made 160 speeches in the summer and autumn of 1890, was a curiosity in American politics. Of Irish birth and New York upbringing, she went to Kansas and, before she was twenty years old, married Charles L. Lease. Twelve years later she was admitted to the bar. At the time of the campaign of 1890 she was a tall, mannish-looking, but not unattractive woman of thirty-seven years, the mother of four children. She was characterized by her friends as refined, magnetic, and witty; by her enemies of the Republican party as a hard, unlovely shrew. The hostile press made the most of popular prejudice against a woman stump speaker and attempted by ridicule and invective to drive her from the stage. But Mrs. Lease continued to talk. She it was who told the Kansas farmers that what they needed was to "raise less corn and more HELL!"

> Wall Street owns the country [she proclaimed]. It is no longer a government of the people, by the people, and for the people, but a government of Wall Street, by Wall Street, and for Wall Street. . . . Money rules, and our Vice-President is a London banker. Our laws are the output of a system that clothes rascals in robes and honesty in rags. The parties lie to us, and the political speakers mislead us. We were told two years ago to go to work and raise a big crop and that was all we needed. We went to work and plowed and planted; the rains fell, the sun shone, nature smiled, and we raised the big crop that they told us to; and what came of it? Eight-cent corn, ten-cent oats, two-cent beef, and no price at all for butter and eggs—that's what came of it. . . . The main question is the money question. . . . We want money, land, and transportation. We want the abolition of the National Banks, and we want the power to make loans directly from the Government. We want the accursed foreclosure system wiped out. Land equal to a tract 30 miles wide and 90 miles long has been foreclosed and bought in by loan companies of Kansas in a year. . . . The people are at bay, and the blood-hounds of money who have dogged us thus far beware!

A typical feature of this campaign in Kansas was the contest between Jerry Simpson and Colonel James R. Hallowell for a seat in Congress. Simpson nicknamed his fastidious opponent "Prince Hal" and pointed to his silk stockings as an evidence of aristocracy. Young Victor Murdock, then a cub reporter, promptly wrote a story to the effect that Simpson himself wore no socks at all. "Sockless Jerry," "Sockless Simpson," and then "Sockless Socrates" were sobriquets then and thereafter applied to the stalwart Populist. Simpson was at this time forty-eight years old, a man with a long, square-jawed face, his skin tanned by exposure on shipboard, in the army, and on the farm, and his mustache cut in a straight line over a large straight mouth. He wore clerical eyeglasses and unclerical clothes. His opponents called him clownish; his friends declared him Lincolnesque. Failing to make headway against him by ridicule, the Republicans arranged a series of joint debates between the candidates; but the audience at the first meeting was so obviously partial to Simpson that Hallowell refused to meet him again. The supporters of the "sockless" statesman, though less influential and less prosperous than those of Hallowell, proved more numerous and triumphantly elected him to Congress. In Washington he acquitted himself creditably and was perhaps disappointingly conventional in speech and attire.

The outcome of this misery, disgust, anger, and hatred on the part of the people of Kansas focused by shrewd common sense and rank demagogism, was the election of five Populist Congressmen and a large Populist majority in the lower house of the state legislature; the Republican state officers were elected by greatly reduced majorities. In Nebraska, the People's Independent party obtained a majority of the members of the legislature and reduced the Republican party to third place in the vote for governor, the victory going to the Democrats by a very small plurality. The South Dakota Independent party, with the president of the state Alliance as its standard bearer, was unable to defeat the Republican candidates for state offices but obtained the balance of power in the legislature. In Indiana, Michigan, and Minnesota, the new party movement manifested considerable strength, but, with the exception of one Alliance Congressman from Minnesota and a number of legislators, the fruits of its activity were gathered by the Democrats.

Among the results of the new party movements in the Western States in 1890 should be included the election of two United States Senators, neither of whom was a farmer, although both were ardent advocates of the farmers' cause. In South Dakota, where no one of the three parties had a majority in the legislature, the Reverend James H. Kyle, the Independent candidate, was elected to the United States Senate, when, after thirty-nine ballots, the Democrats gave him their votes. Kyle, who was only thirty-seven years old at this time, was a Congregational minister, a graduate of Oberlin College and of Allegheny Theological Seminary. He had held pastorates in Colorado and South Dakota, and at the time of his election was financial agent for Yankton College. A radical Fourth of July oration which he delivered at Aberdeen brought him into favor with the Alliance, and he was elected to the state senate on the Independent ticket in 1890. Prior to this election Kyle had been a Republican.

The other senatorial victory was gained in Kansas, where the choice fell on William A. Peffer, whose long whiskers made him a favorite object of ridicule and caricature in Eastern papers. He was born in Pennsylvania in 1831, and as a young man had gone to California during the gold boom. Returning after two years with a considerable sum of money, he engaged in farming first in Indiana and then in Missouri. When the Civil War began, his avowed Unionist sentiments got him into trouble; and in 1862 he moved to Illinois, where after a few months he enlisted in the army. At the close of the war he settled in Tennessee and began the practice of law, which he had been studying at intervals for a number of years. He removed in 1870 to Kansas, where he played some part in politics as a Republican, was elected to the state senate, and served as a delegate to the national convention of 1880. After a number of newspaper ventures he became the editor of the *Kansas Farmer* of Topeka in 1880 and continued in that position until he was elected to the United States Senate. He was a member of the Knights of Labor and was an ardent prohibitionist and, above all, an advocate of currency inflation.

After the elections of November, 1890, came definite action in the direction of forming a new national party. The Citizens' Alliance, a secret political organization of members of the Southern Alliance, held a convention with the Knights of Labor at Cincinnati on May 19, 1891. By that time the tide of sentiment in favor of a new party was running strong. Some fourteen hundred delegates, a majority of whom were from the five States of Ohio, Kansas, Indiana, Illinois, and Nebraska, attended the convention and provided for a committee to make arrangements, in conjunction with other reform organizations if possible, for a convention of the party to nominate candidates for the presidential election of 1892. To those who were anxious to have something done immediately the process of preparing the ground for a new third party seemed long and laborious. Seen in its proper perspective, the movement now appears to have been as swift as it was inevitable. Once more, and with greater unanimity than ever before, the farmers, especially in the West, threw aside their old party allegiance to fight for the things which they deemed not only essential to their own welfare but beneficial to the whole country. Some aid, it is true, was brought by labor, some by the mining communities of the mountain region, some by various reform organizations; but the movement as a whole was distinctly and essentially agrarian.

The advent of the Populists as a full-fledged party in the domain of national politics took place at Omaha in July, 1892. Nearly thirteen hundred delegates from all parts of the Union flocked to the convention to take part in the selection of candidates for President and Vice-President and to adopt a platform for the new party. The "Demands" of the Alliances supplied the material from which was constructed a platform characterized by one unsympathetic observer as "that furious and hysterical arraignment of the present times, that incoherent intermingling of Jeremiah and Bellamy." The document opened with a general condemnation of national conditions and a bitter denunciation of the old parties for permitting "the existing dreadful conditions to develop without serious effort to prevent or restrain them." Then followed three declarations: "that the union of the labor forces of the United States this day consummated shall be permanent and perpetual"; that "wealth belongs to him who creates it, and every dollar taken from industry without an equivalent is robbery"; and "that the time has come when the railroad corporations will either own the people or the people must own the railroads." Next came the demands. Heading these were the monetary planks: "a national currency, safe, sound, and flexible, issued by the general Government only, a full legal tender for all debts," with the sub-treasury system of loans "or a better system; free and unlimited coinage of silver and gold at the present legal ratio of sixteen to one"; and an increase in the circulating medium until there should be not less than $50 per capita. With demands for a graduated income tax, for honesty and economy in governmental expenditures, and for postal savings banks, the financial part of the platform was complete. The usual plank declaring for government ownership and control of railroads and telegraphs now included the telephone systems as well, and the land plank opposed alien ownership and demanded the return of lands held by corporations in excess of their actual needs. Other resolutions, adopted but not included in the platform, expressed sympathy with labor's demands for shorter hours, condemned the use of Pinkerton detectives in labor strife, and favored greater restriction of immigration, the initiative and referendum, direct election of United States senators, and one term for the President and Vice-President.

The platform, according to a news dispatch of the time, was "received with tremendous enthusiasm . . . and was read and adopted almost before the people knew it was read. Instantly there was enacted the mightiest scene ever witnessed by the human race. Fifteen thousand people yelled, shrieked, threw papers, hats, fans, and parasols, gathered up banners, mounted shoulders. Mrs. Lease's little girl was mounted on Dr. Fish's shoulders—he on a table on a high platform. The two bands were swamped with noise. . . . Five minutes passed, ten minutes, twenty, still the noise and hurrahs poured from hoarse throats." After forty minutes the demonstration died out and the convention was ready to proceed with the nomination of a presidential candidate.

No such unanimity marked this further procedure, however. Just before the convention the leaders of the People's Party had thrown the old parties into consternation by announcing that Judge Walter Q. Gresham, of Indiana, would be offered the nomination. Judge Gresham, a Republican with a long and honorable public record, had been urged upon the Republican party in 1884 and 1888, and "Anti-Monopolists" had considered him with favor on account of his opinions and decisions regarding the operation and control of railroads. Just after the adoption of the platform a telegram from the judge announced that he would accept a unanimous nomination. Since unanimity was unobtainable, however, his name was withdrawn later in the day.

This left the field to General James B. Weaver of Iowa and Senator James H. Kyle of South Dakota. Weaver represented the more conservative of the Populists, the old Alliance men. His rival had the support of the most radical element as well as that of the silver men from the mountain States. The silverites were not inclined to insist upon their man, however, declaring that, if the platform contained the silver plank, they would carry their States for whatever candidate might be chosen. The old campaigner proved the stronger, and he was nominated with General James G. Field of Virginia for Vice-President. Unprejudiced observers viewed Weaver's nomination as a tactical error on the part of the Populist leaders: "Mr. Weaver has belonged to the group of third-party 'come-outers' for so many years that his name is not one to conjure with in either of the old camps; . . . his name suggests too strongly the abortive third-party movements of the past to excite much hope or enthusiasm. He is not exactly the sort of a Moses who can frighten Pharaoh into fits or bring convincing plagues upon the monopolistic oppressors of Israel. The wicked politicians of the Republican and Democratic parties breathed easier and ate with better appetites when the Gresham bogie disappeared and they found their familiar old enemy, General Weaver, in the lead of the People's movement."

It may be suspected, however, that even with Weaver at its head this party, which claimed to control from two to three million votes, and which expected to draw heavily from the discontented ranks of the old-line organizations, was not viewed with absolute equanimity by the campaign managers of Cleveland and of Harrison. Some little evidence of the perturbation appeared in the equivocal attitude of both the old parties with respect to the silver question. Said the Democratic platform: "We hold to the use of both gold and silver as the standard money of the country, and to the coinage of both gold and silver without discrimination against either metal or charge for mintage." The rival Republican platform declared that "the American people, from tradition and interest, favor bimetallism, and the Republican party demands the use of both gold and silver as standard money." Each party declared for steps to obtain an international agreement on the question. The Republicans attempted to throw a sop to the labor vote by favoring restriction of immigration and laws for the protection of employees in dangerous occupations, and to the farmer by pronouncements against trusts, for extended postal service—particularly in rural districts—and for the reclamation and sale of arid lands to settlers. The Democrats went even further and demanded the return of "nearly one hundred million acres of valuable land" then held by "corporations and syndicates, alien and domestic."

The directors of the Populist campaign proved to be no mean political strategists. General Weaver himself toured the country, accompanied by General Field when he was in the South and by Mrs. Lease when he went to the Pacific coast. Numerous other men and women addressed the thousands who attended the meetings, great and small, all over the country. One unique feature of the Populist campaign on the Pacific coast was the singing of James G. Clark's *People's Battle-Hymn,* and other songs expressing the hope and fears of labor in the field and factory. Everywhere it was the policy of the new party to enlist the assistance of the weaker of the old parties. In the South, the Populists, as a rule, arrayed themselves with the Republicans against the old Democracy. This provoked every device of ridicule, class prejudice, and scorn, which the dominant party could bring to bear to dissuade former Democrats from voting the People's ticket. One Louisiana paper uttered this warning:

> Oily-tongued orators, in many cases the paid agents of the Republican party, have for months been circulating among the unsophisticated and more credulous classes, preaching their heresies and teaching the people that if Weaver is elected president, money may be had for the asking, transportation on the railroad trains will be practically free, the laboring man will be transferred from his present position and placed upon a throne of power, while lakes filled with molasses, whose shores are fringed with buckwheat cakes, and islands of Jersey butter rising here and there above the surface, will be a concomitant of every farm. The "forty-acres-and-a-mule" promises of the reconstruction era pale into insignificance beside the glowing pictures of prosperity promised by the average Populist orator to those who support Weaver.

The *Pensacola Address* of the Populist nominees on September 17, 1892, which served as a joint letter of acceptance, was evidently issued at that place and time partly for the purpose of influencing such voters as might be won over by emphasizing the unquestioned economic distress of most Southern farmers. If the new party could substantiate the charges that both old parties were the tools of monopoly and Wall Street, it might insert the wedge which would eventually split the "solid South." Even before the *Pensacola Address,* the state elections in Alabama and Arkansas demonstrated that cooperation of Republicans with Populists was not an idle dream. But, although fusion was effected on state tickets in several States in the November elections, the outcome was the choice of Cleveland electors throughout the South.

As the Populists tried in the South to win over the Republicans, so in the North and more especially the West they sought to control the Democratic vote either by fusion or absorption. The effort was so successful that in Colorado, Idaho, Kansas, Nevada, and North Dakota, the new party swept the field with the assistance of the Democrats. In South Dakota and Nebraska, where there was no fusion, the Democratic vote was negligible and the Populists ran a close second to the Republicans.

That the tide of agrarianism was gradually flowing westward as the frontier advanced is apparent from the election returns in the States bordering on the upper Mississippi. Iowa and Missouri, where the Alliance had been strong, experienced none of the landslide which swept out the Republicans in States further west. In Minnesota the Populists, with a ticket headed by the veteran Donnelly, ran a poor third in the state election, and the entire Harrison electoral ticket was victorious in spite of the endorsement of four Populist candidates by the Democrats. In the northwestern part of the State, however, the new party was strong enough to elect a Congressman over candidates of both the old parties. In no Northern State east of the Mississippi were the Populists able to make a strong showing; but in Illinois, the success of John P. Altgeld, the Democratic candidate for governor, was due largely to his advocacy of many of the measures demanded by the People's party, particularly those relating to labor, and to the support which he received from the elements which might have been expected to align themselves with the Populists. On the Pacific coast, despite the musical campaign of Clark, Mrs. Lease, and Weaver, California proved deaf to the People's cause; but in Oregon the party stood second in the lists and in Washington it ran a strong third.

More than a million votes, nearly nine per cent of the total, were cast for the Populist candidates in this election—a record for a third party the year after its birth, and one exceeded only by that of the Republican party when it appeared for the first time in the national arena in 1856. Twenty-two electoral votes added point to the showing, for hitherto, since 1860, third-party votes had been so scattered that they had affected the choice of President only as a makeweight between other parties in closely contested States.

A week after the elections General Weaver announced that the Populists had succeeded far beyond their expectations. "The Republican party," he asserted, "is as dead as the Whig party was after the Scott campaign of 1852, and from this time forward will diminish in every State of the Union and cannot make another campaign. . . . The Populist will now commence a vigorous campaign and will push the work of organization and education in every county in the Union." There were those, however, who believed that the new party had made a great mistake in having anything to do with either of the old parties, that fusion, particularly of the sort which resulted in combination tickets, was a compromise with the enemy, and that more votes had been lost than won by the process. This feeling found characteristic expression in an editorial in a Minnesota paper:

> Take an audience of republican voters in a schoolhouse where a county fusion has taken place—or the press is full of the electoral deal—and the audience will applaud the sentiments of the speaker—but they wont vote a mongrel or democratic ticket! A wet blanket has been thrown!
>
> "Oh," says someone, "but the democratic party is a party of reform!" Well, my friend, you better go down south and talk that to the peoples party where they have been robbed of their franchises by fraud and outrage!
>
> Ah, and there the peoples party fused the republicans!!!
>
> Oh whitewash! Where is thy lime-kiln, that we may swab off the dark blemishes of the hour!! Aye, and on the whited wall, draw thee a picture of power and beauty—Cleveland, for instance, thanking the peoples party for all the favors gratuitously granted by our mongrel saints in speckled linen and green surtouts.

As time gave perspective, however, the opinion grew that 1892 had yielded all that could possibly have been hoped. The lessons of the campaign may have been hard, but they had been learned, and, withal, a stinging barb had been thrust into the side of the Republican party, the organization which, in the minds of most crusaders, was principally responsible for the creation and nurture of their ills. It was generally determined that in the next campaign Populism should stand upon its own feet; Democratic and Republican votes should be won by conversion of individuals to the cause rather than by hybrid amalgamation of parties and preelection agreements for dividing the spoils. But it was just this fusion which blinded the eyes of the old party leaders to the significance of the Populist returns. Democrats, with a clear majority of electoral votes, were not inclined to worry about local losses or to value incidental gains; and Republicans felt that the menace of the third party was much less portentous than it might have been as an independent movement.

✧✧✧

THE *final decade of the nineteenth century is remembered as "the gay nineties." It is a misnomer. Between 1893 and 1897, depression conditions prevailed; farm protest rose to a crescendo as it culminated in the Populist movement; and labor disorders reached peaks of violence in the Homestead and Pullman strikes. The decade finished in a "splendid little war" that introduced the United States into the ranks of empire builders. For the builders of the American dream it seemed a time heavy with portents of a coming catastrophe. Nowhere were the baneful expectations more widely*

proclaimed than in the new farmlands of the Great Plains. Agrarian spokes-
men quoted in wonder figures that indicated that in the quarter of a century
after the Civil War the value of farmlands had declined to between one-third
and one-half of their cost. Their awe increased as they contemplated the
three billion four hundred and twenty-two million dollars of farm mortgages
in the Western states. A nation of yeomen farmers seemed on the verge of
becoming one of tenant farmers.

As the prices of staples such as wheat, corn, cotton, oats, tobacco, and
meat produce steadily sagged, the conviction grew among staple farmers
that a conspiracy of the "money power," housed in the banking houses of
Wall Street and London's Lombard Street, worked without rest to dominate
and exploit the rest of the country. The farm alliances which had been
organized in the 1880's to aid the farmer through collective action entered
politics as the People's party in 1890. Their message had the virtue of
simplicity: it treated the depressed circumstances of agriculture as evidence
of a conflict between "the allied hosts of monopolies, the money power,
great trusts and railroad corporations who seek . . . to . . . impoverish the
people . . . and the farmers, laborers, merchants, and all other people
who produce wealth and bear the burdens of taxation."

In the elections of 1890, both major parties found internal dissension
threatening the foundations of their support. Southern agrarian radicals won
control of eight state legislatures and elected forty-four Alliance candidates
to Congress. In the Great Plains, spellbinding orators like Mary Ellen Lease
declaimed: "It is no longer a government of the people, by the people and
for the people, but a government of Wall Street, by Wall Street and for
Wall Street." Kansas gave a thumping triumph to Populist candidates while
elsewhere in the Plains states they cut deeply into Republican majorities.
The Republican representation in the House of Representatives was re-
duced to a mere 86 while that of the Democrats swelled to 235 and the
Populists sent a 10-man contingent. By 1892, the swelling Populist protest,
now a fully developed political party, insured an overwhelming Republican
defeat and the election of Grover Cleveland. The more than one million
Populist votes had carried Kansas, Colorado, Nevada, and Idaho.

In Nebraska, the once-obscure congressman William Jennings Bryan
won reelection to the House of Representatives, and the Populist message
found a Democratic orator who would in 1896 capture his party's presi-
dential nomination. In addition, the Populist platform of 1892, which com-
plained that the "prolific womb of governmental injustice . . . breeds the
two great classes—tramps and millionaires," set forth a list of demands
which proved a fertile source for subsequent reform agitation. Within little
more than two decades, the call for the direct election of senators and the
income tax would be incorporated into the Constitution. But more im-
mediately, the demand that silver be coined at a ratio to gold of 16 to 1
became the central issue of the election of 1896.

John D. Hicks (1890-   ) wrote the definitive account of the Populist
Movement. He also is the author of the most widely read of all American
history textbooks, The Federal Union. As Hicks indicates, Bryan embraced

the Populist banner and the Populist party accepted him as their spokesman. Although Bryan went down to defeat, the Populist image of justice was to captivate the imagination of the Democrats for almost two decades. It foredoomed them to fall steadily behind in the race for political predominance. As the Republicans took their stand in the urban-industrial America that was coming of age at century's end, the Democrats turned their gaze backward upon an agrarian America that was fast vanishing. It would be a full generation and more before the Republican ascendancy would end. The Populist revolt had not triumphed but it had spelled out in soaring words the dream of an America that never was except in the dreams of men.

THE POPULIST REVOLT

by John D. Hicks

Well before the date set for the opening of the Republican convention, June 16, the Populist leaders received positive assurance that Teller and his silver friends would bolt. Taubeneck, therefore, and a number of other prominent Populists put in their appearance at St. Louis, determined to persuade the bolting Republicans to throw in their lot with the third party. But the Populists were not alone in their desire to obtain help from the silver Republicans. "The Democrats had a large and influential lobby here," Taubeneck wrote to Donnelly, who had found it impossible to be present, "moving heaven and earth to get the bolting Republicans to join the Democratic party and go to the Chicago Convention. Bryan was here the entire week. Bland also had a strong lobby on the ground. We got in touch with the bolting Republicans before the Convention opened, and agreed upon a policy" that permitted the bolting Republicans to maintain a provisional organization; planned fusion with the Populists in the western states on electors, congressmen, and state and local tickets; and proposed that the silver Republicans join the Populists in their July convention. "I think we have received the full benefit of the Republican bolt for our party in the future," Taubeneck concluded. "The Democrats are exceedingly sore; especially the silver wing of the party. They have the arrogance to claim that the bolting Republicans ought to join them and that the Populists ought to endorse their National ticket."

But the definite stand taken by the regular Republicans in favor of the single gold standard worried the Populists. The logic of the situation called for a Democratic indorsement of free silver at Chicago, and the drift of Democratic sentiment in that direction seemed unmistakable. Should the gold wing win control at the Chicago convention, the Populist course at St. Louis would be easy, but suppose the Democrats should name a silver candidate upon a frankly silver platform? What then could the Populists do in the face of the nation-wide demand that the silver forces must unite?

Taubeneck, foreseeing this situation and realizing that an effort would be made by the Democrats "to swallow the People's party," conferred with the Populist leaders on the best course to pursue. Donnelly's advice, vouchsafed even before the Republican nominations had been made, was to induce the Democrats not to make nominations at Chicago but to meet for that purpose with the Populists at St. Louis. This was a fantastic suggestion, for beyond a doubt the Democrats would nominate their own candidates in their own convention. In general, however, western Populists were eager to get together with the Democrats on any possible terms. The southern Populists were obdurate, insisting that the third-party organization be maintained at all costs. Taubeneck told the southerners that he "would go as far as they could to accomplish that end," but he apparently decided that the only way to do it was for the Populists to demand that the Democrats nominate Teller. "We must take a firm stand that we will not endorse the nominee of the Chicago Convention if he should be a straight out Democrat," Taubeneck wrote to Donnelly. "They must take Teller or be responsible for the division of the silver forces at the polls next November."

From the Populist standpoint, there was much to be said in support of the Teller candidacy. Teller's dramatic withdrawal from the Republican convention had advertised him widely and had won great applause from all silverites, regardless of party. He would be far more acceptable to the southern Populists, who had long been allied with the Republicans in local politics, than any Democrat could possibly be. His nomination, moreover, would insure the support of all silver Republicans, whose assistance might be sorely needed, for in case the Democrats and Populists should agree upon any reliable silver man, the gold Democrats would certainly go over to the Republicans. Moreover, with Teller as their candidate, the Democrats and the Populists would both be in the position of having nominated an outsider to head their respective tickets. Neither could look down upon the other. Both organizations could be maintained; separate platforms could be written. Bland, on the other hand, whom the silver Democrats seemed disposed to support, was a strict party man and was regarded by some of the Populists as "especially unsafe upon the questions of national banks and the government issue of all paper money." "Suppose the Democrats give up their favorite sons Boies and Bland," wrote a Minnesota editor, "and the People's party forego the pleasure of nominating their great genius and splendid patriot Ignatius Donnelly, and all unite in the nomination of Henry M. Teller for president?"

There was opposition to Teller, however. It was urged that he represented only the silver corporations, who owned him "soul, body and breeches" and required him to take the step he took at St. Louis. He was not a Populist, never had been, and probably never would be. He had no more interest in the vast majority of the Populistic reforms than if he had been a Democrat or a regular Republican instead of a bolter. Furthermore, his chances of securing either the Democratic nomination or the Populist nomination were not bright. When Taubeneck and some others came out openly for Teller, a Nebraska correspondent wrote to Senator Allen, "Sorry to see those fellows

of yours indorsing Teller—won't do at all. Tail can't wag the dog this time."
Robert Schilling wrote an even more emphatic disapproval to Donnelly: "I
am raising hell about the Teller address. They wanted me to sign it, but I
refused point blank. These fellows ran off after strange gods at every
opportunity. Wonder if the Gresham blunder at Omaha was not enough?"
Nevertheless, when Taubeneck called a conference to meet at Chicago on
the eve of the Democratic convention "to see what can be done towards
getting the silver democrats to unite with us or in some way cooperate so
that we can all vote for one electoral ticket in the next campaign," the weight
of opinion still seemed to be that Teller's name at the head of both tickets
would be the best solution of the problem.

The Chicago convention came over to silver, as had been expected, but
Teller was not its nominee, even though Governor Altgeld of Illinois, "the
Hanna of the Democratic convention," seemed disposed at the outset to
swing the delegates in that direction. Passing by both Teller and Bland, the
convention took Bryan of Nebraska, an out-and-out Democrat, but one
who had long flirted with Populistic doctrines. For vice president, however,
it nominated Arthur M. Sewall of Maine, a well-to-do bank president, railway director, and shipbuilder, who had nothing whatever in common with
the Populists except his belief in free silver.

To say that Populism seethed and boiled after the Chicago results became
known is to put it mildly. Populist sentiment in the West was overwhelmingly in favor of the nomination of Bryan by the St. Louis convention.
Westerners knew that, Democrat though he professed to be, Bryan was in
fact the product of Populism. "We put him to school," Donnelly remarked
later on, "and he wound up by stealing the schoolbooks." True, the Chicago
platform did not go the whole length of Populism, but it did indorse free
silver, "without waiting for the aid or consent of any other nation"; it condemned the bond-selling policy of the Cleveland administration; it demanded
as an offset to the Supreme Court decision invalidating the income-tax
legislation of 1894 an amendment to the Constitution authorizing Congress
to levy such a tax; it urged stricter control of the railway systems by the
federal government; it denounced "government by injunction"; and it
branded Cleveland's recent military intervention in the Pullman Strike at
Chicago as "a crime against free institutions." The Chicago platform so far
as it went was satisfactory, and there were many to argue that the Populists
would do well to take a satisfactory candidate running on a partially satisfactory platform with some chance of being elected rather than to name a
candidate of their own on a platform more to their liking, with the full
knowledge that he had not the slightest chance to win.

The plea, duly fostered by the Democrats, that there should be only one
silver leader in the campaign was enormously effective in the West. Populists
were reminded that they had always professed to believe that principle
should be placed ahead of personal or party advantage. Here was a chance to
prove that they had meant what they said. Let the reform forces be divided
and the gold bugs would continue in control of the national government. Let
all who stood for silver unite, and at least this one reform stood a good

chance of success. "I care not for party names," said Jerry Simpson, "it is the substance we are after, and we have it in William J. Bryan." So also thought Weaver and Allen and a host of minor lights, some of whom had an eye on the loaves and fishes. "Should we be able to endorse Bryan at St. Louis," one enthusiastic Nebraskan pointed out, "and continue the combination for our state offices, . . . we can make a clean sweep." Practical politicians pointed out, too, that the bulk of the Populist vote in the West would go to Bryan, whether he received the Populist nomination or not. Donnelly was told by some of his Minnesota friends that nine-tenths of the Minnesota Populists would vote for Bryan under any circumstances.

Others, however, feared the results of fusion and sounded a note of warning. Peffer of Kansas was afraid of it and came around to Bryan most reluctantly. "There are only two points of which I feel tenacious," he said as the Populists gathered at St. Louis. "The first is to maintain our party organization; the second is to combine the silver vote of the country." A few preferred the frank abandonment of all third-party organization to fusion. "I am in favor of meeting the new democratic party half way," wrote one Nebraska Populist. "If they will give up the name 'Democratic' we should be willing to give up the name 'People's Party.' In union there is strength. Let us all unite as one party with one banner, one name and no fusion. A union is not fusion." A fair number of northern Populists—intransigents such as Donnelly, Coxey, and Weller—protested against the drift towards Bryan. Weller felt that Bryan's nomination at St. Louis would be "construed as a surrender of the People's party movement and the destruction of their present magnificent organization." According to Donnelly, "the Democratic party has now moved up and taken possession of the ground we occupied four years ago. We are glad to see it. This result of the prowess of education is encouraging, but we do not propose to abandon the post of teacher and turn it over to our slow and stupid scholar."

As for the southern Populists, they were almost a unit in their opposition to Bryan. This was not due to any great dislike for the man himself or for his principles. Rather they agreed with Weller that an indorsement of Bryan by the Populists would come dangerously near to ringing the death knell of the party. The Democratic platform, they argued, was a deliberate plagiarism of Populist doctrines, designed not to be carried out but only to win third-party men back to their old allegiance. What had fusion done to the Greenback party a few years before? "Don't be deceived," one Populist editor cautioned his readers. "Experience should teach us to 'fear the Greeks even when bearing gifts.'" Nor could southern Populists forget the rancor that their local campaigns against strongly intrenched Democratic machines had aroused. Men who had turned Populist had been ostracized socially, had been discriminated against in business, had suffered personal insults and even physical injuries. How could they now unite with the enemy? "For God's sake don't indorse Bryan," a Texas Populist wrote to one of the St. Louis delegates. "Our people are firm, confident and enthusiastic; don't betray their trust. Don't try to force us back into the Democratic party; we won't go."

The atmosphere at St. Louis, while the delegates gathered, was heavily charged. Rumors were rife that if the convention indorsed Bryan the mid-roaders would bolt and that if it failed to indorse Bryan those who favored fusion would bolt. The Democrats were on hand, led by Senator Jones of Arkansas, to make sure that the Chicago ticket was indorsed. Hanna's "paid agents" were likewise on hand, or at least were supposed to be, in order to carry the convention against fusion.

Taubeneck was in a most perplexed state of mind. Following the Chicago convention he had been disposed to favor Bryan, but after communicating with Populist leaders all over the country, he had reached the conclusion that not over sixty per cent of the Populist vote could be delivered to the Chicago ticket and that a separate ticket must therefore be constructed. Presently, however, he reversed himself, or, as the mid-roaders contended, he "got in out of the wet," fearing that otherwise he would lose his job in case Bryan were nominated.

Plans of compromise were suggested, the most common being for the Populists to name a separate national ticket but to combine with the Democrats on fusion electoral tickets. After the election all the silver electors could support the candidate of the stronger faction for president and the candidate of the weaker faction for vice president. Senator Jones announced for the Democrats that this would never do; but the number of mid-road delegates appeared to be appallingly large, and clearly some concessions would have to be made to them.

Fortunately for the fusionists there was no obvious mid-road candidate for the presidential nomination. Donnelly of Minnesota and Vandervoort of Nebraska were willing enough, but they lacked followers. Debs was suggested, but he was a Socialist, not a Populist. Allen would have suited many, but he was known to be ardently for Bryan. Mimms of Tennessee, Towne of Minnesota, Davis of Texas, and many others were mentioned, but none aroused enthusiasm. At the end of the first day's session irreconcilables from twenty-one states met together and agreed to support S. F. Norton of Illinois for president and Frank Burkett of Mississippi for vice president; but they had very little reason to prefer these candidates over any of the others. The fusionists, by way of contrast, had only one candidate, and they knew exactly what they wanted.

When the time came for the selection of a temporary chairman of the St. Louis convention, the national committee put forward Senator Marion Butler of North Carolina, as a man who might draw support from both factions. Butler shared with other southerners the view that the Populist organization must be maintained at all costs, but he had come around to the view that the Populists, by nominating Bryan outright instead of merely indorsing him, might retain their separate identity. The Bryanites would have preferred Weaver or Field as temporary chairman, and the mid-roaders talked of Donnelly, O. D. Jones of Missouri, and others; but finally all opposition to Butler died down, and he was selected by acclamation. As keynoter the young North Carolinian—he was still in his early thirties—talked too long and wearied his audience. But his protest against making the Populist party an annex to either of the old parties was well received. "Let us find the truth in the middle way," he counseled.

The compromise on the temporary chairmanship merely postponed the inevitable struggle for supremacy, which came on the matter of permanent organization. After the temporary organization was completed the convention adjourned until eight o'clock in the evening to give the committee on permanent organization time to formulate its report. The mid-road element, still confident that it could control the convention, planned a great demonstration for the evening session, but on reassembling they found that the lights were off. Candles were lighted, but the demonstration fizzled out in the gloom, and Butler adjourned the convention to meet next day at ten o'clock. Twenty-five minutes after Butler had declared the convention adjourned, however, the lights once again burned brightly, and the mid-roaders, remembering that a similar maneuver was reputed to have defeated Blaine for the Republican nomination in 1876, asserted vociferously that they had been the victims of foul play. "The fusion gang manipulated the convention like an expert machine," one irate editor reported. "They even had a string to the electric light switch board, and when darkness was thought to be needed to confound the middle-of-the-roaders, the electric lights were turned off."

Whatever the situation might have been had the lights not gone out, next morning the fusionists were clearly in the majority. The convention call had awarded to each state a delegate for every senator and representative it had in Congress and an additional delegate for each two thousand votes or majority fraction thereof cast for Populist candidates in 1892, 1894, or 1895, the highest vote cast controlling. This gave undue strength to the states where fusion had been undertaken at one time or another and tended to favor the West at the expense of the South. Furthermore, the Bryan propaganda was exceedingly effective, and many who came as mid-roaders presently voted with the fusionists. The majority report of the committee on permanent organization named Senator William V. Allen of Nebraska—a strong advocate of fusion—for the permanent chairmanship, and the minority report named James E. Campion of Maine, a somewhat obscure mid-roader. The vote on adoption of the majority report stood 758 to 564 and fairly stated the ratio of strength between the two contending factions. In taking the chair Allen called attention to the banners that read, "Keep in the Middle of the Road," urging the Populists to go even further and "occupy the whole road." Perhaps his figure of speech was farfetched, but everyone knew that he meant to advocate a union of the silver forces.

The election of Allen as permanent chairman indicated for a certainty the nomination of Bryan, and the contest between the mid-roaders and the fusionists at once shifted to Sewall. It might be argued that Bryan was a Populist in all but name, but by no stretch of the imagination could such a thing be said of Sewall. There was no sounder Populistic doctrine than that the national banks should be abolished, and Sewall was a national banker. Government ownership, or at the very least rigid government control, of the railroads had always been advocated by the Populists, and Sewall was a railway director. Add to these disqualifications such others as that Sewall was the head of one trust, the partial owner of others, an easterner, and a man of wealth, and the reasons why many Populists struck at registering any approval of him whatever seem abundantly clear. Many third-party men who were strongly for Bryan balked at Sewall. "If we elect Bryan," said one of these, "and he should be killed by some assassin by order of the money power, we would want a different man from Sewall."

Nevertheless, the more influential fusionists such as Weaver and Allen advocated nominating Sewall as well as Bryan. In case this were done the Democrats were known to be willing to agree on fusion electoral tickets and Senator Jones, chairman of the Democratic national committee, promised also to give the Populists and the silver Republicans representation on a union executive committee to carry on the campaign. Moreover, the same candidate for president and different candidates for vice president would complicate the situation immeasurably. Senator Jones held that the Populists had no choice but to name both Democratic candidates or neither; and the fusionists among the Populists, mostly of this opinion also, planned to nominate Bryan at once, then adjourn until they could talk the delegates into taking Sewall.

But the danger of a split in the party should Sewall receive the Populist nomination loomed larger as the convention wore on. Butler and others urged the Democrats to drop Sewall and permit the nomination of a Populist as the fusion candidate for vice president, but Jones refused point-blank to consider such a proposition. Then someone suggested that the convention reverse the usual order and name the vice-presidential candidate first. The idea spread like wildfire, and presently a minority report from the committee on rules, advocating this procedure, brought the question directly before the convention.

Naturally enough all the anti-Bryan people supported this modification of the rules. They knew that Sewall would be far easier to defeat than Bryan, and they hoped that with Sewall off the ticket they could yet persuade the convention to nominate a mid-road candidate for president. Others felt that, even if Bryan were to win the nomination for president, the Populists were entitled to their own man for vice president. With a Populist candidate actually named, probably the Democrats could yet be persuaded to withdraw Sewall. Furthermore, with at least a vice-presidential candidate of their own the Populists could preserve their own organization and would be in less danger of suffering complete assimilation by the Democrats. That the man chosen should be a southern Populist was generally conceded. When the matter was brought to a vote, the mid-road element scored a victory. There was much changing of sides, but on every count the minority report was adopted by a majority of about a hundred.

This striking mid-road victory took the breath of the Democratic leaders at St. Louis. Senator Jones telegraphed hurriedly to Bryan, "Populists nominate Vice-President first. If not Sewall, what shall we do? I favor your declination in that case. Answer quick." To which Bryan promptly replied: "I entirely agree with you. Withdraw my name if Sewall is not nominated." And by way of emphasis the Democratic nominee also wired to Chairman

Allen, whom he knew well, "I shall not be candidate before the Populist convention unless Sewall is nominated." Bryan's wire to Jones, which was made public before the vote on vice president was taken, had all the appearance of an ultimatum, and on the strength of this statement Senator Jones gave out the news that if Sewall were not named, Bryan would decline even if nominated. But Senator Allen, as chairman of the Populist convention, refused to take the threat of Bryan's declination seriously. Allen kept to himself the information he had just received, and he declined to permit an announcement of Bryan's attitude to come before the convention, which meantime had launched upon the business of making nominating speeches and was in the midst of a tremendous oratorical orgy.

The nominating speeches put before the convention the names of Arthur Sewall of Maine, Harry Skinner of North Carolina, Frank Burkett of Mississippi, A. L. Mimms of Tennessee, Mann Page of Virginia, and Thomas E. Watson of Georgia. The contest that ensued was in a sense three-cornered. Sewall received the support of the extreme fusionists. Burkett, in particular, and probably all the other nominees except Watson were put forward by the extreme mid-roaders. Watson was the candidate of the compromisers, who, as Donnelly said in a speech seconding Watson's nomination, were "willing to swallow Democracy gilded with the genius of a Bryan" but were unable to "stomach plutocracy in the body of Sewall."

The Watson candidacy was carefully planned. At the end of the first day's session a group of compromisers, foreseeing that if the Bryanites and the mid-roaders could not be brought together, the convention would be hopelessly split, wired Watson of Georgia—as extreme a mid-road Populist as ever breathed or wrote—asking him if he would consent to run on a ticket with Bryan. Watson consented, believing undoubtedly that the Democrats would withdraw Sewall and that the names of Bryan and Watson would head both tickets. Most of the compromisers at St. Louis believed the same thing, and many of them insisted that Chairman Jones of the national Democratic committee had promised them as much.

When the vote was taken it became clear that Watson and the policy with which his candidacy was identified had a large majority in the convention. At sixteen minutes to one on the morning of July 25 his nomination was announced. Most of the Populists were satisfied, but the Democrats sulked. "Wall Street bankers and McKinley managers wild with delight over convention's action yesterday," one New Yorker wired to Allen. "They felt crushed at prospect silver forces being combined. Today they bet ten to one on McKinley and gold."

A long and typically Populistic platform, featuring as usual finance, transportation, and land, had already been adopted, so that all that now remained for the convention to do was to nominate Bryan and adjourn. The one serious obstacle in the way of this program was Bryan's declaration that he would not be a candidate in case Sewall were not nominated. Allen wired Bryan asking that his telegram of declination be withdrawn, but apparently received no answer; so Bryan's name went before the convention along with that of S. F. Norton, on whom the mid-roaders had united for a last stand.

While the vote was being taken, however, word was passed about that Allen had just received and had refused to communicate to the convention a telegram announcing that Bryan would not run if nominated. One delegate asked Allen point-blank if this were true. Allen promptly replied that it was not. Meantime Governor Stone of Missouri asked permission to read to the convention a message that he had received from Bryan, but Allen refused to give Stone the floor, explaining later that the Populist convention could have nothing to do with a purely Democratic negotiation. When the vote was finally counted it showed 1,042 for Bryan to 321 for Norton, with 12 votes scattered. Doubtless as a means of insurance against what Bryan might do, Allen asked and received for the national committee permission to exercise plenary power after the adjournment of the convention. To some observers, however, it appeared that this right of the committee to do all things that the convention might do if it were in session was obtained in order to make it possible later on to "roll" Watson in favor of Sewall.

Apparently there were very few Populists who were entirely satisfied with the outcome at St. Louis. Western Populists were happy at the nomination of Bryan and extremely appreciative of the part Chairman Allen had played in bringing about that result, but they regretted that Sewall's name had been left off the ticket and were deeply concerned as to how they could manage with two vice-presidential candidates. Southern Populists doubted the wisdom of the Bryan nomination and denounced Allen, whom they blamed for bringing it about, in unmeasured terms. "Never did Reed of Maine exercise more autocratic power over the lower house than did Allen in his capacity as presiding officer," one southern editor complained. With Watson the southerners were satisfied, however, and to make way for the fiery Georgian they demanded vociferously that Sewall either resign his place on the ticket or be "taken down." A common opinion was that "Mr. Bryan must take his choice of a running mate. If he is a friend of the people, as he claims to be, he must turn from the millionaire banker and railroad magnate to the poor man, whose heart beats in sympathy with the common people."

Northern mid-roaders found little comfort in anything that the St. Louis convention had done. Some of them held a meeting immediately after the St. Louis convention had adjourned and passed a resolution that Bryan's unsuccessful rival for the Populist nomination, S. F. Norton of Chicago, should be declared the regular nominee in case Bryan failed to accept within thirty days. They were powerless, however, to enforce their resolution and could only lament the unhappy fate that had overtaken their party. "Our convention never should have been postponed until after those of the old parties with the object of catching the crumbs that might fall from their tables," a correspondent wrote to "Calamity" Weller. Donnelly probably felt worse than most of the mid-roaders, for when they had talked at St. Louis of making him their candidate, even the Minnesota delegation had gone back on him. "Our soul is weary of this whole business," he mourned. "We shall retire to our library. . . . In the domain of literature we have a realm of our own . . . and in it we will bestow the remaining years of our life."

Under the circumstances it was not easy for the Populists to organize for the campaign. The St. Louis convention thoughtfully left to the national committee, rather than to the presidential nominee, the task of choosing its own chairman, and the committee replaced Taubeneck with Butler of North Carolina. At once the problem of notifying the successful nominees presented itself. How was Bryan to accept the Populist nomination after having accepted the Democratic nomination? On certain items the two platforms were contradictory. To stand on both of them the versatility of the Nebraskan would be sorely taxed, for he would have to favor redeemable as well as irredeemable paper money and government control of the railroads no less than government ownership. Furthermore, how could Bryan, after all he had said, accept the Populist nomination when to do so implied his approval of Watson for vice-president? Bryan himself passed the word along to Senator Allen, who as chairman of the Populist convention would naturally head the notification committee, that perhaps the notification might best be sent by mail. Further, since the Populists had nominated him after his nomination and acceptance of the Chicago platform, they could not ask him to go beyond that platform or to abandon Mr. Sewall. Ultimately Butler announced that the People's party custom was not to notify its nominees and that no notifications would be made. Bryan therefore never accepted or rejected the Populist nomination. Watson unofficially accepted his nomination many times and refused to get out of Sewall's way, although often besought to do so. The Democratic idea of fusion, he insisted, was "that we play Jonah while they play whale." Small wonder that a correspondent urged Allen to "try and shut off Tom Watson. His egotism and injudicious talk is hurting us." But Watson talked on.

Under the leadership of Butler the Populist campaign was conducted in much closer harmony with the Democrats than the attitude of the St. Louis convention would seem to have justified. Fusion tickets of electors were arranged in twenty-eight states, the number of places allotted to Democrats and Populists following as closely as possible the ratio of votes polled by the two parties in the preceding election. Generally the Democrats got the larger number of electors, only seventy-eight Populist names occurring on the fusion tickets to one hundred and ninety-eight Democratic names.

In the South, where the only fusion that the Populists had ever known had been fusion with the Republicans, "Popocrat" tickets were hard to obtain, but five southern, or near-southern states—Missouri, Arkansas, Louisiana, Kentucky and North Carolina—succeeded in effecting such a combination. In the others the Democrats would give no quarter to the Populists, and even in Watson's own state, Georgia, the Populist ticket was finally withdrawn. Watson's insistence on remaining in the campaign was severely criticized, particularly in view of the fact that, even if Bryan should have been elected, there would probably have been no majority for any one of the three candidates for vice president, and the Republican Senate would surely have chosen Hobart in preference to Sewall.

In those western states where local elections were held in 1896, fusion on state and congressional tickets followed national fusion as a matter of course. This was true not only in the states of the Middle Border, Kansas, Nebraska, the Dakotas, and Minnesota, but also in some of the farther western states, such as Montana, Washington, and Idaho. In Colorado the unhappy experience of the state under Waite militated against any combination of Populists and Democrats. The best the Populists could do was to secure the help of the National Silver party; while the bulk of the Republicans, as silver Republicans, joined forces with the Democrats. In the southern states fusion between the Populists and the Democrats on anything more than the national ticket was altogether too much to expect, except, perhaps, in South Carolina, where the Tillmanites held their lines intact. In Missouri, which may hardly be considered a southern state, the Populist candidate for governor withdrew, and his place on the ticket was not filled. Presumably this was to further the chances of Democratic success. In Arkansas the Populists ran candidates of their own for state offices but made no nominations for Congress. In Tennessee efforts to achieve fusion between the Democrats and the Populists were made, but they were unavailing.

In a number of the southern states the Populists accomplished "what a circus poster would advertise as a great dual feat—they fused with both the Democrats and Republicans. They voted the national ticket with the Democrats and the state ticket with the Republicans." This was not so difficult in Louisiana in view of the fact that the state election came early in the year and was over before Bryan was nominated. A number of Louisiana sugar planters who were out of sorts with the Democratic party because of the tariff law of 1894 joined with the Populists and the Republicans to nominate a full state ticket, which the regular Democrats were able to defeat only by use of the most drastic methods. In some of the parishes there was riot and bloodshed on election day, and the fusionists claimed that they were deliberately counted out. In Alabama the state executive committee of the People's party had met early in the year to consider a program of fusion in the state with the Republicans. "There are some kickers in our ranks against it," one who favored it wrote to Senator Allen. "Without it we are helpless." A strong minority of Alabama Republicans also opposed fusion, but the majority agreed to it, and a complete fusion ticket was finally named for state offices, although in most of the congressional districts each party went its own way. In Georgia no Republican state ticket was nominated. The Republican executive committee advised the Republican voters that they were at liberty to choose as individuals between Populist and the Democratic state tickets; but the chairman of this committee later issued an unofficial circular urging all Republicans to support the Populist ticket. A somewhat similar arrangement existed in Texas, and in North Carolina the Populists and Republicans supported the same candidates for all state offices except those of governor and lieutenant governor. In spite of this apparent disagreement with regard to the leading places on the state ticket, fusion in North Carolina actually went much further than elsewhere. In nearly all of the congressional districts, fusionist candidates received the support of both

parties, and in most of the counties combination tickets for membership in
the state legislature were arranged. Fusion seems ordinarily not to have
extended, however, to candidacies for county offices.

In general, these various fusion measures resulted from a popular demand
and were well received by the rank and file of third-party adherents. Men
who had fought against one another for years rejoiced to "lay aside their
petty differences and unite for the cause of humanity." Bryan was pictured
as less a Democrat than a Populist and his nomination as evidence that, at
least along national lines, the Democratic party was coming around to the
tenets of Populism. Reform journals vied with orthodox Democratic sheets
in their devotion to the "silver-tongued orator of the Platte" and the doctrines for which he stood. "I feel this year we are squarely aligned," one of
Allen's correspondents rejoiced, "the mass against the class, the honest
yeomanry of the land against the pampered owners of wealth, grown
arrogant by sanction of law. I hope and trust the time of our emancipation
has come."

There were nevertheless some doubting Thomases who questioned the
sincerity of the Democrats and feared that the chief result of the campaign
would be the destruction of the Populist party. Especially was this true in
the South, where the unscrupulous methods that the Democrats had long
used against their adversaries were not easily forgotten. "No consent on the
part of the People's Party voters of Texas to support Mr. Bryan," ran one
Southern pronouncement, "can be construed to mean an endorsement of the
corrupt gang in Texas." Southern Populists were also much offended by the
unwillingness of the Democrats to accept the Populist candidate for vice
president. "If Bryan does want our support," the same editor remarked, "he
ought to be willing to adopt the policy which will most certainly assure him
of that support, and that policy is to accept as a running mate a southern
Populist, named by the unanimous vote of the Populist national convention."

On one thing the Populists scored a complete victory. Their crusading
ardor was communicated in full to the Democrats, who, under Bryan's
leadership, treated the country to the most spectacular campaign it had ever
seen. Bryan himself traveled over thirteen thousand miles, visited two-thirds
of the states in the Union, and made during a period of fourteen weeks no
less than four hundred speeches. Lesser lights, Democrats and Populists alike,
imitated him to the best of their ability. Newspapers teemed with news of
the campaign, and editorial writers could think of little else to write about.
The whole campaign was marked by a tensely earnest study of the money
question. According to Professor Woodburn of Indiana University there
had not been such a tremendous interest in any political issue on the part
of the masses since the Civil War. "On the street, in the schoolhouse meeting,
in the debating club, wherever several are gathered together, the money
question has been seriously discussed. Voters have sought anxiously to know
the truth. Men who have never thought about the money question before
have given it their earnest attention." Professor Macy of Grinnell noted
this same "intense and unusual interest in the debate. Men and women sit for

hours listening to a presentation of facts and statistics. . . . Wherever men meet, in shop or by the way, they engage in financial discussion."

It was the tenacious insistence of the "Demopop" campaigners that forced the issue along this line. At the beginning of the canvass the Republicans tried other tactics. Ridicule was a standard weapon, one that William Allen White tried in his famous editorial, "What's the matter with Kansas?"

> We all know; yet here we are at it again. We have an old moss-back Jacksonian who snorts and howls because there is a bath-tub in the State House. We are running that old jay for Governor. We have another shabby, wild-eyed, rattle-brained fanatic who has said openly in a dozen speeches that "the rights of the user are paramount to the rights of the owner." We are running him for Chief Justice, so that capital will come tumbling over itself to get into the State. We have raked the ash-heap of failure in the State and found an old human hoop-skirt who has failed as a business man, who has failed as an editor, who has failed as a preacher, and we are going to run him for Congressman-at-large. He will help the looks of the Kansas delegation at Washington. Then we have discovered a kid without a law practice and have decided to run him for Attorney-General. Then for fear some hint that the State had become respectable, might percolate through the civilized portions of the nation, we have decided to send three or four harpies out lecturing, telling the people that Kansas is raising hell and letting corn go to weeds.

But the Populists had been called names before, and at least for the moment the Democrats were more interested in principle than in persons. The Republicans also tried to draw off the opposition into a discussion of the tariff, but all such efforts proved fruitless. The only thing left to do was to meet argument with argument, and this the Republicans finally did. Such men as Roosevelt and Hanna toured the Populist areas and reasoned earnestly with audiences that had already studied the financial question and understood what the orators were talking about. Tons of literature were distributed, much of which was carefully read and pondered. The fallacies of the silver arguments were painstakingly exposed, and sound money advocates vied with "Professor Coin" in the aptness of their illustrations and the lucidity of their statements. Probably also there was much intimidation of voters. Certainly the silver forces believed that the employees of "Railroads and other great corporations and industrial establishments" were told that, if Bryan won, their wages would be cut and their jobs might be forfeited. Rumors were rife, too, of the unlimited financial resources that the Republicans, under Hanna's leadership, would have at their disposal on election day. But the fusionists themselves, with at least one vested interest—the silver miners—on their side, did not lack entirely the sinews of political war.

The election results were a great disappointment to the fusion forces, who had confidently expected to win. Bryan's vote in the South and the West was magnificent, but even so he lost five states west of the Mississippi River and four states south of Mason and Dixon's Line. Could he have won all or most of these, as optimists among his supporters had hoped, he would have won the election without a single electoral vote from the region east of the Mississippi and north of the Ohio. The Bryan and Watson ticket polled only a little over two hundred thousand popular votes, but the Populist strength was not fairly indicated by this figure, since many Populists voted for Bryan and Sewall. Watson finally received twenty-seven votes in the electoral college, although some regularly chosen Populist electors deserted him for Sewall. In Congress the Republicans won a comfortable majority in both houses over all other parties. The Populists, however, showed an increase. Some twenty-five members of the new House of Representatives classified themselves as Populists, silverites, or fusionists, and in the next Congressional Directory six senators were designated as Populists.

In the West, wherever fusion tickets for state office had been agreed upon, the odds were strongly in favor of the combination. In Kansas, Nebraska, South Dakota, Montana, Idaho, and Washington the fusionists swept everything before them, usually electing a majority in both houses of the state legislature, as well as all the state executive officers. In Colorado, however, the Democratic-Silver Republican ticket emerged far in the lead, and in Minnesota and North Dakota the triumph of the Republicans was complete.

In the South the attempts of the Populists to combine with the Republicans on state offices were more successful than might have been expected under the circumstances. In Georgia, Alabama, and Texas the Populists, with the help of the Republicans, were able, according to the election returns, to poll over forty per cent of the votes cast. But for the frauds, which were as apparent as in the two preceding campaigns, the Populists were confident that they would have won. Tillmanism carried the day in South Carolina as usual; and the combination of Republicans and Populists won a sweeping victory in North Carolina.

The election of 1896 in North Carolina constitutes one of the few outstanding episodes in the history of southern Populism. The legislature of 1895, which had a Republican-Populist majority in both houses, had passed a drastic election law to prevent corruption at the polls. Under the terms of this act, which a Democratic governor had signed, each party was guaranteed a representation on all registration and election boards, and heavy punishments were prescribed for both vote-buying and vote-selling. The law worked reasonably well, and for perhaps the first time since the emergence of the "solid South" non-Democratic voters in a strictly southern state had a chance to show approximately their full strength. The Republican candidates for governor and lieutenant governor were elected, and also the full fusionist slate for the minor state offices. Three Republicans and four Populists out of a total delegation of nine were chosen to Congress, and a Populist-Republican majority was returned in both houses of the state legislature.

So far as the number of Populists elected to office in 1896 was concerned, the third party had done very well, but there was nevertheless abundant reason for discouragement. Populists had been urged to drop everything else for a joint campaign with the Democrats to secure the free and unlimited coinage of silver. They had been assured that, if only they would do this, victory would crown their cause. They had made the sacrifice, had subordinated their party to principle, as requested; but the victory was lacking. Thousands of Populists, moreover, judging by the popular vote, had deliberately gone over to the Democrats, and thanks to the welding influence of a heated campaign against a common enemy, they bade fair to stay where they were. Also, the third-party machinery had suffered from too much Democratic tinkering and would be difficult to repair. Optimists there were to shout that the reform forces were not downhearted, that "just four years after the defeat at Bull Run, General Lee signed the treaty of peace at Appomattox," but the pessimists were much more in evidence. They blamed Butler for his campaign policy of working hand-in-glove with the Democrats. They blamed Bryan and the Democrats for their heartless disregard of Watson. They blamed themselves for ever consenting to an unholy alliance with the enemy. And they conceded freely that the Populist party as a great and independent organization was a thing of the past.

◆§ ξ◆

THROUGH *the nineteenth century the United States was steadily expanding, but until the final decade of that century, Americans assumed territorial accessions would be followed by statehood. The decision to annex the Philippines carried with it the candid admission that Americans did not expect the Oriental archipelago to achieve statehood. Quite the reverse, Americans justified their annexation as fulfillment of the destiny of a great nation "on whose growth and career from the beginning the Ruler of Nations has plainly written the high command and pledge of civilization." It added point to Rudyard Kipling's dedication of his poem "The White Man's Burden" to the United States as tribute to its decision to pick up the burden in the Philippines.*

The debate over annexation of the faraway islands added sharp point to the return match between McKinley and Bryan in 1900. The incumbent President had rationalized his decision to support annexation as necessary to educate the Filipinos, as well as to "uplift and civilize and Christianize" them. The latter point had particular sharpness since the Filipinos were nominal Catholics. His congressional supporters took the same tack and concluded the Filipinos as "Orientals, Malays, instructed by Spaniards" were "not capable of self-government." The justification for lifting the flag over distant land received its fullest expression from Senator Albert Beveridge when he declared, "He has marked the American people as His chosen nation to finally lead in the regeneration of the world."

The anti-imperialists rallied around William Jennings Bryan who believed that the American civilizing mission would be achieved through the force of example. He received particularly poignant support from Southern Demo-

crats who wondered aloud how Americans unable to solve their domestic racial problems were able to justify rationally the incorporation of additional non-whites into the body politic. When it was made emphatic that no one intended to admit them into the national councils, Southerners wondered aloud whether the Republicans were tacitly admitting that their efforts to establish racial equality in the Reconstruction Era were mistaken, and with candor their opponents replied that indeed they had been mistaken.

When the Filipino government headed by Emilio Aguinaldo realized the United States meant to stay as masters, they mounted an insurrection which would continue for almost three years. Before it had ended, thousands of American soldiers and tens of thousands of Filipino irregulars and civilians were casualties. By 1902 American arms had prevailed but at a large price. Part of our justification for intervening in Cuba had been to put an end to the ruthless savagery with which the Spaniards were attempting to repress Cuban rebels, but as the American chief of staff Nelson A. Miles noted in his report of conditions on the islands shortly before the final suppression of the rebellion, we had resorted to the same tactics to achieve our end. Unfortunately, whatever the reason used to justify their building, empires are cemented with blood.

Julius W. Pratt (1888-), long an expert on both American diplomatic and empire building history, analyzed in detail the various reasons used to justify the Spanish-American War. His most significant contribution was to demonstrate how reluctantly the dominant business element of American society accepted the war. He focused instead upon the jingoistic, racist elements of American society. Within that framework, it was widely agreed that the more advanced countries had the obligation "to carry the political civilization of the modern world into those parts of the world inhabited by unpolitical and barbaric races; i.e., they must have a colonial policy." John W. Burgess (1844-1931), author of these words, and whose reputation as an historian was second to none at the beginning of the twentieth century, probably stated the case for American empire building most succinctly when he wrote: "There is no human right to the status of barbarism." The trouble is that when men stoop to barbarism to combat barbarism, it is impossible to distinguish the barbarians.

EXPANSIONISTS OF 1898

THE ACQUISITION OF HAWAII AND THE SPANISH ISLANDS

by Julius W. Pratt

Largely as a result of events in Hawaii, the short session of the Fifty-Third Congress (December, 1894–March, 1895) witnessed a spirited renewal of the debate between the expansionists and the defenders of the administration's "little America" policy. The discussion was opened by Senator Lodge, December 22, with the introduction of a resolution instructing the Secretary of the Navy to inform the Senate why all ships of war had been withdrawn from the Hawaiian Islands, and whether the interests of the United States and its citizens did not require that a war vessel be stationed at Honolulu. In speaking to this resolution, Lodge referred to the correspondence of Admiral Walker, and predicted a royalist rising encouraged by British influence. Fuel was added to the flames when on January 9, 1895, President Cleveland sent to Congress a special message urging that consent be given to the lease by the Hawaiian Government to Great Britain of uninhabited Necker Island to serve as a station for a cable to connect Canada and Australia. The project of a cable to connect Hawaii directly with the United States had been discussed between the two governments as far back at least as 1889 and had been viewed as having decided political implications. That the proposal for a British cable now came to Congress with Cleveland's endorsement seemed to Senators like Lodge to confirm their suspicions both of British designs upon Hawaii and of Cleveland's indifference to them. The same men found further reason for their fears in Cleveland's desire to withdraw from the tripartite Samoan arrangement. In his first annual message (December 4, 1893) he had referred to the Samoan situation as illustrating "the impolicy of entangling alliances with other powers." In May, 1894, he had sent to Congress a long report from Gresham on Samoa, in which the Secretary intimated that the only fruits of the Berlin treaty had been expenses, responsibilities, and entanglements. Now, in his message of December 3, 1894, he had proposed a complete withdrawal by the United States from its engagements there "on some reasonable terms not prejudicial to any of our existing rights." This proposal, coupled with Cleveland's Hawaiian policy, seemed to Senator Lodge ample proof that the administration was bent upon abandoning American interests in the Pacific to Great Britain.

While these matters were agitating the Senate, came the news of the royalist rebellion in Hawaii, which bore out, in part at least, Lodge's earlier predictions. Unfriendly Senators were to a slight degree mollified by the prompt dispatch of the "Philadelphia" to Honolulu, but the opportunity for an intensified attack upon the administration was not lost, and resolutions reflecting various shades of opinion were introduced. Of the hostile resolutions, all condemned, by implication if not directly, the withdrawal of United States warships from Honolulu; one expressed "profound indignation" (later changed to "regret") at the attempt to restore the Queen; two (introduced by Lodge and by Allen of Nebraska) advocated annexation; and one (Lodge's) favored prompt measures for the construction of an American cable to Honolulu and opposed any steps which would permit another government "to secure a foothold or lease upon any part of the Hawaiian Islands." None of these came to a vote. Instead, the Senate adopted as a substitute for Allen's resolution one proposed by Vest, of Missouri, which merely reaffirmed the policy of non-interference for which the Senate had spoken in the preceding May and approved the position taken by the Cleveland administration as embodying that policy. The vote on the substitution

stood 24 to 22, with 39 not voting. It meant little more than an expression of
opinion by twenty-four Senators. Possibly a better index to the attitude of
the Senate was the adoption, February 9, of an amendment to the Diplomatic
and Consular Appropriation Bill providing $500,000 toward the cost of con-
struction of a cable between Hawaii and the United States. The House of
Representatives, however, refused to concur in the amendment, and the
Senate, facing a hint from Senator Blackburn that the President would veto
a bill with this provision, with a resulting need for an extra session, thought
best to yield.

The debate on these various proposals called forth new avowals of their
faith on the part of both expansionist and anti-expansionist Senators. Caffery,
of Louisiana, declared his "unalterable opposition" to incorporating into
the American Union "that heterogeneous mixture of all the nations of the
earth"—Hawaii. Gray opposed annexation in general and that of Hawaii in
particular.

> I believe [he said] that our policy is a continental one, and that we
> are not called upon by anything in our past history or by anything in
> the necessities of our situation to step off this continent in a career of
> colonial aggrandizement. That belongs to a past age; it belongs to other
> forms of government.

On the other side, Teller, of Colorado, reaffirmed his belief in the propriety
of flying the American flag over Cuba—"over that great island and over
other islands." Platt, of Connecticut, visioned the continued westward
progress of the Caucasian race, "carrying civilization and blessing in its
march," and declared his faith that "neither narrow statesmanship nor
political prejudice can prevent or long hinder it in its continued progress
westward, still westward."

But it was Senator Lodge—accused by Gray of having embarked upon a
"scheme of annexation and colonial empire"—who preached with greatest
fervor the twin gospels of expansion and sea power. Lodge, as has been indicated, was active throughout the session, but his supreme oratorical flight
came on March 2, in a desperate effort to save the appropriation for the
Hawaiian cable. He considered this item, he said, "the most important thing
involved in any appropriation bill before Congress," since upon the Hawaiian
Islands depended "a great part of the future commercial progress of the
United States." Lodge thereupon launched upon an exposition of Mahan's
doctrine of sea power.

> The sea power has been one of the controlling forces in history.
> Without sea power no nation has been really great. Sea power consists,
> in the first place, of a proper navy and a proper fleet; but in order to
> sustain a Navy we must have suitable posts for naval stations, strong
> places where a navy can be protected and refurnished.

At this point the speaker exhibited to the Senate a map of the world, upon
which he had marked in red the location of the naval stations of Great

Britain—a line of them on the Atlantic coast of North America and in the neighboring islands, others in European, Asiatic, and African waters—and indicated the relative naval strength of Great Britain and the United States in the Atlantic and Pacific. Pointing to the British stations at Vancouver and in the Falkland and Fiji Islands, he continued:

> In that great triangle marked by these three points Great Britain does not hold a naval station. There in the center of that triangle, in the heart of the Pacific, where I am now pointing, lie the Sandwich Islands. They are the key of the Pacific. . . .

He did not believe that England desired war with us; but we were her natural commercial rivals; she had always thwarted and opposed us; she desired to keep control of the great commercial highways and to put us in a position where we could fight, if at all, only at a disadvantage. We had now the opportunity to strengthen our position against her in the Pacific. Lodge disclaimed any desire to see his country "enter on an unlimited career of acquisition of colonial possessions. . . . But, Mr. President, . . . we hold the citadel of our greatness here on this continent within the borders of the United States, but we should not neglect the necessary outworks."

After another encomium upon the historic role of sea power, the Senator concluded:

> Mr. President, I desire an extra session as little as any man in this body, but I would never vote to strike out that cable as the first step toward the development of American commerce, toward the taking of what belongs as of right to the American people in their onward march. I would never vote to strike it out if it meant ten extra sessions. It is part of a great policy. It is not a mere appropriation of $500,000.

Anxious, apparently, to appeal to a wider audience than that reached by the *Congressional Record*, Lodge formulated his ideas in an article entitled, "Our Blundering Foreign Policy," published in the *Forum* for March, 1895. Characterizing the foreign policy of the preceding two years as "everywhere a policy of retreat and surrender," Lodge denounced Cleveland's attitude to Hawaii at every point, accused him of wishing to give Samoa to Great Britain, and charged him with dabbling ineffectually in the affairs of the Near and Far East, while abandoning true American interests nearer home and permitting the British to violate the Monroe Doctrine in Venezuela. Under Cleveland's leadership, said Lodge, the Democratic Party had abandoned the expansionist policies of Jefferson and Jackson for a policy of retreat coupled with the deplorable heresy of free trade. It had, in fact, become thoroughly "Cobdenized."

Lodge then proceeded to state, in no mincing words, what the foreign policy of the United States ought to be. There should be no further extension on the mainland to the south,

> for neither the population nor the lands of Central and South America would be desirable additions to the United States. But from the Rio

Grande to the Arctic Ocean there should be but one flag and one country. Neither race nor climate forbids this extension, and every consideration of national growth and national welfare demands it. In the interests of our commerce and of our fullest development we should build the Nicaragua canal, and for the protection of that canal and for the sake of our commercial supremacy in the Pacific we should control the Hawaiian Islands and maintain our influence in Samoa. England has studded the West Indies with strong places which are a standing menace to our Atlantic Seaboard. We should have among those islands at least one strong naval station, and when the Nicaragua canal is built, the island of Cuba . . . will become to us a necessity.

Adding to his list of desiderata "a navy strong enough to give protection to Americans in every quarter of the globe," Lodge concluded:

The tendency of modern times is toward consolidation. . . . Small states are of the past and have no future. . . . The great nations are rapidly absorbing for their future expansion and their present defence all the waste places of the earth. It is a movement which makes for civilization and the advancement of the race. As one of the great nations of the world, the United States must not fall out of the line of march.

There can be no doubt that the Massachusetts Senator was, in his own mind at least, defining the political issues of the next campaign. On no issue, not even the tariff, was Republican criticism of Cleveland more bitter than upon his foreign policy. In the *Forum* article Lodge sought rather skilfully to combine the two. Republicans, if Lodge had his way, would stand for a sturdy protection of American interests, at home by the tariff, abroad by a judicious naval and territorial expansion, in contrast with the alleged Democratic policy of free trade and territorial restriction.

Obviously, here was a real issue. It is true that before the year 1895 ran its course, Cleveland was to satisfy even the jingoes in his firm stand for the Monroe Doctrine in the Venezuela affair. It is true that he favored the upbuilding of the Navy, when the state of the treasury permitted, and that he looked not wholly without sympathy upon the Nicaragua canal project. But to all plans for the overseas expansion of American sovereignty he was unalterably opposed. The schemes for acquiring naval bases or insular possessions in the Caribbean, with which President Harrison and his Secretaries of State had dallied, were, during Cleveland's four years, entirely discarded. Such interest as he or either of his Secretaries of State, Gresham and Olney, displayed in the Danish West Indies or the Dominican Republic was aimed solely at preventing those islands from passing under the control, respectively, of Germany and France—in other words at the enforcement of the Monroe Doctrine. Of the acquisition by the United States of the islands, or even of a naval base within their boundaries, there was, apparently, never a thought. Cleveland's attitude on the subject was well summarized in a statement given to the press some months after the close of his term of office.

I regarded, and still regard [he said] the proposed annexation of these [the Hawaiian] islands as not only opposed to our national policy, but as a perversion of our national mission. The mission of our nation is to build up and make a greater country out of what we have, instead of annexing islands.

Cleveland displayed the same conservatism in dealing with the Cuban question, which arose to bedevil his last two years in office as Hawaii had bedevilled the two years preceding. The Cuban insurrection began in February, 1895, and within a few months the yellow press was inflaming the country with exaggerated and one-sided reports of Spanish atrocities. Popular sympathy with a people struggling for their liberty found prompt reflection in Congress, and the long session of 1895-1896 was marked by the introduction of a variety of resolutions expressing sympathy for the insurgents and advocating recognition of their status as belligerents. A concurrent resolution adopted by the Senate in February, 1896, and accepted by the House in April, declared that in the opinion of Congress a state of public war existed in Cuba; that the United States ought to accord belligerent rights impartially to both parties in the conflict; and that "the friendly offices of the United States should be offered by the President to the Spanish Government for the recognition of the independence of Cuba."

Neither in these resolutions nor in the debate upon them can one discover evidence of any clear plan to annex Cuba to the United States. Several advocates of the resolutions expressly disavowed any desire for annexation. Senators and Congressmen, nevertheless, were not unmindful of advantages which the United States might derive from liberating the Cubans, and there was some plain talk of actual annexation, or some relationship closely akin thereto. Mr. Sulzer, of New York, described Cuba as "a natural part of our Geographical domain . . . a possession rich beyond the dreams of avarice and essential to our control of the Gulf of Mexico, our continental supremacy, and our national destiny." Lodge, who a year before had written of Cuba as being a "necessity" to the United States, still retained the opinion that the island was of vast commercial and strategic importance to this country, but he no longer considered absolute possession essential, provided it were "in friendly hands."

> Cuba in our hands or in friendly hands, in the hands of its own people, attached to us by ties of interest and gratitude, is a bulwark to the commerce, to the safety, and to the peace of the United States.

Against all pressure for intervention or for the recognition of the belligerent status of the insurgents Cleveland stood firm. To the concurrent resolution of April, 1896, he paid no attention, viewing it as merely an expression of opinion on the part of the legislative branch. Yet Cleveland was genuinely perplexed as to the best solution of the unfortunate Cuban situation. The suggestion, made by Consul-General Fitzhugh Lee at Havana, that the United States purchase the island from Spain, he thought would not "suit at all, though it is perhaps worth thinking of." It would be absurd to buy the island and turn it over "to the people now inhabiting it"; yet to incorporate it into the system of the United States "would be entering upon dangerous ground." He did everything within his power to avoid the necessity of intervention or of war with Spain; yet in his last annual message he intimated plainly that the United States could not see the struggle drag on indefinitely, and added: "The United States is not a nation to which peace is a necessity." But by the time Cleveland made this cautious admission that war might be the only solution of the Cuban question, he had seen the triumph at the polls of the party which had incorporated in its platform not only a demand for Cuban independence but an endorsement of the program of territorial expansion which for three and one-half years Cleveland had earnestly opposed.

By the end of the year 1896, the United States was unquestionably, in the words Mahan had used in 1890, "looking outward." The Fifty-Fourth Congress, besides showing a tendency to assert American rights in the western hemisphere against all comers, had been ready to lecture the Great Powers of Europe upon their duty elsewhere. It had given enthusiastic support to the President's determination to defend the Monroe Doctrine at all hazards; it had resolved that Cuba ought to be independent, and that the parties to the treaty of Berlin—Great Britain, Germany, Austria-Hungary, France, Italy, and Russia—ought to live up to their obligations by protecting Armenian Christians against Turkish atrocities; and in the last connection it had pledged full support to the President in any action for the protection of American citizens in Turkey. Big navy men dwelt with satisfaction upon this "revival of nationalism" and demanded naval increases which would enable the nation to back up its demands with force. Said one of them:

> Why, Mr. Chairman, a failure at the present time to strengthen our Navy in a superlative degree would be tantamount to making an apology to the world for our actions during the past two months.

Acting in this spirit, the House voted to authorize four new battleships instead of the two asked for by the Secretary of the Navy, and eventually compromised with the Senate on three.

This spirit of aggressive self-assertion found enthusiastic expression in the Republican platform of 1896. "Our foreign policy," declared that document, "should be at all times firm, vigorous, and dignified. . . . We reassert the Monroe Doctrine in its full extent, and we reaffirm the right of the United States to give the doctrine effect by responding to the appeal of any American State for friendly intervention in case of European encroachment." The United States should use its influence to restore peace in Cuba and to give independence to the Cuban people. It should do all in its power to stop the Armenian massacres and to protect American citizens and their property everywhere. And, in order to maintain peace and security at home and "its rightful influence among the nations of the earth," it must have "a naval power commensurate with its position and responsibility."

Such a program clearly called for an isthmian canal and for naval bases at strategic points in relation to it, and the platform was by no means silent upon these points. "The Hawaiian islands should be controlled by the United States . . . ; the Nicaragua Canal should be built, owned and operated by the United States; and by the purchase of the Danish islands we should secure a proper and much-needed naval station in the West Indies." Then, with a glance northward, the platform added:

> We hopefully look forward to the eventual withdrawal of the European powers from this hemisphere, and to the ultimate union of all English-speaking parts of the continent by the free consent of its inhabitants.

In competition with this ambitious program of aggressive foreign policy and territorial expansion, the Democrats could offer only an endorsement of the Monroe Doctrine and a tender of "sympathy to the people of Cuba in their heroic struggle for liberty and independence."

Yet this contrast of foreign policies probably attracted little attention in the ensuing campaign. After all, it was the year of Bryan and the Free Silver menace; and after Free Silver it was the historic debate over the tariff which held second place in popular interest. Even McKinley, the Republican candidate, appears to have given little thought to the foreign policy to which the party imperialists had committed him. A reading of the dry "front-porch" addresses which he delivered during the campaign, reveals scarcely a word upon that theme. Soon after his inauguration he assured Carl Schurz that there was to be no scheming for the annexation of Hawaii, and added: "Ah, you may be sure that there will be no jingo nonsense under my administration." John Sherman, who became his Secretary of State, shared this attitude. To the Hawaiian minister he said, in March, 1897, that "he was opposed to all acquisitions of territory not on the main land. Cuba, Hawaii[,] San Domingo or any other. . . ."

Friends of Hawaiian annexation undertook at once the task of converting McKinley to a belief in that cause. As early as March 15, Senator Frye and John W. Foster, the former Secretary of State, who had negotiated the annexation treaty of 1893, had seen the President and received encouragement. Ten days later, McKinley granted an interview to F. M. Hatch, the Hawaiian minister, and W. O. Smith, of Honolulu, who had been sent to Washington to promote the cause of annexation, listened to their arguments for immediate action, and expressed a great interest in the subject. Hatch and Smith were evidently well satisfied with the result of the interview. The next day Smith was writing:

> The difference between the attitude of the present administration and the last one is like that of the difference between daylight and darkness. The present is the friendly one, waiting for the best opportunity and most favorable means of presenting the matter. The other was irrevocably opposed to it.

Nevertheless, Hatch and Smith had ample cause for worry. Even before Congress convened in special session to revise the tariff, it was evident that sugar interests in the United States would put up a vigorous fight not only against annexation but against even the continuance of the reciprocity treaty. Both McKinley and Mark Hanna, though favorable to annexation, insisted that tariff revision must be put ahead of all else in the special session, and, as it turned out, only the President's personal intervention saved the reciprocity treaty from destruction at the hands of Congress in the course of the new tariff legislation. Meanwhile, the Hawaiian Republic was facing a serious situation in its relations with Japan. The Island Empire had lodged a vigorous protest over the Hawaiian Government's measures to restrict Japanese immigration—restriction to which, as Hatch wrote from Washington, the only alternative was to "abandon the country to Japan"—and a crisis in this quarter seemed rapidly approaching. More than ever before, annexation seemed a matter of life or death to Occidental civilization in Hawaii. "It is the white race against the yellow," said the Honolulu *Star*. "Nothing but annexation can save the islands."

In reality, we may well believe that Japan was unintentionally providing the incentive to annexation which Great Britain had refrained from contributing in 1893. The potential utility of the Japanese attitude was clear to Mr. Hatch in Washington who advised that all newspaper correspondents in Honolulu be kept informed of the Japanese negotiations. Certainly one young member of McKinley's administration reacted in the desired manner. Theodore Roosevelt, Assistant Secretary of the Navy, was almost in a state of panic.

> If I had my way [he wrote Captain Mahan] we would annex those islands tomorrow. . . . I have been getting matters in shape on the Pacific Coast just as fast as I have been allowed. My own belief is that we should act instantly before the two new Japanese warships leave England. I would . . . *hoist our flag over the island leaving all details for after action*. . . . I believe we should build the Nicaragua Canal at once, and . . . should build a dozen new battleships, half of them on the Pacific Coast. . . . I am fully alive to the danger from Japan.

Possibly some of Roosevelt's alarm was shared by his official superiors. At any rate, with work on the tariff bill nearing completion McKinley gave his consent to the negotiation of a treaty of annexation with Hawaii. Secretary Sherman was not at first informed of the decision. The negotiation was placed in the hands of Assistant Secretary W. R. Day, who in turn entrusted the drafting of the treaty to Foster. The treaty thus drawn was signed June 16, 1897, by Secretary Sherman and F. M. Hatch, Lorrin A. Thurston, and Wm. A. Kinney for the Hawaiian Government, and was sent to the Senate on the same day with a report signed by Sherman and a special message from the President. The treaty resembled closely that of 1893, the principal difference being its omission of provision for compensation to the former Queen and the heir presumptive.

On July 14, Senator Davis, from the Committee on Foreign Relations, reported the treaty to the Senate with a resolution consenting to ratification, but no further action upon it was taken before the adjournment of Congress—a result which McKinley had perhaps expected—but the issue was again placed before the public, and, what was perhaps more important, notice was given to Japan of the intentions of the United States. Upon being informed of the signing of the treaty, the Japanese minister at Washington at once protested to Secretary Sherman, complaining that annexation would disturb the international balance in the Pacific and would endanger certain rights of Japanese subjects in Hawaii. The Department of State undertook to mollify the Japanese Government with assurances that all vested rights would be respected by the United States, but in the meantime preparations were made to employ force if it should prove necessary. The commanding officer of the naval force at Honolulu was given secret instructions to do everything in his power to cultivate friendly relations with the Japanese and to promote an amicable settlement of the difficulty; but at the first sign of a resort to force on the part of Japan, he was to take possession of the islands, hoist the United States flag, and proclaim a provisional protectorate. Meanwhile, the commanding officer of the battleship "Oregon," on the Pacific Coast, was instructed to keep his ship coaled and ready to proceed at short notice to Honolulu, and the naval attaché at Yokohama was told to "forewarn Department by telegraph of increase if any of Japanese fleet at Hawaii or other significant movements of Japanese forces." These preparations were made known to Hatch, who, after a conference with the Assistant Secretary of State reported that the United States would give full protection to Hawaii while the treaty was pending. Fortunately, no drastic action was required. The Japanese Government accepted the friendly assurances of the United States and in December withdrew its protest.

Hawaiian annexation was not the only expansionist scheme that revived under the blessing of the Republican platform and the complacency of William McKinley. W. O. Smith had been informed in March that "the Nicaraguan Canal matter [was] to be taken up at the point where it was left when Mr. Cleveland withdrew it from Congress during his first term." Senator Lodge, on March 18, 1897, introduced a resolution calling upon the Senate Foreign Relations Committee to inquire into the chances of purchasing from Denmark the islands of St. Thomas, St. John, and St. Croix. President Heureaux, of the Dominican Republic, recalling the friendly attitude of the last Republican administration, was presently to renew his attempt to dispose of Samana Bay to the United States at a profit to himself. Looking in a different direction and to a much greater distance, Assistant Secretary Roosevelt was initiating those preparations which, in the event of war with Spain over the Cuban question, would launch an attack upon the Philippine Islands and lay an Asiatic empire at the feet of the United States.

The time was not yet ripe for these things; the country was not ready. And, as if in a deliberate attempt to prepare it in spirit for coming events, a group of able writers let loose upon the American public a flood of expansionist propaganda. In *Harper's Magazine* for September and October, 1897, Captain Mahan published two articles entitled, respectively, "A Twentieth-Century Outlook" and "Strategic Features of the Caribbean Sea and the Gulf of Mexico." In the first, he predicted, for the twentieth century, a colossal struggle of European and American against Asiatic civilization and religion. While European armies held the land frontier, American sea power would be the natural defender on the Pacific side, but to function effectively American sea power must hold securely the isthmian canal, the approaches to it through the Caribbean, and its western outpost, the Hawaiian Islands. With its philosophic tone, its strong undercurrent of religious mysticism, and its militaristic lesson, this seemed to Theodore Roosevelt "a really noble article." The second article was an analysis of the relative strategic value of the various naval strongholds, actual or potential, upon the eastern approaches to the isthmus, and reached conclusions highly favorable to Cuba and somewhat less so to Samana Bay and St. Thomas. There was no preaching in this article, but since the author had previously demonstrated that control of the Caribbean was essential to the preservation of Western civilization, his scientific analysis of how that area could be controlled led to practical conclusions which only a dull American could miss.

A civilian who fully shared Mahan's enthusiasm for expansion was Albert Shaw, editor of the *Review of Reviews*. From May, 1897, to February, 1898, the editorial pages of that magazine played frequently upon the importance of annexing Hawaii, constructing a canal, and acquiring or controlling key islands in the Caribbean—all as means toward the eventual domination of the Pacific, which was to be "the theater of great events in the coming century." On the Pacific Coast, the *Overland Monthly*, edited by Horatio Bridge, was equally imbued with expansionist sentiment. Declaring frankly for a breaking away from the ancient tradition embodied in Washington's Farewell Address, the *Overland* announced itself an advocate "of the new doctrine of America's interest in external affairs, whether in the Caribbean sea, the Pacific islands, or the Orient." The subjugation of a continent had kept the American people occupied for a century.

> But now that the continent is subdued, we are looking for fresh worlds to conquer; and whether our conservative stay-at-homes like it or not, the colonizing instinct which has led our race in successive waves of migration is the instinct which is now pushing us out and on to Alaska, to the isles of the sea,—and beyond.

To what extent such literature expressed or influenced public sentiment, it is obviously impossible to determine. It is significant, however, that a Trans-Mississippi Congress, meeting at Salt Lake City in July, 1897, and presided over by William Jennings Bryan, although chiefly concerned with the interests of agriculture, mining, and the development of the natural resources of the West, passed resolutions favoring the construction of the Nicaragua Canal as an American enterprise, the annexation of Hawaii, and the independence of Cuba.

A new spirit of self-assertiveness was animating the American people as the year of 1898 dawned. The elements that would produce a new America were present, but as in the case of certain chemical reactions, heat was necessary to precipitate the new combination—in this instance, the heat of war. This was clearly seen by some as the events of February and March pointed more and more toward war with Spain. It was seen specifically by the Hawaiian minister in relation to the annexation treaty. The united force of the anti-imperialists on principle and the representatives of American sugar interests proved too strong in the Senate to be overcome. After nearly three months of fruitless effort to make sure of the necessary sixty votes, the friends of the treaty, early in March, confessed defeat, and turned to the alternative plan. On March 16, the Senate Foreign Relations Committee reported to the Senate a joint resolution of annexation. Several weeks earlier, Hatch had expressed the opinion that intervention by the United States in Cuba "would carry our treaty through on the jump." Now, referring to the probable action by joint resolution and the prospect that the report on the sinking of the "Maine" would delay matters, he wrote:

> We can well afford to wait until that matter is disposed of. If I mistake not, developments in that connection are sure to help us.

"Developments in that connection" would forward other expansionist plans as well. On January 31, Senator Lodge had written to Henry White, with an apparent prescience that must have startled Lodge himself two weeks later: "There may be an explosion any day in Cuba which would settle a great many things." The explosion he had in mind was presumably political—not the kind that destroyed the "Maine." But some things might be settled even while the explosion was preparing, and the Massachusetts Senator was more than ready to do his part. It was he and Roosevelt who, on February 25, in the absence of Secretary Long, sent off orders to Dewey, in Hongkong, directing him, in the event of war, to begin "offensive operations in the Philippine Islands." Contemporaneously, Lodge's other scheme, for the purchase of the Danish West Indies, seemed on the point of consummation. The consent of the Danish Government was secured, a price of $5,000,000 was agreed upon, and on March 25, 1898, McKinley's Cabinet gave its approval to the proposed transaction. On March 31, Lodge introduced in the Senate a bill giving authority for the purchase and providing the necessary funds. With the bill he submitted a report, drawn by himself, declaring that the islands "occupy a commanding strategic position, and are of incalculable value to the United States," and in the ensuing debate he assured the Senate that he had talked with the President, who deemed the Danish islands of inestimable value in the event of hostilities with Spain. Apparently the purchase would have been consummated at this time but for the unwillingness of the Danish Government to commit what, after war began, it considered would constitute a "diplomatic discourtesy to Spain."

No such scruples deterred President Heureaux of the Dominican Republic, who at this time suggested to the United States consul at Santo Domingo that if the United States cared to take forcible possession of Samana Bay for a base of operations against Spain, he would interpose no serious objection.

This proposal the State Department thought worth referring to the Secretary of the Navy, who replied that his department did not "care to acquire a coaling station in Samana Bay by a process of seizure." We may guess that Roosevelt, had he been in charge, would have answered differently.

McKinley's war message went to Congress on April 11th. On the 19th Congress issued its ultimatum to Spain, and on the 25th declared the existence of a state of war. On the first of May Dewey destroyed the Spanish fleet in Manila Bay. In the interim between the declaration of hostilities and Dewey's opening shot at Manila, an orator in Boston and an editor in San Francisco undertook to interpret the meaning of the war to the United States. On April 27, Albert J. Beveridge delivered an oration upon President Grant at the Middlesex Club in Boston. Declaring that Grant "never forgot that we are a conquering race, and that we must obey our blood and occupy new markets and new lands," the speaker led up to the existing crisis.

> American factories are making more than the American people can use; American soil is producing more than they can consume. Fate has written our policy for us; the trade of the world must and shall be ours. And we will get it as our mother (England) has told us how. We will establish trading-posts throughout the world as distributing points for American products. We will cover the ocean with our merchant marine. We will build a navy to the measure of our greatness. Great colonies governing themselves, flying our flag and trading with us, will grow about our posts of trade. Our institutions will follow our flag on the wings of commerce. And American law, American order, American civilization, and the American flag will plant themselves on shores hitherto bloody and benighted, but by those agencies of God henceforth to be made beautiful and bright.

Rejoicing that the stars and stripes were about to float "over an Isthmian canal, . . . over Hawaii, . . . over Cuba and the southern seas," the orator went on to point out that "the true field of our earliest operations" was Spain's weakly defended island empire in the Philippines: "The Philippines are logically our first target."

In similar strain, the *Overland Monthly*, of San Francisco, in an editorial written before Dewey's victory, predicted the annexation of Cuba, the Philippines, and Hawaii:

> So that almost without knowing it we shall have started forth on our colonizing ventures fully equipped with widely scattered possessions, a navy strong enough to protect them, and a newly roused martial spirit in our hearts made strong and enduring by victory. And if what is bred in the bone breaks out in the flesh, our British ancestry will see to it that we keep what we get, and get more when we can.

The spirit embodied in Beveridge's speech and the *Overland* editorial was apparent to observers across the Atlantic. In the April issue of *Blackwood's Edinburgh Magazine*, "The Looker-on," had commented upon the rising spirit in American affairs, which, with its fleets building, and its enthusiasms kindling, and its hidden spark in the heart of the most orthodox citizen, is preparing as much of a change as we saw in Japan the other day, and perhaps as sudden.

Now, with the opening of the war with Spain, the same writer remarked:

Unless all signs deceive, the American Republic breaks from the old moorings, and sails out to be a "world-power."

&8 8&

THE *Spanish-American War, in the words of Theodore Roosevelt, was "a splendid little war." It had its origins in a multitude of causes. The long destructive Cuban Insurrection of the 1870's had ended in a doubtful peace and erupted again in 1895. As previously, the Cuban rebels could not defeat the Spaniards, but Spanish authority could not suppress the guerrilla hit-and-run attacks. The American reading public obtained a vivid image of the struggle in the yellow journalism of William Randolph Hearst and Joseph Pulitzer. The New York* World *of May 17, 1896, published a typical report: "No man's life, no man's property is safe. American citizens are imprisoned or slain without cause. American property is destroyed on all sides. . . . Blood on the roadsides, blood in the fields, blood on the doorsteps, blood, blood, blood!" When Frederick Remington, the painter of the West, on assignment in Cuba to paint the war for Hearst, concluded there would be no war, his employer cavalierly assured him, "You furnish the pictures and I'll furnish the war."*

The necessary incident to precipitate war came on the evening of February 15, 1898, when the battleship Maine, *paying a friendly visit to Havana, blew up with the loss of 260 American lives. On newspaper banners throughout the nation was emblazoned the slogan: "Remember the* Maine." *The Spaniards were automatically labeled the culprits, although it hardly seems plausible that they would provide the Americans with the perfect justification to intervene. As is now known, the American government had already determined to press Spain to grant independence to Cuba. And Congress, restrained by such conservative businessmen as Mark Hanna who were fearful that war would disrupt the recently returned economic recovery, awaited the report of the eminently respectable Senator Redfield Procter of Vermont. That gentleman upon his return from Cuba in the final days of March of 1898 delivered full confirmation of the distraught condition of the Cubans. It gave the necessary confirmation to Congress that moral imperatives were at stake on the Pearl of the Antilles. On April 25, 1898, in response to a message from President McKinley, Congress acknowledged a state of war.*

What followed was a swift war of conquest during which American forces occupied the Philippines, Cuba, Puerto Rico, and Guam. In less than four months, an American empire was born. Retrospectively the historian was able to say that a small but influential group of businessmen with large holdings in Cuba had helped agitate the war fever. It was also true that thousands of Cuban refugees camped out in American seaports had provided lurid script for the yellow press. But a considerable number of military and naval leaders, most prominent among them Theodore Roosevelt, conditioned to accept the teachings of the naval historian Admiral Mahan, saw in the island acquisitions the foundation of a system of naval bases which would secure American commerce and power. The concern for making the United States a world power was not an inconsiderable part of the motives for war with Spain, as John H. Latané (1870-1932) demonstrated. In his long tenure as professor of American history in the Walter Hines Page School of International Relations at Johns Hopkins, he emphasized the emergence of America on the world scene. He also recognized that the men who made the war in 1898 heartily subscribed to Theodore Roosevelt's assertion: "All the great masterful races have been fighting races, and the minute that a race loses the hard fighting virtues, . . . it has lost its proud right to stand as the equal of the best."

AMERICA AS A WORLD POWER, 1897-1907

by John Holladay Latané

President Roosevelt has said that the most striking thing about the war with Spain was the preparedness of the navy, and the unpreparedness of the army. For fifteen years we had been building up a navy, and for months preceding the war every effort was made, with the resources at the command of the navy department, to put it in a state of first-class efficiency. As early as January 11, 1898, instructions were sent to the commanders of the several squadrons to retain in the service men whose terms of enlistment were about to expire. As the Cuban situation grew more threatening, the North Atlantic Squadron and a torpedo-boat flotilla were rapidly assembled in Florida waters; and immediately after the destruction of the *Maine* the ships on the European and South Atlantic stations were ordered to Key West.

Commodore Dewey assumed command of the Asiatic station January 3, 1898, succeeding Rear-Admiral McNair. The ships were at the time scattered along the coasts of China and Korea. On February 25 the following secret orders were cabled to Dewey: "Order squadron, except *Monocacy*, to Hong-Kong. Keep full of coal. In event of declaration of war Spain, your duty will be to see that the Spanish squadron does not leave the Asiatic coast, and then offensive operations in Philippine Islands. Keep *Olympia* until further orders." This despatch was signed "Roosevelt," then assistant secretary of the navy. On the following day another despatch was sent to Dewey, and also to the commanders of all our squadrons: "Keep full of coal, the best that can be had." The *Olympia*, Dewey's flag-ship, had been ordered home for repairs, but this order was revoked in view of the seriousness of the situation. The *Mohican* was ordered to proceed at once from Mare Island to Honolulu with a large supply of ammunition, to be transferred to the *Baltimore* and conveyed by that ship to Dewey at Hong-Kong.

The battle-ship *Oregon*, which was at Bremerton, on the coast of Washington, was ordered early in March to proceed to San Francisco and prepare for a long voyage. After receiving a supply of ammunition at the latter port, she started, March 19, on the voyage around the Horn that was to make her name immortal in naval history. The *Marietta*, then at San Jose, Guatemala, was ordered to precede the *Oregon* and arrange for coaling.

Both from a political and a military point of view, the blockade of Cuba was the first step for the American government to take, and the surest and quickest means of bringing things to an issue. Cuba was the point in dispute between the United States and Spain, and a blockade would result in one of two things—the surrender of the island, or the despatch of a Spanish naval force to its relief. The navy department had very little apprehension of an attack on our coast, as no squadron could hope to be in condition after crossing the Atlantic for offensive operations without coaling, and the only places where Spain could coal were in the West Indies. The public, however, took a different view of the situation and no little alarm was felt in the eastern cities. A few coast-defence guns of modern pattern would have relieved the department of the necessity of protecting the coast, and enabled it to concentrate the whole fighting force around Cuba. To meet popular demands, however, a Northern Patrol Squadron was organized April 20, under command of Commodore Howell, to cover the New England coast; and a more formidable Flying Squadron, under Commodore Schley, was assembled at Hampton Roads, and kept there until the appearance of the Spanish fleet in the West Indies. The main squadron was stationed at Key West under Rear-Admiral William T. Sampson, who had just been promoted to that grade, and given command of the entire naval force in North Atlantic waters. His appointment over the heads of Schley and other officers of superior rank and longer service created a great deal of criticism, although he was everywhere conceded to be one of the most efficient and progressive officers of the new navy.

A great effort was made before the outbreak of hostilities to purchase war-ships abroad, but with only partial success. It was not so important to add such ships as were for sale to our navy as to keep them from being purchased by Spain. Ninety-seven steam merchantmen, however, were procured at home and abroad, and became cruisers, gun-boats, and colliers. The department also chartered with their crews five ocean liners, the *City of Pekin* from the Pacific Mail Steamship Company, and the *St. Paul, St. Louis, New York*, and *Paris* (the two latter renamed *Harvard* and *Yale*) from the International Navigation Company. One ice-boat and two yachts were loaned, and a number of revenue-cutters and light-house tenders were transferred to the navy department. One hundred and twenty-eight ships were thus added to the navy, and the government yards were kept busy transforming them. To man these ships the number of enlisted men was raised from 12,500 to 24,123, and a number of new officers appointed. The heavy fighting force consisted of four first-class battle-ships, the *Indiana, Iowa, Massachusetts,* and *Oregon;* one second-class battle-ship, the *Texas;* and two armored cruisers, the *Brooklyn* and the *New York.* As against these seven armored ships Spain had five armored cruisers of modern construction and of greater reputed speed than any of ours except the *Brooklyn* and the *New York,* and one battle-ship of the *Indiana* type. Spain had further a type of vessel unknown to our navy and greatly feared by us—namely, torpedo-boat destroyers, such as the *Furor, Pluton,* and *Terror.* It was popularly supposed that the Spanish navy was somewhat superior to the American.

As soon as the Spanish minister withdrew from Washington, a despatch was sent to Sampson at Key West directing him to blockade the coast of Cuba immediately from Cardenas to Bahia Honda, and to blockade Cienfuegos if it was considered advisable. On April 29, Admiral Cervera's division of the Spanish fleet left the Cape de Verde Islands for an unknown destination, and disappeared for two weeks from the knowledge of the American authorities. This fleet was composed of four armored cruisers, the *Infanta Maria Teresa, Cristobal Colon, Oquendo,* and *Vizcaya,* and three torpedo-boat destroyers. Its appearance in American waters was eagerly looked for, and interest in the war became intense.

While this fleet was on its way across the Atlantic, a great battle was fought across the Pacific all unknown to the American people, which was destined to open up a new world to them. Admiral Dewey was at Hong-Kong where his ships had been gathered. On April 7 he was ordered to land all woodwork and stores not necessary for operations; and on April 21 he was informed that the naval forces on the Atlantic were blockading Cuba and that war might be declared at any moment. His ships were at once painted slate-color. On the 24th, the day that Spain declared war, Great Britain issued a proclamation of neutrality, and Dewey at once prepared to leave for Mirs Bay, about thirty miles north of Hong-Kong. On the same day the now celebrated cablegram was sent him by the secretary of the navy: "War has commenced between the United States and Spain. Proceed at once to Philippine Islands. Commence operations at once, particularly against Spanish fleet. You must capture vessels or destroy. Use utmost endeavors." These were the last instructions Dewey received. His squadron left Mirs Bay, April 27, for the Philippines, and three days later Luzon was sighted. As Dewey had heard that the Spanish admiral proposed to take position at Subig Bay, a few miles north of the entrance to Manila Bay, he directed his course thither, but no signs of the enemy were to be seen. Admiral Montojo had indeed taken his squadron to Subig Bay, but, finding that the modern guns provided for its defence had not been mounted, he left twenty-four hours before Dewey arrived, and returned to Manila Bay, where he stationed his ships under the guns of Cavite. Dewey's squadron was superior to that of Montojo, but the Spanish fleet had the support of the shore batteries. Dewey's fighting force was four cruisers and two gun-boats, while the Spanish admiral had two cruisers, eleven gun-boats of antiquated type, and a number of smaller craft.

At 11:30 P.M., April 30, 1898, the American squadron entered the Boca Grande, or south channel, leading into the Bay of Manila, steaming at eight knots, the flag-ship *Olympia* in the lead. When about half through the shore batteries opened fire, but none of the ships was hit; the fire was returned by the *Boston* and the *McCulloch*. The squadron continued its even course across the bay, and at day-break was off Manila, near enough to see the shipping. At 5:15 A.M. they were fired upon by three batteries at Manila and two at Cavite and by the Spanish fleet, which was anchored on a line running almost due east from Cavite. Dewey's squadron quickly turned to the south and proceeded to the attack, the *Olympia* in the lead, followed at distance by the *Baltimore, Raleigh, Petrel, Concord,* and *Boston.* When they had arrived within fifty-six hundred yards, Dewey turned to the captain of the *Olympia* and said, coolly, "You may fire when you're ready, Gridley." With quick response one of the eight-inch guns in the forward turret sent forth its charge, and the battle of Manila Bay had begun. Three times Dewey led his ships to the westward and twice to the eastward in front of the Spanish line and shore batteries, keeping up a continuous and accurate fire at ranges varying from five thousand to two thousand yards. The Spanish ships and batteries returned the fire vigorously but ineffectively.

At 7:35 A.M. the squadron ceased firing and stood out into the bay. When out of range, Dewey ordered, "Let the people go to breakfast." This movement was made under the erroneous impression that the ammunition was getting low in some of the batteries. The opportunity was taken to let the men, who had had nothing but coffee at 4 A.M., refresh themselves. The batteries at Manila had kept up a steady fire, but at this point Dewey sent a message to the governor-general to the effect that if this was continued the city would be shelled; whereupon the Manila batteries ceased firing. At 11:16 A.M. the squadron returned to complete its work, the *Baltimore* leading the column. The duel that followed between the *Baltimore* and the shore batteries is described as the most picturesque scene of the battle. The American fire was overwhelming, and the Spanish flag-ship and most of the fleet were soon in flames. At 12:40 the squadron withdrew and anchored off Manila, leaving the *Petrel* to complete the destruction of the smaller gunboats which were behind the point of Cavite. In this remarkable battle the American ships escaped all but slight injury, and only seven men were slightly wounded. On the Spanish side ten ships were destroyed, three batteries silenced, and 381 men killed, besides numbers wounded.

The *McCulloch* was sent post-haste to Hong-Kong to cable the news to Washington, where it was received early on the morning of May 6. The public had known little of Dewey's movements or instructions, and the suddenness and unexpected character of the news greatly heightened the enthusiasm with which it was received. The eyes of the nation were at once turned to the Orient, and people who had to search closely on their maps in order to find the Philippine Islands were soon discussing glibly the commercial and strategic importance of the group. President McKinley at once appointed Dewey acting rear-admiral, and recommended that he be promoted to the grade of admiral and receive the thanks of Congress.

In spite of his great victory, Dewey's position was critical. A few days after the battle he cabled the department that he could take Manila at any time, but did not have the men to occupy it. Ammunition and men were forwarded as soon as possible, but with the utmost endeavors they did not leave San Francisco before May 21. For more than two months Dewey was left without reinforcements. The most serious cause for embarrassment was the presence in Manila Bay of the war-ships of European powers, which were assigned to duty there after the destruction of the Spanish fleet. Germany, whose interests in the Philippines were very slight, sent five men-of-war, Great Britain three, France one, and Japan one. The German force was stronger than Dewey's, and displayed open sympathy for the Spaniards, committing breaches of international and naval etiquette. They undertook to disregard the blockade and to land provisions. Dewey promptly sent his flag-lieutenant, Brumby, to present his compliments to Rear-Admiral Diederichs, to inform him of his "extraordinary disregard of the usual courtesies of naval intercourse," and to tell him that "if he wants a fight he can have it right now." The German admiral at once disavowed the act, and thereafter treated the Americans with more consideration. No satisfactory explanation of Admiral Diederichs' conduct has ever been given; he was ordered to Manila in answer to an appeal for protection from the German residents, who anticipated trouble from the insurgents, it seems, and not from the Americans. The German admiral, however, not understanding the situation, took his instructions to mean that he was to hold the Americans in check. The state department evidently saw that there was a mistake somewhere, for Andrew D. White, ambassador to Germany at the time, has stated that no explanations were sought from the German government.

The interest of the American people was soon diverted from Dewey and his remarkable achievement and centred once more on the movements of the Atlantic squadron and its efforts to locate the fleet of Admiral Cervera. It will be remembered that the latter left the Cape de Verde Islands, April 29, destination unknown, though rightly believed by our department to be the West Indies. A natural surmise was that he would go to Porto Rico; but if coal enough remained he might push straight ahead to Cuba. That he could get to the coast of the United States without first coaling at some point in the West Indies, whence he would be reported, seemed most improbable. On May 5 Sampson proceeded eastward towards the Windward Passage (between Cuba and Haiti), with the *Iowa, Indiana, New York*, and a number of lighter ships, so as to be in a position to intercept or pursue Cervera in case he should make a dash for the American coast from Porto Rico. This movement was greatly delayed by the presence of two monitors, which, on account of their inferior speed, had to be towed. North of Cape Haitien, shortly before midnight of May 7, he heard from the department that no information had been received as to Cervera's movements. Two American liners, the *St. Louis* and the *Harvard*, had been sent out April 30 to cruise along a north and south line eighty miles eastward of Guadeloupe and Martinique. They met at the middle of the course once a day, communicated, and then went back in opposite directions. In case the enemy was discovered, word was to be sent from the nearest cable station to Sampson and to the department. If by May 10 no information was received, the *Harvard* was to touch at Martinique and the *St. Louis* at Guadeloupe, cable the department and Sampson, wait twenty-four hours for orders, and, if none were received, proceed with all haste to Hampton Roads.

Sampson continued east as far as San Juan, Porto Rico, arriving off that point early on the morning of May 12, having taken eight days instead of five, as he had expected. After satisfying himself that the Spanish fleet was not there, and rather aimlessly shelling the forts for a couple of hours, he sailed off to the northeast until out of sight, then, turning west, hastened back towards Havana. From the log of the *Cristobal Colon* it appears that Cervera's division at noon of May 10, the day the *Harvard* and *St. Louis* were to abandon their patrol, reached a point one hundred and thirty miles east of Martinique, reduced its speed, and sent the *Terror* ahead to reconnoitre. That day the *Harvard*, according to orders, left its patrol station: her commander afterwards stated that he believed another stretch to the south would have revealed the Spanish squadron. On May 11 Cervera's fleet came within sight of Martinique, and that night remained practically motionless. The next morning he probably heard that Sampson was off San Juan, for he put his squadron in motion and started for Curaçao just about the time that Sampson started back for Key West.

News of Cervera's appearance off Martinique was first received at the navy department about midnight, May 12-13, nearly thirty-six hours after the fact. Schley was ordered at once to proceed with the Flying Squadron from Hampton Roads to Charleston, there to receive further orders. When Sampson left Porto Rico he was, of course, in ignorance of Cervera's appearance in the West Indies. The following night he heard from a passing ship the rumor that Cervera was back at Cadiz, and this he cabled to the department. Early Sunday morning, May 15, he received a despatch from Washington telling him that Cervera was at Curaçao the day before, that the Flying Squadron was on its way to Key West, and ordering him to proceed with all possible despatch to the same point. The problem now was to locate Cervera the moment he entered one of his own ports and blockade him, or to pounce on him in case he advanced north from the Caribbean Sea.

The presence of the Spanish fleet at Curaçao caused serious apprehensions as to the fate of the *Oregon*. The last news of her was that she had left Bahia, Brazil, May 9. Her movements were unknown to the navy department, for the question of prescribing her route and sending a detachment to meet her had been carefully considered but abandoned. She was left to shift for herself, and was considered safer if not so closely watched. She reached Barbadoes May 18, and turned up safely off Jupiter Inlet, Florida, on the 24th, ready for service, after a voyage of fourteen thousand miles, one of the most remarkable recorded in history.

Sampson reached Key West at 4 P.M., May 18, several hours after the arrival of Schley. The department had heard that Cervera had munitions of war essential to the defence of Havana, and that his orders were to reach

Havana, Cienfuegos, or a port connected with Havana by rail. As Cienfuegos seemed the only place he would be likely to choose, Schley was ordered there with the *Brooklyn, Massachusetts,* and *Texas,* May 19. He was joined later by the *Iowa,* under Captain Evans, and by several cruisers. The Spanish squadron slipped into Santiago, unobserved by the cruisers on scouting duty, May 19, two days before Schley arrived at Cienfuegos, so that had Cervera known the conditions he could easily have made the latter port. On the same day the department received from spies in Havana probable information, conveyed by the cable which had been allowed to remain in operation, that Cervera had entered Santiago. As we now know, he had entered early that morning. Several auxiliary cruisers were immediately ordered to assemble before Santiago in order to watch Cervera and follow him in case he should leave.

At the same time the department "strongly advised" Sampson to send Schley to Santiago at once with his whole command. Sampson replied that he had decided to hold Schley at Cienfuegos until it was certain that the Spanish fleet was in Santiago. Later he sent a despatch to Schley, received May 23, ordering him to proceed to Santiago if satisfied that the enemy were not at Cienfuegos. The next day Schley started, encountering on the run much rain and rough weather, which seriously delayed the squadron. At 5:30 P.M., May 26, he reached a point twenty-two miles south of Santiago, where he was joined by several of the auxiliary cruisers on scouting duty. Captain Sigsbee, of the *St. Paul,* informed him that the scouts knew nothing positively about the Spanish fleet. The collier *Merrimac* had been disabled, which increased the difficulty of coaling. At 7:45 P.M., a little over two hours after his arrival, Schley without explanation signalled to the squadron: "Destination, Key West, *via* south side of Cuba and Yucatan Channel, as soon as collier is ready; speed nine knots." Thus began the much discussed retrograde movement, which occupied two days. Admiral Schley states in his book that Sigsbee's report and other evidence led him to conclude that the Spanish squadron was not in Santiago; hence the retrograde movement to protect the passage west of Cuba. But he has never yet given any satisfactory explanation why he did not definitely ascertain the facts before turning back. Fortunately the squadron did not proceed very far; the lines towing the collier parted and other delays occurred. The next morning Schley received a despatch from the department stating that all the information at hand indicated that Cervera was in Santiago, but he continued on his westward course slowly and at times drifting while some of the ships coaled. The next day, May 28, Schley returned to Santiago, arriving before that port about dusk, and established a blockade.

Admiral Sampson arrived off Santiago June 1, and assumed direct command of the squadron. The blockade, which lasted for over a month, was eagerly watched by the whole American people. The most thrilling incident was the daring but unsuccessful attempt made by Lieutenant Richmond Pearson Hobson to sink the collier *Merrimac* across the entrance to Santiago harbor, undertaken by direction of Admiral Sampson. Electric torpedoes were attached to the hull of the ship, sea-valves were cut, and anchor chains arranged on deck so that she could be brought to a sudden stop. Early on the morning of June 3, Hobson, assisted by a crew of seven seamen, took the collier into the entrance of the harbor under heavy fire and sunk her. The unfortunate shooting away of her steering-gear and the failure of some of the torpedoes to explode kept the ship from sinking at the place selected, so that the plan miscarried. Hobson and his men escaped death as by a miracle, but fell into the hands of the Spaniards.

As soon as Cervera was blockaded in Santiago and the government was satisfied that all his ships were with him, it was decided to send an army to cooperate with the navy. Hitherto the war had been a naval war exclusively, and the two hundred thousand volunteers who had responded to the calls of the president in May had been kept in camp in different parts of the country. Most of the regular infantry and cavalry, together with several volunteer regiments, had been assembled at Tampa and organized as the Fifth Army Corps, in readiness to land in Cuba as soon as the navy had cleared the way. Conspicuous among these troops was the First Volunteer Cavalry, popularly known as Roosevelt's Rough Riders, a regiment which through the energetic efforts of Dr. Leonard Wood, an army surgeon, who became its colonel, and Theodore Roosevelt, who resigned the position of assistant secretary of the navy to become its lieutenant-colonel, had been enlisted, officered, and equipped in fifty days. It was recruited largely from Arizona, New Mexico, and Oklahoma, and had in its ranks cowboys, hunters, ranchmen, and more than one hundred and sixty full-blooded Indians, together with a few graduates of Harvard, Yale, and other eastern colleges.

Tampa was ill-suited for an instruction camp, and the preparations made by the department for the accommodation and provisioning of such large bodies of men were wholly inadequate. One of the main difficulties was the inability of the commissary and quartermaster departments, hampered by red tape, senseless regulations, and political appointees, to distribute the train-loads of supplies which blocked the tracks leading to Tampa; so great was the congestion that the soldiers could not even get their mail. This condition continued for weeks. The great majority of the troops were finally sent to Santiago to fight under a tropical sun in heavy woollen clothes; lighter clothing was not supplied to them until they were ready to return to Montauk Point, where they needed the woollen. The sanitation of the camp was poor and the water supply bad; dysentery, malaria, and typhoid soon made their appearance. Similar conditions prevailed at the other camps. The administrative inefficiency of the war department was everywhere revealed in striking contrast with the fine record of the navy department. Secretary Alger had been too much occupied with questions of patronage to look after the real needs of the service. Although war had been regarded for months as inevitable, when it finally came the department was found to be utterly unprepared to equip troops for service in Cuba. As the result of this neglect, for which it should be said Congress was partly responsible, it was necessary to improvise an army, a rather serious undertaking!

It had been the original intention to land the Fifth Army Corps at Mariel, near Havana, and begin operations against the capital city under the direct supervision of General Miles; but the bottling-up of Cervera at Santiago caused a change of plan, and General Miles, who still expected the heavy fighting to take place at Havana, selected Major-General William R. Shafter for the movement against Santiago. By June 1 the battle-ship *Indiana*, under Captain Henry C. Taylor, with a dozen smaller vessels, was ready to convoy the expedition. The army was very slow in embarking, and it was not until June 8 that the force was ready to depart. Further delay was caused by the unfounded rumor that a Spanish cruiser and two torpedo-boat destroyers had been sighted off the north coast of Cuba. In order to ascertain whether all the Spanish ships were at Santiago, Lieutenant Victor Blue, of the navy, landed, and by personal observation from the hills back of the city located Cervera's entire division in the harbor. On June 14 the transports, about thirty in number, sailed from Tampa with their convoy. They were crowded and ill-provided with supplies, the whole movement showing lack of experience in handling large bodies of men. The expedition consisted of 815 officers and 16,072 enlisted men, regulars with the exception of the Seventy-first New York and the First Volunteer Cavalry.

While the expedition was *en route* for Santiago the state department received information that the Spanish reserve fleet under Admiral Camara was on its way to the Philippines. Commodore John C. Watson was, therefore, detached from the command of the blockading squadron at Havana and placed in command of a squadron consisting of the *Iowa*, *Oregon*, and four cruisers, which it was widely announced would sail for the coast of Spain immediately. The real intention was that Watson should follow Camara through the Suez Canal and form a junction with Dewey. Camara arrived at Port Said June 26, but his actions here led to some doubt as to his intentions, and Watson's squadron was held pending developments. On June 30 the Egyptian government forced Camara to leave; the ships began their passage through the canal, some of them on July 2, and others on the 5th and 6th. Meanwhile Cervera's ships had been destroyed and Camara was recalled.

The expedition under Shafter began disembarking at Daiquiri on the morning of June 22, and by night 6000 men had with great difficulty been put ashore. No lighters or launches had been provided, and the only wharf, a small wooden one, had been stripped of its flooring: the war department expected the navy to look after these matters. In addition, the troops had been crowded into the transports without any reference to order, officers separated from their commands, artillery-pieces on one transport, horses on another, harness on a third, and no means of finding out where any of them were. By the aid of a few launches borrowed from the battle-ships, the men were put ashore, or near enough to wade through the surf, but the animals had to be thrown into the sea, where many of them perished, some in their bewilderment swimming out to sea instead of to shore.

General Lawton advanced and seized Siboney next day, and Kent's division landed here, eight miles nearer Santiago. General Wheeler pushed on with part of Young's brigade, and on the morning of the 24th defeated the Spanish force at La Guasima, with a loss of 1 officer and 15 men killed, 6 officers and 46 men wounded. During the next week the army, including

Garcia's Cuban command, was concentrated at Sevilla. These were trying days. The troops suffered from the heavy rains, poor rations, and bad camp accommodations. No adequate provision had been made for landing supplies or for transporting them to the camps, so that with an abundance, such as they were, aboard the transports, the soldiers were in actual want.

On June 30 it was decided to advance. San Juan Hill, a strategic point on the direct road to Santiago, could not be taken or held while the Spaniards occupied El Caney, on the right of the American advance. The country was a jungle, and the roads from the coast little more than bridlepaths. Lawton moved out to a position south of El Caney that afternoon, so as to begin the attack early next morning. Wheeler's division of dismounted cavalry and Kent's division of infantry advanced towards El Poso, accompanied by Grimes's battery, which was to take position early in the morning and open the way for the advance towards San Juan. The attack at this point was to be delayed until Lawton's infantry fire was heard at El Caney. After forcing the enemy from this position, Lawton was to move towards Santiago and take position on Wheeler's right. Little was known of the ground over which the troops were to move or the position and strength of the forces they were to meet, consequently they went into battle without knowing what they were about and fought without any generalship being displayed. General Shafter was too ill to leave his headquarters in the rear.

At El Caney, which was surrounded by trenches and block-houses, the Spaniards developed unexpected strength, and held Lawton in check until late in the afternoon, when he finally carried the position. In this fight about 3500 Americans were engaged and not more than 600 or 1000 Spaniards. The American loss was 4 officers and 77 men killed, and 25 officers and 335 men wounded. About 150 Spaniards were captured, and between 300 and 400 killed and wounded.

Meanwhile there had been a desperate fight at San Juan Hill. As soon as Lawton's musket-fire was heard at El Caney, Grimes's battery opened fire from El Poso on the San Juan block-house. This fire was immediately returned by the enemy's artillery, who had the range, and a number of men were killed. The Spaniards used smokeless powder, which made it difficult to locate them, while some of the Americans had black powder, which quickly indicated their position. The road along which the troops had to advance was so narrow and rough that at times they had to proceed in column of twos. The progress made was very slow, and the long-range guns of the enemy killed numbers of men before they could get into position to return the fire. By the middle of the day the advance had crossed the river and lay exposed to a galling artillery and rifle fire. The suffering of the wounded, many of whom lay in the brush for hours without succor, was the most terrible feature of the situation. Hawkins's brigade lost three commanders in fifteen minutes, General Wikoff being killed and Colonels Worth and Liscum wounded.

Finally, after completing their formation and proceeding through brush and cactus in a sweltering heat, many of the troops having been exposed to fire for hours, permission to advance was given. Carroll's brigade took the lead, reinforced on the right by the Rough Riders commanded by Roosevelt, and supported by the First and Tenth regiments of Wood's brigade. The troops charged up San Juan Hill in great confusion, the roughness of the ground and wire-fence obstructions breaking up the formations. Officers and men, detached from their regiments struggled along in groups, but the bravery and pluck of the individual man won the day. The Rough Riders, although raw and inexperienced, acquitted themselves creditably and together with troopers of the First regiment of regulars were the first to reach the intrenchments of the enemy, where they were heroically supported by the Negro troopers of the Tenth Cavalry.

After occupying San Juan Hill the troops were still exposed to a constant fire, and many were discouraged and wanted to retire, but General Wheeler, who, though ill, had come to the front early in the afternoon, put a stop to this and set the men to work fortifying themselves. The next day Lawton came up and advanced to a strong position on Wheeler's right. The fighting was resumed on the two following days, but about noon, July 3, the Spaniards ceased firing. The losses in the three days' fight were 18 officers and 127 men killed, 65 officers and 849 men wounded, and 72 men missing. The condition of the troops after the battle was very bad; many of them were down with fever, and all were suffering from lack of suitable equipment and supplies. General Shafter cabled to the secretary of war, July 3, that it would be impossible to take Santiago by storm with the forces he then had, and that he was "seriously considering withdrawing about five miles and taking up a new position on the high ground between the San Juan River and Siboney." The destruction of Cervera's fleet the same day materially changed the situation.

The advance made by the American troops around Santiago on July 1 and 2 forced the Spanish authorities to come to a decision in regard to Cervera's fleet. Captain-General Blanco insisted that the fleet should not be captured or destroyed without a fight. Cervera refused to assume the responsibility of leaving the harbor, and when ordered to do so went out with consummate bravery, knowing that he was leading a forlorn hope. Sampson seems to have been under the impression all along that the Spanish squadron would attempt to escape at night, but the American ships kept in so close to the shore, with dazzling search-lights directed against the entrance of the harbor, as to render it almost impossible to steer a ship out. On the morning of July 3, at 8:55, Sampson started east to meet General Shafter in conference at Siboney, signalling to the fleet as he left: "Disregard movements commander-in-chief." The *Massachusetts* had also left her place in the blockade to go to Guantanamo for coal. The remaining ships formed a semicircle around the entrance of the harbor, the *Brooklyn* to the west, holding the left of the line, then the *Texas*, next the *Iowa* in the centre and at the south of the curve, then, as the line curved in to the coast on the right, the *Oregon* and the *Indiana*. The *Brooklyn* and the *Indiana*, holding the left and the right of the line, were about two miles and one and a half miles respectively from the shore, and near them, closer in, lay the converted gun-boats *Vixen* and *Gloucester*.

At 9:35 A.M., while most of the men were at Sunday inspection, the enemy's ships were discovered slowly steaming down the narrow channel of the harbor. In the lead was the *Maria Teresa*, followed by the *Vizcaya*, the *Colon*, the *Oquendo*, and the two torpedo-boat destroyers. The *Iowa* was the first to signal that the enemy were escaping, though the fact was noted on several ships at almost the same moment, and no orders were necessary. The American ships at once closed in and directed their fire against the *Teresa*. For a moment there was doubt as to whether the Spanish ships would separate and try to scatter the fire of our fleet or whether they would stick together. This was quickly settled when Cervera turned west, followed by the remainder of his command. At this point Commodore Schley's flagship, the *Brooklyn*, which was farthest west, turned to the eastward, away from the hostile fleet, making a loop, at the end of which she again steamed westward farther out to sea but still ahead of any of the American vessels. The sudden and unexpected turn of the *Brooklyn* caused the *Texas*, which was behind her, to reverse her engines in order to avoid a collision and to come to a stand-still, thus losing position, the *Oregon* and the *Iowa* both passing her. The two destroyers, which came out last, were attacked by the *Indiana* and the *Gloucester*, the commander of the latter, Wainwright, dashing towards them in utter disregard of the fragile character of his vessel. The *Furor* was sunk and the *Pluton* was run ashore. The *Teresa*, struck by several shells which exploded and set her on fire, turned to the shore at 10:15 and was beached about six miles west of the Morro. The *Oquendo* was riddled by shell and likewise soon on fire. She was beached about half a mile west of the *Teresa* at 10:20. The *Vizcaya* and *Colon* were now left to bear the fire of the pursuing American ships, which were practically uninjured. In this running fight the *Indiana* dropped behind, owing to the defective condition of her machinery, but kept up her fire. At 11:05 the *Vizcaya* turned to run ashore about fifteen miles west of the Morro. The *Brooklyn* and the *Oregon*, followed at some distance by the *Texas*, continued the chase of the *Colon*. The *Indiana* and the *Iowa*, at the order of Sampson, who had come up, went back to guard the transports. At 1:15 P.M. the *Colon* turned to shore thirty miles west of the *Vizcaya* and surrendered.

The fight was over, one of the most remarkable naval battles on record. On the American side, though the ships were struck many times, only one man was killed and one wounded. These casualties both occurred on Commodore Schley's flag-ship, the *Brooklyn*. The Spaniards lost about six hundred in killed and wounded. The American sailors took an active part in the rescue of the officers and crews of the burning Spanish ships.

On July 3, General Shafter demanded the surrender of the Spanish forces in Santiago. This being refused, he notified General Toral that the bombardment of Santiago would begin at noon of the 5th, thus giving two days for the women and children to leave the city. Nearly twenty thousand people came out and filled the villages and roads around. They were in an utterly destitute condition, and had to be taken care of largely by the American army, a great drain on their supplies. On the 10th and 11th the city was bombarded by the squadron. At this point General Miles arrived off Santiago with additional troops intended for Porto Rico. He and Shafter met General Toral under a flag of truce and arranged terms for the surrender, which took place on the 17th. Shafter's command was by this time in a serious state of health and anxious to return home. Malarial fevers had so weakened the men that an epidemic of yellow-fever, which had appeared sporadically throughout the command, was greatly feared. The situation was desperate and the war department apparently deaf to all representations of the case. Under these circumstances the division and brigade commanders and the surgeons met at General Shafter's headquarters early in August and signed a round-robin addressed to the secretary of war urging the immediate removal of the corps to the United States. This action was much criticised at the time, but it had the desired effect, and on August 4 orders were given to remove the command to Montauk Point, Long Island. The movement was begun at once and completed before the end of the month.

The surrender of Santiago left General Miles free to carry out plans already matured for the invasion of Porto Rico. He left Guantanamo, July 21, with 3415 men, mostly volunteers, convoyed by a fleet under the command of Captain Higginson, and landed at Guanica on the 25th. Early next morning General Garretson pushed forward with part of his brigade and drove the Spanish forces from Yauco, thus getting possession of the railroad to Ponce. General Miles was reinforced in a few days by the commands of Generals Wilson, Brooke, and Schwan, raising his entire force to 16,973 officers and men. In about two weeks they had gained control of all the southern and western portions of the island, but hostilities were suspended by the peace protocol before the conquest of Porto Rico was completed. The American losses in this campaign were three killed and forty wounded.

The last engagement of the war was the assault on Manila, which was captured August 13, 1898, by the forces under General Merritt, assisted by Admiral Dewey's squadron. This occurred the day after the signing of the peace protocol, the news of which did not reach the Philippines until several days later.

Two controversies growing out of the war with Spain assumed such importance that they cannot be passed by. The first related to the conduct of the war department, which was charged with inefficiency resulting from political appointments and corruption in the purchase of supplies. The most serious charge was that made by Major-General Miles, commanding the army, who declared that much of the refrigerated beef furnished the troops was "embalmed beef," preserved with secret chemicals of an injurious character. In September, 1898, President McKinley appointed a commission to investigate these charges, and the hearings held were sensational in the extreme. Commissary-General Eagan read a statement before the commission which was so violent in its abuse of the commanding general that he was later court-martialled and sentenced to dismissal for conduct unbecoming an officer and a gentleman, though this sentence was commuted by the president to suspension from rank and duty, but without loss of pay. The report of the commission failed to substantiate General Miles's charges, but it was not satisfactory or convincing. In spite of its efforts to whitewash things, the commission had to report that the secretary of war had failed to "grasp the situation." Many leading newspapers demanded Alger's resignation, but President McKinley feared to discredit the administration by dismissing him. Nevertheless, a coolness sprang up between them; and several months later, when Alger became a candidate for the Michigan senatorship, with the open support of elements distinctly hostile to the administration, the president asked for his resignation, which was tendered July 19, 1899. He was succeeded by Elihu Root, a very able and distinguished lawyer of New York.

The other controversy, which waged in the papers for months, was as to whether Sampson or Schley was in command at the battle of Santiago. As a reward for their work on that day, the president advanced Sampson eight numbers, Schley six, Captain Clark of the *Oregon* six, and the other captains five. These promotions were all confirmed by the Senate save those of Sampson and Schley, a number of senators holding that Schley should have received at least equal recognition with Sampson. The controversy was waged inside and outside of Congress for three years. The officials of the navy department were for the most part stanch supporters of Sampson, while a large part of the public, under the impression that the department was trying to discredit Schley, eagerly championed his cause. Finally, at the request of Admiral Schley, who was charged in certain publications with inefficiency and even cowardice, a court of inquiry was appointed July 26, 1901, with Admiral Dewey as president, for the purpose of inquiring into the conduct of Schley during the war with Spain. The opinion of the court was that his service prior to June 1 was "characterized by vacillation, dilatoriness, and lack of enterprise." Admiral Dewey differed from the opinions of his colleagues on certain points, and delivered a separate opinion, in the course of which he took up the question as to who was in command at Santiago, a point which had not been considered by the court. His conclusion was that Schley "was in absolute command and is entitled to the credit due to such commanding officer for the glorious victory which resulted in the total destruction of the Spanish ships." This made matters worse than ever. Secretary Long approved the findings of the majority of the court and disapproved Dewey's separate opinion. Schley appealed from the findings of the court to the president. February 18, 1902, President Roosevelt's memorandum, in which he reviewed the whole controversy, was made public. He declared that the court had done substantial justice to Schley. As regards the question of command at Santiago, he said that technically Sampson commanded the fleet, and Schley the western division, but that after the battle began not a ship took orders from either Sampson or Schley, except their own two vessels. "It was a captains' fight."

The Spanish war revealed many serious defects in our military system, some of which have been remedied by the reorganization of the army and the creation of a general staff. It demonstrated the necessity of military evolutions on a large scale in time of peace, so as to give the general officers experience in handling and the quartermaster and commissary departments experience in equipping and supplying large bodies of troops; it showed the folly and danger of appointing men from civil life through political influence to positions of responsibility in any branch of the military or naval service; it showed the value of field artillery, of smokeless powder, and of high-power rifles of the latest model; it also showed the necessity of having on hand a large supply of the best war material ready for use. While every American is proud of the magnificent record of the navy, it must not be imagined that the war with Spain was a conclusive test of its invincibility, for, however formidable the Spanish cruisers appeared at the time, later information revealed the fact that through the neglect of the Spanish government they were very far from being in a state of first-class efficiency.

VIII

America Becomes a World Power

THE *twentieth century opened with Americans in a high flush of optimism about their future. Prosperity had returned and everyone anticipated an era of the full dinner pail. The debate over empire waxed strong but the reelection of McKinley with his new running mate Theodore Roosevelt firmly placed the American people on the side of the experiment. Beneath the surface there bubbled a growing agitation for reform, one which gave promise of massive social experimentation. It was a time of high elation that had its most succinct expression in Roosevelt's joyous pronouncement, "I feel as fit as a Bull Moose!"*

The undercurrent of despair which had permeated much of the thinking of the early 90's had seemingly faded. No longer did the imagination conjure up as that of the Populist Ignatius Donnelly had the wretched hordes ". . . marching noiselessly as shades to unavoidable and everlasting misery." Instead, the American thinker, contemplating the future with hope, more likely agreed with Lincoln Steffens as he proclaimed, "The radical politics, the thinking of men who are giving their minds to social philosophy, is reaching far into the future, and if the ideas of men are an indication of the course of human action, then the future is secure." Few were prepared to dissent openly from his conclusion, "We are living in a great century, and, after it, there will probably be a still greater era." The final golden flush of an era, moving relentlessly toward the catastrophe of 1914, had blinded all but a few to the profound dislocations that existed concealed beneath the optimism and the great expectations.

The undercurrent of doubt for the future struggled to the surface in moments of vivid illumination such as that of Henry James in his The Princess Casamassima *when the Princess asks in wonderment, "Is everything that is gathering force, underground in the dark, in the night, in little hidden rooms out of sight of governments and policemen and idiotic 'statesmen'—heaven save them!—is all this going to burst forth some fine morning and set the world on fire?" And in counterpoint, she questioned, "Or is it going to sputter out and spend itself in vain conspiracies, be dissipated in sterile heroism and abortive isolated movements?" A shrewd appraisal of the reality that underlay the glittering surface, one that gains in sharpness when added to Henry Adams' illuminating comment about the Boxer Rebellion that rocked Peking in 1900 and disturbed the western world. "The drama acted at Peking . . . was," he wrote, "the most serious that could be offered for . . . study, since it brought [one] suddenly to the inevitable struggle for the control of China, which, in his view, must decide the control of the world." But in a time of portentous events, the new world of the twentieth century, as Adams noted, believed "The value of a Ming vase was more serious than universal war."*

And perhaps because a new century promises a new beginning, Americans greeted with hope the twentieth century. Nostalgia for the seemingly simpler past lingered, but most Americans half understood, "The jocund youth of our people now passes away never to return; the cares and anxieties of manhood's years henceforth are ours." The harsh nineties faded, and with its passing came a large emphasis upon change. Today seemed so much brighter than yesterday, and tomorrow made the mind ache with anticipation. A continent had been conquered in a short century; it seemed likely that a world and even worlds beyond our tiny earth would be in mankind's grasp by the end of another century. The tempo of events sent through some a chill of fear as they wondered whether the human race could come to grips with the accelerating pace of change.

An observer attempting to define the average American at the turn of the century would have had no difficulty in spelling out the physical facts. He was most likely to be of British origin, Protestant in religion, and Republican in politics. The per capita income would in 1911 average $227, and with the return of good times, job opportunities boomed and farm prices rose. The industrial indices read go for broke as total production increased by more than 80 percent, and the national wealth almost doubled in the first decade of the new century. By the eve of World War I the long debtor position in international trade ended. Americans lived in the expectation that the time was not far distant when the dollar would replace the pound as the international measure of monetary value.

The consolidation of American industry continued at a breakneck pace. The bulk of American railroads had been consolidated into six great systems. In 1900, the census reported seventy-three industrial combinations capitalized at more than $10,000,000, most of them dominating more than one-half of production in their fields. The creation of the U. S. Steel Corporation in 1901 placed almost 60 percent of the national steel production under the control of a single corporation. The power wielded by John Pierpont Morgan made that of the usual politician seem picayune by comparison. The cumulative impact of these developments informed the generation coming of age at the turn of the century that the simple equalitarianism that had prevailed in an agrarian America had passed. A society stratified by wealth, ethnic origin, religion, race, occupation, and, in the case of the South and West, by region was taking shape. Dimly forecast was the rise of a class-stratified society that fitted more readily into the classic Marxist mold.

Mark Sullivan (1874-1952), a self-educated newspaperman turned historian, chronicled in six volumes the first quarter of the twentieth century. In his long career as columnist for McClure's and Collier's magazines and the New York Herald-Tribune, he commented upon the passing scene and recorded the changing social habits of a mobile people. His comments ranged from muckraking studies of the patent medicine industry to an exploration of Mary Eddy Baker and her Christian Scientist Church. But in his later days, he concerned himself with exploring gently the daily habits and foibles of his countrymen. It proved a rambling but revealing account.

OUR TIMES, THE UNITED STATES, 1900-1925
THE TURN OF THE CENTURY

by Mark Sullivan

The American of 1900, reading his paper on Monday morning, New Year's Day, or the Sunday paper of the day before, or almost any paper during the year, observed, with some uneasiness, that the head-lines continued to occupy themselves, as they had for a considerable time, with the Philippines, Cuba, Porto Rico, Guam, Aguinaldo, the Igorrotes; words which three years before had had no more meaning to him than to stir old memories of something he had seen in his schoolboy geographies—you couldn't even be confident how to pronounce the names. Now they came close. His favorite politicians demanded that he think about them. Bryan told him we should put them away, Beveridge that we should embrace them. Some of his neighbors were infected with the pride that some newspapers and some orators conveyed in resounding phrases about America, the new world-power. Others, far from satisfied, felt it was an unanticipated result of the war with Spain, not clearly announced on the programme, that had left these waifs of the world on our door-step. They didn't seem to fit the American idea of a family of States, didn't seem quite the sort of folks we could take fully into our family circle, as adopted children should be taken if they are taken at all. We weren't quite sure we wanted them, or what we should do with them. Would it be self-interest to refuse them? Should we follow those who preached that these orphans of the storm were a call to duty? Much advice and exhortation was afloat. It was in February of the year before, 1899, that Kipling had given out his poem:

> Take up the White Man's burden,
> Send forth the best ye breed . . .
> To wait in heavy harness,
> On fluttering folk and wild—
> Your new-caught sullen peoples,
> Half devil and half child.

That poem had a powerful effect on sentimental minds, or minds responsive to the call of adventure; but the average American was probably as much impressed by the less exalted verse which Colonel Henry Watterson —with rather irresponsible neglect to discriminate among the divers varieties of people in our new acquisitions—called to the aid of a strong expression of editorial feeling in the Louisville *Courier-Journal:*

But the riff-raff; Lord, the riff-raff: Injun, nigger, beggar-man, thief—
　　"Both mongrel, puppy, whelp, and hound,
　　　　And cur of low degree."

The Philippines, we felt, were something vaguely Asiatic. As to them, the average American's sentiment was less accurately expressed by the benevolent phrase of the kindly Mr. Taft, "the little brown brother," than by the ballad which that phrase inspired an American soldier, made cynical by closer personal and hostile contact than Mr. Taft as Governor-General had had, to write:

　　He may be a brother of Big Bill Taft;
　　But he ain't no brother of mine.

Hardly less than in our own adventure in the Philippines, America in 1900 was interested in the British effort to conquer the Boers, which, during the early part of that year, was going badly. That fact gave strong satisfaction to the average American. In the form in which the conflict staged itself to the American eye, the Boer was kin to the American himself. He was a free man, economically independent; he was fighting against oppression by highly trained forces, greatly superior in numbers, equipment, organization, and the other leverages of power. The American inevitably thought of the analogy to his own struggle for independence. Recalling that most affectionately held group among all the traditions of his history, Bunker Hill, Valley Forge, George Washington, Israel Putnam, Nathan Hale, he thought of Oom Paul Kruger, Cronje, and De Wet in the same terms.

In the beginning the British papers had talked about the Boers as if they were a mere fly on the track of progress. They had said the British soldiers would eat their Christmas dinner in Pretoria—the Queen sent out chocolate specially stamped for that anticipated celebration. When the Boers administered defeat after defeat to the British, the average American jeered. He applauded stage travesties of the overconfident British. He laughed when the papers lampooned them, in such witticisms as: "The surprise party is the chief amusement of the Boer social season," and: "The Boers are good billiard shots—they are great at reversing the English."

Even so austerely restrained a periodical as *The Review of Reviews*, one so habitually conscious of high responsibility for amity and good manners among nations, reflected, in this case, the emotion of Americans generally in a passage that pointed out "a ludicrous aspect to the heroics and hysterics of the London press":

　　The very same London papers which a few days ago thought the Boers could not and would not fight, and that a few British regiments could go to Pretoria without firing a shot, have now gone to the opposite extreme of regarding the Boer armies as the most formidable ever known in the history of warfare, and are begging their readers to consider that the British Empire is engaged in a life-and-death struggle. . . . This tone merely invites the contempt of the world, while it also provokes the freer expression of enthusiastic admiration for the magnificent stand of the Dutch farmers against such overwhelming odds.

When the British finally conquered the Boers, *Life* (November 15, 1900) said: "A small boy with diamonds is no match for a large burglar with experience." This active sympathy which the average American had for the Boers, coupled with biting disapproval of the British, his hero sentiment for Cronje and De Wet in their rough country clothes as against the spick-and-span military correctness of the British generals, his pleasure at the little armies of Boer irregulars administering defeat after defeat to the much larger armies of British regulars, was more than a mere incident of the news. It had permanent importance, because it was one contribution to a certain mood that was prevalent in America in 1900, a mood of championship for the under dog against the upper, a disposition of the average American to see himself as an under dog in economic situations and controversies in his own country. That prevailing American mood of 1900 determined much that happened after 1900 in our politics and social organization.

If the American, reading the papers of New Year's Day, 1900, was more than commonly reflective over the serious aspects of the news, it was only partly because the sporting page and the comic strip had not yet arrived to overbalance the American newspaper on the side of the merely diverting. It was due also to the presence in the newspapers of that day and in the sermons of the day before, of a spirit of solemnity, occasioned by the coming of a new year and, as some said, a new century.

Throughout 1899 there had been much discussion as to what day and year marked the close of the nineteenth century and the beginning of the twentieth. It was recognized by everybody as a turning-point, a hundred-mile stone. There was a human disposition to sum things up, to say who had been the greatest men of the century just closed, what had been the greatest books, the greatest inventions, the greatest advancs in science. Looking forward, there was a similar disposition to forecast and predict. This appealed to nearly everybody; and to find people disputing the correctness of the date you chose for harking back or looking forward was an irritation. Wherever men met they argued about it. Editorials dealt with it, seriously or facetiously. Contentious persons wrote letters to the papers. School-children were set to figuring. It grew to the vogue of one of those puzzles like "How old is Ann?"

A learned editor, Doctor Albert Shaw, settled the question for his readers in his magazine for January, 1900. With somewhat the air of an Olympian so wise he can afford to be tolerant, he gently rebuked those who were disputing about so clear a thing:

> There has been a curious misapprehension in the minds of many people, and even in print there has been a good deal of allusion to the year now ending (1899) as the closing one of the nineteenth century.

Having thus, in his capacity of commentator on events, recorded a dispute, which, because it existed, one must take account of, Doctor Shaw proceeded with an air becoming to unassailable authority, an air which seemed to say: "Of course, you understand I'm not arguing with you; I'm merely telling you":

> A half-minute's clear thinking is enough to remove all confusion. With December 31 we complete the year 1899—that is to say, we round out 99 of the 100 years that are necessary to complete a full century. We must give the nineteenth century the 365 days that belong to its hundredth and final year, before we begin the year 1 of the twentieth century. The mathematical faculty works more keenly in monetary affairs than elsewhere; and none of the people who have proposed to allow ninety-nine years to go for a century would suppose that a $1,900 debt had been fully met by a tender of $1,899.

*   *   *   *   *

In his newspapers of January 1, 1900, the American found no such word as radio, for that was yet twenty years from coming; nor "movie," for that too was still mainly of the future; nor chauffeur, for the automobile was only just emerging and had been called "horseless carriage" when treated seriously, but rather more frequently, "devil-wagon," and the driver, the "engineer." There was no such word as aviator—all that that word implies was still a part of the Arabian Nights. Nor was there any mention of income tax or surtax, no annual warnings of the approach of March 15—all that was yet thirteen years from coming. In 1900 doctors had not heard of 606 or of insulin; science had not heard of relativity or the quantum theory. Farmers had not heard of tractors, nor bankers of the Federal Reserve System. Merchants had not heard of chain-stores nor "self-service"; nor seamen of oil-burning engines. Modernism had not been added to the common vocabulary of theology, nor futurist and "cubist" to that of art. Politicians had not heard of direct primaries, nor of the commission form of government, nor of city managers, nor of blocs in Congress, nor of a League of Nations, nor of a World Court. They had not heard of "muck-rakers," nor of "Bull Moose" except in a zoological sense. Neither had they heard of "dry" and "wet" as categories important in vote-getting, nor of a Volstead Act; they had not heard of an Eighteenth Amendment, nor a Nineteenth, nor a Seventeenth, nor a Sixteenth—there were but fifteen amendments in 1900, and the last had been passed in 1869.

In 1900 woman suffrage had only made a beginning, in four thinly peopled Western States. A woman governor or a woman congressman was a humorous idea, far-fetched, to be sure, yet one out of which a particularly fertile humorist, on the stage or in the papers, could get much whimsical burlesque. In 1900, the Lower House of Congress, in the spirit of a popular slogan that said "Let the people elect their senators," and stimulated by two recent scandals in the naming of senators by State legislatures in Montana and Pennsylvania, passed, by a vote of 240 to 15, a resolution calling for a constitutional amendment to provide that senators should be chosen directly by the people. In 1900, at Madison, Wis., on August 8, a State convention nominated Robert M. La Follette for governor and demanded that the system of party conventions and caucuses for governor be abolished, and that nominations for political office be made by "direct primaries."

The newspapers of 1900 contained no mention of smoking by women, nor of "bobbing," nor "permanent wave," nor vamp, nor flapper, nor jazz, nor feminism, nor birth-control. There was no such word as rum-runner, nor hijacker, nor bolshevism, fundamentalism, behaviorism, Nordic, Freudian, complexes, ectoplasm, brain-storm, Rotary, Kiwanis, blue-sky law, cafeteria, automat, sundae; nor mah-jong, nor cross-word puzzle. Not even military men had heard of camouflage; neither that nor "propaganda" had come into the vocabulary of the average man. "Over the top," "zero hour," "no man's land" meant nothing to him. "Drive" meant only an agreeable experience with a horse. The newspapers of 1900 had not yet come to the lavishness of photographic illustration that was to be theirs by the end of the quarter-century. There were no rotogravure sections. If there had been, they would not have pictured boy scouts, nor State constabularies, nor traffic cops, nor Ku Klux Klan parades; nor women riding astride, nor the nudities of the Follies, nor one-piece bathing-suits, nor advertisements of lip-sticks, nor motion-picture actresses, for there were no such things.

In 1900, "short-haired woman" was a phrase of jibing; women doctors were looked on partly with ridicule, partly with suspicion. Of prohibition and votes for women, the most conspicuous function was to provide material for newspaper jokes. Men who bought and sold lots were still real-estate agents, not "realtors." Undertakers were undertakers, not having yet attained the frilled euphemism of "mortician." There were "star-routes" yet—rural free delivery had only just made a faint beginning; the parcel-post was yet to wait thirteen years. In 1900, "bobbing" meant sliding down a snow-covered hill; woman had not yet gone to the barber-shop. For the deforestation of the male countenance, the razor of our grandfathers was the exclusive means; men still knew the art of honing. The hairpin, as well as the bicycle, the horseshoe, and the buggy were the bases of established and, so far as any one could foresee, permanent businesses. Ox-teams could still be seen on country roads; horse-drawn street-cars in the cities. Horses or mules for trucks were practically universal; livery-stables were everywhere. The blacksmith beneath the spreading chestnut-tree was a reality; neither the garage mechanic nor the chestnut blight had come to retire that scene to poetry. The hitching-post had not been supplanted by the parking problem. Croquet had not given way to golf. "Boys in blue" had not yet passed into song. Army blue was not merely a sentimental memory, had not succumbed to the invasion of utilitarianism in olive green. G. A. R. were still potent letters.

In 1900, the Grand Army of the Republic was still a numerous body, high in the nation's sentiment, deferred to in politics, their annual national reunions and parades stirring events, and their local posts important in their communities. Among the older generation the memories and issues of the Civil War still had power to excite feeling, although the Spanish War, with its outpouring of a common national emotion against a foreign foe, had come close to completing the burial of the rancors of the war between the

States. Such terms as "Rebel," "Yank," and "damn Yankee," "Secesh" were still occasionally used, sometimes with a touch of ancient malice. A few politicians, chiefly older ones, still found or thought they found potency in "waving the bloody shirt." Negro suffrage was still a living and, in some quarters, an acrimonious issue.

The passing of the questions arising out of the Civil War, and the figures associated with it, as major incidents of politics and life, was one of the most marked of the many respects in which 1900 was a dividing year.

In 1900, America presented to the eye the picture of a country that was still mostly frontier of one sort or another, the torn edges of civilization's first contact with nature, man in his invasion of the primeval. There were some areas that retained the beauty of nature untouched: the Rocky Mountains, parts of the Western plains where the railroads had not yet reached, and some bits of New England. There were other spots, comparatively few, chiefly the farming regions of eastern Pennsylvania, New York State, and New England, where beauty had come with the work of man—old farms with solid well-kept barns, many of heavy stone or brick; substantial houses with lawns shaded by evergreen trees that had been growing for more than a generation, fields kept clean to the fence corners—areas that to the eye and spirit gave satisfying suggestions of a settled order, traditions, crystallized ways of life, comfort, serenity, hereditary attachment to the local soil.

Only the Eastern seaboard had the appearance of civilization having really established itself and attained permanence. From the Alleghanies to the Pacific Coast, the picture was mainly of a country still frontier and of a people still in flux: the Alleghany mountainsides scarred by the axe, cluttered with the rubbish of improvident lumbering, blackened with fire; mountain valleys disfigured with ugly coal-breakers, furnaces, and smoke-stacks; western Pennsylvania and eastern Ohio an eruption of ungainly wooden oil-derricks; rivers muddied by the erosion from lands cleared of trees but not yet brought to grass, soiled with the sewage of raw new towns and factories; prairies furrowed with the first breaking of sod. Nineteen hundred was in the flood-tide of railroad-building: long fingers of fresh dirt pushing up and down the prairies, steam-shovels digging into virgin land, rock-blasting on the mountainsides. On the prairie farms, sod houses were not unusual. Frequently there were no barns, or, if any, mere sheds. Straw was not even stacked, but rotted in sodden piles. Villages were just past the early picturesqueness of two long lines of saloons and stores, but not yet arrived at the orderliness of established communities; houses were almost wholly frame, usually of one story, with a false top, and generally of a flimsy construction that suggested transiency; larger towns with a marble Carnegie Library at Second Street, and Indian tepees at Tenth. Even as to most of the cities, including the Eastern ones, their outer edges were a kind of frontier, unfinished streets pushing out to the fields; sidewalks, where there were any, either of brick that loosened with the first thaw, or wood that rotted quickly; rapid growth leading to rapid change. At the gates of the country, great masses of human raw materials were being dumped from immigrant ships. Slovenly immigrant trains tracked westward. Bands of unattached men, floating labor, moved about from the logging-camps of the winter woods to harvest in the fields, or to railroad-construction camps. Restless "sooners" wandered hungrily about to grab the last opportunities for free land.

One whole quarter of the country, which had been the seat of its most ornate civilization, the South, though it had spots of melancholy beauty, presented chiefly the impression of the weedy ruins of thirty-five years after the Civil War, and comparatively few years after Reconstruction—ironic word.

In 1900 the United States was a nation of just under 76,000,000 people, with dependencies in the West Indies, off the coast of Asia, near the Arctic Ocean, and in the mid-Pacific, all acquired recently, except Alaska. The area of the mainland was 3,026,789 square miles. This expanse of territory reached from 25° north latitude to 49°. Its temperature varied from a winter extreme of 45° below zero in Bismarck, N. D., to a summer extreme of 117° in Phoenix, Ariz., its elevation from the 14,501 feet of Mount Whitney to the sea-level savannas of the Gulf Coast; its climate from the four months of immunity from frost that was good for hard wheat in North Dakota to the practically frostless lands that would raise oranges in Florida and California.

Within this scope of land and climate there was such an abundance and variety of food and other natural resources as made it the most nearly self-sustaining compact nation that then was or ever had been. Within its own borders it reaped every variety of edible grain; raised every kind of vegetable food in common use, except bananas and a few condiments and stimulants, such as cocoa, coffee, tea, and pepper—and even some of these were raised to some extent, and practically all could be raised in any emergency. It produced every kind of meat for common use. From its streams, lakes, and shores it was supplied with nearly every kind of fish or fish product except a few epicurean delicacies, such as caviar from Russia and sardines from the Mediterranean.

Of material for clothing, it had five times as much cotton as all the rest of the world, as much wool as the people desired to raise, and while it imported silk and some linen, it could produce these in any quantity necessary for its own use. Of the raw materials for shelter and for the most exacting and complex needs of modern manufacture of every kind, it had teeming stores. Of woods it had an abundance of all, except a few minor and dispensable ones like mahogany, teak, and balsa. Of minerals it had an abundance of all the more important ones, and also some supplies of tin, manganese, vanadium, and platinum, though it imported most of these. Of vegetable products needed on any large or essential scale for manufacture, it had all except rubber; and it had the soil and climate to produce this if desired.

Not only did this nation have supplies of every kind of natural resource and raw materials abundant for its own use; of most of them, it had stores far greater than those of any other nation; and of many, more than all the rest of the world. Measured by annual output, in 1900 America produced more than half the world's cotton, corn, copper, and oil; more than a third of its steel, pig iron, and silver; and substantially a third of its coal and gold.

Of the physical facts about this country, two had more bearing on its welfare than any others. Externally, it was widely separated from the two old and densely populated continents of the world; from Europe by the Atlantic Ocean; from Asia by the Pacific. Internally, within this nation's whole immensity of territory, there was no boundary, no customs barrier, no variation of language, currency or fundamental law, no impediment to the free interchange of goods and ideas.

The parts of this country were bound together for the purposes of trade and mutual intercourse by almost 200,000 miles of railroad, more than 200,000 miles of telegraph-lines, and more than a million miles of telephone-wire in service.

Though some portions of this country were not as well adapted to the propagation of human stock of the white race, especially to the preservation of infants through their early years, as some European countries less subject to violent extremes of heat and dryness; yet in this respect the people inhabiting this territory had practised much ingenuity in the inventing and perfecting of devices for making artificial ice, pasteurizing milk, heating their homes in winter, and otherwise overcoming local handicaps of climate; and also had equipped themselves generously with physicians and nurses, and institutions for training them, and with hospitals; so that on the whole this territory was admirably adapted to the physical well-being of the human stock that inhabited it.

This human stock was of the white (Caucasian) race, except: about 9,000,000 in whole or part of black (Ethiopian) blood, descendants of a strain originally brought to the country as slaves and later set free and made citizens; about 114,000 of Mongolian stock (90,000 Chinese and 24,000 Japanese); and 237,000 who were in whole or part of the aboriginal Indian blood.

A most important fact about the stock of this nation, for which there was no parallel or precedent among great nations, either of its own time or of the past; an aspect that had many advantages, but which came to be regarded during this quarter-century as having possible perils in excess of its advantages, was the fact that alone among great nations its stock was not indigenous to the soil, was not homogeneous, had no long common history nor any body of common institutions arising out of its own experiences. Its people had come from other countries, either immediately or through near ancestors, all within a period of less than 300 years, and most within a much shorter period. Also, this people recruited its population as much through additions from overseas as through births in its native stock.

As respects the origins of the dominant white race: in 1900, 41,000,000 were reckoned roughly as "native white stock," meaning descendants of stock which had been in America for at least one whole generation. Of this native white stock a large majority derived from the early settlers, who had been chiefly British. Twenty-six millions, or 40 per cent of the total whites, had come very recently from Europe—were either direct immigrants or the children of immigrants. Of this class of recent increments, about 30 per cent were of British stock, 31 per cent of German stock, 4 per cent Swedish, 4 per cent Russian, 4 per cent Austrian, 3 per cent Italian. At this time, however, and for several years after 1900, immigration from Russia, Poland, and Italy was increasing very rapidly; whereas immigration from northwestern Europe was not. Consequently there was a measurable tendency for the British and other northwest European portions of the stock to decline from their numerical superiority in the composition of this people as a whole.

Most of the institutions of this people, their language, their religion, their fundamental laws, their point of view regarding organized society, the relations of the sexes, education and the like, were derived from the same European countries that were the sources of the people themselves. To a greater extent even than the people themselves were British, their institutions were based on British models. English was the common language, universal and mandatory in legislative proceedings, legal documents, and the like; and practically universal in daily use. Exceptions consisted of a few spots in Pennsylvania, where the language in daily use was "Pennsylvania Dutch," a patois derived from the early German settlers of those communities and modified by contact with the English tongue; some communities in the Southwest, where Spanish was in common use, a heritage from the early Spanish settlement of Mexico; a few spots, like part of the Gulf coast of Louisiana, where a remnant of Acadian exiles retained their French tongue after a hundred and forty years; a few other localities, chiefly in New England, where more recent immigrants from French Canada retained their French tongue. Some of the late immigrants from Europe continued to use their native tongues in a few settlements: Italian and Yiddish in New York and other cities of the East; German in some communities in the Northwest, as well as Swedish, Finnish, Polish, Greek. Indian tribal languages were in use in a few scattered places.

In jurisprudence the origin was wholly English, except in Louisiana, where the Napoleonic code of the early settlers was retained. The legislative institutions were based wholly on English models.

In education the traditions were prevailingly British, except that in higher university education there had been for some years a disposition to turn to German models and to import German teachers. Of the modern languages taught in high schools and colleges, other than English, there was more of German than of all others combined.

As respects literature, including poetry and the drama, the origins were almost wholly British. A few Latin and Greek classics were read in high schools and colleges. There was some literature from the French, chiefly novels and philosophy, with a few dramas; some from the German, mostly philosophical; little from the Spanish, except one or two classics; some from Italy; and the beginnings of a literature transplanted from Russia and the Scandinavian countries.

Classical music was an exception to the prevailingly British origins of this people's culture. The only British contributions that could be regarded as within the category "classic" were the comic operas of Gilbert and Sullivan. In this field there was a strong infusion from the German, chiefly the operas of Wagner and the instrumental music of Beethoven, Brahms, and some others. There was also a strong infusion from the Italian, consisting of such operas as Verdi's "Il Trovatore," "La Traviata," and "Aida." There was some classic music of French origin, some of Russian, and a little of Spanish. A few experiments had been made, chiefly by Edward MacDowell, toward building up a characteristic American music based on Indian strains.

Popular music was largely British in origin, and more from Scotland and Ireland than from England. A considerable number of the melodies in popular use came from Negro sources or were based on Negro themes and the Negro imagination. In this particular year, 1900, there was, in instrumental popular music, a vogue for a type known as "ragtime" and the "cake-walk," of mongrel origin.

The religious attachments of this people were almost wholly to denominations accepting the doctrine of the divinity of Jesus Christ. The exceptions, which differed utterly from each other and had nothing essential in common except non-acceptance of the divinity of Christ, were about 1,050,000 Jews, about 75,000 Unitarians, a few hundred believers in Buddhism or some other Oriental religion. A few Indians still followed their original rites.

Within the Christian religion about 12,000,000 were attached to the Roman Catholic faith; about 700,000 to the Episcopal, a few hundred to the Greek Catholic. The remainder belonged to one or another evangelical or reformed denomination—about 6,000,000 Methodists, 5,000,000 Baptists, 1,500,000 Lutherans, 1,500,000 Presbyterians, 350,000 Mormons, 80,000 followers of Christian Science. Except the Mormons and the followers of Christian Science, which sects had originated in America, most of these denominational affiliations had accompanied immigrants to America or been inherited from immigrants. All the immigrant stocks, except the Negro, tended to maintain the religions of the countries from which they came.

The distinctive characteristics of this people, marking them off from some or all other nations, included: a determined faith in the democratic organization of society and the representative form of government; a taboo against kings and aristocracy; separation of church and state; zeal for universal education; an indisposition to maintain a large standing army; a prevailing and growing trend toward the abolition of alcoholic drinks. There was a freedom—at that time—from much of the regulation by government that was common in many other countries, and a vigilance against encroachment by government on the individual, a trait derived from the comparatively recent experiences of most of these people as voluntary exiles from monarchical and other exacting forms of government.

There was a freedom from stratification into castes, social or industrial, accompanied by the absence from the country's political system of any permanent or important labor or otherwise radical political party. Freedom from stratification also led to sociability, an easy approachableness and informality in human relations, not common in nations having one degree or another of caste. The people had independence of spirit, accompanied by the concession of equal independence to others—a trait due to exemption from caste, to the nature of the people, most of whom had been pioneers themselves or in their recent ancestors, and to immunity from great anxiety about making a livelihood, an immunity made possible by the natural wealth of the country. Another national trait was a responsiveness to idealism, greater than was common among older nations where the economic pressure of numbers made unselfishness less easy and where experience had brought disillusionment. The American temperament included adaptiveness, a willingness more prompt than among other peoples to dismiss the old and try the new, a freedom from enthralment to the familiar, which accounted for much of the rapidity of their progress, especially in machinery.

Some minor distinctive institutions included: the celebration of a national holiday known as Thanksgiving, rocking-chairs, a greater fastidiousness about personal cleanliness as measured by the commonness of bathtubs as compared with other countries; ice-water, pie, New England boiled dinner, chewing-gum; baseball, a game calling for unusually quick reactions intellectually and prompt and easy co-operation muscularly; a diversion called poker, indigenous to this nation and containing definite elements of the interplay of psychology not found in ordinary card games.

Of all the characteristics of this people, the most important was freedom of opportunity for the individual, which provided the nation with a constant, rapid, and generous supply of leadership in every line from its own ranks. A national habit of mind, social organization and education, made it as easy for the individual to arrive at leadership from the lowest ranks as for those in the highest ranks to keep it. Certain handicaps, partly legal and partly in the intangible world of social point of view, denied to those already highly placed in wealth or position any great hereditary advantages or rights, or any other security of tenure except what they and their descendants could provide through energy or talent. The same national point of view and practice, together with the great natural wealth of the country and the system of universal free education, made it easy for the talented and the energetic to rise.

In 1900 the President of the United States, William McKinley, was the son of a country lawyer. The greatest ironmaster, Andrew Carnegie, was the son of a weaver—he had come to the United States as an immigrant and had spent his youth as a telegraph messenger-boy. Of the two men who were making the largest contributions to applied science, one, Michael Pupin, had been a shepherd-boy in Serbia, had come to America as an immigrant and worked as a farm-hand in Delaware; the other, Thomas A. Edison, had spent his youth as a newsboy and telegraph-operator. One of the outstanding geniuses in electricity, Charles P. Steinmetz, had come to America to escape persecution for his socialistic beliefs, and had had difficulty, because of physical defects, in passing the immigration authorities, who feared he might become a public charge. The leading railroad operator, James J. Hill, had begun as a clerk in a village store. The richest man in the country, John D. Rockefeller, had been a clerk in a commission house. One of the leaders of literature, Mark Twain, had got his pen-name from his experience as a pilot on a Mississippi River steamboat. A noted journalist, Joseph Pulitzer, had entered America as an immigrant, literally without dry clothes on his back, for he had leaped from a ship in Boston Harbor and swum ashore in order to take advantage, for himself, of the bounty offered to volunteers in the Civil War.

At the same time this American system provided abundant opportunity for those who had been born in the higher ranks to remain there, if they had the character, talent, and energy to endure the competition. In 1900 the man who was just becoming one of the leaders in public life, Theodore Roosevelt, had been born to wealth and in the social environment of the old Dutch families of New York. The man who in 1900 was intrusted with carrying our institutions to our first great dependency, and who was later to be President of the United States and chief justice of the Supreme Court, William H. Taft, was the son of a father who had been secretary of war and attorney-general in cabinets a generation before. The leading educator, Charles W. Eliot, president of Harvard University, had been born in the higher social and business circles of New England. The leading banker, J. Pierpont Morgan, although his power was due to the salience of his personality, had inherited the banking-house of which he was head. One of the leading businesses, the du Pont Company, had been in the hands of one family since its foundation, more than a hundred years before.

Among those who had not yet emerged in 1900 to leadership, but were destined to supply it within the quarter-century to follow; among those who in the opening year of the century were being incubated for leadership through some of the processes which this democracy provided—among these: In 1900, Woodrow Wilson was a professor at Princeton, and had not yet written his history of the American people. William G. McAdoo was practising law in New York and writing the opening chapters of a book on poverty and its prevention, a work for which he had secured practical training through having spent a desperately poor boyhood in the devastated South of the post-Civil-War period, and through, also, his struggles to get a foothold in New York, where he was about to develop the idea of uniting the island of Manhattan with the New Jersey mainland by tunnels under the Hudson River. In 1900, Herbert Hoover, then twenty-five years old, and five years out of Leland Stanford University, through which he had worked his way, was making in China the beginnings of what was to be, before he was thirty-five, a world-wide reputation as an engineer. In 1900, Charles Evans Hughes was in the ranks of young, hard-working, and comparatively unknown lawyers in New York City, spending some of his time as a lecturer in New York University Law School. William E. Borah, then thirty-five years old, was practising law in Boise, Idaho, where he had located because that was the terminus of the longest railroad trip he had been able to pay for when, nine years before, he had started West after completing his legal education. Calvin Coolidge was an obscure lawyer in a small New England town, making his beginnings in politics in fellowship with a local shoemaker.

AN *assassin's bullet put Theodore Roosevelt into the White House, and with his accession to the Presidency the executive office took on unforeseen dimensions. If nothing more, the ebullient Roosevelt brought an unaccustomed youth to the executive office. The staid propriety with which his predecessors had reigned was supplanted by a rambunctious energy that Henry Adams summarized neatly when he wrote, "Roosevelt . . . showed the singular primitive quality that belongs to ultimate matter—the quality that mediaeval theology assigned to God—he was pure act." The nation reacted to his fundamental energy with a mixture of awe, amusement, identification, and some misgivings. They understood that he would propel them forward but they also sensed that he might as easily catapult them into some doubtful ventures.*

But from the moment he entered the White House, he revealed a remarkable ability to use power. He broke with the traditional fear of big business, insisting instead the great corporations were a logical outgrowth of "natural causes in the business world." He argued that their existence assured the United States would "assume the commanding position in the international business world." To confine or disrupt their activities would either cramp or fetter "the youthful strength" of the nation. But he also recognized that such private aggregates of power posed a countervailing challenge to the power of the federal government. To meet this problem, he would institute a system "of supervision and regulation over all corporations doing an interstate business." To emphasize the scope of federal power, he instituted legal proceedings against the proposed Northern Securities Company, a giant holding company formed to administer the major Northwestern railroads, in 1902, his intention being to impress upon the business community the ultimate scope of federal power, but also to avoid disrupting an established enterprise.

To make his point even sharper, he intervened in the 1902 anthracite coal strike to force the mine operators to come to terms with their employees. He did so once he was convinced that the miners had the better case, but he also made it emphatic that his intervention was dictated by the ultimate well-being of the whole community. "The fundamental rule in our national life—the rule which underlies all others—" he declared, "is that, on the whole, and in the long run, we shall go up or down together." In his hands, the Presidency took a large new role, that of tribune of the people. As spokesman for the public interest, he designated the executive office as the one assigned to keep in balance the competing and often conflicting interests that make up American society.

As he explored the reaches of presidential power within the domestic scene, he extended the executive role in determining foreign policy. He did not hesitate to extend his good offices to bring an end to the Russo-Japanese War in 1905. And since his offer was accepted and peace restored, both his own prestige and that of the United States were enhanced. Henry Cabot Lodge writing from Europe concluded, "We are the strongest moral force —also physical—now extant, and the peace of the world rests largely with us." When war with Japan seemed to threaten, he sent the fleet on a round-

the-world tour, declaring afterward, "The sending of the fleet to the Pacific
stopped the Japanese talk of war." He showed an equal willingness to in-
tervene directly into the affairs of Latin-America, justifying his behavior
with the unsubtle comment: "Some time soon I shall have to spank some
little brigand of a South American republic." Such militance convinced
William James, the philosopher, "He is still mentally in the Sturm und Drang
period of early adolescence."

No biographer captured more fully the essential Roosevelt than Henry
Pringle (1898-1958). He had a long career as journalist, serving on the staffs
of the New York Sun, Globe, *and* World, *in addition to a stint as an as-*
sociate editor of the magazine Outlook. *He subsequently held the post of*
Professor of Journalism at Columbia University and during World War II
was chief of the publications division of the Office of War Information.
His biography of William Howard Taft remains the definitive work on the
subject. And his treatment of Roosevelt still sparkles with the obvious
vivacity of the subject. Though hardly a work of reverence, Pringle ex-
plains why a generation prepared to try out new solutions for old problems
accepted him as their natural leader. For in their youthful hope, they rec-
ognized his youth.

THEODORE ROOSEVELT

by Henry F. Pringle

In 1896, Roosevelt praised the manner in which President Cleveland had
been handling the dispute with Great Britain on the Venezuela boundary.
"Primarily," he wrote, "our action is based on national self-interest. In other
words, it is patriotic." This being so, Roosevelt continued, "the limited
number of persons" who would substitute "a kind of milk-and-water cos-
mopolitanism" for patriotic righteousness were "never men of robust character or of imposing personality, and the plea itself is not worth considering."

He was police commissioner in New York City when these sentiments
were expressed. Extraordinary changes altered the map of the world during
the five years which passed before he became President. The ardent advocate
of imperialism, Roosevelt faced problems and dangers resulting from it. The
United States had become a world power. Subjugation of the Philippine
Islands, limited independence for Cuba, a canal across the isthmus at Panama
or at Nicaragua, and naval coaling stations in the Pacific were among the
projects that had to be consummated. There were others, as Roosevelt was
to discover during the seven and one half years of his reign. The balance of
power in the Far East would cause many a troubled moment. An orderly
government had to be imposed on the quasi-comic Republic of Santo
Domingo.

To Roosevelt, the conduct of foreign affairs was essentially simple. The phrase first conceived to describe his attitude toward the New York Republican machine—"Speak softly and carry a big stick, you will go far"—became his slogan in dealing with the governments of Europe and South America. Right was right, and the United States defined and enforced the rules of the international game. Arbitration of disputes was laudable, except when America was a party to the issue. Peace was secondary to honor, and America defined honor. The Monroe Doctrine was the cornerstone of American diplomacy or belligerency; and before President Roosevelt had concluded his interpretations, it had been changed almost beyond recognition. The Roosevelt of 1901 to 1909 had greater wisdom and more discretion than the Roosevelt who had, in 1896, pronounced his theories on patriotism. Fundamentally, he had abandoned none of them.

There is delicious irony in the fact that this was the man who received the Nobel Peace Prize in 1906, and greater irony in the added fact that he deserved the award for his skill and energy in ending the Russo-Japanese War. The countries of Europe, during Roosevelt's Presidency, were far too concerned with the balance of power in the Balkans, in the Far East, and on the Continent itself, to have any stomach for war with the United States. It is idle to say that Roosevelt might have become involved in a long and costly struggle had circumstances been different. Had they been different, he might have been more conciliatory. On the one occasion when he believed war with a major power possible, with Japan between 1906 and 1908, he made valiant efforts to prevent it.

The innate provincialism of Roosevelt's early attitude toward Great Britain and Germany reflected the opinion of his day. Toward the former, as he became President, the hostility was growing less virulent. A story that circulated through Washington in 1902, however, indicates that it was not yet safe for the man in public life to advocate a vigorous handclasp across the sea. One day the President, accompanied by Secretary of War Root, inspected the alterations under way at the White House. They paused in front of a marble mantelpiece on which lions were being chiseled. ". . . Some of our old friends might put a wrong interpretation on the decoration," said Roosevelt, in pretended dismay. Mr. Root looked at the lions critically.

"Well," he said slowly, "we might give them a more subdued expression and then tie a knot in each of their tails. I am sure that arrangement would be satisfactory to most patriotic Americans."

Roosevelt, despite his friendship with Spring Rice, assured himself that he had no illusions about England. "On the whole," he remarked to Lodge in 1901, "I am friendly to England . . . [but] I do not at all believe in being over-effusive or forgetting that fundamentally we are two different nations." A few months earlier he had considered "a combination between Germany and England against the United States as a possibility to be guarded against." In December, 1904, he wrote:

> . . . the average Englishman is not a being whom I find congenial or
> with whom I care to associate. I wish him well, but I wish him well at

a good distance from me. . . . England has been friendly with us since we have grown so strong as to make her friendship a matter of more moment to her than to us. If we quit building our fleet, England's friendship would immediately cool.

England was a source of annoyance, because of her real or imagined attitude of superiority. Germany was considered actually dangerous, not only by Roosevelt but by Secretary of State Hay and by Americans generally. She had been the one important neutral to exhibit overt hostility during the Spanish War, although the facts regarding the Manila Bay incident were probably exaggerated. The seizure of Kiao-chau had been another source of alarm. In April, 1901, Hay had instructed the American chargé d'affaires at Berlin to investigate reports that the German Government contemplated the annexation, contrary to the Monroe Doctrine, of Margarita Island off the Venezuelan coast. Henry White, at the American embassy in London, was convinced that Germany had blocked the sale by Denmark of the Virgin Islands to the United States in 1902, and had designs of her own upon them.

The Kaiser appears to have been aware that the reputation of his country was in danger, but his endeavors to pour oil on the troubled waters of German-American friendship were not signally successful. In November, 1901, he had caused a medal to be conferred upon the President of the United States, and this inspired John Hay to amused contempt. The gift, he wrote, was worth about thirty-five cents and was of dubious artistic merit. Two additional gestures, the visit of Prince Henry early in 1902 and an invitation to have Alice Roosevelt christen a yacht being built for the Kaiser in an American shipyard, seem to have been similarly fruitless. The prince was received with due ceremony, and the future Mrs. Longworth christened the yacht. Roosevelt's private letters, however, continued to reflect a decided irreverence toward the German royal family. Neither Mrs. Roosevelt nor himself "could be dragged to meet Prince Henry if it were not our official duty," he said. He appealed to John Hay, as arbiter in court etiquette, for advice on the state dinner to the Kaiser's brother:

> . . . when we go into the . . . dinner, how in the name of Heaven will we avoid hurting various Teuton susceptibilities? Will the Prince take Mrs. Roosevelt while I walk in solemn state by myself? How do we do it anyhow: I am quite clear that I ought not to walk in with my wife on one arm and the Prince somewhere alongside—but further than this I do not go.

As for the Kaiser's yacht, Roosevelt told Hay that the suggestion had been made that Alice prepare a brief speech for the christening. Her father, however, had hesitated. ". . . The only motto sufficiently epigrammatic that came to my mind," he said, "was 'Damn the Dutch.' "

Against this background of distrust and suspicion must be viewed Roosevelt's handling of his first major problems in foreign affairs: the Venezuela debt friction, in which both Germany and England were involved, and the Alaska boundary dispute with Great Britain.

Cipriano Castro, an "unspeakably villainous little monkey" according to a subsequent characterization by Roosevelt, had achieved the Presidency of Venezuela in 1899 by the traditional South American revolution. His rule, like the administrations of his predecessors, failed to bring an era of peace and prosperity. Large debts had been contracted for public works, and by 1901 the foreign concessionaires were asking their governments for assistance in collecting the bills. They had made repeated attempts to obtain payment, but had been blocked by a tendency on the part of Venezuelan officials to murmur, "*Sí señor . . . mañana*." Nationals of Germany and England seem to have been abused the most, although claims against the Castro government had also been filed by business men in the United States, Italy, France, Belgium, Mexico, the Netherlands, Spain, Sweden, and Norway.

Nothing in the Monroe Doctrine, as it was universally understood in 1901, blocked the path of foreign nations to debt collection. "If any South American country misbehaves toward any European country," Vice-president Roosevelt wrote in July, "let the European country spank it." The chastisement, presumably, could include a blockade, the seizure of customs receipts to satisfy obligations, a bombardment of coast cities; in brief, any form of coercion or destruction. There was but one limitation. The United States could not permit a European country permanently to occupy new territory in Central or South America or in the Caribbean. The Monroe Doctrine, Roosevelt explained in his first message to Congress, had "nothing to do with the commercial relations of any American power . . . we do not guarantee any State against punishment if it misconducts itself . . . provided . . . [this] does not take the form of acquisition of territory."

Italy did not take an active part in the proceedings against Venezuela. In an attempt to arrive at a conclusion of what really occurred during 1901 and 1902 it will be simpler to limit the narrative to the actions of Great Britain and Germany and to ignore, for the moment, Roosevelt's own inaccurate and prejudiced version. The patience of these two powers had been strained by midsummer in 1901. In July, Germany offered to accept arbitration of her claims by the Hague Tribunal, but the self-confident Castro rashly rejected the offer. In December, Baron von Holleben, German ambassador to the United States, informed Secretary of State Hay that coercion against Venezuela might be undertaken. He specified that "the acquisition or permanent occupation of territory" would under no circumstances be considered by Germany. Mr. Hay quoted the President's message to Congress as indication that the United States had no objection to this program.

Great Britain, meanwhile, was nursing grievances which, she believed, were more serious than Germany's. In addition to owing money to her citizens, and refusing to pay, Venezuela had jeopardized British prestige by the seizure of ships flying the Union Jack. Her attitude changed later, but Germany was at first more inclined to conciliation than England. In January, 1902, Count von Bulow, the German Chancellor, asked the Kaiser whether cooperative action with Great Britain against Venezuela could be undertaken. Wilhelm replied that it would be wise to wait until after the visit of Prince Henry to the United States. An offensive, he felt, might further damage the standing of Germany in the United States. Thus it was that England stood by herself during the first half of 1902 in addressing several sharp notes to Castro.

By July of that year, twelve months having passed since Germany's suggestion for arbitration, joint irritation drew the two countries together. Count Metternich, German ambassador at London, informed Lord Lansdowne, the Foreign Secretary, that pressure upon Venezuela seemed to be the only solution. Would Great Britain consent to a blockade? On October 22, 1902, Lansdowne told Germany that England proposed to seize certain Venezuelan gunboats. A blockade, he added, might cause resentment on the part of "other powers," by which he probably meant the United States. Ultimately, both methods of chastisement were used. Final ultimata were delivered on December 7, 1902. Four gunboats were captured by the allies and five ports were blockaded during the next four days. The approach of the German and English warships was enough to break Castro's spirit. When, on December 13, British guns bombarded Puerto Cabello because of a supposed insult to the flag, he scrambled to offer the arbitration he had once spurned.

What was Roosevelt doing, while these belligerent gestures were being carried out? Officially, he was doing little. Privately, through Speck von Sternberg, and probably through conversations with Holleben, he was expressing emphatic disapproval. If the formal diplomatic representations from Washington are examined without relation to the President's confidential negotiations, however, it would appear that his subsequent version of what occurred was romantic to the point of absurdity. On December 5, two days prior to the ultimata, the State Department expressed Roosevelt's hope of a peaceful settlement. Nothing came of this. On December 13, the State Department instructed its representatives at London and Berlin to transmit, "without comment," Castro's belated appeal for arbitration. On December 16, both England and Germany decided to accept arbitration, although with reservations as to certain of the claims against Castro. On the following day, just as acceptance of arbitration was being announced, the United States strongly recommended such action. In other words, Germany and Great Britain had agreed to arbitration before the American State Department had done anything except: first, send a mild suggestion that Roosevelt hoped for peace; second, transmit Castro's appeal "without comment."

Roosevelt's first accounts of the Venezuela episode were in perfect harmony with the facts as they appear in the documents. On April 2, 1903, he said that the sole interest of the United States had been to see that no territory was acquired. Both Great Britain and Germany had given assurances to that end. More than a decade passed. In 1915 William Roscoe Thayer was gathering data for his *Life and Letters of John Hay*. The World War had started. Roosevelt, like Thayer, was ardently pro-Ally. Hay's biographer called on Roosevelt to say that he desired a true version of the Venezuela dispute of 1902 and remarked that any evidence of "German duplicity and evil plotting . . . could not fail to help the American patriotic cause." The former President of the United States, in his own historical writings, had been quite willing to let patriotism's warmth obscure cold fact. He gave Thayer an account of German perfidy in 1902 that substantiated the current conception of the nature of the Hun.

In October, 1915, Thayer published his book. He said that Baron von Holleben had been summoned to the White House and had been told that Admiral Dewey, commanding a flotilla in Caribbean waters, would be ordered to sail unless Germany consented to arbitration within ten days. A week passed without acquiescence by the Kaiser. Then Roosevelt informed the German ambassador that thirty-six hours additional would be allowed before the sharpshooting gunners of Dewey aimed their weapons at the German gunboats off the Venezuelan coast. It was after this that Von Holleben, greatly agitated, announced that arbitration was acceptable to his country. This romantic story, obviously inaccurate in certain details, was promptly attacked by historians; by John Bassett Moore, among others. Challenged, Roosevelt put it in writing.

On August 21, 1916, he addressed a letter to Thayer giving further details. Germany, he wrote, was "the leader . . . the really formidable party in the transaction. . . . England was merely following Germany's lead in a rather half-hearted fashion." This was the first error. England, as the documents clearly show, was the aggressor. "I became convinced," Roosevelt continued, "that Germany intended to seize some Venezuelan harbor and turn it into a strongly fortified place of arms, on the model of Kiao-chau." Perhaps he was, in fact, convinced of this. Why, then, did Roosevelt in April, 1903, state that both Germany and England had pledged nonaggrandizement? Other essential parts of the letter were:

> For some time the usual methods of diplomatic intercourse were tried. Germany declined to agree to arbitrate . . . and declined to say that she would not take possession of Venezuelan territory, merely saying that such possession would be "temporary"—which might mean anything. I finally decided that no useful purpose would be served by further delay, and I took action accordingly. I assembled our battle fleet, under Admiral Dewey, near Porto Rico, for "maneuvers," with instructions that the fleet should be kept . . . in fighting trim . . . I told John Hay that I would now see the German Ambassador, myself, and that I intended to bring matters to an early conclusion. . . .
>
> I saw the Ambassador and . . . asked him to inform his government that if no notification for arbitration came within a specified number of days I would be obliged to order Dewey . . . to the Venezuelan coast . . . and asked him to look at the map, as a glance would show him that there was no spot in the world where Germany in the event of a conflict with the United States would be at a greater disadvantage than in the Caribbean Sea.
>
> A few days later the Ambassador came to see me. . . . I asked him if he had any answer to make from his government . . . and when he said no, I informed him that . . . Dewey would be ordered to sail twenty-four hours in advance of the time I had set. He expressed deep

apprehension. . . . However, less than twenty-four hours before the time I had appointed for cabling the order to Dewey, the Embassy notified me that his Imperial Majesty, the German Emperor, had directed him to request me to undertake the arbitration myself.

It is difficult to separate the truth from the obvious impossibilities of this narrative. Roosevelt gave no dates. The "ten days" of the conversation with Thayer became a "specified number of days." The "thirty-six hours" postponement became "twenty-four hours" earlier. The most important flaw in the account is Roosevelt's theory that his threat forced the acceptance of arbitration by Germany. It will be recalled that arbitration was agreed to on December 16 and announced the following day. Until December 17, the United States, publicly, had not even recommended arbitration. When it did so, Germany had already given way. Further evidence of the passive role that the United States had played is found in a letter from Lord Lansdowne to Sir Francis Lascelles, British ambassador at Berlin. He described a conversation with Count Metternich. Lansdowne said:

> They [Germany] recognized that resort to arbitration would be likely to produce a salutary effect, and they consider that action should be taken on the Venezuelan proposal at once, *without waiting until Washington exchanged the role of post-office* for one of a more active character.

This referred, of course, to the American State Department's action in merely forwarding the Venezuelan requests for arbitration.

Two explanations have been offered. The first is that Roosevelt, fired by the World War and his growing hatred of Germany, imagined the whole thing. The second is that a subsequent conversation with Von Sternberg, who was in Washington in February, 1903, became tangled in his recollection with earlier conferences with Von Holleben. Such a conversation did take place. Germany's earlier acceptance of arbitration had been with definite limitations. For a time, in late January and February, it seemed probable that the negotiations would be broken off. It is a matter of record that Roosevelt made inquiries in February regarding the strength of the German fleet off Venezuela. Moreover, the existing anti-German feeling in the United States had been further inflamed by bombardment of Maracaibo by a German gunboat in January. The British, having learned their lesson, had virtuously refrained from any part in this.

Roosevelt's private letters, however, invalidate both the theory that he had no conversation at all or merely one with Von Sternberg. Official documents can fall short of the truth just as a too dramatic memory can go beyond it. Exactly what occurred will, in all probability, never be known. In the Venezuela controversy, however, Roosevelt was acting as his own Secretary of State. While the State Department served as a mere "post office," the President was conducting diplomatic negotiations of his own. His papers reveal that Von Sternberg had been in Washington during November also, as the Venezuelan crisis developed. He returned to Berlin and on December 15,

1902, was directed by his government "to submit the impressions of my visit."

"Nothing could have pleased me more," Von Sternberg told the President, "because it gave me a chance to tell them the truth. I've told them every bit of it and have used rather plain talk."

Among the subjects discussed, he added, had been Venezuela. Unfortunately, Von Sternberg did not give further details, but it seems wholly probable that he reported Roosevelt's doubts regarding Germany's motives. At all events, Germany consented to arbitrate her claims on the following day. This, of course, is theory. That Roosevelt, however inaccurate his account of it, saw Von Holleben and made strong representations to Germany is demonstrable by a witness who was present. William Loeb, Roosevelt's private secretary, recalled two visits by the German ambassador to the White House during December, 1902, but believed it possible that only two or three days elapsed between them. He remembered saying to the President, following the first conversation:

"You gave that Dutchman something to think about. The trouble is . . . [he] is so afraid of the Kaiser that I don't think he will give a correct picture of your attitude."

Long before the World War poisoned his mind against Germany, Roosevelt wrote letters that offer further substantiation. On August 9, 1903, he said that he had been "steadily engaged in . . . teaching the Kaiser to 'shinny on his own side of the line.'" He told Spring Rice in November, 1905, that during the early part of his term he had felt that "the Germans had serious designs upon South America." "I finally told the German Ambassador," he wrote in June, 1906, "that . . . the Kaiser ought to know that unless an agreement for arbitration was reached . . . I would . . . move Dewey's ships . . . south." Other letters were to the same end; he had threatened Wilhelm.

The final scrap of evidence was an interview granted to the correspondent of the Newark *Evening News* by Admiral Dewey in March, 1903. The winter maneuvers, he said, had constituted "an object lesson to the Kaiser more than to any other person."

A curious circumstance is that the conversation with Von Holleben, which undoubtedly took place, is nowhere mentioned in *Die Grosse Politik,* the enormous mass of German documents published after the war.

In all probability, Roosevelt hastened the acceptance of arbitration by Germany. There is no possible doubt that he dramatized and heightened the part that he played. Arbitration would have come in any event. Germany and England both discovered that coercion of Venezuela had aroused alarm and irritation in the United States. The alliance with Germany had brought a storm of criticism in England. Each country was happy when an opportunity to end the ill-advised excursion came.

To Roosevelt, the affair had one pleasing factor. It resulted in the recall of Von Holleben on "leave of absence." The President had long been conspiring to this end. On January 4, 1902, United States Ambassador Andrew D. White remarked to the Kaiser that Roosevelt was anxious to have Von

Sternberg in the United States. Roosevelt went so far as to mention the matter to Prince Henry when the Kaiser's brother was at the White House. Accused of having used his influence against Von Holleben, Roosevelt insisted that this was "too preposterous for discussion."

The appointment of Von Sternberg followed in due time.

President Roosevelt's next excursion into foreign affairs related to the claims of Canada regarding the southern boundary of Alaska, and Great Britain was his adversary. Interest in this question had been negligible until gold had been discovered in the Klondike in 1896. Then the small strip of land between the coast and British Columbia became exceedingly desirable. Alaska had been ceded to the United States by purchase from Russia, but a treaty between Great Britain and Russia in 1825 had fixed the boundary line with relation to Canada.

Canada's contention, after the gold strike, was that the line was located behind the deep inlets in the jagged coast. This would have left her in possession of the heads, or harbors, of the inlets and given control of important passes to the Yukon River and the gold fields. The American position, of course, was that the strip began at the tips of the arms reaching into the sea and that the inlets were part of Alaska. The matter had been argued prior to Roosevelt's succession to the Presidency. In 1899, Secretary Hay had denounced as "ridiculous and preposterous" the contention that Russia, or any other nation, would have agreed to a boundary that left her merely a few promontories in the Pacific.

In its early stages the dispute was linked with other matters under consideration between the United States and Great Britain, among them the Newfoundland fisheries and revision of the Clayton-Bulwer Treaty. Great Britain, pointing to the fact that the United States had called for arbitration in the first Venezuela episode during the Cleveland Administration, suggested that all these matters be referred to an impartial tribunal. But Hay, with the backing of Lodge, declined to admit that concessions could be made on Alaska. The question was allowed to drift until 1902. Relations between the two countries had in the past been made none the happier by the extraordinary hostility toward Canada exhibited by American politicians. In 1867, Seward had urged the annexation of the Dominion in payment for the damages caused by Great Britain's violations of neutrality during the Civil War. Roosevelt himself had once made violent speeches urging that North America should be inhabited exclusively by citizens of the United States.

If Lodge and Hay were opposed to arbitration in the Alaska matter, Roosevelt was even more emphatic in insisting that the United States, alone, would settle it. Characteristically, although he must have known that the possibility of conflict was grotesque, he made secret preparations for war. In March 1902, instructions went to Secretary of War Root to have "additional troops sent as quietly and unostentatiously as possible to Southern Alaska." Root transmitted to the White House copies of the order dispatched to Brig. Gen. G. M. Randall, in command in the Northwest territory. In July, 1902, Roosevelt told Hay that arbitration was out of the question, that

the Canadian claim was "an outrage, pure and simple . . . to pay them anything . . . would come dangerously near blackmail." A few days later the
President said that he appreciated

> the possibility of trouble . . . [but] Root has been quietly strengthen-
> ing the garrison. . . . In a spirit of bumptious truculence, which for
> years England had resisted . . . the Canadians put in this . . . false
> claim. They now say that trouble may come if it is not acted on. I feel
> like telling them that if trouble comes it will be purely . . . their own
> fault; and although it would not be pleasant for us, it would be death
> for them.

Had Roosevelt continued to oppose arbitration, the Alaska dispute would
probably have dragged on for some time, but in the end would have been
settled in favor of the United States. Instead, he permitted a treaty to be
drafted in January 1903, which provided for six "impartial jurists of repute," three to represent the United States and three, Great Britain and
Canada. The tribunal would meet in London and would fix the line between
Alaska and Canada. This treaty, and Roosevelt's conduct under it, placed
the United States in a bad light throughout the world. If arbitration was
out of the question, no reason for the treaty existed. For the "impartial
jurists," the President selected the rabidly anti-English Cabot Lodge,
Secretary of War Root, and George Turner, former Senator from Washington. Great Britain, however, chose Lord Alverstone, Chief Justice of England, Louis A. Jette, lieutenant-governor of Quebec, and A. B. Aylesworth,
a Toronto attorney.

Roosevelt's appointments, wrote Henry White from London in April,
1903, had "caused a great deal of embarrassment . . . some dismay, as well
as great surprise." Canada's protests to the home government had been
violent and it was, White admitted, "difficult—not to say impossible—for
the British Government to maintain that Cabot is 'an impartial jurist of
repute' or that Root or Turner are impartial in the sense required by the
treaty." Joseph Chamberlain, the British Colonial Secretary, had remarked
that if the United States was so very certain that her position was right, and
he conceded its strength, far greater confidence would have been inspired
by "judges or lawyers not connected with the government." Sir Michael
Herbert, British ambassador at Washington, told his Foreign Office that he
was "disgusted and disheartened . . . everything in this country is sub-
servient to politics . . . really an Ambassador in Washington needs more
than an ordinary stock of patience."

In truth, Roosevelt's "impartial jurists" ill became a nation affecting to
believe in arbitration. The President's attitude was similarly ungracious
later in 1903. To reports that Great Britain might ask for postponement,
he said that she "must be kept right up to the mark." He disliked "making
any kind of a threat," but if England played "fast and loose," he would
break off negotiations, send a special message to Congress, and "run the
boundary as we deem it should be run"; in other words, offer an insult

to British prestige which might have meant war had the issues been less absurd.

"You will, of course, impartially judge the questions that come before you for decision," began the contradictory instructions from the President to the members of the American commission. " . . . In the principle involved there will, of course, be no compromise." By "principle" Roosevelt meant the boundary line itself. He was willing to award to Canada one or two of the uninhabited islands off the coast.

Certainly the evidence was overwhelmingly on the side of the American claims in Alaska. Even British maps, until the dispute arose, had substantiated them. In the Cabinet Room at the White House, Roosevelt told Hay, "stands a globe made in London by the map makers for the Admiralty . . . [which gives] this boundary precisely . . . [as] claimed by us." The tribunal so decided at London on October 20, 1903. Two of the four islands were given to Canada as a consolation prize. The three American commissioners, naturally,voted in favor of the majority decision, while the two Canadians, Jette and Aylesworth, declined to sign it. Lord Alverstone, by voting with the Americans, lived up to the obligations of his high judicial office. Bitterly criticized for his action, the Lord Chief Justice declared at a dinner in London:

> If, when any kind of arbitration is set up they don't want a decision based on the law and the evidence, they must not put a British judge on the commission.

The result, said Roosevelt, "offered signal proof of the fairness and goodwill with which two friendly nations can approach and determine issues."

When he became President, and appreciated the complexities of dealing with the quarrelsome and inefficient governments of the Caribbean and South America, Roosevelt abandoned his earlier lust for the acquisition of territory. In May, 1897, he had favored the purchase of the Virgin Islands, but now he had troubles enough. As President, he would undoubtedly have endorsed adding the Danish West Indies to America's share of the white man's burden, but negotiations to that end in 1902 failed. The President never made it a major issue.

By 1901 the family of dependent nations was ample, even for a Chief Executive who believed in fecundity. It was in an endeavor to apply the Monroe Doctrine to this new world empire that Roosevelt so greatly expanded its meaning. The doctrine, as a matter of fact, had been violated quite openly by the annexation of the Philippine Islands; President Monroe, in his message to Congress on December 2, 1823, said that with "the existing colonies or dependencies of any European power we . . . shall not interfere." But McKinley, at first hesitant, "prayed Almighty God for light and guidance," and evolved a policy which Dr. Lyman Abbott described as "the new Monroe Doctrine, the new imperialism, the imperialism of liberty."

From the start of his first administration, Roosevelt denied that he had any desire to acquire territory. The Monroe Doctrine was equivalent, he wrote Von Sternberg on October 11, 1901, "to Open Door in South America." When, due to incessant revolutions and internal turmoil in Santo Domingo, the subject of intervention arose once more, the President insisted that he wanted to

> do nothing but what a policeman has to do. . . . As for annexing the island, I have about the same desire . . . as a gorged boa constrictor might have to swallow a porcupine wrong-end-to.

The Venezuela trouble in 1902 marked Roosevelt's first amplification of the Monroe Doctrine. This was that the mere threat of territorial aggrandizement by a European power was sufficient to justify intervention. Next came the theory that the smaller nations must not misbehave and thereby annoy Europe. "I think it will have a very healthy effect," he wrote regarding American intervention in September, 1904, Castro of Venezuela being again in trouble. " . . . It will show these Dagos that they will have to behave decently." These utterances, obviously, were private ones. Roosevelt's belief found formal expression in his famous Corollary of 1904, which declared, as the same idea was expressed on another occasion, that the nations of South America "will be happy . . . if only they will be good." A kindly, if stern, Uncle Sam would then find chastisement unnecessary. This, it will be noted, differed radically from the earlier doctrine—if a South American country misbehaved toward Europe, "let the European country spank it."

Santo Domingo, otherwise unimportant in history, brought forth the Roosevelt Corollary. Dictatorships and revolution had reduced the island republic to bankruptcy by 1903. Foreign creditors had persuaded the Government to pledge part of the customs receipts to meet the obligations, but payments had been irregular and threats of intervention were constant. By 1904, the foreign debts totaled about $18,000,000, and in February Roosevelt heard of another revolution. He sent Admiral Dewey to see whether American interests were in danger.

The issue seemed clear to the President. Chastisement by a European power might result in territorial seizure and this would be contrary to the Monroe Doctrine. On May 20, 1904, Roosevelt addressed a letter to Secretary of War Root with the suggestion that it be read at a dinner in New York that night. The sole desire of the United States, this communication said, was

> to see all neighboring countries stable, orderly, and prosperous. . . . Any country whose people conduct themselves well can count upon our hearty friendliness. If a nation shows that it knows how to act with decency in industrial and political matters, if it keeps order and pays its obligations, then it need fear no interference from the United States. Brutal wrong-doing, or an impotence which results in a general loosening of the ties of civilized society, may finally require intervention by some civilized nation, and in the Western Hemisphere the United States cannot ignore this duty.

Read by Mr. Root at the dinner, the letter resulted in widespread praise and condemnation. The President, "rather amused by the yell," insisted that it had been only

> the simplest common sense, and only the fool or the coward can treat it as aught else. . . . If we are willing to let Germany or England act as the policeman of the Caribbean, then we can afford not to interfere when gross wrong-doing occurs. But if we intend to say "Hands off" to the powers of Europe, sooner or later we must keep order ourselves.

This amplification of the Monroe Doctrine was included in the message to Congress in December, 1904. The passage began with reiteration that the United States had no "land hunger" or considered anything save the welfare of her neighbors to the south. With only slight changes in phraseology, Roosevelt repeated the sentiments of the letter to Root. Interference would be a last resort and only because misdeeds had "invited foreign aggression to the detriment of the entire body of American nations."

In December, Roosevelt acted under the Corollary of 1904. Conditions had grown more acute. Commander A. C. Dillingham, a naval officer, was detailed to Santo Domingo to assist the American minister, T. C. Dawson, in effecting an arrangement whereby the United States would supervise customs receipts. It was agreed that forty-five per cent of the total would go to the Dominican Government and the balance to reduce foreign debts. The United States Senate, jealous of its treaty-making rights, was highly irritated when it heard that this protocol with Santo Domingo had been drafted. A prolonged debate ended, despite a special message from Roosevelt, without ratification. The President, however, was more disgusted than dismayed. He was approaching the crest of his power. He ordered that American agents take charge of Dominican customs pending action by the Senate, and this was done. On March 23, 1905, Roosevelt confessed that he did not "much admire the Senate, because it is such a helpless body when efficient work for good is to be done." As for its treaty-making prerogatives:

> The Senate is wholly incompetent to take such a part. Creatures like Morgan [the Senator from Alabama] . . . backed by the average yahoo among the Democratic Senators, are wholly indifferent to the national honor or national welfare. . . . After infinite thought and worry and labor . . . I negotiated a treaty [with Santo Domingo] which would secure a really satisfactory settlement from every viewpoint. . . . The result is that by a narrow margin we find ourselves without the necessary two-thirds vote. . . . The Senate ought to feel that its action on the treaty-making power should be much like that of the President's veto . . . it should be rarely used.

The modus vivendi, as the President's extralegal device for bringing order in Santo Domingo was termed, was in operation for twenty-eight months and the results demonstrated Roosevelt's practicality, but not his reverence for the Constitution. It was, of course, an American suzerainty. Warships were on hand to prevent further internal trouble. In September, 1905, Roosevelt ordered the Secretary of the Navy to preserve the status quo; that is, to put down any incipient revolution. At all events, the plan stabilized Santo Domingo's finances. The foreign debts were paid. The forty-five per cent allocated from the customs revenues to the island Government provided more funds than the total collections under the old regime.

Two additional matters remained. The first was subjugation of the Phillippine Islands. The second was Cuban independence, promised by the United States on the eve of the Spanish War.

A minority among the Filipinos had been reluctant to accept the rule of the United States even after the capture of their leader, Aguinaldo, in March, 1901. The guerrilla warfare continued, accompanied by the cruelties typical of such struggles. It is wholly probable that the American troops on the islands were guilty of atrocities. With fine disregard for ethnological distinctions, they classified the natives as "niggers" and freely administered the so-called water cure to unfortunate captives. On the other hand, it should be recalled that they were fighting men inflamed by futile hopes of freedom and quite without knowledge of the limitations placed, in theory, on civilized warfare. In general, President Roosevelt sympathized with the troops. He told the Grand Army of the Republic that they "fought under terrible difficulties and . . . received terrible provocation from a very cruel and treacherous enemy." For "every guilty act committed by our troops," he said, "a hundred acts of far greater atrocity have been committed by the hostile natives."

"I have taken care," he confided to Von Sternberg, "that the army should understand that I thoroughly believe in severe methods when necessary, and am not in the least sensitive about killing any number of men if there is adequate reason. But I do not like torture or needless brutality."

This robust taste was not shared by the American people, who found this aspect of the new imperialism less pleasing than battles in which heroes such as Dewey and Roosevelt vanquished their foes urbanely and picturesquely. Without Taft as civil governor of the Philippines, the protests might have been important politically. But Taft's appointment—by McKinley— had been a happy one. His sympathy for the small and puzzled brown men, who had looked upon the United States as a savior and then found American soldiers shooting down their brothers, was as large as his huge body. Taft won their confidence immediately. He was sent by Roosevelt to the Vatican in 1902 and settled the long-standing Filipino grievance of land ownership by Dominican and Franciscan friars. The natives placed little trust in these clerics, who recalled the Spanish regime, and the purchase of their land by the United States went far toward bringing harmony on the islands. Roosevelt's advocacy of tariff reciprocity with the Philippines, although it was not approved by Congress until 1905 and even then for only sugar and tobacco, also hastened the day of tranquillity.

To its honor, the Roosevelt Administration resisted all pressure calling for repudiation of the agreement to grant independence to Cuba. Complications, however, stood in the path to complete freedom. Cuba occupied a peculiar position among the countries of the Caribbean. The United States, having brought about liberation from Spain, became her guardian. It was unthinkable, in view of Cuba's proximity to the Isthmus of Panama, for any foreign power to assume even temporary control of her affairs. The United States, therefore, insisted upon its own definition of independence.

This antedated Roosevelt as President. Brig. Gen. Leonard Wood had been appointed military governor in 1899 and American troops were withdrawn two years later. In May, 1902, Tomas Estrada Palma became President of the new republic. Meanwhile, the autonomy of Cuba had been the subject of conferences, and Secretary of War Root had suggested, in January, 1901, that the Constitution of Cuba contain certain vital clauses. It must permit intervention by the United States to maintain order. Cuba must not make treaties that granted special privileges to foreign countries or affected her independence. Naval stations must be offered to her benefactor. Other members of the McKinley Administration took part in drafting the restrictions, but such, in substance, was the proposal offered by Senator Orville H. Platt of Connecticut and called, because with typical senatorial logic it was incorporated in an amendment to an appropriation bill, the Platt Amendment. The Cuban Constitutional Convention realized that this was sovereignty of an abridged nature. The action of the United States Congress in drafting the proposal was a degree highhanded, since such matters were normally left to diplomatic negotiation. Protests, however, were futile. In 1903 a treaty containing the Platt Amendment was signed by the two governments. That same year Cuba leased to the United States Guantánamo Bay and Bahia Hondo on the Cuban coast, for $2,000 a year.

Unquestionably, the Cubans consented to the Platt Amendment the more readily because of promises that commercial favors would be granted by the United States. In his first message to Congress, President Roosevelt said that "morality and national interest" called for reduced tariffs on imports from Cuba. An effective lobby organized by the beet sugar interests caused long delay, but Roosevelt continued to demand action on behalf of Cuba. At last, in December, 1903, reciprocity was authorized at a special session of Congress.

An unsuspected evil inherent in the Platt Amendment was that it constituted a safeguard for dictatorships in Cuba. The island was peaceful for several years, although complaints were frequent that prosperity had not been included among the blessings of freedom from Spain. In September, 1906, however, Roosevelt was compelled to make a public plea for order after charges had been circulated that President Palma had held himself in office through dishonest elections. Intervention, Roosevelt said, would be necessary if Cuba did not put down an incipient revolution. Then followed the familiar story. American troops were landed. Taft, by now Secretary of War, was hurried to Cuba to effect a compromise between the factions. He had a measure of success, but it was not until 1909 that Cuba again assumed the sovereignty to which she was entitled as Queen of the Antilles. Although limited, it was better than none at all.

Roosevelt was still enforcing his Corollary of 1904. Perhaps, with the years, he began to regret the vigor of a Monroe Doctrine which insisted that righteousness justified might. The President had felt no hesitation regarding Venezuela, none regarding Santo Domingo. In 1903 he had "taken Panama," a phrase which crept into Roosevelt's speeches and writings to refute the legalistic justifications by Root and others. But when the insurrection in Cuba came, he moved with reluctance. In February, 1907, he appeared to regret that it had been necessary to interfere at all.

"I am doing my best," he said, "to persuade the Cubans that if only they will be good they will be happy; I am seeking the very minimum of interference necessary to make them good."

In 1906, Elihu Root, who had succeeded John Hay as Secretary of State, was dispatched on a tour of South America for the purpose of convincing the Latin-Americans that no menace to their rights lurked in the Monroe Doctrine. He was received with politeness, even with enthusiasm. But somehow salesmen from the countries of Europe obtained orders where American salesmen failed. The export trade with South America did not increase as it should have done. Certain of these countries, said Roosevelt in his message that year, seemed to suffer from a misapprehension that the Monroe Doctrine attributed superiority to the United States:

> Nothing could be further from the truth. Yet that impression continued to be a serious barrier to good understanding and friendly intercourse, to the introduction of American capital and the expansion of American trade.

But the "Dagos" of Latin-America, as Roosevelt had referred to them in a less formal moment, continued to view the United States with distrust and alarm. Goodwill tours without end were made. Conferences were held. Assurances were given. The irritation persisted. The Monroe Doctrine, as amplified by Roosevelt, might classify them as the wards of Uncle Sam to be smiled upon when they behaved and chastised when they erred. There was, however, no doctrine that compelled them to buy his goods. The loss of foreign trade is sometimes a penalty of imperialism, even when it is benevolent and sanctioned by the Lord. From time to time, as trade with the Americas continued to be disappointing, the State Department sought to break down the prejudices inculcated. The most recent attempt was in December, 1928, while President-elect Herbert Hoover scattered goodwill in person. J. Reuben Clark, Undersecretary of State, compiled a memorandum which declared that "the so-called Roosevelt Corollary" was not

> justified by the terms of the Monroe Doctrine. . . . So far as Latin-America is concerned, the Doctrine is now, and always has been, not an instrument of violence and oppression, but an unbought, freely be-

stowed, and wholly effective guaranty of their freedom, independence, and territorial integrity against the imperialistic designs of Europe.

Mr. Clark did not mention, however, the rape of Colombia. This was the act which did most to terrorize Latin-America during the Roosevelt years. Uncle Sam had already paid $25,000,000 in conscience money because of this.

The story of Panama is replete with heroes and villains. A canal was to be built which would fulfill a dream of centuries and connect the Atlantic and Pacific oceans. In due time it was finished and ships, by the grace of men with slide rules and logarithm tables, steamed from sea to sea. Every step toward realization, wrote Theodore Roosevelt, "was taken with the utmost care . . . was carried out with the highest, finest, and nicest standards of public and governmental ethics." M. Philippe Bunau-Varilla, who played an epic part, said that Reason struggled against Passion and finally triumphed in a mighty war for "Truth, Justice, and National Interest."

Self-hypnosis had again distorted Roosevelt's memory when he praised the ethics whereby the United States effected the preliminaries of the Panama Canal. Hypnosis was all the easier because, as President, he viewed this project as justification for the new Monroe Doctrine. Its construction and defense dominated his Latin-American policy. Roosevelt's belief in the vital need for a canal dated from his first interest in foreign affairs and grew stronger in direct proportion to his imperialistic convictions. "I do wish," he said in October, 1894, "our Republicans would . . . annex Hawaii and build an oceanic canal."

His interest, like that of his fellow citizens, was greatly intensified by the hurried voyage of the U.S.S. *Oregon* around the Horn to join the fleet off Cuba in the Spanish War. Until then a canal had been commendable, but now it was essential. Roosevelt, exiled from national affairs as governor of New York but nursing his hopes for greater glory, considered it in terms of national defense, not economic importance. He had opposed the first Hay-Pauncefote Treaty with Great Britain because it decreed that a canal built by the United States could not be fortified. This, Roosevelt declared, "strengthens against us every nation whose fleet is larger than ours." He objected equally to any provision that permitted foreign governments a voice in the control of the canal. This contravened the Monroe Doctrine. The Senate agreed with Roosevelt, although John Hay was resentful, and negotiations for the revised treaty were on the way to completion when McKinley died.

"I am entirely willing," Roosevelt wrote in July, 1901, "to guarantee . . . neutrality . . . to ships of commerce . . . [but] I insist that the canal be absolutely in our control in a military sense."

Such was the substance of the new treaty signed by Hay and Lord Pauncefote on November 18, 1901, and ratified four weeks later by the Senate. It must have gratified Roosevelt to know that the first important treaty negotiated while he was President terminated the provisions of the

Clayton-Bulwer pact of 1850 whereby Great Britain and the United States agreed to joint control and nonfortification.

One fact became clear with the elevation of Roosevelt to the Presidency. It would be an American canal or none. The day had passed when citizens of France or any other nation could build it.

⌘

No *single person has achieved as dominant a position in American finance as had John Pierpont Morgan before his death in 1913. As representative of his father Junius S. Morgan's London financial house, he engaged in gold speculation during the Civil War and launched a career which would culminate in his building up vast railroad and industrial organizations. Throughout his career a major source of his financial power, one which reflected American dependence on foreign capital, was the ready access he had to the London money market. An American investment recommended by Morgan automatically commanded the confidence of British investors. His reputation received a further boost when an anxious Cleveland eager to maintain the gold reserves of the Treasury turned to him after the Panic of 1893 to stabilize the reserves. Fourteen years later he performed a similar role during the Panic of 1907 for the Roosevelt administration.*

The enormous power he obviously wielded, epitomized by the vast United States Steel and International Harvester Corporations, helped trigger a congressional investigation in 1912 by Congressman Arsène Pujo of Louisiana. The findings of this committee concluded that a "money trust" had been brought into existence through consolidations of banks and trust companies which used their vast resources to establish a system of interlocking directorates to manage insurance companies, railroads, public utilities, and manufacturing corporations. Americans read with amazement that Morgan & Company had a dominant role in 32 transportation systems possessing a total capitalization of $11,784,000,000 and trackage of 150,200 miles in addition to controlling positions in some 34 banks and trust companies and in 10 insurance companies with assets of $4,990,000,000. In the final summarization, the committee noted Morgan and his allies held 341 directorships in 112 corporations having aggregate resources or capitalization of $22,245,000,000.

Once the committee findings were published, Louis D. Brandeis analyzed the implications of its investigation in a series of articles in Harper's Weekly, *which later was published as* Other People's Money. *In it, he spelled out the existence of a "financial oligarchy," the key to whose wealth and power was "Combination—concentration intensive and comprehensive." Within the framework of banking consolidation, they had managed to erect a system of "joint transactions, gentlemen's agreements and 'banking ethics' which eliminate competition among investment bankers." Their consolidation of railroads, public utilities, and industrial trusts had made much of American enterprise dependent upon New York bankers. Control of in-*

surance companies such as the New York Life, the Mutual of New York, and the Equitable guaranteed an inflow of some $55,000,000 of new investment money, even if not a single new policy were issued. "The wealth of the Morgan associates is dynamic," Brandeis concluded somberly. By controlling the depositories of "the people's own money," a financial titan named Morgan seemed dangerously close, in the judgment of many progressives, to control of the people.

Lewis Corey (1891-1953), a Marxist historian, has written what remains still the best extant study of Morgan's activities. The tone of indignation that runs through his treatment conveys something of the sense of outrage and fear that shook the Progressive Era when it learned that the American people had provided their masters with the means for their subjugation.

THE HOUSE OF MORGAN

by Lewis Corey

In 1907 J. Pierpont Morgan was seventy years old, and many believed he had retired. They misjudged Morgan. Almost up to the moment of his death he was aggressively active, dominating the House of Morgan. Of a friend who retired from business and shortly died, Morgan was reported to have said: "If he'd kept at work he'd have been living yet." The story is probably apocryphal; in one form or another it appears in the biography of every American captain of industry and finance. Yet it characterizes Morgan and the businessmen of whom he was the ideal, and the type. The man expressed a cycle of civilization, with his absorption in business (which meant power, the chance to impose himself on others), his glorification of things, and his eternal big black cigar. Then came the great panic of 1907, yielding Morgan the supreme moment of his power.

Although actively in the financial whirl, Morgan, along with other important financiers, was unaware of the developing panic. After the depression of 1904, business developed unprecedented activity and prosperity flourished. Financiers rationalized the "boom" and insisted panics could not arise any more owing to the control imposed by industrial and financial concentration (as they did after the depression of 1921). But they miscalculated, and Morgan with them.

Industry was still unregulated, there being no machinery to adjust production and consumption and prevent industrial crises. Prosperity, as usual, by concentrating profits and income, produced reckless speculation, particularly in rail stocks. E. H. Harriman, with the money secured from the sale of Union Pacific's holdings in Great Northern and Northern Pacific, plunged into the market buying immense blocks of rail stocks (to enlarge his railroad empire) and inflating prices. The Standard Oil oligarchy again busily manipulated the market, concentrating on Amalgamated Copper the price of which rose to 115 and then crashed to 52, the turnover being 30,000,000 shares in one year. Increasingly large issues of new securities, of more and more doubtful types, aggravated the speculative mania. Financial strain developed. The "undigested securities" of which Morgan spoke soon became indigestible. Unscrupulous financiers used the resources of banks and insurance companies in stock-jobbing schemes and speculation.

The whole financial situation was unsound. An aggravated, but characteristic, expression of the situation was the Morse-Heinze group. Charles W. Morse (afterward sent to prison) accumulated a large fortune out of the American Ice Co., charging extortionate prices, manipulating its stock and bribing public officials. Morse organized an overcapitalized and unsound combination of Atlantic coastal lines (buying from J. P. Morgan & Co. a railroad in order to get control of one steamship company) and then acquired a series of banks in New York City, using the collateral of one bank for loans to buy other banks. An ally of Morse, F. Augustus Heinze, had large industrial and financial interests, in control of United Copper and the Aetna Indemnity Co. This Morse-Heinze group was in the forefront of the speculative movement using the resources of financial institutions for stock-jobbery and speculation, but it was powerful, amassing millions, and the envy of lesser magnates.

In March 1907, the approaching financial storm threw out warnings. Prices broke severely on the New York Stock Exchange—"frightful" declines, according to Wall Street. Production and earnings were slackening, and this necessarily affected the inflated prices of stocks. The situation was aggravated by large financiers being forced to liquidate owing to their many issues of "indigestible securities."

The financial community refused to recognize the facts and insisted that President Roosevelt's "policy of hostility against all corporations and their securities, particularly railroads," was responsible for the disturbances in the stock market. Morgan and three other important financiers called upon the President to discuss the situation, the conference being interpreted as "satisfactory" by Wall Street.

But the industrial and financial situation was inherently unsound, and neither Roosevelt nor Morgan could change it. Stock prices broke again in August, seriously affecting banks that had bought stocks in the March disturbance, expecting to sell at higher prices but could not. To ease the money situation the Treasury distributed $28,000,000 to banks in the smaller cities. Business failures increased and many corporations crashed. In October United Copper shares collapsed and cleaned out F. Augustus Heinze. The Mercantile National Bank, under Heinze's control and which financed his speculations, was seriously affected by the break in United Copper. Help was given by the other banks only on condition that Heinze and the directors retire. This was done and the Mercantile National reorganized. By now the situation was uncontrollable. The Knickerbocker Trust Co., under Morse control, financing his speculations and an affiliate of Heinze, was in an insolvent condition. Its suspension was threatened when the National Bank of Commerce refused to act any longer as its Clearing House agent. There was a run on the bank—"one young woman, it was observed, paced nervously up and down until the bank opened." At a conference in Morgan's office, representing a concentration of financial forces, the ultimatum went forth that the Heinze-Morse interests must withdraw from all financial institutions before they could expect aid. This was done, and Knickerbocker's new president appealed personally to Morgan for help, who answered: "I can't go on being everybody's goat. I've got to stop somewhere." At another conference the decision was "thumbs down" on Knickerbocker Trust. After the conference Morgan said:

"We are doing everything we can, as fast as we can, but nothing has yet crystallized."

Asked about Knickerbocker Trust, Morgan replied:

"I don't know anything about that; I am not talking about that."

Under Morgan's direction organization and plans were being developed to meet the crisis. On October 20, in spite of underlying uneasiness, Wall Street was confident, Jacob H. Schiff saying: "The trouble is over and the general situation sound." Within three days banks began to crash and panic broke loose on the Stock Exchange.

Secretary of the Treasury George B. Cortelyou rushed to New York and held conferences with Morgan, Perkins, Baker, Stillman and others. Government accepted the Morgan dictatorship—an inescapable decision. There was no central banking institution under government control to mobilize the banks' resources in the crisis. In spite of financial centralization by Morgan and others, the nation's banking system was incompletely co-ordinated, reserves being scattered in the vaults of thousands of banks which distrusted each other and did not or could not effectively co-operate. There was a scramble for money by the banks and no central institution to provide and distribute the money. Co-operation and centralized organization had to be improvised in the midst of the panic, while banks crashed, necessarily by the House of Morgan, the most powerful of financial institutions, and under control of the only man with sufficient financial authority, J. Pierpont Morgan. What a properly organized banking system would have done automatically Morgan had to do in an improvised and dictatorial style. Cortelyou accepted Morgan's dictatorship, testifying in the Money Trust investigation:

UNTERMYER: What was Mr. Morgan's relation?
CORTELYOU: Mr. Morgan's relation to it was that, by the consensus of opinion, he was regarded as the leading spirit, I think, among the businessmen who joined themselves together to try to meet the emergency.
UNTERMYER: He was the representative of the banks, was he, in a sense?
CORTELYOU: He was the representative of the general business of the community.
UNTERMYER: Mr. Morgan was the general in charge of the situation?
CORTELYOU: He was generally looked to for guidance and leadership.
UNTERMYER: And the banks acted under his direction and took his instructions?
CORTELYOU: For the time being, I suppose that was true.

The Treasury deposited $42,000,000 without interest, in banks under control of or affiliated with the House of Morgan, the disposal of which for purposes of relief was determined by a series of conferences under final authority of Morgan himself.

J. P. Morgan and Co. were in shipshape condition to meet the crisis, having learned from the experience of 1903-4 to maintain a high degree of liquidity in their resources. In the persons and institutions of Morgan and his chief lieutenants, George F. Baker of the First National Bank and James Stillman of the National City, was concentrated an immense money power which dominated all the other banks and the general situation. They necessarily determined measures to meet the crisis, and Baker and Stillman unquestioningly accepted Morgan's authority. With royal generosity Morgan afterward said to his son (who was not in New York during the panic): "Of course, you see, it could not have been done without Mr. Baker; he is always ready to do his share—and more."

It was Morgan's supreme moment, the final measure of power and its ecstasy. President Roosevelt, the scourge of "malefactors of great wealth," accepted Morgan's financial dictatorship through the Secretary of the Treasury. One after another Morgan's antagonists came to him, offered their resources and asked his orders—John D. Rockefeller, Edward H. Harriman, Jacob H. Schiff, Thomas F. Ryan, and after them came presidents of banks, railroads and industrial combinations. To a reporter Harriman said: "This is no time for words. It's action now." All of them asked Morgan's orders, which he issued in his sharp, abrupt manner. Conference after conference was held, usually in Morgan's library. While the lesser masters of money discussed plans in the library, in a small adjoining room Morgan sat in massive truculent silence, playing solitaire and smoking his eternal big black cigar. Aloof, masterful, majestic. The lesser masters of money coming to some decision, Morgan would stroll in, listen, usually answer "yes" or "no." Or they gave him a sheet of paper upon which they had set down their resources or needs, which Morgan might tear up, silently. Then the master of money went back to his solitaire and eternal big black cigar, until called again. Or, in more important conferences, Morgan sat with the others, silent, listening, usually speaking only to impose his will. Yes, it was Morgan's supreme moment.

Call money on the Stock Exchange shot skyward and its president, R. H. Thomas, discussed the situation with Stillman. Thomas testified in the Money Trust investigation:

UNTERMYER: You spoke to Mr. Stillman of the money stringency?
THOMAS: Yes. . . . He recommended me to go to Mr. Morgan and tell him the exact story I had told him, Mr. Stillman.
UNTERMYER: Did you go to Mr. Morgan's office?
THOMAS: Yes . . . Mr. Morgan said, "We are going to let you have"—I think these are his words—$25,000,000. Go over to the Exchange and announce it." I said, "One suggestion, Mr. Morgan, I would like to make." He said, "What is it?" I said, "It is this: That you divide this money up among several people, as I think it would have a better

effect in bringing in money and meeting the emergency." He said, "That is a good suggestion, Perkins, divide that up in lots among several people." And I proceeded to the Stock Exchange.

Morgan's decisive influence in the crisis was determined by personality plus the financial dominance of the House of Morgan. There were, first of all, the banks, railroads and industrial corporations under direct Morgan control or influence, the officers of whom were accustomed to accept Morgan's orders. This largest of the financial groups was bound with other groups by the community-of-interest system which operated under over-lordship of the House of Morgan, the whole representing an amalgamation of financial forces dominated by J. Pierpont Morgan. Then there was the factor of personal prestige. Morgan was the businessman's ideal, solid, sub-stantial and successful, silent and masterful, inspiring confidence in men who might dislike and fear him. Once the panic assumed the dimensions of un-reasoning stampede, inspiring confidence in lesser men constituted much of Morgan's contribution to the restoration of normal conditions.

While banks crashed and the cries for help multiplied, the improvised organization directed by Morgan mobilized the available money and dis-tributed it to banks and other financial institutions. J. P. Morgan & Co. announced they would anticipate all interest and dividend payments payable through the firm, particularly the Northern Pacific dividend of $2,700,000 in furtherance of the movement to relieve the monetary tension. John D. Rockefeller deposited $10,000,000 in one trust company and pledged fifty more. The banks imported gold from Europe. Money was poured into the Stock Exchange, Morgan ordered the bears not to sell, and James R. Kenne was engaged to prevent another market crash. By October 28 the newspapers reported the situation "getting back to normal."

In these operations first consideration, of course, was given to institutions under the control or influence of the House of Morgan, its affiliates and allies. There were protests from some of the smaller trust companies that money placed in Morgan's hands was being withheld, that they were re-ceiving no relief. There was a run on the Trust Company of America, but its president's appeals for help were brushed aside by Morgan, whose attitude was: "There are too many: wipe them out." At one of the conferences where trust-company relief was discussed Morgan said, bluntly:

"Why should I get into this? My affairs are all in order. I've done enough. I won't take all this on unless—" and then a gesture signifying "unless I get what I want out of it."

James Stillman disagreed, favoring immediate trust-company relief. But the situation was delicate: none dared challenge Morgan directly, except Stillman, who knew, however, that if Morgan definitely said "no," the deci-sion was final, the others being compelled to accept. Stillman knew his Morgan, the man's arrogant pride and dislike of yielding. Diplomacy was necessary to placate Morgan's pride, or it might prevent him changing his opinion. After an all-night struggle, in which finesse matched itself against massive power, Stillman conquered. The trust companies were promised relief.

The panic was almost over when it was reported to Morgan that one of the most important brokerage firms in the city would go bankrupt unless aided immediately. The brokers, Moore & Schley, held a large block of stock of the Tennessee Coal, Iron & Railroad Co., pledged as collateral by a syndicate including John W. Gates and Oliver H. Payne, and which could not be easily sold as the stock's market was limited. It was suggested that relief might assume the form of the United States Steel Corporation buying Tennessee Coal & Iron, issuing in payment its own bonds which were more negotiable than the stock. A midnight conference in Morgan's library considered the suggestion. Gary and Frick opposed purchase, Frick proposing instead that they loan Moore & Schley $5,000,000. Morgan insisted on purchase. There being a problem of legality under the anti-trust laws, Gary and Frick were sent to Washington to secure President Roosevelt's approval, which was granted.

United States Steel's purchase of Tennessee Coal & Iron was justified on the ground that it checked the panic, Roosevelt maintaining that "my action" in approving the purchase produced "stoppage of the panic." But did it? The panic was practically over. Moore & Schley could have been saved by other means, by a direct loan, by some of the millions which had appeared to help the banks and stock market. At the government investigation of the Steel Trust in 1911 Gary testified:

> LITTLETON: Suppose, instead of buying Tennessee Coal & Iron, you had loaned United States Steel bonds to Moore & Schley for the purpose of saving the situation, would you not have effected the same result?
>
> GARY: It is possible. That was not suggested, however. We offered to lend them five or six millions and take stock of Tennessee Coal & Iron as collateral security. But they came back with the statement that that would not answer the purpose.
>
> LITTLETON: You could have loaned the bonds without any embarrassment to the Steel Corporation?
>
> GARY: We could.
>
> LITTLETON: And if the bonds, when exchanged, were the means of saving Moore & Schley they would have been just as efficient means when loaned, would they not?
>
> GARY: They would.

Relief for Moore & Schley was necessary: other purposes determined the *form* of the relief. Tennessee Coal & Iron, the leading iron and steel concern in the South, owned immense reserves of coal and iron ore in Alabama. It was the potential basis for another large steel combination; in fact, plans had been made to combine with two other companies but were never completed. In buying Tennessee Coal & Iron, United States Steel acquired an important competitor and became the most powerful single factor in the Southern iron industry. In normal times the purchase would have been impossible, considering the attacks being made on United States Steel as a monopolistic combination. The panic provided the opportunity for an unusually sharp business stroke on the great value of which Gary expatiated within a few months and which added 600,000,000 tons of iron ore and 1,000,000,000 tons of coal to the reserves of the United States Steel Corporation.

The panic was over. . . . Revelations appeared of the dishonest use of trust-company funds by officers and directors. . . . There was a crop of arrests, and another crop of suicides. . . . President Charles T. Barney, of Knickerbocker Trust, although himself solvent, committed suicide owing to "loss of prestige." . . . Howard Maxwell, another trust-company president, slit his throat. Arrested on a charge of grand larceny for using trust funds in stock deals, Maxwell, penniless, was abandoned by all his friends, who declined to help raise bail. These friends offered to pay the funeral expenses, but the widow scornfully rejected their offer: "I do not want the help they now offer—too late." . . . In New York City there were 100,000 unemployed and probably 3,000,000 in the nation. "Men are eager to work for 35¢ a day," and bread lines were overwhelmed by the needy. . . . In the midst of the panic Andrew Carnegie, seventy years old and enjoying his gold, said: "All is well, since all grows better." . . . Morgan and Baker went to Washington to confer with President Roosevelt and report the end of the panic. . . . Industrial depression continued for almost two years. Clever businessmen organized the "Sunshine Movement," urging people to think prosperity as a means of restoring prosperity. But in spite of the magic potency of sunshine prosperity declined to prosper.

J. Pierpont Morgan received the formal thanks of the financial community for his work during the crisis. "The man of the hour," said the press, praising his "genius for dealing effectively with intricate problems of business and finance." Lord Rothschild issued a bulletin: "Morgan's latest action fills one with admiration and respect." The panic produced many failures and changes in financial power and alignments, but—"Morgan still reigns!"

*   *   *   *   *

During and after the 1907 panic it was freely charged that dominant financial interests, particularly the House of Morgan and its affiliates, deliberately engineered the crisis in order to crush competitors and magnify their own power by larger centralization and control. Denunciations flamed forth in Congress and the press, intensifying popular discontent and strengthening the developing movement for government regulation of corporate combinations.

While the criticism was unjustified, economic forces beyond the control of the financial magnates producing the panic, the magnates facilitated its coming and sharpened the disaster by their reckless promotions, unscrupulous use of other people's money and frenzied speculation.

And when the panic broke loose most of the magnates were frightened, helpless, their morale shattered. Men formerly dominant, austerely aloof, as if carved of granite, now ran like a flock of sheep after the Morgan bellwether.

The panic, moreover, revealed the incapacity of finance, as the unifying expression of business, to insure economic security. Fooling themselves and the public, the magnates believed they were creating a system in which panics could not occur. After the Steel Trust organization John B. Claflin said at a bankers' dinner where J. Pierpont Morgan was an honored guest: "With a man like Mr. Morgan at the head of a great industry, as against the old plan of many diverse interests in it, production will become more regular . . . and panics become a thing of the past." But the 1907 panic, only six years later, was as bad as the panics of 1857 and 1873 when Morganization was still in the future. Morganization, the centralization of industry and finance imposing financial control over industry, introduced co-ordination and regulation, but it was largely coordination of control and regulation of profits, and only partly unification of the nation's economic life. The production and distribution of goods was still determined loosely by markets, prices and profits, still unregulated in terms of balancing production and consumption, still competitive in the struggle after larger and larger profits— booms, depressions and panics being the consequences. Morganization, the community of interest and control, measurably prevented business disturbances produced by buccaneers waging war on each other and by unrestrained competition, but it did not and could not prevent the more serious cyclical disturbances of business.

This limitation of the power of financial centralization, and of finance itself, appears in the "stoppage" of the panic. Morgan and other bankers stabilized the financial situation: by the end of 1907 Wall Street was again "normal" and security prices rallied. But financial stabilization did not revive business prosperity; during the first nine months of 1908 commercial failures increased and production declined. The dynamics of business revival and prosperity lay in the creative force of production and consumption, not in financial centralization and control.

The great bankers, in whom financial control was centralized, neither originated nor introduced fundamental economic changes, most of which developed without their aid. They scarcely participated in the development of railroads and steamships, the first telegraph line was constructed by Congressional appropriation, and they only slightly assisted the development of the steel, telephone, electric and automobile industry. Bankers, by the very nature of their institutional function, usually appear in an enterprise *after* it is established and successful. Finance is regulative, not creative. The creative force is in industry itself. Money, which is finance, conveniently expresses the relationships between one industry and another, between production and consumption. Under business enterprise money becomes the supreme power, usurping the function of determining production and consumption; and Morganization, by the control of money, usurped financial control of industry. In this control inhered a measure of regulation, but it neither insured prosperity nor prevented panics. For that, larger unification and social control of industry are necessary.

While the financial magnates did not engineer the 1907 panic to crush competitors and magnify their own power by larger centralization and control, that was, however, exactly what happened.

The panic crushed many financial combinations, such as Morse-Heinze, their holdings being acquired by the survivors. Banks consolidated to increase their resources, prestige and power. Although James Stillman retired from active control of the National City Bank, his successor, Frank A. Vanderlip, continued its aggressive policy of expansion, extending the Bank's control of trust companies and increasing its affiliations with large institutions in other cities. Harriman, apparently bent upon creating a money power capable of competing with J. P. Morgan & Co., used the immense resources of Union Pacific to develop his own system of financial centralization and control. He spent $130,000,000 buying stock in other roads, becoming a director in twenty-seven railroads with a mileage of 39,354, including control of two lines to the Atlantic. He then snatched Erie from the House of Morgan. Developing his plans, Harriman acquired large interests in the Guaranty Trust Co. and the Equitable Life Assurance Society. Now the mightiest single factor in railroads, pursuing imperialistic plans in Asia and developing formidable financial power, Harriman loomed as a direct and threatening competitor of Morgan. But Harriman's end approached. His railroad manipulations aroused investigation and action by the national government—"actively and openly aided by apparently invincible Wall Street alliances, and secret enemies in his own camp almost as strong." Moreover, Harriman was incapable of institutionalizing his system, as Morgan did: everything, with him, seemed to require the personal touch. Worn out, he died in 1909, and the Harriman system collapsed.

Meanwhile the House of Morgan, emerging triumphant out of the panic, consolidated its system. Immediately after the panic Morgan's Bankers Trust Co. absorbed the Trust Company of America (and the Mercantile Trust in 1911). Within three months of Harriman's death Morgan and his associates bought his stock in the Guaranty Trust along with Mutual Life's holdings. Tightening his control of New York Life, Morgan proceeded, in 1910, to buy control of Equitable Life, becoming dominant in the three largest insurance companies. Under complete control of the House of Morgan, with Henry P. Davison and William H. Porter (both Morgan partners) and George F. Baker as voting trustees and Davison and Thomas W. Lamont as directors, Guaranty Trust absorbed six other trust companies. The Guaranty and Bankers Trust companies were the first and second largest in the country, with combined resources of $357,000,000.

Control of larger financial resources meant larger financial control over industry. In 1909 J. P. Morgan & Co. reorganized the Chicago Great Western Railroad, Morgan and Baker becoming two of the three voting trustees and Charles H. Steele a director. Another Morgan partner became a director in the Westinghouse Electric Co. (reorganized by the Morgans after the 1907 panic), the competitor of General Electric, community of interest being established. The House of Morgan extended its influence in the American Telephone & Telegraph Co., Davison becoming a director and the Morgans marketing, between 1906 and 1912, $299,000,000 of the company's securities, largely used to buy up independents and secure control of Western Union.

But the years immediately after the 1907 panic, which marked the end of a period, were characterized by stabilization, not expansion. Speculation and manipulation broke loose again on the Stock Exchange, for a time forcing the prices of many stocks above the levels of 1907 and 1906, but business depression prevented any considerable speculative movement. Financial adventures almost ceased, there being scarcely any large combinations or promotions (except the attempt of the New York, New Haven & Hartford Railroad, under Morgan's direction, to monopolize New England's transportation facilities). Sobered by the panic and its aftermath, and by Theodore Roosevelt's campaign against the "malefactors of great wealth," finance and Big Business concentrated on consolidating their conquests. The death of Harriman, the only man capable of disputing Morgan's supremacy (the rapier and the broadsword!) eliminated the only threat to the system of community of interest which now flourished undisturbed under overlordship of the House of Morgan.

The National City Bank merged in a larger community of interest with the House of Morgan, while Standard Oil, its former aggressive masters retiring and put on the defensive by government action, was in no mood to struggle for larger power, satisfied to maintain itself. Morgan, apparently eternal, was still active, but most of the other magnates of an embattled age were either dead or retired. There was none to dispute J. Pierpont Morgan's supremacy in the system of financial centralization and control, over which towered the House of Morgan, now unchallenged in its mastery (except by the government).

By 1912 Morgan's system of financial centralization and control appeared definitely in all its essentials.

At the basis of the system was institutionalized control of financial resources, of money and credit. By means of voting trusts, stock ownership and directorships J. P. Morgan & Co. controlled or dominated three national banks (exclusive of First National), three trust companies and three life-insurance companies, with large aggregate resources. (J. P. Morgan & Co. held deposits of $162,491,000, one-half by seventy-eight interstate corporations in thirty-two of which the Morgans were represented by directorships, marketing $1,950,000,000 of their securities between 1902 and 1912.)

By means of stock ownership, voting trusts and directorships J. P. Morgan & Co. dominated ten great railroad systems, with mileage of 49,000 and had close financial affiliations with eighteen other railroads, three street railway corporations and one express company (besides control of the International Mercantile Marine Co.).

By means of voting trusts, stock ownership and directorships J. P. Morgan & Co. dominated five great industrial corporations—United States Steel, General Electric, American Telephone & Telegraph, International Harvester and Western Union. In addition the Morgans held directorships in nine more industrial corporations and had close financial relations with eleven others (including Western Electric and American Fruit).

In all, the Morgan partners held seventy-two interlocking directorships in forty-seven of the largest financial and other corporations with more than $10,000,000,000 in resources or capitalization. The House of Morgan, moreover, completely dominated the Bankers Trust, Guaranty Trust and National Bank of Commerce, whose officers and directors held upward of 300 interlocking directorships, many of them in corporations not under direct Morgan control or influence.

This control of the House of Morgan was enlarged by its affiliate, the First National Bank, four of whose officers held forty-six directorships in thirty-seven corporations, some interlocked with and others independent of direct Morgan control. The Morgans and their affiliates constituted the supreme financial combination and power, upward of $18,000,000,000 in corporate resources or capitalization being under their control or influence.

George F. Baker, president of the First National Bank, an efficient money-making machine probably twice as rich as Morgan, was one of the dominant factors in the system of financial centralization and control. The most secretive of the masters of money, his contempt of public opinion was equal to Morgan's. "It is none of the public's business what I do," said Baker. Of First National's 100,000 shares of capital stock, Baker and his son owned 25,000, J. P. Morgan & Co. 14,500, Henry P. Davison and Thomas W. Lamont 1,000 shares each, and James J. Hill 3,900, making the Morgan interest almost as large as Baker's. Morgan, Davison and Lamont were First National directors and Morgan a member of the executive committee. In spite of being unknown to the public, Baker was almost as powerful as Morgan, under whose direction, however, he always worked willingly and harmoniously.

Trailing the House of Morgan and its affiliates was the National City Bank, five of whose officers held thirty-two directorships in twenty-six corporations. After the 1907 panic rivalry between Morgan and Stillman largely ceased, more intimate community of interest being established: J. P. Morgan & Co. in 1909 acquired large holdings of National City stock (becoming the largest stockholder next to Stillman and his son), and two years later National City acquired large holdings in Morgan's National Bank of Commerce. Competitive struggle for supremacy merged in institutionalized co-operation under overlordship of the House of Morgan.

The interlocked Morgan-Stillman-Baker combination held a total of 341 directorships in 112 of the dominant financial and other corporations with aggregate resources or capitalization of $22,245,000,000 as follows:

Thirty-four banks and trust companies—118 directorships; resources, $2,679,000,000 (13 per cent of all banking resources).

Ten insurance companies—30 directorships; resources, $2,293,000,000 (57 per cent of all insurance resources).

Thirty-two transportation companies—105 directorships; capitalization, $11,784,000,000; mileage, 150,000.

Twenty-four industrial and commercial companies—63 directorships; capitalization, $3,339,000,000.

Twelve public-utility companies—25 directorships; capitalization, $2,150,000,000.

Other investment houses, banks and trust companies were creating minor combinations of their own. In all, 180 individuals representing eighteen financial institutions in New York, Boston and Chicago (including J. P. Morgan & Co., the Morgan affiliates and allies, Kuhn, Loeb & Co., Lee Higginson & Co., Speyer & Co. and Kidder, Peabody & Co.) held 746 directorships in 134 corporations with aggregate resources or capitalization of $25,325,000,000—dominating the economic life of the nation.

In this centralization of industry and finance the House of Morgan was the dominating factor. There were shades of control in the system. Not all affiliated corporations were dominated as completely as Morgan dominated United States Steel. But within the system as a whole, of which the pivot was the House of Morgan, definite and complete control prevailed in its larger aspects.

There was nothing peculiarly American in financial centralization and control. In Europe, particularly Germany, the centralization was infinitely larger. Five or six German great banks institutionalized an almost complete control of financial resources, regulating industry, determining general policy, national and international, and dominating the government with which they worked in full agreement. Larger financial centralization in Germany, France and England was a result of three factors: industrial and financial combination did not meet with any substantial resistance, the struggles of imperialism demanded unification and centralized manipulation of financial resources, and governments encouraged the centralization of industry and finance.

In the United States, on the contrary, industrial combination and its accompanying financial centralization and control aroused intense resistance. The Granger, Populist and Bryan movements glorified small-scale industry and insisted on restoring competition, while European revolt usually assumed the form of socialist acceptance of large-scale industry and proposals for its socialization. American resistance did not prevent the development of financial centralization and control, but compelled the adoption of comparatively loose and incompletely institutionalized forms.

The system of community of interest, and the emphasis on financial centralization and control operating by means of 180 interlocking directors, disproportionately stressed the personal factors, making centralization appear as if simply the work of predatory financiers. But community of interest meant much more than that. Centralization was the inevitable product of large-scale, concentrated capitalism, developing new institutions and functions; class resistance and government prohibitions interfered with centralization assuming completely institutional aspects, compelling it in many cases to adopt the looser forms of community of interest and personal relationships in order to evade legal restrictions and avoid public antagonism.

These conditions provided an opportunity for the personal dictatorship of J. Pierpont Morgan. In any system where relationships are not completely institutionalized authority becomes more personal than institutional, favoring the emergence of dictatorship. While an institutional development, the system of financial centralization and control was compelled to function partly on the personal basis of community of interest, in which Morgan usurped dictatorship. He was not the most constructive of the captains of industry and finance, Wall Street placing him below Harriman and Hill in that respect, but Morgan had the advantage of being a financier, and finance was the concentration point of the system. He was not the most brilliant of financiers, as such, Baker and Stillman being at least his equals, but Morgan had the advantage of being more of a ruler, supremely capable of imposing himself by personal authority where the others depended largely upon institutional power. And, finally, Wall Street trusted Morgan where it would not trust anybody else. Dependability is a necessary quality of sustained dictatorship.

The basis and distinctive financial feature of Morgan's system of centralization and control was the development by banks and other financial institutions of investment functions and their penetration of industry. The critics of centralization urged separation of functions, insisting that a bank should limit itself to commercial business, not realizing that integration of industry and finance compelled banks to assume investment functions.

National banks were not directly authorized by law to engage in investment-banking operations, but they did just the same. When the government challenged the practice, the First National Bank (in 1908) organized a separate company, the First Security Co., to carry on investment operations. First National declared a dividend of 100 per cent which was issued to stockholders in the form of stock ($10,000,000) in the new security company, the two institutions having the same directors, the president, vice-president and cashier of the bank being trustees of the security company. The organization agreement, between George F. Baker representing the trustees and J. Pierpont Morgan representing the stockholders, made bank and security company inseparable. Within four years the First Security Co., in addition to paying regularly 12 to 17 per cent dividends, accumulated surplus equal to 40 per cent of its capital. The idea of a security company owned by and inseparable from the bank, carrying on investment operations forbidden under the National Bank Act, was adopted in 1911 by the National City Bank in its organization of the National City Co., the $10,000,000 stock of which was secured by the bank paying a 40 per cent dividend to stockholders.

The organization of security companies constituted evasions of legal restrictions upon national banks, imposed, however, by the needs of developing industry and finance. Large-scale industry required larger, more unified banking facilities, and erased the old distinctions between commercial and investment operations. Corporate combinations, their ownership and management separated by the multiplication of stockholders, required contacts and unity with each other, which financial centralization and control provided. Morgan's system, operating by means of a complex (if incomplete) institutionalized mechanism for the control of financial resources and corporate industry, was the expression of a new economic order, of concentrated capitalism, and its need of a measure of unity and regulation. As the sensitive expression of the new order, finance imposed unity and regulation upon corporate industry (since society in the shape of its government almost completely rejected the task).

But while necessary under the conditions of concentrated capitalism, the system of financial centralization and control had its predatory aspects and abuses, while it limited the scope of small-scale competitive enterprise. Revolt against the system developed, and against the House of Morgan and its affiliates as the system's most characteristic representatives.

REFORM *has been to America what revolution has been to much of the rest of the world. Americans had their Revolution in 1775 and have accepted generally Lincoln's conclusion that the nation that resulted was "conceived in liberty and dedicated to the proposition that all men are created equal." They have also believed that their land was mankind's last best hope. Given the foregoing, it is hardly surprising to find that when obvious abuses arose, Americans took the stance that tinkering rather than a major overhaul would correct the system. It has rarely been assumed that the basic institutions are at fault, but rather their violation by corrupt men that disrupt their proper functioning. So it was that the anti-slavery crusade of the antebellum period concluded that a conspiracy of slavocrats to dominate the federal government accounted for the maintenance of slavery. And as the industrial dislocations of the later nineteenth century radically altered the economy, and demonstrated the unworkability of rural mores in an increasingly urbanized society, reformers denounced "malefactors of wealth" and demanded the return of the government to the people.*

It was within the framework of the foregoing assumptions that the Progressives operated. "We have made up our minds to square every process of our national life again with the standards we so proudly set up at the beginning and have always carried at our hearts," Woodrow Wilson announced in his first inaugural address. Thus change in America comes to preserve the already revealed truths; its purpose is always to restore and is by implication conservative in its intent. If any one political philosopher explains the American approach to change, it is Edmund Burke who saw in change the necessary response to the needs of a society evolving in time, but who also insisted that the past exerts its claims, allowing no man to ignore its circumscribing impact.

At the heart of the Progressive concern was the overweening claims of the individual; these they feared, if left unchecked, would erode the foundations of society. Too frequently, private interests pushed off their obligations on the public, forgetting, as S. S. McClure noted, "that we are all the people; that while each of us in his group can shove off on the rest the bill of today, the debt is postponed; the rest are passing it on back to us." Within the confines of McClure's Magazine and other contemporary journals, a new form of journalism which received from Theodore Roosevelt the uncomplimentary description of muckraking worked to expose the corruption of American life. The assumption used to justify the effort was elementary: let the people know and they will correct the abuse and make society clean again. With this belief underlying their effort, the Progressives ranged across American life, seeking out the wrongs and proposing the cures.

Thus Upton Sinclair nauseated a generation with his description of the Chicago stockyards and created a demand for the passage in 1906 of the Pure Food and Drug Act. The campaign against child labor accelerated as a result of John Spargo's unnerving The Bitter Cry of the Children *(1906) and the first children's court got underway in Denver as a result of Ben Lindsey's efforts. Ray Stannard Baker exposed in his* Following the Color Line *(1908) the tragic plight of the Negro, exposed as he was to systematic violations of his civil rights and economic exploitation. By 1910, such agitation had resulted in the establishment of the National Association for the Advancement of Colored People. It specifically rejected the idea of gradualism in achieving Negro rights, arguing instead for the immediate political, economic, and social equality of the black man. Within the city such reformers as Lawrence Veiller brought much-needed reforms in housing. The attack upon the dumbbell tenement construction was given its most succinct justification in Veiller's blunt assertion that every man had a "God-given right to light and air." Concern for the plight of the underprivileged received its most touching expression in Robert Hunter,* Poverty *(1904), when he wrote: ". . . the process of Justice is to lift stony barriers, against which the noblest beat their brains out, and from which the ignoble (but who shall say not more sensible?) turn away in despair." To restore justice, a traditional American value, to its supremacy was the objective of most Progressives. It is this effort that set the tone of their time.*

Few working historians have been more productive than Richard Hofstadter (1916-   ), a two-time Pulitzer Prize winner. Presently the De Witt Clinton Professor of History at Columbia University, he has given particular attention to intellectual and social history. His explorations of the techniques of sociology, political science, and social psychology and their application to history has made him a pioneer of the interdisciplinary approach to historical analysis. It is probably correct to say that he explores the outer edges of historical research and in the process points the way to tomorrow's history.

THE AGE OF REFORM

by Richard Hofstadter

Progressivism, at its heart, was an effort to realize familiar and traditional ideals under novel circumstances. As I have emphasized, the ordinary American's ideas of what political and economic life ought to be like had long since taken form under the conditions of a preponderantly rural society with a broad diffusion of property and power. In that society large aggregates had played a minor role. Corporate businesses were then just emerging, and they had not yet achieved the enormous size and national scope which they acquired during the closing decades of the nineteenth century, when the Progressive generation was still growing up. Political machines, though an important feature of American life since the days of Aaron Burr, had not played the massive managerial role that they now assumed in American cities and states, and in any case had appeared less formidable threats to civic virtue and democratic politics than they now seemed to be in the corrupting presence of the great corporations. The American tradition had been one of unusually widespread participation of the citizen in the management of affairs, both political and economic. Now the growth of the large corporation, the labor union, and the big impenetrable political machine was clotting society into large aggregates and presenting to the unorganized citizen the prospect that all these aggregates and interests would be able to act in concert and shut out those men for whom organization was difficult or impossible. As early as 1894 William Dean Howells, who had grown up in a small Midwestern community, remarked that the character of American life had undergone a drastic change. "The struggle for life," he said, "has changed from a free fight to an encounter of disciplined forces, and the free fighters that are left get ground to pieces between organized labor and organized capital." Ray Stannard Baker, writing in *McClure's* almost a decade later, pointed out that a number of well-knit local combinations of capital and labor had recently been organized, and gave voice to the fears of the potential victims: "The unorganized public, where will it come in? The professional man, the lecturer, the writer, the artist, the farmer, the salaried government employee, and all the host of men who are not engaged in the actual production or delivery of necessary material things, how will they fare? . . . Is there any doubt that the income of organized labor and the profits of organized capital have gone up enormously, while the man-on-a-salary and most of the great middle class, paying much more for the necessaries of life, have had no adequate increase in earnings?" The central theme in Progressivism was this revolt against the industrial discipline: the Progressive movement was the complaint of the unorganized against the consequences of organization.

Of course there was a problem underlying this effort that did not escape the most astute contemporaries, including many who sympathized deeply with the Progressives. The processes of modern technology and machine industry—not to speak of the complex tasks of civic life—make organization, specialism, hierarchy, and discipline utterly necessary. The Progressives, object though they might to the many sacrifices of traditional values that the new society demanded, did not seriously propose to dismantle this society, forsake its material advantages, and return to a more primitive technology. Nor did they always make the mistake of thinking that the revolt against organization could go on without itself developing new forms of organization. They were trying, in short, to keep the benefits of the emerging organization of life and yet to retain the scheme of individualistic values that this organization was destroying. In order to understand them sympathetically, then, it is important to think of them not as stupid or incapable men who fumbled a simple task, but as men of reasonable and often indeed of penetrating intelligence whose fate it was to attempt, with great zeal and resourcefulness, a task of immense complexity and almost hopeless difficulties.

Long before the Progressives arose some Americans had seen that organization had its disadvantages and dangers, but it was in the Progressive era that the social types expropriated and alienated by the new organization reached a new peak in numbers and a pitch of restiveness such as they have not shown since. Many historians have pointed out that Progressivism appealed powerfully to small businessmen who were being overwhelmed or outdistanced by great competitors. It also appealed—as all the rhetoric about the trusts and the consumer made evident—to the new middle class of technicians and salaried professionals, clerical workers, salespeople, and public-service personnel that multiplied along with the great corporations and the specialized skills of corporate society. This was by far the most rapidly growing stratum in the population. From 1870 to 1910, when the whole population of the United States increased two and one-third times, the old middle class—business entrepreneurs and independent professional men—grew somewhat more than two times; the working class, including farm labor, grew a little more than three times; the number of farmers and farm tenants doubled. But the new middle class grew almost eight times, rising from 756,000 to 5,609,000 people. When we compare the latter figure with the 3,261,000 independent enterprisers and self-employed professionals, we have some notion of the relative strength of these two strata of the population from which Progressivism drew so much of its urban following.

A large and significant political public had emerged that was for the most part fairly well educated, genteel in its outlook, full of aspiration, and almost completely devoid of economic organization. It had no labor unions, no trade associations; its professional societies were without bargaining power. It had only political means through which to express its discontents. While it could not strike or fix prices or support expensive lobbies, it could read the muckraking magazines, listen to the Progressive orators, and vote. I suspect that this class was recruited in very large measure from people who had either risen upwards or moved sideways in the social scale—of Yankee farmers' sons who had come to the city, of native workmen's children aspiring to white-collar respectability—of people, in short, who had been bred upon the Horatio Alger legend and the American dream of success and who had not given up hope of realizing it. Today the white-collar class is more apathetic and more self-indulgent; it hopes chiefly for security, leisure, and comfort and for the enjoyment of the pleasures of mass entertainment. But in the Progressive era this class still lived within the framework of the old ambitions. While it resented the swollen wealth of the tycoons and the crass impersonal conditions of economic life under the corporate economy, it none the less maintained a half-suppressed feeling of admiration and envy for the captains of industry who had after all done no more than fulfill the old dream of heroic personal ascendancy. This may explain why the very journals that ran the devastating muckrakers' exposures of the predations and excesses of the corporations also published hero tales about the outstanding figures of American industry. It may also explain why the same Progressive periodicals, and even the Socialist periodicals, that pilloried the evils of American society, tore into its established ideas, and offered blueprints for progress and reform were full of little individualistic advertisements intended to tell clerks how they could improve themselves and "get ahead"— so that simply by moving one's eye from left to right, from one column to the next, one could pass from the world in which the Beef Trust or Standard Oil was being exposed and denounced, to the world in which "You Too Can Be a Certified Public Accountant."

The discontent over the trusts expressed familiar ideals of entrepreneurship and opportunity which great numbers of Americans were quite unwilling to abandon. In the old society upon which American ideas of the right and the good had been founded, the fluid capital of the middle classes had commonly found an outlet in investments over which the investors exercised a large measure of control. The typical business unit of the early and middle nineteenth century was owned by an individual or a small group, was limited in size by the personal wealth of the individuals who controlled it, and was managed either directly by them or by their agents. As the corporate form of organization grew and a large market in corporate securities was developed, the savings and investments and insurance of the substantial middle class, and with these more and more of the power to make the vital economic decisions of society, passed into the hands of the masters of corporations and the investment bankers. The restlessness of the Progresive era owed much of its force to a class of substantial property-owning citizens whose powers of economic decision had been expropriated by the system of corporate organization.

It would be misleading to imply that the development of the corporation eliminated profitable direct small-scale investments. Quite the contrary, for the urbanization of the country brought a growing need for the work of service industries that are usually organized in small units, and such lines of enterprise continued to offer much opportunity for small investors who were satisfied to operate profitably on a small scale in marginal lines of business. But such enterprises could not absorb more than a part of middle-class savings; and after 1870 the decisive and strategic lines of enterprise that called the tune for the economy as a whole, that afforded the richest profits and aroused the highest excitement in the entrepreneurial imagination, passed increasingly under the corporate form of organization. Confined in the pre-Civil War period to a few types of industries, the business corporation had taken a new lease on life as a consequence of the Civil War. The necessities of war finance and the success of Jay Cooke in reaching the domestic investor with government securities had awakened men to the possibilities of a domestic investment market. In the period after the war this market had grown swiftly, spreading from the railroad and banking fields into public utilities, mining and quarrying, manufacturing, and eventually merchandising. By 1900 there were estimated to be 4,400,000 stockholders in American corporations; by 1917, 8,600,000.

One area in which middle-class savings became a focus of poignant conflict was that of life insurance. As a major pivot of finance, life insurance was a product of the post-Civil War era. Life-insurance protection in the United States, which amounted to $5.47 per capita in 1860, rose to $40.69 in 1885, and to $179.14 in 1910. The aggregate of insurance in force rose by 577 per cent between 1870 and 1896, while the total admitted assets of the insurance companies rose by 958 per cent. With these changes in the size of the business came internal changes in company policy. The adoption of the so-called deferred-dividend contract made available to the insurance managers large undistributed surpluses that did not have the legal status of liabilities in the companies' accounts. These surpluses, supposedly to be distributed at the end of stated periods to policyholders, were drawn upon by the managers of some of the large companies and used for speculative purposes through subsidiary companies. The exposure of these life-insurance practices in the work of the New York State legislature's Armstrong Committee and in such books as Burton J. Hendricks's *The Story of Life Insurance* made it painfully clear to the policy-holding public that even in the citadels of security they were being shamelessly and ruthlessly gulled.

A thought most galling to middle-class investors was that the shrinkage in their own power and the growth in the power of the "plutocracy" were based upon their own savings—that, as Louis D. Brandeis put it, "the fetters which bind the people are forged from the people's own gold." The American had been brought up to accept as "natural" a type of economy in which enterprise was diffused among a multitude of firms and in which the process of economic decision, being located everywhere, could not be located anywhere in particular. Now it was shocking to learn that this economy had been self-destructive, that it was giving way to small bodies of men directing great corporations whose decisions, as Woodrow Wilson protested, were "autocratic," who could concentrate in themselves "the resources, the choices, the opportunities, in brief, the power of thousands." The poor stockholder, Wilson continued, "does not seem to enjoy any of the substantial rights of property in connection with [corporate stocks]. He is merely contributing money for the conduct of a business which other men run as they please. If he does not approve of what they do, there seems nothing for it but to sell the stock (though their acts may have depreciated its value immensely). He cannot even inquire or protest without being told to mind his own business—the very thing he was innocently trying to do!" The Pujo Committee investigators underlined this argument when they revealed that none of the witnesses that appeared before them was able to mention a single instance in the country's history in which stockholders had either successfully overthrown the management of any large corporation or secured an investigation of its conduct.

People readily acknowledged that in spite of all this they were prosperous. But many of them could not help feeling that this prosperity was being obtained on false pretenses, that it was theirs in disregard of sound and ancient principles, and that for this disregard they would in good time come to grief. It had been their tradition to believe that prosperity and economic progress came not through big or monopolistic businesses—that is, through the gains and economies of organization—but rather through competition and hard work and individual enterprise and initiative. They had been brought up to think of the well-being of society not merely in structural terms—not as something resting upon the sum of its technique and efficiency—but in moral terms, as a reward for the sum total of individual qualities and personal merits. This tradition, rooted in the Protestant ethic itself, was being wantonly defied by the system of corporate organization.

In 1905 Judge Peter S. Grosscup of the United States Circuit Court of Appeals published in *McClure's* an article that reveals, coming as it did from a man of impeccable conservatism, how widespread this concern was. Although Grosscup acknowledged that the nation was enjoying a prosperity and power such as it had never seen before, he expressed his fear that it was losing its soul. It was the intangibles that worried him. Neither the prosperity nor the power was in danger, but "the soul of republican America . . . is individual opportunity. . . . The loss that republican America now confronts is the loss of individual hope and prospect—the suppression of the instinct that . . . has made us a nation of individually independent and prosperous people." The country was in the midst of a trend that, if not deflected, would eventually reach a point at which "the acquisition of property, by the individuals who constitute the bulk of the people, will cease to be one of the opening and controlling purposes of their lives. This means that, as a republican political institution, America will have lost the spirit which alone promises it life. It means social and, eventually, political revolution." The widespread apprehension about corporations was not merely a consequence of anxiety over high prices. It was rather the result of an "intuitive perception that, somewhere, something is wrong—that in the face of the future there is a disturbing, even sinister look." What was wrong was that the corporation was putting an unbearable strain on the institution of private property, upon which the civilization of the world rested; for it was the desire and the hope of acquiring private property upon which the entire moral discipline of an individualist society must rely. The nation was at a crossroad leading on one side to corporate paternalism and on the other to state socialism—both fatal to individual liberties. Fortunately there was another path that could still be taken: "Individual Opportunity—the opportunity, actual as well as in theory, to each individual to participate in the proprietorship of the country."

Grosscup proposed, in short, to reverse the entire process by which the individual had been expropriated. This he thought could be done if the matter was taken out of the hands of the states and vested in the federal government, if "stock-jobbing" and stock-watering were prevented (that is, if the corporation was "regenerated"), and if the "road to proprietorship" was opened to the wage-earners of the country. How such proprietorship could be made possible he did not say.

Grosscup was expressing an attitude toward economic life that was to appear with increasing frequency down to the end of the Progressive era. While the great theoretician and technician of this protest was Louis D. Brandeis, its master spokesman in politics was Woodrow Wilson, whose campaign speeches in 1912 provide us with a magnificently articulate expression of the whole impulse. Like Grosscup's article, Wilson's evocative speeches express the tendency of the middle-class public to think of the economic order not quite so much as a system organized for the production and distribution of goods as a system intended to stimulate and reward certain traits of personal character. The public to which Wilson appealed had been brought up on the nineteenth-century ideal of opportunity and the notion that success was a reward for energy, efficiency, frugality, perseverance, ambition, and insight. In their thinking, people competed—or ought to compete—in the exercise of these qualities, and success ought properly to go to those who had the most of them. The metaphor they most often and most significantly used in describing their economic ideal was that of a race—"the race of life," as it was commonly called. What Wilson was pointing to—and what he refused to accept as a governing principle for American industry—was the fact that this race was no longer being run. It had once been true that a man could "choose his own calling and pursue it just as far as his abilities enable him to pursue it." America had been committed to "ideals of absolutely free opportunity, where no man is supposed to be under any limitations except the limitations of his character and of his mind . . . where men win or lose on their merits." By various means the new system of organization had destroyed this body of ideals. But: "America will insist upon recovering in practice those ideals which she has always professed."

Wilson saw that Americans were living under "a new organization of society," in which the individual had been "submerged" and human relations were pervasively impersonal. Wilson's hero, the rising individual entrepreneur of classical economics and of earlier days of diffused property management, had been done in by just such impersonal organization. This entrepreneurial hero—referred to by Wilson as the "beginner," the "man with only a little capital," the "new entry" in the race, "the man on the make"—was the figure for whom he was particularly solicitous. For Wilson was profoundly interested, he said, in "the constant renewal of society from the bottom," upon which the genius and enterprise of America had always depended. And while it was true that the country was still prosperous, the "middle class is being more and more squeezed out by the processes which we have been taught to call processes of prosperity. Its members are sharing prosperity, no doubt; but what alarms me is that they are not *originating* prosperity." The real treasury of America lay in the ambitions and energies that were not restricted to a special favored class but depended upon the inventions and originations of "unknown men." "Anything that depresses, anything that makes the organization greater than the man, anything that blocks, discourages, dismays the humble man, is against all the principles of progress." According to the ideals of individualism, then, the acknowledged power and prosperity of the country had been achieved by means that must in the long run be considered retrogressive. For was it not true that the big fellows had narrowed and stiffened the lines of endeavor, cut the little man off from credit, and shut the markets against him? This process had gone so far that men were about to forget "the ancient time when America lay in every hamlet, when America was to be seen in every fair valley, when America displayed her great forces on the broad prairies, ran her fine fires of enterprise up over the mountainsides and down into the bowels of the earth, and eager men were everywhere captains of industry, not employees; not looking to a distant city to find out what they might do, but looking about among their neighbors, finding credit according to their character, not according to their connections, finding credit in proportion to what was known to be in them and behind them, not in proportion to the securities they held that were approved where they were not known."

While the worst forebodings of the Progressives were not to be realized, one must see with sympathy the view of affairs taken by the men of their generation whose historical consciousness had been formed on the American experience with individual enterprise. The drama of American history had been played out on a continent three thousand miles wide and almost half as long. Great political issues had been fought out over this terrain, great economic risks taken on it, fantastic profits exacted from it. The generation that had not yet passed from the scene had produced and admired, even as it resented and feared, a Carnegie, a Rockefeller, a Hill, a Harriman, a Morgan. America had engendered a national imagination keyed to epic dimensions, a soul unhappy without novelty and daring, raised on the conquest of a continent, the settlement of an immense domain, the creation within the life span of one man of a gigantic system of industry and transportation. Its people had pioneered, improvised, and gambled their way across the continent. And now were its young men to become a nation of employees, at best of administrators, were they to accept a dispensation under which there was nothing but safe investment, to adapt themselves passively to a life without personal enterprise even on a moderate scale? How, then, was the precious spiritual bravura of the whole American enterprise to be sustained? And if it could not be sustained, what would become of America? The Progressives were not fatalists; they did not intend quietly to resign themselves to the decline of this great tradition without at least one brave attempt to recapture that bright past in which there had been a future.

*   *   *   *   *

Representing as they did the spirit and the desires of the middle class, the Progressives stood for a dual program of economic remedies designed to minimize the dangers from the extreme left and right. On one side they feared the power of the plutocracy, on the other the poverty and restlessness of the masses. But if political leadership could be firmly restored to the responsible middle classes who were neither ultra-reactionary nor, in T.R.'s phrase, "wild radicals," both of these problems could be met. The first line of action was to reform the business order, to restore or maintain competition—or, as the case might be, to limit and regulate monopoly— and expand credit in the interests of the consumer, the farmer, and the small businessman. The second was to minimize the most outrageous and indefensible exploitation of the working population, to cope with what was commonly called "the social question." The relations of capital and labor, the condition of the masses in the slums, the exploitation of the labor of women and children, the necessity of establishing certain minimal standards of social decency—these problems filled them with concern both because they felt a sincere interest in the welfare of the victims of industrialism and because they feared that to neglect them would invite social disintegration and ultimate catastrophe. They were filled with a passion for social justice, but they also hoped that social justice could be brought about, as it were, conspicuously. Men like Roosevelt were often furious at the plutocrats because their luxury, their arrogance, and the open, naked exercise of their power constituted a continual provocation to the people and always increased the likelihood that social resentments would find expression in radical or even "socialistic" programs.

Writing to Taft in 1906 about the tasks of American political leadership as he envisaged them for the next quarter century, Roosevelt declared: "I do not at all like the social conditions at present. The dull, purblind folly of the very rich men; their greed and arrogance, and the way in which they have unduly prospered by the help of the ablest lawyers, and too often through the weakness or shortsightedness of the judges or by their unfortunate possession of meticulous minds; these facts, and the corruption in business and politics, have tended to produce a very unhealthy condition of excitement and irritation in the popular mind, which shows itself in part in the enormous increase in the socialistic propaganda. Nothing effective, because nothing at once honest and intelligent, is being done to combat the great amount of evil which, mixed with a little good, a little truth, is contained in the outpourings of the *Cosmopolitan*, of *McClure's*, of *Collier's*, of Tom Lawson, of David Graham Phillips, of Upton Sinclair. Some of these are socialists; some of them merely lurid sensationalists; but they are all building up a revolutionary feeling which will most probably take the form of a political campaign. Then we may have to do, too late or almost too late, what had to be done in the silver campaign when in one summer we had to convince a great many good people that what they had been laboriously taught for several years previous was untrue."

Roosevelt represented, of course, the type of Progressive leader whose real impulses were deeply conservative, and who might not perhaps have been a Progressive at all if it were not for the necessity of fending off more radical threats to established ways of doing things. The characteristic Progressive thinker carried on a tolerant and mutually profitable dialogue with the Socialists of the period, perhaps glancing over his shoulder with some anxiety from time to time, to be sure that Marxian or Fabian ideas were not gaining too much ground in the United States, but chiefly because in this age of broad social speculation he was interested to learn what he could from Socialist criticism. Fundamentally, however, the influence of such criticism was negative: if the Socialist said that the growing combinations of capital were natural products of social evolution and that the challenge they represented to democracy must be met by expropriating their owners, the typical Progressive was only spurred all the more to find ways of limiting or regulating monopoly within a capitalist framework; when the Socialist said that the grievances of the people could be relieved only under Socialism, the typical Progressive became the more determined to find ways of showing that these grievances were remediable under capitalism. In these ways the alleged "threat" of Socialism, much talked about in the Progressive period, actually gave added impetus to middle-class programs.

At bottom, the central fear was fear of power, and the greater the strength of an organized interest, the greater the anxiety it aroused. Hence it was the trusts, the investment banking houses, the interlocking directorates, the swollen private fortunes, that were most criticized, and after them the well-knit, highly disciplined political machines. The labor unions, being far weaker than the big businesses and the machines, held an ambiguous place in Progressive thinking. The Progressive sympathized with the problems of labor, but was troubled about the lengths to which union power might go if labor-unionism became the sole counterpoise to the power of business. The danger of combinations of capital and labor that would squeeze the consuming public and the small businessman was never entirely out of sight. The rise in the price of coal after the anthracite strike aroused much public concern. And wherever labor was genuinely powerful in politics—as it was, for instance, in San Francisco, a closed-shop town where labor for a time dominated the local government—Progressivism took on a somewhat anti-labor tinge.

Where the labor movement was of no more than moderate strength, and where it clearly represented the middle-class aspirations of native workers and of business unionism, it was readily accepted, if only as a minor third partner in the alliance between agrarians and the urban middle class that constituted the Progressive movement. Those Progressives who lived in the midst of industrial squalor and strife seem to have felt that the best way of meeting the "social question" was through means more benevolently disinterested than those of direct labor action. Here again the ideal of the neutral state came into play, for it was expected that the state, dealing out evenhanded justice, would meet the gravest complaints. Industrial society was to be humanized through law, a task that was largely undertaken in the state legislatures. In the years following 1900 an impressive body of legislation was passed dealing with workmen's compensation, the labor of women and children, hours of work, minimum wages for women, and old-age pensions. Even when much allowance is made for spottiness in administration and enforcement, and for the toll that judicial decisions took of them, the net effect of these laws in remedying the crassest abuses of industrialism was very considerable. Today it is perhaps necessary to make a strong effort of the imagination to recall the industrial barbarism that was being tamed—to realize how much, for instance, workmen's compensation meant at a time when every year some 16,000 or 17,000 trainmen (about one out of every ten or twelve workers so classified) were injured. The insistence that the power of law be brought to bear against such gratuitous suffering is among our finest inheritances from the Progressive movement.

Progressivism was effective, moreover, not only for the laws it actually passed but for the pressure it put on business to match public reform with private improvements. American business itself had entered a new phase. Before the 1890's it had been too much absorbed in the problems of plant construction, expanding markets, and falling prices to pay much attention to either the efficiency or the morale of its working force. American plant management had been backward. But in the early twentieth century thoughtful American businessmen, pressed by the threat of union organization, condemned by muckrakers, and smarting under comparisons with the most efficient managers in Europe, began to address themselves to poor working conditions and employee morale and to the reformation of their haphazard shop methods. Between 1900 and 1910, 240 volumes on business management were published. Frederick Winslow Taylor's interest in efficiency was popularized among businessmen. The emerging business schools, nonexistent in the country before 1898, provided numerous new agencies for discussion, education, and research in the field of management. Employers began to study personnel problems, consider devices for cutting fatigue and improving work conditions, and launched in some cases upon their own welfare and pension programs and profit-sharing schemes. Much of this was resisted by labor unions as an attempt to set up a system of paternalistic control, and much was indeed associated with the fostering of company unions. Few employers went as far as Edward A. Filene in encouraging labor participation in managerial decisions. But the whole Progressive atmosphere did help to give rise to a system of private welfare capitalism alongside the statutory system of business regulation that was growing up. During and after the first World War this private system developed with notable rapidity.

So far as those important intangibles of political tone were concerned in which so many Progressives were deeply interested, they won a significant victory, for they heightened the level of human sympathy in the American political and economic system. One of the primary tests of the mood of a society at any given time is whether its comfortable people tend to identify, psychologically, with the power and achievements of the very successful or with the needs and sufferings of the underprivileged. In a large and striking measure the Progressive agitations turned the human sympathies of the people downward rather than upward in the social scale. The Progressives, by creating a climate of opinion in which, over the long run, the comfortable public was disposed to be humane, did in the end succeed in fending off that battle of social extremes of which they were so afraid. Thanks in part to their efforts, the United States took its place alongside England and the Scandinavian countries among those nations in which the upper and middle classes accepted the fundamental legitimacy of labor aspiration and labor-unionism, and took a different path from those countries of the Continent where the violence of class antagonism and class struggle was heightened by the moral rejection of Labor. To realize the importance of the change in the United States itself, one need only think of the climate of opinion in which the Pullman strike and the Homestead strike were fought out and compare it with the atmosphere in which labor organization has taken place since the Progressive era. There has of course been violence and bloodshed, but in the twentieth century a massive labor movement has been built with far less cost in these respects than it cost the American working class merely to man the machines of American industry in the period from 1865 to 1900.

Although the Progessives were thus capable, except in special instances, of coming to terms with the organization of labor, the objective problem as well as the confusing mixture of feelings involved in their approach to business organization gave them far greater trouble. While the Progressive citizen was alarmed at the threat to economic competition and political democracy, he was also respectful of order, aware of prosperity, and cautious about launching any drastic attack upon propertied institutions. While he was hostile to private business power, he also admired bigness, efficiency, and success. While he was devoted to the moral virtues and believed in the material benefits of price competition, he was also willing to reckon with social change, and he worshipped that god of progress which the consolidation of business was said by many men to represent.

The Progressive discussion of the so-called trust or monopoly question is therefore filled with all that uneasiness and inconsistency which we may expect to see when men find themselves enmeshed in institutions and practices that seem to be working to considerable effect but that violate their inherited precepts and their moral preferences. When a social problem is, in its largest aspects, insoluble, as this one was, and when the feelings aroused over it are as urgent as the feelings of the Progressive generation, what usually happens is that men are driven to find a purely ceremonial solution. Among later generations, which do not approach the problem in the same way or have feelings of the same urgency about it, such ceremonial solutions are a temptation to the satirical intelligence. But we must be wary of falling too readily into that easy condescension which one may feel when speaking with hindsight about the problems of an earlier age. Since we no longer experience with anything like the same intensity some of the Progressives' anxieties or their sense of loss, we have outgrown the problem of business organization that they faced: and in so far as we recognize it as a real problem—as we do, for instance, in relation to the preservation of democracy—we have by no means solved it.

From the very beginning, at any rate, when the Sherman Anti-Trust Act was passed in 1890, it was recognized by most of the astute politicians of that hour as a gesture, a ceremonial concession to an overwhelming public demand for some kind of reassuring action against the trusts. Senator Orville Platt was candid enough to say at the time that it was just the result of a desire "to get some bill headed: 'A Bill to Punish Trusts' with which to go to the country." Before the time of Theodore Roosevelt's presidency very little attempt had been made, and negligible results had been achieved, in employing the act to check business consolidations, and the Supreme Court had already made it clear that enforcement would be no simple matter. T.R., as we have seen, dramatized the issue in his Northern Securities prosecution, which was followed in time by a few other selected prosecutions of comparable public-relations value. The readiness with which his reputation as a "trust-buster"—a reputation that despite all the efforts of the historians still clings to his name—grew up around these prosecutions is itself striking testimony to the public's need to believe in the effectiveness of action in this sphere; for not only did T.R. fail to prosecute many trusts, and fail to check the accelerating business consolidation that occurred during his administrations, but he did not even believe in the trust-busting philosophy and he was utterly and constantly candid in saying so in his presidential messages and other public statements. He inveighed regularly and with asperity against attempting "the impossible task of restoring the flintlock conditions of business sixty years ago by trusting only to a succession of lawsuits under the antitrust law. . . ." "The man who advocates destroying the trusts," he said early in his presidency, "by measures which would paralyze the industries of the country is at least a quack and at worst an enemy to the Republic." Lacking faith in the viability or workability of all efforts to restore the old competitive order, he urged, as did those Progressive intellectuals who followed the lead of Herbert Croly, that the whole system of organization be accepted as a product of modern life, and that such efforts as must be made to control and check overgrown organization be carried out along the lines of the counter-organization: "A simple and poor society can exist as a democracy on a basis of sheer individualism. But a rich and complex industrial society cannot so exist; for some individuals, and especially those artificial individuals called corporations, become so very big that the ordinary individual . . . cannot deal with them on terms of equality. It therefore becomes necessary for these ordinary individuals to combine in their turn, first in order to act in their collective capacity through that biggest of all combinations called the government, and second, to act also in their own self-defense, through private combinations, such as farmers' associations and trade unions."

These remarks come as close as a brief statement could do to foreshadowing the important developments in this sphere since Roosevelt's time. It was his belief that while business combinations should be accepted and recognized, their affairs, their acts and earnings, should be exposed to publicity; and that they should be subject to regulation and be punished when they were "bad." The Bureau of Corporations, which was created at his instance in 1903, did in fact carry out useful studies of the conduct of a number of major industries, including lumber, meatpacking, oil, steel, and tobacco. Roosevelt seems to have thought of the Bureau of Corporations as the tentative beginning of a somewhat more effective system of regulation, whose ultimate form was, not surprisingly, rather vague in his mind. As time passed, however, he put more and more emphasis on the distinction between good and bad trusts. Monopoly power itself was not to be the object of concern, but only such monopoly or near-monopoly as was achieved or maintained by unfair methods. This distinction might be difficult to realize satisfactorily in positive law—but such a consideration seems not to have concerned him. The facilities of the Antitrust Division of the Department of Justice were limited to five attorneys working with a budget of about $100,000 a year. By definition, since only a handful of suits could be undertaken each year, there could hardly be very many "bad" businesses. Such was the situation as T.R. left it during his presidency.

Despite the efforts of President Taft to put some force into the antitrust movement, public dissatisfaction continued to grow, as the appetite for the regulation of business consolidation seemed to enlarge with such small evidences of success as the politicians were able to produce. There was a growing awareness of the danger of what Wilson called "a combination of the combinations"—the union of all the great business interests under the leadership of the chief investment banking houses. More and more Americans were coming to the conclusion that what had been done thus far did not go nearly deep enough. The view expressed by Herbert Croly, T.R., Charles H. Van Hise, and some others that monopoly must be accepted and regulated may have had widespread appeal among many lawyers, intellectuals, and the more sophisticated businessmen, but it was probably not the predominant sentiment among those who had strong feelings about the matter. The idea of Brandeis, Wilson, La Follette, and Bryan that a real effort should be made to restore, maintain, and regulate competition rather than regulate monopoly seems to have been more congenial to the country at large, to most of the reformers, and especially to rural people and small businessmen in the West and South, where Populist anti-monopoly traditions had some strength. No doubt it was this large public that Vice-President Thomas R. Marshall had in mind when he declared in 1913: "The people were told in the last campaign that trusts were a natural evolution, and that the only way to deal with them was to regulate them. The people are tired of being told such things. What they want is the kind of opportunity that formerly existed in this country."

This remark summarizes the issue of business consolidation as it had been dramatized in the election campaign of 1912. Both Wilson and Roosevelt ran on platforms so generally Progressive that only their difference on the trust issue clearly marked them off from each other. The issue, as Brandeis put it, was regulated competition versus regulated monopoly, and although it was vigorously debated in these terms, giving strong expression to the feelings of the two schools of thought, it is doubtful that the difference was in fact as sharp as the debate made it seem. To be sure, men like Wilson and La Follette at times seemed really to believe that the tide of business consolidation could be swept back by Sherman Act methods. La Follette declared in 1912 that "the executive could have saved the people from the appalling conditions which confront us today, if all the power of this government had been put forth to enforce the [Sherman] Anti-Trust law." Wilson asserted in the same year that the community of business interests by which the United States was in danger of being governed was "something for the law to pull apart, and gently, but firmly and persistently dissect"—a threat that raises the image of a surgical president, perhaps with Brandeis and La Follette in attendance, exercising his scalpel over the palpitating body of the American business community.

In fact Wilson's approach was not so straightforward or unequivocal as this menacing surgical metaphor suggests—for he too recognized that "the elaboration of business upon a great co-operative scale is characteristic of our time and has come about by the natural operation of modern civilization," and admitted that "we shall never return to the old order of individual competition, and that the organization of business upon a grand scale of cooperation is, up to a certain point, itself normal and inevitable." While he believed deeply in the little entrepreneur and in competition, he rested his hope in what he called "free competition," not in "illicit competition." Free competition was anything that promoted the victory of superior efficiency, while illicit competition was the use of unfair means to surpass competitors by firms that were not actually more efficient. Wilson had to admit that free competition, too, would kill competitors, and that these competitors would be just as dead as those killed by illicit competition. But in such cases the net result would be good, because it would add to the total efficiency of the nation's production. Thus a big business that grew big through superior efficiency was good; only one that grew big by circumventing honest competition was bad. "I am for big business," said Wilson in one of his more inscrutable sentences. "and I am against the trusts." But no one, not even Brandeis, knew how to define or measure superior efficiency, or to draw a line in the progress toward bigness beyond which a business would lose rather than gain in efficiency. While it was possible to draw up a list of business practices that most honest men would agree to condemn, no one knew a constructive or responsible way of dissolving great businesses that had already grown up by employing just such practices. No one knew how to make empirical sense out of Wilson's distinction between the big business he favored and the trusts he disliked. And no one could be sure that there was any real working difference between the distinction T.R. made between good and bad trusts and the distinction Wilson made between free and illicit competition.

A Progressive voter who felt impelled to take a rational view of the trust question might well have been confused, and may have wondered whether the warm debate expressed a really profound difference between the candidates. In fact, by the time of the 1912 campaign the decisions of the Supreme Court had already whittled the Sherman Act down to the point at which it was no longer possible to imagine that the law could be— without a juridical revolution—an instrument for a broad frontal attack on business consolidation. What remained was the possibility that particular businesses guilty of flagrantly unfair competition could occasionally be singled out for action—a procedure not signally different from the Roose- veltian distinction between good and bad trusts. What is perhaps most worthy of comment is that the further anti-trust legislation of the Wilson administration, the Clayton Act and the creation of the Federal Trade Commission, did not include any provisions aimed at circumventing the Supreme Court's extremely damaging approach to anti-trust suits. Nor was any serious effort made by Wilson to launch a vigorous policy. Under him the Antitrust Division was expanded, but only to eighteen men—and even this was done only after wartime conditions had sent prices sky-high. (The most elementary policing of the economy, more recent experience has shown, calls for a staff of well over ten times as many attorneys.) Wilson also disappointed those who hoped that the Federal Trade Commission would become an effective agency of regulation by choosing commissioners who were either ineffectual or primarily interested in making the agency useful to business. Brandeis, who had helped to draft the act creating the Federal Trade Commission, later dismissed its management under Wilson as "a stupid administration."

No one who follows the trust question at the level of both public dis- cussion and legislative action can fail to be impressed by the disparity between the two: the discussions were so momentous in their character and so profound—for nothing less was at stake than the entire organization of American business and American politics, the very question of who was to control the country—and the material results were by comparison so marginal, so incomplete, so thoroughly blocked at all the major strategic points. It is impossible not to conclude that, despite the widespread public agitation over the matter, the men who took a conservative view of the needs of the hour never lost control. It was not merely that, on the main issues to be adjudicated, the Supreme Court stood with them, but that the executive leaders who occupied the White House and the sober gentry of the Senate were in the final analysis quite reliable. It proved impossible for men like Bryan and La Follette, who did not enjoy the confidence of at least large segments of the business community, to find their way to the White House; and the considerable influence that these men had through- out the country was carefully filtered through the hands of more con- servative politicians before it was embodied in legislative or administrative action. A leader like Theodore Roosevelt, and with him several prominent Republicans, who understood the urgency of Progressive sentiments, knew also how to act as a balance wheel between what he considered to be the

most irresponsible forces of left and right. (In 1912 George Roosevelt remarked to him that whereas earlier he had been the progressive leader of
the conservatives, he was now the conservative leader of the progressives.
" 'Yes, Yes,' T.R. muttered, as he rocked back and forth in his favorite rocking chair, 'that's it. I have to hold them in check all the time. I have to
restrain them.' ")

Historians have long been aware how T.R., while enjoying the support
and indeed even on occasion whipping up the sentiments of the insurgent
forces in American life, turned for advice in the solution of his problems
to the great conservative leaders in the Senate and to the great spokesmen
of Eastern industry and finance capital; and how much support he accepted
for his campaigns from the financial interests whose custodians these men
always were. Woodrow Wilson had a different temperament, and in his
administration the same forces worked in a somewhat roundabout way. To
preserve his own sense of integrity, Wilson had fewer direct dealings with
the captains of industry and finance; but his closest adviser, Colonel House,
became a personal agent through whom the needs and views of capital
could be expressed to the White House, and House's diary records frequent
conferences with J. P. Morgan, Felix M. Warburg, Henry Clay Frick,
Francis L. Higginson, Otto H. Kahn, and Frank Vanderlip. Moreover,
when a depression developed late in 1913 which grew more serious in the
following year, Wilson himself began openly and assiduously to cultivate
the support of business, began to welcome bankers and business leaders
back to the White House, and issued unequivocal reassurances to the effect
that the wave of reform legislation was nearing its end. Progressive intellectuals, who were familiar with the praise Herbert Croly had lavished
upon the circumspect Roosevelt, must have been bemused to see this editor
scold Woodrow Wilson in 1914 for his failure to go very far with the program of Progressive reform.

But to say all this about the ceremonial function of the agitation over
big business should not divert us from our search for its other uses. The
relations of the reform movement to business were not limited to the effort
to restore competition or check monopoly. There were other, more pragmatic reforms under consideration; and it was the effect of all the monitory
writing and speaking, and all the heated agitation over the trusts and their
threat to democracy and enterprise and liberty, to throw big business and
the vested interests on the defensive and to create a climate of public
opinion in which some reform legislation was possible. The Progressives
may not have been able to do much about business consolidation, but they
did manage, in the Hepburn Act, to take the first step toward genuine
regulation of the railroads, a thing long overdue; they did manage, in the
creation of the Federal Reserve System, to establish a more satisfactory
system of credit subject to public control; they did bring about, in the
Underwood tariff, a long-sought downward revision of duties; and on a
number of fronts, both state and national, they won other legislative reforms of real value to farmers and workers and the consuming public that
would have been far more difficult to achieve in a social atmosphere unaf-

fected by the widespread demand to challenge the power of big business.

In a number of ways the problem of business consolidation now presents itself, even to liberals and reformers, in different forms from those in which it appeared to the men of the Progressive generation. Fewer men by far experience the passing of independent entrepreneurship with the same anguish. The process of capital formation has changed in such a way as to reduce the importance of the investment banking houses and thus to lay the specter of the money trust. Product competition has in some respects replaced the old price competition. The great distributive agencies, themselves giant concerns, have given consumers some protection from the exactions of monopoly. Big business has shown itself to be what the Progressives of the Brandeis school resolutely denied it would be—technologically more progressive than the smaller units it has replaced. The political power of capital has been more satisfactorily matched by an enormous growth in labor organization. The very dissociation of ownership from control, so alarming to the Progressives, has created a class of salaried managers who have a stake in their own respectability and civic comfort that is as large as or greater than their stake in profits-at-any-cost. It is conceivable that such men may continue to show more industrial flexibility than the hard-pressed entrepreneurs of old-fashioned enterprise could afford.

None the less, subsequent generations of Americans still owe a great debt to the anti-trust inheritance they hold from the Progressive era. The rise of big business may have been inevitable, but if so it was salutary that it should have taken place in a climate of opinion that threw it intermittently on the defensive. Even Thurman Arnold, whose name is conspicuously identified with the argument that the chief effect of the anti-trust rhetoric "was to promote the growth of great industrial organizations by deflecting the attack on them into purely moral and ceremonial channels," had to concede, when he elaborated this thesis in *The Folklore of Capitalism*, that the same anti-trust rhetoric, by encouraging the notion that great corporations could be disciplined and made respectable, had something to do with the fact that they finally did become respectable; and that without the presence of hostile laws the pricing policies of big business might have been a good deal more unfavorable to the public interest. His own subsequent career as Assistant Attorney General in charge of the Antitrust Division of the Department of Justice was, in a broad historical sense, built upon intangibles of sentiment inherited from the Progressives and their anti-monopoly predecessors. For even though he and the other planners of the latter-day New Deal movement against monopoly planned no such general assault on bigness as was foreshadowed in the more exalted campaign talk of the Brandeis-Wilson school, they did rely upon political sentiments that the Progressives had nourished and strengthened. Franz Neumann, examining the conditions that led to the collapse of the Weimar Republic and the rise of the Nazis in Germany, pointed out that in Germany there had never been anything like a popular anti-monopoly movement such as the United States experienced under Theodore Roosevelt and Woodrow Wilson, that the middle classes had not been articulate against the cartels and the trusts, and that labor, looking at concentration through Marxist eyes, had consistently favored it. This, he suggests, weakened the opposition, within the business order, to authoritarian controls. This comparison suggests another respect in which the anti-trust tradition has justified itself. Paradoxically, while hostility to big business and finance has on occasion led to local authoritarianism and to unhealthy modes of rebellion, it has also been one of the resources upon which American democracy has drawn. So, after all, even the overblown rhetoric of the anti-trust movement finds its place, and even the Progressive charade of anti-monopoly takes on a function that goes beyond mere entertainment. No doubt the immediate material achievement was quite small in proportion to all the noise; but there are many episodes in history in which intense struggle has to be waged to win modest gains, and this too must be remembered before we pass too severe a judgment on the great Progressive crusade against the trusts.

REFORM agitation has most often found its eloquent exponents among members of the middle class. Populism, although agrarian in its audience, obtained its leadership largely from among the small-town middle class; Progressivism derived its leadership from the urban middle class, particularly that element whose roots were in the professions. It is not, therefore, surprising that the chief arena of their protest was the city, or that much of its most productive leadership directed its attention to urban problems. For in the close confines of the city, the dislocations and abuses that plagued life refused to be concealed from view. The gulf that separated reality from traditional morals and ethics yawned so wide there that only a man bent upon playing the ostrich could ignore the divergence.

Since urban problems rarely had a ready precedent to which reference could be made for their solution, Progressive mayors and their followers settled for the pragmatic solution. It unsettled men of the cloth when Cleveland's Tom Johnson allowed houses of prostitution to stay in business so long as their madams agreed to operate with restraint and refuse to pay graft. But as one farseeing minister noted, Johnson was "trying, not to enforce Christianity, but to make it possible." Within the teeming ghettos of the city, the immigrant inhabitants and their children, torn loose from their past loyalties, and denied access to the main stream of American life, raged against one another as they flung themselves against psychic walls without exit. Jane Addams recognized the breakdown of communications between the immigrant generations and the no less real absence of communications across the barriers into the surrounding alien native life. Within her settlement house, she worked to restore the whole man, one who could recognize in the city and its industries not imprisonment but emancipation. The machine freed man from backbreaking labor and gave him a new release to rediscover his creative energies as an artisan.

The city which in the American environment existed circumscribed by rural prejudice and suspicion required that Americans be reeducated to meet its challenge and its problems. All of history testified to the fact that civilization found its fulfillment in the city. But no less certainly, the city spawned social problems, made acute by the omnipresent isolation which condemned every man to make his way alone in what a later social critic would describe as "the lonely crowd." To combat the corrosive impact of urban isolation, the Progressive called for the creation of a sense of community which would restore the lost art of face-to-face intercourse. "No one knows," the philosopher John Dewey said, "how much of the frothy excitement of life, of mania for motion, of fretful discontent, of need for artificial stimulation, is the expression of frantic search for something to fill the void caused by the loosening of the bonds which hold persons together in immediate community of experience." Within the city a Great Society had emerged, but, as Dewey argued, what was really needed was a "Great Community," one which would restore the happy concourse of a simpler past while exploiting the promise of the city.

Harold U. Faulkner (1890-   ) achieved his greatest reputation as an economic historian. His particular forte has been the changing economic system that led to an abandonment of laisser-faire, imperfect though its application in reality was, and the emergence of large-scale enterprise regulated by government in response to the needs of society.

THE QUEST FOR SOCIAL JUSTICE, 1898-1914

by Harold Underwood Faulkner

To many thoughtful men in the opening years of the twentieth century it seemed that America in making her fortune was in peril of losing her soul. What had become of that precious concern of the Fathers, the "general welfare," when affairs of far-reaching social significance were settled outside legislative halls by contests between big business and little business, between capital and labor, between urban business interests and the embattled farmer? The infection indeed had spread to the legislatures themselves where the enactment of important laws was too often dictated by powerful lobbies which did not hesitate to employ outright corruption and bribery to accomplish their purposes. Despite the occasional victories of labor big business was in the saddle, and it was the unorganized and inarticulate public that was being whipped and spurred. The tocsin of revolt sounded in 1896 against "Wall Street" had been hushed by the bewildering new interests and the outburst of prosperity which came with the Spanish-American War. The death of Henry George in the midst of the New York mayoralty campaign of 1897 stilled the voice of the most acute critic of American economic life. Yet the fires of revolt, though burning low, were not quenched. Soon they were to blaze forth into hot and consuming flame.

Nowhere were conditions so bad as in state and municipal politics. Here the party machinery was at the beck and call of railroad and corporation interests which understood all too well the means whereby legislators were made their pliant tools. Indeed, bribery was so common in political life that Judge H. S. Priest of Missouri affirmed extenuatingly that it was, "at the most, a conventional crime," and the grand jury for one of Folk's trials declared,

> We have listened to the confessions of State senators, and were we at liberty to make known all they have told us, the recital would appall and astound the citizens of this State. . . . Our investigations have gone back for twelve years, and during that time the evidence before us shows that corruption has been the usual and accepted thing in State legislation, and that, too, without interference or hindrance.

"That bribery exists to a great extent in the elections of this state," said Governor L. F. C. Garvin of Rhode Island in a special message to the legislature in 1903, "is a matter of common knowledge." Indeed, General Charles R. Brayton, boss of the Rhode Island "system," freely admitted that he was "an attorney for certain clients and looked out for their interests in the legislature," adding that he was retained annually by the New York, New Haven and Hartford Railroad Company and by other prominent corporations doing business in the state. Such corporations as the railroad just mentioned held the legislature of not one but a half-dozen states in the hollow of their hands.

Although the people exercised the forms of democracy, wherever they possessed anything worth stealing "interests" were at work in the state legislatures to take it away. A reform wave in Ohio in 1905 helped purify the legislature of that commonwealth, but how far even this body fell short of perfection is clear from one member's description of the last day of the session.

> Enmities were forgotten and by a tacit agreement each member was permitted to call up some bill that bore his name and if it was not too controversial it was permitted to pass. Thus members had something to show their constituents. These last hours were pandemonium. Many of the law-makers were drunk. . . . Scores of bills went through by gentlemen's agreement. Nobody knew what they contained and nobody cared. . . . I came away from the legislature with scant respect for the laws of the land. I had seen how they were made. Some were frankly bought and paid for. . . . Only occasionally were bills in the public interest forced through by the pressure of public opinion, and they were so crippled with amendments that they were of little value.

How recreant to its trust a state legislature could be was dramatically illustrated in 1907 by the amazing exposure of the graft involving millions of dollars connected with the building of the new Pennsylvania state house.

With the multiplying evidences of public betrayal before their eyes the voters, jarred out of their apathy or complacency, resolved upon drastic measures to reform the law-making departments of their governments. The years from 1898 to 1914 were years of almost ceaseless constitutional tinkering, and the one constant thought in the minds of the members of the conventions was to curb the powers of the legislatures. Five states framed new organic laws, in addition to those of the new states of Oklahoma (1907), New Mexico (1912) and Arizona (1912), and the comprehensive revisions made in Ohio (1912), Vermont (1913) and other states. More than fifteen hundred amendments to state constitutions were, in fact, proposed between 1900 and 1920, of which three out of five were adopted. New York, which had accepted a new constitution in 1894, wrote a modern and scientific revision in 1915 which was voted down. Of the other states where the movement failed, an interesting example is Connecticut. Its legislature, under the control of rural delegates chosen through a "rotten-borough" system, acceded to the popular clamor for a constitutional convention, but made certain that the rural delegations would control it. The resulting constitution offered little relief from existing abuses and was voted down in 1902.

In general, these constitutional changes reveal an effort to strengthen the power of the executives, centralize administration and increase popular control over the government. So far did the tendency go that one expert queried whether it would "ultimately prove worth while to retain an expensive legislature to exercise its small residue of petty powers"; and when the movement had about run its course, another was led to assert that the "most serious impediment to a right kind of legislature and a proper kind of legislators seems to me to lie in the fact that they are individually and collectively powerless." But if the new constitutions erred in reducing too radically the functions of the legislative branch, they made long strides in the direction of greater executive efficiency and in the perfection of democratic machinery.

Of the democratic innovations the initiative, the referendum, the recall, the primary system, woman suffrage and the popular election of United States senators stand out. By means of the initiative a small percentage of the voters acquired the power of forcing upon the legislature the consideration of a measure, and by the referendum they could take it out of the hands of the legislature and compel its submission to the people. As early as 1898 South Dakota under Democratic-Populist leadership adopted an amendment providing for the initiative and referendum, and its example was followed two years later by Utah. But the widespread interest resulted when Oregon committed herself to the experiment in 1902. In the next ten years fifteen other commonwealths followed her lead with some form of state-wide initiative and referendum. Though the movement slowed up after 1912, Mississippi, North Dakota, Maryland and Massachusetts joined the procession between 1914 and 1918.

An even more radical innovation was the recall, a device for enabling dissatisfied voters to force a public official to submit himself and his policies to the test of a new election. First appearing in the Los Angeles city charter of 1903 and embodied in the Seattle charter of 1906, the recall spread most rapidly in the field of municipal government. Oregon gave it state-wide application in 1908, and ten other states followed before the close of 1914, of which all but one were west of the Mississippi. The whole question was given wide publicity in 1911 when President Taft vetoed the resolution authorizing the admission of Arizona to the Union because of a clause in the constitution permitting the recall of judges. Though Arizona was forced to withdraw the clause, she reinserted an even more drastic provision after she had been safely admitted. Roosevelt in 1912 went so far as to approve the Colorado plan for the recall of judicial decisions, a stand which did more than anything else to alienate the conservatives in the campaign of that year. The recall, as a matter of fact, has not been used with the same frequency as the initiative and referendum, the average through the country being not more than six recall elections annually in the past twenty years.

This generation was not content, however, to lock the barn door after the horse was stolen: it was determined that there should be a proper keeper of the stable. To this end it took steps to remove the choice of candidates from the machine-ridden party conventions and place it in the hands of the people. Wisconsin in 1903, under the influence of La Follette, was the first state to adopt the direct primary for all nominations and Oregon followed two years later. By 1915 the system, in some form or other, was recognized in all of the states and adopted in its state-wide form in at least two thirds. Before interest in this innovation subsided, at least twenty of the states extended their laws to include preferential presidential primaries.

Another important political change, facilitated by the primary system and further strengthening popular control of the government, was the direct choice by the people of United States senators. The Populist party had demanded it in the nineties, the Democratic party was on record for it from 1900 on, and the legislatures of more than two thirds of the states favored it before the Senate itself showed any interest. The demand was in part the result of the democratic tide sweeping the country and in part due to very definite abuses. Corruption was rife in the choice of senators by the legislatures and the feeling was strong that the Senate represented the special interests rather than the electorate. Bryce asserted in 1888 that "some, an increasing number, are senators because they are rich; a few are rich because they are senators," and there was little a decade later to revive the faith of the people in the upper house. Tired of waiting, and quite contrary to the letter and spirit of the federal Constitution, twenty-nine states by 1912 had framed a method whereby electorates might indirectly work their will. In Oregon and Nebraska, for instance, the members of each party chose senatorial nominees in the primaries and these names were then submitted to all of the voters in the general election. The candidates for the state legislature were required to indicate on the ballot whether or not they would support the popular choice. Invariably they said they would do this, with the curious result that in 1908 a Republican legislature in Oregon was committed to the election of a Democrat, George E. Chamberlain. As members selected by popular choice began to take their seats in the Senate, that august body could hold out no longer. The Seventeenth Amendment passed both houses in 1912 and on May 31, 1913, became part of the Constitution.

The political reformation we have traced and the social legislation which followed in its wake were not obtained without strenuous effort and valiant leadership. In Oregon, where so many democratic innovations were tried out that the whole movement came to be called the "Oregon system," the battle was led by William S. U'Ren, a gentle but persistent crusader. Born in Wisconsin of parents who had emigrated from Cornwall, U'Ren had spent his boyhood in his father's blacksmith shop and upon various frontier farms. After studying law in Denver he had wandered about the West in search of health and opportunity until a reading of George's *Progress and Poverty* led him to a life of political reform. U'Ren held public office only once, but as secretary of various voters' organizations he was a leading influence behind the adoption of the Australian ballot (1891), the registration law (1899), the initiative and referendum (1902), the direct-primary law (1904), the corrupt-practices act (1908) and the recall (1910). "In Oregon," asserted a contemporary observer, "the state government is divided into four departments—the executive, judicial, legislative and Mr. U'Ren—and it is still an open question who exerts the most power." Quite opposite in type from the self-effacing U'Ren was the battling politician, Robert M. La Follette, who, as part of a lifelong struggle against special privilege, won the governorship of Wisconsin in 1902, 1904 and 1906, forced a direct-primary law through the legislature, and rescued his state from railroad domination by championing a tax-equalization law and the establishment of a railroad commission.

If Oregon was the outstanding example of progressive politics on the Pacific Coast and Wisconsin in the Middle West, the boss-ridden state of New Jersey toward the end of the reform period rather unexpectedly assumed that role in the East. A reform agitation had already been started in the state Republican party by Everett Colby and George L. Record when the Democratic machine nominated Woodrow Wilson, then president of Princeton, for governor in 1910. "I earnestly commend to your careful consideration," said the newly elected governor in his inaugural address, "the laws in recent years as adopted in the State of Oregon, whose effect has been to bring government back to the people and to protect it from the control of the representatives of selfish and special interests." To the dismay of the politicians he proceeded straightway to demolish the reactionary Democratic machine in the state and took the lead in a thoroughgoing campaign for reform. His achievements embraced a strong public-utilities law, a workingmen's compensation act, a sweeping primary law including presidential preferential primaries, a corrupt-practices act governing campaign expenditures and methods and effective legislation for restraining corporate abuses. Long the refuge of trusts, New Jersey was at last brought by Wilson's efforts into line with the antitrust legislation of other progressive states.

La Follette and Wilson were but outstanding examples of the new type of political leaders who were springing up in many parts of the country. Roosevelt, elected governor of New York state upon his return from the Spanish-American War, injected a cleaner atmosphere into New York politics and secured a reenactment of the civil-service law, much labor legislation, improvement in the conservation laws and the appointment of better state officials. Charles Evans Hughes, who served two terms after defeating William Randolph Hearst for governor in 1906, gave New York state an efficient and distinctly reform administration, achieving among other things a commission to control public utilities, a law prohibiting race-track gambling and the enactment of a primary law. Even the Tammany governor, William Sulzer, made a stand for a far-reaching primary system, an action which so enraged the party bosses that they secured his impeachment and removal in 1913 on the charge of making a false statement in reference to his campaign fund. In Missouri Folk carried his fight for clean government, begun in St. Louis, to the entire state and was elected governor in 1904. Albert B. Cummins, governor of Iowa from 1902 to 1908, secured the better regulation of railroads and the direct primary, while Hiram W. Johnson, who had come to the fore as the result of his activities in prosecuting San Francisco grafters, won the Republican gubernatorial nomination in 1910 on the slogan, "The Southern Pacific Railroad must be kicked out of state politics."

It is true many of these men found their quickest road to political preferment through the adoption of new rules of the game favorable to themselves, but with political conditions as bad as they were there was little reason in most cases to doubt their sincerity. With the exception of John P. Altgeld, governor of Illinois (1893-1897), there was hardly a state executive who stood out during the nineties as the representative of a better political day; yet within a decade of Altgeld's retirement to private life amidst a storm of abuse, the people of the various states were placing in the gubernatorial chairs men whose schemes of reform were more radical than Altgeld's.

If conditions in the states cried for reform, those in the great cities were, if possible, even worse. Such centers were likely to be ruled by political machines of the lowest order, which found no type of graft too petty to exploit. In New York the widespread toils of Tammany Hall reached out in an alliance with the underworld. In Philadelphia the Republican machine, controlled by the state bosses, Matthew S. Quay and Boies Penrose, maintained power by the most scandalous election frauds and grew fat by "selling out" the people to the public-utility companies. In Pittsburgh Christopher L. Magee and William Flinn attained a finesse in robbing the city which enabled them to control it for years with an appearance of keeping within the law. In St. Louis Edward R. Butler ("Colonel Ed") acted as go-between for the franchise grabbers and the city council, supervising the distribution of graft while the councilmen turned over municipal property to private interests. Farther to the north Mayor Albert Alonzo ("Doc") Ames of Minneapolis boldly allied himself with commercialized vice, even allowing his police force to cooperate with thugs in perpetrating robbery upon the citizenry. On the Pacific Coast the labor government of Ruef and Schmitz turned the city of San Francisco over to the grafters after the fire of 1906.

It made little difference where one went, whether the older, thickly populated immigrant cities on the Eastern seaboard or the newer frontier cities of the West, the story was the same—inefficiency and corruption extending from the city through the state governments even into the national legislature, and behind the politicians to the business men and great corporations. It was customary—and convenient—to blame the evil conditions on the newly arrived immigrants, but Mrs. Older has pointed out that the San Francisco reformers received their best aid from Irish and German Americans and their greatest opposition from the descendants of New England and Southern aristocrats, while Lincoln Steffens, who studied the conditions from coast to coast, found little to choose between the hill-town Yankee of Rhode Island who regularly sold his ballot and the newly arrived immigrant who, hurried through the formalities of naturalization, was lined up at the polls to vote as ordered. One of the most corrupt and at the same time contented cities was Philadelphia, which boasted of a higher percentage of native-born Americans than any other large city, yet the graft ran all the way from the city councilor, who took fifty thousand for a vote, to the police captain who pocketed the miserable earnings of a prostitute. An idea of the extent to which graft was carried may be seen in Pittsburgh, where disorderly houses were safe from interference only when rented from a ward syndicate, furniture for them bought from the "official furniture man," beer purchased from the "official bottler," liquor from the "official liquor commissioner" and clothes from the "official wrapper maker."

The traditional leadership for broader popular rights, so long borne by the rural frontier, had begun to pass with the failure of Populism. Though it was the newer states that led in democratic legislation in the new century, Western radicalism reached out to Eastern radicalism—a radicalism emanating from the population centers. Long regarded by political philosophers as sores on the body politic, the great city now began to stand forth as "the hope of democracy." Thus at a time when municipal corruption was at its height reformers began to spring up here and there—in Toledo, Cleveland, Detroit and elsewhere—to battle for the restoration of government to the people. As in the case of state misrule, the disease bred its own antidote.

Of the new municipal leaders, one of the most picturesque and forceful was Samuel M. Jones, who in 1897 became mayor of Toledo, Ohio. Brought to America at the age of three, he had won a fortune as an oil pioneer and as manufacturer of improved apparatus for oil wells. A big sandy-complexioned Welshman with a ready smile and a rich gift of humor, Jones's one ambition in his later years was to improve the lot of mankind. His factory he conducted on the principles of the Golden Rule and as mayor he sought to carry the same ideal into municipal affairs. His philosophy was that of the Tolstoyan anarchists; his quarrel was with society which produced the evildoer, not with those who had fallen foul of the law. "I don't want to rule anybody," said Jones; "nobody has a right to rule anybody else. Each individual must rule himself." In his administration he showed his zeal for social justice by advocating the public ownership of public utilities and the abolition of the private-contract system of doing city work. He took the clubs away from the policemen, telling them that theirs was to help, not to hurt; he introduced free kindergartens into the public schools, established public playgrounds for the children, instituted free concerts in the parks and secured an eight-hour day for city employees.

His attempt to apply Christian principles to municipal politics brought about his speedy repudiation, not only by the Republican machine but also by the churches. "Every one was against him," says Howe, "except the workers and the underworld." Nevertheless "Golden-Rule" Jones was re-elected three times on an independent ticket, and the impetus which he gave to nonpartisanship in politics was salutary and lasting. When he died in office in 1904, he was succeeded the following year by his disciple and former secretary, Brand Whitlock, whose philosophy was very close to that of Jones and who carried on the administration of the city in much the same spirit. Among the many things which Whitlock accomplished during his four successive terms was the securing of a new city charter providing for the initiative, referendum, recall and direct nominations.

When in 1901 Cleveland elected Thomas Lofton Johnson for its mayor, the new democratic movement was strengthened by the accession of one of the ablest men which the period produced. In the savage economic competition of the eighties and nineties Tom Johnson, the son of an impoverished Confederate colonel, had risen to fortune as a steel manufacturer, a manipulator of street railways and the inventor of street-railway apparatus. At the height of his business career, however, he was completely captured by the economic philosophy of Henry George, and relinquished his business activities to work for the single tax and other reforms. As congressman (1891-1895) he could do little, but as mayor of Cleveland for eight years a field was provided for his remarkable talents. Johnson's energies were chiefly expended in bringing the street railways under municipal control and in reducing the fare to three cents, but his program included city planning, a reassessment of city real estate and many other reforms. He was, as Steffens expressed it, the "best mayor of the best governed city in the United States." Endowed with keen intellect and a magnetic personality, he was never more at home than in handling a hostile audience; his charm and utter sincerity won him the support of young and able lieutenants—such men as Newton D. Baker, Frederic C. Howe, Peter Witt, Fred Kohler and Harris R. Cooley. Like Jones, his opposition came from the "interests" and others in high places. Cleveland gained enormously from Johnson's administration, though his defeat in 1909 by a few hundred votes prevented a full fruition of his program. Much was saved two years later, however, when the voters returned to the Johnson ideals by electing Newton D. Baker as mayor.

Jones and Johnson were only the most famous of the prophets who were endeavoring to lead the citizens of the great American municipalities out of the wilderness of political inefficiency and corruption. Joseph W. Folk between 1900 and 1904, as district attorney and later governor, attacked municipal corruption in St. Louis. Ben Lindsey fought to shake the rule of the bosses in Denver. In Minneapolis Hovey C. Clarke, foreman of the grand jury for the summer term of 1902, almost single-handed uncovered the graft of the Ames ring, forced the district attorney to prosecute the leaders, and freed the city from their toils. In Jersey City Mark Fagan fought valiantly to free the city from railroad and public-service domination. The election of the Socialist, Emil Seidel, as mayor of Milwaukee in 1910 opened a new era for that city. Even New York in one of its periodic uprisings against Tammany elected Seth Low mayor in 1901.

Of the efforts to reform municipal conditions perhaps the story of San Francisco is the most astonishing, although there was little that was unusual in the graft disclosed there. In 1901 Eugene E. Schmitz, a member of the Musicians' Union and candidate of the Union-Labor party, was elected mayor. The real head of the city government, however, was an unprincipled lawyer, Abram Ruef, who dominated the mayor and dictated policies to the board of supervisors, the legislative branch of the government. Unfortunately for the Ruef-Schmitz machine, an honest man, William H. Langdon, had been elected district attorney; and Langdon with the backing of Fremont Older, editor of the *Bulletin*, Rudolph Spreckels, who guaranteed the expenses, James D. Phelan, later United States senator, and other public-spirited citizens began investigations. For this purpose Francis J. Heney, prosecutor in the Oregon land-fraud cases, was made assistant district attorney and William J. Burns was hired to do the detective work. Thrown into a panic, the machine hastily secured the suspension of the district attorney, but Langdon ignored the action and continued his work. Indictments were eventually obtained against Ruef and Schmitz for taking money from "French restaurants," or assignation houses, since the more serious charge, that of distributing the slush funds of the great public-utility concerns, though generally known, could not be proved. In spite of powerful backing and an array of high-paid legal talent Schmitz and Ruef were convicted of extortion and sentenced to jail.

The real fight, however, had just begun, for as soon as the prosecutors began to attack the bribe-givers as well as the bribe-takers the massed influence of California wealth and power was thrown against them. The higher courts freed Ruef and Schmitz, and only after a long legal battle was Ruef sent back to jail; at least one jury was tampered with. Fremont Older was kidnaped and barely escaped with his life, while an attempt was made on Heney's life during a recess in one of the trials. Newspapers were subsidized to fight the prosecution; even Hearst's *Examiner*, which posed as the enemy of corruption, threw its powerful influence against the prosecution and allowed the cartoonist, "Bud" Fisher, to poke daily fun at it in his series of "Mutt and Jeff" comic strips. The prosecution, forced to enter politics in self-defense, carried the 1907 election, but was unable to do much against the corporation bribe-givers. Though Louis Glass, manager of the Pacific States Telephone and Telegraph Company, was found guilty of bribery, efforts to convict General Tirey L. Ford and Patrick Calhoun of the United Railroads failed, and when the reformers lost the campaign of 1909 the graft cases were speedily dismissed. Even Ruef would probably have escaped further confinement if the election of Heney's assistant, Hiram W. Johnson, as governor in 1910 had not precluded the possibility of a pardon. The old regime returned in San Francisco, as it usually did elsewhere, but the three-year battle against intrenched corruption had stirred the people sufficiently to bring a state-wide victory for the progressive forces in 1910.

The leaders for municipal improvement in most cases were partial to some particular reform. Thus, Jones and Johnson were firm believers in the municipal ownership of public utilities. All the reformers, however, were one in their belief that what was needed first of all was the elimination of corruption, a return of power to the people and the development of efficiency in municipal administration. In this they were assisted by various nonpartisan organizations composed of men interested in better government. The National Municipal League, formed in 1894, offered in 1900 a general program which included city home rule, government by experts, the establishment of official responsibility through the simplification of governmental machinery and full publicity of accounts, and the protection of the city's property from the raids of franchise grabbers. It also proposed specific constitutional amendments and drew up a model municipal-corporations act. In carrying out this program the League's exertions were soon augmented by nonpartisan associations of voters and "city clubs," which sprang up in many large centers to study municipal problems and assist the cause.

To put these efforts on a more scientific basis, bureaus of municipal research were established in many of the leading cities, including New York, Philadelphia, Chicago, Rochester, Detroit, Cincinnati, Minneapolis, and temporarily in other places. The prototype of these organizations was the New York Bureau of Municipal Research established in 1906 through the enthusiasm of R. Fulton Cutting and maintained during the first six years by private contributions aggregating upwards of five hundred thousand dollars. Under the direction of Henry Bruere, Charles A. Beard and Frederick A. Cleveland the New York bureau not only maintained a staff of experts to advance efficient government and promote scientific methods of administration, but established in 1911 a school, likewise supported in its early years by private subscription, for the training of experts in municipal government. Soon the College of the City of New York and the University of Cincinnati began to offer practical courses in municipal administration, research agencies were established in various universities, and the whole subject of municipal government was taken up with greater seriousness in the colleges and graduate schools. For the first time in American history trained intelligence was being brought to bear upon the complex problems of the city. It was high time, for under the new conditions of American life successful government of the cities was essential to national welfare.

The demand for more efficient municipal government received unexpected impetus from a catastrophe in the South. More than once in history has an event tragic and disastrous at the time worked in the end to further social progress. Confronted with the necessity for instant and efficient action, the community sloughs off its outworn precedents and customs and rises to new heights of cooperative activity. In 1900 Galveston was visited by a great tidal wave and storm which in a single night drowned one sixth of the population and destroyed one third of the property. In desperation the citizens threw aside their unwieldy government and put the task of rehabilitation in the hands of a commission of five. The commission form of government thus improvised was made permanent in the new charter of

1901. As amended in 1903, it placed the government in the hands of five elected commissioners who, at open meetings and by a majority vote, should enact municipal ordinances, make appropriations, determine all appointments and award contracts. The four main city departments were to be each under the direction of one of the commissioners, while the fifth, who was to be the mayor-president, was to exert a coordinating influence on all of them. The new plan was so successful that the near-by city of Houston adopted one somewhat similar in 1905.

Soon these experiments began to attract attention in other parts of the country. James G. Berryhill told his fellow citizens in Des Moines of the improved conditions in Galveston; a committee of Kansas citizens visited Texas to study the results; and in October, 1906, George Kibbe Turner published a magazine article on the subject which provoked widespread discussion. In 1907 the growing interest began to produce results. Iowa passed a general act authorizing the adoption of the commission form by cities of over twenty-five thousand, and Des Moines immediately inaugurated the system, adding new features in the form of popular checks on the activities of the commission. The commission form had been attacked as autocratic, but the Des Moines plan proved that efficiency and democracy might be skillfully blended.

Hoping to approximate even more closely the efficiency of big business, certain variations of the commission form, known as the city-manager or commission-manager, were evolved, the essential feature being the employment of a manager to run the government, while the people's representatives or commissioners merely supervised in much the same manner that a board of directors supervises the president of a corporation. Although this method was authorized by the New Mexico legislature in 1909 and inaugurated in Staunton, Virginia (1908), Sumter, South Carolina (1912), and other places, its most notable experiment was at Dayton, Ohio. Under the privilege granted by the home-rule amendment made to the Ohio constitution in 1912, Dayton was already evolving such a scheme when the severe flood of March, 1913, inundated the city. As at Galveston some years earlier, the exigencies of the situation speeded the adoption of the new plan, which demonstrated an efficiency in the work of rehabilitation that continued in the normal years to follow. By 1912 commission government in some form had been adopted by two hundred and ten communities, and it was still growing in favor. It was especially popular in Texas and in sections of the Middle and Far West, but examples were also to be found in New England.

One excellent result of the movement was the impulse given to the demand for municipal home rule—the right of cities to frame their own charters. The power which the state legislature had assumed over cities in days when American civilization was primarily agricultural and rural had outlasted its usefulness. On the one hand, the state legislatures needed to be freed from handling the details of many purely local problems and, on the other, the cities needed greater autonomy for looking after their own special concerns. "Whenever we try to do anything," complained George R. Lunn, the Socialist mayor of Schenectady in 1913, "we run up against the charter.

It is an oak charter, fixed and immovable." Furthermore, reformers often found themselves powerless as long as the system they fought extended into the state legislatures and grafting politicians sought aid and protection there. Tom Johnson, for example, finding his efforts to remake Cleveland continually balked by the invisible government in the state legislature, made a state-wide campaign for the principle of home rule; the defeat of his candidacy for governor in 1903 delayed, but did not permanently prevent, its achievement. Only four states had home-rule provisions in their constitutions before 1898, but by 1915 they were joined by Colorado, Oregon, Oklahoma, Michigan, Arizona, Ohio, Nebraska, Texas and Maryland. As this enumeration shows, the movement was limited almost entirely to the Middle and Far West. As a step in the same direction, however, other states passed general acts giving cities the option of forming commission governments according to a standard pattern.

While the improvement in municipal government was notable, it was not universal nor was it continuous. Reform efforts were likely to be spasmodic; even in a reform age it was not easy to keep the electorate ceaselessly vigilant. Thus New York, after electing Seth Low mayor in 1901 and enjoying a brief respite of honest government, turned back to Tammany in 1903 with the election of George B. McClellan, and in the following years was in frequent turmoil over police-graft scandals and the attempts of Tammany to rewrite the city charter. In some cities, as Philadelphia and Pittsburgh, little effort was made to oust the corrupt rings. Even in the "reform cities" the old interests, hungry for power and ever watchful for opportunities, managed to creep back. Nevertheless some of the gains were too great to be lost, a new sense of civic responsibility was awakened in the urban populations, and an impetus to good government was given from which the next generation was richly to benefit.

Though the movement for political reform was in general from the bottom up, the national parties also made their contributions. Indeed, it might be said that in the nineties the discredited Populists had anticipated most of the demands which were carried to victory and popular acclaim by the anointed leaders of the early years of the new century. Roosevelt, to mention no lesser person, was the direct heir and beneficiary of the Populism he had once so bitterly assailed. Suddenly finding himself the leader of a party which had completely succumbed to special privilege during the leadership of Hanna and McKinley, he strove mightily to give it a distinct progressive tone. In this his personal inclinations fitted nicely with political expediency. The nation was ready for a swing to the left, and Roosevelt gave voice to the unspoken aspirations of the common man with an accuracy achieved by few politicians. Instinctively he responded to the widespread desire for a better civilization and, rushing to the head of the movement, he rose to unprecedented heights of popularity as the reform wave surged onward. Assemblyman, police commissioner, civil-service reformer, historian, assistant secretary of the navy, roughrider, governor, vice-president—the exemplar of the strenuous life with a long career of public service behind him—Roosevelt typified as have few others the ideal of his generation. What the many would like to be, he was, and his unerring journalistic sense enabled him to dramatize his actions and discomfit his enemies. Children in the nursery played with Teddy Bears, and leading intellectuals considered him one of the greatest men of his day. The very initials T. R. came to have an almost magic symbolism.

From the point of view of uncompromising progressives, like La Follette, his devotion to the progressive cause had in it an element of charlatanry, while many of his political associates accused him of ingratitude, insincerity and personal ambition. To his friends, however, his railroad legislation, his prosecutions of the trusts, his efforts in behalf of pure-food laws and conservation, placed him in the forefront of the newer statesmen. Whatever may be the final opinion as to Roosevelt's contribution to the newer America, his domestic policies while president were aggressive and forward looking. Not only was he personally influential in the enactment of progressive legislation, but he helped give momentum to forces in our national political life which his more conservative successor in the White House could not stop.

With the great mass of voters the Rooseveltian policies were undeniably popular, representing as they did the hopes of a new political and social era, and the voters had no hesitancy in supporting William Howard Taft, whom Roosevelt had handpicked as his successor in 1908. Although the Taft administration saw the fruition of much advanced legislation and the president himself was far from the whole-souled reactionary which his political enemies pictured him, it was not long before Taft found himself out of touch with the more progressive of the Roosevelt followers. The tariff issue, which his predecessor had so skillfully and persistently avoided, proved, in particular, to be his undoing, and the Democratic success in the 1910 elections was a strong indication of the growing unpopularity of his regime.

As the Taft administration drew stormily to a close, the progressive movement, which had been steadily growing in strength, reached its climax. Roosevelt, returning from a hunting trip in Africa, threw in his lot with the insurgent Republicans and, in a famous speech on "The New Nationalism" delivered at Osawatomie, Kansas, assumed an advanced progressive position. The insurgents, planning to contest the renomination of President Taft, first rallied around La Follette, and then, scenting victory in the air, they stampeded to their old idol, Roosevelt. Though Roosevelt had asserted he would not run again, he yielded to the importunities of his friends and the promptings of his own ardent nature, and on February 26, 1912, announced that he would accept the nomination if it were offered to him by the Republican national convention. To many the future of political and social reform seemed to rest on the outcome of the ensuing campaign. Charging from state to state in his whirlwind campaign, Roosevelt undoubtedly won the indorsement of the rank and file of the Republican voters, but in the nominating convention he was flattened by the same "steam-roller" which but four years before had so efficiently cleared the way for Taft. Hot with wrath and loud in their cries of fraud, the Roosevelt delegates launched the Progressive party, nominated their chief for president and wrote a platform which epitomized the hopes of reformers. "We stand at Armageddon, and we battle for the Lord," shouted Roosevelt in concluding his keynote speech to a convention which in its fervor resembled an old-time religious revival.

Flushed with the hope that the Republican schism might open the way for victory the Democratic party met to choose their candidate. The political bosses in the convention labored under no illusion that they were battling for the Lord, but the more liberal element under the leadership of Bryan succeeded in mastering the situation and in nominating Woodrow Wilson on a liberal platform. The Socialist party which had grown steadily in power during the previous decade again nominated its hero, Eugene V. Debs, on a platform more radical than that of the Progressives. Even the Republicans were forced to promise reforms which in an ordinary campaign might have given their platform a complexion of liberalism.

For the progressive voter the millennium in national politics seemed to have been reached. Each of the platforms was progressive and three out of the four candidates were reformers—even crusaders. However the election turned out, it appeared, for once, that the cause of reform would win. Reckoned by the popular vote Wilson was elected as a minority president, but gauged by public sentiment as well as by the decision of the electoral college he represented a majority. For the only time perhaps in its history the nation contained a progressive majority and the new chief executive stood for that group.

The Underwood tariff with its income tax, the Clayton antitrust act, the federal-reserve act and other important legislation which marked the early years of Wilson's presidency may have stopped short of the full progressive program, but they represented an extraordinary advance. The nation had made vast strides since the complacent plutocracy of the McKinley era and since the days when the Populists had been repudiated as dangerous radicals. A "social consciousness" had developed which demanded not only clean politics but a better world in which to live. If the battle waged across a long front can be epitomized in the lives of a few men such as Tom Johnson, Robert La Follette or Theodore Roosevelt, the fact remains that their efforts would have been largely futile had they not represented the aspirations of the common man.

⤙ ⤚

THE *election of Woodrow Wilson in 1912 was determined less by the appeal of the Democratic party to the nation and more by the split of the Republican party. Theodore Roosevelt had handpicked his successor Taft in 1908, had him elected, and then went off on a safari. When he returned in 1910, he soon expressed first private and then public dismay at Taft's literal implementation of trust-busting and his less than enthusiasm for con-servation. The more radical elements of the Republican party were disen-chanted with Taft's catering to the conservative party leadership. The rift widened until in the late winter of 1912 Roosevelt announced his intention to wrest the Republican nomination from the incumbent. With lashing invective, Teddy denounced Taft as "disloyal to our past friendship, disloyal to every canon of ordinary decency," and guilty of "the grossest and most astounding hypocrisy." When Taft men rammed through the renomination of their man at the Republican convention, Roosevelt led his followers into a new Progressive party. It is hardly surprising to read that Woodrow Wilson, then Governor of New Jersey, wrote: "Nothing new is happening in politics, except Mr. Roosevelt, who is always new, being bound by nothing in the heavens above or in the earth below. He is now rampant and very diligently employed in splitting the [Republican] party wide open—so that we may get in!"*

It was a prophetic statement. Not only did Wilson get in, but the Demo-cratic party gained a solid legislative majority. With it Wilson set to work to implement a program designated as a New Freedom. Its objective was to preserve traditional American economic practices by restoring through gov-ernment regulation "competition." He spoke for the small entrepreneur against the confining limitations of the giant aggregates of industry and finance. He did not mean to destroy the existing giants, he meant merely to establish a better balance between the great and the small. As he explained it, "By setting the little men of America free, you are not damaging the giants."

What followed was a veritable flood of legislation. The Federal Reserve Act created a more flexible currency and strengthened the banking system. The Underwood Tariff overhauled the prohibitively high tariff rates. The Clayton Anti-Trust Act buttressed already existing trust regulating legisla-tion and gave minimal support to labor organizations. And finally the Fed-eral Trade Commission Act was created to more effectively regulate corpo-rate practices. All in all, it was an impressive performance. Although sub-sequent reform legislation was passed, an external event intruded to disrupt the even flow of American life. In a distant place called Sarajevo, a husband and wife were murdered. The date was June 28, 1914. In the month that followed, the long European peace ended and World War I began. Four years of savage bloodletting followed. Both President and nation struggled "to avoid the sort of numbness that comes from deep apprehension and dwelling upon elements too vast to be yet comprehended or in any way controlled by counsel." They sought also to keep their neutrality, but failed.

William E. Leuchtenburg (1922-   ), a brilliant narrative historian at Columbia University, has made his specialty twentieth-century America. His Franklin D. Roosevelt and the New Deal (1963) is the best single-volume account of that tumultuous experience. In the piece that follows he defines the dilemma that faced Wilson as the European war expanded to en-velop America.

THE PERILS OF PROSPERITY 1914-32

by William E. Leuchtenburg

In the autumn of 1815 the *Northumberland*, bearing the captive emperor Napoleon Bonaparte, dropped anchor before Saint Helena Island and opened a century of peace in western Europe. During that century, democracy and the rights of man won their greatest triumphs. Universal suffrage and public education, scientific marvels and social reforms, manifested a belief in the perfectibility of mankind. Localized wars there were—bloody enough in the case of the American Civil War and the Franco-Prussian struggle—yet war itself appeared more and more to be an anachronism, a dying institution. "It looks as though this were going to be the age of treaties rather than the age of wars," declared a leader of American peace forces in 1912, "the century of reason rather than the century of force."

In the early years of the twentieth century the menace of war grew—"incidents" in Africa, fighting in the Balkans—but not the general war that men had come to fear; and because it did not come, it lost its power to frighten. In 1913 Dr. David Starr Jordan, director of the World Peace Foundation, observed: "What shall we say of the Great War of Europe, ever threatening, ever impending, and which never comes? We shall say that it will never come. Humanly speaking, it is impossible." Even the assassination of Archduke Franz Ferdinad, heir to the Austro-Hungarian throne, by a young Bosnian terrorist in June, 1914, did not seem to mean war. "Never since Christ was born in the Manger," wrote a Maine newspaperman as late as July 30, "was the outlook for the universal brotherhood of man brighter than it is today."

Through the summer of 1914, Americans watched the growing war crisis almost with indifference. When, after weeks of gestures and countergestures, Britain sent her ultimatum to Germany, Secretary of Agriculture Houston recorded, "I had a feeling that the end of things had come. . . . I stopped in my tracks, dazed and horror-stricken." To the very last hour, war seemed unbelievable; when it came, it struck with a stunning sense of finality.

The only reasonable explanation was that Europe had gone berserk. The European powers, declared the *New York Times*, "have reverted to the condition of savage tribes roaming the forests and falling upon each other in a fury of blood and carnage to achieve the ambitious designs of chieftains clad in skins and drunk with mead." If the war had any rational cause at all, Americans thought, it could be found in the imperialist lust for markets. "Do you want to know the cause of the war?" asked Henry Ford. "It is capitalism, greed, the dirty hunger for dollars. . . . Take away the capitalist," Ford asserted, "and you will sweep war from the earth." Americans rejoiced in their isolation from Old World lunacy; and, after the initial sense of horror, their chief feeling was one of gratitude that they were not involved. "We never appreciated so keenly as now," wrote an Indiana editor, "the foresight exercised by our forefathers in emigrating from Europe."

President Woodrow Wilson urged a course of complete neutrality: he even asked movie audiences not to cheer or to hiss either side. The war, he said, was one "with which we have nothing to do, whose causes cannot touch us." Wilson cautioned the American people to be "impartial in thought as well as in action," but the impossibility of this soon became obvious. German-Americans and Irish-American Anglophobes cheered on the German cause. To many of the progressives, Britain suggested monarchy, privileged classes, and their ancient enemy Lombard Street (seat of international financiers). Germany (the Wisconsin reformers' model for a generation) suggested social insurance, the university scientist, and municipal reform. But sympathy for the Central Powers was on the whole a minority feeling. Overwhelmingly, American sentiments went out to the Allies.

Men who as schoolboys had read Gray and Tennyson, who knew Wordsworth's lake country as though they had tramped it themselves, who had been stirred by stories of Sir Francis Drake and Lord Nelson, could not be indifferent to the English cause. Nor did any nation evoke a greater sentimental attachment than France, the country of Lafayette, the land which had come to the aid of the Colonists in their struggle for independence.

At the same time, Americans had nervously eyed German militarism ever since the accession of Kaiser Wilhelm II in 1888. When Germany invaded Belgium in the early days of the war, Americans were outraged not only by the invasion of a neutral nation but by Chancellor Bethmann-Hollweg's tactless remark that the treaty with Belgium was "just a scrap of paper." The Machiavellianism, the glorification of brute force by the Germans, seemed amply proven by events like the sack of Louvain and, although in later years their influence was greatly exaggerated, by atrocity tales like those of the crucified Canadian and the Belgian babies with their hands severed. The execution of Nurse Edith Cavell, the destruction of the Cathedral of Rheims, and the mass deportation of French and Belgian civilians to forced labor completed the picture of a Prussian militarism which in its deliberate *schrecklichkeit* menaced Western civilization. Nevertheless, despite the indignation over Belgium, the United States had no thought of intervening. Even the bellicose Theodore Roosevelt, who would soon be the leader of the war hawks in America, wrote: "Of course it would be folly to jump into the gulf ourselves to no good purpose; and very probably nothing that we could have done would have helped Belgium."

As the struggle in Europe settled down to a war of attrition between great land armies, it quickly became clear that victory would go to the nation which could maintain control of the seas. Britain, the great naval power of the world, lost no time in taking advantage of its strategic position. In November, 1914, England mined the North Sea, seized American vessels carrying noncontraband goods to neutral nations, and forced all merchant ships to thread a narrow channel under British control. The Allies attempted nothing less than a gigantic blockade of the Central Powers; if they could prevent neutral merchantmen, in particular American ships, from carrying vital materials to Germany, they could force the Central Powers to sue for peace.

The United States could have taken a strong line with Britain, for Britain did not dare provoke a serious quarrel with her chief source of supply while she was involved in a desperate war. President Wilson, however, was unwilling, at a time when the Germans had overrun Belgium, to deprive Britain of her naval superiority. With England under such pressure, he felt a strong stand by the United States against Britain would be an unneutral act. Moreover, Wilson could not help but be influenced in his definition of "neutrality" by his own sympathies for the British cause, however much he tried to control them. Wilson had modeled his career on the example of English statesmen, he was an extravagant admirer of British government, and he actually courted his second wife by reading passages from Bagehot and Burke.

Wilson's closest advisers were firmly committed to the Allies. Robert Lansing, first Counselor and then Secretary of State, deliberately delayed the resolution of disputes in order to avoid a showdown with Britain. By May, 1915, Lansing was convinced that American democracy could not survive in a world dominated by German power. Wilson's alter ego, Colonel Edward House, was scarcely less pro-Ally, while, whenever notes of protest were sent to London, the strongly pro-British ambassador Walter Hines Page watered them down. On one occasion, Page took an American protest to Sir Edward Grey and said: "I have now read the dispatch, but I do not agree with it; let us consider how it should be answered!" The result was the same as if the United States itself had embargoed all trade with Germany. Commerce with Germany and Austria fell from $169 million in 1914 to $1 million in 1916.

The outbreak of war in Europe at first produced a serious economic recession in this country, but by the spring of 1915 Allied war orders were stoking American industry and opening up new markets for farm products. Boom times came to the United States as trade with the Allies jumped from $825 million in 1914 to $3,214 million in 1916. Before the war was many months old, the Allied cause and American prosperity became inextricably intertwined. When Allied funds quickly became exhausted, the United States confronted the alternatives of permitting the Allies to borrow funds from American bankers or of allowing purchases to fall off sharply, with the probable consequence of a serious depression. At the outset of the war, Secretary of State William Jennings Bryan had warned that money was "the worst of all contrabands because it commands everything else," and Wilson, anxious about the country's gold reserve, had banned American loans and let it appear that he shared Bryan's concern. In March, 1915, however, Wilson and even Bryan relented and permitted the House of

Morgan to extend a large credit to France. By the time the United States entered the war, the Allies had borrowed over $2 billion.

In February, 1915, Germany struck back at the Allied blockade by declaring a war zone around the British Isles and announcing that German submarines would destroy all enemy vessels in the area. Neutral ships in the war zone would be in danger, the Germans warned, since the British often flew neutral flags. Wilson responded to the German declaration in the strongest terms through a State Department dictum to Berlin that the Kaiser's government would be held strictly accountable for loss of American life or damage to American vessels. Under this pressure, the Germans were eventually forced to back down from their veiled threat to sink American ships. Not until 1917 would German-American relations be troubled by a menace to American lives and property on *American* ships. Instead, diplomats were faced with a new problem: the right of Americans to sail on the ships of belligerent nations.

The Germans did not yet have enough submarines to do serious damage to British commerce; yet even a few submarines could strike terror by attacking passenger ships. In March, a German U-boat ambushed a British liner and caused the death of one American aboard. Americans, however, continued to travel on British liners, which carried munitions into the war zone, and Wilson brushed off attempts to ban such travel. On May 7, 1915, came the inevitable tragedy. The queen of the Cunard fleet, the *Lusitania*, unarmed but carrying a small amount of munitions, was torpedoed off the Irish coast; eighteen minutes later it sank with a loss of 1,198 lives, 128 of them American.

The United States was horrified by the sinking. Yet few Americans wanted war, and, with the country divided, Wilson was determined to avoid a rupture with Germany. "There is such a thing as a man being too proud to fight," the President said, to the disgust of Theodore Roosevelt and the bellicose nationalists. "There is such a thing as a nation being so right that it does not need to convince others by force that it is right." Nonetheless, Wilson sent three vigorous notes to Germany. In June, Germany, fearing war with the United States, ordered submarine commanders to spare all large passenger liners, including those of the enemy, but in August a German U-boat commander violated orders and sank a British White Star Liner, the *Arabic*, with the loss of two American lives. When Wilson sent another strong protest, Germany replied with assurances that the *Arabic* incident would not be repeated, that no unresisting passenger ship would be sunk without warning or without care for the safety of passengers and crew.

The submarine wrought havoc with Wilson's neutrality policy and ultimately brought the United States into the war. It was an accepted principle of international law that no naval vessel would destroy an enemy merchantman without first giving warning and providing for the safety of passenger and crew. This was reasonable enough when merchant vessels were defenseless, but in the late summer of 1915 the British started arming merchantmen and ordering them to attack; a single shot could destroy a fragile submarine. A U-boat commander could not distinguish an armed from an unarmed vessel, and Britain and Italy were arming even their passenger liners. Wilson himself recognized the difficulty for a time. "It is hardly fair," he wrote Colonel House in October, 1915, "to ask submarine commanders to give warning by summons if, when they approach as near as they must for that purpose, they are to be fired upon."

On February 10, 1916, the Germans, not unreasonably, announced they would sink all armed merchantmen. Once the issue was forced, Wilson took a stern line. When Democratic congressional leaders called on him at the White House to protest going to war for the right of Americans to travel on armed ships, Wilson declared that Germany would be held strictly accountable. When another group of House Democratic leaders asked him what would happen if the Germans sank an armed vessel on which Americans were traveling, Wilson told them he would break relations with Germany and that this might well mean war.

In adopting this course with regard to armed merchantmen, Wilson was taking an inconsistent, an unrealistic, and, in view of his acquiescence in Allied transgressions, an unneutral line. Yet the Allied and the German maritime policies were not strictly comparable. Although the legality of the British system was uncertain, the British were able, because of their almost absolute control of the seas, to exercise controls in an orderly manner. If Britain seized American ships, the United States always had recourse to law and could obtain an indemnity; nothing would restore the loss of life from the ships Germany sank. Wilson felt justified in protesting mildly against seizure but issuing ultimatums about sinkings. Moreover, granting that passenger liners sometimes carried munitions and that they were after a time armed, the German policy of sinking passenger ships was intolerable. The U-boat that deliberately fired on the *Lusitania* did not fear attack, for the *Lusitania* was unarmed; it was not concerned with the cargo, for the amount of ammunition aboard was insignificant. The Germans were using terror as a weapon. They ruthlessly took the lives of noncombatants and they exulted over their acts. Decades later, one has a sense of horror at the fate of the passengers. At the time, in a world not yet hardened to Lidice and Belsen, the German campaign of terror seemed unbelievably barbaric.

After Wilson's second *Lusitania* note, Secretary of State Bryan, fearing it might provoke war, resigned and was succeeded by the strongly pro-Allied Robert Lansing. Out of office, Bryan took the leadership of the peace forces in America. Convinced that Wilson was risking war for the right of a few Americans to travel on belligerent vessels in a war area, Bryan headed a movement to prohibit Americans from sailing on such ships. "Germany has a right to prevent contraband going to the Allies," Bryan had written Wilson, "and a ship carrying contraband should not rely upon passengers to protect her from attack—it would be like putting women and children in front of any army." When Germany announced it would sink all armed merchantmen, strong support developed in Congress behind resolutions introduced by Senator Gore of Oklahoma and Representative

McLemore of Texas, supported by Bryan, to warn Americans not to travel on belligerent ships destined for war zones. In the House, the sentiment was 2-1 in back of the resolutions, but President Wilson brought such enormous pressure to bear against them that they were sidetracked in March. "Once accept a single abatement of right," wrote Wilson sternly, "and many other humiliations would certainly follow."

In that same month, March, 1916, a U-boat torpedoed an unarmed French channel steamer, the *Sussex*, with heavy loss of life; no Americans were killed, but several were seriously wounded. This clear violation of the German promises made after the *Arabic* incident created a diplomatic crisis. Wilson appeared before Congress on April 19 to read an ultimatum to Germany that unless it abandoned unrestricted submarine warfare against all vessels, even armed belligerents, the United States would sever diplomatic relations. The Kaiser, convinced he did not yet have enough submarines to risk war, decided to appease Wilson. Germany replied on May 4, 1916, that her submarines would no longer sink merchantmen without warning and without humanitarian precautions, so long as they did not resist. But, the Germans added, this so-called "Sussex pledge" was conditioned on the United States persuading the Allies to give up their blockade of Germany. If the United States did not, Germany would retain freedom of action.

Wilson chose to ignore the German conditions and to accept the pledge. He thereby achieved a great (however temporary) diplomatic triumph. The main threat of war—the German submarine—was removed. At the same time, Wilson had adopted such a strong line that if Germany resumed submarine warfare, which, given the continuation of the British blockade, she was likely to do, the United States would almost certainly be plunged into war. The decision for peace or war was taken out of the hands of the United States and given to Germany.

For nine months after the "Sussex pledge" not only did relations with Germany greatly improve but American diplomats were mainly troubled by the British. American public opinion, incensed by the ruthless suppression of the Irish rebellion of April 24, 1916, particularly at the execution of Sir Roger Casement, was angered still further by British intensification of economic warfare. The British opened American mail, dealt cavalierly with American diplomatic protests, and blacklisted American firms suspected of trading with Germany. By July, 1916, President Wilson was confiding to Colonel House: "I am, I must admit, about at the end of my patience with Great Britain and the Allies." By the autumn of 1916 it appeared that the United States might be drifting toward an open break wih Great Britain.

As the 1916 Presidential election approached, Wilson's Republican critics made a strong bid to defeat him by arguing that in his attempt to preserve peace he had sacrificed national honor. In their effort to dislodge Wilson, the Republicans had the support of the head of the Progressive party, Theodore Roosevelt, who viewed Wilson as a "demagogue, adroit, tricky, false, without one spark of loftiness in him, without a touch of the heroic in his cold, selfish and timid soul." When the Republicans nominated Charles Evans Hughes for the presidency (Hughes had distinguished himself first as governor of New York and then as Supreme Court Justice), Roosevelt secured the Progressive nomination for him as well.

One of the ironies of the 1916 campaign is that the Republicans attacked the President for a lack of concern with preparedness and Americanism at the very time when Wilson was under fire from radicals and reformers precisely because they thought he had become so chauvinistic. When Martin Glynn, former governor of New York, prepared his keynote address for the Democratic convention in June, Wilson instructed him to emphasize Americanism and the flag, and Glynn dutifully did so. The delegates, however, sat unresponsively as he went through his spread-eagle remarks. Glynn also felt called on to give some defense for Wilson's series of diplomatic notes, which the Republicans had scored as un-American timidity, and he cited a number of historical precedents for Wilson's actions. Fearing he would tire his audience with further examples, Glynn started to pass on to another subject, but delegates rose from their seats and shouted, "No! No! Go on!" An old campaign war horse, Glynn rose to the occasion. Each time he cited an example from the past when, provoked to the point of war, a President sent a diplomatic note instead, the crowd would shout, "What did we do? What did we do?" And Glynn would shout back, "We didn't go to war! We didn't go to war!"

The developments at the Democratic convention caught Wilson by surprise. On the very day of Glynn's speech, Wilson had led a preparedness parade in Washington with a flag draped over his shoulder. He felt exceedingly uneasy about the new Democratic slogan. ("I can't keep the country out of war," Wilson protested to Secretary of the Navy Daniels. "They talk of me as though I were a god. Any little German lieutenant can put us into the war at any time by some calculated outrage.") Despite his doubts, Wilson made good use of the peace appeal by charging Republicans with being a war party and by implying that, if he were elected, he would keep the country out of war. On the combined appeals of peace, prosperity, and progressivism, Wilson eked out a victory. The passion for peace proved so strong that Hughes was frequently forced to soft-pedal his attacks on Wilson's foreign policy, while Roosevelt's belligerent nationalism was a handicap rather than an asset. The Republicans, noted the *Saturday Evening Post* after the election, "woefully misread the public mind. They thought it was truculently heroic, and writhing under a sense of national disgrace, when, in fact, it was merely sensible. . . ."

Wilson's victory in 1916 was almost universally interpreted as a mandate for peace. As peace sentiment in America reached an astonishingly high pitch, Wilson made a bold attempt to bring the war to an end. All through the war, Colonel House had crisscrossed Europe in search of a formula for peace. Early in 1916, House and Sir Edward Grey, the British Foreign Secretary, drafted a memorandum providing that Wilson, on hearing from the Allies when the time was opportune, would call a peace conference. If the Germans refused to attend such a parley or if they would not agree to reasonable terms, the United States would "probably" enter the war on the side of the Allies. Wilson's adamant stand against Germany in regard to armed merchantmen early in 1916 stemmed mainly from a desire to maintain his usefulness as a mediator by not antagonizing the Allies. In May, 1916, all the President's careful plans were blown sky high when the Allies decided not to pursue further the program outlined in the House-Grey agreement. Wilson's ultimatum of April, 1916, had given Britain and France reason to believe that a break between Germany and the United States was imminent; once America intervened, they had high hopes of winning a total victory over Germany. Moreover, the Allies were unwilling to risk a peace conference at a time when Germany held Belgium, northern France, and much of eastern Europe, without a firm pledge from the United States to fight unless Germany evacuated these areas.

Wilson, irked by the Allied rebuff, now decided on independent mediation without prior consultation with the Allies. To make clear his independence from the chancelleries of London and Paris, Wilson adopted a severe line with the Allies. He won legislation from Congress in September, 1916, to permit him to deny clearance and harbor facilities to nations that discriminated against American commerce and to use force to carry out these powers. He got the Federal Reserve Board to caution American bankers to use care in financing the Allied war trade. When Germany was derelict in upholding the "Sussex pledge"—in two cases, which Berlin held were "mistakes," American lives were lost—the President disregarded the provocations.

Wilson had decided on a bold change of policy to free himself from the tangle of maritime rights. He wanted greater maneuverability than a foreign policy geared to German submarine attacks offered. In the last eight months of 1916, Wilson said almost nothing about freedom of the seas, his chief concern since 1914, and stressed instead the impact of the war on democratic ideals and the future of Western civilization. The only way to avoid American involvement in the war, the President concluded, was direct American mediation, even at the cost of surrendering the tradition of American isolation from Europe's quarrels. In a speech in Omaha in October, 1916, Wilson counseled: "When you are asked, 'Aren't you willing to fight?' reply, yes, you are waiting for something worth fighting for; you are not looking around for petty quarrels, but you are looking about for that sort of quarrel within whose intricacies are written all the texts of the rights of man; you are looking for some cause . . . in which it seems a glory to shed human blood, if it be necessary, so that all the common compacts of liberty may be sealed with the blood of free men."

On December 18, 1916, Wilson sent identical diplomatic notes to the belligerent capitals asking them to state their war aims and to indicate upon what terms they would be willing to end the war. Since Germany, for reasons of her own, had made a peace feeler six days before, Wilson's message was received with dismay in Allied circles. Sir Henry Wilson fulminated, "That ass President Wilson has barged in and asked all belligerents for their terms." Lord Northcliffe told Page, "Everybody is mad as hell." If Germany desired a reasonable peace, Wilson had given her the opportunity. But the Germans were interested in a peace conference only as a

device to split the Allies. At the very least, Germany was determined to
control Belgium. "Albert shall keep his Belgium, since he too is King by
Divine Right," the Kaiser advised Prince von Bülow in the autumn of 1916.
"Though, of course, I imagine our future relationship as rather that of the
Egyptian Khedive to the King of England." The Germans, whose dreams of
glory included acquisition of the Belgian Congo, a large indemnity from
France and England, and the end of British naval supremacy, aimed at noth-
ing less than the destruction of Allied power.

On January 31, 1917, the German ambassador, Count von Bernstorff,
informed the State Department that on the following day Germany would
resume unrestricted submarine warfare. U-boats would sink all ships, passenger and merchant, neutral and belligerent, armed or unarmed, in the war
zone. With the British blockade squeezing off supplies and with the war
deadlocked, Germany staked everything on one great effort. She knew that
the result would almost certainly be war with the United States, but she
reasoned that the submarine campaign would end the war before the United
States could give any more aid than it was already giving as a neutral. Wilson promptly broke off diplomatic relations with Germany.

American ships, fearing submarine attack, clung to port, refusing to sail
unless they were armed. As wheat and cotton piled up on Atlantic piers,
railroads were forced to embargo shipments to the seacoast. If Wilson accepted the German submarine policy, he would have to permit a blockade
of American ports by the German navy; with ships rusting at their piers,
factories, in the absence of markets, would throw men out of work and
farmers would suddenly be plunged into a devastating depression. We had
permitted the Allies to cut off our trade with Germany; could we afford to
permit Germany to cut off our trade with the Allies as well? Yet Wilson
refused to ask Congress for authority to arm ships. When on February 23
cabinet officers urged him to do so, he attacked them for attempting to
revive the code duello. Two days later, however, Wilson changed his
mind; from Ambassador Page he had received a dispatch that made him
angry clear through.

Page's dispatch enclosed a message which the British Secret Service had
intercepted and decoded from the Under Secretary of the German Min-
istry of Foreign Affairs, Alfred Zimmermann, to the German minister to
Mexico. The Zimmermann telegram read: "We intend to begin on the first
of February unrestricted submarine warfare. We shall endeavor in spite
of this to keep the United States of America neutral. In the event of this
not succeeding, we make Mexico a proposal of alliance on the following
basis: make war together, make peace together, generous financial support
and an understanding on our part that Mexico is to reconquer her lost territory in Texas, New Mexico, and Arizona." Japan was also to be invited by
Mexico to join in the plan.

On February 26, 1917, Wilson asked Congress for authority to arm
American merchantmen and to carry on an undeclared naval war. When
a group of eleven senators led by Robert La Follette of Wisconsin fili-
bustered the bill to death, the President, after attacking his opponents as a

"little group of wilful men" who "had rendered the great government of the United States helpless and contemptible," went ahead and armed the vessels on the authority of an ancient statute of 1797. In March the first American merchantmen left port with orders to shoot on sight.

Still there was no war. Wilson had the clearest grasp of what war would mean. (Page had written him of the "shells and acres of bloated human bodies, careless of sun or rain, giving off stench.") The terrible campaign of the Somme in 1916 had cost the Germans some 500,000 men, the British 400,000, the French 200,000, and Wilson shrank from throwing American lives into the same inferno. Moreover, Wilson wished to avoid war because, he told Secretary Lansing, it was necessary that the United States keep itself intact so as to maintain the dominance of "white" civilization. At a cabinet meeting in February, Wilson declared, according to Secretary Houston, that if "in order to keep the white race or part of it strong to meet the yellow race—Japan, for instance, in alliance with Russia, dominating China —it was wise to do nothing, he would do nothing and would submit to . . . any imputation of weakness or cowardice." Late in February, when U-boat marauders had been roving the seas for days, the President was still opposed to war. Wilson could not sleep. His face was ashen. He was racked with doubt.

Yet he had reached the point of no return. A few hours before Wilson asked Congress to arm merchantmen, a German submarine torpedoed without warning the Cunard liner *Laconia* with the loss of twelve lives, including those of two American women. On March 12 an unarmed American merchant vessel was sunk without warning; on March 18 U-boats sank three more unarmed merchantmen with heavy loss of life. When this news came, the last member of Wilson's cabinet to hold out for peace capitulated and advocated an American declaration of war. Wilson himself, incensed by the Zimmermann note and angered by the sinkings, was given a new reason for war by the Russian Revolution, which by removing the last despot among the Allies made the war at last seem a clear-cut fight between democracy and autocracy.

On April 2, 1917, on a black, wet, Washington evening, Wilson went before Congress to declare that a state of war already existed with Germany. He had decided on war; yet he would make it a holy war, a war of service to mankind. No other kind of war was tolerable. It would be a struggle of democracy against autocracy, for it was only autocrats who could sanction such fiendish acts as the U-boat commanders had committed. "The world must be made safe for democracy," Wilson proclaimed. "Its peace must be planted upon the tested foundations of political liberty." Congress burst into applause, and men rushed forward to congratulate him. "My message today was a message of death for our young men," the white-faced Wilson remarked afterward to his secretary. "How strange it seems to applaud that."

In both houses of Congress a small band of progressives spoke out against war, convinced that the country was entering it at the behest of financial interests. "We are going into war," declared Senator George Norris of Nebraska, "upon the command of gold." But they were drowned out by the cry for war. Two days after Wilson's message, the Senate voted war 82-6, and early on Good Friday morning the House adopted the war resolution 373-50. On April 7 the New York *Tribune* headlined the end of the long months of fretful neutrality: AMERICA IN ARMAGEDDON.

Why did the United States enter World War I? In later years millions of Americans became convinced that America was led into war by a conspiracy of bankers and munitions makers or was hoodwinked by British propaganda, but neither Wall Street nor Reuters (the British news service) played a decisive role. The United States entered the war because it saw no alternative when faced with unrestricted submarine warfare. Wilson's critics have argued that it was his quixotic insistence on neutral rights that provoked the Germans to the point where they had no choice other than to unleash the submarine and precipitate war. It is an argument which, although mistaken, has considerable substance. Wilson treated World War I as though he were dealing with the War of 1812, ignoring the way in which the submarine had completely altered the nature of armed conflict. He contended that an American citizen had the right to travel on an armed ship, including ships which carried munitions, and had the right to look to his own country for protection. But the citizen in fact had none of these rights under international law and still less under cold common sense.

Wilson conducted his foreign policy by rules of war which neither Germany nor Britain respected. Neither country wanted war with America, but either would have gone to war with America rather than face defeat. Neither pursued her course out of respect for American principles of neutral rights. Both took calculated risks as to whether violating American rights at the cost of American intervention would or would not be a wise policy. The Dutch treated armed merchantmen as warships and interned them. If the United States had done the same, the British would have stopped arming merchantmen, and the Germans could have afforded to (and might have been coerced to) obey rules of safety.

When the United States submitted to the British blockade and, in effect, blockaded Germany herself, when the United States at the same time served as the Allied base of supplies, the submarine became indispensable to Germany. When Wilson attempted to dictate the terms on which Germany could wage war, terms which would have resulted in German defeat, war between Germany and the United States became almost inevitable. Like the hero of a Greek tragedy, Wilson spun his own fate by holding Germany to strict accountability, and he pushed the nation toward war by a merciless logic.

If war had come as a result of Wilson's ultimatum of April, 1916, the responsibility for war would have rested almost wholly on the President. But to censure Wilson for America's entrance into war in April, 1917—as revisionist historians have done—is to overlook completely the important developments in the year following Wilson's ultimatum. Convinced that a drastic change of direction in foreign policy was needed, Wilson shifted to a position of almost absolute impartiality toward the Allies and the Central

Powers. At the same time, he attempted to bring the war to an end before European civilization was damaged beyond repair. It was too late. Neither the Allies nor Germany could afford to wage such a devastating war any longer. Yet, so terrible had been the loss of life, neither side felt it could justify ending the war on any terms save total victory.

Of Wilson's neutrality in the autumn of 1916 there can be no question. If the Germans had not sabotaged Wilson's peace moves, the President might have used economic pressure to compel the Allies to modify their methods of warfare. If the Germans had been content merely to resume submarine attacks on armed merchantmen in 1917, Wilson, despite his earlier statements to the contrary, would almost certainly have acquiesced. But the Kaiser, his appetite whetted by the promises of his military and naval advisers, insisted on unrestricted U-boat warfare against all vessels, neutral as well as belligerent.

The German decision of 1917 gives a perspective to Wilson's neutrality policies that was not available at the time. It seems likely that Germany would have unleashed its submarines the moment it had enough built to make such a tactic feasible. It would have done so irrespective of American policy. Once Germany declared unrestricted warfare on all vessels, the United States would have been forced, as the price of peace, either to suffer without retaliation heavy loss of life at sea or to end its trade with Europe. An embargo on American commerce would have been even less practicable in 1914 than it had been during the Napoleonic wars. Once the Germans had enough U-boats, they could not have been stopped from declaring unrestricted warfare by anything less than a strong show of American force—and American force was not great enough in these years to be effective—or by total American collaboration. World War I was a revolutionary effort to change the distribution of power in Europe. Since Germany believed, probably correctly, that it could not overthrow Allied supremacy without destroying American commerce, it is not clear that there was any policy open to the United States which would not ultimately have led to American intervention.

Apart from the issue of neutral rights, it is impossible, even at this distance, to know whether American entry was a wise decision, for we do not know what the consequences would have been if the United States had not entered. With power balanced on the Continent and the Atlantic controlled by Great Britain, the United States had been able to avoid huge armament expenditures, heavy taxation, a large standing army, peacetime conscription, and expeditions to fight localized wars. A German victory—and without American entrance a German victory was a distinct possibility—presented certain threats. It is by no means clear that a Germany which dominated both the Continent and the Atlantic would have been as benign as Britain had been and continued to be. Over all this conjecture hangs our later knowledge of the menace of Nazi power. The Germany of the Kaiser was certainly not the Germany of Hitler; yet there were enough elements of later German nationalism in the Hohenzollern Empire to give one pause. One thing was certain: if the Allies won, American interests would be safe.

No one could say for certain then or now what would happen if Germany won the war.

All this, of course, is largely historical hindsight. Although a few men like the career diplomat Lewis Einstein and Secretary Lansing thought in terms of the menace of German power to the Atlantic System, they were in a minority. Lansing in fact kept his views to himself and argued for action against Germany on quite different grounds. Whatever the merits of the case, the United States did not go to war for reasons of self-preservation. Wilson himself did not feel that Germany menaced American security, while Roosevelt's bellicosity was more the product of an adolescent derring-do than of an understanding of the realities of power.

American entrance into the war cannot be seen apart from the American sense of mission. The United States believed that American moral idealism could be extended outward, that American Christian democratic ideals could and should be universally applied. This sense of national mission was combined with a new consciousness of national power. The United States was aggressively peaceful. Admiral Mahan had compared the duty of America to repress evil abroad with that of the rich to wipe out slums; this view carried with it the assumption of unique American virtue, which had the ironic effect of making it the duty of "peace-loving" Americans to resort to killing to impose virtue abroad. The culmination of a long political tradition of emphasis on sacrifice and decisive moral combat, the war was embraced as that final struggle where the righteous would do battle for the Lord.

&ᶜ ᶜ&

POWER *makes its possessors appear to be hypocrites, for it compels contradiction between the word and the deed. No President demonstrates this fact more completely than Woodrow Wilson. And in no instance was the contrast between word and deed sharper than in his reaction to the Mexican Revolution. But it was not the result that Wilson had intended. He had wanted to normalize relations between Mexico and the United States, and he wanted to assure the Mexicans that we would respect their revolution.*

The difficulty in maintaining balanced relations between the two countries had its roots in the long history of American-Mexican hostilities. No Mexican could for any length of time suppress his antagonism toward and fear of the Gringo to the north. The size and the power of the Colossus of the North left Mexico in the shadow: it was not a pleasant position for a proud people. When in 1910, a coalition of reformers and revolutionaries under the idealist Francisco I. Madero overthrew the dictatorship of Porfirio Díaz, and then launched an experiment in democratic government, counterrevolutions succeeded one another until February 18, 1913, when Madero was overthrown and murdered. When Wilson entered the White House, General Victoriano Huerta, the author of Madero's assassination, was

Mexico's provisional president. Wilson received a double shock when he learned the American ambassador Henry Lane Wilson had played a major role in the overthrow of Madero and was also pressing the State Department to recognize Huerta. The new President determined to use his influence and power to remove Huerta. But he did not fully understand who in Mexico could provide the leadership which would allow the distracted country to complete its journey from a medieval system built on "aristocracy, exploitation, and peonage" to a "modern civilization" based on popular self-government. He did not understand that the fate of Madero or Huerta were but passing incidents in a vast revolution which would rank among the major upheavals of the twentieth century.

Nonetheless, the good intentions of Wilson toward Latin America received touching expression on October 27, 1913, at Mobile, Alabama. There he denounced the exploitation of Latin America by "foreign capitalists" and pledged no further territorial aggression by the United States on her southern neighbors. He climaxed his address with a call to Americans: "We must prove ourselves their friends, and champions upon terms of equality and honor." To demonstrate the sincerity of that intention, Wilson refused to recognize the Huerta government, a decision which the shrewd Mexican promptly exploited. Huerta appealed to Mexican antagonisms toward the United States, support of him was equated to a defiant thumbing of the nose at the pretensions of Washington, D.C. When it became obvious that Huerta was not going to fall, and that the impending arrival of German munitions was likely to strengthen his government, Wilson ordered on April 21, 1914, the Navy to occupy Veracruz. In a day-long battle, several hundred casualties were sustained, but American forces held the city. Wilson found that he had united all Mexicans against him. Only the mediation of Argentina, Brazil, and Chile prevented the rift from degenerating into open warfare, but at the same time, Wilson's opposition to Huerta sealed his fate. On July 15, 1914, Huerta stepped down and little more than a month later revolutionary forces occupied Mexico City.

For a brief moment, Wilson and the outside world thought the Mexican upheaval had reached a fruitful conclusion, but they underestimated the depth of the upheaval. The Mexican Revolution still was far from its end, and Wilson would be compelled to intervene again, converting his appeal for friendship into an ironic commentary upon the steadily worsening relations between the two countries. Ray Stannard Baker (1870-1946), a muckraking journalist, was designated Wilson's official biographer. Between 1927 and 1940, he wrote an eight-volume study of Wilson's life, the final two volumes winning the Pulitzer Prize in biography for 1940. Previous to writing the biography, he and William E. Dodd edited The Public Papers of Woodrow Wilson *(six volumes, 1925-26). The result was a readable but uncritical biography of the 28th President of the United States that still remains valuable. It is being superseded by the monumental effort of Arthur S. Link (1920-   ) which in its five published volumes brings Wilson to the eve of World War I. If the size of a biography is the measure of a man's importance, then undoubtedly Wilson was an important man.*

WOODROW WILSON: LIFE AND LETTERS

by Ray Stannard Baker

No sooner had Woodrow Wilson entered the White House, with visions of a reconstructed America, than he found that he must turn his attention to the great blue globe that filled one corner of his quiet study. The present writer retains in his mind's eye a vivid picture of the President standing there, turning the globe with one finger, tracing out the relationships of America with Europe, with Mexico, with Japan and the Philippine Islands. It was a symbol of preoccupations that were unexpected when he came into office, of duties for which he had never deliberately prepared.

It is certain that he knew little in detail of the complications in Mexico— still less, probably, of other Latin-American conditions. We have heard him remarking that it would be the irony of fate if his administration had to deal chiefly with foreign affairs when his own preparation had been so exclusively in domestic problems. But he had a sound background of historical knowledge, and he came to the consideration of the Mexican question with certain broad preconceptions, based upon his own researches. In his *History of the American People*, we find him indulging in no derogation of the Mexican people. He says of the invasion of General Scott's soldiers during the war of 1846:

"They fought men as brave as themselves, a subtile, spirited race, tenacious to the last of all that it could hold. . . ."

He speaks of the Mexican war as "inexcusable aggression" upon the part of the United States, and in another place contrasts our attitude toward Mexico with our attitude toward the Great Powers:

"With England, which was strong, we were ready to compound differences; from Mexico, which was weak, we were disposed to snatch everything, conceding nothing."

During the month previous to his inauguration the American press was filled with the news of the crisis in Mexican affairs. On the day that the report came of the arrest of Francisco Madero, then President of Mexico, and the seizure of power by Huerta, Wilson told a group of newspaper correspondents that he did not believe any harm would come to the deposed President. We know how deeply he was shocked by the news that soon followed of the cold-blooded assassination of Madero, and Pino Suarez, the Vice-President, with the implication that Huerta, directly or indirectly, was responsible for the crime. It was the sort of thing that stirred Wilson's nature, with its passion for orderly and democratic processes, to the depths. Behind his Mexican policies lay a substratum of strong feeling, of deep indignation.

President Taft not only refrained from any action that might embarrass the new President but assisted him in every way possible in dealing with the complicated heritage of woe. Even before Wilson was inaugurated, Secretary Knox instructed Assistant Secretary of State Wilson to advise him of the status of Mexican affairs. We find, also, that he began at once to receive letters and memoranda concerning Mexican problems, mostly from interventionists, or from those who had property interests at stake. All the recent reports from the American ambassador in Mexico, Henry Lane Wilson, together with the comments of the experts of the State Department, were placed in his hands. He studied Taft's policies relating to the shipment of arms into Mexico, his inquiries being so keen that we find him a little later assuring A. A. Adee, Acting Secretary of State, that his questions "implied no criticism whatever."

His consideration of Ambassador Wilson's reports not only gave him much concrete knowledge of immediate conditions, but, in opening to him the Ambassador's mind, filled him with a profound sense of distrust. The Ambassador was, of course, an appointee of the Taft administration, and was a strong advocate of Mr. Knox's "dollar diplomacy," which Wilson abominated. He was the "spearhead" in Mexico of "the larger business elements" that feared a "general dislocation of their advantageous position," and, as we now have reason to believe, had "actively abetted" the "handful of military plotters" who had overthrown Madero. When Madero was deposed on February 18th the Ambassador began to work vigorously for the recognition of the new regime "now installed and evidently in secure possession." After Madero and Suarez were assassinated on February 22nd, the Ambassador attempted to brush the "incident" aside as of no international concern:

"I am disposed to accept the government's version of the affair and consider it a closed incident, in spite of all current rumours. The cooperation of the department in this direction will be of infinite value."

The Taft administration, however, had refused to move precipitately in the matter of recognition, and soon drew rein upon the indiscreet Ambassador:

". . . you will . . . be carefully guided by the President's direction that, for the present, no formal recognition is to be accorded those *de facto* in control, except upon specific instructions from the department to do so."

Secretary Knox had also been mindful of the fact that while the Ambassador was ready to consider the murders a closed incident, the American press was not:

"With practical unanimity the American press treated as inadequate the explanations made by the Huerta regime in regard to the death of Madero and Pino Suarez, and is consequently expressing its horror thereat. Having by inadequate precautions made possible that horrible occurrence, those responsible cannot expect to escape public suspicion, and this department is naturally obliged to express itself on that painful subject pending the results of the promised thorough judicial investigation."

Undoubtedly Wilson also saw the despatches showing that the British government would refuse to recognize the Huerta government because of the circumstances surrounding the death of Madero and Suarez. Instead of considering their deaths a closed incident, the British minister, Stronge, had "raised the question of the government's culpability in the death of Madero as a reason for withholding recognition." It must also have been clear to Wilson that Taft had resisted the strongest kind of representations from hotheaded interventionists in the United States who were seeking both recognition and a "show of force."

There was also plain evidence in the despatches that the Ambassador, failing in his effort to secure immediate recognition for Huerta from the Taft administration, had pursued the extraordinary course of seeking to win submission within Mexico to the Huerta administration so that it might on the strength of its effectiveness command the good will of the new President of the United States. To the American consul at Hermosillo he wrote on the 26th:

"You should exert yourself without ceasing to bring about the general submission to the provisional government. . . . Move actively in this matter. . . . The provisional government is being generally adhered to throughout the republic and is showing great firmness and activity."

On the day after the inauguration, the Ambassador was assuring the new Secretary of State, Mr. Bryan, that "the states which have submitted represent 90 per cent of the people of Mexico and order has been reestablished over three fourths of the territory they represent."

But the President was soon to see the reports from our Mexican consular officers, as well as many letters from men who had some authority to speak upon conditions, which told quite a different story. It was plain that there was widespread horror in many parts of Mexico over the assassination of Madero, who was looked upon as a liberator, and that the spirit of revolt against Huerta, much wider spread than Ambassador Wilson disclosed, was increasing daily. Carranza, then governor of the state of Coahuila, had telegraphed to President Taft on February 26th:

"The Mexican nation condemns the villainous *coup d'état* which deprived Mexico of her constitutional rulers by cowardly assassination. . . . I am certain that both the government of your excellency as well as that of your successor will not accept the spurious government which Huerta is attempting to establish upon crime and treason, but will proceed with circumspection towards the social and political interests of our country."

There was another aspect of the situation which came forcibly to Wilson's attention—the attitude of Latin America generally. Reports from ambassadors, ministers, and consular agents in Central and South American countries gave current opinion regarding the Mexican situation, and all showed much unrest, much suspicion and fear of the "giant of the North"—Yankee meddling, Yankee materialism, the implications of the Knox doctrine of "dollar diplomacy."

Mexico, in short, was part of a complex of problems which involved all of Latin America: what was needed was a policy applicable to the entire situation. As we have already seen Wilson set forth his views in the extraordinary pronouncement of March 11th which so offended the hierarchy of the State Department and astonished the diplomats. While there was no direct reference to Mexico, his attitude toward Huerta could not be doubted:

"Cooperation is possible only when supported at every turn by the orderly processes of just government based upon law, not upon arbitrary or irregular force. . . . We can have no sympathy with those who seek to seize the power of government to advance their own personal interests or ambitions."

It gave him also the opportunity to declare what was to be the essence of his foreign policy, that his evangel of democracy was to be applicable to the world as well as to America.

"We hold, as I am sure all thoughtful leaders of republican government everywhere hold, that just government rests always upon the consent of the governed, and that there can be no freedom without order based upon law and upon the public conscience and approval. . . . We shall lend our influence of every kind to the realization of these principles in fact and practice, knowing that disorder, personal intrigue, and defiance of constitutional right weaken and discredit government and injure none so much as the people who are unfortunate enough to have their common life and their common affairs so tainted and disturbed."

The President's pronouncement of March 11th, together with the failure to follow his urgent demands for the recognition of Huerta, were bitterly disappointing to the Ambassador. He had no belief whatever in the President's idealistic purposes. He had no confidence in the success of any sort of rule in Mexico that was not based upon force. As he wrote to Secretary Bryan on March 12th:

". . . unless the same type of government as was implanted here by General Porfirio Diaz is again established, new revolutionary movements will break forth and general unrest will be renewed."

Conditions in Mexico, indeed, rapidly grew worse. Before the end of March a revolution against Huerta, headed by Carranza, was in full swing. To complicate matters still further, the British government reversed its earlier decision, and announced its purpose of recognizing Huerta as "interim President." It was quite likely that other governments would follow suit, thus strengthening the hands of the dictator and weakening the prestige of the new administration in the minds of Latin-Americans.

Wilson soon realized that the situation was highly complicated, and that he must have far more comprehensive information regarding it. He had lost confidence in the Ambassador and he was bewildered by the babel of reports and advice from other sources. He therefore adopted his favourite device of sending a special agent whom he thought he could trust to make special inquiries. He chose William Bayard Hale, a brilliant journalist who was, however, temperamentally unfitted for such a task. He wrote to him on April 19th:

"I think that the situation of affairs in Central and South America is very much more difficult to get the threads of than the situation in California, and with the full acquiescence of Mr. Bryan I am writing to ask if you would be willing to undertake a tour of the Central and South American states, ostensibly on your own hook, in order that officially and through the eyes of an independent observer we might find out just what is going on down there.

"Will you not be kind enough to regard this inquiry as strictly confidential?"

Other agents with more or less uncertain credentials, one an old friend of Mr. Bryan's, W. H. Sawtelle, also went into Mexico and like Hale, having small knowledge of the language, and little historical background, soon began to add to the confusion of counsel.

At some time, also, during the crowded months that followed, Wilson managed to acquire, from books and reports, many of them read and analyzed for him by Mrs. Wilson, a considerable knowledge of the history and problems of Mexico. It was the instinctive method of the scholar to seek a sound foundation for action in the present through knowledge of the past. It is plain from his speeches and interviews that he saw the conflict not primarily as a contest between ambitious men seeking power, plunder and privilege. It was the struggle of a down-trodden, poverty-stricken people against the oppressions of a landlord and ruling class, a people who were seeking emancipation from a feudal system bordering on slavery. Diaz, during his long rule, had brought order out of chaos by iron-handed severity, mistaking the tangible wealth of his country for its welfare, but in establishing a school system, he "raised up," as Wilson expressed it, "the instrument that brought about his own destruction. . . ." Wilson considered that it was out of the civilian revolt that followed, founded upon this new public opinion, that Madero, a sincere if impractical leader, had arisen to power in 1911. He saw in the succession of events a similarity to the French revolution. ". . . my passion is for the submerged eighty-five per cent of the people of that Republic who are now struggling toward liberty."

Events would not, however, await deliberate investigation such as the President desired. He was not only being urged to act by the Ambassador and by angry resident Americans, but he was soon made aware of the complicated interests of great American banks, railroads, industries—the very class of men who had opposed him in New Jersey and whom he knew he would have to oppose in seeking tariff and currency legislation.

Early in May, James Speyer, the New York banker, called upon John Bassett Moore, Counsellor of the State Department, expressing his anxiety regarding a $10,000,000 loan to Mexico which was to mature in June. Huerta was making no preparation to pay it. Speyer suggested that without recognition from the United States, Huerta would have serious trouble in getting funds, his government might collapse, and in the resulting disorder, the United States might have to intervene. This matter was immediately brought to Wilson's attention.

One of the powerful railroad leaders of the United States, Julius Kruttschnitt, chairman of the board of the Southern Pacific Company, whose lines ran down through the border states into Mexico, was also deeply concerned. Through Colonel House he sent the President an able and temperate statement of conditions prepared by Judge D. J. Haff of Kansas City, who had had long experience as attorney for American interests in Mexico. This communication was understood to meet the approval of the interests represented by the Phelps, Dodge Company, the Greene Cananea Copper Company, Mr. Doheny of the Mexican Petroleum Company—the greatest oil interest in Mexico—and others. In short, this was the proposal of the "Big Interests" regarding the Mexican situation. It is so important that liberal extracts are here presented:

"The Constitutionalists steadfastly refuse to recognize Huerta or to treat with him. The United States government, therefore, has a great opportunity, by acting quickly, of presenting a plan to Huerta agreeing to recognize him on condition that he call an election at an early date, October 26th being too remote, and that he guarantee a fair election in all those states of which he has control, the Constitutionalists to do the same and to participate in the election. The Constitutionalists, on the other hand, to agree that in consideration of this election being called and being fairly held, hostilities shall be suspended, and that they will loyally support the President who shall be chosen as a result of such election.

"We do not think it necessary to insist that Huerta shall resign and some other interim President be appointed in his stead. . . . He is the *de facto* President at the present time, and is a man of energy and executive ability, is in command of the army and is, better than any other person, able to carry out such an agreement; and we feel certain, from our knowledge of the situation on both sides and the temper of both sides, that both the Federalists and the Constitutionalists would welcome the friendly intervention of . . . our government. . . . If this is not done, war will continue until the country is absolutely exhausted, banditism will grow and increase until there will be no security for human life and private property whatever. . . . The losses now amount to millions of dollars per day and the situation cannot much longer be sustained.

"In addition to that fact foreign nations are becoming restive and are seeking to undermine the influence of the United States in Mexico. The British government has already recognized Huerta in a most marked manner by autographed letter from the King due to the efforts of Lord Cowdray . . . who has the largest interests outside of American interests in the Mexican republic. He is using his efforts to obtain a large loan in England, and we are informed that he has succeeded on condition that the English government would recognize Huerta, which has been done. If Mexico is helped out of her troubles by British and German influence, the American prestige will be destroyed in that country and Americans and the commerce of the United States will suffer untold loss and damage. On the other hand, if the Huerta government falls as the result of the hostility of the American government or its inactivity in the present crisis, it will make us morally responsible for consequences too frightful to contemplate. . . .

"Our ambassador in Mexico is, in my opinion, the man to attempt this work. It might be found necessary to send a special envoy to treat with the Constitutionalists, while entrusting our ambassador in Mexico to treat with the Huerta government."

While much of the advice in this letter ran contrary to the President's in-

clinations, since he profoundly distrusted both Huerta and the American ambassador, the letter made a strong impression upon him. This was heightened
a few days later by a visit from Judge Haff himself, who was introduced
by Wilson's old friend Cleveland H. Dodge. Dodge's approval always went
far with the President. Judge Haff enlarged upon his former statement and
Wilson was so far convinced that he began to consider the temporary recognition of Huerta on condition that a fair election be held soon and a constitutional President be chosen. He therefore prepared or partially prepared
a statement to be sent to Huerta through Ambassador Wilson—working out
the main points in his own stenographic notes. Since this document has not
before been published it is here inserted in full:

"Please represent to Huerta that our understanding was that he was to
seek an early constitutional settlement of affairs in Mexico by means of a
free popular election, and that our delay and hesitation about recognition
has been due to the apparent doubt and uncertainty as to what his plans
and purposes really were. Our sincere wish is to serve Mexico. We stand
ready to assist in any way we can in a speedy and promising settlement
which will bring peace and the restoration of order. The further continuation of the present state of affairs will be fatal to Mexico and is likely to
disturb most dangerously all her international relations. We are ready to
recognize him now on condition that all hostilities cease, that he call an
election at an early date, the twenty-sixth of October now mentioned being, in our judgment, too remote, and that he absolutely pledge himself as
a condition of our action in his behalf that a free and fair election be secured
by all proper machinery and safeguards. Upon this understanding this Government will undertake the friendly office of securing from the officials of
the states which are now refusing to acknowledge the authority of Huerta's
government an agreement to cease hostilities, maintain the status quo until
the election shall have been held, and abide by the result of the election if
it be held freely and without arbitrary interference of any kind as we have
suggested. It should be intimated to Huerta that the Government of the
United States is not likely to assent to any method of settlement secured
by the Government of Mexico making interest with European Governments to lend their countenance and assistance in consideration of special
advantages accorded their citizens or subjects."

Having prepared this communication, however, Wilson hesitated to send
it. Huerta, encouraged by the recognition of Great Britain and other European and Latin-American governments, was becoming more arrogant and
dictatorial. He even announced his intention of refusing diplomatic recognition to the American representative in Mexico. Wilson began to doubt,
even if the truculent dictator agreed to his proposals, whether he would
carry them out. How could such a man be trusted to hold a fair election or
to make way for a new President chosen by the people? Once he was
recognized, even as an interim President, would there by any way of dealing with him if he failed in his promises, short of armed intervention?

Recognition, indeed, was the core of the problem. All of the argument in favour of recognition was of course based upon the historical practice of accepting a *de facto* government. Wilson was undoubtedly thoroughly acquainted before he came into office with the traditional American diplomatic procedure in this regard: and he was certainly fully informed afterwards. It was a policy that had been instituted, like so many other fundamental American practices, by Thomas Jefferson.

Jefferson said with reference to the French revolution:

"It accords with our principles to acknowledge any government to be rightful which is formed by the will of the nation substantially declared."

The right of revolution, by virtue of which the American nation came into being, was too precious to be limited. How else could a people free itself from tyranny? There were numerous pronouncements by later Presidents or Secretaries of State supporting the validity of this position.

Later, there began to be doubts. Unlimited revolutions were beginning to endanger American residents in Mexico, injure American commerce, and irritate the governments of Europe. A tendency developed to reinterpret the phrase "will of the nation substantially declared." In 1858, a constitutionally elected President having been turned out, President Buchanan, an experienced diplomat, took a firm stand, refusing to recognize any government in Mexico until it was "obeyed over a large majority of the country, and by the people, and was likely to continue."

When Porfirio Diaz came into power by a revolutionary movement in 1876, the same problem arose and President Hayes declared that although the United States government was "accustomed to accept and recognize the results of a popular choice in Mexico, and not to scrutinize closely the regularity or irregularity of the methods" by which those results were brought about, the United States would in this instance wait "before recognizing General Diaz as the President of Mexico until it shall be assured that his election is approved by the Mexican people, and that his administration is possessed of stability to endure and of disposition to comply with the rules of international comity and the obligations of treaties." It was not until April, 1878—sixteen months after Diaz came into power and nearly a year after all the other powers represented had acted—that the United States granted recognition.

It will thus be seen that in the mere fact of delayed recognition or even of concern as to whether the people really supported the new regime, Wilson's position involved nothing unprecedented.

It is plain from the letters and documents that Wilson's interest in Mexico went further and deeper than the mere problem of recognition. America was to serve the really best interests of Mexico: how could it do that by saddling the nation with a bloody tyrant? How could it stop short of positive assistance to the 85 per cent of the people who were down-trodden? In short Wilson was not content to follow the course so eagerly and promptly urged by the great business interests; he was thinking of a kind of moral intervention in behalf of new democratic institutions in Mexico and the welfare of the Mexican people. It may have been "idealistic"—it may have been impractical, it may even have been "meddling"—it was what Wilson had most deeply and sincerely in his mind. As he said in his notable pronouncement of March 11th:

"The United States has nothing to seek in Central and South America except the lasting interests of the peoples of the two continents, the security of governments intended for the people and for no special group or interest, and the development of personal and trade relationships between the two continents which shall redound to the profit and advantage of both and interfere with the rights and liberties of neither."

We have a beautiful glimpse of the real problem that lay in Wilson's mind in an argument that took place between the legalists and the moralists in a cabinet meeting on May 23rd, when the question came up as to whether Wilson's proposed message to Huerta should be sent:

"Mexico loomed up at the cabinet meeting, May 23rd, as an ugly problem. Several members expressed themselves as being in favour of the recognition of Huerta. The President and Bryan were opposed to recognition. I emphatically opposed it as immoral. I asserted that the Huerta government was bad both in origin and in purpose, that neither Huerta nor his crowd had any interest in the Mexican people; and that recognition would probably make us indirectly responsible for a large loan to Huerta which would fasten him upon the Mexicans. It was replied that he would get the money anyway and hold the people down, and that, if he did so and suppressed the revolutionists, we would have to recognize him. I said that this would not necessarily follow and that, if it did, we would not be responsible for him. It was agreed that Bryan should sound the English and French ambassadors, to see if their governments were back of the loan and to warn them that they could not enforce a loan guaranteed by a pledge of customs duties."

Having delayed in sending the message to Huerta which he had worked out, Wilson finally set it aside altogether. This decision started a new movement on the part of Mr. Kruttschnitt and the oil interests that supported him. They now avoided suggesting recognition but asked that the administration use its good offices in bringing about an election at an early date and in composing the differences between Huerta and the revolutionaries of the North.

By this time Hale's reports had begun to come in, and they were vigorously critical of the provisional government and especially of Ambassador Wilson. The President read them carefully and transmitted them to Bryan, his accompanying notes indicating that he placed no little dependence upon the information they conveyed. He was also hearing much unfavourable news from other quarters, some of it dealing with the activities of American financial interests in Mexico of which in the past he had known little or nothing. How far, after all, could he follow the advice of men who, however able, were far more concerned with the stability of their investments than with the welfare and good government of the Mexican people? Nevertheless something had to be done. Conditions were steadily growing worse: the Ambassador was sending urgent telegrams:

". . . although I have been his [the President's] personal representative at this post for three months, I have not been put in possession of the attitude of the administration on the question of recognition."

On June 14th, after a conference with Secretary Bryan and Secretary Garrison, definite instructions were forwarded to the Ambassador—the first outright declaration of the new administration. It is impossible to say who made the original draft; in the President's hands it was corrected and improved upon in his characteristic way. While it contained certain of the ideas of the earlier proposed message, it avoided any promise whatsoever of recognition. Wilson began by emphasizing the profound distrust of the American government:

". . . it is convinced that within Mexico itself there is a fundamental lack of confidence in the good faith of those in control at Mexico City and in their intention to safeguard constitutional rights and methods of action."

It goes on to say, however:

"If the present provisional government of Mexico will give the Government of the United States satisfactory assurances that an early election will be held, free from coercion or restraint, that Huerta will observe his original promise and not be a candidate at that election and that an absolute amnesty will follow, the Government of the United States will be glad to exercise its good offices to secure a genuine armistice and an acquiescence of all parties in the program. It would be glad, also, to be instrumental in bringing about any sort of conference among the leaders of the several parties in Mexico that might promise peace and accommodation."

While these instructions gave the Ambassador the information he had asked for, they did not satisfy him or cause him to alter his attitude toward Huerta. He continued to press the American government for recognition of the provisional authorities and, worse still, was indiscreet enough to invite Huerta to dine at the American embassy. The President and Bryan were shocked, and the former wrote on the memorandum from Hale that conveyed this information:

"I think Wilson should be recalled."

The Ambassador, perhaps not unnaturally, bitterly resented Hale's presence in Mexico. Hale lacked those quiet, unobtrusive, tactful methods that were so much a part of Colonel House's equipment as a presidential emissary. His evident position of authority embarrassed the Ambassador and excited irritation and confusion among the Mexican officials. The Ambassador protested to Washington against his interference in Mexico City and later on Hale reported that he believed himself in danger of arrest by the Huerta authorities.

Nevertheless Hale's reports had much influence upon the President and no doubt served to hasten the recall of the Ambassador.

"The document from Hale is indeed extraordinary. I should like . . . to discuss with you very seriously the necessity of recalling Henry Lane Wilson in one way or another, perhaps merely 'for consultation' until we can have a talk with the man himself."

And on July 3, 1913, the President again wrote to Secretary Bryan:

"After reading Hale's report and the latest telegrams from Henry Lane

Wilson, I hope more than ever you will seriously consider the possibility of recalling Wilson, as I suggested in a recent note, and leaving matters in the hands of O'Shaughnessy, who, you will notice, is commended as a perfectly honest man by Hale."

Another aspect of the complicated situation—the attitude of foreign governments—caused Wilson constant anxiety. The recognition of Huerta by Great Britain was a disappointment to him. It had been followed by similar action by Spain, China, Italy, Germany, Portugal, Belgium, Norway, Russia, and later by most of the Latin-American states. The arrival of the Japanese ambassador in Mexico City in July was marked by demonstrations which indicated the anti-American feeling in the capital city, and added greatly to Huerta's truculence.

In the case of Great Britain both Wilson and Bryan were satisfied that the oil interests headed by Lord Cowdray were largely responsible for the recognition of Huerta, and there was much to confirm their belief. Page wrote home in July that the Mexican minister in London had told him that the influence of the British oil interests was great because of the contract of the British navy with Cowdray's company. Disorder was not only endangering vested interests but, long continued, it might threaten sources of supplies for British ships.

It is unfortunate, in this connection, that there should not have been prompter understanding and better diplomatic cooperation between the two governments. It is possible that much confusion, much loss, much bloodshed, might have been avoided. The British Foreign Secretary, Sir Edward Grey, was, like Wilson, a liberal in opinion: the two men, if brought together, would have found that they held many beliefs in common. Even though, as an experienced diplomat, he might have doubted its expediency, Grey would have appreciated and sympathized with Wilson's effort to found his policy in Mexico upon ethical principles rather than upon selfish national interest. In his memoirs, criticizing German policy because it was based upon "a deliberate belief that moral scruples and altruistic motives do not count in international affairs," he declares:

"Surely the conclusion is irresistible that a policy which rules out all moral purpose except national interest has a fatal lack of what is essential to enduring success."

But there was no adequate machinery for bringing about such an understanding. The crisis came in the unfortunate interval between two administrations. Owing to the overturn in American politics, and the accession to power of a party that had not held office for sixteen years, those in control of foreign affairs at Washington were novices. Wilson, as we have seen, had, in the beginning, little knowledge either of Mexico or of diplomatic technique. Bryan, although he had travelled in Mexico, probably had still less: and Wilson in any event expected to be his own Secretary of State. Page, the new ambassador in London, and Colonel House were no more experienced. It takes time even for the ablest men to master such complications as those presented by the Mexican situation. Wilson might, indeed, have consulted more fully the experts of the State Department; he might even have followed their advice with confidence that if he was making no progress, he was making no serious mistakes. But both he and Bryan had come into office with progressive ideas, and they distrusted the silent, slow-moving, often extremely useful and powerful permanent bureaucracy of the State Department, traditional to the marrow of its bones, which for three administrations had been working under Republican control. It was probable indeed that these under-secretaries and experts, full of old knowledge, looked with long-suffering indulgence bordering on indignation at such pronouncements as those made by Wilson early in March. Impractical, amateur, idealistic! In any event, why not play safe by following traditional practice? Wilson did not realize the inert power of this bureaucracy, which in every changeable democratic government, here and elsewhere, must be reckoned with. Almost at the beginning he had had, as we have seen, a noteworthy example of the feeling of the bureaucracy in the indignant resignation of the Assistant Secretary.

It was for this reason, in part, that Wilson began the practice of using extra-diplomatic agents, of whom Colonel House was the outstanding example. He was determined not to allow his administration to slip into the "rut of mere legalism." But the employment of such "special" or "secret" ambassadors as House, Hale, Lind, and others, while it had certain advantages and yielded Wilson much information secured by men who shared, or seemed to share, Wilson's liberal views, tended to paralyze the normal relationships and understandings between the American State Department and the foreign offices of other governments. It was to have a profound effect not only in the Mexican affair but later, and far more seriously, in the World War.

Colonel House, for example, with the sincerest intention of helping Wilson, may have added to his difficulties by attempting to explain to Sir Edward Grey what he himself plainly did not understand, concerning Mexican affairs. It was an extraordinary situation. House had talked with Wilson soon after the President's conference with Judge Haff when the message proposing the temporary recognition of Huerta pending an early constitutional election was under consideration—the message which, as we have seen, was never sent. Soon afterwards he sailed away to Europe. There is no evidence that he was in any way informed regarding the swiftly changing situation; and yet when he met Sir Edward Grey for the first time on July 3rd, he set forth Wilson's position regarding Mexican affairs with complete assurance. Since House was Wilson's personal representative—he had letters that were undeniable credentials—Grey had no cause for doubting what he said. House gives an account of his meeting with Grey in his diary:

"I told him the President did not want to intervene and was giving the different factions every possible opportunity to get together. He wished to know whether the President was opposed to any particular faction. I thought it was immaterial, as far as our government was concerned, which faction was in power, if order was maintained. I thought our government would have recognized Huerta's provisional government if they had carried out their written promise to call an election at an early date and abide by its decisions."

House was here vitally misconstruing Wilson's purposes. While he was right in saying that Wilson did not wish to intervene, to proceed with the assertion that "it was immaterial . . . which faction was in power, if order was maintained," was to misinterpret, fundamentally, Wilson's chief purposes, as revealed in the record. It implied that the President's diplomacy was exactly that of Henry Lane Wilson, and the oil and financial interests, which were clamouring for immediate recognition, and whose sole interest was in "order," no matter how attained. Incidentally House referred, quite erroneously, to the "written promise" of the provisional government "to call an election at an early date"—when there had never been any such agreement.

After hearing House's exposition of the President's views it was not unnatural that Grey should add the great weight of his influence in urging Wilson to recognize Huerta as the provisional head of the Mexican government, letting the matter of recognition come up *de novo* for both powers after the Mexican election on October 26th. If Grey had known what Wilson's position and ideals really were he might possibly have pursued a different course, for opinion in England was much divided. Ambassador Page reported to Bryan on July 25th that a widespread feeling existed "among intelligent men in both political parties that the British government made a mistake in recognizing Huerta. Opinion divides itself along financial rather than party lines."

Page was also beginning to interpret Wilson's real purposes and ideals to Grey and intimating that the President was "unlikely at this time to recognize the Huerta government." Grey remarks in his memoirs:

"Page saw an ideal in the Mexican policy of President Wilson. I was ready to sympathize with the ideal, and to believe in the moral purpose of the policy; but I did not believe that morally there was much to choose between Huerta and his opponents. That was the difference between us. Had I realized then, as I came to know afterwards, how devotedly Page cared for an ideal of right in public affairs, how indifferent he was to anything else but that, I should have been less reserved and more frank in our Mexican conversations."

Confused no doubt by their want of understanding of the Washington attitude, and pressed by their own oil interests, the British now sent Sir Lionel Carden to take charge of the British legation in Mexico City. A more displeasing appointment could scarcely have been made. Carden had been serving for several years in the British legations in Central America and the West Indies, was an economic imperialist in viewpoint, and notoriously anti-American. Secretary Knox had twice intimated to the British government that his recall from Cuba would be gratifying to the United States, but the suggestion was rebuffed and Carden knighted.

By July Wilson had not only gone beyond the point where he was willing even to consider a provisional recognition of Huerta, but he was beginning to feel, more strongly than ever before, that his real opponents were the oil men and other vested interests in Mexico, both American and British. He remarks:

"I have to pause and remind myself that I am President of the United States and not of a small group of Americans with vested interests in Mexico."

Ambassador Wilson was becoming more sharply urgent: ". . . I am obliged again to urge upon the President the pressing necessity for some action of a drastic and convincing kind that will convince this government and this people that our nationals must be protected in life and property, and that the barbarous and inhuman warfare which has now been waged for three years shall cease."

The President's response was to call the Ambassador to Washington for "consultation relative to the Mexican situation"—with his removal in the background. He reached Washington on July 25th, and on the 28th met the President at the White House. We have the Ambassador's account of the conference:

"The President was affable and pleasant in his demeanour, revealing that charm of manner that characterized his earlier public life. Without referring to the memorandum which I furnished him, he asked for a brief summary of the Mexican situation, and as I proceeded, commented, as I thought, irrelevantly. I noticed a certain inflexibility of preconceived views which rendered discussion and a faithful presentation of the situation difficult. He impressed me as being under the influence of opinions other than those which I had been reporting to the department and as having perhaps a different version of the events that had occurred in Mexico. . . . The President's questions suggested a lack of knowledge of the psychology and facts of the situation in Mexico, and it was quite evident that he had not availed himself of the information accessible to him at the Department of State."

On August 4th Secretary Bryan informed the Ambassador that the President had decided to accept his resignation since it was apparent that there was a wide divergence in their views as to a Mexican policy.

Why should the President have retained in office even for five months an ambassador who was so obviously out of sympathy with the views and purposes of the new administration? In the first place, no doubt, the President had supposed that his representative in Mexico—an ambassador being the mouthpiece of the government in power—would promptly accept the implications of the pronouncement of March 11th and especially the instructions of June 14th, and do his best to cooperate. This, indeed, he had the right to expect. When it became clear that the Ambassador was not only opposed to the purposes of his chief, but doing his best to defeat them—and yet clinging to his office—it is probable that the President hesitated to recall him, thinking that a change at such a critical time would have the effect of magnifying the seriousness of difficulties which he hoped to bring to a speedy termination. Moreover, he was evidently loath to act quickly in a situation of which he was, as yet, so little informed. There was another, and personal or temperamental, aspect of the situation. Wilson intensely disliked changes in personnel; all through his administration he seemed to have preferred to go on working with an official who was under fierce attack or whom he distrusted, rather than to face the difficulty of appointing and educating a new one. This characteristic had its valuable aspects, since it assured many a loyal, honest, hard-driven office holder that the President would back him to the last ditch. On the other hand, sometimes in important matters, the want of cooperation, the mutual distrust, militated against efficient action. We shall see, in future, many instances illustrative of this characteristic of the President.

The resignation of Ambassador Wilson ended the first phase of the Mexican crisis, so far as the President was concerned. He was now to take hold of the problem with new energy and a new programme. Rightly or wrongly he began to see that Huerta himself must be removed before anything constructive could be done. No real peace, or order, or stability was possible so long as the control rested in the hands of a tyrant who was in no way responsible to the people and against whom a large portion of the people were in actual rebellion. Peace had in the past too often been purchased by suppression. To recognize Huerta was to give moral support to despotism and to put a premium upon revolutions. To fall in with the purposes of the "dollar diplomatists," to accept the doctrine of order by force, after proclaiming the new day and the new freedom in the United States, would make him a "living illustration of a horrible incongruity."

Huerta, however, had no intention of resigning. Two days before Ambassador Wilson stepped out of office he announced through his Minister of the Interior:

"General Huerta will not resign. Much less will he permit nationals or foreigners to take a hand in a question in which is involved his honour and that of the nation."

If he could be determined, he had to face a President at Washington who had ideals and was Scotch. On the next day, August 3rd, Wilson declared in a private letter that he must now consider "what is to be done in Mexico, how that murderous Castro is to be choked off and kept in cold storage."

The struggle was to deepen.

⚜ ⚜

"It's an awful thing to be President of the United States," Wilson wrote less than two years before his inaugural. "When a man enters the White House," he added, "he might as well say, 'all hope abandon, ye who enter here.'" As he would learn in Mexico, so he would learn elsewhere that a President is not necessarily his own master. When he entered the White House, he had noted playfully that the worst thing that could happen would

be if he were obliged to concentrate on foreign affairs before his domestic problems were solved. It was exactly what happened.

The Mexican Revolution would have provided more than enough foreign distraction, but in July of 1914, the long peace inaugurated a century earlier at the Congress of Vienna came apart. The assassination of the Archduke Franz Ferdinand and his consort at Sarajevo set the Vienna government on a path to settle finally the Serbian problem. In the wake of that decision, the rest of Europe plunged over the brink into four years of World War, which when it ended had destroyed the Habsburg, Hohenzollern, Romanov, and Ottoman Empires. It opened the Russian Revolution, an event the full implications of which are still unplumbed, and put the United States into the front rank of world powers.

But when the war opened, Americans simply were not prepared for it. Wilson, as catastrophe overtook the world, struggled with the tragedy of his first wife's death. When he finally found time to concentrate upon the expanding upheaval, he pleaded: "The United States must be neutral in fact as well as in name during these days that are to try men's souls." He understood that the ethnic variety of Americans would put severe tugs upon their loyalty as they wished one or another nation "to succeed in the momentous struggle." He also worried lest our entry into the war undermine "every reform we have won."

For a little more than thirty-three months, the administration tried to maintain neutrality, as both England and Germany subjected the United States to endless and in the presidential judgment "unnecessary provocations." As the scale of the European war escalated, Wilson concluded: "Both sides are seeing red on the other side of the sea, and neutral rights are left, for the time being, out of their reckoning altogether." When the Lusitania was sunk on May 7, 1915, by a German submarine, the nation responded with horror, but Wilson turned aside from the swift riposte. To an assemblage of new citizens he declared instead: "The example of America must be a special example. The example of America must be the example not merely of peace because it will not fight, but of peace because peace is the healing and elevating influence of the world and strife is not." He went on to add a peroration which struck the imagination of friend and foe: "There is such a thing as a man being too proud to fight. There is such a thing as a nation being so right that it does not need to convince others by force that it is right." Within less than two years of that declaration, Wilson would appear before Congress and call for a declaration of war. He would justify it as necessary to make "The world . . . safe for democracy." It would leave some doubt as to how sincere he was when he made his earlier pronouncement.

Walter Millis (1899-   ), long a journalist on such newspapers as the Baltimore News *and the* New York Herald Tribune, *has made a specialty of military history. His treatment of the Spanish-American War in* The Martial Spirit *(1931) is a hilarious account of a war that proves even war can be comic. One detects through all of his work a skepticism about the military profession, and never more so than in* Road to War.

ROAD TO WAR; AMERICA, 1914-1917

by Walter Millis

In the second inaugural of Woodrow Wilson there was little to suggest the splendors of that great day, four years before, when Democracy had returned to the White House and the bright sun of the New Freedom had dawned over a happy land in a world at peace. It was across chasms more profound than those of time that one had now to look back into that far-off age. Its innocent sunshine could now be seen—when it could be seen at all—only as a traveller, pressing onward through a storm, sometimes sees a shaft of light against some serene mountain peak that he has left far behind him. Could one have really believed in those days that the sunshine would last forever, that Privilege was dead and war a grotesque anachronism? Had Theodore Roosevelt actually been a battler for the Lord; and was it really Woodrow Wilson who had once said: "I tell you, ladies and gentlemen, I take off my cap to Bob La Follette. . . . Taunted, laughed at, called back, going steadfastly on. . . . I love these lonely figures"?

Even the day was wintry, though a pale sun broke through after the speechmaking began. As the parade came down Pennsylvania Avenue the customary plumes and gold lace, the absurdly brilliant uniforms of the militia and the marching clubs, were noticeably absent. For the first time since the Civil War the troops were there with the thought that they might be needed. National Guard regiments in field service equipment lined the Avenue—a duty which had always been left to the police in the past—and near the Capitol a machine gun was mounted and ready on the pavement. The President's four-horse carriage (it was the last time that a horse-drawn vehicle was to be used for an inaugural parade) was surrounded as it advanced by a hollow square of thirty-two secret service men, and the troop of regular cavalry which acted as escort rode in olive drab. No one was allowed within the Capitol grounds unless he carried a pass. The inaugural address was brief, and largely a repetition of what had gone before.

But in New York City that evening a wildly enthusiastic mob was pouring into Carnegie Hall to denounce the recalcitrant Senators for the crime of having tried to save them from the most terrible war in history. "The Rev. Dr. Lyman Abbott was greeted with roars of approval when he called the filibustering Senators 'Germany's allies.' " "Traitors! Hang them!" came the answering shouts from the audience. The Hon. James Beck devoted his legal talents to the proof that the President had a right to arm merchant ships anyway, and the cheers resounded. They cheered the proposal that Mr. Root should be made Secretary of State and Mr. Roosevelt Secretary of the Navy; and at every declaration that Germany was at war with the United States already they yelled and waved their little American flags in an orgy of patriotism.

Spring Rice reported that the action of the eleven "Iscariots, as they are called" was "an evident proof of the direct authority exercised by Germany in Congress. . . . Rumors of plots and discoveries of plots by German-Americans are rife, and some of them authenticated." The second great "conspiracy scare" was in fact now fully under way, as the precautions of the inaugural bore witness. Again there were everywhere visions of great armies of trained German reservists arising suddenly, as from the dragon's teeth, out of the heart of the nation. Bombs were discerned under every country bridge, and every tennis court was already a German gun-emplacement. In the War Department and the Council of National Defence they were furiously at work upon the vast mobilization plans; while Mr. Roosevelt, who hoped to get a division, was "as yet holding in; but if [Wilson] does not go to war with Germany I shall skin him alive. To think of the folly of having cursed this country with the really hideous misfortune of four years more of Wilson in this great and terrible world crisis."

On March 9, the Friday after the inauguration, Mr. Wilson issued the call for the extra session which was now unavoidable. But he set the date for April 16—over a month away. In the meanwhile, however, could he continue simply to do nothing about the merchant ships? It was also on March 9 that an anxious, and perhaps slightly disingenuous, cable arrived from Mr. Page: "I find that continued delay in sending out American ships, especially American liners, [!] is producing an increasingly unfavorable impression. . . . There is a tendency even in high government circles to regard the reasons for delay which are published here as technicalities which a national crisis should sweep aside." That Sunday, March 11, was "War Sunday" in New York churches. The New York Federation of Churches had decided to "mobilize its Christian strength behind President Wilson." The ministers proclaimed the holy war from many pulpits. In Brooklyn Dr. Newell Dwight Hillis brought his congregation to its feet in un-ecclesiastical cheers with his sermon: "Why We Should Go to War With Germany." A resolution in favor of conscription and pledging support for war was adopted by 158 congregations in the city. "Our churches," said the Rev. Charles A. Eaton in the Madison Avenue Baptist Church, "have been preaching what amounts to a moral asphyxiation. Pacifists afflict the country. . . . They make me want to swear, pray, laugh and weep." It was a performance echoed in countless other cities. On the Monday it appeared that organized labor would not be behind organized religion, when Mr. Gompers summoned the American Federation of Labor chieftains to Washington to decide upon labor's attitude in "the impending crisis." It was to take them but a day to pledge labor's services to the cause without reservation. Before they had done so, however, President Wilson, on Monday evening, March 12, formally announced that naval guns and gun crews would be supplied to American merchant ships even without Congressional authorization.

On the same day the American steamer *Algonquin* was sunk without warning off Plymouth. No lives were lost; but it constituted the second in a series of "overt acts" that were now to come in an ever more rapid succession.

From the preceding November down to that moment, President Wilson had clung consistently to his policy of preserving the United States from war by buying a peace in Europe with an American guaranty of a world peace system. Now, he was without the means to develop it farther. Should he attempt to continue in that course, his authority would be at an end— at a moment when his four-year term of office was just beginning. Mr. Wilson was not a man easily to accept a loss of personal power. But if he now felt that the re-establishment of his command over the situation was a matter of absolutely vital importance to the nation which he represented, one can hardly ascribe the feeling wholly to personal egotism.

He had endeavored to retain command by making peace; and the peace solution lay shattered before him. There remained the alternative—the easy, the profoundly tempting alternative—of making war. The more vigorously he intervened the more complete a hold would he regain over Allied policy; while as for his own public, no ruler ever wields so absolute a power as that of the head of a modern democratic state leading his people into war. Yet President Wilson—and it is the fact which has earned him his great place in human history—was not willing to sentence perhaps hundreds of thousands of his countrymen to death or mutilation on the battlefield for the utterly barren satisfaction of taking revenge upon the Germans. The lives lost at sea could not be restored by the sacrific of countless others. The military defeat of Germany could not return the submarine into the brains of its inventors, nor solve the baffling intricacies of sea war and neutral right for which the Entente was quite as much responsible as were the Germans. Simple victory over the Central Powers would not in itself serve any American national interest remotely commensurate with the human costs of a large-scale intervention in Europe. If President Wilson was to take this one tempting exit from the *impasse* at which he had arrived, he must find some reason that would make it worth while for the common men and women who would pay the price. But it was just here, as chance would have it, that the war solution assumed its most tempting aspect.

The great vision of a world remade, of peace, justice and equal opportunity enthroned among the nations, of the armies disbanded and the old curse of war lifted at last from the scarred backs of men, arose to beckon him forward. He would have been more than human had so vast a role not appealed to his personal ambition. Yet if his egotism was at work, it was an egotism which all sides had been earnestly striving to arouse through the past two years. It was Mr. Lloyd George who, speaking as Prime Minister of Great Britain, had just told him that he must save the Allies from themselves, that "he must help make peace if the peace made at that conference is to be worth keeping." Is it strange that such promptings should have had an effect? Jane Addams saw the President in those days and remembered the conversation:

> [He said that] as head of a nation participating in the war, the President of the United States would have a seat at the peace table, but that if he remained the representative of a neutral country he could

at best only "call through a crack in the door." . . . The foreign policies which we so extravagantly admired could have a chance if he were to push and defend them, but not otherwise.

On March 15, the Czar of Russia abdicated and the news of the Russian revolution reached the United States. Germany had won the greatest, the most nearly decisive, victory in her whole four years of effort. Yet, so strong were the Entente propagandas and so imperfect was the American understanding of the war that it was received by our public as only another augury of the early success of the Allies. Was not "autocracy" the great enemy, and had not the unusually extreme form of autocracy in Russia always constituted one of the most obvious and embarrassing weaknesses of the Allied cause? It was so no longer. The Czarist court, it was now everywhere discovered, had throughout been pro-German at heart; its over-throw would only release the full energies of the Russian people and nerve their armies to fight with redoubled vigor for freedom, justice and human-ity. The fact that a chief reason for the overthrow was the weariness of the Russian people with fighting of any sort escaped our editors. It also escaped our statesmen; and the Russian revolution supplied only a fresh impulsion toward our own entry into the conflict.

The ten days from March 11 to March 21 would seem to have been the decisive period. They had opened with "War Sunday," with the orders to arm the merchantmen, with the sinking of the *Algonquin* and Mr. Gomper's rallying of labor to the cause of militant patriotism. The Russian revolution was an accomplished fact by Thursday, the 15th. On Friday there came the startling discovery of something that looked, in the heated atmosphere of the moment, almost like revolution in the United States. The powerful rail-way brotherhoods—key trades unions which did not belong to Mr. Gomper's A.F. of L.—had been waiting for the Supreme Court to determine the con-stitutionality of the Adamson eight-hour law, a Federal enactment which they had won some time before under threat of a strike. It was known that the Court was about to hand down its decision. On Friday evening the rail-way unions abruptly called their strike throughout the nation, with the demand that the provisions of the Adamson act be granted them by the owners regardless of the constitutionality of the law. On the verge of a war in which transportation would be all-important, it was an unnerving crisis.

Some, at any rate, of the railway executives felt that it would be grossly unpatriotic of them to enter the European struggle burdened with an eight-hour day; and as they mobilized the war passion to defeat the union demand they were convinced that they were "standing out for a principle" which was "the very foundation of practical patriotism." The brotherhoods, on the other hand, had no intention of seeing their own interests sacrificed upon those altars of patriotism which were to bring so rich a yield to most of its high priests. The week-end passed in a high tension. Secretary Lane, active in the negotiations, thought that "we came near to having something akin to a civil war." It was a close thing; but in the end the patriotism of the brotherhoods was to prove more practical than that of their employers, and they got their eight-hour day. On Monday the Supreme Court (which may also have been mixing practicality with its patriotism) upheld the act with a five-to-four decision.

On the Saturday that the railway executives and the government were struggling with the brotherhoods, the Council of National Defence was taking another great step toward industrial mobilization. The Munitions Standards Board was set up that day under Mr. Frank A. Scott of the Warner & Swazey Company. It was to develop into the chief agency of munitions procurement upon our entry into the war. It was also on this Saturday, the 17th, that the War College tore up all its tables of munitions requirements to rewrite them upon a larger scale. The new schedules were based upon an army of 1,000,000 men fighting under European trench war conditions.

During this same week-end there came the definite news of the famous German retreat upon the Hindenburg Line. On their war maps, our public saw the black lines, so long and so tragically immobile, suddenly leap forward at the rate of whole miles a day. The cities of Bapaume and Péronne, upon which every mind had been fastened all through the terrible last half of 1916, but which had continued to stand inaccessible behind the heaps of dead, now fell within a week. The public had heard about "strategic retreats" too often to believe that this was in fact one of the true strategic retreats of the war. Hopes leapt high again, bringing new fuel to the war fever. Only later was the grim irony to sink in and the truth to appear that the Entente had again suffered what was in reality a severe reverse.

Finally, it was together with all these events that three more American steamers—the *Vigilancia, City of Memphis* and *Illinois*—were sunk in quick succession on Friday, Saturday and Sunday. In two of the sinkings there was no loss of life, but fifteen men, six of them American citizens, were drowned with the *Vigilancia.* "Prepare! prepare! prepare!" the Reverend S. Parkes Cadman was shouting at a Y.M.C.A. meeting in Brooklyn that Sunday. In the remoter wilds of Kansas and Missouri a newspaperman, Mr. Edward G. Lowry, was finding the hinterlands still opposed to war but ready "to follow the President." In Washington the bureaucracy had worked itself into an almost unbearable state of tension, and was exerting all its influence to hurry the President forward. "Armed neutrality" was becoming a byword and a joke. On Monday, March 19, with the news of the latest sinkings, the War Department suspended further demobilization of the National Guard troops returning from the border, while Secretary Daniels was reported to have convened the Navy General Board "for discussion of plans of co-operation with the Entente."

Colonel House, content to await the inevitable in his New York apartment, heard from one visitor in the early days of that week that "something akin to a panic" was developing at the capital and that there was a "feeling in Government circles that if the President did not act promptly, a strike would come about in Cabinet and official circles." On Monday another friend called the Colonel twice by telephone from Washington. "He is disturbed at the President's inertia, and he and Lansing want me to come to Washington to see if I cannot stir him into action." On Tuesday still another visitor was "disturbed" at the lack of activity. "He believes there will be an unfavorable reaction against the President unless he formulates a plan . . . and follows it vigorously." That evening House summoned Captain Guy Gaunt to give him a private explanation of the delay. The President, House said, was "rather hesitating about the attitude the new Congress may adopt," and House himself was "loath" to advise his chief, for the interesting reason that "if he goes wrong he will lose influence with him." On the other hand, the Colonel explained that the Cabinet "is for war and is trying to force the issue"; and Downing Street was secretly reassured with the extraordinary hint that the Administration, while "uncertain of Congress," was "anxious about *danger of cooling down of public feeling.*" Was it partly for this reason, perhaps, that at the regular Tuesday Cabinet that day the "disturbance" had already reached the point of open rebellion?

According to Mr. Houston, it was the President himself who opened the discussion by asking flatly whether he should advance the summons to Congress and what he should say to it. There was silence, until Mr. Houston sprang into the breach:

> Germany is now making war on us. . . . We ought to recognize that a state of war exists. What can we do: We can get a big army and navy started. We can further prepare financially. . . . First of all, find out from the Allies just what aid we can most quickly and effectively give. . . . We were drifting. . . . Call Congress and ask it to declare that a state of war existed. . . . War could not be waged mildly.

Secretary Baker thought "that immediate steps should be taken . . . to raise a great army and that universal training should be inaugurated." Secretary McAdoo supported Houston. "Lansing said little or nothing, as usual." William B. Wilson, Secretary of Labor and one of the pacific faction, "said that he had reluctantly made up his mind that action had to be taken. We were at war." Secretaries Gregory and Redfield, also of the milder wing, "expressed the same opinion." Two remained; both had been hesitant in the past.

> The President said: "Burleson, you and Daniels have said nothing,"
> Burleson replied quietly: "We are at war. I am in favor of calling Congress at the earliest moment."
> Daniels gave us the views of the naval experts.

The Cabinet, as Secretary Lane put it, was "at last a unit. We can stand Germany's insolence and murderous policy no longer. Burleson, Gregory, Daniels and [William B.] Wilson were the last to come over." Confronted with this unanimity among his advisers, the President appears to have said little. He did let drop one idea: "If our entering the war would hasten and fix the [revolutionary] movements in Russia and Germany, it would be a marked gain to the world and would tend to give additional justification for the whole struggle." When they broke up they did not know what his decision would be. But next morning small doubt remained. On Wednesday, March 21, a new Presidential proclamation advanced by two weeks the date for convening the extra session. It was now summoned for April 2—a week from the following Monday.

"It is either war or it is submission to oppression," Mr. Elihu Root told the Union League Club of New York. "There is no question about 'going to war.' Germany is already at war with us." That convincing slogan, so nicely calculated to relieve those who uttered it of any necessity for thought and any responsibility for the consequences, now re-echoed everywhere through the press. It was proclaimed by editorial pages in New England and in Southern California, in the cotton South and the industrial Middle West. So unanswerable did it seem that the chief debate turned not upon the question of war but upon the magnitude of the war effort that we should put forth.

The Governor of Connecticut, a pillar of the Baptist Church, was already mobilizing the clergy of his state to take a census of its human war material. The Governor had not forgotten, he explained, that "our God is the God of Love," but he felt that "this country has a mission to perform in the world." So, no doubt, did the American Peace Society, the oldest of the American pacifist organizations, with a history stemming directly from the horror and exhaustion which the Napoleonic Wars had left behind them. It, too, was now "standing behind the President," while the Springfield *Republican* congratulated it for being such a "good loser." On Thursday, the 22d, there was still another huge rally in Madison Square Garden in New York. Again Mr. Root was a chief speaker:

> All history teaches us that the rich and defenceless peoples, the peoples who are too luxurious, too fond of their comfort, their prosperity, their wealth, their ease, to make sacrifice for their liberty, surely fall a prey to the aggressor. So Rome fell. . . . So Persia fell. . . . So poor, peaceful China fell, three hundred years ago. . . .

Mr. Root, like Mr. Lloyd George and Mr. Wilson, wanted the United States to enter the war in order to attain a place at the peace table, but for a different purpose.

> I hate war, but I welcome the coming of the inevitable at the beginning. . . . I say that upon the issue of the war in Europe hangs the question whether America shall, at the close of that war, be turned into one armed camp, or whether America shall be a subject nation. There is no nation on earth—not England nor France, nor Belgium nor Italy nor Russia, with a greater stake in the success of the Allies in this war against German militarism than the United States. We are able to hold this peaceful meeting—with a few weak explosions—and why? Because we are protected by the navies and armies of the Allies!
> *A Voice:* That's a lie! (Followed by the ejection of the interrupter.)
> One thing more. . . . Every true American heart should respond with joy, amid its sorrow, to the feeling that if we enter this war . . . we shall be fighting over again the battle of American democracy, along

with the democracy of England, the democracy of France, the democracy of Italy, and now, God be praised, the great democracy of Russia; fighting for the principle of free self-government against the principle of old-time autocracy and military power.

"Enough has been said and hinted," Spring Rice was advising his Government next day, "to justify the assertion that the die has been cast and that this country has drifted into war." Already Colonel House had sent off a glowing message, through an English visitor: "Tell them we are with you to the finish of our resources in supplies, money and men. We are prepared to go the whole hog. . . . Give my warmest regards to my friends over there, Lloyd George, Balfour, Asquith and Grey. Tell them all I am thinking of them all every hour." It was a melting sentimentalism not shared by the more hard-headed agents of Great Britain; and together with Spring Rice's report of Friday, the 23d, there went another from one of the British "representatives" in the United States who was "in close touch with events at Washington":

> It looks as if W[ilson] would in fact help us *pretty* well: almost all he can: but I think he will try not to be *technically* an ally. He's the most agile pussy-footer ever made, and when any serious decision is taken alwas tries to unload the responsibility on to someone else. . . . But it does seem as if the Huns had fairly driven him into a corner out of which he can't possibly wriggle!

The private communications of the British, however, were safe from interception. It was on this same Friday that Mr. Lansing finally ordered Mr. Whitlock to withdraw with all his staff from Brussels, leaving the Belgian Relief in the hands of the Dutch. In the Friday Cabinet, during the same hours, the time was consumed with "routine matters of preparation." The reporters were told afterward that the President and his Cabinet had now decided upon an "aggressive warfare" in addition to the mere protection of American shipping. Next day the great industrialists of our Council of National Defence were formally demanding a conscript army of 1,000,000 men; while Secretary Baker was engaging to urge "strongly" upon the President their decision in favor of a draft as opposed to volunteer enlistment.

One bellicose mind was conceiving even stranger plans. On the day after the submarine declaration Mr. Roosevelt had filed his request with Mr. Baker to be notified "at once" if there was any chance that there would be a war. The notification had never arrived. With all the fierce excitement of preparation now going forward on every side, Mr. Baker, it seemed, was taking no interest in the great, the long-cherished project of a personal Roosevelt army. Desperately, the former Colonel of the Rough Riders appealed to his old friend, Senator Lodge, to circumvent a hostile Administration by getting direct authorization for the plan from Congress. Nor was that all:

> Meanwhile, I have notified Jusserand of the facts, and told him that if either Congress or the Administration declares that a state of war

exists, I shall take an expeditionary infantry division to France (under the American flag) on my own account if his Government thinks it worth while to pay for us. If his Government does not, I shall try whether Canada would like to pay for an American division (under our flag)—I understand that they need more men.

There could be no more eloquent testimony to the extraordinary psychology of the moment than the fact that a former President of the United States could advance this remarkable and distinctly treasonable proposal. But perhaps it is a question whether Mr. Roosevelt—a prey to a raging furnace of emotion within his own breast, fed by war madness, by ambition, jealousy and disappointment—was by this time altogether rational. And Secretary Baker knew, as Marshal Joffre was soon to tell him, that in the real war upon which the American people were now about to embark, "it cost from ten to fifteen thousand lives to train a major-general."

Nor was Mr. Roosevelt the only independent and ambitious soldier. On March 24 the axe, poised for so long above the insubordinate neck of General Wood, fell with a cruel abruptness. In his stronghold at Governor's Island the general was suddenly notified that his command was to be divided up, and he was politely offered his choice between the task of defending Charleston, South Carolina, from invasion or exile to the even more "important" and remote commands at Hawaii or Manila. Incredulous, the general telephoned to the Adjutant-General for confirmation of this order, and was told that it was final. He hung up. "Wood's comment was, 'I guess he thinks he's got me now.'" And he had. Preparedness, after all, is not war.

There was to be a storm of protest from the general's adherents, and the Republicans sought patriotically to exploit it as another means of hamstringing Mr. Wilson. "We can conceive of no service to the Government more worth while at the moment," the Boston *Transcript* severely observed, "than that its head shall be made to understand, with all the speed and solemnity possible, that his attack upon a citizen soldier of the character, courage and capacity of Leonard Wood is looked upon at home and abroad as a national disgrace." But in war one does not make heads of governments understand things—it is the other way around.

In his Brooklyn church on Sunday, March 25, the fire-eating Rev. Newell Dwight Hillis was suggesting that the eagle upon the Great Seal of the United States should be replaced by a tortoise, with the motto: "God made every creeping thing." It is true that when Senator Wadsworth, at another meeting in Brooklyn, cried for war to the hilt and the immediate despatch of a regular division to France, the utterance "curiously" drew "quite a number of hisses." But they were drowned at once in roars of applause. The quiet seclusion of East Fifty-Third Street was being broken that Sunday morning as the pacifists—Amos Pinchot, Paul Kellogg, Lillian Wald—led a last forlorn hope against Colonel House himself. But the Colonel easily put them off. At his Embassy in London Mr. Page was already at war, setting his whole staff to "asking everybody what the Americans can best do to help the cause along," and cataloguing the results for the guidance of Washington. Most of the British leaders talked ships, naval patrols and credits, but the military men, significantly enough, wanted "an expeditionary force, no matter how small."

The Sunday passed. A bare week now remained before the Congress would convene. President Wilson turned to call the National Guard back into service as a defence against that long-anticipated uprising of the pro-Germans (which never happened), but what his Message would be no one knew—not even the President, for it was as yet unwritten. Colonel House at last began to feel some anxiety. Through all the critical period since the break with Germany the President had rather noticeably failed to call his adviser into consultation. The Colonel, convinced of the inevitability of the outcome, had been satisfied to wait; but the strain seems to have been growing more severe, for he now wrote suggesting that it might be well for the President to see him. There was no reply. On Monday, however, the Colonel had a long conference with Mr. Howard Coffin, one of the industrialists of the Council of National Defence, which disturbed him so much that he resolved to go at once to Washington. He thought the war preparations required attention; he was also "anxious to talk with [Mr. Wilson] concerning his message to Congress." Thus self-invited, the Colonel reached the White House on Tuesday afternoon. His doubts, he found, had been unnecessary. What the President asked him was whether the Message should call for a declaration of war or should announce that war already existed and merely request the means to wage it.

Colonel House immediately advised the latter course, for "I was afraid of an acrimonious debate if he puts it up to Congress to declare war"—as the Constitution would seem to have required. At any rate, the main point had evidently been decided. Yet the President, strangely enough, seemed not to share his adviser's mood of cheerful relief. "He was not well, and complained of a headache." The Colonel sought to restore him to a proper frame of mind and nerve him for the slaughter with the old, old argument that he should act "in a creditable way so that his influence would not be lessened when he came to do the great work which would necessarily follow the war." But perhaps the President, standing upon that somber verge, had a clearer realization of how distant, how unattainable, those splendid visions really were. He said that "he did not believe he was fitted for the Presidency under such conditions." House answered with ready encouragements—fighting a world war would be easier, even, than such peacetime achievements as the passage of the Federal Reserve Act or the Panama Canal tolls repealer. "He listened with a kindly and sympathetic attention, and, while he argued with me on many points, he did it dispassionately." It is possible that for the time being the Colonel, like Mr. Page, no longer counted.

Next morning, Wednesday, the President played golf. While he was on the links Mr. McAdoo arrived to see House—breathing fire and desolation. "McAdoo wants war—war to the hilt. He said his appetite for it was so strong that he would like to quit the Cabinet, raise a regiment and go to the front. All three of his sons have enlisted." So perhaps Mr. McAdoo, too, had remembered the splendors of San Juan Hill. When Mr. Wilson returned he called in Colonel House to show him, at last, the first rough notes of the

Message which had to be delivered five days later. House "approved" them and returned to New York.

In the War Department, in the Council of National Defence and among the passionate patriots of preparedness, the pressures which were to take an A.E.F. of 2,000,000 men to Europe were rapidly being worked up. The most that Allied opinion was suggesting at the time was a relatively small American contingent for the Western Front; indeed, it is possible that some, even, of the military men were still a little cautious about inviting an American intervention on too great a scale. Yet "this did not change the War Department's policy, which had been formed before we entered the war. We went on with our plan for a great army." In the Cabinet on Friday, March 30, the President was still raising that obstinate question about the "sentiment of the country," but they assured him that although there would presumably be "a great many disaffected individuals," no "situation would develop which could not be readily handled." So far had we already come in our war against militarism and autocracy. When the Cabinet rose, the members felt confident that the President was going to ask, not for a declaration of war, but for the more compelling "declaration of a state of war," and that the nation would "pledge all its resources to the prosecution of the struggle to a speedy end." Next day, Saturday, the Council of National Defence was adopting a resolution by Secretary Lane providing that all the military contracts should be written on the basis of a three years' program. "We may win in two years," Mr. Lane thought. "If we had the nerve to raise five million men at once we could end it in six months." Could they?

That Saturday evening fell. Within less than forty-eight hours, the Congress would be in its place and waiting. According to Winkler:

> On the night of March 31, the President stirred restlessly in his bed. Finally he rose, donned bathrobe and slippers and took his small typewriter out on the south portico of the White House. Mrs. Wilson, hearing him, slipped into the kitchen and prepared a bowl of milk and crackers which she silently placed at his side. There, in the stillness of the night, Wilson wrote his War Message.

Sunday morning came—the last Sunday of that peace which the President had striven courageously, if perhaps mistakenly and too tardily, to maintain. In Vienna, Count Czernin was devoting it, by a rather tragic irony, to a public call for a conference and a negotiated settlement among the war-weary peoples. In London Mr. Page was pouring out another of his endless letters:

> The Administration can save itself from becoming a black blot on American history only by vigorous action—acts such as these: . . . We must go in with the Allies. . . . We must sign the pact of London —not make a separate peace. . . . (1) The Navy—full strength, no "grapejuice" action. (2) An immediate expeditionary force. (3) A larger expeditionary force very soon. (4) A large loan, at low interest. (5) Ships, ships, ships. (6) A clear cut expression of the moral issue.

The day wore on. The bellicose Lane was writing happily to his brother. The die was cast. Even in the Far West they were standing behind the President, for Mr. Lane had collected telegraphic reports on the local feeling there and the replies had all been in that sense. "Yet none came back," Mr. Lane added, "that spoke as if they felt that we had been outraged or that it was necessary for humanity that Germany be brought to a Democracy. There is little pride or sense of national dignity in most of our politicians." Mr. Lane had a better spirit and a clearer understanding of the needs of humanity.

At about the same hour the freighter *Aztec*, the first armed American merchantman to sail from the United States, was foundering in the dusk and a stormy sea off the island of Ushant. She had been torpedoed, efficiently and without warning; one of her boats was smashed in launching and there was a heavy loss of life. Her two five-inch guns—our first answer to the U-boat—had not fired a shot; their crews had not seen even the track of the torpedo, much less the submarine which discharged it. As the *Aztec*'s people were drowning in the cold, black seas off Finisterre, the pacifist forces in New York that Sunday afternoon were organizing for one last, desperate effort—a mass descent upon the capital in the morning. But at Columbia University a group of patriotic professors were hastily preparing a counter-demonstration. Professor Walter B. Pitkin was rushed off to Washington as an advance guard; several ministers—Dr. William T. Manning, Dr. George R. Van de Water and Dr. Karl Reiland—were enlisted as aids; reinforcements were summoned from Yale under Professor Henry V. Farnum, and a statement was issued by the committee through Professor Charles A. Beard: "The hour has struck to put an end to the Prussian oligarchy. . . . Every advocate of peace at any price . . . is now playing into the hands of Prussian militarism."

There was one minister of the Gospel who refused to be swept away by the tides of war emotion. At the Church of the Messiah at Park Avenue and Thirty-Fourth Street, the Rev. John Haynes Holmes's morning sermon had been a passionate declaration of faith: "If war is right, then Christianity is wrong, false, a lie. . . . No order of a President or a Governor will persuade me or force me to this business of killing. . . . Other clergymen may pray to God for victory for our arms. I will not. In this church, if nowhere else, the Germans will still be included in the family of God's children." It gave his trustees a bad afternoon. "Dr. Holmes is an idealist," one of them explained to the reporters, but this was not "the time to put his idealism into practice. We are not going to lie down and let Germany or anybody else wipe up the floor with us. . . . The Church of the Messiah is going to fight first . . . to protect American right and American lives, and after we have protected them we will go on with our ideals." Elsewhere that Sunday the churches overwhelmingly agreed, not with Dr. Holmes, but with his trustees. Throughout the nation the pulpits were mobilized for the Christian conflict; and even in the remote fastness of the Rocky Mountain states (where the politicians might be backward) the clergy were holding flag-raising services and proclaiming the holy war. The nation as a whole, whatever it may actually have wanted, was now standing behind the President; the War Message was written and ready; only a few hours remained before the irrevocable step would be taken. But in all the moral fervor and war hysteria of the moment there was one statesman who retained a clearer and a sadder understanding of what the great crusade was in reality to imply. That man was Woodrow Wilson, President of the United States.

As the day dragged on, Mr. Wilson despatched a sudden summons, not to Colonel House, but to Mr. Frank I. Cobb, who presided so ably and so loyally over the editorial page of the New York *World*. Mr. Cobb could not get to Washington until after midnight, and it was about one o'clock on Monday morning when he finally reached the White House:

> The "old man" was . . . sitting in his study with the typewriter on his table. . . . He looked as if he hadn't slept. . . . For nights, he said, he'd been lying awake going over the whole situation. . . . He said he couldn't see any alternative, that he had tried every way he knew to avoid war. . . . I told him his hand had been forced by Germany, that so far as I could see we couldn't keep out. . . . "Yes," he said, "but do you know what that means? . . . It would mean that we should lose our heads along with the rest, and stop weighing right and wrong." . . . The President said a declaration of war would mean that Germany would be beaten and so badly beaten that there would be a dictated peace, a victorious peace.
>
> "It means," he said, "an attempt to reconstruct a peacetime civilization with war standards, and at the end of the war there will be no bystanders with sufficient power to influence the terms. There won't be any peace standards left to work with. There will be only war standards." . . .
>
> He went on to say that so far as he knew he had considered every loophole of escape, and as fast as they were discovered Germany deliberately blocked them with some new outrage. . . . He had no illusions about the fashion in which we were likely to fight the war. He said when a war got going it was just war, and there weren't two kinds of it. . . . We couldn't fight Germany and maintain the ideals of government that all thinking men shared. He said we would try it, but it would be too much for us.
>
> "Once lead this people into war," he said, "and they'll forget there ever was such a thing as tolerance. To fight you must be brutal and ruthless, and the spirit of ruthless brutality will enter into the very fibre of our national life, infecting Congress, the courts, the policemen on the beat, the man in the street." . . . He foresaw too clearly the probable influence of a declaration of war on his own fortunes; the adulation certain to follow the certain victory, the derision and attack which would come with the deflation of excessive hopes, and in the presence of world responsibility. But . . . it was just a choice of evils.

The President foresaw it all, down even to the bitter end. Yet Mr. Wilson, no less than his countrymen, was the prisoner of his own policies, of fate, of human limitations. He was powerless to check the course of history now.

What he could do was to strive to turn this moral disaster to the highest possible ends. He could still dedicate himself to the task of salvaging, if it was possible, that settlement of justice, humanity and reason for which all sides had convinced themselves that the Great War was being waged. President Wilson knew how enormous now would be the difficulty of an attempt "to reconstruct a peacetime civilization with war standards." But he would try.

The sky paled. The morning of April 2, 1917, was dawning.

As President Wilson and Mr. Cobb were talking in the White House, "one thousand militant pacifists, each armed with a white tulip" were crowding the railway station in New York, ready to take the night train for Washington. "They are going," according to one hostile account, "to keep the nation out of war, and 14,000 other flower bearers from the rest of the United States are going to help them do it." Colonel House, hurrying likewise for the night train, must have passed through the curious spectacle. The lights glared over the crowd; the white tulips waved their pathetic way through the gates, and the trains trundled off in the darkness toward Washington. In their mail-cars there went the morning editions, whose headlines already assumed that it was all over:

CONGRESS READY TO DECLARE STATE OF WAR NOW EXISTS; COUNTRY IN MILITANT MOOD

The day came in raw and stormy. President Wilson had sat late with his visitor, but he was up much earlier than usual. Before breakfast the White House reporters saw a messenger emerge with a sealed envelope—it was the War Message, in the President's own typescript, on its way to the public printer. Mr. Tumulty was at the White House an hour before his usual time; Colonel House arrived for breakfast, but the President was already leaving for the golf links with Mrs. Wilson, and House saw him "for a moment only." Until Congress should be convened and organized there was nothing to do but to kill time. Mr. Wilson spent the whole morning playing golf. Colonel House motored with Mr. Polk of the State Department, or answered anxious telephone inquiries from Mr. McAdoo as to whether the War Message would prove adequate. The Colonel, who had himself seen only the rough notes for it as yet, felt certain that it would "meet every expectation." Outside the whole city was clothed with flags—a sufficient indication of what Washington expected—while on Capitol Hill the Senators and Representatives were collecting in their offices, waiting for the opening of the session, which was fixed for noon.

The pacifist host, led by Dr. David Starr Jordan, was milling about the Capitol in the damp weather, considerably at a loss. They had tried to organize a parade and had been sternly refused a police permit. They had tried to see the President and had been denied; they had tried to storm the State, War and Navy Building and had been repelled by the heavy guards posted there. Most of them drifted back to the other end of Pennsylvania Avenue, to invade the Senate and House office building or sit about on the

Capitol steps, watching one of their number who bore a solemn banner: "Is this the United States of Great Britain?" Senator La Follette tried to get authorization for them to hold a formal demonstration, but failed; and no one else paid very much attention until, shortly before noon, there arose a sudden fracas in one of the corridors of the Senate Office Building.

Six or seven Massachusetts pacifists, among them Mrs. Anna May Peabody, the Rev. Paul Harris Drake and Mr. Alexander Bannwart, a youngish man of German-Swiss parentage, had penetrated to the door of Senator Henry Cabot Lodge himself to make their protest, as his constituents, against a declaration of war. The Senator was busy. They insisted. The Senator, stepping to the door, consented at least to hear them. "There followed the usual pacifist harangue" ending with the argument that Massachusetts senti- ment was strongly against war. With dignity Mr. Lodge replied "that he alone could be judge of sentiment in Massachusetts"; the pacifists, unsup- pressed, told him that war was cowardly. "National degeneracy and cowardice," Mr. Lodge answered, "are worse than war," and backed toward the office door. The heroic episode which followed has been recorded in Mr. Lodge's own words:

> They were very violent and very abusive, and I was engaged in back- ing away from them and saying that we must agree to differ when the German member of their party said, "You are a damned liar," and he hit me and I hit him. Then all the pacifists rushed at me and I thought I was in for a bad time, but my secretaries sallied forth to my rescue and there was a mixup.

Mr. Bannwart was thirty-six and athletic; the Senator was spare and sixty- seven, but according to some witnesses he floored the traitor with his first blow. The secretarial reinforcements came pouring out of the office; a gallant Western Union messenger, passing through the corridor, sprang into the fray. "I saw an old man in a fight," he modestly told the reporters after- ward, "and I thought it my duty to help him." The help, at all events, was efficacious. "The pacifist who attacked me got badly beaten up and it all ended very comfortably and without hurt to me"; the mauled and bleeding Bannwart was finally borne off to custody by the Capitol police, and the thrilling news ran through the Senate Office Building that Senator Henry Cabot Lodge, striking our first blow for freedom, had personally punched a pacifist in the nose. "I am glad that I hit him," Mr. Lodge concluded. "The Senators all appeared to be perfectly delighted," and Mr. Lodge himself was momentarily a national hero.

The forces of peace had been routed at the beginning. Other Senatorial doors were hastily closed upon them; the police presently broke up an incipient demonstration on the Capitol steps, and ultimately they adjourned to a public hall for a conventional and impotent mass meeting. The hall, as it happened, was next door to a National Guard armory, and the young citizen soldiers—whose lives, after all, they were trying to preserve—booed and jeered them as they went by. Later there were some other meetings and speechmakings, but it was not of the slightest use, and before the day was over the peace army was dissolving.

At noon Congress convened; it was to require the whole afternoon, however, to complete the organization of the House of Representatives, and the serious business could not begin until evening. Among the members taking their seats for the first time there was one who attracted particular attention —Miss Jeannette Rankin, Representative from Montana and the first woman to sit in the Congress of the United States. As to the attitude of the statesmen there was little doubt, although it was, perhaps, rather less than unanimous. One newspaper survey discovered that the Congressmen "are beginning to look upon defence of our trade routes as merely incidental. The members of the House of Representatives, all fresh from home, now interpret the sentiment of their communities to mean that when the United States enters the war it will be as a great democracy aiding in the overthrow of an autocracy of the worst sort"; while a poll revealed seventy-six of the Representatives for war as against only fifteen definitely opposed. Yet there were twenty-five others who were doubtful or noncommittal, while one lingers over the curious detail that this survey showed a two-to-one sentiment against sending any troops to Europe, or even formally joining the Entente alliance.

In the House the routine business droned on; the Senate was temporarily in recess. In New York that afternoon a crowd stopped to mob a pacifist speaking from a cart-tail, but there was little excitement. Far away in Brussels Mr. Whitlock was paying his farewell visit to General von Bissing, whom our newspaper readers had known so long as the ogre of the Belgian occupation:

> *"Vous partez donc?"* *"Oui, Excellence!"* And then in a kind of rage he almost roared: *"Et pourquoi?"* . . . He said that he was sorry to see me go.

The Germans gave them every courtesy; while the Belgians gathered in silent crowds at every street corner and before the railway station to wave farewell. The train finally rolled away toward Switzerland with Mr. Whitlock and his staff, and another famous mission was at an end. In the White House they whiled away the time. Mr. Wilson finally read his message to the Colonel, and the adviser noted happily that none of the Wilson papers had pleased him more. Superficially the President seemed calm, but House's trained eye could detect "signs of nervousness." The afternoon lengthened; until word came at last that Congress would be ready at eight-thirty, and they sat down to an early dinner in order to be in time. Only House and the members of the family were there, and they talked "of everything excepting the matter in hand." Beyond the windows the evening fell, in mist and a soft rain; the crowds were already lining the avenue to cheer the President on his way to the Capitol, while a troop of United States cavalry was drawing up as an escort to safeguard his passage—from the embattled pacifists!

By nightfall two more troops had been thrown around the Capitol; the whole building was swarming with secret service men, Post-office inspectors and police, and it was impossible for any pacific disturber to "get within pistol shot" of the place. The House galleries were filling again with a brilliant assemblage of the authorized; the Representatives were taking their places; the Supreme Court was seated, this time, directly before the Speaker's desk; the Cabinet was on one side, while behind them the Diplomatic Corps, in full evening dress, occupied a place upon the floor of the House for the first time in anyone's memory. In an atmosphere of intense excitement the House was called to order; two minutes later the doors were flung open, and the Vice-President entered, followed once more by the Senate, marching two by two, with every man—or almost every man—"wearing or carrying a small American flag." Solemnly that impressive and patriotic spectacle moved down the aisle to the seats reserved. Senator La Follette was flagless; so was Senator Vardaman, but there was no time to check up on the others, for a moment later the Speaker was announcing: "The President of the United States."

The chamber had never witnessed an ovation such as that which followed. The Supreme Court rose en masse to lead the applause; the Senate, the Representatives, the packed galleries, stood up to clap and then to cheer. Mr. Houston glanced back at the Diplomatic Corps and "bowed to Spring Rice and Jusserand, who were expectant and happy." Not for two minutes could the demonstration be quelled. "At eight-thirty-five o'clock tonight," the New York *Times* correspondent was writing as the cheers resounded, "the United States virtually made its entrance into the war. At that hour President Wilson appeared before a joint session. . . ." The noise died at last; and as the President opened the sheets of note paper before him an intent and absolute silence fell. Without looking up the President began:

> Gentlemen of the Congress: I have called the Congress into extraordinary session because there are serious, very serious, choices of policy to be made, and made immediately. . . .

The opening paragraphs were a brief recital of the submarine controversy and the failure to check the progress of that "cruel and unmanly business." The "German submarine warfare against commerce," the President said, "is a warfare against mankind." Chief Justice White, prominent in the foreground, was seen to give a vigorous nod of approval. The voice went on: "The challenge is to all mankind. Each nation must decide for itself how it will meet it. The choice we make for ourselves must be made with a moderation of counsel and a temperateness of judgment befitting our character and our motives. . . . But armed neutrality, it now appears, is impracticable." On the Chief Justice's face there appeared an expression of profound satisfaction. The President continued, pointing out the weaknesses of that solution, the practical certainty that it could only lead to the war it had been designed to prevent. And then—did he draw a breath?—"There is one choice we cannot make, we are incapable of making: we will not choose the path of submission—"

At the word, the Chief Justice, "with an expression of joy and thankfulness, dropped the big soft hat he had been holding, raised his hands high in the air and brought them together with a heartfelt bang; and House, Senate and galleries followed him with a roar." The President finished the sentence: "—and suffer the most sacred rights of our nation and our people to be ignored or violated," and then swept on:

> With a profound sense of the solemn and even tragical character of the step I am taking and of the grave responsibilities which it involves, but in unhesitating obedience to what I deem my constitutional duty, I advise that the Congress declare the recent course of the Imperial German Government to be in fact nothing less than war against the Government and people of the United States; that it formally accept the status of belligerent which has thus been thrust upon it; and that it take immediate steps not only to put the country in a more thorough state of defence but also to exert all its power and employ all its resources to bring the Government of the German Empire to terms and end the war.

The Chief Justice rose to his feet, "leading the Supreme Court and the entire assembly. His face was a study. It worked almost convulsively and great tears began to roll down his cheeks." Behind him "the Senators and Representatives were cheering. . . . Heflin of Alabama sprang to his feet. In a second the whole Democratic side of the House was up after him, and then Ollie James of Kentucky rose in his turn, followed immediately by the Democratic side of the Senate . . . cheering at the top of their lungs." The tension was broken in a fierce tide of emotion. From that moment until the end the Chief Justice "was vigorously applauding everything"; the others were not behind him. The President went on to catalogue the measures which such a declaration as he asked would call for—the "mobilization of all the material resources of the country," further great naval expansion, an immediate addition of 500,000 men to the Army, to be raised by conscription, with subsequent increases as rapidly as the men could be trained. It made no difference. Whatever some of them may have thought in saner moments, they cheered it all now; they even cheered as the President turned to the attempt to fix the great effort which he was invoking upon the highest of ends:

> Our object . . . is to vindicate the principles of peace and justice in the life of the world as against selfish and autocratic power, and to set up amongst the really free and self-governed peoples of the world such a concert of purpose and of action as will henceforth ensure the observance of those principles. Neutrality is no longer feasible or desirable where the peace of the world is involved and the freedom of its peoples. . . . We have seen the last of neutrality in such circumstances. We are at the beginning of an age in which it will be insisted that the same standards of conduct and of responsibility for wrong done shall be observed among nations and their governments that are observed among the individual citizens of civilized states.

Could they have failed to realize that the duties and responsibilities of that new age must apply to the United States equally with other peoples? There was, at any rate, no sign of dissent; and the President changed his theme. "We have no quarrel," he went on, "with the German people"—just as he had long before announced, upon the verge of a lesser war, that we had no quarrel with the people of Mexico. "We have no feeling towards them but one of sympathy and friendship." He launched into a long denunciation of the crimes their government, however, had committed—crimes of spying, intrigue and propaganda of which "self-governed nations" could never, of course, have been guilty. "We are glad, now that we see the facts with no veil of false pretence about them, to fight thus for the ultimate peace of the world and for the liberation of its peoples, the German peoples included; for the rights of nations great and small and the privilege of men everywhere to choose their way of life and of obedience. The world must be made safe for democracy." In the tide of the President's rolling prose the phrase might have passed without accent had not Senator John Sharp Williams of Mississippi, who had been listening intently and in silence, "instantly seized the full and immense meaning of it. Alone he began to applaud, and he did it gravely and emphatically" until one after another took it up and the whole Chamber burst into another uproar. It died again, and President Wilson passed on at last to his peroration:

> It is a distressing and oppressive duty, Gentlemen of the Congress, which I have performed in thus addressing you. There are, it may be, many months of fiery trial and sacrifice ahead of us. It is a fearful thing to lead this great peaceful people . . . into the most terrible and disastrous of all wars. . . . But the right is more precious than peace, and we shall fight for the things which we have always carried nearest our hearts—for democracy, for the right of those who submit to authority to have a voice in their own governments, for the rights and liberties of small nations, for a universal dominion of right by such a concert of free peoples as shall bring peace and safety to all nations and make the world itself at last free. To such a task we can dedicate our lives and our fortunes . . . with the pride of those who know that the day has come when America is privileged to spend her blood . . . for the principles that gave her birth and happiness and the peace which she has treasured. God helping her, she can do no other.

It had taken him just thirty-six minutes. As the last words fell, another hurricane of cheering swept the Chamber. Secretary Redfield was near Jusserand; his hand met that of the Ambassador and "grasped it firmly. I shall not forget the expression of his eyes." Everyone was on their feet again, shouting, clapping, waving the American flags they had brought or tearing the minature emblems from their lapels to wave them too. All but one:

> Senator Robert Marion La Follette, however, stood motionless with his arms folded tight and high on his chest, so that nobody could have an excuse for mistaking his attitude; and there he stood, chewing gum with a sardonic smile.

The President walked quickly from the desk. People crowded around him as he went with their congratulations. Senator Henry Cabot Lodge, fresh from that magnificent appeal for a new world order of peace and international responsibility, "shook his hand warmly and said: 'Mr. President, you have expressed in the loftiest manner possible the sentiments of the American people.'" Mr. Houston, an almost equally determined war hawk, poured out his congratulations. The President "smiled, thanked me and passed on." Behind him, within five minutes after he had left the desk, the House was being called to order to adopt a rule making possible the swift passage of the great war appropriations bills. In the Senate, Mr. Stone was summoning the Foreign Relations Committee for 10 o'clock next day to draft the declaration of war. "I am against a declaration of war," said the Senator, who had fought against it so long, "but when it is declared I will be a war eagle screaming as loud as the rest. Blood is thicker than water." By that time the President was out of the crowd and glare, on the way back to the White House through the darkness and the rain.

Beyond the radius of that fierce mass hysteria at the Capitol it did not seem, for some reason, so exciting. Perhaps the nation had discounted it all too long; perhaps the statesmen had been more deeply moved by mere dramatic suggestion than they quite realized themselves. In New York the city editors found it hard to work up anything worthy of the day. The streets were calm, except at Carnegie Hall, where there had been a pacifist meeting. Someone remembered that next day would be the eightieth birthday of Mr. John Burroughs, the celebrated naturalist; and a reporter routed out the old man by long distance telephone. He was found to be "awaiting patiently the entrance of the United States into war. . . . He particularly wished to live to see the day when militarism was crushed." Before the bulletin boards in Herald Square only some hundred loungers could be counted; and they appeared to receive the news without enthusiasm. In the more elegant atmosphere of the Metropolitan Opera House, however, there was a response more fitting to the occasion, though even there it required a little stimulation. Ambassador Gerard, who was in the audience—the piece was De Koven's "The Canterbury Pilgrims"—heard the extras being shouted between the acts. He was in the act of telephoning Mr. Swope of the *World* for confirmation of the news, when one of the directors of the opera company passed. Mr. Gerard told him what had happened and demanded that he do something—"order the news read from the stage, for example, and The Star-Spangled Banner played." The reply was disappointing. "No," the director said, "the opera company is neutral." Shocked, the former Ambassador hurried back to his box, "and stepping to the front, called on the house to cheer President Wilson. There was, for a moment, surprise at such unconventional action, but the whole house soon broke into cheers, "and as the orchestra responded then with The Star-Spangled Banner on its own account, "conventionalism was dead." It ended in a queer climax. When the last act curtain rose upon the dying cheers, they could see that Margarete Ober, the German singer playing the Wife of Bath, was nervous; and the action had progressed for only a moment or two when she collapsed in a dead faint and had to be carried from the stage. The opera went on without her.

But in the White House, as on the streets, the feeling was subdued. For a time they talked it all over again in the Oval Room, "as families are prone to do after some eventful occasion"—the President, Mrs. Wilson, Margaret Wilson and Colonel House. The Colonel told him how great was the position he had taken; Mazzini, the Colonel thought, was the one modern statesman who could approach the grandeur of these policies. Mr. Wilson protested, citing Webster, Lincoln, Gladstone; but the Colonel begged to differ. Apparently, Mr. Wilson let go, and they broke up. "I could see the President was relieved that the tension was over and the die was cast. I knew this would happen." But if one dares to trust Mr. Tumulty's memory, there was another scene in the White House that night, when the secretary talked alone with his chief in the Cabinet room. The applause from the sidewalk crowds as he had driven to the Capitol returned to the President's ears. "My message today," Tumulty remembers his saying, "was a message of death for our young men. How strange it seems to applaud that." And afterward, in the secretary's account, the President broke down and wept, with his head on the Cabinet table.

⚜

Once in the war, the United States set to work to makes its presence felt. The Germans who had calculated that with the collapse of Russia they would be able to turn their eastern armies westward and win the war did so in the expectation that the Americans would be unable to interfere decisively. It proved a gross miscalculation. Without the world quite realizing it, there had grown up in the western world a giant industrial power, one that would justify the description of "arsenal of democracy." The American intervention also came at a critical moment in the fortunes of the western powers. A war-weary France, its armies almost bled dry at Verdun, and mutiny running rampant in ten of its divisions, almost despaired of victory. A combined Austrian-German offensive smashed the Italian army in mid-autumn of 1917 at Caporetto; to save the Italian army from total collapse, French and British reinforcements were sent into Italy to bolster their quaking ally. With the Russian surrender at Brest-Litovsk in early spring, the Germans smelled the sweet scent of victory.

Between March and July of 1918, the German armies launched five great offensives, their target the breaking of the Western Front, the annihilation of the French and British forces, and the capture of Paris. But even as the first German assault along the Somme was launched on March 21, more than 300,000 American soldiers were in France; seven months later as the war drew to its close, more than 2,000,000 Yanks had reached the front. In a nationwide draft, an army had been mobilized and trained, while at the same time both industry and agriculture were put on a round-the-clock operation.

The American genius for organization revealed itself in the establishment of a huge storage depot near Bordeaux, the shipment of whole trains to man French railroads, and the building of a vast gasoline tank farm and refrigerating plant in central France that required 20,000 men for its operation. The bulk of the munitions used until almost the end of the war was obtained from the French and the British. To an extent, this form of equipment resulted from the use of doughboys to plug gaps in Allied lines and to relieve exhausted French divisions, but despite the dispersion of these forces, the American commander John Pershing insisted on maintaining his army's identity. The presence of fresh, dynamic American forces sent sagging Allied morale soaring and German morale plummeting. The war of exhaustion that had threatened to overtake the British and French took its toll instead from the Germans who lost heart. Even as they did so, their allies in Central Europe and the Balkans gave up the fight, and even as the western allies prepared for a final year of war, Berlin sued for an armistice. The war had ended, the task of making a durable peace remained, one which would convert into reality Wilson's plea for "a peace without victory."

Samuel Flagg Bemis (1891–   ), long a Professor at Yale University, is beyond a doubt the grand old man of diplomatic history. His study of Jay's Treaty *(1923) and* Pinckney's Treaty *(1926) are definitive on those subjects. His two volume biography of* John Quincy Adams *(1949-1956) is likely to remain not only standard but is also a monument to the art of biography. Few historians have achieved quite the eminence in a single field as he has; it is a tribute to the thoroughness of his research and the judiciousness of his scholarship.*

A DIPLOMATIC HISTORY OF THE UNITED STATES

by Samuel Flagg Bemis

The United States in 1917 went over to the Allied cause unconditionally, wholeheartedly, overwhelmingly.

It is the unconditional feature of that decisive intervention which most concerns the historian of American diplomacy.

That the intervention was decisive we are told by British and French historians. They say that it marked the turning-point of the war. They declare that, without this intervention, which followed the collapse of Russia, Germany would have won the war. We may believe this.

This is not the place to say much about military participation in the last eighteen months of the World War: the immediate joining of the American and British fleets; the bridling of the submarine with mine barrages and destroyer convoys; the industrial and financial mobilization of the nation; the conscription and training, behind the protection of secure sea power, of a civilian army of 4,000,000 men; the transport of 2,000,000 American troops to transfuse the bleeding man power of France and the British Empire; the collapse of the Central Powers in the autumn of 1918 before these freshened odds. It is rather the diplomatic history of the United States during this most terrible of wars which concerns us here: (1) the relations with the nations associated in the war against Germany and Austria-Hungary, (2) the evolution of the American peace program, (3) the pre-Armistice negotiations, (4) the negotiation of peace at Paris, (5) the rejection by the United States Senate of the League of Nations and with it of the Treaty of Versailles, (6) the separate peace with the enemy, (7) the aftermath issues of neutral rights and the freedom of the seas.

The declaration of war against Germany and against Austria-Hungary did not in itself signalize departure from the traditional policy of the Fathers, from the Farewell Address and the Monroe Doctrine. The United States was careful to avoid any alliance with the partners in war. President Wilson studiously referred to them as "associates." He spoke of the "Allied and Associated Powers." Other associates rather than allies, like the United States, were, of course, those Latin-American nations which followed the call of the United States to declare war against Germany, namely: Brazil, Cuba, Costa Rica, Guatemala, Haiti, Honduras, Nicaragua, and Panama. In the Far East, another associate, China, declared war in order to be able to defend her interests at the peace negotiations. Fighting by the side of the Allies, the United States studiously refrained from those infringements on neutral rights against which it had complained to Great Britain and to Germany. It is true that the United States helped to lay the barrage of mines across the northern entrance to the North Sea, thus aiding to shut German submarines out of the Atlantic, but we must remember that the caveat (rather than protest) filed against Great Britain on mined war zones in February, 1917, had acknowledged that this subject was "unsettled" in international law. The United States cooperated with the Allied blockade not by the use of naval force but rather by domestic embargoes, allocation of bunker fuel, and the wide extension of contraband, without distinction of conditional contraband. There were no naval captures of neutral ships and cargoes, no prize court decisions.

The first question to come up between the Allies and the United States concerning the conduct of the war was the command of the American troops at the front. In their desperate need for man power to stem the final offensive of the Germans on the western front the British and French requested that American troops, as they arrived, be brigaded into the British armies. There was of course something reasonable to be said for this: time seemed of the essence in the general strategical situation, with Russia now out of the war and Germany preparing for a knock-out offensive before an American army could appear in force; the British commanders had more experience; and the English language would make the command easily possible. Insuperable and highly proper reasons forbade the use of American troops to fill the British ranks. National pride alone made it impossible—there were the old historical issues dating back to before impressment; further, to have accepted a British command would have destroyed the national identity of the American army and have greatly diminished American influence in the making of the final peace. So President Wilson insisted that, except for a few diversions in emergencies, the troops of the United States moved to the front as an army under the command of an American General, subject later, of course, like the British armies and those of the Allies, to the Generalissimo of the Allied and Associated forces, Marshal Foch. For this unity of command, indispensable to victory, the United States was an unswerving advocate.

It would have been quite possible, and honorable, for the United States to have restricted itself to the maritime sphere, to defending the freedom of the seas, the violation of which had brought the Republic into the war. Toward the fighting on the continent of Europe it could have remained in only a state of war, like Brazil and Cuba, without sending an army to Europe or raising from its citizens huge loans for support of the Allies. At least this full endeavor could have been withheld until there was some sort of agreement upon the terms of a victorious peace which would be won now only by full American co-operation. That an explicit understanding of such a nature was not made a prerequisite by the Government of the United States showed diplomatic ineptitude. It meant that the United States gave without stint of its treasure and its manhood, of its power and its soul, with no guaranty that its ideals or its interests would be written into the peace of victory. That the Allies were prepared to expect some such demand as a reasonable condition of full American participation is indicated by the British mission led by Arthur Balfour which came to Washington in April, 1917, and the French mission which immediately followed. Balfour had full details about the secret treaties which the European Allies had made among themselves marking out the share which each was to have in the final victory.

These treaties were generally unknown in the United States when it entered the war although American diplomatic advisers like Colonel House knew the general nature of the contents of at least the European ones—they were published in the press in November—and had apprised the President; and Secretary of State Lansing knew at least of the Anglo-Japanese accord of 1915 with regard to the conquered German islands in the Pacific. These treaties, which molded the final peace, were not so bad as some publicists have painted them. It is instructive to note that where they were followed there was no sore point left in the subsequent peace settlement. Students of the war have excoriated the treaties as proof of the naked imperialistic designs of the Allies as contrasted with the hypocrisy of their professions of fighting for the defense of democracy and the rights of small nations. That the treaties were tinctured with imperialism and selfishness is without question; but many commentators do not notice the obvious fact that these treaties were not the cause of the European War; they were negotiated *after* the war had already commenced. This holds true at least for the Allied powers which went to war in 1914. No spoils treaty antedated the war. In the cases of Italy and Roumania, the secret treaties by which they entered the conflict represented what the Allies had to promise to them in advance in order to bring them over.

There were five of these treaties or understandings, or groups of such, made to solidify the enthusiasm of the original Allies and to bring new ones into the circle.

(1) Russia secured her claims by a treaty with Great Britain and France made in March, 1915, at the beginning of the Allied attack on the Dardanelles. By this the two western Allies agreed that Russia might annex Constantinople and the Asiatic shore of the Bosporus and the Dardanelles, leaving free transit of the straits for the merchant ships of all nations. Russia on her part agreed to the separation of the Caliphate from Turkey and to sharing with France and Great Britain an influence over other portions of the Turkish Empire, reserving to England particular influence in the neighborhood of the Suez Canal and the Gulf of Persia—the British buffer of influence in Persia also was to be extended. These partitions of the Turkish Empire were marked out with more precision—conformable to the later mandates to France and Great Britain—in supplementary understandings (the Sykes-Picot agreement of May 16, 1916, and the agreement at St. Jean de Maurienne, April 17, 1917), reserving for Italy (in conformance with the Treaty of London) a share in the region of Adalia (which the entrance of Greece into the war later stopped her from taking, after the European peace). Thus did the Allies imperturbably dispose of the territory of Germany's Turkish ally, that vigorous "sick man of Europe" near whose bedside the European powers for a century had been waiting either so anxiously or so eagerly.

(2) Italy's claim to expansion had been recognized in principle by the Treaty of London (April 26, 1915) which brought, or bought, that nation into the war. The Central Powers had been willing to promise a redemption of Italy's irredentist population at the end of the war, but not to deliver immediate occupation of the territory concerned. Ardent to weaken their enemy, the Allies promised the irredentist territory with strategical control of the Adriatic and of the Alpine passage into Austria, specifying a line which delivered over to Italy a Slavic and an Austrian *irredentum* at the head of the Adriatic and on its eastern shores.

Italy was also to have the strategic part of Albania, unchallenged government of the Dodecanese Islands in the Eastern Mediterranean, and a share in the partition of the Turkish Empire.

(3) Roumania was in a most favorable position for bargaining: the Central Powers offered her the irredentist province of Bessarabia, Russian; but the Entente Allies offered her the larger and more populous irredentist part of Hungarian Transylvania and even the Banat of Temesvar, where there was a numerous Serb population. After much wavering Roumania accepted the Allies' offer (Treaty of Bucharest, August 8, 1916), and entered on their side, only to be speedily crushed and occupied during the remainder of the war by German, Austro-Hungarian, and Bulgarian troops. Her separate treaty of peace in 1918 abrogated the obligations of the Allies.

(4) In the Far East, Japan and Great Britain by mutual understanding had divided up the conquered German islands in the Pacific: at the outset of the war British forces occupied those islands south of the Equator; Japan

took over those north of that line. When it became apparent that the United States might enter the war Japan reached an understanding (February–March, 1917) with Great Britain, France, Italy and Russia, sanctioning her claim to the transfer of all German rights in the Chinese province of Shantung, and, of course, to the islands north of the Equator.

(5) Finally there was the arrangement between France and Russia, also made (March 11, 1917) after the United States had broken relations with Germany, just on the eve of the first Russian Revolution. Each gave the other a free hand in arranging its frontier on the side of Germany—this meant at least Alsace-Lorraine for France and the Polish provinces for Russia.

Such were the famous secret agreements which Arthur Balfour presumably had in his portfolio, with their boundaries drawn on a large map, when he hurried to Washington in April, 1917, to secure full American participation in the war on the continent of Europe. To his surprise he found the United States enthusiastic for winning the war first and talking peace only afterward. Congress was appropriating (April 24, 1917) $7,000,000,000, of which $3,000,000,000 was to be loaned to Allied governments, the first great credit of a total which rapidly amounted to $7,296,000,000 before the armistice of November 11, 1918, and $2,170,200,000 more after it.

The President felt it would be a pity to let Balfour go home without a thorough discussion of the peace terms of the Allies. Colonel House thought it would be inadvisable at that time to have a general discussion with *all* the Allies: "If the Allies begin to discuss terms among themselves," he wrote to the President, "they will soon hate one another worse than they do Germany and a situation will arise similar to that in the Balkan States after the Turkish War. It seems to me that the only thing to be considered at present is how to beat Germany in the quickest way." Balfour easily concurred in House's sentiments. During the Balfour mission peace terms were nevertheless canvassed in long conferences. To Colonel House Balfour showed his map with the territorial lines of the secret treaties drawn on it. With the President and House, he went over the same ground. Russia had now collapsed, and the British spokesman did not defend her claims in Washington: Constantinople might be a free city, and Poland a resurrected state, though it would be a problem to find an outlet for that state to the sea. Roumania could have Bessarabia (Russian). As to the surviving Allies, the British Secretary insisted on keeping the bargains made with them. There appears to have been no mention of the freedom of the seas.

Upon House's request, Balfour promised to furnish copies of the secret treaties and agreements, but he returned to London without any new American demands. With the sequent French, Belgian and Italian missions which had hurried to the United States, there was no discussion of peace terms, so far as we know.

President Wilson had agreed with his confidential adviser that it would not be well to disturb Allied unity before the enemy with any discussion of peace terms. He seems to have felt that his defense of immutable prin-ciples, together with American military and financial power, would be so unchallengeable at the final peace conference that he could brush aside these secret agreements by the force of his prestige and that of his country. In this he was sadly mistaken. Having neglected the opportunity presented by the Balfour mission, at a time when it would have been a fatal mistake for the Allies to have cooled the military ardor of America, the President's crystallizing American peace terms began to conform more and more to the obligations to each other of the surviving Allies—objectives which themselves were of no mean service to the principle of nationality—and more and more he was forced to fall back on the unexceptionable principle of a League of Nations as the protected refuge for his peace policy and the sanctuary of his hopes for the future.

There was no longer any doubt that the United States would use all of its resources to help win the war. The Allies had found an ideal Associate, better than a real ally who would have extracted an equivalent for his sacri-fices. A national conscription act passed Congress, May 18, 1917. A few weeks later the President promised Arthur Balfour a million and a half American troops on the western front by the end of 1918. The diplomats settled down now to the difficult task of gearing American resources to the military requirements of the Allies. In August the President rejected as impossible the Pope's proposal to the belligerents for a peace without victory on the basis of mutual restoration, disarmament, organization for future arbitration, indemnity for civilian damages, general condonement, "com-munity" of the seas, with a negotiated settlement of territorial questions like Alsace-Lorraine and the Trentino. These would have been ideal Wil-sonian terms the previous January.

We recall again that during the American Revolution, following the Declaration of Independence and the signature of the French alliance, the United States refused the British terms of home-rule within the Empire, terms with which they would have been so content as colonies of Britain before July 4, 1776. So now in 1917 President Wilson, launched on the war without stint or condition, insisted on a peace with victory where six months previously he had declared there could be no peace with victory.

A peace of victory, would it be really possible? The military situation had steadily blackened. The near collapse of Italy after the Austrian vic-tory of Caporetto, in the autumn of 1917, eased the Central Powers on that flank. American troops could not appear in force before the summer of 1918. The collapse of Russia was made complete and definitive by the Bolshevik Revolution of November, 1917. Straightway the Russian revolu-tionists began the negotiation of a separate peace (signed at Brest-Litovsk, March 3, 1918) which assured the Central Powers a free hand in regulating and expanding their eastern frontiers for future penetration beyond, and complete liberty to concentrate their whole war efforts on the western front of battle. The Bolsheviki in December, 1917, tore open the archives of the Czar and published to the world the secret treaties by which the Allies after the beginning of the war had pre-arranged a territorial settlement of Europe and the Near East. It was an appeal to the laboring masses of the Allied countries to repudiate a war for what the revolutionists now branded as imperialistic ambitions hitherto masked by moral professions. In France mutiny was brewing among the weary patriotic troops. In Flanders the German high staff, nervous at popular restiveness, and disappointed by the Allies' checking of the submarine campaign, were preparing for a last mighty offensive to break through into France before their man power should give out in face of the American reinforcement.

It was in this black winter of the war that the Allies looked desperately for some moral impetus to their cause which would hold their peoples fighting together against complete military disaster. It was then that President Wilson made his notable pronouncement to the Congress (January 8, 1918) of Fourteen Points for a peace acceptable to the United States. The Fourteen Points were formulated by the President and Colonel House, after the latter had become convinced that the President must take a hand himself in a liberal crystallization of Allied war aims, if the Russians were to be kept in the war, and the morale shoved up of the Allied peoples. House had studied carefully the previous expressions of the Allies' terms of peace, as they had been conveyed to him in his contact with Sir Edward Grey and Arthur Balfour, and as they had been proclaimed by Great Britain and France in January, 1917. If we bear in mind the new Russian situation, the Fourteen Points did not conflict seriously with the secret treaties which Balfour had discussed in the White House. They proposed if possible to remake Europe along boundaries of nationality which perhaps would break up the Austro-Hungarian Empire and destroy the military strength of the Central Powers. The American emphasis came in a demand for the freedom of the seas and insistence on a League of Nations to organize peace after the war with a general guaranty thereafter of political independence and territorial integrity to great and small states alike. The authors of the Fourteen Points carefully phrased them so as to be useful under any of the three following conditions: (1) complete victory, (2) a stalemate war and a peace of compromise, (3) defeat. Witness the use of the words *must* and *should* which we have italicized:

The program of the world's peace, therefore, is our program, and that program, the only possible program, as we see it, is this:

1. Open covenants of peace, openly arrived at, after which there shall be no private international understandings of any kind, but diplomacy shall proceed always frankly and in the public view.

2. Absolute freedom of navigation upon the seas, outside territorial waters, alike in peace and in war, except as the seas may be closed in whole or in part by international action for the enforcement of international covenants.

3. The removal, so far as possible, of all economic barriers and the establishment of an equality of trade conditions among all the nations consenting to the peace and associating themselves for its maintenance.

4. Adequate guarantees given and taken that national armaments will be reduced to the lowest point consistent with domestic safety.

5. A free, open-minded, and absolutely impartial adjustment of all colonial claims, based upon a strict observance of the principle that in determining all such questions of sovereignty the interests of the populations concerned *must* have equal weight with the equitable claims of the government whose title is to be determined.

6. The evacuation of all Russian territory and such a settlement of all questions affecting Russia as will secure the best and freest cooperation of the other nations of the world in obtaining for her an unhampered and unembarrassed opportunity for the independent determination of her own political development and national policy and assure her of a sincere welcome into the society of free nations under institutions of her own choosing; and, more than a welcome, assistance also of every kind that she may need and may herself desire. The treatment accorded Russia by her sister nations in the months to come will be the acid test of their good will, of their comprehension of her needs as distinguished from their own interests, and of their intelligent and unselfish sympathy.

7. Belgium, the whole world will agree, *must* be evacuated and restored, without any attempt to limit the sovereignty which she enjoys in common with all other free nations. No other single act will serve as this will serve to restore confidence among the nations in the laws which they have themselves set and determined for the government of their relations with one another. Without this healing act the whole structure and validity of international law is forever impaired.

8. All French territory *should* be freed and the invaded portions restored, and the wrong done to France by Prussia in 1871 in the matter of Alsace-Lorraine, which has unsettled the peace of the world for nearly fifty years, *should* be righted, in order that peace may once more be made secure in the interest of all.

9. A readjustment of the frontiers of Italy *should* be effected along clearly recognizable lines of nationality.

10. The peoples of Austria-Hungary, whose place among the nations we wish to see safeguarded and assured, *should* be accorded the freest opportunity of autonomous development.

11. Rumania, Serbia, and Montenegro *should* be evacuated; occupied territories restored; Serbia accorded free and secure access to the sea; and the relations of the several Balkan states to one another determined by friendly counsel along historically established lines of allegiance and nationality; and international guarantees of the political and economic independence and territorial integrity of the several Balkan states *should* be entered into.

12. The Turkish portions of the present Ottoman Empire *should* be assured a secure sovereignty, but the other nationalities which are now under Turkish rule *should* be assured an undoubted security of life and an absolutely unmolested opportunity of autonomous development, and the Dardanelles *should* be permanently opened as a free passage to the ships and commerce of all nations under international guarantees.

13. An independent Polish state *should* be erected, which *should* include the territories inhabited by indisputably Polish populations, which *should* be assured a free and secure access to the sea, and whose political and economic independence and territorial integrity *should* be guaranteed by international covenant.

14. A general association of nations *must* be formed under specific covenants for the purpose of affording mutual guarantees of political independence and territorial integrity to great and small states alike.

The President and Colonel House studiously went over the whole document after they had first drafted it, qualifying it with their *musts* and *shoulds*.

The Fourteen Points, it proved, were to be interpreted under conditions of complete victory and solely by the Allied and Associated Powers, with the defeated enemy reaching desperately to the Wilsonian principles in the hope to save at least something. In these circumstances it was easy for the victors to interpret *should* to mean *must*.

The final German offensive in the west failed in July, 1918. The Turkish, Bulgarian and Austrian allies began to crack all along their respective fronts and at home. With the victory now surely in sight, the Allies themselves were reeling with exhaustion. During 1918 there took place a series of long-distance exchanges of peace views in the shape of pronouncements from the rostrums of the different governments. These varied in their force according to the military situation. At no time were the Allies driven to accepting a "peace by compromise and negotiation" which the Central Powers offered. Meanwhile President Wilson in public addresses had piled the Fourteen Points with further general principles of durable peace which included: the destruction or at least reduction of arbitrary power capable of upsetting the peace of the world, satisfaction of "well-defined national aspirations," prohibition of especial leagues or embargoes within the proposed League of Nations, no secret treaties, self-determination for peoples and territories whose sovereignty was in question, and, finally, "impartial justice."

The end of the war suddenly appeared when Bulgaria signed an armistice of military surrender and occupation, September 29, 1918. Already Austria-Hungary (September 16, 1918) had proposed to the enemy a discussion of peace by all belligerents. Facing complete collapse, and in panic at the furious and general advance of the Allies and Associates all along the western front, General Ludendorff and the Field Marshal von Hindenburg, the German Chief of Staff, urgently advised the Government to sue for peace and to try to salvage something by an appeal to the Wilsonian principles. On October 6, Germany, and on October 7, Austria-Hungary, transmitted to the United States (instead of to the Allies) a request for an armistice. With victorious troops exultantly pushing through on all fronts the President made the most of his advantage, and kept control of the preliminary moves for peace. He used in a masterly way the strategy of delay. In a correspondence with Germany he insisted that he must know that he was treating with a government that really had the support of the people; to Austria he replied that the recent recognition of the belligerency of Czechoslovakia by the United States had modified Point X, which stressed "autonomy" for the peoples of Austria-Hungary: now it was the Czechoslovaks themselves, and also the Jugoslavs, who must themselves judge of their own rights and destiny.

Before the discussion with the United States could be completed the crumbling and vanishing Austro-Hungarian Empire signed (November 3, 1918) an armistice with the Italians, technically with the Allied and Associated Powers. The Wilsonian principles, therefore, were not made a certain condition of peace in the Austro-Hungarian surrender. The historic but volatile empire had suddenly exploded before it could securely seize hold of them. Turkey had accepted a controlling British armistice, October 31, 1918, before its appeal to Wilsonianism could be heard and transmitted to the Allies.

A frantic constitutional reformation of the German Government did not prevent the proclamation of a socialist republic in Berlin, but it induced President Wilson at least to transmit to the triumphing Allies the German request for an armistice, making it first well understood to Germany that it must be an armistice of complete surrender. The Kaiser abdicated (November 9, 1918), fleeing ignominiously to Holland. The Central Powers, who had almost grasped the fringe of victory's robes in the spring of 1918, were now at the mercy of their enemies.

Germany had appealed to the United States for peace on the basis of President Wilson's pronouncements, particularly the Fourteen Points. The President had leisurely consented to transmit the appeal to the Allies. He had left it unreservedly to the commanding generals in the field, notably to Marshal Foch, the Generalissimo of the Allied and Associated armies, whether the military situation justified an armistice. Foch replied yes, if Germany agreed to an effectual disarmament he was ready to sign. In view of obstinate public ignorance it is necessary to emphasize what British and French historians and statesmen have repeatedly pointed out; that President Wilson did not interfere with the command in the field and force them to agree to an armistice without further invasion and the complete pulverization of Germany. It was Marshal Foch who dictated the military terms of the armistice and was completely content with it, as were the other commanders, except Pershing. The French General said: "One makes war only to get results." In the military and naval surrender of Germany and her allies the results would be obtained, so far as they could be had by war.

It was for the Allies to decide among themselves what political conditions they would attach to the military surrender. Could they all agree to the Fourteen Points and later pronouncements of President Wilson as the fundamental basis of peace, to be interpreted to suit themselves in the condition of complete victory, then to be dictated to Germany? Were there any other conditions to attach to the Fourteen Points before accepting a German surrender?

In the important pre-Armistice negotiations between the United States and the Allies, conducted by Colonel House as the personal representative of the President, Great Britain reserved her interpretation of Point 2, the freedom of the seas, the historic American principle. Prime Minister Lloyd George said he could not give up control of a means which had enabled the Allies to win the war, notably by transporting American troops to

France. Premier Clemenceau of France agreed to this; and on his part insisted on specifying broadly for "reparation for damages." He insisted that there must be compensation by Germany, "for all damages done to the civilian population of the Allies and their property by the aggression of Germany by land, by sea and from the air." House, and Wilson behind him, contented themselves with a general understanding that Point 2 might be made the subject of future discussion with the Allies. With these, two essential modifications, the significant emasculation of the freedom of the seas, and the sweeping provision for reparation, the Fourteen Points and the subsequent pronouncements of the President became by the terms of the Armistice of November 11, 1918, the agreed basis of the peace to be negotiated between the Allied and Associated Powers and Germany.

The negotiation of the Armistice had taken place while the American congressional elections of 1918 were approaching. Republicans and Democrats during the war had put away their political opposition in common patriotic endeavor. It had been the Republican spokesmen who had been more aggressive in demands on Germany than the Administration, more forward for war. During the war they had at least equaled their old political adversaries in their demand for the utmost national exertions. Including the two ex-Presidents, Roosevelt and Taft, they had demanded, during the autumnal political campaign, the election in November, 1918, of a Republican Congress to push through the war and control a peace of unconditional surrender by the enemy. Roosevelt in particular contemned the Fourteen Points as "soft."

President Wilson feared that if the Republicans should secure control of Congress they would sweep away his program for peace. He was nervous about reports of large sums of money being spent by his political opponents to carry the elections, notably in Michigan. A friend asked him, in a long conversation in the White House (September 13, 1918), what he would do in case he should lose the elections. Would he resign the Presidency, following his well-known convictions about responsible government? It was recalled to him that he had planned to resign that high office in case Mr. Hughes, the Republican candidate for the Presidency, had been elected in November, 1916, thus allowing the President-elect to come into office immediately without waiting until March 4. "I cannot do it," Woodrow Wilson now said, "on account of the world-wide situation, in which American influence is very important and may be decisive. It happens to be a case where, even if defeated by the people, I shall have to try to obtain the objects for which we went to war."

It was this fear which led the President into what has been generally regarded as a strategical misstep. But for this mistake he might have kept his position as the leader of a politically undivided nation. He could have appealed to the voters to return senators and representatives, of whatever party, who would support him in finishing the war and settling the peace. With the end of the war in sight, he issued a public appeal for the election of a Democratic majority in both houses of Congress in order that he might be wholly unhampered in the approaching negotiations. It is true that

President McKinley issued a similar call, successfully, in 1898. But it was unnecessary for President Wilson and unwise. Some of his political advisers counseled against it. The appeal invoked a partisan issue where previously there had been little for the public to discern between the two parties united in war. The country was normally Republican—Wilson had come to power and stayed in power only because of the division of his Republican opponents; now, with the war over, they united to meet his challenge.

The elections resulted in a clear Republican majority for the new Senate (and House too) which would meet after March 4, 1919, to consider the treaties of peace. Ex-President Roosevelt, presuming to speak for a reunited and victorious Republican Party, declared to the world after the election: "Our allies and our enemies, and Mr. Wilson himself, should all understand that Mr. Wilson has no authority whatever to speak for the American people at this time. His leadership has just been emphatically repudiated by them. . . ."

The world cried for peace. The overturn of three great empires, Germany, Austria-Hungary, and Russia, and their satellites, displayed throughout the eastern half of Europe a panorama of confusion, anarchy and chaos. The question of the hour was how to shape the machinery of procedure directly, and efficaciously, to dictate peace quickly on the terms of the Allied and Associated Powers, terms couched as yet in the very general Wilsonian principles. France had suggested to the United States, in a memorandum to Washington of November 29, 1918, that the five great victors (the United States, Great Britain, France, Italy, Japan) should sweep the table clear of all previous special agreements arrived at by some of the Allies only, and straightway agree among themselves on the principal bases of peace. The small belligerents, the neutral states, and the new states in formation could be called in for consultation as their special interests were touched on one by one. In subsequent conferences, after a preliminary peace had been dictated, garnished with the invocation of moral principles, all the nations could meet in a congress to work out the permanent organization of world peace in a League of Nations. Colonel House and Secretary Lansing were inclined to favor some such procedure. President Wilson did not even answer the French proposal. He had his mind first on a League of Nations. He was determined that it should be interwoven with the peace treaties, and that he himself would take the American delegation to Paris to make sure that this was done; otherwise the peoples of the embattled nations might be overreached by the more sophisticated spokesmen of their governments. He did not realize that actually the peoples could be more uncompromising than their spokesmen.

If repudiated by the electorate of his own homeland, it was at the apogee of his prestige in the world that Woodrow Wilson surveyed the European shore from the bridge of the *George Washington*. He arrived in Europe as a true friend of mankind, closer to the principles of Christian charity and justice than any statesman in history. The new great ideal seemed really possible. If only he could bring Europe to agree to a peace of justice resting on the foundations of a league of democratic nations which would execute and regulate the treaties of peace, he was convinced that the opposition of Congress at home would have to yield to the force of public opinion. By the gospel of his principles he would overbear the Republican politicians in the Senate, as abroad he expected to sweep aside whatever obstacles the Allies' secret treaties presented to the application of his Fourteen Points.

The American Peace Commission consisted of executive agents appointed without the advice and consent of the Senate, a custom which had been engrafted by practice to the American constitutional system by virtue of the President's control over diplomatic negotiations. In the language of the treaties which he later signed, the President was "acting in his own name and by his own proper authority." Very unwisely he did not include in the Commission, according to traditional practice, representatives from both parties in that Senate which would be called upon to ratify his treaties. He was also criticized, even by his own Secretary of State, for jeopardizing his dominant position in the world by descending into a conference with the foreign statesmen in Europe. One of the real advantages of the American diplomatic system has been the reserve power which the President, back home across the ocean, has had to stiffen the demands of his plenipotentiaries in the give and take of negotiation; and back of this, and despite the shocking abuse of it by party politics, lies the still greater reserve power of the Senate in the right to advise and consent, by a two-thirds majority, to the ratification of any treaty. These advantages the President, in his convictions, threw away by going to Paris at the head of a personal executive delegation. The other members were: Secretary of State Robert Lansing; Colonel Edward M. House, the President's constant political mentor; General Tasker H. Bliss; and Mr. Henry White, veteran career diplomatist of pale Republican allegiance, who had never made any public statement hostile to the President. The latter was the only Republican on the Commission, and through him Senator Lodge, leader of the Republican Senate and chairman of the Committee on Foreign Relations, unsuccessfully tried to speak to the Allies behind the back of the President.

A shipload of officials of the State Department, intelligence officers, specialists and secretaries accompanied the Commission. The "experts" had been recruited quietly from academic and other walks of life under the direction of Colonel House. Organized unostentatiously under the name of The Inquiry, after the immemorial habit of professors everywhere they had diligently assembled during the previous twelve months a mass of facts and information of a special nature for the advice of the diplomatists who were to discuss the intricate political, territorial and economic questions of several continents. These specialists played an important part in drafting the non-debatable articles of the peace treaties and in fortifying the plenipotentiaries in the diplomatic disputations.

At the Peace Conference at Paris, which opened January 12, 1919, met the plenipotentiaries of twenty-seven nations, enemies of Germany or of her allies, or nations, like five of the Latin-American states, who had severed relations with Germany. There had never been such a diplomatic gathering in history. Even the Congress of Vienna, once consecrated to the principle of Legitimacy as the Paris Conference was now consecrated to the principle of Nationality, could not approach its vast importance. It was the focus of seething national rivalries, resentments, despairs, ambitions, triumphs. President Wilson, it must be generally conceded, was the only statesman of the great powers who had no selfish national interest to serve, no particular necessitous war bargain to fulfill. Each of the other war-weary nations, except for those like the South American Republics which had been only nominally at war, had some special right or attachment to protect, some vital or profitable interest to secure. Among the actual fighting belligerents only Canada stood in the American relationship, but she had her responsibilities to the British Empire. How can we blame the plenipotentiaries for not having made a perfect peace? The marvel is that they agreed to any peace at all.

Able participants, conscious of the historic importance of the occasion, have pictured the highlights of the momentous gathering and its vivid personalities: Clemenceau, who presided, the dauntless Premier of France, acclaimed by his compatriots as the Father of Victory, seventy-eight years old, ancient, wrinkled, with his black skull cap, his gray-gloved and imperturbably folded hands, his fringe of white hair, a tiger statesman, frank exponent of the balance of power, fighting first and always to sustain his rescued France; Lloyd George, Prime Minister of Great Britain, crystal of perspicacity, indomitable dynamo of human energy, the parliamentary chiefs of the daughter Dominions arrayed at his side, a prime minister conspicuously serving the interests of the British Empire but a sincere striver for permanent reconciliation with the enemy—providing no fleet were left him; Orlando, the Italian Premier, virile, ardent, eloquent, little concerned with anything but the questions which affected Italy; Saionji, aged Elder Statesman of Japan, who as a lad had fought in feudal wars with bow and arrow—quiet, inscrutable, intervening only to protect Japan's winnings and to make sure her position as an equal among the Great Powers; finally, Woodrow Wilson, President of the United States of America now come to Europe, his eager academic countenance alive with success, the crusader for organized world peace.

It had been the President's first thought that all the Allied and Associated Nations, great and small, should meet together at the conference to interpret and apply the Fourteen Points. The small nations would welcome the League more unconditionally. For all the powers, big and little, to meet equally to dispose of issues, proved impossible. The Big Five (the United States, Great Britain, France, Italy, and Japan) therefore agreed that their chiefs of state and foreign ministers should meet in a Council of Ten, settle things, and prescribe articles to be ratified at the plenary sessions of the Conference. Smaller powers would be consulted as their interests were touched. In reality this Council of Ten was an *alter ego* of the Supreme Allied War Council which had developed in recent months to deal with inter-allied war interests. The Council of Ten appointed representative commissions, fifty-two in number, to study and report on particular questions. The meetings of the interpreters and experts proved too cumbersome, and too public, for frank and expeditious settlement of delicate subjects. Eventually a Council of Four: Wilson, Lloyd George, Clemenceau and Orlando, began to meet confidentially together with only one secretary—sometimes none—to keep their records. Here the main points of the peace were settled. These meetings were really continuing the method instituted at the time of the conferences on the impending armistice, when Clemenceau, Lloyd George, Orlando and House had settled essential points before they were treated in the Supreme War Council. Orlando quit the Four, when later in disposing of Austria-Hungary they would not award Fiume to Italy, so the last weeks of the conference were under the diplomatic tribunal of the Triumvirate of the chiefs of state of the United States, Great Britain and France. Thus it was the principal powers which arranged the peace, as France had proposed after the armistice; but it was only after Wilson had persuaded them to agree on the League; on the other hand there had been no sweeping aside of the secret treaties as France at first was willing to suggest.

The history of the Conference can be divided into three stages. The first extended from January 12 to February 14, 1919, on which date President Wilson left Paris for a visit to the United States to attend to his constitutional duties at the close of the Congress. During these weeks Wilson's insistence forged the first draft of the League of Nations, setting aside, until the great Covenant could be agreed upon, the final decision of the crucial territorial and political questions that were being examined by the commissions. The second stage was the interval of the President's absence, a month, during most of which Lloyd George was in England to attend to pressing duties at home, and Clemenceau lay stricken by the attack of an anarchist. It had been agreed that during the President's absence discussion should proceed on the territorial and political questions. During this period much important work was done by the special commissions appointed to consider territorial, economic and other technical questions. The third and final stage was from March 14, when the President returned to Paris, until the signature of the Treaty of Versailles. This was the period in which the Four, and then the Three, made the most important decisions on the great issues among the victorious Allies and Associates.

When Wilson returned to Paris on March 14 these paramount questions, though clarified by discussion, still remained to be settled. In the intimate discussions which followed among the Four, with Japan included where she so desired, it boiled down to this, from the American point of view: President Wilson, in his endeavor to mold the peace settlement to the matrix of the principles of his pronouncements as interpreted by the American delegation under his leadership, found himself obliged to make compromises with the special demands of the great Allies and their commitments to each other. He reached this point not only through the necessity of bargaining with the Allies but also after the conclusions of his own advisers that his principles were inapplicable in their entirety.

Great Britain and the Dominions wished to keep the colonies they had conquered from Germany in Africa and on the Pacific. A Dominion spokesman, General Smuts of South Africa, had proposed the system of mandates for the regions detached by the war from the Ottoman Empire, but he did not apply that also to Africa and the islands of the Pacific. Nobody on that side of the Atlantic thought of returning to Germany any of these conquests, despite Point 5, "a free, open-minded and absolutely impartial adjustment of colonial claims." This, in victory, was interpreted by all the victors to mean the claims only of the victors to the colonial spoil. To adjust the colonial question, Wilson acceded to the compromise suggestion of a graded mandate system for all the conquered colonies, as well as for Asia Minor and Mesopotamia. The appointed mandatory under the direction of the League of Nations, in each instance, proved to be either the conqueror, or the beneficiary of a secret treaty. Men have sneered at this as an hypocritical disguise of annexation; at least it was an appeal to an international control of backward peoples and colonial areas, stakes of imperialistic contention. The efficacy of the system would depend on the strength of the League of Nations.

◆❦ ❧◆

WHEN *the First World War began, Elihu B. Root, former Secretary of State, wrote the British political scientist Lord Bryce: "I can see already the dawning of a vague hope that [the war] means the beginning of a new era, the passing away of the old military dynasties, an immense extension of the principles of popular government, and the establishment of international relations on the basis of a peace which is something more than a military truce." When the war ended, such expectations soared, all the more so as one reactionary government after another fell. "An edifice of lies collapses, a system of dynastic power, which has been a plague to the world ever since it started on its infamous course," proclaimed one European newspaper, "has reached its term in world history." The expanding revolution in Russia reinforced the belief that the idea of the nation-state was on the verge of receivership. Americans who had originally greeted the Russian Revolution as a triumph of democracy still harbored the hope, despite the Bolshevik seizure of power, that out of the internal confusion that shook the old Russian Empire a liberal democracy would emerge. Woodrow Wilson nursed the belief that only the failure of the western Allies to abandon the narrow war aims of nation-state politics during the war had prevented the Russians from enlisting once and for all in the democratic camp. He meant at the peace negotiations to assure that a concert of world power would be created to guarantee the "political independence and territorial integrity to great and small states alike."*

It was with this objective in mind that Wilson went to Europe to represent the United States at the Paris peace negotiations. His certainty that he carried with him the backing of humanity was reinforced by the surging enthusiasm of hysterical mobs who thronged the capitals of Europe to give him a greeting without parallel in history. From a distance, many American reformers shared the belief of The New Republic *that "He has engaged the attention, and can depend upon the support, of the people." But cheers carry little weight in the chancellories of the world; when the hard business of negotiating the peace began, the men who shaped the peace were aware that in Europe, at least, the measure of the peace would be in the gains they could display to their home constituencies. Somehow men like Clemenceau of France, Lloyd-George of Great Britain, and Orlando of Italy had to make the enormous sacrifices of their people productive of concrete results. Underwriting their objective was the awesome toll of more than 5,000,000 dead: the leaders of Europe no less than Wilson were determined that their dead should not have died in vain. The tragedy of the treaties that made up the Peace of Paris (1919) was that the Europeans bargained territory to secure themselves against further attack, and to insure themselves doubly strove to confine the future power of Germany, while Wilson worked to create a community of interest that would loom larger in the future than the single state or nationality. It was a Progressive aim writ large, worthy of the most elevated imagination, but it missed its target because the home folk, as Wilson learned, were not yet prepared to embrace so large a vision.*

Nevertheless, the American President who went to Versailles had few illusions about the difficuties he would face there. Shortly after America entered the war, he had written Colonel House, "England and France *have* not the same views with regard to peace that we have *by any means." He added significantly, "When the war is over we can force them to our way of thinking, because by that time they will, among other things, be financially in our hands. . . ." He was no less certain that any peace negotiated would have to be final. "The Past and Present are in deadly grapple," he declared, "and the peoples of the world are being done to death between them." To end this haunting specter, "The settlement must be final. There can be no compromise. . . . No halfway decision is conceivable." Once at the peace table, Wilson learned what he had already been warned to expect, that his "League of Nations plans [were] not taken seriously by the heads of state in Europe." For a time he believed he could reach "the peoples of Europe over the heads of their rulers," but as the negotiations dragged out, he made endless concessions always with the view to save his League of Nations, but held fast to the proposition that his nation was "but one of the champions of mankind."*

It was a glorious view but once abroad Wilson found that yesterday's hope is today's disappointment. His triumphal journey through the Allied capitals proved ephemeral. "When he stepped from his lofty pedestal and wrangled with the representatives of other states upon equal terms," Colonel House subsequently concluded, "he became as common clay." His League upon which he set such store would be reluctantly accepted abroad and turned aside at home. The Senate refused to ratify the treaty, and Wilson set forth to convince his people that the time had come to embrace internationalism. "The isolation of the United States is at an end, not because we chose to go into the politics of the world, but because by the sheer genius of this people and the growth of our power we have become a determining factor in the history of mankind," he pleaded, "and after you have become a determining factor you cannot remain isolated, whether you want to or not." But it was a message that went unheeded. At Pueblo, Colorado, he concluded, "I proposed nothing whatever at the peace table at Paris that I had not sufficiently certain knowledge embodied the moral judgment of the citizens of the United States." That night, the fragile health of the man began to fail, and the argument was left to those who opposed him. The League was repudiated and so was Wilson. It would take a second war, more devastating than the first, to put Wilson's vision on the road to perhaps more than ephemeral fulfillment.

Thomas A. Bailey (1902-   ), Professor of Diplomatic History at Stanford University, has a lively style and a forthright presentation. One hardly is left in doubt on where he stands, nor is he timid in posing the controversial opinion. His peppery approach to diplomatic history translates the highflown propositions of the diplomat into the language of the layman.

WOODROW WILSON AND THE GREAT BETRAYAL

by Thomas A. Bailey

While Wilson was purging his Cabinet and laying down the law to the Allies, the senators were languidly moving toward a reconsideration of their previous action. Finally, on February 9, the Senate formally voted to reconsider the treaty, and the members entered upon a rehash of their old arguments with little evident relish. Vice President Marshall wearily remarked to the news correspondents, "Boys, why don't you just take your files on this treaty debate and print them over again?"

Yet an atmosphere of optimism pervaded the capital: this time the treaty must not be allowed to fail. Even the "irreconcilables" were privately conceding defeat. One of them remarked that, now they had "raised all the Cain possible," he would not be surprised to see most of them voting for ratification. Borah sneered that the only essential difference between the Lodge and Hitchcock reservations to Article X was the difference between "unless" and "until," and with all his oratorical talents he poured scorn upon the heads of the "unlessites" and the "untillites."

Senator Hitchcock was revealing an auspicious willingness to compromise. Lodge, on his part, agreed to accept the bipartisan conference changes on nine of the original fourteen reservations. But the stumbling block was a more satisfactory reservation regarding Article X. Hitchcock emphatically declared that the new proposal of both Lodge and the "mild reservationists" was worse than the original. By February 17 the Democratic leader was deeply discouraged; he feared that "we may come out at the same hole we went in."

Hitchcock openly blamed the Republicans. The Democrats, he complained, had agreed to accept two versions of a reservation on Article X which came so close to the original Lodge reservation that many senators could see no real difference between them. Whereupon the irrepressible Borah summed the situation up neatly: The Democrats had come nine-tenths of the way toward compromise; they were admitting that the remaining one-tenth amounted to little or nothing. Then why not, after having gone this far, go the whole way?

The Senate at first moved with gratifying speed. Between February 21 and March 7 it adopted or revised eight of the fourteen so-called Lodge reservations.

The withdrawal reservation was approved as it stood (45 to 20), with Lodge vainly trying to secure a joint resolution of Congress, *as Wilson desired*, rather than a concurrent resolution.

The reservation declining to accept a League mandate without the consent of Congress carried by the overwhelming vote of 68 to 4. Wilson had conceded that there was no real objection to this.

The reservation on Shantung was changed (48 to 21), as the Democrats had urged in the bipartisan conferences, to a more tactful version, with the words "China" and "Japan" omitted.

These three reservations all received a two-thirds vote, quite in contrast with the narrow margins of November. Strong Democratic support was mustered for all of them, which indicated that Hitchcock would be unable to hold his followers completely in line on the final vote. Nevertheless a feeling of hopelessness overtook the Senate by the end of February. The "irreconcilables" were voting the reservations on, as before, but they would vote against the whole thing at the end, and barring a surrender by Wilson they would be joined by enough Democrats to defeat the treaty.

The blast that chilled the Democrats, and indirectly the Republicans, came from the White House. About the last week in February, Senator Glass of Virginia (Democrat) was delegated to visit the convalescing President and ascertain whether he would pocket the treaty if it should be approved with the Lodge reservations. Wilson emphatically told Glass that he would, according to a newspaper account which is confirmed by their private correspondence. This being the case, why waste more time?

Late in February, Hitchcock told the reporters that he expected the present attempt at ratification to fail, but he was "quite confident" that there would be another one which would succeed. This was incredibly purblind. Only by the grace of a tidal wave of public opinion were the Democrats having their second chance; such tidal waves would not roll up indefinitely. Henry White talked with Hitchcock and was vexed by his "light and airy way" of referring to the treaty, and of expecting that another deadlock would force the Republicans to yield.

Hitchcock's confidence may have been bolstered by Borah, who was declaring that he intended to present a strong anti-League plank at the coming Republican convention, and bolt the party if it was rejected. The prospect of another Republican schism was highly tempting to the Democrats. Why should either Hitchcock or Wilson yield too much in the way of compromise and get the League issue out of the way, when there was this high political premium on continued deadlock?

During the first week in March the debate over reservations was alternately listless and heated. The "bitter-enders" were again cheerful. Everywhere there was a feeling that the treaty white elephant should be dragged from the Senate floor and pushed into the coming campaign. There seemed to be no other way to get rid of it.

Yet the debate ground on, to the amusement of well-filled galleries. Having made up their minds to kill the treaty, the senators could not decide on a prompt and decent burial. Borah baited the Democrats by charging that they would all finally surrender and be in there voting for the Lodge reservations at the end. This naturally hardened Democratic resistance, as did the rumor that the President, if his followers surrendered, would head a third party in the approaching campaign and ruin their chances of reelection.

Lodge was at his wit's end. He had endorsed most of the changes which the Democrats had pushed in the bipartisan conferences, and had succeeded in getting some of them adopted. But the "irreconcilables" were threatening to bolt if he gave ground on Article X; the "mild reservationists" were threatening to bolt if he did not; and the Democrats were under orders from the White House to vote down whatever was agreed upon. On March 4 Lodge flared up and said that since the Democrats seemed unwilling to support some of the amendments which they had presented in the bipartisan conferences, he would offer no more. He solemnly admitted for the first time that the treaty had "fallen by the wayside."

Yet to the very end a few of the faithful never gave up hope that some compromise might be worked out on the reservation to Article X. Senator Simmons of North Carolina (a Democrat) was one of these, and he enlisted the support of Senator Watson (a Republican), who in turn secured the assent of Lodge to a part of the plan.

Simmons was anxious to talk with the President about his proposal. On or about March 5 (the letter is undated), Hitchcock wrote directly to Wilson urging that Simmons be called to the White House, and giving reasons why. At the bottom of this letter is a brief notation in the writing of Mrs. Wilson, presumably dictated by the President and sent on to Hitchcock. The note curtly said that it would be folly to undertake individual interviews. (Wilson was probably thinking of the fruitless conferences with individual senators back in July.)

The upshot was that Senator Simmons and his fellow compromisers were not permitted to see Wilson, and Senator Watson records that Simmons was much vexed. The President was probably vexed, too: why should people be constantly bothering him about compromising on Article X, especially since he had already made it clear that he would not compromise?

Wilson's Olympian seclusion from the Senate during these critical days is puzzling. Senator Glass, a warm friend, seems to have been the only one whom he did consult, though others were reported as anxious to see him. There can be no doubt that he was physically able to talk with individual senators, and might have done so if his mind had been open and if he had realized the importance of keeping in touch with developments in the Senate.

Evidently Wilson had reconciled himself to the rejection of the treaty, and looked forward to a triumphant vindication at the polls.

The President fired another verbal bombshell, on March 8, 1920, when he addressed a communication to Senator Hitchcock setting forth his objections to the Lodge reservations. The letter was in the nature of a reply to Hitchcock's request that Wilson see Senator Simmons and one or two of his colleagues.

No devitalizing reservation to Article X, Wilson insisted, would be acceptable, for Article X was a moral obligation—a sacred pledge to our gallant boys. Without this article we should get nothing out of the war but regrets for having gone in. Either we should enter the League fearlessly, accepting responsibility for world leadership, or we should retire "as gracefully as possible" from the concert of powers.

Wilson went on to say that at Paris he had run afoul of "militaristic" forces, particularly those of France, and they had fought Article X. The Lodge reservation would be a victory for them.

The President further explained that "practically every so-called reservation" was a "rather sweeping nullification" of the actual terms of the treaty. He had heard of "reservationists" and "mild reservationists," but he could not understand the difference between "a nullifier" and a "mild nullifier." In concluding, Wilson expressed the wish that Hitchcock would communicate these views to his fellow Democrats in the Senate for their guidance. In brief, reject the Lodge reservations because they nullified the treaty.

This letter is one of the most striking that Wilson ever wrote. In his discussion of Article X he soared again into the empyrean idealism of his Fourteen Points and other war addresses. But he was clearly out of touch with reality. Some of the things he said were no doubt true but they would not get the treaty approved. It was, for example, a gross exaggeration to assert that practically every one of the proposed reservations was in effect a sweeping nullification of the treaty.

The letter disclosed not only a stubborn mind, but a closed mind. By the day that Wilson wrote these instructions, *about half of the Lodge reservations had not yet been voted upon* (including that to Article X), and in general they were the less important ones. The others were still taking shape, and were subject to amendment. The reservation to Article X was still being hammered out, and at the time Wilson sent the letter there was still a lively hope of some kind of compromise along the lines of the Simmons-Watson proposal. Yet Wilson *vetoed all the rest of the reservations without even waiting to see what they were going to be.*

The reverberations from this March letter were both national and international.

The wavering Democrats were beaten back into line by the crack of the Wilsonian whip. Most of them, especially those up for reelection, did not care to go before the voters and admit that they had defied the sickbed wishes of their great President.

Some of the more reasonable Democrats, like Owen of Oklahoma, were forced to choose between Wilson and Lodge, and they sadly chose Lodge. Owen openly announced that he would fall in behind any leadership that would take us into the League, with or without reservations.

The "mild reservationists," who had not completely abandoned hope of a compromise on Article X, were again slapped in the face. They were branded as "nullifiers," when in their judgment they were trying to save the treaty from a stubborn zealot who would destroy it.

The "irreconcilables" were delighted. Senator Brandegee, "overjoyed and exultant," hastened with a copy of the letter to Mrs. Alice Roosevelt Long-worth. It meant that the angered "mild reservationists" would stand with the "bitter-enders" in voting reservations onto the treaty. Senator Moses sacrilegiously rejoiced that he, an "irreconcilable," had been united in the holy bonds of "political wedlock" with Senator Kellogg, a "mild reservationist," by the Reverend Woodrow Wilson.

The "Lodge reservationists" were now more determined than ever to carry through their program with dispatch, and dump the dead treaty on Wilson's doorstep. Lodge snorted that the President's letter contained some "delightful" passages, especially on French militarism and imperialism. He rose in the Senate several days later to explain that he had meant this sarcastically.

The French were stunned by the attack upon their militarism. Wilson had promised them security through the League and the Security Treaty. The League was dying; the Security Treaty was dead. Could France be blamed, after this betrayal, for building up a strong system of alliances and trying to safeguard herself against future aggression?

The French Ambassador in Washington, Jules Jusserand, promptly sent a note of remonstrance to Acting Secretary of State Polk, who forwarded it to Wilson. The President replied on March 15 that he resented Jusserand's rushing in, and expected Polk to have a frank and firm talk with him. Wilson evidently was piqued because Jusserand was piqued. The same trace of asperity that had crept into the Lansing and Adriatic notes again had come to the surface.

Across the Atlantic, the French press flared forth in anger. It was shocking to learn that Article X had been devised to hold France in check. It was hypocritical for America (who had not reduced her armaments) to blame France (after betraying her) for maintaining large armies. Some of the less moderate French journals referred to the maunderings of a sick man. The Paris *Midi* said bluntly, "The American nation is directed by an idiot." The Paris *Matin* quoted *Harvey's Weekly* as saying, "No, Mr. Wilson had not become insane; *he* is just as he always was."

The London *Globe*, the first English paper to break silence, wondered if Wilson was now physically or temperamentally capable of dealing with a complicated international situation which demanded give-and-take. His illness had aroused the sympathy of the whole world; his recent petulant outbursts elicited "a certain degree of sympathy for the United States."

On March 8, the day that Wilson wrote his disturbing letter, the weary senators, convinced of the futility of what they were doing, unanimously adopted a motion to limit debate. Most of the remaining reservations were rapidly carried through, all of them by lopsided if not overwhelming votes, all of them with some Democratic support, and one of them without debate. The six-to-one reservation, in revised form, was approved 57 to 20, *with 17 Democrats supporting it.*

By March 10 the crisis was approaching on Article X. There were rumors that the Simmons-Watson proposal might yet win enough votes. Even Lodge alarmed the "irreconcilables" by presenting a watered-down version of his own reservation, though he admitted he had changed the phraseology and not the basic principle. Senator Reed then told the story of the boy who was fishing for suckers: when they would not bite, he merely reversed the same worm on the hook, saying, "Oh, these are just fish I'm after; they don't know much."

Senator Hitchcock took the trouble to send the new Lodge reservation to the White House about March 12 with a note (undated) saying he assumed it would be unacceptable. Wilson curtly noted on the bottom of the page that the senator was quite right, and returned it. The "irreconcilables," by threatening dire things, were finally able to force Lodge to accept an amendment to his revised reservation on Article X which, if anything, made it more sweeping. In this form it was adopted on March 15 by a vote of 56 to 26, *with 14 Democrats voting for it.*

The irate Senator Simmons taxed Lodge with twice having surrendered on Article X when agreement was in sight, and with twice having entered into an alliance with the "irreconcilables." Lodge replied that the Republican senators had been "endeavoring to act together." Then, with an acid thrust at Wilson, he added: "We cannot conduct matters on this side of the aisle as they are conducted on that side. *We have no one to write us letters.*"

Simmons snapped back that no one had to write Lodge letters. All that was necessary was for Borah, the leader of the "irreconcilables," to "tell" the Massachusetts senator what to do.

Borah then spoke up for the "irreconcilables" to say that they were standing four-square with Wilson in seeking "to defeat the treaty." "There is just as much of an understanding between the President of the United States and myself as there is between the Senator from Massachusetts and myself."

On March 18, appropriately enough the day after St. Patrick's Day, an astonishing development occurred. Senator Gerry of Rhode Island, a stalwart Democrat, proposed a fifteenth reservation putting the Senate on record as favoring self-determination and independence for Ireland.

This was the acme of legislative absurdity. Ireland was completely irrelevant to the subject matter of the treaty. The fourth Lodge reservation warned other powers to keep out of our domestic concerns, and now we were rushing headlong into those of Britain. Such an indefensible irrelevancy would give Wilson complete justification for pocketing the entire treaty, even assuming that he would not have done so anyhow. Finally, the British would be strongly impelled to object to the Irish reservation and perhaps defeat or delay final ratification.

It was crystal-clear by this time that the only chance of securing ratification lay in the Lodge reservations. The last-minute Ireland dodge was but a transparent trick by the Democrats to make the preceding fourteen reservations so offensive that not even the Republicans would vote for them. The regular Democratic senators apparently did not want agreement, and they preferred to take their chances in the coming campaign, unless they were allowed to put the stamp of their own interpretation on the treaty. From now on the Democrats were hardly in a position to accuse the "irreconcilables" of bad faith in voting for reservations with the plain intent of later voting them down.

Lodge frantically sought to wriggle out of this diabolically clever trap. He finally proposed a recess so that he might rally his demoralized ranks. But the outspoken Ashurst of Arizona (Democrat) cried out in piercing tones against further delay. The Senate, he shouted, should either take this treaty in a pair of tongs and drop it into the Potomac, or ratify it without more palaver or delay, for the people were heartily tired of it. This sally brought such a tremendous outburst of applause from the packed galleries that not even the stern hammerings of the presiding officer could check it.

The Irish reservation carried by the close vote of 38 to 36, with the "bitter-enders" and *over half the Democrats present voting for it*, among them men like Hitchcock who had consistently opposed the Lodge reservations. Such are the mutations of politics.

Just before the final vote, on March 19, the Senate adopted without record vote a Lodge amendment to the preamble of the original reservations. This provided for silent acquiescence by all the Allied powers, rather than explicit written acceptance by three of the major four. (It will be remembered that Wilson had strongly objected to the original reservation because it required written consent.)

By this time it was hardly accurate to speak of the "Lodge" reservations. That regarding Ireland was vehemently opposed by the Massachusetts senator. Others had been revised to meet Democratic objections and had received strong Democratic support, notably the preamble, the Shantung reservation, and the League-expense reservation. Lodge seemingly was willing to yield more than this but was repeatedly beaten back by the "bitter-enders." Generally speaking, the revised Lodge reservations (except for that on Ireland) were more tactful, less likely to wound foreign sensibilities, and more carefully worded.

Throughout the debate Hitchcock consistently presented substitute reservations, and was as consistently voted down. A careful analysis of his proposals shows that in principle, if not in phraseology, they differed little if any from the corresponding ones of Lodge. The difference was not so much between tweedledum and tweedledee as between Democratic political face and Republican political face. Throughout the debate, repeated and unabashed references to the impending campaign again demonstrated that the curse of party politics was ever present.

As the hour again approached for the crucial vote, it was apparent that the tide of public opinion, even within Democratic ranks, had begun to turn strongly against the uncompromising President. This was quite in contrast with November, when Wilson had radiated something of the aura of a martyr. But the Lansing and Adriatic affairs, combined with the peremptory letter to Hitchcock, had caused the President to appear in a less lovely light.

When it became clear that the choice was either a reserved treaty or nothing, all but the most partisan and stubborn shrank from the terrifying responsibility of giving the country and the world nothing. Men like Herbert Hoover, William Jennings Bryan, and ex-President Taft begged Wilson not to throw away nine-tenths of a loaf because he could not get the whole loaf. Personal friends of the President added their voices to the swelling chorus.

Highly significant was the defection in March of a number of the most influential Democratic newspapers. The Cleveland *Plain Dealer* turned a somersault and reluctantly declared for the Lodge reservations. The Brooklyn *Eagle* was sadly urging the senators to ignore the President and vote their own convictions. The powerful New York *World*, an unflagging defender of the League, now belittled the Lodge reservations, and while insisting that Wilson was right in principle, admitted that on occasion every statesman must yield to expediency. The President's position, from this point of view, was "weak and untenable."

The Louisville *Courier-Journal*, which carried on the violently outspoken tradition of "Marse Henry" Watterson, had long been, like the other Democratic newspapers, a foe of reservations. It now reversed itself and urged ratification on "the best terms possible." The St. Louis *Post-Dispatch* (nominally Independent, though strongly Democratic in its leanings), had supported the treaty all along with great vigor. It now parted company with Wilson because he was "endangering the cause"—and the cause was greater than any man or any party.

It was in this changing atmosphere that, on March 19, 1920, the Senate prepared for the final vote. The galleries were jammed; the air was electric; but the excitement was less tense than in November. Barring some kind of miracle or last-minute shift, the treaty would be rejected.

Several of the senators took the floor to make their final arguments. Among them was Senator Walsh of Montana, who contributed one of the few really impressive speeches of the entire debate. He would reluctantly vote for reservations, partly because the influence of Article X had been exaggerated, but primarily because there was no alternative.

The zero hour had now arrived. The question was on agreeing to the resolution of ratification with the Lodge reservations incorporated. With stentorian tones the clerk began to call the roll. Three of the first four Democrats turned against Wilson and voted for the treaty. Then came the name of Senator Culberson of Texas, a Democrat who had grown gray in the service and who was high in the esteem of his colleagues. If he too voted

"Yea" he might touch off a Democratic stampede. His face was perplexed, but after a moment's hesitation he voted "Nay." (Later in the street he turned to a friend, and after speaking in the highest terms of Walsh's speech, remarked, "You know, for a minute in there I didn't know how to vote.")

The roll call continued. Some of the Democratic stalwarts stood fast; others deserted. Then came the name of Hitchcock. If he voted with Lodge, he might yet start a stampede among the remaining Democrats. But he remained true to Wilson's leadership and voted "Nay." (Some years afterward he told Dr. Nicholas Murray Butler that he was the man who had really defeated the treaty, at "virtually the command" of Wilson. "It was," Butler reports him as saying, "the mistake of my life.")

When the votes were all tallied, the count stood 49 to 35, which meant that the treaty, *though commanding a simple majority this time*, lacked seven votes of the necessary two-thirds. Twenty-one Democrats went over to the Lodge camp, but twenty-three remained loyal. If seven of the twenty-three had followed the others, the treaty would have carried. Thus twenty-three old-line Democrats, acting at the behest of the uncompromising Wilson, joined with the "bitter-ender" Republicans to bring about the second and final defeat of the treaty.

The "irreconcilable" Brandegee turned to Lodge and said, "We can always depend on Mr. Wilson. He never has failed us."

Once the treaty was rejected, the Senate passed the customary motion (47 to 37) to return it to the President. No effort was made, as in November, to approve the treaty without reservations, or with the Hitchcock reservations. All this was regarded as completely hopeless.

Yet a feeble attempt was made to reconsider the vote of rejection. It was generally felt that such a motion would be acceptable, once the wheel-horse Democrats had stuck by their guns and Wilson long enough to salve their consciences and stay in the good graces of their constituents. The loyal Democrats could then support a motion to reconsider, and leave the final decision up to the President.

The press reported that the administration Democrats had worked out a "deal" with the "mild reservationists" to carry a vote to reconsider. Senator Robinson (Democrat) actually made such a motion. Senator Watson moved to table it, but this maneuver lost 43 to 34, with the "mild reservationists" joining the Democrats.

The president of the Senate pro tempore (Senator Cummins of Iowa, Republican) thereupon declared the Robinson motion to reconsider out of order. He expressed misgivings as to the soundness of his ruling, and plainly invited an appeal from the decision of the chair. If such an appeal had been made, the loyal Democrats doubtless would have combined again with the "mild reservationists" to declare the Robinson motion in order, and there would have been a final chance to save the treaty. Incredible though it may seem, *not a single one of those who professed to favor the treaty with reservations*, either Republicans or Democrats, *rose to challenge the chairman's questionable ruling.*

Then Lodge came forward. He said that since some of the senators obviously wanted another chance to vote, he would propose unanimous consent for a motion to reconsider, and in this way give the Democrats one more opportunity to approve the treaty with his reservations. But Hitchcock flatly objected to unanimous consent, and Lodge's last attempt to revive the pact had to be dropped. The Treaty of Versailles was never again formally considered in the Senate of the United States.

It is clear that, if those Democrats who voted against the treaty had really wanted a second chance, they could have had it. The conclusion must be that they did not want it. The twenty-three loyal Democrats were standing so steadfast that another roll call would obviously have been a waste of time. Wilson was insisting that he would rather have the treaty thrown into the tumult of politics than have it approved with the Lodge reservations; so the administration Democrats, for whatever reasons, gave their crippled leader what he wanted.

As before, the "irreconcilables" met at the home of Mrs. Longworth for a victory supper. But the affair was not a great success; they were all tired and suffering from the feeling of an anticlimax. "For weeks," says Mrs. Longworth, "it was really comic how we missed having the League to fight about."

Bright and early the next morning after the final vote, the secretary of the Senate appeared at the White House Executive Offices with the big bound volume of the official treaty, wrapped securely in brown paper and tied generously with red tape. The President had personally presented it to the Senate for approval; the senators could not agree on a resolution of ratification, so they were sending it back.

The next move, as Lodge explained, was up to the President. If he wanted to resubmit the treaty, the Senate would treat it as new business. If he wanted to toss it into the campaign, then the Republicans would gladly meet him on the hustings.

The treaty was now dead, as far as America was concerned. Who had killed it?

The vital role of the loyal Democrats must be reemphasized. If all of them who professed to want the treaty had voted "Yea," it would have passed with more than a dozen votes to spare. If the strait-jacket of party loyalty had not been involved, the necessary two-thirds could easily have been mustered.

In the previous November, the Democrats might have voted against the treaty (as they did) even without White House pressure. But this time pressure had to be applied to force them into line, and even in the face of Wilsonian wrath almost half of them bolted. On the day of the final balloting the newsmen observed that two Cabinet members (Burleson and Daniels), possibly acting at the President's direction, were on the floor of the Senate, buttonholing waverers. The day after the fateful voting Hitchcock wrote Wilson that it had required the "most energetic efforts" on his part *to prevent a majority of the Democrats from surrendering to Lodge.*

Desertion of the President, as we have seen, is no light offense in the political world, especially when he has declared himself emphatically. Senators do not ordinarily court political suicide. Wilson still had the patronage bludgeon in his hands, and having more than a trace of vindictiveness, he could oppose renegade senators when they ran again, and in fact did so.

Many of the loyal Democrats were up for reelection in 1920. They certainly were aware of the effects of party treachery on their political fortunes. They knew—or many of them knew—that they were killing the treaty; they made no real effort to revive it; they must have wanted it killed—at least until after the November election.

One striking fact stands out like a lighthouse. With the exception of Hitchcock of Nebraska, Johnson of South Dakota, and Thomas of Colorado, *every single one of the twenty-three senators who stood loyally with Wilson in March came from south of the Mason and Dixon line.* Only four of the "disloyal" twenty-one represented states that had seceded in 1860-1861. At the polls, as well as on the floor of the Senate, decent southern Democrats voted "the way their fathers shot." As between bothersome world responsibility on the one hand, and loyalty to President, party, section, and race on the other, there was but one choice. Perhaps world leadership would come eventually anyhow.

Democratic senators like Walsh of Montana and Ashurst of Arizona were not from the South. When the issue was clearly drawn between loyalty to party and loyalty to country, their consciences bade them choose the greater good. Ashurst had gone down the line in supporting Wilson; but several days before the final vote he declared, "I am just as much opposed to a White House irreconcilable as I am to a Lodge irreconcilable."

A word now about public opinion.

In March, as in November, more than 80 per cent of the senators professed to favor the treaty with some kind of reservations. All the polls and other studies indicate that this was roughly the sentiment of the country. Yet the senators were unable to scrape together a two-thirds vote for any one set of reservations.

The reaction of many newspaper editors, as before, was to cry out against the shame of it all—this indictment of the "capacity of our democracy to do business." We had astonished the world by our ability to make war; we now astonished the world with our "imbecility" in trying to make peace. How could we blame other countries for thinking us "a nation of boobs and bigots"? The Louisville *Courier-Journal* (Democrat), referring to our broken promises to the Allies, cried that we stood betrayed as "cravens and crooks," "hypocrites and liars."

Partisan Republican newspapers loudly blamed the stiff-backed Wilson and his "me-too" senators. Two wings of "irreconcilables"—the Wilsonites and the "bitter-enders"—had closed in to execute a successful pincers movement against the treaty. The New York *Tribune* (Independent Republican) condemned the "inefficiency, all-sufficiency and self-sufficiency of our self-named only negotiator," Woodrow Wilson. If the treaty died, said the *Tribune*, "the handle of the dagger that pierced its heart would bear the initials 'W. W.' "

If Republicans scolded Democrats, Democrats scolded Republicans. Lodge and his cheap political tricks were roundly condemned, and the general conclusion was that "the blood of the Treaty stains the floor of the Republican wigwam." A few of the less partisan Democratic journals openly conceded that Wilson's obstinacy had something to do with the final result. William Jennings Bryan asserted from the platform that this "most colossal crime against our nation and the civilized world in all history" made his "blood boil." He began a vigorous campaign against the two-thirds rule in the senate. "A majority of Congress can declare war," he cried; "it ought to be as easy to end a war as to begin it."

The leading liberal journals, as before, were sadly happy. They rejoiced that the result would clear the way for a renovation of the treaty, but they regretted that the pact had been defeated as a result of partisanship rather than as a result of the betrayal of Wilson's promises.

An impressive number of the more discerning editors deplored the fact that the issue was now in the dirty hands of politicians. An electoral referendum, it was felt, would merely confuse the issue; such a canvass could not possibly reveal anything more than was already known, namely, that *an overwhelming majority of the people wanted the treaty with some kind of reservations*.

Is it true that the invalid in the White House really strangled the treaty to death with his own enfeebled hands?

It is seldom that statesmen have a second chance—a second guess. They decide on a course of action, and the swift current of events bears them downstream from the starting point. Only rarely does the stream reverse itself and carry them back.

In November, Wilson had decided that he wanted deadlock, because he reasoned that deadlock would arouse public opinion and force the Senate to do his bidding. The tidal wave of public opinion did surge in, and Wilson got his second chance. But he threw it away, first by spurning compromise (except on his terms), and then by spurning the Lodge reservations.

There had been much more justification for Wilson's course in November than in March. In November he was sick, secluded, was fed censored news, and was convinced by Hitchcock that the strategy of deadlock was sound. In March, he was much improved in health, far less secluded, more in touch with the press and with the currents of opinion, though probably still not enough. He consulted even less with the Senate, presumably because he had made up his mind in advance to oppose the Lodge reservations. In November, there was a fair possibility of reconsideration; in March, it was clear that the only possibility lay in making the League an issue in the coming campaign. Wilson, with his broad knowledge of government and politics, should have seen that this hope was largely if not completely illusory. Perhaps he would have seen it had he not been blinded by his feeling for Lodge.

The evidence is convincing that Wilson wanted the issue cast into the hurly-burly of politics. He could not accept Lodge's terms; Lodge would not accept his terms. The only possible chance of beating the senator—and this was slim indeed—was to win a resounding mandate in 1920.

Yet this strategy, as already noted, meant further delay. At Paris, the feeling at times had been, "Better a bad treaty today than a good treaty four months hence." Europe was still in chaos, and increasingly in need of America's helping hand. Well might the Europeans cry, "Better a treaty with the Lodge reservations today than a probable treaty without reservations after the election." Or as Dr. Frank Crane wrote in *Current Opinion*, "It is vastly more needful that some sort of League be formed, *any sort*, than that it be formed *perfectly*." (Italics Crane's.)

Yet Wilson, for the reasons indicated, could not see all this clearly. Four days after the fatal vote he wrote Hitchcock, praising him for having done all in his power to protect the honor of the nation and the peace of the world against the Republican majority.

Mrs. Wilson, no doubt reflecting her husband's views, later wrote, "My conviction is that Mr. Lodge put the world back fifty years, and that at his door lies the wreckage of human hopes and the peril to human lives that afflict mankind today."

To the very end Wilson was a fighter. When the Scotch-Irish in him became aroused, he would nail his colors to the mast. He said in 1916 that he was "playing for the verdict of mankind." His conception of duty as he saw it was overpowering. He once remarked that if he were a judge, and it became his duty to sentence his own brother to the gallows, he would do so—and afterwards die of a broken heart.

It is well to have principles; it is well to have a noble conception of duty. But Wilson, as he became warmed up in a fight, tended to get things out of focus and to lose a proper sense of values.

The basic issue in 1920 was the Hitchcock reservations or the Lodge reservations. Wilson accepted those of Hitchcock while rejecting those of Lodge, which, he said, completely nullified the treaty and betrayed his promises to the Allies and to the American dead.

This, as we have seen, was a gross exaggeration. Minds no less acute than Wilson's, and less clouded with sickness and pride, denied that the Lodge reservations completely nullified the treaty. To the man in the street—in so far as he gave the dispute thought—there was little discernible difference between the two sets of reservations. How could one decry statements which merely reaffirmed the basic principles of the Constitution and of our foreign policy? To a vast number of Americans the Lodge reservations, far from nullifying the treaty, actually improved it. This was so apparent to even the most loyal Democrats in the Senate that Wilson could barely keep them in line.

In the final analysis the treaty was slain in the house of its friends rather than in the house of its enemies. In the final analysis it was not the two-thirds rule, or the "irreconcilables," or Lodge, or the "strong" and "mild reservationists," but Wilson and his docile following who delivered the fatal stab. If the President had been permitted to vote he would have sided with Borah, Brandegee, Johnson, and the other "bitter-enders"—though for entirely different reasons.

Wilson had said that the reservation to Article X was a knife thrust at the heart of the Covenant. Ironically, he parried this knife thrust, and stuck his own dagger, not into the heart of the Covenant, but into the entire treaty.

This was the supreme act of infanticide. With his own sickly hands Wilson slew his own brain child—or the one to which he had contributed so much.

This was the supreme paradox. He who had forced the Allies to write the League into the treaty, unwrote it; he who had done more than any other man to make the Covenant, unmade it—at least so far as America was concerned. And by his action, he contributed powerfully to the ultimate undoing of the League, and with it the high hopes of himself and mankind for an organization to prevent World War II.

IX

Challenge and Response

WOODROW WILSON *had led his country into war to make the world safe for democracy, but even as he did so he wondered whether the intolerance born of wartime hyperpatriotism would not undermine democracy at home. He soon had his answer as chauvinists resorted to tar-and-feather parties and other assorted niceties to compel conformity. The long-smoldering agitation against unrestricted immigration took new life. The idea of America as a melting pot diminished as anti-immigrationists such as Madison Grant charged that southern and eastern Europe dumped "their human flotsam" into "our jails, insane asylums and almshouses."*

When the war ended and Europe resorted to its usual haggling over the spoils, America, prepared by its President for a New Jerusalem, reacted with vigor to reembrace its traditional isolation. As the outside world seemed bent upon embracing the new revolutionary doctrines of rampaging Bolshevism, and as strikes disrupted the war-imposed labor peace, Americans moved to reclaim their lost tranquillity. Nativist sentiments prevailed as the drive to restrict immigration culminated in the National Origins Act of 1924 which closed the golden door proclaimed by the Statue of Liberty. The Ku Klux Klan burned its crosses as a warning to Catholic, Jew, and Negro to keep their places. The foreigner without and within was put on notice that native America meant to reclaim past virtues, that in the words of Theodore Roosevelt the United States had only "one soul loyalty," and that was Americanism.

American historians have concerned themselves at some length with the recurring outbreaks of nativism. R. A. Billington, The Protestant Crusade *(1938), deals with the Know-Nothing movement of the 1850's and John Higham,* Strangers in the Land *(1955) carried the story from 1860-1925. The repressive impact of nativism during the twenties is succinctly put by Preston W. Slosson (1892-   ). He suggests some of the compensating features of the Great Crusade on American life but it is more like an echo, weak and hollow, in the aftermath of his previous recitation of aggressive nationalism. Most historians today are inclined to agree with Higham that whereas the nativism of earlier periods produced only marginal changes in American life, that of the twenties changed forever both the social structure and habits of mind of the United States.*

THE GREAT CRUSADE AND AFTER, 1914-1928

by Preston William Slosson

The outstanding spiritual phenomenon of the times was the remarkable intensification of nationalism. By one decision this generation closed the door to most European and all Asiatic labor. By another the American people placed themselves outside all international unions for world peace. But the same spirit showed itself in humbler forms as well—in a dramatic revival of nativism, in an aggressive watchfulness against unconventional political doctrines, in an exaltation of the virtues of the "Nordic" race, in an extraordinary revival of popular interest in American history and, in general, in a glorification of "one-hundred-per-cent Americanism." In large measure this efflorescence of nationalism was a product of the war. The epoch which witnessed the climax and collapse of Pan-Germanism and the rebirth of a dozen nationalities in central and eastern Europe was one of intense national feeling everywhere. In many countries, such as Fascist Italy and the states of the Balkans, the Danube and the Baltic, as well as among the insurgent students of China and Hindustan, the fever rose many degrees higher than in the United States. Its evil side, so tragically illustrated in the Old World, was only feebly reflected in the New. And yet, relatively to the immediate past, the United States was keenly and intolerantly patriotic after 1914.

The direct influence of the war showed itself at first in self-pleasing contrasts between war-torn Europe and peaceful, prosperous America, and later, as active propaganda was carried on by foreign governments among immigrant Americans, in a fear that the integrity of American citizenship was endangered by alien sympathies. Though in the actual test of battle most of the recent comers proved as loyal as the sons of the *Mayflower,* the years of hesitation which preceded the abandonment of neutrality were so marked by "hyphenism" and the echoes of Old World feuds as to awaken pardonable misgivings that a divided allegiance might appear in times of crisis. Theodore Roosevelt spent his last energies in appealing for a united nation. He popularized the phrase, "one-hundred-per-cent Americanism," though in his mouth it meant a common allegiance by men of all races and not, as so often misused, the supremacy of a single racial type. But as the passions of war mounted the man of foreign accent became as much suspected as the man of foreign sympathies. To be sure, the popular feeling against the "Hun" quickly evaporated after the war, but it left behind it a residual dislike of aliens and "radicals" and a general suspicion of greedy and unscrupulous European diplomacy.

The controversy over the peace treaty, which the press in general represented as a victory of France and England over the United States, and that over the League of Nations, portrayed by the same papers as a trap set by Old World diplomats for American armies and dollars, heightened the distaste for international politics engendered by the war. Other influences as well helped to discredit President Wilson's foreign policy. Thus, many German Americans and pacifists could not forgive the war itself; Italian Americans disliked the president's opposition to Italian claims east of the Adriatic; some Irish Americans, powerful in the president's own party, feared lest the League might augment the power of the British Empire. Certain leaders of liberal thought, represented by the *Nation* and the *New Republic*, who had given a general, though hesitating, support to the Wilson administration, now broke with it on the ground that the peace contained many injustices which might provoke new wars. They were joined by men of exactly opposite habit of thought who believed that the whole idea of a League of Nations was a mirage of pacifism that might lead the nation to neglect its military security. Still others opposed the president because they disliked him personally, or were his opponents in the game of party politics, or disapproved of his rather high-handed disregard of the opinion of the Senate.

But, when all is said, the chief opposition to the Treaty of Versailles was simply dislike of playing world politics. Faced with the question of ratification, the Senate expressed its hostility to the treaty by drawing up lists of reservations, unacceptable to the president, which aimed to restrict American participation in the League's activities and to limit the jurisdiction of the League over American foreign policy. The opposition centered its fire particularly on Article Ten of the Covenant, guaranteeing against external aggression the territorial integrity and political independence of member nations. The rejection of the treaty in 1920 and the negotiation of a separate peace with the enemy countries in the following year marked a complete reversal of the tendency to identify the United States with the "concert of the Powers" which began with President Roosevelt's first administration. The United States declined a proffered mandate over Armenia, withdrew its forces from the guardianship of the Rhine, refused to conclude a proposed defensive alliance with Britain and France, and weighted down the proposal to join the Court of International Justice with reservations which brought on interminable discussion. The department of state, relieved of responsibility for the political stability of Europe, devoted its attention mainly to routine national business, such as the settlement of war debts with former associates in the World War and the policing of disorderly Caribbean republics.

Some qualification must be made to the assertion that the United States pursued from 1920 to 1928 a policy of isolation from world politics. In a conference held in Washington (1921) the chief naval powers of the Pacific agreed to a limitation of capital battleships and promised to respect each other's insular dependencies within the Pacific area. They agreed also to respect the integrity and existing commercial rights of China. The Coolidge administration sent frequent "observers" to European conferences and cooperated with the purely humanitarian and nonpolitical activities of the League of Nations. Private individuals did much more than the national government. Though the United States failed to join the World Court, Elihu Root assisted in its organization and John Bassett Moore and Charles Evans

Hughes served on its bench. Charles G. Dawes, later vice-president, Owen D. Young and other financial experts helped devise the plan eventually adopted for the payment of German reparations. An American committee, including General Tasker Bliss, Professor James T. Shotwell, David Hunter Miller and other prominent citizens, proposed methods of procedure in cases of international aggression which were later incorporated into the Geneva Protocol of the League of Nations and thence, indirectly, into the Locarno Pacts and similar regional agreements. Even the League itself—though still the *bête noire* of the politicians—employed many American citizens in its service.

The deadlock between the Senate and foreign governments with reference to the terms of admission of the United States to the Court of International Justice, and the failure to arrive at an understanding with Great Britain for the limitation of cruisers and other minor war craft, led the Coolidge administration to seek for some new expression of pacific intentions. Frank B. Kellogg, secretary of state, combining a hint from the French statesman Aristide Briand with the desire expressed by Senator William E. Borah of Idaho for the "outlawry" of war, negotiated a series of treaties with other Powers for "the renunciation of war as an instrument of national policy." In August, 1928, representatives of the Powers met at Paris to approve the antiwar pact. One notes, however, that the multilateral antiwar treaty did not commit the United States to any positive action to associate with other nations in the forcible maintenance of world peace. It was an expression of pacifism rather than of internationalism.

The panic over Russian Bolshevism, needless though it was, served almost as much as the war itself to bring about an antialien sentiment. The activity of so many East Europeans in radical labor agitation and the boast of the Russian revolutionists that their agents were active in all parts of the world undermining the foundations of capitalist society, caused many to see in every humble immigrant a potential spy or rebel. The civil war in Ireland, also, caused some Americans to hate England as an oppressor, and others to hate Ireland as a disturber, and both alike to deplore the injection of the feud between the Orange and the Green into American life. It is not surprising that European dictatorships, civil wars and class struggles made many Americans feel that their peaceful, wealthy and stable country stood on another and higher level than the rest of the world. So the eagle screamed again as loudly as in the days of Andrew Jackson. The *Chicago Tribune* flaunted in each day's issue the arrogant motto, "Our country, right or wrong," and the Hearst papers, perhaps to recover a reputation for patriotism somewhat damaged during the war, lost no opportunity to contrast the virtuous American with the sinister European and the quite demoniac Asiatic.

With the bulk of the press, however, the fault was rather ignorance than malice. Although the war had greatly increased the space given to international events, very few papers had foreign correspondents of their own. Domestic affairs, except during the actual prosecution of the war, at all times held the spotlight. Nor did the trickle of daily news items from the Associated Press and similar agencies supply the lack of historical background in the editor's mind. For example, the separate representation of the British Dominions in the League of Nations Assembly, really an expression of the insurgent nationalism of those self-governing commonwealths, was everywhere presented by the press as a mere trick to secure extra votes for London. Disturbances in Mexico were represented as caused by intrigues from Moscow. A particularly persistent error was the tendency to lump Europe together as a unit in contrast to America and blame the whole continent for conditions characteristic of only the more backward nations. It must have been highly exasperating to a Swiss to find "Europeans" scolded as militaristic and imperialistic, or to a Norwegian to hear that Europe was a home of despots and dictators ruling over an oppressed and illiterate proletariat.

But if the postwar American was supercilious, the postwar European was in an even more dangerous mood. At least half the insults, and those the sharpest, were flung westward across the Atlantic. This was partly the bitterness of poverty, for many nations were poorer than they had been in 1913 and not one of them had quite attained the standard of living prevailing in the United States. There was now a new style in criticizing the Americans. In the days of Dickens and Matthew Arnold the United States had been pictured to unfriendly eyes as a crude, backwoods encampment devoid of all civilized comforts. The accusation was still of materialism, but of a materialism triumphant in its own sphere and embodied in industrialism. Englishmen spoke of the United States much as a Hindu critic might have spoken of Victorian England at the height of her complacency and commercial power. "By 'modern civilization' I mean American civilization. . . . America leads the pack, and if we want to know whether the pack is heading for heaven or for hell, we shall be well advised to examine the direction taken by the leader," said one of the most savage critics.

"Spiritually the country is a corpse, physically, a terrific machine. Materialism is the tyrant which rules from ocean to ocean, and its backwash is superstition and an effervescing froth of cranks." Again, "As the present tendency to superficiality increases, as the vigour of the race is divided more exclusively between money getting and pleasure getting and all life is measured in terms of the pay envelope and the dance floor, that part of the American brain that should be devoted to the acquisition of knowledge, the appreciation of beauty and the exercise of wisdom will atrophy." In a similar vein, though with milder temper, spoke the peripatetic German philosopher Count Keyserling, and the Hindu prophet Gandhi. Materialism was the modern devil, and the United States therefore the modern inferno.

Even more sympathetic foreign observers contrived to widen the Atlantic gulf of misunderstanding. Hilaire Belloc's *The Contrast* (1923) was not wholly hostile, but his assertion that the difference between the United States and Europe was greater than that between any two European countries played all too easily into the bad American habit of treating Europe as a unit. André Siegfried in somewhat similar fashion summed up America with a gentle sigh as a strange continent peopled by incomprehensible Puritans. Rudyard Kipling, once the idol of the American reading public, sneered at the American war effort and compared the United States to the laborer who had come at the eleventh hour to the vineyard but demanded a full day's wages. Indeed, the two debates, "who won the war?" and "who will pay the war debts?" caused more international hostility than anything else. Insistence on collecting war debts caused Uncle Sam to be dubbed in certain foreign newspapers "Uncle Shylock." On a few occasions American tourists were hissed and pelted in the streets of Paris. Such incidents, absurdly exaggerated by the press, crystallized into the common saying that "America is hated by every European country."

The effect was to drive the American back on his own pride. He felt that he had done his full share in the war, which was none of his making, and that he had been more than generous after the peace. The rapid transition from being called "soldier of humanity" and "savior of civilization" in 1918 to being called "Uncle Shylock" in 1921 made him feel that he had been wasting beneficence on ingrates. Henceforth he would keep his sons and his money at home. As for the sinfulness of material comfort, it was recalled that the fox who could not reach the grapes had found them to be sour. At any rate, none of the numerous lecturers on American materialism refused their fees.

A similar defensive reaction was called forth by the hostile and unsympathetic depiction of American life by Americans of native or foreign birth. No doubt H. L. Mencken, Sinclair Lewis and the thirty authors of *Civilization in the United States* performed a useful service in puncturing national complacency, but their manner of doing it merely transformed complacency into irritation. Just as the average American refused to recognize himself in the European mirror as a calculating dollar-worshipper, so he refused to recognize himself in the Greenwich Village mirror as a gloomy, hypocritical Puritan incapable of humane culture. Any competent psychologist could have told the critics that an indiscriminate assault upon a national sentiment makes the nationalist more set in his ways than ever. If his very virtues are derided as faults, he will erect his very faults into virtues.

The fact that the outbreak of the war had temporarily turned aside the flood of immigration led to a reexamination of the traditional national policy of encouraging all who were discontented with their lot to seek a better home in America. Despite an increasing amount of restrictive legislation in recent years the gates at Ellis Island still stood wide in 1914. The criminal, the contract laborer, the anarchist, the polygamist, the physically or mentally diseased, the pauper with no visible means of support, the Oriental coolie, were all debarred. But there was no fixed numerical barrier. Immigrants might come in whatever numbers economic conditions should determine. But as the sparsely populated parts of the country became more thickly settled and the alien competed with the native-born laborer in the great urban centers, the question became increasingly acute whether the future of America could be wisely intrusted to the children of the more recent comers in preference to the children of the men and women whose forefathers had long been here. The problem was rendered more urgent by the change in the national composition of the later arrivals, for in recent years hundreds of thousands of bread seekers from Sicily, Naples, the Slavic and Magyar parts of Austria-Hungary, and the Jewish Pale in Poland and western Russia had formed the bulk of the newcomers. The annihilation of distance by means of transportation had brought the whole world to the doorstep of Uncle Sam.

The new immigration contained much that was valuable to American life, much that it had traditionally lacked. It must be remembered that the earlier German and Irish arrivals had provoked nativist feeling. The southern Italians were, as a group, lighthearted, thrifty, temperate and hard working. The Polish Jew combined with his marked aptitude for commerce a thirst for learning and a zeal for social reform. The Slav and Magyar undertook the hardest and heaviest tasks of mine and mill. Without these new additions to the working force of the nation the economic progress of the new century must have been slower and costlier. Many regarded the prospect with as little dismay as Dr. Abraham Flexner, scientist and educator, who declared, "Far from regarding the mixed composition of races in this country as unfortunate, I regard it as a distinct advantage of which not enough use has been made. Every one of the stocks represented in the American people has made to this country its own unique contribution in the establishment of the native culture."

But there was another side to the question. Even granting the good qualities of the new immigrants, could they be assimilated to American life in such quantities and in such variety? A million aliens a year, settling in compact racial blocks in the slums of the great cities and rarely coming into touch with the real life of the nation, might in time reduce the United States to a mosaic of nationalities as unstable as Austria-Hungary. The immigrants from southern and eastern Europe rarely understood English on their first arrival and often could not read or write in any tongue. They were accustomed to a meager livelihood and could underbid alike native American labor and the immigrant from the more prosperous countries of northwestern Europe. The trade unions advocated laws restricting European and excluding Asiatic immigration. In this they were supported not only by the nativist prejudice which intolerant men always feel against a foreigner, but also by the more considered judgment of statesmen who believed that a temporary stimulus to industry would be too dearly bought if it impaired either the racial quality or the standards of living of the nation. As Dr. H. H. Laughlin expressed it, "immigration is a long-time investment in family stocks rather than a short-time investment in productive labor."

The first important attempt at restriction was to bar the illiterate. The proposal was certainly not a new one, for a literacy test had been vetoed by three presidents, Cleveland, Taft and Wilson. It finally became law in 1917 in spite of President Wilson's continued opposition, based mainly on the ground that literacy was a test of opportunity and not of inherent ability. The comprehensive act of 1917 summed up the existing laws on immigration and added the important provision (section 3) that, with certain exceptions such as very near relatives, "all aliens over sixteen years of age, physically capable of reading, who cannot read the English language, or some other language or dialect" should be denied admission. Congress might have rested content with this measure, which clearly favored northwestern Europe as compared with the rest of the continent, had not the close of the World War and the general poverty which succeeded it in central and eastern Europe threatened an exceptionally high tide of immigration. Facing this contingency Congress determined to add to the existing restrictions a fixed numerical quota for each nation.

The emergency law of 1921 limited the annual immigration from any transatlantic country to three per cent of the number of its nationals resident in the United States as determined by the census of 1910. The new plan met with so much popular favor that in 1924 a more drastic measure reduced the quota from three to two per cent and based it on the census of 1890, choosing that date as the turning point when the old immigration from the British Isles, Germany and Scandinavia was beginning to be largely supplemented by the new immigration from southern and eastern Europe. It was further provided that after July 1, 1927, the annual quota of any nationality should be such proportionate share of one hundred and fifty thousand as inhabitants of that national origin bore in 1920 to the entire population of the United States. But the national-origins basis was not brought into effect until 1930 because of difficulties in making a satisfactory analysis of the very mixed blood of the American nation. Not everyone was subject to the quota restriction, as foreign-born wives and children of American citizens, travelers and students, Canadians, Mexicans and other natives of American countries were exempted. To prevent the tragedy of broken homes and disappointed hopes, American consular officers abroad were directed to see that intending immigrants obtained certificates before starting for the United States.

One difficult question involved in the law of 1924 was the exclusion of Japanese labor. As a highly civilized Great Power with a respectable army and navy Japan did not like to be classed with powerless China. But the Far Western states feared Japanese immigration quite as much as Chinese, regarding both as too alien in race ever to become merged into the general body of American citizenship. Since President Roosevelt's time a "gentleman's agreement" between the American and Japanese governments had prevented Japanese of the laborer class from coming to the United States. But in spite of the protests of Japan and the misgivings of President Coolidge Congress insisted on definitely barring Japanese immigration by law. The dread of a new racial problem on the Pacific Coast prevailed over all diplomatic and political considerations, though the general immigration law would have admitted only 146 Japanese per year.

The new quota system of 1924 favored most the British Isles and Germany. Great Britain and Ireland together could send about 62,000 immigrants a year and Germany over 50,000; no other nation exceeded 10,000. This meant, among other results, that the late enemy was favored over all but one of America's recent associates in the war. Italy's great flood of immigration sank to a mere trickle of less than 4000 a year. All southern and eastern Europe together could scarcely muster 20,000. In but one respect did the non-Nordics win an advantage. Owing to the fact that American republics did not come within the restrictions of the quota, thousands of Mexicans crossed the border to meet a demand for cheap labor no longer supplied from Europe. Negroes also moved north to take industrial positions that formerly would have gone to Italians or Slavs, but in the latter instance this was a matter of migration within the nation, not of immigration into it.

Apart from the decrease in immigration and the change in its national character there was a significant change in the occupations of the newcomers. For the period 1911-1914 three times as many unskilled laborers came to the country as skilled, while in 1925 and 1926 the two classes of immigrants were about equal in number. If allowance be made for emigration, the decrease in unskilled labor becomes even more evident. The number of immigrant farmers increased both relatively and absolutely. The economic effects of the quota law were therefore much greater than the mere restrictions on number would indicate. Immigration practically ceased to be a factor affecting wages in the labor market.

Inevitably the law worked many individual hardships, surprisingly little latitude in its interpretation being allowed to the port officials. As an example, one might mention the case of Professor Peter M. Jack of the University of Michigan. Called from Scotland to occupy the chair of rhetoric, he was delayed for months on the technicality that he had not practiced his profession for two years immediately before applying for admission. Even the rich and titled found it hard to pass the jealously guarded gate. The Countess of Cathcart discovered that a divorce case involving the charge of adultery was construed as "moral turpitude" within the meaning of the law. The Countess Karolyi of Hungary was barred from fear of Bolshevist propaganda, a charge which showed the color blindness of the authorities to the different shades of European socialism.

On the other hand, much was done to protect the admitted immigrant from mistreatment and exploitation. Many immigrants had become bad citizens through fraudulent notaries, banks, employment agencies and the like, often conducted by men of their own nationality who were in a position to take advantage of their confidence. To cope with such evils state agencies were established, notably the Massachusetts bureau of immigration founded in 1917 "to bring into sympathetic and mutually helpful relations the commonwealth and its residents of foreign origin, to protect immigrants fron exploitation and abuse, to stimulate their acquisition and mastery of the English language, to develop their understanding of American government, institutions and ideals, and generally to promote their assimilation and naturalization." Elaborate Americanization programs, greatly stimulated by the war, were undertaken by municipalities, employers, schools and welfare agencies of all sorts.

Unfortunately not all Americans were tactful Americanizers. During the war occurred such incidents, based on mutual misunderstanding, as the stoning of a Czech patriotic meeting by the local Loyalty Legion which ignored any fine distinction between a foreign language spoken by allies and one spoken by enemies. In another instance an Armenian immigrant, almost pathetically ready to admire all things American, tells what happened when he gave his name to a grammar-school teacher.

"She looked at it for a moment and then turned to me and said, 'Oh, give that up and change your name to Smith, Jones or a name like that and become Americanized. Give up everything you brought with you from the Old Country. You did not bring anything worth while anyway.' I was shocked by her idea of Americanization and thought to myself: 'The Turkish sword did not succeed in making me become a Turk, and now this hare-brained woman is trying to make an American out of me. I defy her to do it.' After that I was more of an Armenian patriot than I had ever thought of being."

Many of the foreign-born, like this Armenian, became increasingly sensitive and resentful in the face of forcible Americanization. The motion-picture industry found it impossible to present a villain or a stock comic character of any nationality on the films without being deluged by complaints from compatriots who conceived their national sentiment insulted. When Claude G. Bowers in his keynote speech at the Democratic national convention of 1928 accused the Republican administration of degrading the American farmer to the status of a Rumanian peasant, the American Rumanian Association sent a solemn note of protest, declaring, "The state of the Rumanian peasant is not so out-of-date as to justify a party taking it as an example of misery."

The controversy over immigration aroused a keen interest in problems of population. This interest concentrated upon three momentous questions: Was America in danger of having too many people? Was she in danger of having too many inferior individuals? Was she in danger from the presence of inferior races? Books on all these themes multiplied and found an eager market. That these important scientific questions should have awakened so much popular interest was a tribute to the public intelligence, although unfortunately quite unqualified journalists and propagandists obtained as good an audience as the men of scientific training.

The first question, that of quantity, had been in the minds of educated men at least since the days of Malthus. Obviously a country could be too crowded for its economic good, like modern Sicily, or insufficiently peopled for proper development, like modern Alaska. As compared with most European countries the United States was still underpeopled, but the cheap land was almost gone, the cities crowded, the birth rate of the native stock falling, and the balance of exports shifting from food-stuffs and raw materials to manufactured goods. Careful students of the population question, such as Professor Edward M. East of Harvard, challenged the popular optimism which regarded America's capacity for numerical growth as practically unlimited.

The second question, that of quality, was the problem of eugenics. As we have seen, the falling birth rate had affected chiefly the educated and thrifty classes who demanded much of life for their children. Fears were widely expressed that the recent marked progress in popular education and material well-being had done nothing to improve the real physical, mental and moral qualities of the individual; that the civilized man differed from the savage only in training and equipment. The eugenics record office, under the direction of Dr. C. B. Davenport, and the studies by Professor Lewis M. Terman and others on psychological tests in the schools and the army, furnished a wealth of material which was utilized in a crusade for eugenics by such popularizers of science as Albert E. Wiggam.

But the third problem, that of race, bore most directly on the new nationalism, for it threw into contrast the pioneer American stock with other races seeking American opportunities. It was in this field, therefore, that science was most endangered by current political controversy. So widespread was the discussion of anthropological problems in the press that technical terms which had been before the war the monopoly of a few score research workers were now familiar in every crossroads cracker-barrel debate. Popular talk on race in the United States had once been in terms of "white men" and "niggers," or, at a higher social level, discussed in terms of language groups: "Anglo-Saxon supremacy," "the Latin races" and the "Slavic peril." But magazine science replaced the talk of "wops," "kikes," "sheenies," "dagoes," "greasers" and "Dutchies," with disquisitions on "Nordics," "Alpines," "Mediterraneans," "cephalic index" and "atavism."

The favorite was the Nordic, the tall, long-headed, fair-haired, blue-eyed son of the Vikings. Most anthropologists seem agreed that, quite apart from present advantages of environment, the Nordics are an inherently energetic group with a high average of ability, perhaps because many of the lazy and stupid were eliminated by natural selection in the cold winters of the Baltic forests. So much might reasonably be conceded. But it is the fault of popular journalism to take more out of an idea than science puts into it. With such writers as Madison Grant and Lothrop Stoddard, the Nordic became almost the sole author of human progress, and America was warned that her future destiny depended on keeping the pure Nordic gold of her population from being debased by Alpine roundheads and swarthy Mediterraneans. At a still lower level, what might be termed the Ku Klux Klan school of anthropology not only identified the old-stock American with the Nordic (in itself a very questionable piece of guesswork), but assumed that the Protestant religion, the English language, the institutions of democracy, and the moral qualities of truth, honor and respect for womanhood were all bound together in a magic and inseparable racial tie. Such notions had no standing whatever in the courts of science, but they are of importance to the historian because they were widely credited on Main Street.

The rise of the Ku Klux Klan was perhaps the clearest manifestation of the popular belief that Americanism was no longer—as it had been for Jefferson and Lincoln—a gospel to all the nations, but a national secret which could not be shared with those "not of the blood." When the shadow of impending war hung over a yet neutral America, Colonel William J. Simmons, preacher, salesman and amateur organizer of fraternal societies, determined to revive the Reconstruction organization. On an autumn night in 1915 he led a band of associates, including three members of the original

Ku Klux Klan, to the top of Stone Mountain, Georgia, for this purpose. At first the order was hardly more than a sentimental and patriotic reminiscence, an attempt to throw Southern tradition into the scale against alien influence at a moment of national crisis. For four or five years it remained small and mainly sectional; probably it had no more than five thousand members. But in 1920, when Edward Clarke and Mrs. Elizabeth Tyler took over the financial management, it was put on a business basis and began a nation-wide membership campaign. The ten-dollar membership fee was divided: four dollars to the local Kleagle, one to the King Kleagle of the state, fifty cents to the Goblin of the district, and $4.50 to the headquarters of the Invisible Empire at Atlanta. The boom was now of giant dimensions. By 1925 perhaps four or five million Americans had placed their names on the rolls of the organization. In December, 1922, Hiram Wesley Evans, a Texas dentist, became the new Imperial Wizard and Emperor in succession to Simmons.

The Ku Klux Klan was essentially a protest of American nativism against the pressure from alien races, creeds and social ideals. Though there was no organic connection with the original Ku Klux Klan of the days of reconstruction following the Civil War—its spiritual father was rather the Know Nothing party of the mid-century—the new organization copied, or rather adapted with slight variations, the robes, the mask, the ritual and the secret-society language of its titular predecessor. Its slogan was "native, white, Protestant" supremacy and it was directed quite as much against the Catholic, the Jew and the alien white immigrant as against the colored man.

The Klan, however, turned to other purposes as well. Indeed, the chief source of its strength seems to have been that it was all things to all men. In one state it would be chiefly a champion of the prohibition law against the bootlegger; in another a stern censor of morals, sending warning notes and even flogging expeditions to punish men and women who had violated the seventh commandment. Often it denounced internationalism and pacifism, demanding a strong navy and abstention from the wiles of the League of Nations and the World Court, or insisting on a more militantly patriotic tone in school histories. Here and there it allied with the Fundamentalists and denounced evolution as "European infidelity." For brief periods in certain states the Klan was a political machine, concerned chiefly in bestowing local offices on its members and their friends. And, finally, to many Americans it was merely another secret society whose imposing ritual, with its Imperial Wizards, Kleagles, Klaverns, robes, signs and burning crosses in the night, afforded the same harmless pleasure that a Greek-letter fraternity brings to the college boy. In the processions of Klansmen who marched in solemn file through the streets of the national capital and many other great cities, there was a sprinkling of alarmed patriots, fanatics and political schemers, but the rank and file were just average Americans who would join any organization whatever that professed vaguely patriotic aims and promised a social good time.

The anti-Romanist propaganda on which the Klan more and more concentrated was the revamping of an old phobia which dates back to Bloody Queen Mary and the Book of Martyrs. It had been continued in America by the strongly Protestant character of early American Christianity and had found new fuel to feed on in the vast expansion of Catholicism of more recent years. New York and other Eastern centers had long since fallen into the hands of clannish groups of immigrant politicians, usually Roman Catholic Irish or Italians. Many old-stock Americans were also alarmed by the rapid growth of Roman Catholic organizations, such as the Knights of Columbus, with over seven hundred thousand members in 1928, or puzzled by the legal complexities of dual allegiance to the pope in spiritual matters and to the nation in civil matters. Finally, the refusal of many Catholics to enter the public schools and their support of a complete system of Catholic schools and colleges offended people who believed that the "little red school-house," supported by public taxation, was the most potent agency in Americanizing the immigrant. Out of such miscellaneous material a night-mare was fashioned. One paper found in the honors paid to Columbus a "brazen defiance of the fact that America was not discovered by a Roman Catholic but by a Norseman who landed in Vinland nearly five hundred years before the Pope's agent raised the cross of Inquisition at San Salvador." The motion pictures, too, were revealed as a huge conspiracy. "Jews and Roman Catholics own 95 per cent of the big producing and distributing companies. . . . This accounts for so much papal propaganda being dis-played before American audiences." Rome also controlled, so Senator Heflin of Alabama asserted, most of the press!

In the years from 1920 to 1922, when the Klan had become a huge profit-making machine, slipping from the bewildered founder into the hands of practical men who "sold hate at ten dollars a packet," occurred the period of greatest violence. Under the protection of the mask and the added pro-tection of a secret membership list sinister elements entered the Klan and used it for their own purposes. Between October, 1920, and October, 1921, revelations by the *New York World* showed four killings, one mutilation, one branding with acid, forty-one floggings, twenty-seven tar-and-feather parties, five kidnapings and forty-three persons driven into exile. Klansmen said, and no doubt with much truth, that the majority of these outrages were not by Klansmen at all but by private individuals assuming the robe and mask to disguise their identity; yet it was the existence of the robe and mask that made these crimes possible. In 1922 two mutilated corpses charged to the Klan were discovered in the swamps near Mer Rouge, Louisiana. Hardly less merciless were the factional fights within the Klan. In 1923 William S. Coburn, an opponent of Wizard Evans, was murdered by Philip Fox, an Evans adherent. By the new "Western Method" of recruiting the recommendation of a single Klansman would now admit a new member. Little or no discrimination was used in filling the ranks, and membership became a convenient refuge for criminals who wanted protection and politicians who wanted a ready-made "machine."

Politically the Klan became a power in the North as well as the South. It was a major issue in gubernatorial contests in Texas, Louisiana, Oklahoma, Maine, Kansas and Indiana. It made war on Judge Ben B. Lindsey, the na-tionally known reform judge of the juvenile court in Denver, Colorado. It loaned its support to the agitation for doing away with Catholic parochial schools by requiring all children to attend the public schools. In 1924 the fight in the Democratic national convention to have the Klan denounced by name in the party platform threatened a disruption of the party and contributed to its defeat. As a compromise the convention adopted a general affirmation of civil liberty and religious equality without specific mention of the Klan. The Klan fought in 1924 the nomination and in 1928 the election of Alfred E. Smith of New York as presidential candidate because of his religion. In general, the order was Democratic in the South and more frequently Republican in the North, though it often controlled factions in both parties.

The most amazing story in the political history of the Klan was that of the dictatorship of David Curtis Stephenson over the state of Indiana. Indiana was not a Southern state with bitter memories of Reconstruction to excuse a racial panic, nor an illiterate backwater where political apathy might permit an unrepresentative minority to seize power. On the contrary Indiana was a typical Mid-Western commonwealth, well balanced between agriculture and industry, active and alert in politics, served by excellent schools, distinguished for its literary output. A foreign and Catholic element existed, but in much smaller degree than in such states as New York or Massachusetts. Here, if anywhere, the old America was safe, and white, Protestant, Nordic, Gentile supremacy unendangered. Yet by the arts of salesmanship, the shrewd exploitation of rumor, Stephenson had thousands of honest villagers believing that the papal crown had been imposed as a watermark on the paper money issued by the government, that the pope planned within a decade to leave Italy and establish himself within the United States, and that every time a Catholic child was born an extra rifle was placed in the vaults of the local cathedral.

Stephenson captured the Republican state machine, forced the two senators from the state to adopt a friendly attitude towards the Klan, and elected his candidate for governor, Ed Jackson. But he desired to be more than a boss: he wished to stand in the limelight as senator and perhaps some day as president. His vanity brought him to disaster. Thinking himself above the law, he kidnaped a girl, terrified her into suicide, and was sentenced to imprisonment for life. Governor Jackson was indicted for bribing ex-Governor Warren McCray, himself a convicted felon. Several members of the Indianapolis city government were indicted for bribery or election frauds. Judge Clarence Dearth, an active Klan agent, was impeached, though not convicted, on charges of oppression in office. The Klan was now in disgrace throughout the state and its honest, patriotic members left the Stephenson organization in horror when they found out how their credulity had been abused. By 1928 there were less than seven thousand active Klansmen in all Indiana.

As late as 1927 an epidemic of floggings took place in Alabama under the protection of Klan politicians, but on the whole the story of the Klan from 1923 to 1928 was one of political intrigue rather than of violence. Both, however, had done their work in making the Klan unpopular. In an effort to regain credit with the public and remove the reproaches which secrecy had cast upon its doings, Wizard Evans chose Washington's birthday, 1928, as the occasion to ordain that henceforth "no mask or visor shall be upon the helmet of the regalia of any Klansman." A new degree was created, the Knights of the Great Forest, and all Klansmen required to assume it. Thus terminated the subterranean days of the Ku Klux Klan. No longer a mysteriously threatening "invisible Empire," it was revealed as little more than an organization for propaganda against alien and Roman Catholic influences.

The campaign against the Jew in America was far less active than that against the Roman Catholic, although the two were yoked together in the formal denunciations of the Klan—truly a strange association in view of their centuries of opposition to each other. One of the dupes of the anti-Semitic propaganda was Henry Ford, the automobile manufacturer, by nature a kindly man and seemingly one of the last to cherish a racial or religious feud. Yet his newspaper, the *Dearborn Independent*, became simultaneously spokesman for Mr. Ford and for reactionary Europeans who traced all the social ills of modern times to "international Jewish finance." On the basis of an alleged "protocol of the elders of Zion," repeatedly exposed by historians on both sides of the Atlantic, a Jewish conspiracy for the subjugation of the Gentile world was charged. It is possible that some of Mr. Ford's personal experiences with Jewish bankers and business rivals may have affected his attitude in the matter, but his zeal in the cause was without question, though eventually, when faced with court action, he dropped the campaign.

Chauvinism found another target in "unpatriotic" schoolbooks. The same type of unhistorical mind that could believe in the enthronement of the pope or the elders of Zion on the ruins of American liberty found it equally easy to believe in an Anglo-Saxon conspiracy for bringing back the United States into the British Empire. The elements in this conspiracy were the late Cecil Rhodes and his Oxford scholarships, the Sons of St. George, the English-Speaking Union, the Sulgrave Institute, the "multiform Carnegie institutions," the universities and the writers of textbooks dealing with the American Revolution. Charles Grant Miller, vocal in the Hearst papers which were always ready for a chance to "twist the lion's tail," was the chief spokesman of the protest against the Anglo-Saxon conspiracy, and he easily obtained the indorsement of veterans' organizations, patriotic-hereditary societies and some of the more irreconcilable racial groups. The politicians began to be interested. Oregon and even liberal Wisconsin enacted a law forbidding the use in public schools of textbooks defaming or misrepresenting the heroes of the War of Independence or the War of 1812. Mayor John F. Hylan in New York and Mayor William H. Thompson of Chicago gravely conducted investigations of textbooks alleged to be over-friendly to the British cause in 1776. The spirit of these inquiries is indicated in the report of the committee to investigate school histories in New York in 1922, from which we learn that "strictly speaking the textbook writer is not a historian. . . . It is for the teacher to determine what material is needed. It is for the textbook writer to supply it. . . . Truth is no defense to the charge of impropriety."

The opposite spirit of American historians was well expressed in a resolution adopted by the council of the American Historical Association:

> In the opinion of this Association, the clearly implied charges that many of our leading scholars are engaged in treasonable propaganda and that tens of thousands of American school teachers and officials are so stupid or disloyal as to place treasonable text-books in the hands of children is inherently and obviously absurd. . . . Genuine and intelligent patriotism, no less than the requirement of honesty and sound scholarship, demand that text-book writers and teachers should strive to present a truthful picture of past and present . . . criticism of history text-books should therefore be based not upon grounds of patriotism, but only upon grounds of faithfulness to fact. The real charge against the historians was not that they were propagandists but that they refused to be.

It would, however, be a gross injustice to the American public of the period to say that they were interested only in the censorship of history. There was a more positive and pleasing side to the general interest in the national past. Single-volume texts on American history appeared annually, and were supplemented by studies in series such as *The Chronicles of America, The Pageant of America* and the *Dictionary of American Biography*. Biography was especially popular. Certain authors made an effort, sometimes with more zeal than discretion, to "humanize" George Washington, so that he would be liked as a man instead of being revered as a marble statue. Abraham Lincoln, who never needed humanizing, was an even more popular subject—the records of the Library of Congress show about eight new books or booklets on Lincoln for each year of the period 1914-1928. A corresponding cult for General Robert E. Lee as the central figure of the Epic of the South reached comparable proportions. Hamilton, Jefferson, Marshall and many lesser heroes, especially Western pioneers and unconventional figures in the social history of the country, were reportrayed for the new generation. "A glance over a bookshelf which holds some new American biographies that I have read in the past year or two," said a critic,

> shows George Washington and Billy the Kid, Thomas Jefferson and Wild Bill, Aaron Burr and Jesse James, William Lloyd Garrison and Brigham Young, Poe and P. T. Barnum, Carl Sandburg's Lincoln, Bill Nye, Andrew Jackson, Commodore Vanderbilt, John Paul Jones, Margaret Fuller, Benjamin Franklin, Henry Ward Beecher. What a hash! But they are all good biography. Not a plaster saint on the list. They are written scientifically, trying first of all to get at the truth about the man and set it forth.

Some of the most successful motion-picture films likewise dealt with American history: the Oregon pioneer in "The Covered Wagon," the building of the Union Pacific in "The Iron Horse," an earlier generation of

Gothamites in "When Old New York Was Young." There was a notable
revival of interest in the "Paul Bunyan" legends of the north-woods lumber
camps and similar American folklore. Colonial furniture became more than
ever the fashion among the wealthy, and prices were paid for counterpanes
and obsolete lamps that would have gone far to purchase a spinning machine
or furnish a house with a complete installation of electric lights. State historical societies rescued from oblivion traditions of the pioneers. Historic
homes, such as Thomas Jefferson's Monticello estate, were refurnished for
public exhibition. Many excellent monuments—from the Lincoln Memorial
in Washington, D.C., to the sculptures in honor of the Confederate army
on Stone Mountain—commemorated heroic deeds of the past. A typical
venture by America's most typical citizen was Henry Ford's restoration of
the Wayside Inn of Longfellow's poem, and his "village of yesterday" which
aimed to "assemble a complete series of every article used or made in
America from the days of the first settlers." Through the munificence of
John D. Rockefeller, Jr., work was begun to restore the old town of
Williamsburg in Virginia to its colonial appearance.

If this chapter has been mainly a chronicle of the absurdities and extrava-
gances of American nationalism, the fact should not be taken to imply that
there were no compensating gains. One should reckon on the credit side
the devotion of all classes and all sections of the country to a common cause
in the World War, the extension of federal aid to education and welfare
work, the increased civic pride which made many an ugly mill town a
garden city. H. G. Wells in the years before the war criticized the American chiefly for his lack of any "sense of the state"—he was too individualistic, selfish, preoccupied with his private business, to think of the nation.
No such charge was brought against the postwar American citizen, indifferent, perhaps, to party politics but immersed in a tangle of civic duties and
welfare movements. Public spirit there was in abundance; only instruction
was needed to harness it to useful tasks.

❦ ❧

IT *was said once that if the Papacy could survive the Renaissance Pope
Alexander VI, it could survive anything. An American might well conclude
that if the Presidency could survive Warren G. Harding, it too could survive anything. Few men have been more unfit for the office they were
elected to than the 29th President of the United States. William Allen
White described his predecessor as "a frozen flame of righteousness"; Alice
Roosevelt Longworth, Theodore's acid-tongued daughter, dismissed Harding as "a slob." Even by his own admission, the former Senator from Ohio
ought never to have been elected President. Any question about the wisdom
of that conclusion is removed by a brief contemplation of the scandals that
rocked Harding's administration; all of them revealed after his sudden death
in August of 1923.*

Something of the lurid nature of Harding's Presidency was suggested by one historian who wrote in the mid-sixties of the four scandals of Harding: 1. Did he know how shamefully his friends had abused his confidence? Apparently yes. 2. Did he father an illegitimate daughter by Nan Britton? Yes, and evidently he indulged in other extramarital adventures. 3. Did he have Negro blood? Probably. 4. Did his wife or someone else cause his unexpected death? No. But as the four items suggest, Harding's personal life was that of a weak, self-indulgent man. In fairness, it should be added that he possessed a fundamental decency that made his tragedy all the more shocking.

Historians have shied away from telling of the Harding tragedy. For one thing, a good part of the documentation was destroyed either by his wife after his death or by his faithless friends who had the good sense to know that it might send them to prison. For another, the Roaring Twenties with its swirl of social change and persistent commitment to retrogressive values presents too complex a kaleidoscope for easy analysis. One might say that the colorful incident in its plentitude has obscured historical vision. It has been left to the journalist and the novelist, less inhibited by the strictures of documentation, to tell Harding's story. Few have done it with greater verve than Samuel Hopkins Adams (1871-1958), a novelist turned social historian. The history he relates is of the sort that the human imagination would quail at inventing, but then truth is often stranger than fiction.

INCREDIBLE ERA

THE LIFE AND TIMES OF WARREN GAMALIEL HARDING

by Samuel Hopkins Adams

Everyone wished well to the incoming President. The stalwart figure, the handsome, genial face, with its kindliness of glance, its smiling mouth, its frank expression, the patent humanity, simplicity, and sincerity of the man, made up a picture of typical Americanism which filled the eye. No President ever enjoyed a greater initial popularity. Much was in his favor at the outset; a hope in all sections of public opinion and in many a faith that he would be able to restore equilibrium and prosperity through establishing that "era of good feeling" which he had forecast; the personal friendship of the congressional leaders; and not least, the strong favorable prejudice of the Washington correspondents, who understood and liked him as he understood and liked them, in the caste-fellowship of working newspapermen. No other President up to his time met with such consideration or was treated with equal tolerance for his blunders. I do not mean to imply that news was distorted in his favor. But wherever his course was dubious, he received the benefit of the doubt in fullest measure, and charity covered, as long as it was possible, a multitude of errors which, had he been regarded with a less affectionate lenity, would have stood against his official account.

In a moment of optimism, the President-elect had expressed the opinion that government, after all, was a pretty simple business. He was now to put that hopeful theory to the test. Friendly counsellors thought the prospect more dubious.

"Never has any President come to the tremendous office with so much unfinished business and so many fresh problems of moment," warned the *Philadelphia Public Ledger*.

Due to Wilson's collapse, post-war economic complications, and the "quarrelsome inertia" of Congress, the mechanism of government was practically stalled. Vital readjustments were necessary. Business men were demanding, "What is to be done to restore good times?" The unemployed were crying, "When do we get our jobs back?" The more decent-minded of a public, now widely given over to the lawlessness of evasion, impatiently wanted to know, "When does Prohibition begin to prohibit?" All voices joined in the wail, "Reduce the cost of living." More specifically, constructive action was required on waning national finances, taxation, disarmament, tariff, the peace treaties, and the League of Nations.

Looking beyond our borders, the view was no more reassuring. Our relations with Mexico were touchy. Senator (now Secretary) Fall and the oil barons had been pressing for intervention. There was unrest in Cuba. War clouds were forming in the Orient where Japan and Russia were making faces at each other. Europe's diplomacy of tooth and claw was fostering those inequities and engendering those vengeances which now, a generation after, are liquidating themselves in a new and more dreadful blood-bath. Germany was prone. Soviet Russia, an unknown quantity, was knocking at our door for recognition. England was peevish at us for our Yankee smartness—a little more sharp than honest—in the matter of Panama Canal tolls. Foreign cartoonists delighted in picturing Uncle Sam as a Shylock because we exhibited the shocking bad taste of wanting our cheerfully loaned money back.

People looked to the Administration to set everything right.

"The whole world hangs upon Mr. Harding's every word," declared the *Advocate of Peace*.

Mr. Harding had no helpful word to contribute. His inaugural address was vague where it should have been definitive. He was feeling his way, leaning upon others. "Ike" Hoover, a shrewdly analytical judge of men, commented upon the ease with which Harding's congressional cronies were able to convince him that whatever they wanted was right. He followed others because he lacked a program. Domestic dilemmas and foreign complications alike were obscure to a mind which had never found occasion to be studious or analytical. Harding simply didn't know what it was all about.

His pathetic admission to one of his secretaries illustrates the confusion of a mind appalled by the mass of material presented for its digestion. The immediate subject of his consideration was tax reform over which Wall

Street was at odds and the party financial sharps wrangling among themselves.

"I can't make a damn thing out of this tax problem," he complained. "I listen to one side and they seem right, and then—God!—I talk to the other side and they seem just as right, and here I am where I started. I know somewhere there is a book that will give me the truth, but hell! I couldn't read the book."

On tariff his brain was little if any clearer. He announced that he was for "a two-cent tariff" and his puzzled supporters looked at one another and asked in pained voices what the devil he meant by that. Poor President! Before he had been in office a week, twenty thousand pages of expert opinion on subjects of prospective legislation were dumped on the desk before his stricken eyes.

He astounded an interviewer, Bruce Bliven, with this obiter dictum:

"The United States should adopt a protective tariff of such a character as will help the struggling industries of Europe to get on their feet."

Fearful that something had gone wrong with his hearing, Mr. Bliven asked for a repetition and took down the words as the President repeated himself verbatim. He published it in the *New Republic*, as spoken.

Arthur S. Draper, correspondent of the *New York Tribune*, had come back from Europe to conduct a round-table on "Foreign News" at the Williamstown Institute of Politics. While in London he talked confidentially with such men as Lord Robert Cecil, Sir John Simon, Austen Chamberlain, Ramsay MacDonald, and leading editors and publishers. After a press conference at the White House, he was detained to see the President. He had expected to have a talk of fifteen or twenty minutes with Harding and Secretary Judson C. Welliver, but the President swept it aside by saying:

"I don't know anything about this European stuff. You and Jud get together and he can tell me later; he handles these matters for me."

On learning, however, that Mr. Draper had encountered a former *Marion Star* man in London, the President was much interested and held him in talk to hear all about his old employee.

"Jud and I had a long lunch together," writes Mr. Draper, "and he told me how difficult it was to get the President interested in foreign affairs. . . ."

Harding's own self-estimate is pertinent. To David Lawrence he expressed the humble conviction that he was "a man of limited talents from a small town. . . . Oftentimes, as I sit here, I don't seem to grasp that I am President."

In his official capacity the new President bore himself with dignity and gravity. Members of his Cabinet were struck with his seriousness; he seemed to them to be approaching his heavy task with a full appreciation of its import. He was eager to win and hold the respect of men whom he recognized as his mental superiors. Without question this was his instinctive attitude toward at least three of his official family. The dignified Secretary of State, the unobtrusively forceful Secretary of Commerce, the shy but impressive Secretary of the Treasury were, to him, Mister Hughes, Mister Hoover, Mister Mellon; or, more simply, Mister Secretary.

From them, rather than from his intimates, Daugherty and Fall, he took his official tone. The stage was set for statesmanship, and the President readily took on the form and color of his environment. He was sorely and righteously offended when the late Will Rogers, in a radio burlesque of a Cabinet meeting, represented him as boasting of his golf and interrupting discussions of weighty affairs to telephone an inquiry about the baseball score. Jokes about his drinking and poker parties flicked him on the raw. He thought them unseemly.

His Cabinet had the appearance of a great asset, in the beginning. It could be roughly divided into two groups: the officially loyal—Hughes, Hoover, Mellon, Wallace, Denby, Weeks, and Davis; and the personally devoted—Daugherty, Hays, and, so far as anyone then knew, Fall. Fortunately or unfortunately, according to the viewpoint, Harding had a weak Congress to deal with. Leadership was lacking in the Senate. Lodge, the titular leader, was slipping. Penrose, the most powerful intellect and the most skilful manipulator in the body, pottered about in clothes grotesquely too large for a form shrunken by the dissipation and disease that was soon to carry him off. Knox, Smoot, Warren, and McLean of Connecticut all wielded influence rather than authority. Factional dissensions split the majority party.

In the lower house Speaker Gillett had passed the peak of his power, as had Fordney, chairman of the Ways and Means Committee. Nicholas Longworth and James R. Mann, neither of whom was identified with the Harding crowd, were forces to be reckoned with. While the House was more conservative than the Senate, there was enough insurgency in both to cause legislative uncertainty and, for a time, legislative impotence.

All signs were set for positive action by the Executive. A Wilson, a Roosevelt, a Cleveland would have taken full advantage of such conditions, perhaps over-advantage. Harding had modelled himself upon the inert and negative McKinley. By his own interpretation of his function, he was there to serve the nation through the party; the leaders of the party with an indubitable mandate as leaders of the nation, would show him how best to proceed. One of his secretaries viewed him at this time as "voluntarily allowing the power of the Executive to fall lower than it has for the last twenty-five years," while at the same time giving him credit for being "of great virility . . . conscious of his present power . . . of undoubted courage." From this estimate another of his secretaries, Mr. Welliver, differs in part. He thinks that President Harding "never appreciated the extent or effectiveness of the moral force he might have wielded."

Mr. Crawford's words, "voluntarily allowing," express President Harding's conscious attitude of mind. He saw himself as one of an aggregation, all committed to the same end. There is a legend that, after the election he said to a little group of political friends:

"We're in the Big League now, boys. We're going to play ball."

From every member of his Cabinet, his secretariat, his Administration, he confidently expected the same teamwork which he meant to and did contribute within the limitations of his conception and his capacity.

Not all of his team-mates were as altruistically disposed. They were out for the spoils. Ever amenable to party demands, the President responded. One of his first acts was to cheer the faithful by an executive order shifting thirteen thousand postmasterships from the protection of the Civil Service regulations, under which Wilson had placed them. "The spoils system is back in high speed," snapped the *New York Times*. If one may believe Harding's assurances to the Academy of Political Science in New York, nothing was further from his intentions; he promised that economy and efficiency would prevail in the Administration. Perhaps he did not mean to be taken too literally. Postmaster General Hays, however, seems to have accepted the pronouncement in good faith. He organized his department for service, thereby mitigating the effect of the executive order and disappointing many hungry office-seekers.

As Senator, Harding had adopted a *laissez-faire* policy. Now he was in a position where slackness was impracticable. Neither lazy nor negligent toward his new duties, he nevertheless did not bring an efficient method to their performance. The task was too big for him. Instinctively he leaned upon others. "Ike" Hoover wrote of him:

> He never seemed to be very concerned with the fate of a measure under consideration, depending more on these so-called friends to take care of his interests.

Penrose had expressed the will of the party leaders in saying, "We are going to put in a man who will listen." Harding was willing to listen; he had always a well-grounded ear; now he was more than ever anxious to hear counsel. But the powers that had elevated him had nothing valuable to say to him. When they did speak, it was in voices so diverse and discordant that the result was confusion. On tariff, on taxation, on the sorry heritage of war their program was threatening to bog down because of intra-party squabbles. Sensing that he was more popular than they, the leaders hoped that he might assert the authority and prestige of his office to restore order. Would he come to the aid of the party?

This was outside the bargain. He had not expected the Best Minds to delegate their functions. Worse, the Senate, forum of said Best Minds, was dividing into mutually recriminative factions, acting like a lot of unruly children. Even in the House, when he turned to it as the more conservative body, sour notes impaired the party harmony.

Harding could go to the front for his friends. He was ready to stand up and fight on such issues as the defence of a Daugherty or a Forbes. But to battle for a principle was beyond his political tradition.

Republican newspapers were clamoring for tax revision. Responsive to their arguments, the schedule-makers put taxation first on the legislative programme and tariff last. Before election Harding had declared for heavier rates on large incomes. Secretary Mellon converted him.

As one of the world's richest men, Mr. Mellon logically and conscientiously conceived his official duty to be the conservation and protection of wealth. Under his influence the President reversed himself and advocated a maximum impost of thirty-two per cent. This was bad politics. The memory of the "quickie" millionaires of the war still rankled. Pointing out that the House would insist upon a severer ratio, Congressmen Fordney and Longworth persuaded Harding to accept an increase to forty per cent, which they thought they could carry through. They were mistaken. Led by the malcontents of the Middle West, where large fortunes are comparatively rare, the "wild asses of the desert," as Senator George Moses was to call them in a spirit of irritability rather than of tact, took the bit in their insurgent teeth and ran out on their President. The fifty per cent maximum in the new income imposts was his first major defeat.

After the tax bill was enacted, no one liked it. It was nobody's child, everybody's stepchild. In both houses the Democrats sneered and the Republicans snarled. The pro-Administration *Herald* thought it "a thoroughly bad job."

Although permanent action on the tariff was postponed, something had to be done to carry on. The Emergency Tariff Bill became a law on May 27, 1921. It was a sorry makeshift, a compromise arrived at by the familiar pull-devil, pull-baker method. It was no more popular than the tax effort.

Harding put forth two pet projects of his own, the Department of Public Welfare and the Ship Subsidy Bill. Congress was not kindly disposed. It declined to recognize the President's leadership in the field of legislation. The Senate was becoming critical of his "personal" appointments, which it regarded as encroaching upon its own prerogatives; it asked questions about his tampering with the Civil Service. Presumably as indication of independence, it turned down both Public Welfare and Ship Subsidy. Harding accepted the rebuffs. He was not a fighting man.

Compensation and comfort were found in the success of the Budget and Accounting Bill. When, with the President's support, it became law, he appointed Charles G. ("Hell-and-Maria") Dawes, Budget Director. For the first time business system was introduced into, and a business check set upon, government expenditures. The effect was swift and definite. Within six months taxes were reduced at the rate of a round billion a year, notwithstanding which the public debt was cut down in about the same ratio.

Another mark to the credit of the President (though entered on the debit side of his political ledger) was his stand on the Soldiers' Bonus. For a time he showed a disposition to play safe. Acridly reminded by the *New York Times* that if he expected to stem the raid on the Treasury and enlist help from legislators it must be "by the application of some pressure other than that of an arm around their shoulders," he announced his opposition and fought so valiantly that he delayed the passage of the bill for a year.

At the end of six months' incumbency, President Harding was able to felicitate himself upon economies initiated, tariff and tax problems on the way to solution (here he was overoptimistic), and prosperity returning. Well-disposed, as a whole, Washington correspondents concurred in his self-approval. Mark Sullivan, casting up half-yearly accounts, decided that the President had "undersold himself to the public." He admitted that Mr. Harding had not taken over leadership, but saw no evidence of subservience to the senatorial cabal, and credited him with "good housekeeping and business management."

"No one doubts that the present Administration will make a record never equalled before," he wrote, a forecast sadly borne out by subsequent developments, though not within the meaning of Mr. Sullivan's encomium. He also estimated as "the best Cabinet we have had in a generation" a body of men which was to see one of its members a convicted criminal, and two others dismissed in disgrace.

All this is cited, not in disparagement of Mr. Sullivan, whose reputation for perspicuous observation and honest evaluation is established, but to show how eager was the desire and hope for a successful administration. Ninety-five per cent of the nation, probably, would have endorsed his estimate.

Confusion and obstruction were threatening, but not yet obvious. The "era of good feeling" which Harding had invoked was still in progress. Praise and support were plentiful; criticism mild to the point of charity.

Had the President chosen to assert himself positively at this time, he might possibly have established real leadership, though it is doubtful whether he would have had the force to maintain it. The party guides were still unable to get together on any of the "three T's that all spell Trouble," tariff, taxation, and treaties. The House was battling the Senate on duties. West was hostile to East. Bloc was at sword's point with bloc on almost any issue. Under the incitement of Fighting Bob La Follette, twenty-seven senatorial recalcitrants had formed a working coalition. They held the balance of power. They could neither be bought nor bluffed. Penrose, the trusted adviser and "trouble-shooter" of the Old Guard, discouraged, disgruntled, and misanthropic, angrily admitted his impotence and cursed that of his colleagues. The spirit of rebellion spread to the lower House where a band of insurgents, less powerful and close-knit than their Senate congeners, were nevertheless capable of making trouble in plenty. All of this the President, as titular leader of the party, was called upon to face.

It might have been worse. However perturbed and divided the Best Minds might be, however troubled and muddled the presidential thinking, the nation was still favorably inclined. In the early fall elections, Massachusetts and New Mexico remained sturdily Republican. Harding was encouraged.

*   *   *   *   *

Nineteen-twenty-one, passing into nineteen-twenty-two had seen President Harding full of vigor, zest, and purpose. Nineteen-twenty-two, giving way to nineteen-twenty-three, found him a changed man, a man beginning to break, to lose faith in himself and confidence in his regime. Those nearest him noticed a despondency and indecision in his bearing. He took no action without councils and conferences. The most optimistic of his supporters could not fail to perceive that there was no leadership in him.

The November elections had served as a sharp reminder of responsibility, a warning of dissatisfaction on the part of the electorate. With losses of sixty-nine seats in the House and seven in the Senate, though the Republicans retained a nominal majority, the Administration had lost control, since the insurgent wing, growing in assertiveness as well as authority, more than ever held the balance of power. Among the leaders the feeling of slipping control approached melancholia.

This applied chiefly to Washington. Out through the country opinion of Harding was still favorable. His veto of the bonus, sustained by the Senate, commended him to the far-sighted conservatives. So confirmed a liberal as William Allen White published a commendatory article asserting his belief that "our President is ruling the nation and doing a better than fair job." Samuel G. Blythe noted captious criticism in certain quarters and called for a fair deal for the President. The intellectual and moral leaders of Republicanism exhibited a growing respect for Harding as the Administration progressed. Elihu Root, who, late in 1920, "did not believe that Harding was of big enough calibre for the Presidency," changed his mind and wrote:

> I knew him very slightly at the time he was elected and I was afraid he was going to be too anxious to please everybody, but he has shown himself to have a decision of character and cheerful courage that are most gratifying. I have stopped having depressing thoughts about him and have turned my private, individual worry current on to Congress which is not quite holding up its end.

In party circles nobody had any conception of the extra-political activities beneath the not-yet-abnormally troubled surface of Washington.

Responsive to the worries of those about him, the President called a secret emergency meeting of trusted advisers, to bring about better teamwork. Among those invited were Lodge, Smoot, Brandegee, McCumber, Longworth, Fordney, Speaker Gillett, and Everett Sanders. Vice-President Coolidge was not there.

The project of holding caucus on important votes was brought up. It annoyed Lodge who sensed in it a slur on his titular leadership of the Senate. He was holding conferences whenever necessary, he pointed out. In rebuttal, some of the others charged that he was slack about taking his associates into his confidence. The undercurrent of sentiment and expectation was that here was the President's opportunity to take over command. He did not do so. The caucus idea was dropped. The meeting had accomplished nothing except to demonstrate the slow party disintegration.

Among the Best Minds there was disaffection. Senator Brandegee split sharply from the President on his League and treaty policies, if they may be so termed. Harding's personal appointments had always irked the Senate. Now one of them brought about a difference with his Secretary of the Treasury. Friendship and the fact that they used to steal melons together in boyhood apart, there had been no discernible reason for the appointment of Neighbor Daniel R. Crissinger to be Comptroller of the Currency. When it was proposed to advance him to the important and responsible post of Governor of the Federal Reserve System, Secretary Mellon protested. Harding stiffened. That was his invariable attitude where friendship was put to the test. The appointment went through and proved one of the worst in a bad list. To Crissinger's ignorance and ineptitude, as later evinced, Mark Sullivan attributes a considerable share of the responsibility for the mad bull market which culminated in the crash of 1929.

The tariff was not working well. Farm prices had slumped, in spite of high duties on agricultural products. But the farmers could not reasonably object when the manufacturers, seeking their share, demanded higher duties. The result was "an extreme of protection which few had thought possible," as Professor Taussig put it. The Fordney-McCumber bill had introduced the so-called "flexible provisions" empowering the President to increase or decrease rates. This was another burden. He lacked expert knowledge of the intricate subject.

In all these controversial fields he strove to bring about the easiest and most peaceable settlements. Whether or not he was yet aware of his condition, he lacked the physical stamina for a fighting program. In January he suffered a sharp attack of influenza, followed by digestive disorders and kidney symptoms. The condition was not so severe as to occasion alarm, but it left the patient still further depressed. He would have been grateful for a let-up in the pace, and set about adjusting his personal habits to a more restful basis.

A pistol shot shattered the hope of respite. Charles F. Cramer, whose wife had warned him by telegram of the corrupt dealings at Perryville, came back to Washington and found himself hopelessly involved through his partnership in the Forbes side-deals. When he learned that, in spite of the well-meant clean-up, there would be a senatorial investigation, he knew that he had reached the end of his rope.

The Cramers were living in the Wyoming Avenue house. The President was on genial terms with the quiet, industrious, middle-aged lawyer and his high-spirited young wife, known to her intimates as "Bonnie." He was an occasional visitor to the home which had once been his.

Forbes had left Washington, but would be called back to testify. Cramer realized that there was no hope of his escaping the witness stand. Thinner of skin than his chief, he could not face the test.

On March 11 he finished his day's work at the office, came home to dinner, and devised an errand of pretended importance which required his wife's presence in New York. She left on the midnight train. After seeing her off, he went home and shot himself through the head. The body was not found until morning. Shortly after the discovery an agent from the Department of Justice was on the spot. Burns's men had a habit, in those troublous days, of arriving early when anything untoward occurred and revelations might threaten.

Washington throbbed with rumors. The most persistent one dealt with the activities of the agent on the spot. The story took several forms, all alike in essentials. The version which presents the highest degree of probability, since it comes through the secret service (not, however, Gaston B. Means!), is this. The Federal Bureau of Investigation man examining the premises, found on a bedroom mantel several letters in the suicide's handwriting, one of which was addressed to President Harding. Taking it to the

Department of Justice for instructions, he was ordered to deliver it personally into the addressee's hand.

It was early. The President, still out of condition from his illness, was not up. Roused, he put on a dressing-gown and came to the Blue Room to meet the messenger. He was pale and shaky. The agent said:

"Mr. President, I have a letter for you."

"Who's it from?"

"Charles F. Cramer. You know that Mr. Cramer is dead."

"Yes; I know."

"Here is the letter, sir. It was found in his room."

Harding stared at the messenger. His face worked. "Take it away. I don't want it."

The operative bore the letter back to the Department of Justice, where it was destroyed.

Capital gossip of the day was busy with two subjects of prime importance. One rumor was that several Cabinet resignations were pending; the other that the President was worn out and would not seek a renomination. It may have been this latter which impelled Harry M. Daugherty to a gratuitous action. He gave out this statement for publication:

> The President will be a candidate for renomination. He will be op-posed by only one other candidate except for one man who always is and always will be a candidate. . . . The President will be renominated and re-elected because the country will demand it.

The strategy of Daugherty's timing would appear to be sound. What more likely, when the President was dispirited and discouraged, sensitive to criticism and wounded by reflections upon his Administration which he considered unjustified, than that a summons to future battle would restore his flagging forces?

Political seers generally regarded the hat-in-the-ring challenge as pre-mature and probably unauthorized. There is no evidence that at this time Harding wished another term, though afterward there was some conven-tional talk of his having desired an "endorsement" at the hands of the people. Reports that there had been an actual quarrel between the two friends over the issue were erroneous, though Harding considered that there had been too much precipitancy. However, for better or worse, Harding was now a candidate. To the duties of the Presidency, he had added the burden and test of being a formal candidate.

As for the whispers about a Cabinet break-up, they were justified not by the five resignations which the wiseacres prophesied, but by one alone. Albert B. Fall resigned at the end of his second year and went openly into the oil business.

Much criticism has been directed against those who sat in Cabinet meetings with Fall for having lifted no voice in reprehension of his corrupt deals, the special targets being Secretaries Hughes and Hoover, and Vice-President Coolidge. What Hughes and Coolidge thought of Fall at this time is not known. But Hoover is on record. Within a few days after the resignation, he wrote a letter, beginning, "My dear Fall," and continuing:

> In my recollection that department has never had so constructive and legal a headship as you gave it.

As an engineer Hoover was better equipped to judge of the operations of the Interior than any other of his colleagues. The inference would seem to be either that the writer of the letter had some ulterior motive—and this would be far to seek—or that the retiring Secretary of the Interior had so cleverly concealed his trail of malfeasance that no suspicions had been aroused. Doctor Hubert Work, who later succeeded Fall, an amiable and ineffective person, did little or nothing to correct the abuses.

Before Daugherty's hat-in-the-ring gesture, a presidential "voyage of understanding" across the continent and up into Alaska had been projected. Now that he was a candidate, there was added reason for Harding's showing himself to the people. The journey would afford the ailing couple a complete change and two months' absence from the thousand daily pressures of the Capital. It was a surprise to Washington circles to learn that Harry Daugherty and Jess Smith, that inseparable pair of White House intimates, were omitted from the tentative list for the tour. Whispers revived that the President was still displeased with his too forehanded nominator. As for Jess, nobody understood his exclusion: he was supposed to be riding high, wide, and handsome in the official parade.

He was not. Somewhere the President had heard what, to every insider in town had been jocular gossip for many months, that Jess was swanking around town like a turkey-cock, acting as if he considered himself the National Government. It shocked the President.

"I am informed," said he to Harry Daugherty, "that he is running around with a gay crowd, attending all sorts of parties, using the Attorney General's car at all hours of the night."

The charge, with slight alterations as to the car, might justly have been alleged against the presidential critic himself, less than a year before. But Jess, however invulnerable in his own magnificent conception of himself, did not enjoy presidential privilege. His career of splendor was over.

How blackened the Smith name was, Jess discovered only when Harry Daugherty brought him the incredibly bad news that he was expunged from the White House roster. He was further advised that, for the good of all concerned, it would be well that he should leave Washington. It was a brutal blow to poor Jess. So far as he knew, everything was lovely. He was having a wonderful time. He was living the life of Riley. To be sure, nosy Senators with their fool questions about him had jockeyed him out of his special quarters in the Department of Justice Building, but he was still the Attorney General's "bumper," with all the dignity, prestige, and immunity of the great office back of him when people with cash to trade for favors were to be impressed. Money was pouring in upon him; such money as he had never dreamed of out in Ohio. People practically forced it upon him.

No misgivings as to the ethical bearing of these transactions seem ever to have troubled his simple soul.

And now this! What had he ever done to his great and good friend, the President, that all should be taken from him! He faced a life from which the glory was departed, a career turned to dust and ashes. Washington Court House, after this greater Washington, was a place of exile, of outer darkness to which he was being committed as if he were a criminal. What was it all about? Graft, to his mind, was a normal principle of politics. Everywhere in the record it stands out that Jess Smith was, in all such matters, morally imperceptive. He did not know right from wrong, nor distinguish between foul money and fair.

He sank into black depression. His health was not good. A diabetic tendency, aggravated by his far from hygienic personal habits, had so undermined his system that after an appendectomy the wound failed to heal. Refusal to accept the sentence of exile did not occur to him. Harry Daugherty had told him he must go. That was final. Whatever Harry said must be right. For his wounded spirit there was but one refuge, Ohio, where he could rejoin Roxy Stinson. Thither he went, and presently Daugherty followed. There was a party at the shack on Deer Creek.

Daugherty had not been well. In February, the solicitous Jess had reported him "still very weak. I don't see how he is going to be able to go South next Monday." At the shack he hoped to get rested. After luncheon he was accustomed to take a nap.

Early one afternoon a caller arrived on business which Jess deemed important enough to warrant an interruption to the Attorney General's slumbers. Daugherty was furious. He berated his alarmed "bumper" and even threatened to go back alone in the car leaving Jess to his own resources, though he relented later. Jess was like a whipped puppy.

"Harry has turned on me," said he to Roxy, in tears.

Back in town he bought a revolver and cartridges at Carpenter's hardware store, to the surprise of the merchant who knew his morbid dread of fire-arms.

"This is for the Attorney General," he explained.

At the next meeting with Roxy, he seemed quiet and calm. He told her that everything was all right.

What follows lacks satisfactory explanation. Why should Jess, banished by presidential fiat, have ventured back to Washington? Possibly to pack his belongings, though he had had ample time for that before. In any case, he went back and established himself in the Daugherty-Smith apartment at the Wardman Park Hotel. He did not pack. It would have been superfluous.

Harry Daugherty did not stay at the apartment with him, but spent the night at the White House. Concerned as to his old friend's condition, he arranged for Warren F. Martin, his official secretary, to remain at the apartment.

This was the night of May 29. In the morning of Decoration Day, Mr. Martin was awakened by a sharp noise near-by. At first he sleepily thought that a door had slammed or that something heavy had fallen. Unable to drop off again, he rose and went into the living-room, beyond which was Jess's bedroom. As usual, the door was open; Jess had gone to bed with his fears of loneliness. He now lay, curled on the floor, his shattered head in a metal waste-basket.

The news was telephoned to the White House. It was a ghastly day, followed by a more ghastly evening when half a dozen pallid people sat around, trying to make conversation, and Harry Daugherty groaned from time to time. Justified though the President was in banishing Jess Smith as a measure of protection, the act must have now appeared to him as at least a contributory cause of the suicide.

Suicide? Was it suicide? All Washington was asking itself the question. The shot in the early morning silence of the Wardman Park Hotel was the starting gun for a rush of surmises, queries, alarms. The ugly word "murder" was on the tongues of men wherever they gathered to discuss the tragedy.

For the safety and mental peace of many important people, Jess Smith dead was indubitably preferable to Jess Smith alive. He had splurged too much; that sort of thing attracts attention and eventually starts inquiries. He knew too much. He talked too much. He had been loose of tongue and braggart of claims in circumstances where silence is the only safety. Worse, his actions for some weeks had given indication of queerness. His mind seemed, at times, to be abandoned to vagaries. There was speculation as to whether drink and dissipation might not be undermining him. An irresponsible Jess Smith who might "spill" could do incalculable damage, could spoil the most profitable and promising graft which had been developed for many years. Furthermore, he had been dealing on a large scale with desperate characters and had not always carried out his bargains with them. Suppose they decided that he had double-crossed them? Suppose, again, he was viewed in the light of a potential threat by people in established and profitable positions? Any well-informed person on Pennsylvania Avenue could tell you offhand a dozen people who would breathe easier with the Ohio grafter out of the way.

There were circumstances in connection with the death that were dubious. No autopsy was performed. The Department of Justice took efficient charge and all was hushed up as soon as possible. One curious fact that came out was the destruction of a mass of papers. Somebody had burned them. Testimony was adduced which seems to indicate that Jess himself was the incendiary. Harry Daugherty supported this theory. It was far from conclusive.

"To my surprise," he wrote, "I found that Jess had destroyed all my house accounts and my personal correspondence. In fact, there was hardly anything left pertaining to my personal affairs."

There were investigators in Washington who would have liked to go through those Smith-Daugherty records.

In so far as suspicion attached to the nature of Smith's death, Daugherty's alibi, had he needed one, was impregnable. He was asleep in the White House at the time.

Charles F. Cramer's suicide had been a sensation. Coming soon after it,

Jess Smith's fate, so similar, was ominous. Putting one and one together, the gossip-mongers surmised an E. Phillips Oppenheim plot to put away such people as knew more than it was safe for them to know. Who would be the next? they asked. The Veterans' Bureau counsel was comparatively obscure, with connections that were narrowly bound within his own department. But the Ohioan was one of Washington's show figures. Through his association with the Attorney General he had become a power. He was known to be well within the charmed circle of White House habitués, a chum of Ned McLean's, hail-fellow with half the Cabinet, and a boon companion of President Harding's. It was not yet known that he had fallen from that high estate.

In a personal sense his passing was a shock to a wide circle of most curiously heterogeneous friends and acquaintances. This ignorant, unlettered, boorish, genial, garrulous, back-slapping drugstore sport from the sticks, arrayed in the smartest apparel purchasable, and pervading official and semi-official drawing-rooms like a shambling butterfly, touched a responsive chord in widely diverse natures. The list of those who wrote or wired condolences comprises such names as T. Coleman Dupont, Will Hays, Mark Sullivan, John Hays Hammond, John Oliver La Gorce, Albert D. Lasker and Wayne B. Wheeler, the Anti-Saloon leader. What did they see in him? Those whom I have asked find themselves at a loss to explain. His friendliness, his spontaneity, his overflowing juvenile zest in the splendid expansiveness of existence, without other qualities to back them would seem hardly enough. To this extent he casts illumination upon the Harding environment, that in no other administration of modern times could a Jess Smith imaginably have attained such position and recognition.

That Harry M. Daugherty was shocked and grieved by the fate of his associate is well attested. Yet according to Roxy Stinson, who was practically Jess's widow, he did not attend the funeral.

Was Smith murdered? The suspicion, so widespread at the time, is still firmly believed by many of the survivors of that unsavory era. Several times in the course of her testimony, Roxy Stinson patently tried to implant the idea that her ex-husband did not die by his own hand. But other statements by her constitute the strongest indication of suicide; indications amounting, I think, to practical proof. He was "down," physically and mentally. His brief career of glory had reached its end in bitter reproof if not open disgrace. The shining radiance of presidential favor was withdrawn. His protector and idol, Harry Daugherty, had exhibited an unprecedented harshness toward him. Their ways had parted. Life held little for the transplanted playboy.

His mind had shown signs of weakening. At times he succumbed to excesses of unreasoning terror, believing that he was followed by mysterious persons with obscure and terrifying intent. He dreaded to be out after dark. Returning from an evening engagement with Roxy, he would insist on walking in the middle of the street. People on railroad trains who did not know of his existence were objects of alarmed suspicion. "They have put the spot on me," he said to Roxy, but added darkly that he knew what to do. Everything was going to be all right. To all this she testifies.

It was all planned in his quivering mind, she believes, when he bought the weapon at Carpenter's store, to take back to Washington with him. All points to suicide motivated by a mixture of hallucination, dread of unknown threats, physical depression and nervous humiliation from the circumstances of his unhealed wound, and incapacity to face a future in which jail was one of the possibilities. It must have been a powerful, perhaps an insane, impulsion which drove the timorous, inconclusive Jess, with his intuitive horror of guns, to send a bullet into his brain.

So died the Happy Grafter.

Two grisly tragedies within the close circle of his intimates accentuated Harding's desire to be quit of Washington. Meantime a brew of other troubles was coming to a boil.

AMERICANS *elected Harding their President by a margin equaled only by Franklin D. Roosevelt in 1936 and Lyndon B. Johnson in 1964. They unknowingly elected a second President in his running mate, Calvin Coolidge. Unknown outside of Massachusetts in 1919, he soared to national prominence in that year, when as Governor of the Old Bay State, he intervened in the Boston police strike, as it already fell apart, by wiring Samuel Gompers of the A.F. of L.: "There is no right to strike against the public safety by anybody, anywhere, anytime." He seemed and proved to be the embodiment of the laconic Yankee. Once in the Presidency, he provided a staid propriety, a virtue particularly valued by a Republican leadership unnerved by the revelations of the Harding peculations.*

Something of the aura of the surface tranquillity that concealed the vast social changes of the twenties is traceable to the President Americans affectionately dubbed Silent Cal. He understood how to reign rather than rule. His mind, what there was of it, rarely rose above the obvious. The legatee of a party half-committed to reform, he propelled the Republican Progressives into an opposition that ended for some only with their joining the New Deal. He commanded the loyalty of the standpatters, the men who saw tomorrow in the yesteryear of McKinley. But they were a dwindling handful in a world where change was everywhere evident. Harding and Coolidge, between themselves, managed to reveal the bankruptcy of nineteenth-century small-town and rural values. And Coolidge earned that cruelest of epitaphs delivered when Will Rogers, told of Coolidge's death, asked: "How do you know?"

In the hands of William Allen White (1868-1944), the superb Kansas editor, the incongruity of Coolidge is made amply evident. Long privy to the innermost secrets of the Republican party, White combined his privi-

leged knowledge with the journalist's gift for the vivid incident, the color-
ful detail, and the penetrating insight. He belongs to the increasing number
of journalist-historians who give perspective and depth to immediate events.
Where historians fear to tread, journalists are obliged professionally to enter.
And those who truly know their business end up writing history.

A PURITAN IN BABYLON

by William Allen White

Calvin Coolidge, at Plymouth in his shirt sleeves and work clothes was doctoring a sick maple tree when the news came to him that Harding was ill. There also was a man of sensibility and not without imagination, whose manifestations he always held in check. When the heart throb between him and the Presidency began to tremble, his own heart may have skipped a beat.

Thursday, August 2, the Coolidges told the newspapermen who were writing of Coolidge's doings that summer, that they were starting Friday morning for a few days motoring trip to visit Frank Stearns at Swampscott, Massachusetts. They were expecting to spend Friday night enroute at the baronial estate of Guy Currier, at Peterboro, New Hampshire. He will be recalled as that old friend of Coolidge's Boston days who as the bipartisan leader of the political forces of New England conservatism had given Coolidge a helping hand in many of his earlier upward journeys. It was a grand palace the Guy Curriers kept there at Peterboro, befitting a man who soon was to leave an estate of three million. The newspapermen noted the Currier visit, and left Ludlow in the afternoon. Nothing held them in Plymouth.

The nearest telegraph office to the Coolidges was at Ludlow twelve miles away on a rough mountain road. No telegrams came for them that day, and no news of President Harding later than Tuesday was available; but that news was most encouraging. Thursday night at the usual early bedtime for Plymouth, the Coolidge household went to bed. At half past ten in Plymouth the Vice President sank into a deep sleep. It was half past seven in San Francisco.

Then the doctor who had been at Harding's bedside all day left the sick room and meeting Raymond Benjamin, an old friend, in the lobby of the Palace Hotel, chatted with him awhile. The doctor explained that he was leaving his patient because he was so much better and the doctor was going for a walk. Benjamin suggested that he join him at dinner and when the doctor declined Benjamin strolled up Market Street to a little French restaurant where he dined leisurely, reading the evening papers, rejoicing that the tide had turned in the President's illness. As Benjamin came into the street at eight o'clock he found it in turmoil. Newsboys were crying the President's death. It had come that suddenly.

Dr. Ray Lyman Wilbur, at that time President of Stanford University, a physician of the highest standing, declared that death had come to the President from an embolism. Because his death was sudden, because obviously those near him knew that he was not putting up a fight, many theories, some of them scandalous, were whispered about after his death. But if death came as a welcome release, how is not important. At 7:30 Thursday evening his nurse coming into the room found him dying. A minute and it was over. It took an hour to arouse the nation.

After midnight into the graveyard quiet of the town of Plymouth, Vermont, came a chugging automobile. It stopped at the white roadside cottage where the Coolidges slept. A man dashed around the headlights and pounded on the door of the Coolidge house. A match flared out, a coal oil lamp was lit, and a head appeared at a bedroom window. Colonel John Coolidge asked sharply:

"What's wanted!"

Breathlessly the telegraph messenger who had come from Bridgewater, the nearest night station of the Western Union, cried:

"President Harding is dead and I have a telegram for the Vice President."

Colonel Coolidge aroused his son and daughter-in-law, dressed hurriedly, brought the messenger into the house, and taking the message to his son's room, read it in the lamplight—a communication from George B. Christian, secretary to President Harding, informing the Vice President of the President's death. With this was a telegram from Attorney General Harry Daugherty advising the Vice President to qualify as President with as little delay as possible. The heart throb between Calvin Coolidge and the Presidency had stopped. His first thought in a flash came:

"I believe I can swing it."

He had looked over the job for two years, had seen how Presidential failures come. He knew his own qualities. He was not afraid. There was exultation in whatever shock, or sorrow the moment may have brought. Here was dramatic, poetic justice: that Calvin Coolidge should have that first fine flare of exuberant self-respect, and have that eager zest in the very scene, indeed staged in the very home where for some sad reason in his childhood his spirit had been broken in shyness, and where either by blood or environing circumstances his whole nature had been turned inward behind a flinty mask!

Here the story slows down. After that first self-reliant moment when the news of Harding's death flashed into the life of Calvin Coolidge, the tempo of his normal life began. He and Mrs. Coolidge dressed, and as they dressed, the Vice President decided what to do. His stenographer came up from Bridgewater in a car a few minutes behind the first telegraph messenger. The Vice President soon had a message on the way to Mrs. Harding. In an hour, Ludlow knew of Harding's death. The few reporters still lingering at Ludlow appeared about two o'clock. Telegraph linemen were tapping the telephone trunk line at Plymouth Union. At 2:30 the Vice President was talking to Secretary Hughes who advised him to come to Washington at once. It was Mr. Coolidge's idea—having a taste, if not for large drama at least for a homely cast of characters of the obvious sort—that his father, who was a Notary Public, should administer the oath which would make Calvin Coolidge President of the United States. So there in the little room, half-living-room, half-office, where Colonel John Coolidge kept his daily accounts and transacted his scant business, eight people saw a President inducted into office. What a beginning for the new President! How superbly he made his entrance into his role—the American classic—from poverty to the White House. The scene was so commonplace, so simple, that with one bizarre touch it might have been prepared as a travesty on democracy itself. Around the President and his father were Congressman Porter H. Dale, L. L. Lane, of Chester, President of the New England Division of the Railway Mail Association, Captain Daniel D. Barney, of Springfield, Vt., Herbert P. Thompson, Commander of the Springfield Post of the American Legion, Joseph H. Fountain, editor of the *Springfield Reporter*, Erwin C. Geisser, Mr. Coolidge's stenographer, and Joseph McInerney, his chauffeur. It was 2:47 by the old fashioned clock on the mantel, a rococo clock with a pressed wood front, the worst of the seventies. A typewritten oath had been dictated by the Vice President which his father held. As the father read, his voice broke. His son repeated the words, phrase by phrase, after him. When the last phrase was spoken, the Vice President put his hand on the open Bible and with decent solemnity added:

"So help me God!"

The new President turned to his wife, put his arm around her. She had been crying. The emotional impact of the news was too much for her. His father held out his hand. The son grasped it for a moment, let it drop, turned away wordless. Yet if that blood clot which closed Harding's life had only taken another turn in the artery—had delayed its course another day—the new President would have taken his oath under the glowing lights of Guy Currier's spacious parlors, surrounded by every bauble of sophisticated luxury that a millionaire's country palace could assemble, with one of the first score of America's veiled political prophets as the new President's host and sponsor. Knowing in his heart of this day's narrow squeak that might have spoiled his humble entrance to power and glory, how this sharp self-centered Yankee must have wetted his lips to throw surreptitious kisses to his Lady Luck for this good turn!

As it was, after the oath was administered to the new President, he beckoned to his stenographer. The two went to the dining-room and President Coolidge dictated a brief statement to the country indicating he would carry through the Harding policies. He expressed a desire that the members of the Cabinet should remain in office to help him, and closed with the faith "that God will direct the destinies of our Nation."

While this ceremonial was progressing under the lamplight in the Coolidge home, hired motorcars from all over the region bearing newspapermen, shiny cars bringing public officials, rattletraps conveying townsfolk from Ludlow and Bridgewater, were coughing like a herd of paleolithic beasts as they came charging up the hill roads from all directions to Plymouth. Before dawn the village street was packed with autos.

Farm houses began to light up. But characteristically, at three o'clock the President blew out the lamps in the Coolidge home and went back to bed. When he got up three hours later, the street before the house was filled with townsfolk from Plymouth, from Ludlow, from Plymouth Notch, and the Union, from all over the adjacent hills. When he appeared at the doorway, he would not make a speech. He greeted his friends simply, with innate good taste. After breakfast he went across the field to the little family cemetery on Galusha Coolidge's farm, where he paused for a time in front of the marble headstone where his mother lay buried. There he stood bareheaded, and silent. Before seven he bade his father goodbye, and he and Mrs. Coolidge started across the hills to Rutland, followed by a long train of newspapermen, local politicians, old friends. That also was a simple, homely American scene. At no time did events get out of key or tempo with the slow, strong rhythm of the Coolidge spirit. He dominated it. At Rutland, Governor Redfield Proctor, surrounded by a crowd of Vermont statesmen, greeted the new President and went with him in a day coach to Albany where he changed cars for New York City. There a private pullman car appeared.

Yet in it no plumed knight was this new President. He was evidently nervous. He wore his second best suit and a golf cap and sat for a time on the divan with Mrs. Coolidge and one of the reporters. Occasionally he would wander aimlessly, nervously through the group of politicians in the car, then duck into his stateroom for a few minutes. At every stop he was on the rear platform waving kindly greetings to the crowd. A photographer snapped him shaking hands with a boy.

Mrs. Coolidge was deeply moved. Her eyes were on the President watchfully. She could not have been unmindful that his nervousness was sometimes staging him awkwardly. She might have feared that the train of mourning by some unconscious gaucherie of the new President would be turned into a journey of triumph which she knew and he naturally realized would be most unfortunate. But their nerves were taut. For he was unused to pageantry and the arts of kings. Thus they came out of the mountains, down the Hudson Valley to New York City, crossed the town from the Grand Central to the Pennsylvania Station and arrived in Washington. They went to their old quarters at the New Willard.

The new President was not so important a figure as the body of the dead President. A spontaneous emotional upsurge of affection for a lovable man, an emotion which Warren Harding would have understood perhaps better than Calvin Coolidge, was moving the heart of the nation. As the funeral cortege spanned the continent, while the Vice President was coming down out of the Green Mountains to the Potomac, tens of thousands of people, perhaps ten times ten, were lining the railroads, crowding at the stations, to pay a last tribute to the dead President. The American people knew little of the scandal that was hovering about the White House, knew nothing of the tragedy of their President's life which made him a shining mark for death.

On the funeral train from Washington to Marion, Ohio, the new President and Mrs. Coolidge felt for the first time the power of the new office. They also began to know its distraction. They were the center of a vast polite pulling and hauling. The train was crowded with Republican statesmen who suddenly had to make their wants known to a new figure in the White House. After two years untroubled by patronage, Calvin Coolidge all at once found himself in the midst of the heaviest patronage pressure area in the world. Every man who approached him might well be under the suspicion of wanting something. When Chief Justice Taft stooped over and kissed Mrs. Coolidge's hand, just after the train left the Washington station, he felt it necessary to explain that "there could be no suspicion of the infusion of the spirit of royalty into the function because of that courtesy." He explained to his wife that he had no office to seek and added of Mrs. Coolidge: "She is very nice." But he continued: "There was a good deal of political talk on the train, even talk of the nomination in 1924" and "Senator Spencer, of Missouri, was voluble on the subject." The Chief Justice makes it plain that when he could get a word in edgeways with the President, he warned the President that Mr. Spencer had the appointment of a federal judge up his sleeve. Every Senator, every Representative, had his little pet scheme to promote, and the Chief Justice noted, with mounting resentment, a Senator who "kept nudging up close to Coolidge to promote the appointment of his judge." There on the train, amidst the shoving and jostling of the new President, began Taft's four year campaign for a high class judiciary. He told the President that the Senator wanted a judge "so that he can appoint receivers or counsels to receivers in the courts." The new President promised the Chief Justice that he would not yield in such cases, and the Chief Justice, being wise and a bit sophisticated, in his letter to Mrs. Taft, expressed something more than a shadow of a doubt about the new President's high resolve.

Amid the whirlpool of self-interest that made the vortex around the new President, the Chief Justice, who was a superb old gossip, picked up and brought to the President on the train after the funeral in Marion this choice bit, that "Charles Evans Hughes had declared that he would not run for the Presidency and that was final." Such a bit of information to take to Calvin Coolidge was worth something. Incidentally the Chief Justice found that in Marion they looked askance at the Coolidges because "they were the successors of the town's great man." They wanted to know "why it was necessary to bring the Stearnses of Boston to Marion, whom Harding did not like, nor they Harding."

The social vampires started to sink their suckers in the new President. A young military aide was fired and an order issued rescinding the discharge. In Washington, the Chief Justice notes that the Ned McLeans, rich social satellites with a newspaper back of them, who had led the gaiety in Harding's White House, began to woo the new President. The night when Mrs. Harding started back from Washington to Marion with her husband's body, the McLeans entertained the Coolidges at their country place and advertised it extensively in the morning *Post*. And the *Post* also printed the story "that Mrs. Harding had to follow her husband's body from the station in the private car of a friend." The Chief Justice explained that as a matter of fact Mrs. Harding had asked the White House people not to send a car for her because she was going in the McLean car. Whereupon the new President soured upon the McLeans. He said nothing at the time, but later to the White House staff, he wrote the word "Finis" at the end of the McLeans' social dominance of his administration.

When Calvin Coolidge turned away from the Harding tomb, in Marion, Ohio, he was President with full powers. The white light beat upon him without a flicker. He and Mrs. Coolidge returning from Marion went again to the New Willard; Mrs. Harding to the White House. The Coolidges made it plain that she must not be hurried in assembling her belongings and leaving the White House.

While the new President waited in the New Willard, he wrote *billets-doux* to his old friends. One to a Northampton politician read:

DEAR GEORGE—
I know you will be thinking about me. I am all right.

Nothing more. Just that!

When at last, after ten days alone in the White House, Mrs. Harding had packed her last trunk, closed her last valise and had put all her personal belongings into the White House car which took her to her hotel in Washington, another White House car was sent immediately to the New Willard for President and Mrs. Coolidge. Their sons were still in New England. It was midafternoon when the new President and his wife alighted from their car and walked quickly across the portico to the doorway of the White House. He wore the proper afternoon garb. She was dressed in black, a color that he particularly disliked, but mourning for Harding was necessary.

Just beyond the doorway in the spacious hall that divides the two wings of the mansion, they stopped for a moment, perhaps to gather themselves, to realize this new realm, the new life, the new magnificence that was upon them. They gazed possessively around for a moment, looked up at the portraits of their predecessors. Some hint, some intaking breath of the sheer power and glory of the greatest elective office on earth was thrilling through them. They walked a few steps into the hall and stood undecided. An usher approached them to guide them to the elevator if they preferred to avoid the stairs. Still shyly they stood for another second. The President turned to his wife and said:

"Now you run upstairs, mamma."

He turned into the little anteroom to greet the head usher, Irwin H. Hoover, known for forty years there as Ike Hoover. The President said:

"I understand how things are around here. I want you, yourself, to keep right on as you are. There will be no change so far as you are concerned. But one thing: I don't want the public in our family rooms on the second floor so much as they have been."

Briefly he indicated that Hoover should expect a change in the gaiety and informality that the Hardings had encouraged. He said:

"I want things as they used to be—before!"

Indicating that he meant the simple and dignified hospitality of the Wilsons which President Coolidge knew only by hearsay. That was his simple answer to a serious and sophisticated social problem, the problem that faces every President who is bedevilled by the rich residents of the Capital city to make the White House a rendezvous of fashion. No such problem had faced him in Boston. In Washington, he had only his common sense and invariable good taste to guide him.

Having delivered his oracular comment, he turned from the head usher and walked back into the hall. There he stood surveying his new domain with a comprehending eye, like an assessor setting down a list of goods and chattels. The head usher standing by him, caught almost a smile, and then slowly draining the moment to its dregs he walked to the elevator and went to his room. In those nine words, "I want things as they used to be—before," the new President changed the whole social aspect of the White House. No more poker, no more Forbes and Fall and Daugherty, no more butterflies clustering around the younger Senate set and the rich idlers of the Capital, no more trash in the White House.

He arose at half past six the first morning and for a few months made it his White House rising hour. He went for a walk in the White House grounds before the servants were up. He looked over the whole menage himself with the same critical eye which he used when as lieutenant governor he trotted over the penal and charitable institutions of Massachusetts. He had taken the Massachusetts post-graduate course in public kitchens. But that first morning, waiting for the day to begin, he installed his mother's portrait on his desk and sat down, the confirmed sentimentalist, to write a love letter to his old friend, the shoemaker philosopher of Northampton which was to pass through Shoemaker Lucey to posterity, guided by the President's far-seeing eye.

The White House,
Washington, D.C.
MY DEAR MR. LUCEY:
    Not often do I see you or write to you, but I want you to know that if it were not for you I should not be here. And I want to tell you how much I love you. Do not work too much now and try to enjoy yourself in your well earned hour of age.
                                Yours sincerely,
                                CALVIN COOLIDGE
    August 6, 1923.

The sentimental mood being upon him, he turned to his other and more powerful sponsor, Guy Currier, of Peterboro, New Hampshire, the grand vizier of New England politics, as it related to all business in New England. He remembered the engagement to visit Peterboro, the engagement broken by President Harding's death. All the business of his place of power did not crowd from his mind the recollection of that engagement, so he wrote with his own hand this note to Mrs. Currier:

The White House
Washington, D.C.

August 7, 1923.

MY DEAR MRS. CURRIER:

We were very much disappointed at not coming to your house and seeing the presentation of the play.

Tell Mr. Currier that Pres. Smith spoke most complimentary of him. With every good wish, I am,

Cordially,
(Signed) CALVIN COOLIDGE

Mrs. Guy Currier,
Peterboro, N.H.

The note to James Lucey found its way into print. Being a rather perfunctory social billet and being politically of no consequence, the note to Mrs. Currier did not find its way into print for several years after his death.

Then, President Coolidge clicked off the current of his sentimentality but not until he had arranged that his first White House guest should be former State Senator Richard W. Irwin of Northampton who had given him "the singed cat" letter sixteen years before. Whereupon he turned to the business of the day.

His faithful friend, Frank Stearns, who had followed him to Washington became a sort of a spiritual buffer to the President who needed Stearns. He sent for Stearns five times during his first Presidential days; one time was a hurry-up call. And after each summons the President let his friend sit there while the President went about his work. Stearns figured it out, probably correctly, that in the new environment with the new duties and a new world pressing down upon him, the President wanted one familiar, dependable, immovable, restful object near him. During all of Coolidge's White House years, Stearns left his business and became the President's silent monitor. Stearns said grace at the White House table. Otherwise it went unspoken. Stearns and Mrs. Stearns often sat quietly with the Coolidges in the evening. And on occasion, he and the President retired to the Presidential study where Lincoln had sat, and Stearns, smoking his cigar, mutely sat by while the President babbled about his troubles and trials. Stearns offered no advice, rarely interjected a syllable of comment. Once in some moment of aberration Stearns told Coolidge that he had been asked to recommend a Judge, and named him. The Boston merchant mentioned the request casually and with no idea of pushing it. But the fact that Stearns had even been approached irritated Coolidge. He snapped out:

"What do you know about the qualifications a man should have to go on the bench?"

"Nothing!"

"What do you know of this man's qualifications?"

"Nothing!"

"Well then, I advise you in the future not to meddle in things you know nothing about."

It was that relation, a sort of father and son relation, one in which the son has a right to be as impolite as he pleases and the father does not care, a relation in which the generic father realizes that the boy takes after his mother and lets it go at that. Stearns who had no idea of meddling, was not peeved. He was merely amused at the younger man's jealousy and pique. There was no political bond between them. It was purely psychological, a desire for comradeship on the President's own terms. And no account of the Coolidge administration, and of Coolidge the inner man, may be written without some relation of this strange association made necessary by a repressed man's urgent need for a confessor. As Mrs. Coolidge has written, he did not respect her education, he never talked things over with her, probably felt that he could not, or should not for some vain reason. And because he knew human nature well, he dared not talk casually to the men he met officially. He was not the kind to make confidants of men who he felt were his inferiors, his office force for instance. Yet human nature could not stand the strain of utter isolation in the White House, so Stearns became the father confessor of the tight-mouthed Puritan with a constricted heart. Stearns, living in the White House, found the new President took many of his problems from the executive offices to the residential section of the White House. He was forever studying questions, reading statistics, cramming for interviews with Congressmen like a student for examination. It was his technique to be ready for visitors before the visitors came. He had the figures. They had a general idea. He persuaded his visitors. He had a retentive mind for facts. Writing was a chore to him. Over and over he worked upon the verbiage of a speech to get the phrases balanced, even to make the syllables click with a metallic rattle trippingly on the tongue. But Stearns remained at the end as he was those first days, the psychological vessel of release. He asked Stearns for no advice, sent him on no errands, told him no secrets. After a thing had happened, he liked to gas about it to Stearns, but disliked questions. Stearns knew his heart, knew how kind he was, and how flinty of skin.

Calvin Coolidge in the White House was the same shy, imprisoned soul who had puzzled men in Boston, who had held them at arm's length in Northampton, who had baffled them in Amherst, who had let them alone in Ludlow, and amused but never warmed their hearts at Plymouth. At Washington he slapped no man on the back, he pawed no man's shoulder, he squeezed no man's hand, gave no man the glad come hither with his "pretty keen eyes." Yet in the secret places of his heart that almost puerile sentimentality waxed fat and warm.

The new President took over the Harding cabinet. Indeed, at no time in his administration, even when he was elected to serve as President in his own right, did he make any notable changes in his cabinet. Men came and went—Secretaries of State Hughes, for instance, and Kellogg, Attorneys General Stone and Sargent, Secretary Wilbur of the War Department, Secretaries Wallace, Gore and Jardine of Agriculture. Two major figures in the cabinet remained through his administration: Herbert Hoover, who represented, if anyone did, the liberal sentiment; and Andrew Mellon, who was the archetype of the complacent, convinced, class-conscious plutocrat. Mellon was advertised in politics as the richest man in the world, which he was not; and certainly the appellation "the greatest Secretary of the Treasury since Alexander Hamilton" was sheer adulation. It was characteristic of Calvin Coolidge that he kept two men so widely different in viewpoints in his cabinet through all the years. In times of crises they gave widely different advice. Instinctively, in those times, he would turn to the man who represented the militant power of concentrated wealth. Indeed, so completely did Andrew Mellon dominate the White House in the days when the Coolidge administration was at its zenith that it would be fair to call the administration the reign of Coolidge and Mellon.

Coolidge's first cabinet meeting in the White House lasted just fifteen minutes. He cancelled three consecutive weekly Cabinet meetings and instead of discussing matters in the full Cabinet he had long conferences with various Cabinet members during the first month of his White House occupancy. He made Bascom Slemp his secretary early in his occupancy of the White House.

It is easy to understand why he called Bascom Slemp to the White House as his secretary. Slemp was a Virginia politician, a former Congressman, the son of a Congressman in a Republican district. He was familiar with Republican politics in the southern states. He had handled patronage there for the Republican National Committee. Political purists sniffed and did not like the odor of Slemp's transactions. But he knew his way around in Washington. His party status had not been questioned. His personal integrity was not at issue, however keenly his political activity had been criticized by those who had no great love for the Republican party. Slemp was the man whom President Coolidge needed, a liaison officer between the White House and the Republican organization in Congress and in the National Committee, a man "diligent in his business" who should stand before kings. From the Democratic press, from the independent press, from the Progressive group in Congress and out, a storm of protest rose over Slemp, but it beat vainly upon the White House. The new President knew exactly what he wanted and he had it. He specified in his preliminary arrangements with Slemp that he should keep no notes, copy no papers, write no intimate memoirs. Bascom Slemp lived up to the letter and spirit of his contract.

Calvin Coolidge, of course, took color from his times. He felt that he was the head of the party of talent and wealth and that talent meant, of course, acquisitive talent which produced and owned the wealth of the land—the Hamiltonian idea made perfect. Bascom Slemp meant successful party manipulation in the interest of talent and wealth. After the World War the reaction in American social and political thinking snapped back beyond Wilsonian idealism, back even beyond Taft's chuckling *laissez-faire* complacence, back of Roosevelt to the Hanna period that followed the Spanish-American War and its rising imperialism.

On one of his earlier visits to the White House in September, the Chief Justice wrote to Mrs. Taft that the President asked the Chief Justice what he thought should be done now. "I told him I thought the country was delighted to have a rest before Congress" . . . met, and that "with approaching and present prosperity the people wanted to be let alone." The next day when the Chief Justice took a group of Circuit Court Judges on a pilgrimage to the White House, he noted that one of the Democratic Judges declared that Coolidge was "the most insignificant looking man he had ever seen in the Presidential chair," but the Chief Justice thought he appeared to great advantage. And the day after that, Harry Daugherty dropped in for a chat with the Chief Justice and after talking over the appointment of certain federal judges in the lower courts, the Chief Justice, not unlikely inspired by his two recent visits to the White House, hinted that it might be wise for Daugherty to retire and found "that he has no intention of retiring. Indeed he is very sensitive on the suggestion." A day or so later, the Court "put on its silk hats and three button cutaways" and went to see the President. And Justice Taft felt "that it was a bit tepid to hang around the White House." He added with fine irony: "He was as interesting as usual!" No subconscious self-interest in Taft's heart could conceal the sad aridity of the Coolidge personality.

Yet Coolidge, the politician, was the Yankee throw-back to McKinley's era. "Coolidge's political philosophy grew to be that of the mid-nineteenth century, the optimistic ideal of democracy as the final solution of all problems, the cure of all evils," wrote Gamaliel Bradford, who understood him, and added, "there may still be something to be said for this theory but it can hardly be said to denote advanced thinking from the twentieth century point of view. It can hardly be said that Calvin Coolidge had much to do with the twentieth century." Which truth makes it more amazing that in this time of reaction democracy, obeying some deliberate instinct—or if you will by some almost unbelievable coincidence—carefully turned the clock in the White House around twenty-five years and then slammed down in the seats of the mighty a man to match the nation's beclouded mind.

Anyway the times called for a nineteenth century tolerance of official malfeasance in Washington in the autumn and winter of 1923. At that moment certain rich men, lumped by New England as "crude westerners"— Sinclair, Doheny, Fall and the oil men, were beginning to appear in the newspaper headlines. The annoying shortcuts to the accumulation of wealth, which these oil magnates were taking, seemed to trample down formal plans of legal usage and ancient custom. The oil scandals were beginning to blacken the front pages of sensational newspapers. Instinctively the new President rejected this gossip. Among those near the President who contended that the oil scandal when it first appeared was a plot of the Democrats and Progressives to discredit a Republican administration, was Chief Justice Taft. His distrust of the Progressives who had caused his defeat in 1912, was excusably bitter. One could not blame the Chief Justice if he doubted the sincerity of the Progressives or the validity of their oil scandal. That he tried to bring the President to his way of thinking, his letters to his family seem to show. And it is also obvious that for several months, Taft's view was reflected in the White House attitude.

The Democrats and Progressives were, from the Coolidge viewpoint, discrediting the whole theory of immanent democracy—that brains are wealth and wealth is the chief end of man. Yet the ways of these western oil barons did not affect his philosophy. Before he had been five months in the White House he declared in a public speech that "the business of America is business." So the activities of the oil mongers could hardly be explicitly condemned offhand even if for the moment they were discrediting the Hamiltonian ideal. But business men did those things more carefully in New England, more circumspectly, within due process of law and generally without crass bribery. There greed was deodorized. Certain Amherst, Williams, Dartmouth, Yale and Harvard alumni who wore braid on their morning coats, and who encased their legs in mouse-colored trousers, burned academic incense in charnel houses. So when Coolidge came to the White House, Sinclair and Doheny and Fall and the western oil men with sludge on their boots were for the moment barred, while the manicured associates of Kreuger and Toll were admitted. The bankers of New York and New England who were pyramiding shares and evidences of ownership and obligation of the railroads, of utilities, of mills, even of the oil wells, and of the mines were welcome. Had not the President said:

"For all the changes which they [the people] may desire, for all the grievances they may suffer, the ballot box furnishes a complete method and remedy!"

In that first year of the Presidential administration of Calvin Coolidge, his countrymen were more interested in their new ruler than in the whims of the various markets. For he was a rare bird. His strange ways in the White House made news. America was passing into an urban civilization and here was the first farm boy to enter the White House for a generation, and barring McKinley, the first since Garfield's day. America smiled when Calvin Coolidge first came there and tried to sit in a rocking chair on the front porch under the great white columns. As Mayor, State Senator, Governor, even as Vice President, he could rock in his porch chair at Northampton and at Plymouth without exciting the multitude. But a crowd gathered in Washington whenever he brought his rocking chair out after dinner and he had to give up the country habit. Irwin Hoover, head usher of the White House, recalls the President parading about the family quarters in his old fashioned nightshirt disporting his spindle shanks, in his rooms, much to the embarrassment of the White House entourage!

How exactly he fitted into the mid-Victorian picture of political rectitude, how like a ghost he came back from Lincoln's Day! The President liked to snoop about the kitchen and the pantry. Mrs. Jaffray the White House housekeeper declares that the President liked to talk over the menus of meals with her and she sent the day's menus up to the President. He didn't like the custard pies made in the White House. Once he suggested that Mrs. Howard Chandler Christy, whose husband was painting the Presidential portrait, go to the kitchen and make some apple pies which he ate with a relish but without comment until Mr. Christy had finished his portrait when he declared that the portrait was almost as good as his wife's pies and let flattery stop at that. Mrs. Jaffray made up a special recipe for his custard pies and his muffins. When the Prince of Wales came to lunch at the White House, the President worked out the menu which Mrs. Jaffray called one of the most extraordinary official luncheons "we ever had at the White House." It was composed of both fruit cup and clear soup, fairy toast, speckled trout, broiled chicken, a mixed salad, strawberries, ice cream, salted almonds and White Rock, and the Prince in one of the voluminous silences that adorned the meal remarked:

"What a marvelous chef you have, Mrs. Coolidge!"

Coolidge liked breakfast food but could not endure manufactured brands, so every few weeks the White House cook would buy a peck of wheat and a quarter of a peck of rye, mix it, and boil a portion of it for the President's breakfast, whole wheat and whole rye. Mrs. Jaffray remembers that once while she was in Mrs. Coolidge's bedroom just before an elaborate state dinner, the President popped in from downstairs. By way of making conversation the White House housekeeper asked him how he liked the dining room and he admitted it was all right. And then she asked him about the kitchen and he cackled:

"I don't see why we have to have six hams for one dinner. It seems like an awful lot of hams to me."

She explained there would be sixty people and that Virginia hams were so small that no more than ten people might be served with one ham. He reiterated:

"Well, six hams looks like an awful lot to me!"

So she closed the debate and left the room and shortly after quit her job. A sophisticated cook working for an old fashioned countryman would have her baffled moments!

Naturally the President slept in a double bed. Twin beds probably seemed new fangled and citified. He liked pets and being a man of routine he generally appeared in the White House from his day in the executive office at the same hour daily. A signal from the executive office sounding in the residential portion of the White House always precedes the President's departure from one section of the structure to another. His favorite cat, a big yellow tabby, hearing the gong sound which heralded his approach, used to stand waiting for him at the door. He would pick her up and drape her like a foxfur from his shoulders to her great delight and go carrying her into the family presence where there were always dogs and birds and various household livestock reminiscent of the barnyard of his early days. He even had a pet coon. And when some admirer sent him a moth-eaten bear, he put it into the Washington zoo and visited it with some regularity to see that it was well cared for.

The social life which the Coolidges instituted when they came to the White House was simple but dignified. No other mistress of the White House in the memory of men living in her day had more charm and brought more adequate training to her task than Mrs. Coolidge. Looking back at those first days of '23 and '24, she set down a dozen years later the fact that she was graduated from a co-educational State University and had taught a year in a deaf school and then had established her own home on Massasoit

Street in Northampton where she remained until the Coolidges left for Washington and were installed in a suite of rooms at the New Willard.

When she came to the White House, it is well to remember that at the first White House reception she wore her best dress made by the town's dressmaker in Northampton, and her utter lack of pretense was the secret of her charm.

She had no official duties in Boston, no executive residence. At the New Willard when Coolidge was Vice President, the Coolidges entertained only formally under the culinary guidance of the Willard chef. But she remembers that when the appalling prospect of assuming her White House responsibilities faced her, she shrank from the task with fear and inner trembling. But she did it splendidly.

Writing to Mrs. Frederick J. Manning during the autumn which followed Harding's death, Chief Justice William Howard Taft commented upon Mrs. Coolidge's anxiety to please. He saw she was not quite certain of herself, yet he was sure that "when she gets entirely at home at the White House she will be a worthy First Lady." He looked forward to "a lovely social season in Washington this winter. The Coolidges expect to do all that is required of them."

However, Mrs. Coolidge was never a part of the President's political family. Over and over in her reminiscences in *Good Housekeeping*, which appeared in 1935, she reveals the fact that she scarcely knew or knew but casually, the members of the President's Cabinet; their wives—yes; Senators' wives, Congressmen's wives, diplomats' wives, of course; but the President drew her into no councils. She did her job. He did his. She spent the money. He went over her bills! She remained to the end the farm wife who looked after the chickens and pigs, butter and eggs, the garden and the kitchen and never fretted about the crops and the live stock.

Yet no more affectionate and dutiful husband ever came into the White House than Calvin Coolidge. And the President's pride in her was beautiful to see. In his family he was a disciplinarian and a strict one. This is revealed by John's reminiscences though Mrs. Coolidge recalls that he only spanked the boys once and that was with a flat hairbrush. When they wrote for dressing gowns from their school, he asked why their nightgowns wouldn't do, and Mrs. Coolidge wangled the money for dressing gowns out of her private allowance. The President was always her problem child. Again and again in those curious comments upon Coolidge stories printed in *Good Housekeeping*, in 1935 she reveals the fact that he had a crusty temper which broke easily. Yet also it is obvious, looking at him through her eyes, that he carried no grudges, that he made up quickly. His son John, reminiscing about him, recalls that the President was a tease. He loved that gay hyperbole of language, part irony, part satire, which dances gaily, sometimes a bit puerilely, around its victim. The word "kidding" expresses it. He even liked to deceive himself and held up his lefthand virtues to mild derision. But he was not always so eager to be the butt of another's joke. It depended upon the joke, and who played it. He was what is known as a practical joker. He found and rang the front doorbell of the White House in his first few weeks. It had rarely been rung, for a footman or usher standing near the door usually greeted the caller before he could ring. A literal White House servant named Mayes, faithful but without humor, was the butt of many of Coolidge's practical jokes. When Judge and Mrs. Hughes were at the White House early in Coolidge's administration, the President rang for Mayes and told him to knock at the door of Judge Hughes's room and see if the Judge was ready for a shave and a haircut. Poor Mayes was worried. He submitted the matter to Mr. Stearns complaining that Hughes had never been shaved, and Stearns would not countermand the order. Mayes knocked gently and when Judge Hughes did not respond, hurried away. It was Mayes who explained to a friend of Taft that he noticed the newspapers were commenting on the fact that Mrs. Taft wore a skirt too short. When she came to the dinner for the Supreme Court, Mayes carefully measured her dress with his eye and found that it was nine inches from the floor. Then he added to Judge Taft's friend: "You and I know what a fine woman Mrs. Taft is and we know that when she wears short skirts, it is not because she is a sport but because she is in fashion." With such a man in the White House, Coolidge had a source of continual delight.

At odd times the President used to press all the buttons on his desk at once and sound half a score of alarms over the White House and bring the servants to him for the sheer fun of it, like the little boy playing at Plymouth, who never entirely died in his heart. Inside him that little boy—sentimental, mischievous, sometimes inconsiderate and cruel—never grew up!

Yet he did not trifle with serious matters. He thought them out as best he could. Bascom Slemp pictures the President in that day—"thinking and thinking and thinking." That line shows Coolidge at his best. Certainly he talked loquaciously to his friends after he had thought. Now this kind of man, money-honest, old-fashioned, self-respecting, conscientious, in short a homely soul, is not the kind to gloss over the misdeeds of the rich vulgarians who were caught in the various scandals of the Harding days. We must remember also that he was sensitive to public opinion once it had set and hardened. By the late winter of 1923, American public opinion seemed to be definitely turned against Fall, Doheny, Sinclair and Daugherty and their associates in the oil scandals. So President Coolidge was ready to act.

But for the orgy of commercial speculation that was beginning to riot over the land he had no words of public rebuke, no dramatic warning. In the presence of thieves stealing the people's birthright in naval oil, even while he knew that in his cabinet men sat who had connived at the rascality, he was dumb. In Heine's study of Shakespeare's "Cleopatra," there is a brilliant portrayal of the contrast between the dark, solemn, austere, mysterious, dreary land of Egypt and the gay, frivolous, trifling Persian harlot who ruled over it. In a striking paragraph about Calvin Coolidge, Gamaliel Bradford declares that: "It would be possible to make an equally effective contrast between the mad, hurrying, chattering, extravagant, self-indulgent harlotry of twentieth-century America and the grave, silent, stern, narrow, uncomprehending New England Puritanism of Calvin Coolidge. And Heine caps his climax with the exquisite comment, 'Wie witzig ist Gott.' "

During his first months in the White House, when President Coolidge went across the land, he observed that national economic and industrial progress had run in a parallel course to the line of progress which he saw while he shuttled from Northampton to Boston and back during the two decades of his public service. Electrical invention had been knitting all industry in all America into a close class-conscious structure, into interlocking directorates, into industrial homogeneity. Here was a new fiduciary invention—produced by electrical financial welding, highly effective, highly possessive rather than creative. The savings mounting in the banks of the little Massachusetts towns were but replicas of mounting savings in tens of thousands of various institutions, trust companies, building and loans, insurance companies, savings banks, mortgage companies all over his America. These savings, by the legerdemain of new business methods and morals had become one lake of capital, placid on the surface, sustained in its waterline by constant springs in the hills while it was being drained slowly into Wall Street. It was a lake of debt—bonds, mortgages, preferred stock, all sorts of curious evidences of obligation were dumped into the lake replacing the fluid capital drained off the cash reserves. Thus as the machines to make machines had been creating industrial debt in plant expansion, the secondary machines themselves were speeding up consumption, piling up goods and chattels at the factory doors. The economic problem of perpetual motion seemed to be solved. Production had been hooked up to the golden machine of perennial credit. We were making wealth by making debt which made more wealth to make more debt. And Calvin Coolidge, President of the United States, with German mysticism in his heart, looking out from the portico of the White House across the lawn at Andrew Jackson's statue, which should have given him a shudder, viewed America to the westward and saw that it was good.

His daily routine was light and comparatively easy. He rose early, breakfasted at eight, went to work at nine, quit at half past twelve, lunched lightly, went back to work at half past two or three, quit in mid-afternoon. His schedule was set in steel. It clocked from minute to minute. In his office he was rarely ruffled. But he was not a hard worker. He delegated his tasks. His relations with public men were much as they had been in Boston—wooden and graceless. But public men themselves were ordinarily not expansive—in Boston! A Yankee of the Coolidge type was unusual but understandable there and forgivable. In Washington, President Coolidge had succeeded five gracious men: Harding, whose one talent was his charm; Wilson, who was charming at times but grim on occasion; Taft, who was always amiable, who breathed frankincense and myrrh; Theodore Roosevelt, who was a gay and happy sprite when he was not one of the devil's own imps; and McKinley, suave, smooth, diplomatic, a trained politician, the second oldest profession in the world which had for ten thousand years learned the philandering arts of the oldest profession. But Coolidge had the sour manners of a stern and rockbound New England spinster. Washington hailed him with curiosity and delight, a new specimen of a rare species. There was no accounting for him by any of the rules of the game laid down in American politics. He was silent when it served his ends, but loquacious, even gabby when he wished to talk.

Three major matters lay on the desk of the new President which demanded his attention between August, 1923, when he came to the White House, and December, when he would have to face the new Sixty-eighth Congress. They were, first in importance, the oil scandals, second, his first Presidential message, and third, a decision about his own Presidential candidacy at the Republican National Convention, in June, 1924, less than a year ahead. Let us take them up in reverse order:

Evidently the decision that he would seek the Presidential nomination of his party was made early. For before Congress met, in December, less than four months after the new President had crossed the portals of the White House, his nomination seemed assured. When he chose Bascom Slemp as his Secretary, the choice was an announcement. Bascom Slemp, a former Congressman from Virginia, the son of a Republican Congressman, was a politician. He went to work on the Southern delegates. The New Englanders had rounded up the North Atlantic Seaboard. He called in John Adams, of Iowa, Chairman of the Republican National Committee, and his committeemen, working with the western Senators, who in 1920 had supported Harding, conservative westerners led by Senator Smoot. They went to work on the West as Slemp had taken over the South, and the New England Senators under Moses were in charge of New England. Chief Justice Taft, whose familiarity in the White House colored his views, wrote to his wife that Lodge could be counted on to do "the Jingo thing," which was true of the Senate under his leadership, and the President built his plans for the Republican Presidential nomination largely ignoring the Republican Senatorial leaders. He gave Bascom Slemp plenary powers. The plan had its drawback. Justice Taft, gossiping in a letter to his wife, tells of a rich Republican who came to Taft worried about making his contribution through Slemp. The rich man wanted the President himself to know about it and be properly appreciative, because chuckled Taft, "Of course while he said he did not wish anything and was only anxious to save the country from the Reds, his wife had let out to me some months ago that she would like a diplomatic post!"

But really Theodore Roosevelt in 1904 had made the same direct appeal to the people over the heads of politicians as Coolidge made in 1924.

Coolidge clashed with Lodge and the Senate jingoes. They favored Japanese exclusion, increased pensions and a soldiers' bonus. He opposed these things.

In spite of all his Yankee cunning, another Congressional group he could not control was the Progressive group. They also had a legislative program and were seeking a Presidential candidate; a score of Senators, or more, mostly westerners with at least eight leaders. The leaders included Senators La Follette, Borah, Johnson, of California, Kenyon, of Iowa, Capper, of

Kansas, Ladd, of North Dakota, Norris, of Nebraska, and Smith W. Brookhart, of Iowa. They were forming what was known as the Farm Bloc. They were backing an agricultural bill known as the McNary-Haugen bill, which provided for an equalization fee to market surplus agriculture and to subsidize agriculture by stabilizing the home market. They were also fighting a rear guard action against the retreating railroads that for fifty years had been the particular devils of American reform politics. The railroads had flourished under the curses of the Grangers, of the Greenbackers, of the Populists, of the Rooseveltians and of La Follette. This progressive group, which Vice President Coolidge had met in the Senate, was strong enough in December, 1923, in the House, to delay for three days, when the new Congress met, the election of Congressman Gillett, of Massachusetts, as Speaker, and Congressman Nicholas Longworth, of Ohio, as floor leader. This progressive group, to all intents and purposes, was a third party deeply different in aim from the Republican party, able to ally itself with the Democratic party when the Democratic party saw the advantage of yielding to progressive principles and making a majority to harass the flank of the Republican phalanx. These progressives were blood-bred martyrs. They sought trouble. Turmoil was their meat and drink. The spotlight was ever their strongest weapon. Inevitably Coolidge, however earnestly he tried, would fail to tame them. For in the long run they would distrust his methods and suspect his aims. He had no personal quarrel with them. Yet the progressive congressional leaders did not long maintain cordial relations at the White House. At first, Hiram Johnson, George W. Norris and La Follette came and went and Brookhart when he pleased, but their days there were numbered. Between them and the President was an inevitable clash of temperaments. This was not true of progressive Senator Capper. When Mrs. Capper died, the President and Mrs. Coolidge asked Senator Capper to come to the White House after her funeral and live for a time. Yet for all his waving olive branches, the progressives sensed that Coolidge was a party man first and would only go with them so far as they could command a Republican majority. Capper had voted a score of times to defeat administration projects. Capper was the head of the Farm Bloc. When the President finally vetoed the McNary-Haugen bill, he used such emotional language that the message cracked with malicious static. Yet the President kept trying to placate the Progressives. During that first White House year, he appointed Governor Gifford Pinchot as coal mediator in a struggle in the bituminous coal region of Pennsylvania and western Virginia. He pardoned all of the prisoners convicted under the espionage act. Whatever he could do as a pious party stepmother for these impish party orphans—or worse—he did—everything but giving them the key to the pantry. He had his Presidential nomination bagged. But he had it with the sullen opposition of many Progressives and without much help from the regular Senatorial leaders, Harding's friends—the Senate cabal of 1920.

When it came to his second objective which was his first Presidential message to Congress, he was fairly sure of himself. He recommended adherence to the World Court. Many, probably, most of the Progressive

Senators were internationalists. But that did not break their lines. Neither did his declaration in favor of recognizing Russia, nor his fair words for the farmer. A few days later the President let Secretary of State Hughes wipe out the implications of the President's fair words to Russia. That episode irritated the Progressives. Yet his message had many mellow spots, which should have attracted the Progressives. But they sensed his inner attitude of conservatism. They were intransigent—"agin the government," and so remained to the end of his term, a quarrelsome, militant, uncompromising group the like of which was never known on any New England land or sea. This group was on the whole without either distrust or enthusiasm for the nominee.

Perhaps the rise of this Progressive bloc in the Senate was rooted in the decay of Republican leadership. That decay began with the introduction of the direct primary and the direct election of United States Senators by the people. Senators elected by the state legislatures were beholden for their election to forces which controlled legislatures—generally those forces which would pay lobbyists to organize and direct legislatures—capital in its corporate forms. The Senate, which McKinley knew, had vanished. It is not fair to assume, indeed it is most unfair to presume that the Senators of the later day, coming directly from the people, were more nobly patriotic than those Senators coming from legislatures directed by the benevolent despotism of the last half of the nineteenth century. Probably the state legislators on the whole, discounting the scandals and the flagrant corruption of the times, were men of more intelligence, of more parts and consequence, than their successors in the days of Wilson, Harding, and Coolidge. It was not a question of patriotism, not a matter of erudition. In the days of Grant, Cleveland and McKinley, Americans of the highest vision were looking toward an expanding America. They were interested in problems of production. So were all the people. But when the primary came, and when the direct election of United States Senators was achieved, problems of production were secondary problems. The people—particularly the people of the agrarian West were interested in problems of distribution. So the complexion of the Senate changed—not in patriotism, not in honesty, not in nobility, but in aims, aspirations, purposes. It was a new world.

Calvin Coolidge, as Vice President, knew the Senate in the beginning of a decline. Senator Penrose, titular leader of the Senate, was dying. He had inherited his scepter from Nelson Aldrich and surrendered it to Henry Cabot Lodge. When Lodge came to power, he was sated with glory. The Lodge whom Vice President Coolidge knew had refreshed his spirit with a victory over President Woodrow Wilson in the contest for the American entrance into the League of Nations and the World Court. But Lodge was old and proud. The sublimated vanity of the conscious patrician gaited him in his public appearance. His hold slackened upon his Republican Senatorial associates. Despite the diligence which had energized his earlier life, he seemed lazy. The progressive Senators were younger men, chiefly westerners —outlanders to Lodge. Their creed, an inheritance from Theodore Roosevelt, revised by the elder La Follette, was gibberish to the Massachusetts

Brahmin and the open liaison with the Democrats which the Republican Progressives flaunted in the Senate sickened him. They were living in open sin and Leader Lodge could do nothing more effective than to brand them with the Scarlet Letter. Which pleased and amused them and helped them at home in the hustings.

Often, perhaps generally, men of Lodge's caste of mind who appear in high places in politics are encrusted by a protective innocence. They put out of their minds the knowledge of how the mechanics of politics reinforces the shaky foundations of any jerry-built capital structure. But Calvin Coolidge was no innocent. He knew from the hour a bill was drafted in a lobbyist's office, how it was conceived, gestated, born and nourished into maturity. In the White House he played the game with the most astute regular Republican parliamentary leaders. He lost sometimes, but they knew that he knew their tricks and wiles. Often he had gone up and down the backstairs of Massachusetts politics, yet unsmudged with scandal.

Still this is important: His political advancement unquestionably came because he was willing to accept political favors from men who might much more conveniently have given him money for political attitudes and for political actions which from his own viewpoint were fundamentally right. He too often saw justice in the policy of those who use government as a shield for economic privilege. He sometimes stood for the public interest. But the Coolidge quality that endeared him to the Congressional leaders of his party was his slant toward the dollar once it was legally galvanized as an "investment." Men of wealth, seeking to put the gold plate of authority upon legalized past deeds and deals which were built upon sand, found Calvin Coolidge in Washington, as in Massachusetts, generally willing to accept their claims as rights. He asked few questions. Generally speaking, property once it had gathered itself under a charter and was guarded by a silk hat, was sacrosanct to him.

On the whole therefore, the regular caucus Republicans in Congress were pleased with his message and accepted his leadership. He tried to lead where they delighted to follow. Moreover they realized he was not squeamish about this political alignment at home and in Washington. He was not offended by the knowledge that certain of the congressional leaders were beholden to representatives of the major commodity industries in their states—oil, steel, transportation, food, textiles, communication, banking, copper, coal, insurance, lumber. He declared in his speeches that "the business of America is business." It was plain that in his first message he had consecrated his country under the moral government of an orderly universe, to profits.

So much for the first two items of business on the new President's desk: his presidential nomination and his message to Congress. The oil scandal was not so easily dismissed. No cry of alarm, no exclamation of wrath rose in public and little in private from the new President to rebuke those who were touched with the tar of the various scandals which the Harding administration had produced. To Coolidge, Harding was a Republican President who should be shielded in his mistakes. So at first, President Coolidge gave no encouragement to those who were fighting to uncover the scandals in the Interior and Navy Departments. It was evident from the start that he would "go along" with the party leadership.

❦ ❧

THE *Roaring Twenties was a golden time when many Americans concluded eternal prosperity had finally been discovered. But appearances can be deceptive. In the din of the national boom, numerous pockets of poverty were overlooked. The farmer, the coal miner and the textile worker lagged far behind the remainder of the economy. All three segments were plagued with overproduction. But they were not alone in their difficulties. Deep social problems plagued the American cities which, according to the federal census of 1920, had outstripped the countryside as a place of residence for Americans. Although manufacturing soared, rapid shifts in consumer interest frequently sent more than one industry into unexpected tailspins. "Technological unemployment" was a neat euphemism for large-scale instances of workers being dismissed because machinery had stripped them of their skills. Once unemployed, workers were left to struggle along as best they could. America alone of industrial giants lacked even the rudiments of a social security system; a condition made all the more telling when it is remembered that even Czarist Russia provided some social insurance. The unemployed, the unemployable, the destitute, were all left to shift for themselves in a country that still believed that the poor were not blessed but marked instead with the curse of Cain.*

More than one economist concluded during the twenties that the rich grow richer and the poor grow poorer. It was a description confirmed by census figures that revealed the top 10 percent of the population received almost a third of the national income while the bottom 10 percent eked out considerably less than 2 percent of the total. And as production grew, Americans learned to buy on time, living, as some critics warned, today on tomorrow's income. But the need to encourage consumption led public officials and spokesmen for private enterprise to draw a vision of two cars in every garage and the not too distant time when every American would be or about to become a millionaire. With such encouragement, the public indulged in speculative orgies in Florida land purchases and in the stock market. Prices rose on the market until all relationship between dividends and quoted prices ceased. Paper fortunes underwrote the golden aura of the twenties, only to disappear when the bubble burst in 1929. Suddenly the American people awoke to find they could not cash in fool's gold.

The exact circumstances of the Great Depression are still a matter for both historical and economic dispute. Little systematic analysis in either discipline has been applied to explain what happened. Historians as well as such social economists as John K. Galbraith have settled for the vivid word portrait. But from what exists, a remarkable image of the disintegration of a society's morale emerges. The historians dealing with the process have added their own indignation at the stupidity with which the crisis was handled until the inauguration of the New Deal. They have tended to emphasize the personal responsibility of the incumbent administration and have fastened upon Hoover and the Republican Party the label of indifference. It would be interesting to contemplate what might have happened if Alfred E. Smith rather than Herbert Hoover had been in the White House in 1929. As any evaluation of the twenties reveals, the foibles, blunders, and expectations of the twenties were nonpartisan. But since most of the historians who have dealt with the depression have been partisans of the New Deal, they have accentuated Republican responsibility. The Republicans and their defenders have not helped their case by too frequently resorting to a blanket defense of the old order.

Curiously enough, Herbert Hoover made a point which helps, when divorced from his obvious partisanship, to place the depression in proper perspective. It was worldwide in its impact. The American experience was simply more emphatic than most. Even a partial catalogue of the human woe makes for unnerving reading. In city after city, the pressures upon welfare reached "a disaster basis," and the "slow starvation and progressive disintegration of family life" reported from Philadelphia applied to most cities. More than a third of the population fitted the description of Fortune magazine when it wrote: "They haven't starved yet. They get along somehow." The need was indeed awesome.

Dixon Wecter (1906-1950), whose career was all too brief, not only graphically defines the dimensions of the depression, but also does it in a language of pulpit indignation. Yet, there is throughout his work an underlying theme of optimism, one that transcends disaster. Thus he concludes: "Disaster helped Americans to recollect that only through cooperation could the cart be pulled from the mire." But then Americans have always managed to extract from their worst experiences proof that progress is inevitable.

THE AGE OF THE GREAT DEPRESSION, 1929-1941

by Dixon Wecter

In mid-October, 1929, the average middle-class American saw ahead of him an illimitable vista of prosperity. A newly inaugurated president, Herbert Hoover, had announced soberly in the previous year that the conquest of poverty was no longer a mirage: "We have not yet reached the goal, but given a chance to go forward with the policies of the last eight years, and we shall soon with the help of God be within sight of the day when poverty will be banished from the nation." This was the economic promise interwoven with what a popular historian soon would call the American Dream. More complacently, Irving Fisher and the other economists in the confidence of Wall Street assured the citizen that he was dwelling upon "a permanently high plateau" of prosperity.

This upland of plenty—more tangible than the Beulahland dear to the old Protestant hymnal—appeared to be the final triumph of a great industrial development dating from the Civil War. The aftermath of America's latest war had seen the arrival in strength of mass production, to compound the wonders of the new technology. Even now, in this third week of October, 1929, with the president and other notables in attendance, Henry Ford was sponsoring the "Golden Jubilee of Light," honoring Edison and the fiftieth birthday of the incandescent lamp. Motor cars, bathtubs, electric refrigerators, radios, were the touchstones of progress. Keeping up with the Joneses, under the spur of fashion and advertisement, demanded nothing less than the latest model. Pressures of salesmanship urged even the duplication of luxuries—two cars in every garage—in a consumer's market already displaying symptoms of surfeit, not because all Americans were gorged with worldly goods, but because buying power was unevenly distributed.

The nation's policies and institutions were closely enmeshed with the prosperous middle class. "The suburban community is the dominant American group," one observer wrote in the summer of 1921. The increasing stress upon the solidarity and good fellowship of certain organizations—fraternal orders, business men's luncheon clubs, Legion conventions—and the moral meddlesomeness of others like the Anti-Saloon League bred a regimentation which he feared as foreshadowing "the group from which the Fascisti of the future will be drawn, if there are Fascisti." That Babbitt might ever doff his natty silk shirt for one of brown or black was problematical; but the cult of conformity, in so far as it boosted material success, was in the saddle. Cotton Mather, Ben Franklin, Peter Parley and Horace Greeley would have understood the spirit of the times, even though old maxims of drudgery and penny pinching seemed to have been bypassed for quicker ways to wealth.

Time, liveliest weekly of the decade, in January, 1929, hailed Walter P. Chrysler as "Man of the Year," because during the past twelvemonth he had introduced the public to Plymouth and DeSoto cars, bought out Dodge Brothers for one hundred and sixty million dollars and begun to build "the world's tallest skyscraper, a 68-story colossus." Now, on the cover of *Time* for October 14, 1929, appeared the face of William Wrigley, Jr., to be followed in successive weeks by Harry F. Guggenheim, Ivar Kreuger, Samuel Insull and Thomas W. Lamont—heroes all. The last issue before the Wall Street crash carried a triple-page announcement of the new magazine *Fortune*, at the "unique price of $10 a year," which proclaimed the "generally accepted commonplace that America's great achievement has been Business." Other large advertisements featured Babson's *Reports* ("Your Dollars—Are They Continuously and Efficiently at Work?"), the Hamilton watch ("Can you tell a successful man by the time he carries?"), Robert I. Warshow's new book *The Story of Wall Street* ("These giants march through its pages . . . like the adventurers of the middle ages . . . Daniel Drew, Jim Fisk, Jay Gould, Vanderbilt, Hill, Harriman . . . and the many others whose exploits have astounded the nation"), and the investment services of a firm to collapse in 1932 leaving millions in defaulted bonds, S. W. Straus & Co. ("He invests his modest earnings in good sound securities"). They represented the stimuli which beat incessantly upon the mind of the average magazine reader.

Masses of Americans who bought their first bonds in the liberty loans of 1918 had lately turned to more speculative issues. Advertisements flaunting high prices instead of bargains—from $45,000 apartments of Park Avenue and bathrooms equipped with "Crane Louis XVI Trianon Fittings Gold-Plated," down to $2.50 lipsticks and razor blades at three for fifty cents—set the sumptuary scale for a generation of easy money. To keep abreast of the traffic in this climb to the highlands of permanent prosperity, the stock market was the obvious vehicle. In 1920 there had been 29,609 stockbrokers in the United States; within ten years they had jumped to 70,950. It was commonly observed that a great many citizens no longer read the front page of their newspaper, but turned hurriedly to the financial columns. Tabloid papers and tip sheets offered investment advice to amateurs. Over the radio flowed the voice of the "Old Counselor," steady as a deacon, intoning the wisdom of Samuel Insull's own brokers.

Popular interest was growing about the mystery of business cycles. Whether they were ruled by overproduction or underproduction, banking operations, innovations in method, hysterias of hope or panic, or perhaps sun spots, was not clear. Guessing was garbed in the robes of prophecy. Wishfulness took priority over planning. Optimists believed that the old laws of economics had been arrested; others conceded that rainy days might come, but after every storm the skies must clear—if everybody, as the season's most popular song exhorted, would keep his sunny side up. Above all, recession was the abnormal thing. Prosperity needed no explanation. Nor was it the monopoly of so-called leisured classes, or the Republican party, despite their effort to claim all the credit.

> If a man saves $15 a week, and invests in good common stocks, and allows the dividends and rights to accumulate, at the end of twenty years he will have at least $80,000 and an income from investments of around $400 a month. He will be rich. And because income can do that, I am firm in my belief that anyone not only can be rich, but ought to be rich.

So declared John J. Raskob, chairman of the Democratic national committee, in the summer of 1929. Employees were encouraged to invest in the stocks and bonds of their employers—a system regarded somewhat vaguely as the American equivalent of profit sharing, or perhaps social security.

Much of this buying of stocks was on margin, which meant that investors, including the small fry with little cash but big hopes, put up about a fourth of the price. The broker advanced the rest by borrowing from banks. This precarious credit structure of brokers' loans had trembled in February, 1929, when the Federal Reserve Board ordered member banks not to lend money for such speculative purposes. But private bankers, led by Charles E. Mitchell, had promptly unlocked their millions for speculation and given a further fillip to the great bull market and the age of confidence upon which it was built. This caused another spasm of activity, unwarranted by any such tangibles as consumer demand, gains in productive efficiency or real earning of the stocks in question. While the rich were growing richer, several million citizens with small incomes were raiding their savings, reducing their immediate purchasing power and mortgaging their future in order to speculate. Ninety per cent of these market transactions in the twenties, it has been estimated, were gambling ventures rather than permanent investments.

Almost imperceptibly a shift had occurred in economic control, from the industrial capitalism of an earlier day to finance capitalism. Exploitation of investors and frequent duplicity in bookkeeping were among the less lovely traits of the new order. The holding company—an avatar which sprang from the slain dragon of the "trusts" late in the previous century—now flourished mightily. It permitted control by a small group of stockholders over a widely scattered empire of interlocking or even loosely related interests, like Samuel Insull's three-billion-dollar domain in utilities. The power exercised by the holding company, particularly in the utility field, was often so disproportionate to its size that Franklin D. Roosevelt as president well described it as "a ninety-six-inch dog being wagged by a four-inch tail."

These concerns were sometimes pyramided one upon another, towers of Babel reaching to the skies and equally tremulous at the base. Not infrequently they were used to mask the true state of corporate finances from the eyes of regulatory authorities or the public. A New York state bank called Bank of United States, in January, 1930—almost a year before its spectacular failure brought down the roof upon nearly half a million depositors—concealed its growing weakness by creating a dummy company, the Bolivar Development Corporation, capitalized at one hundred dollars, to buy and sell the stock of still another dummy conjured by the Bank into making the motions of prosperity. Deceived by this solemn farce, the outsider was slow to suspect that many a façade of granite and marble had become a hollow shell of indebtedness and precarious bookkeeping.

Another development in the pathology of Wall Street was the mushrooming in the latter twenties of so-called investment trusts, whose function was to invest moneys loaned to them and to distribute the net return to their stockholders or beneficiaries. Some were "rigid," i.e. confined to a restricted list of securities, but many were "flexible," which meant that the selection of securities for investment was left wide open. In practice they were little better than gambling establishments in which the innocent patron intrusted his stakes not even to a fellow player picked at random but to the croupier—whose main interest, of course, was to represent "the house." Four and a half million Americans, it was reported, handed over part or all their savings to investment trusts, eventually losing about a third of their capital, or a total of three billion dollars.

The overexpansion of credit was a prime cause of the disasters that followed 1929. The First World War began a process which reckless financing continued to accelerate. In the background loomed the huge structure of long-term debt in the United States—a public debt, federal, state and municipal, of thirty-three billion dollars, and corporate and individual debts of one hundred billion—which demanded expanding markets and world pros- perity for successful carrying. A relatively small reduction in buying power, or backsliding of prices, could send tremors along the whole length of this mountain chain. The grand operations of credit, a new force of such power that one economist likened it to the prime movers of physics, were still im- perfectly understood and recklessly abused. The average American in 1929 had little notion of credit on the imperial scale, such as the growth of inter- national financing dependent upon a constant transfusion of credit from have to have-not nations, nor even the magnitude of eight billion dollars' credit in the form of brokers' loans which Wall Street recorded at its all- time crest of September 3, 1929.

The common man knew more about overexpansion of credit in such homely shapes as installment buying. Intensive campaigns to break down "sales resistance"—often insufficient purchasing power among small citizens —led to new extensions of the time-payment plan for cars, clothes, electric washers, refrigerators, furniture, jewelry. In effect it was a loan from pro- ducer to consumer, because the latter lacked cash, and the former, with his urgent need for sales, preferred this method to that of increasing mass purchasing power by cutting prices and boosting wages. By 1929 felicity on the installment plan had lured its tens of millions. In the harsh light of the Great Depression, such aspects of the system as inflated prices and exorbitant carrying charges, along with misrepresentation of the product, would be- come all too plain. Certain state laws, like those of New York and Kentucky, held a still more pernicious trap, sprung during the early thirties, by which a debtor's entire wages could be attached until the account was cleared.

Meanwhile important business enterprises were being concentrated in fewer hands. The forging of chain stores all over the nation was no less significant than recent big mergers in the automotive industry. Centralized industry made every metropolis the center of a regional web, and each of these networks fitted into a national pattern for making, selling and dis- tributing commodities. The economy of a continent had never been so highly integrated, nor its equilibrium so sensitive. The frontier, the farm, the village and Middletown had at last been engulfed by the rise of the city. As never before, urban industrialism called the tune. In 1870 wage and salary workers had made up about half the working population; now they composed four fifths. An interdependence unknown to old-fashioned America had become the basic economic fact. The fabric of industrial and corporate life, joined to the structure imposed by labor unions and labor legislation, had imper- ceptibly altered the flexibility of *laissez faire* into something more rigid, less accommodating.

These sweeping changes had hardly entered the consciousness of the average citizen. In his own mind he was never more loyal than in 1929 to the doctrine of individualism and unhampered private enterprise. Clashes be- tween theory and practice, like the potential friction of capital and labor, remained almost inaudible so long as the nation's economic mechanism ran with the oil of prosperity.

Not, indeed, that the prosperity of the twenties was consistently sound. To the later view it resembled a hectic flush rather than the bloom of health. Agriculture still groaned from its dropsical overexpansion in 1917-1918. Along with bituminous coal mining and textiles, it belonged to a clinical ward known as the "sick industries." Great was the industrial turnover; a sense of insecurity about jobs had been rising for several years. Even in 1926 the unemployed were estimated at 1,500,000; by 1929 their number had swelled to upwards of 1,800,000. Unperceived by the optimists, joblessness and poverty had come to be chronic social problems in the United States—neither a passing crisis nor one readily met by efforts of private charity. The ratio of private to public funds for such purposes was diminishing, as public relief expenditures gradually mounted. Sixteen major cities which in 1911 had spent $1,500,000 on public charity were by 1928 spending $20,000,000 annually.

Flaws in banking practice might also have been suspected. During the six years prior to the October crash of 1929 bank failures occurred at an average rate of nearly two a day, but since the delinquents were minor institutions, chiefly in small towns, scant publicity resulted. Nor was the output of goods commensurate with the capacity to produce. At least twenty per cent of the country's resources were not being utilized, to the loss of about fifteen billion dollars in national income, or one fourth of the goods and services it was actually producing.

Yet beyond question the major shortcomings of the American economy lay not with production but consumption. Already in the early autumn of 1929 financial pages gloomed over "heaviness" in automobiles and radios, slackening of the building trades, disappointment along the new frontiers of aviation. Much of America's productive effort and income had lately gone into luxuries and durable goods, whose purchase could be postponed without affecting daily needs. At the first storm warnings these goods would pile up in warehouses, causing wheels to stop turning and huge areas of joblessness to appear. This was one reason why the Depression following 1929 was unparalleled for severity and duration.

Even in 1929 the purchasing power of the American people looked ill-balanced, an anomaly soon to be pointed up by quotation of Carlyle's phrase, "poverty in the midst of plenty." Between 1923 and 1928, while the index of speculative gains rose from 100 to 410, the index of wages advanced from 100 to a mere 112. Naturally enough, too little income went for consumer goods in proportion to the torrents that flowed into investment channels and the call-money market, into the making of new capital equipment for future production and into the savings of the well-to-do. Never before had so large a share of the national income been saved and invested as in this decade, nor had current production ever outstripped current consumption so spectacularly. The National Survey of Potential Product Capacity later described the period from 1923 to 1929 as an "orgy of saving" among the rich.

Two thirds of the country's savings were made by families with incomes over $10,000 a year. Those with less than $1500, comprising forty per cent of the population, actually paid out more than they earned. Six million families, one fifth of the nation, fell below even $1000. Making provision for a rainy day seemed less than feasible when one was already drowning. Up to the income bracket of $5000, American families had to spend a disproportionate amount merely to get sufficient food; hence among those nine out of ten families "not in a position to enjoy a liberal diet," substantial savings could hardly be expected. In presenting the extremes of the economic spectrum a study by the Brookings Institution observed that the twenty-four thousand families which received over $100,000 apiece in 1929 enjoyed a total income three times as great as that of the six million poorest families. In other words, the average income among the top group was six hundred and thirty times that in the bottom one.

Orthodox economists argued that savings led to more capital equipment and superior efficiency and, in turn, to lower production costs, lower prices and greater purchasing power for the masses. It was plain by 1929, however, that this chain of causation had developed weak links. Mass buying power was unable to absorb the nation's output, not alone because wages had advanced comparatively little but because retail prices took virtually no cut between 1922 and 1929. Savings achieved by improved technologies were not being handed on to the consumer in the form of lower prices. They were diverted into dividends, reserves, bigger salaries and bonuses. Various shapes of monopoly, like trusts in disguise, mergers, combinations in mining and manufacturing, helped keep prices up, even while new machinery, better production methods and services of "efficiency experts" increased the overall output of American labor by more than a third in the decade after the First World War. In some trades, like the automobiles, productive efficiency was reported to have tripled.

But from this plenitude the average consumer gathered only the crumbs, and even the producer reaped merely a shortsighted advantage. To reckon profit not for a day or season, but upon a broad and long-term base of buying power, might have proved wiser. Posterity would probably agree with the retrospective view of Hoover who, after praise for the technologists, remarked:

> When we fully understand the economic history of the 'twenties, we shall find that the debacle which terminated another apparently highly prosperous period was largely contributed by a failure of industry to pass its improvement (through labor-saving devices) on to the consumer.

Some others were less inclined to praise the engineers than to damn them. Their ingenuity, it was charged, had supplanted men with machines. The effect of invention in upsetting group equilibrium was, of course, no novelty. In the past, management had sometimes shown reluctance to scrap old equipment for new; more often, labor feared the "immigration of iron men." Naturally at the first threat of spreading unemployment the machine was indicted, for this generation was less apt than its forefathers to accept all calamities as mysterious visitations of Providence. Soon, in the wake of apprehensions that technology had done its job too well, came a flock of ideas about social engineering. Could not the same magic which had rid the factory of waste and inefficiency do the same for society? This hope—newer to American life than the invincible faith in applied science—led from Hoover the "Great Engineer" to Technocracy, the National Recovery Administration, the Tennessee Valley Authority, the National Resources Committee and other concepts of a managed economy. Few could have foreseen in 1929 all the paths of this projection. Nevertheless in that year the fundamental balances of a vast industrial civilization were slipping: the precarious relations between wages and prices, production and consumption, machines and manpower.

Upon this world of uneasy prosperity the first blow fell in late October. Like the sound of gunshot which starts an Alpine avalanche, a minor panic on the New York Stock Exchange began on the twenty-third among stocks that speculators had pushed to fantastic heights. The next day, "Black Thursday," saw hysteria rampant. Brokers wept and tore off their collars trying to keep abreast of selling orders; sight-seers jammed the Wall Street district, ogled the arrival of great bankers in their limousines before the House of Morgan, and under the rumor of mass suicide gathered to watch an ordinary workman on a scaffolding in morbid expectation of his plunge.

At first it appeared that the magicians of finance had arrested disaster, but just as the public cheered them and breathed more easily, another sickening lurch sent the market to new depths, spreading conviction that these wizards had merely propped the falling timbers long enough to get out from under. October 29 set a lurid record for sales, a total of 16,410,000 shares. At the month's close fifteen billion dollars in market value had been wiped out, and before the end of the year losses reached an estimated forty billion.

After the first shock official optimism took over. A generation taught to be "a bull on the United States" was conditioned to respond. Upon feeling the initial jolt, many seemed as incredulous about the real gravity of the situation as the passengers of a luxury liner ripped below decks by an iceberg: the boat listed only a trifle at first while the band played on. Manhattan's dapper mayor, "Jimmy" Walker, asked the movies to show nothing but cheerful pictures. The patient was recommended to try the hair of the dog that bit him: *True Story Magazine* ran big advertisements in the newspapers urging wage-earners to buy more luxury items on credit. "Wall Street may sell stocks, but Main Street is buying goods," came a cheery assurance from the *Saturday Evening Post*. A Manhattan jeweler in early November put on display a $750,000 pearl necklace, while the Shuberts revealed plans for a $15,000,000 theater-hotel on Broadway. "Forward America, Nothing Can Stop U.S.," shouted the nation's billboards. And over the radio Julius Klein, assistant secretary of commerce, announced that only four per cent of the people had been adversely affected. A tuneful hit called "Happy Days Are Here Again" was copyrighted on November 7 for one of the new talking pictures appropriately named "Chasing Rainbows"; three years later it would become the campaign song of the New Deal. And early in 1930, with skies growing blacker, makers of a cheap radio brought out a "prosperity model."

The solvent of American humor began early to attack the crisis. Grim jokes arose about the complimentary revolver given with every share of Goldman Sachs, or the room clerk's query of every registrant, "For sleeping or jumping?" A little later, when mass unemployment began to steal the headlines from Wall Street, bravado succeeded flippancy. Billboards began to ask, "Wasn't the Depression Terrible?" The departing owner of a ruined shop scrawled upon the door "Opened by mistake" if he were a humorist, or "Busted and disgusted" if possessed by the blues. Trained in the cult of the stiff upper lip, of singing in the rain, Americans hated to admit that things were not as they had always been. The International Association of Lions Clubs observed the week of October 19, 1930, as Business Confidence Week. Prosperity was just around the corner; perhaps the corner was one already turned.

For a while the momentum of the great bull market carried certain enterprises. The year 1931, for example, saw the opening of the world's finest luxury hotel, the new Waldorf-Astoria in Manhattan, and completion of the tallest of all skyscrapers, the Empire State Building of one hundred and two stories topped by a "mooring Mast" for airships—but functionally as useless as the metallic needle surmounting its nearest rival, the new Chrysler Building. Many floors in each of these grandiose business palaces remained spectrally vacant in the times ahead. The same year saw publication of architects' plans for New York's most impressive cluster of buildings, Rockefeller Center, which the next two years consummated. Housing broadcasting studios, ornate movie and music halls, foreign-trade syndicates and other business enterprises upon a scale never before attempted, this group culminated in the austere gray seventy-story shaft of the R.C.A. building.

Some critics of architecture prophesied that these would be the last dinosaurs of America's metropolitan era, convinced that such vainglory had overreached itself, promoting little save congested traffic, overcrowding and colossal debts. Like many other vanities of the century, perhaps the skyscraper too was bankrupt. At any rate, the nation's outlay for new construction fell sixty per cent between 1931 and 1932 as the momentum of prosperity ground to a dead stop. By 1933 architects were doing less than a seventh of the business they had enjoyed in 1928.

Gala openings and soothing statements no longer fitted the temper of the times; the smile of official optimism slowly froze into something that resembled a *risus sardonicus*. In 1931 Edward Angly garnered the more fulsome assurances of Wall Street and Washington into a little book with the derisive title *Oh Yeah!* Early in the following year appeared a new magazine called *Ballyhoo*, its first issue packaged in cellophane as a touch of commercial parody. Within six months it rocketed to a two-million circulation largely by debunking the specious salesmanship of the twenties.

The public, seeking a scapegoat for its bitterness, found one with the help of a shrewd publicist hired by the Democratic party, Charles Michelson. Old newspapers were called "Hoover blankets," jack rabbits "Hoover hogs" and the shanties of starvation rising on outskirts of cities "Hoovervilles." A large share of popular odium also fell upon the shoulders of rich and weary Andrew Mellon, lately toasted by business as the "greatest secretary of the treasury since Alexander Hamilton." In February, 1932, Mellon was glad enough to relinquish his portfolio and be kicked upstairs as ambassador to Britain.

As President Coolidge had said in the palmy days, the business of America had indeed been business. But now the luxuries and amusements, the bustling sense of power which cloaked life's essential materialism for the prosperous urban or suburban citizen, were suddenly stripped away. This greatest of economic reverses gave millions of citizens the jolt of taking a downward step in the dark when expecting an upward one. A nation used to regarding prosperity as a habit found itself startled, then incredulous, more than a little helpless and finally resentful. It made the situation no easier that the adversary was invisible, and unlike a domestic or foreign foe, invulnerable to ridicule, ballots or bullets.

But the reality of this enemy admitted no doubt. His unseen stature could be measured by the two yardsticks of income and employment. The loss of earnings, chiefly paper profits, had first taken the spotlight. A few moths had singed their wings; so what? But as early as the spring of 1930, when the Federal Council of Churches set aside April 27 as "Unemployment Sunday," the crisis had assumed breadth as well as depth. Soon, lowered income and unemployment were seen in constant interaction, forcing the national economy into a descending spiral. White-collar workers began to take salary cuts, laborers to find discharge slips in pay envelopes. The city felt the shock first. Initial symptoms were not ostentatious: postponement in buying that new car, or breaking ground for a new home; surrender of small apartments by young couples moving in with parents; a drop in pleasure travel and theater attendance; more business for the cleaner, invisible mender, shoe-repair man, less for tailor and haberdasher.

A few grimmer signs appeared early, upon a small scale. In late February, 1930, Seattle, Los Angeles and Chicago witnessed minor demonstrations of the unemployed, in which Communists usually had a hand. In the same month bread lines in the Bowery were drawing two thousand daily. In March Milwaukee opened a municipal soup kitchen. The summer of 1930, as happened seasonally through the Depression, brought a measure of relief. Food was fresher, more plentiful and cheaper; clothing, fuel and shelter offered problems less acute. But the descent of winter in 1930-1931 inaugurated harder times, with New York City appropriating a million dollars for direct relief and Lloyd's of London announcing that for the first time on record they were selling riot and civil-commotion insurance in quantity to American clients.

Outside the city, harbingers of the crisis were less newsworthy. Farmers had known nothing but depression since the Armistice boom burst, and even though their plight continued to worsen, they had the gloomy satisfaction of long conditioning. Smaller industrial cities and towns, however, were reluctant to admit the fact of hard times, which in many citizens' eyes was either a Manhattan gamblers' fiasco or else just a state of mind. They congratulated themselves upon a firmer foundation. Notwithstanding that every fourth factory worker in Muncie, Indiana—the Middletown of sociologists—had lost his job before the end of 1930, men of substance in that community kept insisting to the end of 1931 that the Depression was "mainly something we read about in the newspapers." Still feeding upon the gospel of keeping up appearances, a delegation of local business men in 1932 persuaded General Motors not to board up the windows of its abandoned Muncie plant, which stood in clear view of the passing trains. The philosophy of the peptomists died hard.

As the average citizen could see for himself, working capital and jobs were closely interlocked, and upon their joint scarcity the years of depression hinged. What happened to income may be shown briefly. National income dwindled from eighty-one billion dollars in 1929 to less than sixty-eight in 1930, then cascaded to fifty-three in 1931 and hit bottom in 1932 with forty-one. Correspondingly, the country's estimated wealth over this span shrank from three hundred and sixty-five billion to two hundred and thirty-nine, a loss representing diminished values in real property, capital and commodities. Much of the nation's physical plant, of course, rusted in idleness and disrepair. These three years took a toll of eighty-five thousand business failures with liabilities of four and a half billion dollars and the suspension of five thousand banks. Nine million savings accounts were wiped out, and wage losses upwards of twenty-six billion dollars sustained.

While the debt structure of the American economy remained little changed—only 3.5 per cent less money being paid out in interest in 1932 than in 1929—in other fields deflation proceeded furiously, making long-term debts more crushing than borrowers had anticipated when incurring them. The volume of money paid as salaries dwindled 40 per cent, dividends 56.6 per cent, and wages 60 per cent. Early in the crisis, at the Hoover administration's earnest request, major industries made few cuts in pay rates, but by drastic reduction of working hours and days they contrived to slash pay rolls about 40 per cent between 1929 and September, 1931. Since a workingman's family had to live on the money he brought home, this procedure looked better in the headlines than in private.

For the country at large, per-capita realized income (adjusted to the cost of living) tumbled from $681 in 1929 to $495 in 1933. At the apex of the economic pyramid the number of persons reporting an annual income over a million dollars fell from seventy-five in 1931 to only twenty the next year. Despite repeated assurances from government circles and high finance that the recession had reached bedrock—the "terminal trough," forcasters liked to call it—the general course of business after the Wall Street crash plunged fitfully downward for more than three years.

Many industries and small businesses denied even lip service to the administration's plea for maintenance of wage rates. A growing backwater of unemployment led department stores to pay clerks as little as five or ten dollars weekly. Investigation of a group of working girls in Chicago showed the great majority toiling for less than twenty-five cents an hour, a fourth for less than ten cents. Makers of ready-to-wear dresses, confectionery employees and cannery workers were among the classes exploited most callously. First-class New York stenographers' salaries fell from $35 and $45 a week to $16; domestic servants were obliged to labor for room and board plus ten dollars a month. As usual, unskilled workers had been the shock troops, followed by white-collar workers and technicians. Professional classes felt the jar a little later, as teachers' and ministers' salaries were cut or fell into arrears, and the practice of other groups declined, with fees increasingly hard to collect. Even in 1936 physicians' incomes were still from eighteen to thirty per cent below their 1929 level, lawyers' between eighteen and thirty-eight per cent.

Turning from lowered income and diminished working capital to the other side of the coin, one comes upon the face of total unemployment. In April, 1930, President Hoover ordered a house-to-house survey of this situation, the first federal census of unemployment in the nation's history. In all, slightly more than three million employables were reported out of work, against forty-five million persons gainfully employed. But the tide was rising fast, and a special census by the department of commerce in January, 1931, based upon sampling, disclosed more than six million unemployed. Before the end of that year almost all appraisers agreed that the ten-million mark had been passed, and 1932 saw the addition of four or five million more. Thanks to seasonal factors and local flurries of advance or retreat, the national picture shifted constantly; unemployment tended also to propagate itself, with wives and older children of idle men now joining in the scramble for any crumbs of odd jobs. Exhaustion of savings and losses in modest investments drove aged folk to participate in the frantic search and be counted.

This cycle brought forth its changing tokens and symbols. If the still cheerful desperation of 1931 was crystallized in the song "Life Is Just a Bowl of Cherries," the grimmer abasement of 1932 was epitomized by "Brother, Can You Spare a Dime?" appealing on behalf of casualties like the jobless war veteran or the discarded builder of an industrial empire. The most memorable symbol of the great unemployment, and of pride in facing it, came to be the apple. In the autumn of 1930 the International Apple Shippers' Association devised a scheme to dispose of surpluses. It offered to sell the fruit on credit to the jobless, to retail at five cents apiece. By early November six thousand apple sellers had taken their stand on the sidewalks of New York, and the idea soon spread elsewhere. In this early phase of the Depression, the stubborn self-reliance of America—the poor as well as the rich—bridled at the notion of direct relief or a dole, as had been practiced since the First World War in Britain. But this meager toll upon the passing throng soon lost its novelty. In 1931 Manhattan began to forbid apple selling upon certain streets. By 1932 people were reported to be "sick of apples."

Those who could lift their eyes from this bleak domestic picture to scan the international horizon could draw at least some solace from the proverbial fellowship of misery. President Hoover himself at first was inclined to lay the ultimate blame upon causes outside the United States. In the war of 1914-1918 and its aftermath he saw the wellspring of this bitter draught. Waste and destruction, loss of manpower, war debts and taxes, inflation and subsequent devaluation, the greed and imperialism of others, together with the fears and new spending bred by rearmament, were the malign heritage of a struggle "for which our people had no blame." And so far as America was concerned, these complications sprang from the days of Woodrow Wilson, "this war having come on during a Democratic administration."

If this analysis seemed overcomforting—presenting the American people in the classic role of innocents at home and abroad—at least none could deny that the Depression was fast spreading over an economically interdependent world. Nations were seen to be roped together like mountain climbers in the bonds of loans and debts, cartels and tariffs, and quick communication whether of hope or panic. The footing of countries mainly agricultural tended to give way first, with the industrial powers slipping later but more spectacularly. By the spring of 1929 or slightly earlier, Australia, Brazil, the Orient, the Near East, Argentina, Canada and Poland were showing symptoms of decline, while Germany's chronic postwar depression deepened. Later than the United States to feel the shock were Great Britain, France, Czechoslovakia, Switzerland and the Scandinavian countries. A second wave, beginning about 1931 and more severe than the first, likewise affected all these lands, and did not begin to recede until around the spring of 1933.

In most places similar factors had been at work, although the shape and gravity of the crisis varied a good deal. A look at the global picture, however, showed that Americans had not been the only dupes of hit-or-miss prosperity, the Republicans not the sole villains of 1929, nor the Democrats the exclusive heroes of 1933.

Refusal to admit this fact of economic interdependence was never shown more clearly than by the Hawley-Smoot tariff of June, 1930, in itself an aggravation of the crisis. The armistice of 1918 found the United States for the first time in history, a great creditor country. At the same time its citizens' private investments abroad were growing so rapidly that from a prewar total of three billion dollars they had swollen to fourteen by 1932. A mighty producing nation, America naïvely construed foreign commerce as the right to sell, with little or no obligation to buy in exchange. Indeed, the nightmare of foreign dumping led both farmers and industrialists to clamor for the highest protective rates yet known and to obtain them in 1930 at an average of forty per cent. President Hoover wished to limit the bill chiefly to a few agricultural commodities, but he was overborne.

Abroad the Hawley-Smoot act was interpreted as a declaration of economic war. It met such prompt retaliatory tariffs, quotas and anti-American embargoes that by 1932 twenty-five governments had joined in the reprisal, thus halving the volume of United States exports. The vicious spiral held another twist. To escape this threat of boycott, American manufacturers during the first two years of the Hawley-Smoot act set up two hundred and fifty-eight separate factories in foreign countries, including seventy-one across the Canadian line.

What the average American thought about these matters depended largely upon his region, politics and business. Southerners had always been taught to regard high tariffs as iniquitous, but in the industrial North and agricultural Midwest "protection" still exercised its charm. No doubt many solid citizens would have echoed an editorial in Middletown's press: "The difference between good times and bad times in the United States, so far as history indicates, is the difference between an adequate protective tariff for the products of our farms and our factories and an inadequate tariff." When regression rather than improvement followed, Middletown's editor stuck doggedly to his line, ridiculing the "mistaken" view that "conditions in Europe have something to do with America's coming out of the depression."

Within the United States the twenties had seen a remarkable increase in the number and influence of trade associations, by which rival producers pooled statistical information, credit standards, cost formulae, and the like, and sought to curb unfair marketing practices. To this extent they were beneficent, and so impressed Hoover as secretary of commerce and as president. But not infrequently they sought by their definition of "fair" and "unfair" price policies to achieve price control while sailing to the leeward of the Sherman antitrust act, and sometimes the effect was to eliminate the small independent operator. Their growth was further indulged by a series of Supreme Court decisions which an earlier progressivism would have eyed with suspicion as entering wedges for native cartels and capitalist syndicalism.

Although domestic cartels remained illegal under federal law, in the international sphere certain American concerns benefiting by the concentration of economic power—DuPont, United States Steel, General Electric, Westinghouse, Bendix Aviation, Diamond Match, Anaconda Copper, Standard Oil of New Jersey—entered into agreements in the twenties and the thirties with foreign producers often to restrict production in order to raise prices and increase profits, and still more commonly to divide world markets and exchange patents. In hampering free enterprise cartels tended to constrict the flow of supplies, retard foreign and domestic trade and prevent the introduction of new products and improvements (such, for example, as the "everlasting" match usable many times).

Their effect upon prices may be illustrated by the fact that in 1914 the cost of quinine sulfate was twenty-five cents an ounce, but after Merck joined the international cartel the price rose to seventy-five cents by 1941. The imposition of production quotas is suggested by the fact that, while in 1930 domestic aluminum production exceeded a hundred thousand metric tons and that of Germany was only thirty thousand, in 1934, three years after Alcoa entered the cartel, the American output had fallen to thirty-three thousand tons and the German had risen to thirty-seven. In the Depression their effect apparently was to aggravate unemployment and underconsumption. Later in the thirties cartels began to attract unfavorable notice from Senate investigating committees and the antitrust division of the justice department because of their alleged threat to the national security. On the whole, the shapes assumed by the internationalism of Big Business seemed as futile as those of economic nationalism in promoting the greatest good for the greatest number.

Lurking in the background of the ordinary American's insularity remained the old issue of unpaid debts from the First World War. Here, he believed, was proof that in dealing with foreigners he and his compatriots always got trimmed. Isolation was best. Other persons saw the urgency of war debts and reparations as strangling the economy of Europe and ultimately harming the creditor as well. President Hoover's decision in June, 1931, to sponsor a moratorium on intergovernmental war debts was hailed in some circles as a great contribution to good will and recovery, by others as a ruse to help the bankers and holders of foreign bonds. By the time of Franklin D. Roosevelt's inauguration, practically all the war debts were in hopeless default. Popular grievance over these unpaid bills did much to feed the pacifism of the mid-thirties and impede the international education of Americans.

The period 1929-1941 began with a domestic debacle which stemmed from many causes, but perhaps the most basic was selfish blindness to the bond between group welfare and the satisfactions of the individual. Disaster helped Americans to recollect that they were one nation and that only through cooperation could the cart be pulled from the mire. This period closed upon the eve of American participation in a global war which had been bred largely by the equally stubborn refusal of many nations to admit the tie between their security and the good estate of all—the concept of one world. About the commonalty of man and the commonweal of nations revolved the great debates, the most significant activity, of these dozen years. Even in his daily life the average American could not help being profoundly affected by the outcome.

◄§ §►

THE *twenties witnessed a time of confidence made more confident by the constant reassurances of authoritative sources that all was well. When the depression came, the Hoover administration struggled to bolster public confidence. As economic conditions worsened, though administration reassurances continued, even its closest friends realized Hoover and his confidants doubted their own words. The first achievement of Franklin D. Roosevelt was his success in striking the right note in his inaugural address of March 4, 1933. Although all facts seemed to contradict his optimism, he assured the nation that all it needed to fear was fear itself, and the people listened. In the one hundred days that followed, a surge of legislation, unmatched in legislative annals until the first session of Lyndon B. Johnson's 89th Congress, transformed the nation. In a spectacular sequence of experiments (some critics viewed them as spur-of-the-moment brainstorms) Roosevelt launched a large effort to distribute the fruits of American productivity more equitably. He also made it obvious that he intended to preserve the American system of capitalism with its devotion to free enterprise and the sanctity of private property.*

It was an intent that seemed to radicals both timid and conservative if not openly reactionary. The Great Depression had seemed to critics of the left as demonstrating the accuracy of Karl Marx's prognosis of the future of capitalism. The surge of energy released in the New Deal, they felt, did not precipitate the radical innovations required, but provided instead the stopgap improvisations of desperate men trying to salvage a bankrupt economic system. The whole objective of Roosevelt's program, and many left wing critics refused to acknowledge it was pragmatic, seemed intent upon forestalling an impending socialist revolution.

It is this large criticism from the left that reinforces the conclusion of most historians that the New Deal intended the conservation of traditional institutions through necessary reforms. In a situation that seems retrospectively to have been ripe for revolution, the New Deal channeled discontent within the framework of accepted political techniques. It expanded the definition of constitutional powers to make ever more flexible the scope of federal power. It took care to maintain the traditional state and local powers by implementing them in the development of federal powers. By demonstrating that the American system could provide acceptable solutions to urgent problems, it contained grievances that might well have budded into revolutionary agitation, and it also subverted the expectations of the left.

Roosevelt's consistent willingness to indulge in "bold, persistent experimentation," to abandon, without apology, a program that did not work, and to try, in its place, something new reveals his essential pragmatism. Basil Rauch (1908-   ) recognized that this willingness to accommodate to altering circumstance explains the steadily more radical social experimentation of the New Deal. He concluded that two distinct New Deals occurred: the first, between 1933 and 1934, emphasized institutional reforms within capitalism; the second, between 1935 and 1937, responded to the welling popular pressures for social reform that culminated in the creation of social security and insured the rights of labor. More recently historians have emphasized the personal reluctance with which Roosevelt greeted these reforms, particularly those involving labor. But as James MacGregor Burns noted, Roosevelt, ever the politician, never allowed his personal predilections to override a popular program. Throughout the New Deal experiment, its makers employed a single test of worth: does a program work? It is their link with the abiding American past, for, from the first settlements, an affirmative answer to this question proved the worth of a program.

THE HISTORY OF THE NEW DEAL, 1933-1938

by Basil Rauch

A few hours before the inauguration of the new President, Governor Lehman proclaimed a holiday which closed the banks and stock exchanges of New York. All the states had then declared holidays, but only federal authority could close the Federal Reserve Banks or stop the loading of gold on fast liners for Europe. The vast machinery of the country's economic life ground to a virtual stop. The people of the United States never faced a more dangerous economic crisis or looked more anxiously to a Chief Executive for economic salvation than on March 4, 1933, when Franklin D. Roosevelt, under gray, rainy skies, took the oath of office as the thirty-second President of their country.

The Inaugural Address, which went out over the radio a few minutes after one o'clock, was the first of many dynamic appeals and actions which were to transform the nation's anxiety into hope. "First of all, let me assert my firm belief that the only thing we have to fear is fear itself." This might have differed little from the Hoover pleas for confidence. It was followed by a daring analysis of the source of economic ills such as had not been heard from a President since Andrew Jackson's veto of the Bank Bill:

> Plenty is at our doorstep, but a generous use of it languishes in the very sight of the supply. Primarily this is because rulers of the exchange of mankind's goods have failed through their own stubbornness and their own incompetence, have admitted their failure, and have abdicated. Practices of the unscrupulous money changers stand indicted in the court of public opinion, rejected by the hearts and minds of men. . . .
>
> Stripped of the lure of profit by which to induce our people to follow their false leadership, they have resorted to exhortations, pleading tearfully for restored confidence. They know only the rules of a generation of self-seekers. They have no vision, and when there is no vision, the people perish.
>
> The money changers have fled from their high seats in the temple of our civilization. We may now restore that temple to the ancient truths. The measure of the restoration lies in the extent to which we apply social values more noble than mere monetary profit.

Then came the promise of action:

> Restoration calls, however, not for changes in ethics alone. This Nation asks for action, and action now.
>
> Our greatest primary task is to put people to work. This is no unsolvable problem if we face it wisely and courageously. It can be accomplished in part by direct recruiting by the Government itself, treating the task as we would treat the emergency of a war. . . .

"Hand in hand with this" was envisaged a redistribution of population from industrial centers to rural areas, a movement which would be helped by raising farm prices, preventing foreclosures, reducing the cost of government, unifying relief activities, and planning for and supervising transportation, communications, and utilities.

The placing of what were to be the civilian conservation corps and farm resettlement activities in the center of his program, to which all else would be merely contributory, was, perhaps, dictated by the President's need to focus on solutions of the main problem of unemployment. The First New Deal was to be dominated by other means to that end. But the National Industrial Recovery Act was not yet formulated, and emphasis on the monetary policy would have created fantastic opportunities for gold speculators. He did promise "strict supervision of all banking and credits and investments, so that there will be an end to speculation with other people's money; and there must be provision for an adequate but sound currency."

A warning was clearly given that the relative importance assigned by the Hoover administration to foreign and domestic policies would be reversed:

> Our international trade relations, though vastly important, are in point of time and necessity secondary to the establishment of a sound national economy. I favor as a practical policy the putting of first things first. I shall spare no effort to restore world trade by international economic readjustment, but the emergency at home cannot wait on that accomplishment.

Thus economic nationalism as a temporary expedient for recovery was foretold, and Secretary Hull and the "internationalists" were left to exercise patience while Professor Moley and the "nationalists" had their day. That the policy would be temporary and only economic was suggested by the pregnant statement of political foreign policy:

> In the field of world policy, I would dedicate this Nation to the policy of the good neighbor . . . the neighbor who respects his obligations and respects the sanctity of his agreements in and with a world of neighbors.

Liberals were later to profess they found the germs of fascism in the First New Deal. Perhaps they found cause for suspicion in the evocation of the "regimented" moods of wartime:

> If we are to go forward, we must move as a trained and loyal army willing to sacrifice for the good of a common discipline. . . . We are, I know, ready and willing to submit our lives and property to such discipline, because it makes possible a leadership which aims at a larger good. This I propose to offer, pledging that the larger purposes will bind upon us all as a sacred obligation with a unity of duty hitherto evoked only in time of armed strife.

But the President found that "action . . . is feasible under the form of government which we have inherited from our ancestors." Changes in emphasis and arrangement are possible without loss of the essential form of the Constitution, and have proved it to be "the most superbly enduring political mechanism the modern world had produced."

The nature of such possible changes was defined. "It is to be hoped that the normal balance of Executive and legislative authority may be wholly adequate," but if Congress fails to act of its own volition or under recommendation:

> I shall not evade the clear course of duty that will then confront me. I shall ask the Congress for the one remaining instrument to meet the crisis—broad Executive power to wage a war against the emergency, as great as the power that would be given to me if we were in fact invaded by a foreign foe.

The nation could not doubt that a new spirit had begun to move across the land. That democracy could be weakened by a vigorous attack upon the evils that beset it was a thesis developed by conservatives as well as radicals only after the attack had begun to succeed. Meanwhile, all groups, particularly bankers and Congress, begged to be commanded.

The President immediately summoned the new Congress, which was Democratic by large majorities and ready for strong leadership, to meet in special session on March 9, when Secretary Woodin had promised to have ready an emergency banking bill. Powers of the President were found in the Trading with the Enemy Act of 1917 to issue before the banks opened on Monday, March 6, a proclamation which suspended all transactions in the Federal Reserve and other banks, building and loan associations, and credit unions, and embargoed the export of gold, silver, and currency until March 9. And the leading bankers of the country were called to a meeting with the President and his subordinates.

The bankers were in a chastened mood. They had lost confidence in themselves. Three and a half years of attrition ending in the rout of the previous weeks, the disgrace for malpractices of many of their leaders ending in the collapse of the public prestige of their calling, and the forceful lesson that their power and privileges derived ultimately from the power of the people's government brought them to Washington eager to do its bidding. They had lost the cohesion of a vested group, and could not agree on what should be done. Some wanted a nationwide issue of fiat money or scrip; some wanted currency issued against their banks' frozen assets; some proposed that the state banks be forced into the Federal Reserve Banks to become government-owned banks of deposit; still others advocated a government guaranty of all bank deposits; and there was talk of nationalizing all the banks to bring them under government ownership and operation.

The bankers' confusion and willingness to give up responsibility to the government was an extraordinary display of the effects of loss of security on a class ordinarily quite self-reliant. If the administration had been bent upon achieving radical reforms as a condition of recovery, it could have had them. A drive for "socialism" of the kind the Brains Trust was accused of planning would have taken advantage of the discredited position and collapsed morale of the bankers to put through nationalization of the country's banks. As it was, a conservative solution, highly acceptable to bankers and businessmen, and symptomatic of the policies of the First New Deal, was decided upon. An ironic aspect of the decision was that, in deference to the bankers' sensibilities, the "radicals" of the Brains Trust who had helped draw the plan up were kept out of the bankers' sight.

The Emergency Banking Bill provided only such government controls against export and hoarding of gold, silver, and currency, and against the reopening of unsound banks as would assist private bankers to regain control of the situation. Further panic was forestalled by providing for the issuance of Federal Reserve notes on the security of assets of sound banks, so that the latter could immediately reopen for business. Thus the money changers who had fled from their high seats in the temple were invited to return under government escort. Socialists could deplore the loss of an opportunity by the government to install itself in their seats.

The temper of the new Congress was illustrated by its almost unanimous passage of the Banking Bill within four hours of its introduction on March 9, the Bill having been represented by a newspaper in the House where only the party leaders had read it. The only protest against the Bill was made in the Senate by seven Western progressives led by Senator La Follette, who voted against it on the ground that it strengthened the great New York bankers' control of the country's economy. The Act had been signed by nine o'clock that evening, and the arduous work began of reviewing the condition and licensing the reopening of banks across the country, work which was said to have condemned Secretary Woodin to his untimely death.

The next morning the President fulfilled the campaign pledge which had most pleased conservatives. He sent to Congress legislation to balance the budget by reducing the normal expenditures of the government, particularly in the fields of veterans' benefits and federal salaries. The businessman's thesis, that extravagance by the Hoover administration was a leading hindrance to recovery, was accepted by the President, and instrumented until in 1934 Congress began to pass appropriations over his veto. Later, when he recommended expenditures for unemployment relief which piled up larger deficits than those of the Hoover administration, he insisted on the distinction between "normal" expenditures, in which economy was pledged and fulfilled until Congress overrode his vetoes, and those which carried out his other pledge that he would not practice economy "at the expense of starving people." The Economy Bill was passed on March 11 over the protests of a small group of progressives against catering to "millionaires."

On Sunday evening, March 12, the President made his first "fireside chat" over the radio to the people of the country. The actions taken to solve the crisis he explained in plain terms in order to help dispel the clouds of public fear. His assurance that unsound banks would not be allowed to open created confidence in the banks which did open. Before another week was out most banks had been allowed to open, deposits and hoarded gold were re-turned, stock prices rose 15 per cent on Wall Street, and the dollar rose in foreign exchange markets. By the end of the year losses of bank deposits had been reduced to slightly over one billion dollars, owing to the failure of 1,772 banks which the Treasury had refused to license. Practically no licensed banks failed.

The swift and successful solution of the banking crisis, the clearing away of danger and fear as if by magic, launched the administration on a high tide of public enthusiasm and support. The mass of small depositors found that the new administration had suddenly made their banks safe. Newspapers were filled with hopeful portents and plans for general recovery. Within a month, legal beer of 3.2 per cent alcohol content was made to flow where home brew and worse had been before. Within a year, Prohibition was an evil memory. Congressmen were made to understand that their constituents would not tolerate opposition or delay in carrying out the program of the deliverer in the White House. Not the least important cause of the almost universal support which the administration received during the next six months was the assurance which the Emergency Banking Act and the Econ-omy Act gave to creditors, businessmen, and bankers that conservative solu-tions were acceptable to the President. The confidence for which Hoover had pleaded for three years had been restored within two weeks by Roose-velt. And most remarkable was the fact that Hoover's main purpose had been deliberately maintained:

> Those who conceived and executed [the policies of the first week] were intent upon rallying the confidence, first, of the conservative busi-ness and banking leaders of the country and, then, through them, of the public generally.

Only a seemingly minor clause in the Emergency Banking Act looked toward developments feared by conservatives. This clause granted the Presi-dent authority to take whatever steps he deemed necessary in regard to gold, silver, and foreign exchange. The Executive Order which authorized the reopening of the banks forbade transactions in foreign exchange and the withdrawal from banks or export of gold or gold certificates except as au-thorized by the Secretary of the Treasury for legitimate and normal require-ments. These restrictions on the free operation of the gold standard were in-tended not only to prevent hoarding and speculation, but to be "a step to-ward permitting the dollar to become adjusted in an orderly manner to a position with reference to other currencies that would be more in accord with our goal of increasing domestic and foreign trade."

The decision had already been made to devaluate the dollar by reduction of its gold content. The purposes of this policy will be examined hereafter; now it is sufficient to note that the President's course was devised to strike a middle path between those who wanted the gold standard maintained at all costs and the extreme inflationists. The crisis had weakened the former group but strengthened the latter, especially in Congress. At his first press conference, the President read a little lesson on monetary theory which made it clear that the United States would maintain some but not all of the requisites of a gold standard. On the other hand he defined the "unsound" currency against which he was pledged, as "printing press" money. He admitted that the government was moving towards a managed currency, but would not allow correspondents to report his words. While conservatives feared any "tinkering" with the gold standard which would reduce the purchasing power of money paid by debtors to their creditors, the advocates in Congress of inflation through issuance of money which would be "unsound" even by the President's definition were gathering their strength to force their policy on the administration. The struggle came to a climax during the debate over the Agricultural Adjustment Bill, for the farmers were still, as they had been since colonial times, the chief advocates of inflation.

The President had decided to hold Congress in special session beyond the immediate banking emergency, in order to put through a group of basic recovery measures while the atmosphere of emergency helped to minimize opposition. Unemployment and farm relief were announced as his objectives. Before the legislative mills had ceased to grind at the end of the famous "hundred days" a large number of important laws had been passed.

On March 16 a draft of the Agricultural Adjustment Bill was sent to Congress with a message urging its passage in time to restrict the spring planting of crops in accordance with its provisions. The Bill was the product of the President's campaign pledge, and of general agreement among farm and administration leaders to experiment with the Voluntary Domestic Allotment Plan, but its provisions were so broad that either one, or both, of two methods might be used. The more conservative and nationalistic scheme, sometimes called the Clair Plan, found its chief advocate in George N. Peek. He had been associated with General Hugh S. Johnson in the Moline Plow Company of Illinois, where both had learned the lesson that farmers who were not prosperous could not make industry prosperous by buying its products. Much thought and search for the solution of the problem had finally brought them to Washington in early spring of 1933 with plans which were incorporated into the First New Deal, Johnson's in the program for industrial, and Peek's in the program for agricultural recovery. The plan which Peek advocated aimed to give the farmers the benefit of tariff protection which their surpluses ordinarily denied them because they had to be sold in foreign markets whose low prices therefore determined prices in the American market. The plan was to allot money received by the government from agricultural import taxes to every farmer in an amount proportionate to the percentage of his crop which would be sold in the domestic market. No curtailment or regulation of the farmer's production would be required except in years and areas of superabundant yield, when farmers would be called upon to destroy a portion of the growing crop in order to qualify for their money allotments. High tariffs would be maintained, and ordinary surpluses would be marketed abroad with the same aggressive help of the government which had supported the export of manufactures during the Republican administrations. Peek claimed that this scheme would minimize bureaucratic control of the farmer while giving him those benefits of economic nationalist policy which industry already enjoyed.

With the substitution of an excise tax on processors of farm products as the source of money benefits to be paid to farmers, Peek's scheme was incorporated in the Rainey Bill and passed the Senate in 1932. Then it was quietly shelved in the House. He and leaders of the main farm organizations thereupon supported the candidacy of Roosevelt because they had been led to believe that their plan would be adopted by him. According to Peek's account, after the election professors and lawyers led by Rexford G. Tugwell and Jerome Frank, and the "mystical idealist," Henry Wallace, took control of farm legislation for the new administration and wrote a bill which embodied the alternative scheme for carrying out the Domestic Allotment Plan. This scheme was for acreage control by the government and would abolish the farm surplus, even in normal years and before the crop was planted, by paying rentals to farmers on acreage taken out of production. Cooperation by farmers was voluntary, but few were likely to refuse to receive checks for not cultivating a percentage of their acres, and Peek believed the scheme to be "collectivist" because it entailed "regulation" of the farmers, as well as "internationalist" because it would benefit the whole world by removing the American surpluses from the international market and thereby raise the world price of farm commodities. It was linked to low tariff and other internationalist ideals and, Peek was convinced, would not work.

He insisted early in March that the dispute be carried to the President, but the latter sided with the Wallace group and acreage control. Nevertheless, the President was unwilling to abandon the "nationalist" features of the Peek scheme as yet, so the terms of the Agricultural Adjustment Bill were made broad enough to permit either scheme or both to be carried out, and Peek himself was promised the office of administrator of the law. The dispute was also aired before the Senate Committee on Agriculture and Forestry. The broad terms of the Bill, Peek's announcement that he was opposed to acreage control, and the understanding that he would administer the Bill according to his own plan permitted the problem to be passed over and postponed.

The Domestic Allotment Plan was supported chiefly by larger farmers who produced the staples subject to export, such as wheat and cotton, which would be included in the Plan. These farmers constituted the strength of the Farm Bureau Federation, the National Grange, and several other organizations which wielded great influence on the Congressmen of the bi-partisan Farm Bloc. Peek's statement that these farm organizations had little to do with the Agricultural Adjustment Bill must be taken in the narrow sense of actual participation in its writing, because limitation of farm production by a scheme such as the Domestic Allotment Plan had long been their chief demand, especially since the failure of Hoover's Marketing Act. On the other hand, the National Farmers Union and the Farmers National Holiday Association represented the smaller farmers and tenants who were less dependent on staple crops and therefore less interested in the Domestic Allotment Plan.

These two organizations held conventions to pass unanimous resolutions condemning the Agricultural Adjustment Bill. The homespun President of the Farmers Union, John A. Simpson, conducted a vigorous campaign against it over the radio and before the Senate Committee. He considered both acreage control and tariff equalization to be unworkable, and mere palliatives in any case. The fundamental problem was that

> 40 or 50 per cent of farmers are sinking out in the middle of Old River Mortgage and the first thing is to throw him a lifesaver. . . .
>
> A privileged few now hold the obligations of the great mass of the people to the extent that any time they want to foreclose they can make about 120,000,000 of us propertyless. You have got one way to remedy that thing, and that is to make the dollar cheap enough so that the farmer, the little business man, the professional man, everybody, can pay their debts.

Representative Lemke of North Dakota declared that Simpson correctly expressed the sentiments of 85 per cent of all farmers. Certainly the advocates of the Bill did not explain what it would offer to the smaller, diversified-crop farmers and tenants. Whatever soundness there was in the arguments of Simpson, they were eagerly taken up by inflationist Congressmen, among whom representatives of silver-producing states were important. The former hoped to reduce the value of the money which would be used to pay off farm mortgages, and the latter hoped to find a market at the mints for silver. Thus the descendants of the Populist farmers and of the Silver Senators of 1896 reproduced the alliance which had gone down to defeat with William Jennings Bryan in the great free-silver campaign. This time the alliance succeeded in exacting an inflationary amendment as the price of its support of the Agricultural Adjustment Bill.

The administration feared an amendment which would make uncontrolled inflation mandatory and defeat its plan for a managed currency. Senator Wheeler of Montana introduced an amendment providing free coinage of silver at a ratio with gold of sixteen to one, far above the market price. This measure was defeated in the Senate by a vote of 43 to 33 on April 17, but the President knew that more than ten more Senators were prepared to vote for other inflationary devices. The House overwhelmingly favored inflation. The problem became one of limiting and controlling the movement: it could not be stopped. When Senator Thomas of Oklahoma introduced an amendment designed to win the support of all varieties of inflationists, the President had it rewritten and then did not oppose its passage. The Thomas Amendment gave permissive power to the President to inflate or alter the currency by one or more of several devices: free coinage of silver at a ratio to gold fixed by the President, unlimited issuance of paper currency, and devaluation of the gold content of the dollar. None of the devices was mandatory, and it became possible for the President to use the one which was necessary to establish a managed currency while ignoring those which would produce an "unsound" money system. One of the President's conservative advisers, Director of the Budget Lewis A. Douglas, believed that the amendment was "the end of Western civilization," but it possibly saved the country from the uncontrolled inflation upon which many Congressmen were intent. Another amendment provided that compensating duties might be imposed to prevent higher domestic farm prices from leading to increased imports.

While Congress debated the Agricultural Adjustment Bill, unrest in the Corn Belt rose to new heights. The Farm Holiday Association, led by Milo Reno, organized strikes by farmers who refused to sell, or allow anyone else to sell, produce at the prevailing low prices. These measures of desperation accomplished little, because the market was too favorable to buyers for sellers' strikes to succeed. More effective was the frustration of farm mortgage foreclosures. Crowds of farmers forced sheriffs to accept bids of a dollar or two at foreclosure auctions, and then turned the farms back to their original owners. At LeMars, Iowa, on April 27, District Judge Bradley refused to promise a mob of farmers that he would sign no more foreclosures, and was dragged from his courtroom and hung by a rope until he was unconscious. States passed mortgage moratorium laws. On May 4, a conference of farm leaders voted for a national strike, which was postponed only at the request of the President that the new farm legislation be given a chance to create recovery by orderly methods. After a special message by the President to Congress another amendment was added to the farm bill, under which farm mortgages would be refinanced at low interest rates by the federal government.

When it was finally passed as an administration measure and signed on May 12, the Agricultural Adjustment Act was an omnibus which gave the farmers of the country their three main demands of the preceding half-century and longer; protection against the ruinous effect on prices of their surplus crops, inflated currency with which to pay their debts, and cheap credit. No law had promised the farmer so much since the Homestead Act of 1863. If the law did not introduce Utopia, it was not for lack of willingness by the administration to heed the farmer's voice in the spring of 1933.

Unemployment relief was the second immediate objective of the administration. On March 21, the President sent a message to Congress asking for three types of legislation, none of which departed far in principle from the relief policies of the Hoover administration. Two of the requests were quickly met by establishment of the Civilian Conservation Corps which provided 250,000 unemployed young men with little more than subsistence wages as workers in the national forests, and the Federal Emergency Relief Administration which made grants to the states for direct relief. The CCC was a type of public works activity which the Hoover administration had not developed, while the FERA grants were gifts as contrasted with the loans to the states for direct relief which Hoover had inaugurated in June, 1932. The third request was met in Title II of the National Industrial Recovery Act passed in June. This Title established the Public Works Administration and was a simple expansion of the Hoover policy of providing employment by the construction of public buildings, roads, and other traditional federal works. The appropriations for the CCC, FERA, and PWA exceeded the outlays for relief by the preceding administration, but they did not approximate the great expenditures which began in 1935, when, for the period of the Second New Deal, a fundamentally new relief policy was inaugurated to provide federal employment at security wage scales to all employables. Meanwhile a relief policy acceptable to conservatives was intended to mitigate the worst suffering without solving the unemployment problem.

Title I of the National Industrial Recovery Act was intended to solve the broad problem of industrial depression and unemployment. Contrary to general impression, this most significant experiment of the First New Deal was not improvised by the President or the Brain Trust. The occasion of its passage may be called fortuitous, but its policies are traceable to theories and practices of organized industry and labor during the preceding decades, and it was only one more experiment in the world-wide movement by advanced industrial countries in the twentieth century away from laissez-faire individualism.

Over the years both of the main groups dependent upon factory production had worked out programs for the improvement of their own position in the industrial system. The depression was an incentive to each group to work more aggressively for its own program as a cure for the ills which afflicted the system, and they both demanded that the government adopt and enforce their programs. Before the depression, labor had chiefly depended on non-political union activity to achieve its aims of shortening the hours of work and raising wages. The depression created a great surplus in the labor market which was unfavorable to the bargaining power of unions. They lost membership and became virtually useless in achieving benefits for labor. In this situation workers looked increasingly to state and federal legislation as the only practicable means of achieving the labor program. Laws to improve labor's position were presented as being in the public interest because they would increase employment and production by increasing the purchasing power of the mass of the population. Manufacturers, on the other hand, had since the First World War developed to a high level the use of trade associations to formulate codes of fair trade practice which should minimize competition, support prices, limit production, and divide markets. These codes suffered from two weaknesses: their legality under the antitrust laws was doubtful, and the courts had not clarified the issue; and agreements by corporations to observe the provisions of a code were voluntary and unenforceable. The latter weakness permitted the collapse of the codes during the depression when the search for vanishing markets led manufacturers to revive the whole arsenal of savage competition. The opinion grew among businessmen that the codes of the trade associations must be exempted from the antitrust laws and enforced by government authority. Since this would raise prices and restore profits, production would be expanded and employment restored, wherefore the scheme was held to be thoroughly justified by the public interest.

The two programs were incompatible to the degree that each group intended to win the lion's share of advantage from an industrial revival. They could be reconciled only by a mutual determination to share the benefits of recovery. Until President Roosevelt came to power there was little hope of obtaining such an agreement.

Meanwhile the two groups worked separately. An important victory in the labor campaign for state legislation was won with the New York minimum-wage law of April, 1933. By that time the fight for a federal maximum-hours law was well underway. In December, 1932, Senator Black of Alabama introduced a bill which would limit the hours of work in factories to thirty per week. Early in January, President Green of the American Federation of Labor told a Senate Committee that labor would resort to a general strike if necessary to compel adoption of the thirty-hour week: "A lot of employers understand only one thing—force, and this change can only be brought about either by legislation or force."

The Black Bill attracted little attention until a committee of the Chamber of Commerce issued a "Report on Working Hours" recommending that a forty-hour week be adopted by industry, that it be only temporary and voluntary, and vigorously opposing any legislation on the subject. As if in defiance of the Chamber, the Senate suddenly passed the Black Bill on April 6. Chairman Connery of the House Committee on Labor added a provision for a boycott of imports produced by foreign industries whose laborers worked more than thirty hours per week. This he considered necessary to prevent dumping of foreign goods in the United States when domestic labor costs were suddenly raised by the thirty-hour rule. Such a boycott would wreck at one blow Secretary Hull's plans to reduce tariff rates and the London Economic Conference which was scheduled to meet in June. Nevertheless, there were signs that the House would pass the Black-Connery Bill with a large majority.

This precipitated in a form unwelcome to the administration the whole question of its industrial recovery program. On April 4 the President had decided, after considering many conflicting plans offered by industrialists and others, to postpone the question because "thinking in business and government circles on the subject had not yet crystallized sufficiently." Now he immediately appointed a Cabinet committee headed by Secretary Perkins to "work out a substitute for the Black Bill."

Secretary Perkins carried the findings of her cabinet committee to the hearings on the Black-Connery Bill, and proposed them as "suggestions" of the administration. She declared that the Bill, while not an administration measure, represented a general policy which had the sympathy of the President. The suggestions were that a minimum-wage provision be added to the Bill to prevent employers from cutting wages when they reduced the hours of work, and to bring substandard wages up to a minimum level; that some flexibility be permitted in the hours provision to suit the needs of seasonal industries; and that power be vested in the government to restrict production to prevent it from again outrunning consuming power and forcing the cut-throat competition and low prices which would make obedience to the hours and wages provisions impossible. The whole should be administered by the Department of Labor.

Organized labor heartily endorsed the plan, although it was inclined to fear that minimum wages would become maximum wages unless an amendment guaranteed the right of collective bargaining. But the Perkins suggestions were a shock to employers. The President was "aghast at the commotion" they caused. A hundred leading industrialists met in Philadelphia on April 11 to protest against the Bill, and similar meetings were held in other cities. Manufacturers were accused of coercing their employers to oppose the Bill. Leaders of the main organizations of business, including President Henry I. Harriman of the Chamber of Commerce, President James A. Emery of the National Association of Manufacturers, and Robert Lamont of the Iron and Steel Institute, appeared before the House Committee to register their protest. Immediately when the aggressive opposition of business began to be felt, the President directed Moley to obtain plans from business groups which they would favor as substitutes for the Black-Connery-Perkins Bill. On May 1, the administration leader Senator Robinson announced that the Bill was no longer supported by the administration. The House Committee continued its hearings nevertheless, indicating that it might be impossible to divert the movement for a recovery plan based exclusively on the labor program.

The business plan for recovery which was formulated by the administration under these circumstances had been officially adopted by the Chamber of Commerce as early as April, 1931, when its annual convention urged that the government modify the antitrust laws to permit industry to limit competition, raise prices, and restrict production. This would provide the guaranty of profitable operation of factories which was indispensable to recovery. The trade associations were the instruments best fitted for the organization of the proposed controls, but their inability to enforce their own codes of fair-trade practices demonstrated the need to find stronger sanctions than they possessed. In December, 1931, the Chamber announced that it favored a national economic council, not under government supervision, to enforce codes drawn up by the trade associations.

The specter of government regulation of business was being fought valiantly, but the deepening depression and further collapse of the trade associations' codes brought businessmen to admit in desperation the need for governmental authority to bring order out of the chaos created by destructive competition. In June 1932, after another convention, the Chamber of Commerce launched a nation-wide drive to win support for relaxation of the antitrust laws and "government approval" of trade association codes. At this stage businessmen hoped that the power of government could be used in their favor without submitting to government regulation or even supervision.

At about the same time, Roosevelt and the Brains Trust began to collect plans for the organization of new relations between government and industry. Many variations on the theme of government authority behind trade agreements were gathered together and filed. To these Moley turned when the President suddenly needed to placate business fears of the Black-Connery-Perkins Bill. Moley handed over to General Hugh S. Johnson the task of integrating them in one plan. At the same time the President authorized Senator Wagner of New York, Secretary Perkins, Assistant Secretary of Commerce John Dickinson, Donald Richberg, Rexford Tugwell, and others to work independently on the same problem.

While all were at work, business leaders who were appearing before the House Committee on Labor complemented their protests against the Black-Connery-Perkins Bill with proposals which finally added to the business program for suspension of the antitrust laws and codes of "fair competition" the admission of the need for government supervision. On May 3, two days after the administration had ended its support of the pro-labor Bill, the Chamber of Commerce convention met in Washington and voiced further strong protests against it. But it became clear to the convention that the administration was struggling to avoid passage of the Bill and needed support. Speakers explained that the government might be forced to regulate industry directly unless business cooperated with it to make concessions to labor under a system of self-government by industry with government supervision. The President himself addressed the convention to appeal for concessions to labor in return for government aid in the suppression of cut-throat competition. The convention promptly resolved in favor of the President's plan.

After these developments it remained for the framers of the new Bill to work out details such as the degree of government control which "supervision" would require, and the exact nature of the concessions to labor which would be demanded of employers in return for the suspension of the antitrust laws. In the end, the President ordered all those whom he had assigned to draw up plans to shut themselves in a room until they could agree on a single draft of a bill.

Their product was the National Industrial Recovery Bill. It was based on the assumption that labor and industry would share the benefits of recovery, and to this end both interests were granted government support in the achievement of their programs. In the famous Section 7A, labor was promised the inclusion in industrial codes of unspecified minimum-wages and maximum-hours rules, and was guaranteed the right of collective bargaining with employers through representatives freely chosen by employees. For businessmen, limitation of production and exemption of codes from the antitrust laws were provided. The question of the degree of government control in the drawing up of codes was left to a tug-of-war between the trade associations which were given the right to formulate them, and the government which could reject them and promulgate codes on its own motion. Violators of code agreements could be prosecuted before the federal courts and punished. The President was left free to establish whatever administrative agencies he deemed necessary. The Bill was considered by the President to be a deliberate step away from the philosophy of "equalitarianism and laissez faire" which Hoover's failure and his own election had proven to be "bankrupt." Ideally, the system envisaged would consist of separate institutions of self-government for both labor and industry, with the government requiring them to cooperate and preventing either one from injuring the other or the public.

The draft was sent to Congress on May 15. The Black-Connery-Perkins Bill was dropped, and hearings were held on the substitute by both houses. Senator Wagner sponsored the new Bill, and he and Donald Richberg represented the administration at both hearings. In the Committee on Finance hearing Senator King of Utah asked Senator Wagner whether the Bill was "drawn largely from the philosophy of Mussolini or the old German cartel system," and Senator Wagner denied it, but to the House Committee on Ways and Means Donald Richberg admitted that the Bill encouraged manufacturers to fix prices immune from prosecution, and thus to achieve the same ends as cartels did in Europe. He stated that the trade associations wanted the antitrust laws suspended in order to legalize codes of fair competition chiefly to end unfair competition in the use of labor. However, since labor unions and labor contracts had already been exempted from the antitrust laws by the Clayton Act of 1914, Congressmen questioned whether the proposed law was motivated by a desire to raise wages as much as by a desire to raise prices. Answering this, President Harriman of the Chamber of Commerce, who had been in close consultation with the authors of the Bill, admitted that a price rise was the primary motive. Some business leaders believed that Section 7A made too great concessions to labor. President James A. Emery of the National Association of Manufacturers and R. P. Lamont of the Iron and Steel Institute frankly spoke their fear that Section 7A would cause labor unions and collective bargaining to thrive and "individual bargaining" to perish. That the Bill left the way open for the building of company unions and thus avoidance of collective bargaining presently became apparent to businessmen and lessened their opposition to Section 7A.

The most important amendment made by Congress provided that the President might limit, prohibit, or make conditions governing imports when the new law caused rises in prices which invited foreign goods into the American market. In this way the economic nationalist implications of the Bill were recognized, and tariff provisions made which matched the compensating duties of the AAA. Businessmen had advocated a manufacturers' sales tax as the source of new revenue needed to service the borrowing of $3,300,000,000 for the public works program which was authorized in Title II of the Bill, but the administration's recommendation to increase income, corporation, excess profits, and gasoline taxes was carried out by Congress.

The National Industrial Recovery Act was passed by large majorities and signed on June 16. The President said that history would probably record it as "the most important and far-reaching legislation ever enacted by the American Congress. . . . Its goal is the assurance of a reasonable profit to industry and living wages for labor." Thus were added to the farmers the second and third main interest groups to whom the administration during the First New Deal tried strenuously to grant their main demands.

The chief purpose of the AAA and NIRA was recovery. They dominated the First New Deal, and the administration's first crusades were organized around them. Three other laws were passed during the Hundred Days the chief purpose of which was reform rather than recovery. These attracted less attention at the time, but their greater permanence and their capacity for organic growth make them significant. Each of the three laws had been promised in the Democratic platform, and was a specific application of the reform traditions which had been interrupted when Woodrow Wilson left the White House.

The Tennessee Valley Authority Act of May 18 was a victory for those who, without discussing socialist theory, insisted that the government own and operate for the benefit of the people hydro-electric plants on the great waterways of the nation in order to prevent private corporations from exploiting these vast resources for private profit. Republican administrations had nowhere shown themselves more ineffective than in their inability to find any solution other than shutting down the government's great wartime power and munitions plant at Muscle Shoals. Senator George W. Norris of Nebraska had conducted a relentless struggle to end the waste of power on the Tennessee River and to place it at the service of the people of the region. The TVA was a personal victory for him as well as for the public policy which Roosevelt had painstakingly developed while Governor of New York.

The law created a corporation with a board of three directors appointed by the President with the consent of the Senate. This body was vested with the power of eminent domain to build dams and power plants with the purpose of developing the Valley economically and socially. It was empowered to produce, distribute, and sell electric power and nitrogen fertilizers to the people of the region and to industry, and to sell explosives to the United States government. Flood control, navigation, proper use of marginal lands, reforestation, and the general welfare of the region were within its sphere. Direct competition with private power companies was authorized by the erection of transmission lines to farms and villages not otherwise supplied with electricity "at reasonable rates." The widespread opposition which the latter feature of TVA might have aroused in normal times was distracted by the dramatic events of the Hundred Days on other fronts, and also by the cloud which had passed over the private utility companies with the collapse of the Insull holding company pyramid and the revelations of widespread abuses. As it was, the full development of opposition was postponed until the success of TVA was assured, when the only question which remained was whether the costs of a federal corporation on which TVA power rates were based constituted fair competition with private companies, or even a fair yardstick by which the rates of private companies might be measured. To the people of the Valley and the manufacturers who moved in to use the cheap power, the question was fairly academic. Wendell Willkie was to attract his first admiring attention from the business world when, as President of the Commonwealth and Southern

Power Company, he drove a particularly sharp bargain in the sale of facilities to the TVA. His victory might well be called Pyrrhic. The general success of TVA encouraged federal development of similar sites in other regions. When war came again, the nation did not lack vast power facilities for munitions, aluminum, and a thousand other purposes.

The Securities Act of May 27 originated in the conviction of liberals over many years that a federal "blue-sky" law was needed to protect the public from fraud and misrepresentation in the issuance, manipulation, and sale of stocks and other securities. The depression had thrown glaring light on the unscrupulous purposes behind many securities issues, the devious methods by which insiders rigged the stock market, and the deceptions practiced by high-pressure salesmen who gulled the small investor. Correction of these abuses was a part of the Democratic platform. Confusion of counsel separated regulation of securities issues and sales from the allied problem of stock-exchange regulation, postponed action on the latter until 1934, and resulted in a bill drawn chiefly by Felix Frankfurter and hastily passed without hearings by Congress. Its main provisions were that new issues of securities be registered with the Federal Trade Commission along with a statement of the financial position of the company, and that the same information be given to all purchasers of the issue. "Let the seller beware!" was substituted for the older slogan: misrepresentation was made subject to prosecution. Whether or not this Truth-in-Securities Act was cumbersome, as its revision in 1934 argues, and hindered the flotation of new issues in 1933, it was of less pressing importance than the regulation of stock exchanges. In the absence of the latter reform, a speculative Wall Street boom, garnished by all the abuses of the pre-depression era, threatened to discount recovery before the administration's program could be put into effect and purchasing power be increased to keep pace with rising prices.

The Glass-Steagall Banking Act of June 16 established three reforms which most bankers as well as liberals had come to believe were necessary to prevent repetition of the abuses which had aggravated the boom, the depression, and the banking crisis. Investment banking was separated from commercial banking so that affiliates could no longer be used by bankers for speculation with their depositors' money. The Federal Deposit Insurance Corporation was established to afford a government guaranty of bank deposits under $5,000, and thus remove the motive for runs on banks by small depositors such as had occurred prior to March 4. The Federal Reserve Board was given powers over interest rates and other factors which would enable it to prevent excessive speculation with borrowed money.

The TVA, the Securities Act, and the Banking Act were all sustained by the Supreme Court, while the chief recovery laws, AAA and NIRA were invalidated. This remarkable fact, usually forgotten at the time of the struggle over the President's court reorganization plan, made the reform legislation of the First New Deal more important for the future than the recovery legislation which was at the time the administration's chief concern.

The three reform laws which were passed during the Hundred Days were also distinguished by their compatibility with the purposes of the recovery program. On the other hand, reforms which had been promised in the sphere of economic foreign policy, especially tariffs, were not reconcilable with the domestic recovery measures.

❧ ☙

ROOSEVELT *won an overwhelming victory at the polls in 1936. Within a year, he seemed to have reached political ebb tide. His effort to secure a friendly Supreme Court through the Court Packing proposals failed; his efforts to institute further reform legislation floundered; and his effort to cut back on government expenditures to assure a balanced budget sent the economy into a tailspin. Unemployment rose sharply, and by Roosevelt's own testimony, one third of the nation was ill-housed, ill-clad, and ill-fed. Five years of New Deal experimentation left the nation still far from its goal of full economic revival and full employment.*

It was with such bleak conditions as a background that Roosevelt found himself compelled to face up to a worsening international crisis. In Europe, Adolf Hitler, who had preceded Roosevelt into office by barely a month, systematically dismantled the 1919 Peace of Paris, a process aided and abetted by the British policy of appeasement. In the Far East, Japan launched its campaign to gain preeminence in China. Within a short time, following the December 12, 1937, Japanese attack on the American gunboat Panay *as it patrolled the Yangtze River, the United States seemed headed for a collision with Japan. Even before this crisis, on October 5, 1937, Roosevelt proposed that the nations of the world combine to quarantine the aggressor powers. Evidence mounted that the Roosevelt administration contemplated a shift from its previous quasi-isolationist policies.*

The outbreak of general war in Europe on September 1, 1939, put a further dent in American isolationism, but when the German blitzkrieg overwhelmed France in June of 1940 and seemed on the verge of invading Great Britain, Roosevelt abandoned any pretense at neutrality. Fearful of the consequences of having to face a world dominated by Hitler and Japan, the United States gave all possible aid to both Great Britain and China. The power of the Pacific fleet was committed to shoring up the crumbling Southeastern Asiatic empires of France, the Netherlands, and Great Britain. Thoughtful observers realized that if the United States were to persist in her policies she would end up on collision course with both Japan and Germany. As the nation supported a peacetime draft, traded destroyers to Britain for bases, extended increasingly large aid under Lend-Lease to Britain and her allies, China, and then to the Soviet Union, the economy surged ahead to end at last the Great Depression.

The abandonment of isolationism provoked a bitter debate that only ended with Pearl Harbor. It also provided the circumstances of a major historical debate. A small group of historians including Charles A. Beard, Harry Elmer Barnes (1889-   ), and Charles Callan Tansill (1890-1965) charged Roosevelt's foreign policy worked deliberately to force Germany and Japan to attack the United States. It was their contention that this alone would overcome the isolationist sentiments of the American people. It also allowed, Beard contended, the New Deal to escape the consequences of its economic failures. Right-wing critics of the New Deal, and more especially of Franklin D. Roosevelt, found in these interpretations further proof of their conviction that 1933 had inaugurated an abandonment of traditional American institutions and beliefs.

Defenders of administration policy immediately before the outbreak of World War II have accepted his critic's charges that Roosevelt's policies risked war but they have denied that he deliberately provoked war. William L. Langer (1896-   ) and S. Everett Gleason (1905-   ), both active diplomatic historians who have had extensive involvement in formulating foreign policy, insist that a fair analysis of prewar American diplomacy requires an understanding of the intent of foreign policy. They define it as primarily an effort to define the national interest abroad. In the process, a discrimination between those issues which are vital and those which are secondary must be drawn. Once an interest is judged vital, the full power of the nation must be committed, if necessary, to its defense, even if in the end war alone can maintain it. In their judgment, it was the fundamental import of the American interests under challenge by both Germany and Japan that made it necessary for Roosevelt to risk war in their defense.

What were these interests? Militarily in 1940 the United States was not prepared for war when France capitulated to Hitler's legions. Aid to Britain was dictated by self-interest. Their resistance to Nazism would allow us time to prepare our own defenses. The chance that Britain would be forced to surrender its fleet to Germany left the United States with the uncomfortable prospect of having to face alone the combined naval might of Japan and a triumphant Germany. Churchill assured Roosevelt that under no circumstances would such an event be permitted to happen. To the critics of Roosevelt's European policy, his defenders would reply that behind the shield of first British and then Russian resistance, America was allowed a necessary breathing spell to mobilize its own defenses.

In the Pacific Ocean, American policy had always emphasized our need to maintain our naval preeminence. As Japan revealed its intentions to challenge our supremacy, Roosevelt worked to confine Japan's imperial designs, using Tokyo's dependence upon imported raw materials to maintain its industrial plant as a way to inhibit Japanese aggression. Far from seeking to provoke Japan, the American policy of restricting exports of petroleum, scrap iron and other strategic materials intended to deprive Japan of the sinews of war. But once Japan determined to establish its suzerainty over Southeast Asia, nothing short of an American withdrawal could prevent war. There is a certain wisdom also in considering what manner of a world we would be living in if Hitler and the Japanese war lords had triumphed. In a world grown infinitely smaller since 1939, we need only consider that whatever our choices, technological advances had foredoomed isolationism. To think otherwise would have been to play the ostrich.

BACK DOOR TO WAR

The Roosevelt Foreign Policy, 1933-1941

by Charles Callan Tansill

HITLER LAUNCHES A BLITZKRIEG ALONG THE WESTERN FRONT

Before the Nazi armed forces had scored an important success in the Norway campaign, President Roosevelt began a series of endeavors to keep Italy out of the war. On April 29 he sent a telegram to Mussolini in which he expressed his deepest satisfaction with reference to "the policy of the Italian Government in exerting every effort to prevent war from spreading to southern and southeastern Europe." A further extension of the area of hostilities would bring into the war "still other nations which have been seeking to maintain their neutrality." He could see "no reason to anticipate that any one nation or any one combination of nations" could successfully "dominate either the continent of Europe . . . or a greater part of the world." He earnestly hoped that the powerful influence of Italy would continue to be exercised "in behalf of the negotiation of a just and stable peace."

When Ambassador Phillips conveyed this message to Mussolini he was informed that "Italy, Germany and Russia did not desire an extension of the war." The Duce then expressed the opinion that "Germany could not be beaten" and that an Allied naval blockade would be "completely ineffective." The President should realize that the political system created by the Treaty of Versailles had been liquidated. In the new system Germany "would willingly permit a new independent Polish State" to be erected but it would not have the "old boundaries which were completely without justification." Germany was "also willing that a new Czechoslovakian state be reestablished." Last, but not least, certain important concessions should be given to Italy.

Throughout this conversation Mussolini appeared to go "out of his way to be friendly." He requested Ambassador Phillips to "thank President Roosevelt cordially" for his message and he seemed to be "extremely appreciative of it."

In his diary, Count Ciano had a somewhat different story to tell. He noted that the Duce received the Roosevelt message with "ill grace" and that he said "little or nothing to the American Ambassador." Mussolini then sent a brief note to the President in which he argued that responsibility for World War II did "not fall upon Germany but upon the initiatives of the Allies." As far as he knew, Germany was "opposed to a further extension of the conflict, and Italy likewise." With reference to the President's belief that "an extension of the war fronts" might have a serious effect upon the

Western Hemisphere, he called attention "to the fact that Italy has never concerned itself with the relations of the American republics with each other and with the United States (thereby respecting the Monroe Doctrine), and might therefore ask for 'reciprocity' with regard to European affairs."

Ciano regarded this note as "cutting and hostile." It was certainly not conciliatory. The Duce was "literally exalted" by the news of Hitler's victories in Norway. In a letter describing his success the Führer complained that the "excessive rapidity" of the advance of his troops had not "permitted his involving the English forces more effectively" so as to "destroy them completely." He intimated that he would have to "obtain a victory in the West as soon as possible" because of "hidden threats of American intervention."

On this same day (May 4) the German General Staff issued a statement that awakened instant apprehension in Belgium and the Netherlands. The charge was made that those countries had not maintained an impartial neutrality. It was also alleged that on January 12, 1940, some extended discussions had taken place in Breda "between Dutch, Belgian, French and British staff officers." These discussions were supposed to have been for the purpose of aiding British and French forces to launch an "attack on the Ruhr."

Alleging the necessity of anticipating this Anglo-French invasion, the German Government began a blitzkrieg upon the Western Front. News of this attack came to President Roosevelt early on the morning of May 10 when Ambassador Cudahy telephoned the White House to report that a large German air force was already over Luxemburg en route to Belgium and the Netherlands. Later during the morning "President Roosevelt and Secretary Hull called from time to time asking for latest developments." Cudahy replied that the news was "entirely reassuring." But King Leopold, of Belgium, was not so confident about the situation. Fearful of the outcome of the German invasion he sent a hurried telegram to President Roosevelt expressing the ardent hope that he would support with all his "moral authority the efforts which we are now firmly decided to make in order to preserve our independence." The President could only reply that he and the American people cherished the strong desire that "policies which seek to dominate peaceful and independent peoples through force and military aggression may be arrested, and that the government and people of Belgium may preserve their integrity and freedom."

In Rome, Ambassador Phillips told Ciano that the German blitzkrieg was "bound to stir America profoundly." It had already stirred the Pope who had sent telegrams to the "rulers of the three invaded states." This act had incensed Mussolini who blurted out to Ciano that the Papacy was "a cancer which gnaws at our national life." If necessary he would "liquidate this problem once and for all." Later the Pope evidenced a "clear-cut intransigency" and remarked that he was "even ready to be deported to a concentration camp."

Into this tense and ominous atmosphere in Rome the President once more intervened by sending another note to Mussolini. Rumors that the Duce was "contemplating early entry into the war" had given him "great concern." Most Americans believed that the whole world faced a "threat which opposes every teaching of Christ, every philosophy of all the great teachers of mankind over thousands of years." Therefore, as the President of the United States he made "the simple plea that you, responsible for Italy, withhold your hand, stay wholly apart from any war and refrain from any threat of attack."

Ciano noted that the new communication from the President was not in a "covertly threatening style." It was rather a "discouraged and conciliatory message." Allusions to the "Gospel of Christ" would have "little effect upon the mind of Mussolini," who was convinced that Germany would win the war. As an ally of Hitler, Italy could secure rich spoils of war.

ROOSEVELT REGARDS NEUTRALITY AS AN OUTMODED CONCEPT

While the President was pleading with Mussolini to remain neutral in the great conflict that was wrecking Europe, he himself was pushing America down the road to war. On April 26 it was reported that the Anglo-French Purchasing Commission could obtain planes of almost any type then being produced for the armed forces of the United States. This news encouraged the French Premier, Paul Reynaud, to send to Washington (May 14) the startling request that the American Government arrange for the sale or lease of old destroyers. On the following day Winston Churchill, who displaced Chamberlain as Prime Minister on May 10, sent a more ambitious request that was quite breath-taking:

> All I ask is that you [President Roosevelt] should proclaim non-belligerency, which would mean that you would help us with everything short of actually engaging armed forces. Immediate needs are: First of all, the loan of forty or fifty of your older destroyers; . . . Secondly, we want several hundred of the latest types of aircraft; . . . Thirdly, anti-aircraft equipment and ammunition. . . . Fourthly, the fact that our ore supply is being compromised from Sweden, from North Africa and perhaps from Northern Spain, makes it necessary to purchase steel in the United States. . . . I should like to feel reasonably sure that when we can pay no more, you will give us the stuff all the same. Fifthly, . . . the visit of a United States Squadron to Irish ports . . . would be invaluable.

The President replied that he could not make a deal concerning the destroyers "without authorization from Congress." Moreover, America "needed the destroyers" for its "own defences." Churchill greatly regretted this negative answer but he still hoped to get "at the earliest possible date" the largest possible number of Curtiss P-40 fighters. In conclusion he sounded a loud note of alarm that he knew would profoundly affect the President. If Britain were "left by the United States to its fate," there was a definite danger that the British fleet might be turned over to the Germans as a bargaining point.

We have already noted that in 1939, while Chamberlain was still Prime Minister, Churchill began his momentous personal correspondence with President Roosevelt. It has been stated that one of the first cablegrams sent by Churchill to Roosevelt was phrased in a most grandiloquent manner. The gist of it has been given as follows: "I am half American and the natural person to work with you. It is evident we see eye to eye. Were I to become Prime Minister of Britain we could control the world."

Churchill states that he sent "nine hundred and fifty" of these cablegrams to the President and received "about eight hundred in reply." His relations with the American Chief Executive "gradually became so close that the chief business between our two countries was virtually conducted by these personal interchanges between him and me. . . . As head of the State as well as Head of the Government, Roosevelt spoke and acted with authority in every sphere."

It is obvious that Churchill regarded Roosevelt as an American dictator who had little concern for the opinions of Congress and the American people. With reference to the matter of war the Churchill cablegrams reveal that he believed that Roosevelt could plunge America into the conflict in Europe at any time he desired. The French Cabinet apparently had the same viewpoint.

The urgency of Churchill was translated into hysteria by Premier Reynaud. On May 18, Bullitt was informed by Alexis Léger, Secretary-General of the French Foreign Office, that Reynaud was about to request President Roosevelt to ask Congress for a declaration of war against Germany. Bullitt frankly informed Léger that such a request would be worse than useless: Congress would almost unanimously vote against such a declaration. The President then talked to Bullitt over the telephone and instructed him to say that "anything of this nature was out of the question." But Reynaud continued to press for the impossible. On May 22 he told Bullitt that the German tide was growing more menacing every minute. There was grave danger that the French public would insist upon a separate peace with Germany. In that event a German victory over Britain "would be destroyed by air bombardment" and the "American Army would be able to offer little resistance." Prompt action by the American Government was "the only real guarantee that Hitler would not some day be in the White House."

A week later the Reynaud appeals grew more frantic. On May 28 he warned Bullitt that he had convincing evidence that "if France and England were conquered, Hitler would move almost immediately against the United States." The American fleet should be sent at once to the Mediterranean so as to exert pressure upon Mussolini to stay out of the war.

The President did not send the fleet to the Mediterranean but he decided to permit American pilots to fly planes, ordered by the Allies, to Halifax and other ports in the Canadian maritime provinces. Before this decision the Dominion had been designated as a combat area and American nationals had not been allowed to enter it in aircraft belonging to belligerent nations. The President then urged Churchill to send additional planes to France but he was told that Britain needed all available aircraft for defense against expected German attack. Ambassador Bullitt became furious over this negative reply from Britain and he confided to Secretary Hull his belief that the British Cabinet "might be conserving their air force and fleet so as to use them as bargaining points in negotiations with Hitler."

Both the President and Secretary Hull discounted these observations of Bullitt. They were certain that while France "was finished," Britain, with the aid of American supplies, could withstand a German assault. It was imperative, therefore, that these supplies be rushed at once to British ports. Joseph C. Green, chief of the Division of Controls, brought to Secretary Hull's attention an old statute of May 12, 1917. The language of this statute could be interpreted so as to authorize the exchange of army and navy aircraft for new models of a more advanced type. Arrangements were made with a Buffalo concern to deliver to them fifty planes belonging to the Naval Reserve squadrons in exchange for planes of a "superior type." These planes were then rushed to Britain. But Churchill wanted more than planes. In order to meet his importunate requests, the President turned to the Acting Attorney General, Francis Biddle, who conveniently ruled that the Secretary of War had the right to sell surplus war supplies to "any corporation or individual upon such terms as may be deemed best."

General George C. Marshall, as Chief of Staff, now came to the front and directed his Chief of Ordnance and his Assistant Chief of Staff to survey the entire list of American reserve ordnance and munitions stocks. On June 3 he approved these lists. The first list was a lengthy one:

> It comprised half a million .30 calibre rifles out of two million manufactured in 1917 and 1918. . . . For these there were about 250 cartridges apiece. There were 900 soixante-quinze field guns with a million rounds, 80,000 machine guns and various other items. . . . On June 3 all the American Army depots and arsenals started packing the material for shipment. . . . By June 11 a dozen British merchant ships moved into the bay [Raritan] and anchored, and loading from lighters began.

But this flood of war matériel reached the Allies too late to stop the rapid German advance. On May 15, General Winkelman, the Dutch Commander in Chief, signed articles of capitulation. German pressure upon Belgium rapidly mounted. When General Giraud's Army in Holland was completely crushed and the French Ninth Army collapsed on the Mézières-Dinant front, it was evident that a crisis had arisen. After the news of the British retreat to Dunkerque was brought to King Leopold he realized that the situation had become critical. On May 27 the demoralization of the French military forces was so rapid and complete that he decided the time had arrived to ask the German High Command to state its terms for a suspension of hostilities. The blunt answer called for unconditional surrender. The King felt compelled to comply with this grim demand, and at 4:00 A.M. on the following day the Belgian Army obeyed a cease fire order from headquarters.

THE PRESIDENT MAKES A THIRD PLEA TO MUSSOLINI
TO STAY OUT OF THE WAR

Before the bad news from Belgium was received in the United States, the President decided to make another plea to Mussolini to stay out of the war. In this third communication to the Duce, Roosevelt offered to act as a mediator between Hitler and the Allies. Ambassador Phillips was instructed to deliver this message to Mussolini personally, but Count Ciano bluntly informed him that this was not possible. When Ciano finished reading the President's plea he was asked by Phillips as to the nature of the reply: "He said with conviction—'it would be a no' and he went on to explain that Mussolini's position was not merely a question of securing Italy's legitimate aspirations but that the Duce was determined to carry out his obligations under his alliance with Germany." Later in the day Ciano sent for Ambassador Phillips and confirmed the statements he had made during the morning meeting. Mussolini desired to preserve his "freedom of action" and was not disposed to "enter into any negotiations which . . . would not be in the spirit of Fascism."

Although to Sumner Wells the "horizon looked extremely dark," Roosevelt thought that the clouds might take on a silver lining if he could persuade Mussolini to stay out of the war. On May 30 he made his fourth appeal to the Duce. Ambassador Phillips was instructed to call upon Count Ciano and once more emphasize the fact that the entrance of Italy into the war would "immediately and prejudicially affect" the interests of the United States. While the American Government had never "asserted any political interests in Europe," it had "asserted its clearly defined interests of an economic and property character. Through the extension of the war to the Mediterranean region and the inevitable destruction of life and property . . . the legitimate interests of the American people will be gravely curtailed." Inasmuch as the relations between the Italian and American people had always been particularly close, it was hoped that nothing would be done adversely to affect them.

On June 1, Ciano informed Ambassador Phillips that the Duce did not agree "with the point taken by the President with regard to the interests of the United States in the Mediterranean" and he maintained that the United States had the same interest in that area as Italy had, for example, "in the Caribbean Sea." The decision had "already been taken to enter the war."

REYNAUD MAKES A LAST APPEAL TO ROOSEVELT
FOR IMMEDIATE MILITARY ASSISTANCE

It had long been realized in Paris that Italy would probably enter the war as soon as Hitler's armies had gained important successes. The early collapse of the Netherlands and Belgium had made a deep impression upon the mind of Mussolini who was intent upon securing some of the spoils of war. Ambassador Bullitt knew this fact only too well and for this reason he begged the

President to consent to the delivery of some old destroyers that would strengthen French naval forces in the Mediterranean. The President's reply remained negative: "Any exchange for American destroyers probably inacceptable because of enormous sea area which must be patrolled by us and would require Congressional action which might be very difficult to get. Our old destroyers cannot be sold as obsolete as is proved by fact. All of them are now in commission and in use or are in process of being commissioned for actual use. "

Churchill was critical of the President's continued refusal to send old destroyers to the Allies. On June 5 he remarked to Mackenzie King that although the American Chief Executive was an excellent friend he had sent "no practical help" to Britain. He had not expected any military aid from the Americans "but they have not even sent any worthy contribution in destroyers or planes." It would be expedient "not to let Americans view too complacently the prospect of a British collapse, out of which, they would get the British Fleet and the guardianship of the British Empire."

On the day that Churchill sent this letter to Mackenzie King, the Germans began the final phase of the Battle of France. In five days they blazed a path to Paris. With a crushing defeat staring him in the face, Reynaud sent another plea to President Roosevelt. Its tone was quite epic but there was a strong feeling that the French Premier was like some frightened boy whistling loudly as he walked down a very dark alley: "For six days and six nights our divisions have been fighting without one hour of rest against an army which has a crushing superiority in numbers and material. Today the enemy is almost at the gates of Paris. We shall fight in front of Paris; we shall fight behind Paris; we shall close ourselves in one of our provinces to fight and if we should be driven out of it we shall establish ourselves in North Africa to continue the fight and if necessary in our American possessions." To make matters even worse, at this tragic hour Italy had "stabbed France in the back." The Allies were in desperate straits and required at once all the material support of the United States "short of an expeditionary force."

Reynaud's allusion to Italy's entrance into the war was turned by Roosevelt into a sharp thrust at Mussolini. That evening, in an address at Charlottesville, Virginia, the President alluded to the sweep of the tides of war across the Continent of Europe and the consequent menace to America of such a martial flood. Then, adopting a graphic phrase from Reynaud's plea earlier in the day, he suddenly remarked with dramatic intensity: "On this tenth day of June, 1940, the hand that held the dagger has struck it into the back of its neighbor." This unexpected interpolation directed at the Duce indicated the President's bitterness towards a dictator to whom he had made four futile pleas for nonintervention.

But Reynaud needed more than bitter allusions. Churchill rushed to France and tried to recall to Marshal Pétain the glorious stand of the Allied armies in the spring of 1918. The Marshal replied very quietly "that in those days he had a mass of manoeuvre of upwards of sixty divisions; now there was none." In 1918 there had been "sixty British divisions in the line." In 1940 the story was tragically different and Pétain was "haunted" by the grief he felt "that Britain, with her forty-eight million population had not been able to make a greater contribution to the land war against Germany."

The remarks of Marshal Pétain irritated Churchill considerably. On June 12 he sent to President Roosevelt the latest news from the French front and in this communication he permitted his resentment to color his message: "The aged Marshal Pétain, who was none too good in April and July, 1918, is, I fear, ready to lend his name and prestige to a treaty of peace for France." This was the moment for the President to "tip the balance in favour" of the best and longest possible French resistance. In the White House it was believed that Reynaud's arm might be strengthened by brave words and bright promises. The Premier was assured that the American Government was "doing everything in its power" to make available to the Allied powers the war matériel they so urgently needed. The "magnificent resistance of the French and British armies" had profoundly impressed the American people.

When Ambassador Kennedy brought to Churchill a copy of this Presidential salute to Allied courage, the Prime Minister pressed for its immediate publication. It could play a "decisive part in turning the course of world history." At the very least it would "decide the French to deny Hitler a patched-up peace with France." In a hurried note to Reynaud, Churchill indicated the compromising character of the Roosevelt message. If France, on the basis of this assurance from the American Chief Executive, would continue in the war, it should be obvious that the United States was "committed beyond recall to take the only remaining step, namely, becoming a belligerent in form as she has already constituted herself in fact."

The President realized the truth of this Churchill statement. He had already committed beyond recall the United States to take part in the war then raging in Europe but he could not afford in the summer of 1940 to let this fact become known. His campaign for re-election as President would soon take shape and he knew he could not hope for success if the voters knew that he was secretly putting America into World War II. He quickly sent word to Churchill explaining that he could not agree to the publication of his message to Reynaud. The Department of State saw in such publication the "gravest dangers." Churchill would not take this "disappointing telegram" as a final answer from the White House. On June 15 he frankly told the President that events in Europe were moving "downward at a pace where they will pass beyond the control of American public opinion." Eventually America would enter the struggle; why not now? It would be expedient to remember that if the Churchill Government fell a new cabinet might give the British fleet to Hitler. What would the United States do in that event? There was desperate need for the delivery of thirty-five destroyers at once. This matter should not be delayed.

Reynaud realized that he could not wait for several months until American assistance reached France. It was now or never. On June 14 he sent a message to Roosevelt that plumbed the depths of despair. German troops had just burst into Paris. Would it pay France to "continue to sacrifice her youth in a hopeless struggle"? Unless America could rush to France's aid with armed force she would "go under like a drowning man and disappear after having cast a last look towards the land of liberty from which she awaited salvation." When Roosevelt replied with a warm encomium upon the "resplendent courage" of the French armies but with no promise of immediate military aid, Reynaud requested Churchill to release his Government from its obligations not to negotiate a separate peace. The Prime Minister hastened to France in a vain effort to save the situation, but Reynaud had resigned by the time he reached Bordeaux. Marshal Pétain now assumed the burden of leadership and forwarded to Berlin a request for an armistice.

On June 18, Ambassador Biddle was assured that the French fleet would "never be surrendered to the enemy." After receiving this comforting news Secretary Hull instructed the American representatives in Berlin and Rome that the government of the United States "would not recognize any transfer, and would not acquiesce in any attempt to transfer any geographic region of the Western Hemisphere from one non-American power to another non-American power." Germany would not be permitted to occupy any French islands in the Caribbean.

THE DESTROYER DEAL

The fall of France imparted a sense of urgency to the Administration's program for aiding Britain by the sale or lease of war matériel. The President's qualms about constitutional limitations slowly disappeared under the drumfire of repeated requests from Churchill. Moreover, he brought into his Cabinet certain new members who were not averse to a prowar inclination. This was particularly true of the new Secretary of War, Henry L. Stimson, who was a notorious war hawk. It is apparent that after June 1940 the Administration embarked upon a phony bipartisan policy that pointed directly to American intervention in the European conflict.

This policy was given a green light on June 10 when Senator Sheppard offered an amendment to a pending defense bill authorizing the War Department to exchange unserviceable or surplus materials for others of which there was a scarcity. Senator Clark, of Missouri, declared that the purpose of the amendment was "an evasion of international law and of the Neutrality Act." But the amendment was adopted by a large majority and the measure finally became law on July 2, 1940.

In the meantime Senator David I. Walsh had sponsored legislation that would provide against any "limitation or reduction in the size of our Navy." The Act of June 28, 1940, embodied the ideas of Senator Walsh. It was not long, however, before the fertile mind of Benjamin Cohen, special assistant to the Attorney General, found several loopholes in this act. The President still had wide powers he could use without previous consultations with Congress. This opinion of Mr. Cohen was shrewdly argued but the Chief Executive "frankly doubted" if it would "stand up." He also feared that Congress was "in no mood at the present time to allow any form of sale."

These doubts were dissolved under the impact of pressure from Churchill.

On June 24 he wrote to Mackenzie King and once more emphasized the danger that if England fell there was the possibility that Hitler would get the British fleet. Four days later, in a letter to Lord Lothian in Washington, he repeated this disturbing thought which should be repeated to Roosevelt. He also complained that Britain had "really not had any help worth speaking of from the United States so far." After more than a month of silence he wrote again to the President (July 31) to inform him that the need for destroyers had "become most urgent." The whole fate of the war might rest upon the speed with which these destroyers were delivered. He was confident that the President would not "let this crux of the battle go wrong" for want of the much-needed warships. When Lord Lothian spoke of an exchange of naval bases for destroyers, Churchill indicated his preference was for an indefinite lease and not an outright sale.

Churchill's cablegram to the President (July 31) had led to a Cabinet meeting in the White House on August 2. There was immediate agreement that "the survival of the British Isles under German attack might very possibly depend on their getting these destroyers," but there was also recognition that legislation would be "necessary" to authorize any deal concerning the destroyers. If the British Government would give positive assurances that the British fleet "would not under any conceivable circumstances fall into the hands of the Germans," the opposition in Congress would be "greatly lessened." Perhaps William Allen White would work upon Wendell Willkie, Joseph Martin, and Charles McNary and thus divide the Republican ranks! When the President talked with White over the telephone he elicited a promise from the famous editor to get in touch with Willkie at once.

There was no doubt in Churchill's mind that any transfer of American destroyers to Britain would be a "decidedly unneutral act by the United States." It would justify a declaration of war by Hitler. Such action would be eminently agreeable to Churchill who would ardently welcome American help in the struggle against the dictatorships. But the situation had to be handled carefully. When Lord Lothian (August 6) cabled that the President was exceedingly anxious for a pledge that the British fleet would not be turned over to the Germans in the event that Britain fell, Churchill refused to give one. The British nation would "not tolerate any discussion of what we should do if our island were overrun." It would be best to couple the transfer of destroyers with the lease of naval and air bases in Newfoundland and on some British islands in the Caribbean.

On August 13 the essential paragraphs in this agreement were worked out during a conference between the President, Secretaries Knox, Morgenthau, and Stimson, and Sumner Welles. In the meantime William Allen White had received assurances from Wendell Willkie that he would "not make a campaign issue of the transfer." The services of General Pershing were next enlisted. The old warrior warned the American public in a broadcast that Britain needed immediate aid. This could best be given by placing at the disposal of the British and Canadian governments "at least fifty over-age destroyers which are left from the days of the World War." Admirals Yarnell, Standly, and Stirling supported this viewpoint.

On August 16, President Roosevelt issued a statement that he was negotiating with the British Government for the acquisition of naval and air
bases. Nothing was said about a deal for destroyers, Senator David I. Walsh
was still showing strong opposition to such a transaction. With the hope of
changing the Senator's opinion in this regard the President wrote him a
letter with the familiar salutation, "Dear Dave." He assured the Senator
that the British islands were "of the utmost importance to our national defence as naval and operating bases." After reminding him that Jefferson in
1803 had purchased Louisiana "without even consulting Congress," the
President then expressed the hope that there would be no further opposition
to a deal that would be the "finest thing for the nation that has been done
in your lifetime and mine."

"Dear Dave" did not fall for this bait so he was later smeared as a loose
character. But even so stanch a New Dealer as Secretary Hull had doubts
about a destroyer deal and he regretfully informed Lord Lothian that in
order "to meet the wishes of your Government an amendment to these
provisions of law [the United States Code and the Act of June 28, 1940]
may be necessary." But this would take time and Britain's need was immediate. In the meantime Churchill on August 20 had announced in Parlia-
ment that negotiations were in progress for leasing air and naval bases in
Newfoundland and on British islands in the Caribbean to the United States.
Two days later he explained to President Roosevelt the difficulties that
would attend any exchange of letters that would admit "in any way that the
munitions which you send us are a payment for the facilities." The dispatch
of war matériel to Britain should seem to be "a separate spontaneous act on
the part of the United States, arising out of their view of the world
struggle." But Sumner Welles informed Lord Lothian that under existing
legislation it was "utterly impossible" for the President to send destroyers to
Britain as a spontaneous gift; they could be sent only as a *quid pro quo*.

On August 23 the President confessed to Secretary Hull that the negotiations with Britain "on the bases and destroyers have bogged down. Please
see what you can do." In an extended conference among the President, Secretary Hull, and Lord Lothian the matter was further explored. Secretary
Hull made it clear to the British Ambassador that the President "had no
authority whatever to make a gift of public property to any Government or
individual." But Attorney General Jackson had no trouble finding convenient
loopholes in existing legislation. His assistant, Ben Cohen, had also discovered
them some months previously. The Act of June 15, 1917, made it unlawful
to send any ship out of the United States that was "built, armed or equipped
as a vessel of war, with any intent or under any agreement or contract . . .
that such vessel shall be delivered to a belligerent nation." This restriction
did not apply "to vessels like the over-age destroyers which were not built,
armed, equipped as, or converted into, vessels of war with the intent that
they should enter the service of a belligerent."

Mr. Jackson blandly pushed aside the pertinent provisions of the Treaty
of Washington (May 8, 1871) and Article 8 of the Hague Convention XIII
of 1907 which required that a neutral government take measures to prevent

the departure from its jurisdiction of any vessel intended to engage in belligerent operations, if the vessel was specially adapted within the neutral's jurisdiction to warlike use. The one precedent that Mr. Jackson adduced to support his contention concerning the transfer of destroyers was a most dubious one. Indeed, the opinion of the Attorney General was distinctly "phony" and was based upon the familiar dictum: "What's the Constitution between friends."

The way was now prepared for the destroyer deal. On September 2 notes were exchanged between Secretary Hull and Lord Lothian which first recited that the British Government, freely and without consideration, granted to the United States a lease for the "immediate establishment and use of naval and air bases and facilities" on the Avalon Peninsula and on the southern coast of Newfoundland, and on the east coast and on the Great Bay of Bermuda. The second item dealt with the establishment by the United States of air and naval bases on certain British territory in the Caribbean (Bahamas, Jamaica, Saint Lucia, Trinidad, Antigua, and British Guiana) in exchange "for naval and military equipment and material which the United States Government will transfer to His Majesty's Government." The leases would run for a period of 99 years. At the same time Churchill also gave an assurance that the British fleet would not be scuttled or surrendered. This assurance was not to be published.

From the viewpoint of international law the destroyer deal was definitely illegal. As Professor Herbert Briggs correctly remarks: "The supplying of these vessels by the United States Government to a belligerent is a violation of our neutral status, a violation of our national law, and a violation of international law." Professor Edwin Borchard expressed a similar opinion: "To the writer there is no possibility of reconciling the destroyer deal with neutrality, with the United States statutes, or with international law." The whole number was correctly described by the *St. Louis Post-Dispatch* in a pertinent headline: "Dictator Roosevelt Commits an Act of War."

PROPAGANDA PUSHES AMERICA TOWARDS INTERVENTION

During the years 1914 to 1917, British propaganda played a significant part in preparing the American mind for intervention in the World War. In the period prior to American intervention in World War II the British Government did not have to bear a heavy burden of propaganda: there were thousands of Americans who eagerly assumed this responsibility. The colorful story of these merchants of death has been told in such detail that it will be given merely a brief mention in these pages.

Rev. Harry Emerson Fosdick gave Roosevelt an excellent cue when he remarked that "of all the ways for Christians to make a war seem holy, the simplest way is to get Jesus into it." The President followed this tip on January 4, 1939, when he addressed Congress on the state of the nation. Storms from abroad were challenging three institutions "indispensable to Americans, now as always. The first is religion. It is the source of the other two—democracy and international good faith. . . . We have learned that

God-fearing democracies of the world which observe the sanctity of treaties and good faith in their dealings with other nations cannot safely be indifferent to international lawlessness anywhere. They cannot forever let pass, without effective protest, acts of aggression against sister nations."

The belligerent implications of these words were not lost upon members of Congress who fully realized the dangers and futility of embarking upon a holy war. Their fears were heightened when the President enlarged upon the same theme in an international broadcast under the auspices of the Christian Foreign convocation: "Today we seek a moral basis for peace. . . . It cannot be a moral peace which the early Christians preached meant meeting and overcoming those forces in the world which had set themselves against the brotherhood of man and which denied the equality of souls before the throne of God."

Catholic leaders did not respond to this summons to enlist the churches in a movement towards intervention. Catholic cardinals like O'Connell and Dougherty were strongly opposed to America's entry into World War II, and the Catholic press was outspoken in its criticism of the implications in the President's policy. The *Catholic World* thought Americans "were in no position to save anyone. We shall be lucky to save ourselves. . . . What kind of madness has got hold of those who advocate our settling the quarrels of the world, changing the habits of nations that have been fighting for the last thousand years? Who do we think we are?" The *Ave Maria* was equally opposed to intervention: "The people of this country do not want war at this moment; they can see no transgression against our safety or honor to justify a war. . . . They have no commission, human or divine, to challenge aggression not directed against them."

The *Ave Maria* was particularly sharp in its criticism of William Allen White, famous Kansas editor, who was "doing everything humanly possible to get us into the European conflict." It was certainly true that White had been very busy in the fight against fascism. He was a member of the Union for Concerted Peace Efforts, the American Committee for Non-participation in Japanese Aggression, the National Refugee Service, the Council Against Intolerance, and the Non-partisan Committee for Peace through the Revision of the Neutrality Law. This last organization was an active pressure group in favor of sabotaging existing neutrality legislation.

After this work had been carried to a successful conclusion, White helped to launch the Committee to Defend America by Aiding the Allies. The implications of this movement should have been evident to him. In December 1939, Robert Sherwood wrote to White to express the view that "it was necessary for the United States to intervene in a military way to check aggression by dictators." In his reply White remarked that he had always stood with Sherwood "in spirit" but had been constrained "by an old man's fear and doubt when it comes to lifting my voice for war."

In the spring of 1940 after this new organization had begun its activities, White became feverish in his anxiety to speed the gift of munitions of war to the hard-pressed Allies. In July he and the members of the Committee to Defend America by Aiding the Allies bent every effort to secure the "re-

lease of fifty or sixty over-age but recently reconditioned American destroyers to England." When the President failed to show any great enthusiasm to
push through a destroyer deal, White felt that "he had, as it were, lost his
cud." Contact was made with large numbers of influential persons throughout
the United States and they were urged to exert pressure upon the Chief
Executive. The committee with its six hundred local chapters and thousands
of volunteer workers was able to inundate the Capitol in Washington with a
flood of letters and telegrams favoring the destroyer deal. The President
owed a big debt to White who was so naïve as to believe that America
could walk halfway down the road to war and then stop.

This naïveté was clearly indicated on December 20, 1940, in a letter
he wrote to Roy Howard of the Scripps-Howard newspaper chain. He
assured Howard that "the only reason in God's world" he was a member
of the Committee to Defend America by Aiding the Allies was to keep
America "out of war." Some of the war hawks on the committee deeply
resented White's letter to Howard. When Frederick McKee flew to Em-
poria to persuade White to issue a statement that he was "not for peace at
any price," he was met with a flat refusal. But White then showed his mental
confusion by signing a round-robin letter to the President urging him to do
"everything that may be necessary to insure defeat of the Axis powers."
This letter, as the committee recognized, had "more warlike implications
than the repeal of the neutrality law or the convoy issue." But there were
still some lingering doubts in the mind of Clark Eichelberger who wired
White on December 26 about the "unfortunate repercussions" of the letter
that had appeared in the Scripps-Howard newspapers. It was at last apparent
to White that he had failed to understand the real intentions of the Committee to Defend America by Aiding the Allies. Its real drive was towards
war, not peace. In his letter of resignation he confessed that he was "amazed"
that he was "so far behind the procession," but he would go "no faster nor
no further." He had been used as a convenient façade by an organization
that had talked of peace while rushing down the road to war. He was the
symbol of millions of Americans.

LEND-LEASE—BACK DOOR TO INTERVENTION IN WORLD WAR II

It was entirely fitting that lend-lease legislation should have a prelude of
promises by the President that American boys would not be sent abroad
to die along far-flung frontiers. It had been evident to the President in the
summer of 1940 that American involvement in World War II might be just
around the corner of the next year. Senator Wheeler had read between the
lines of the President's pronouncements and when he saw the word *war*
written in bold letters he tried to block such a contingency by a strongly-
worded plank in the Democratic platform. But the pledge to keep out of
"foreign-wars" was nullified by the pregnant phrase—"except in case of
attack." It would not be difficult for an Administration seeking war to
push one of the Axis powers to the point where an attack was inevitable.

But the American people, like William Allen White, had to be fooled by pacific phrases. When the election currents in the fall of 1940 appeared to be making a turn towards Wendell Willkie, the President made some new pledges at Philadelphia on October 23: "To every man, woman and child in the nation I say this: Your President and your Secretary of State are following the road to peace. . . . We are arming ourselves not for any purpose of conquest or intervention in foreign disputes." A week later, in Boston, his pledge became more specific: "While I am talking to you mothers and fathers, I give you one more assurance. I have said this before, but I shall say it again and again and again: Your boys are not going to be sent into any foreign wars."

Robert Sherwood who helped to prepare this Boston speech had some qualms of conscience in later years: "For my own part, I think it was a mistake for him [the President] to go so far in yielding to the hysterical demands for sweeping reassurance, but, unfortunately for my own conscience, I happened at the time to be one of those who urged him to go the limit on this. . . . I burn inwardly whenever I think of those words 'again—and again—and again.' "

In the spring of 1941 these fires of conscience were burning very low in the President's entourage. Under the impact of appeals from Churchill in England the entire structure of American neutrality was finally demolished by the legislative bomb of lend-lease. This bomb was many months in the making. On November 6, 1940, Churchill wrote to Roosevelt to express his profound relief at the election results: "I feel you will not mind my saying that I prayed for your success and that I am truly thankful for it. . . . I must avow my sure faith that the lights by which we steer will bring us all safely to anchor." Those lights would lead America into the war.

On December 8, 1940, Churchill sent another long letter in which he outlined in great detail the pressing needs of Britain. In Churchill's eyes these needs were also America's needs because Britain was fighting for "the survival and independence of the British Commonwealth of Nations." Therefore, America should rush to Britain war matériel of specified kinds together with the gift or loan "of a large number of American vessels of war." It was useless to expect Britain to pay for these loans. The moment was approaching when the British Government would "no longer be able to pay cash for shipping and other supplies." The few dollars Britain had left were badly needed for domestic requirements. It would be wrong "in principle" for Britain to be "divested of all saleable assets, so that after the victory was won with our blood, civilization saved, and the time gained for the United States to be fully armed against all eventualities, we should stand stripped to the bone." America should bear a large part of the financial burden for a new crusade in Europe.

Roosevelt received this communication while he was cruising in the Caribbean. When he returned on December 16 he signified his ardent approval of aid to Britain at America's expense. On the following day, at a press conference, he recited an interesting parable:

Suppose my neighbor's house catches fire and I have a length of garden hose four or five hundred feet away. If he can take my garden hose and connect it up with his hydrant, I may help him to put out the fire. Now what do I do? I don't say to him before that operation, "Neighbor, my garden hose cost me fifteen dollars; you have to pay me fifteen dollars for it." No! What is the transaction that goes on? I don't want fifteen dollars—I want my garden hose back after the fire is over. . . . What I am trying to do is to eliminate the dollar sign.

What he really meant to say was that he was trying to eliminate the dollar sign so far as Britain was concerned. The American taxpayers would have it before their anxious eyes for the next generation. But before they had time to make any estimates, a lend-lease bill was introduced in the House of Representatives. It bore the significant number H.R. 1776. In that year we declared our independence from Britain; in 1941 we put it into grave peril by giving Britain a blank check which Churchill filled in with great gusto and then sent back to Washington for Roosevelt's indorsement. Harry Hopkins was the contact man in this regard and while still in Britain he heard Churchill's famous broadcast in which the following dangerous nonsense was beamed to rapt American listeners:

It seems now to be certain that the Government and the people of the United States intend to supply us with all that is necessary for victory. In the last war the United States sent two million men across the Atlantic. But this is not a war of vast armies, firing immense masses of shells at one another. We do not need the gallant armies which are forming throughout the American Union. We do not need them this year, nor next year, nor any year that I can foresee.

These assurances of Churchill were of the same stripe as the Roosevelt assurances during the last days of his campaign for re-election. He probably remembered Lord Northcliffe's sharp indictment of the American masses during the World War: "What sheep!" They could be sheared once more for British benefit by constant repetition of the old propaganda line about Britain fighting America's fight. Roosevelt repeated this line on December 29 in a "fireside chat" to the American people. Aid to Britain was now a question of "national security." If Britain were conquered, "all of us in the Americas would be living at the point of a gun."

On the following day the President summoned to the White House, Secretary Morgenthau and Arthur Purvis, head of the Anglo-French Purchasing Commission, to discuss the details of lend-lease legislation. On January 2, 1941, Edward Foley, Morgenthau's general counsel, and his assistant, Oscar Cox, began the arduous task of drafting the bill. When opposition to the bill developed in certain circles in the State Department, Secretary Knox remarked to Morgenthau in his best serio-comic manner: "Let's organize a hanging bee over there someday and hang the ones that you and I pick out." Some of the clique around the President probably would have regarded the matter of a hanging bee very seriously when Senator Wheeler began a series of blasts against lend-lease legislation. On January 4, 1941, he asked some very pertinent questions: "If it is our war, how can we justify lending them stuff and asking them to pay us back? If it is our war, we ought to have the courage to go over and fight it, but it is not our war." A week later, in a radio broadcast, he feathered a shaft that evoked an immediate cry of pain from the sensitive President. He regarded the lend-lease program as "the New Deal's 'triple A' foreign policy—to plow under every fourth American boy." The President deeply resented these prophetic words and denounced the Wheeler comment upon lend-lease as the "rottenest thing that has been said in public life in my generation."

Although Admiral Stark expressed on January 13 the opinion that "we are heading straight for this war," the lend-lease program was sold to the American people as a form of peace insurance. On March 11, 1941, the lend-lease bill was signed by the President, and it was not long before a forecast of Senator Taft was proved correct: "I do not see how we can long conduct such a war [undeclared war] without actually being in the shooting end of the war."

HITLER IS ANXIOUS TO AVOID CONFLICT WITH THE UNITED STATES

This "shooting end of the war" was greatly feared by Hitler who strove in every way to avoid any incident that might lead to war with the United States. In order to conciliate public opinion in neutral countries, submarine commanders, from the very beginning of the war, had been directed "to conform to the Hague Convention." Passenger lines were not to be torpedoed even when under escort.

In September and October 1939, Hitler had high hopes that America might be induced to accept the role of mediator and thus bring to an early close a war that he had entered with many misgivings. In a previous chapter we have dealt with the mission of William Rhodes Davis to Berlin for the purpose of arranging mediation. It is apparent that Berlin took this mission quite seriously. In Hitler's speech of October 6 there were evident indications of his readiness to accept Roosevelt as mediator, and on the following day Mr. Kirk, American chargé d'affaires in Berlin, cabled to Secretary Hull that "someone close to Hitler had conveyed the thought that the President might use Hitler's speech as the occasion to send a confidential message to him endorsing his 'efforts toward peace.'" On October 9, Kirk cabled that a German press spokesman informed him that Germany "would certainly accept from the President a suggestion for a truce and negotiations toward peace and intimated that Germany might take part in a conference somewhere far removed from the war theater"—which some interpreted to mean Washington.

The terms of peace that Germany would present to such a peace conference were made known to the President and Secretary Hull through the long letter that William Rhodes Davis had sent to the Chief Executive. General Göring had spoken to Mr. Davis (October 3) in the following terms:

You may assure Mr. Roosevelt that if he will undertake mediation, Germany will agree to an adjustment whereby a new Polish State and the new Czechoslovakian independent government would come into being. . . . As for myself and my Government, I would be glad to attend and in the event of such a conference I would represent Germany. I agree that the conference should be in Washington.

At this time Germany was already profoundly disturbed by the way the Russians were acting in Poland. During the meetings of a peace conference in Washington there would be an opportunity to focus the eyes of the world upon the ills of Europe and attempt to remedy them. If the President had possessed real courage and vision he would have welcomed these German overtures and staged a peace conference that would have saved both Poland and Czechoslovakia. But he and Secretary Hull were fearful that a move towards peace might benefit Hitler and discourage the Allies so they rejected the German peace feelers and thus prepared the way for eventual Red domination over both those countries. In the long chapter of historical might-have-beens, Roosevelt plays a prominent and dismal part.

Roosevelt's rejection of the idea of a peace conference in Washington did not put an end to Nazi efforts to conciliate the United States. Hitler was exceedingly anxious not to have war with America. This fact is clear in the testimony given during the Nürnberg trials. Ribbentrop insisted upon the pacific disposition of the Führer concerning the United States, and Weizäcker confirmed this fact: "No German desired to be at war with the United States or looked for trouble in that direction. . . . We were not to let ourselves be provoked to be the ones who bring the conflict to the open daylight. Wherever there would be unfriendly acts, . . . we would not be the ones who start."

The German press, under strict instructions, stopped its sharp criticism of the United States and of prominent American officials. Nazi officials became increasingly careful about any statements that might offend American sensibilities, and the German chargé d'affaires in Washington (Dr. Hans Thomsen), in a press release, went so far as to call President Roosevelt "high-minded" and to praise his admonitions of neutrality. In April 1940, General Walther von Brauchitsch assured representatives of the press that he had always admired the youthful strength of the United States and its people to which he attributed the "gigantic success of the new continent."

The new American neutrality law (November 4, 1939) gave certain satisfaction to Hitler who assured leading Nazis that it would render the United States harmless. Under this law the waters around the British Isles and the entire European coast from Bergen to the Spanish border were closed to American ships. These restrictions pleased the Führer who decreed on December 30, 1939, that American crews were to be treated "with the greatest consideration." In this same spirit Admiral Raeder issued instructions that American ships were not to be pursued or sunk in order that "all difficulties which might result from trade war between the United States and Germany might be avoided at the very beginning." But this German policy of conciliation was sorely tried by incidents arising out of the establishment of a neutrality zone announced by the Panama Conference, October 3, 1939. This safety belt around the Americas south of Canada varied in width from 300 to 1000 miles. Belligerents were warned to refrain from naval action within that area, but no armed forces were stationed along the safety belt to enforce this regulation.

In order to conciliate America the German Admiralty issued orders designed to prevent naval engagements within the safety belt. When the Admiralty wished to recede from this position, Hitler refused to permit any change of orders. Moreover, the Führer adhered to this conciliatory policy even when American vessels adopted a course that must have enraged him. In December 1939 the German liner *Columbus* left Veracruz and was closely trailed by the U.S.S. *Tuscaloosa* which constantly broadcasted her position. This action compelled the Nazi captain to scuttle his ship some 450 miles east of Cape May. The same tactics were pursued by the U.S.S. *Broome* in trailing the *Rhein*, which also was scuttled by her captain. The freighter *Idarwild* was followed by the *Broome* until it was destroyed by H.M.S. *Diomede* (November 1940), with the *Broome* standing by to watch the result of her pursuit. The German Government refrained from filing any protest at these actions.

At a naval conference on March 18, Admiral Raeder was finally able to secure an important concession from the Führer. This took the form of a new blockade order (March 25, 1941) which not only included Iceland but went as far as the waters of Greenland. The first naval incident in the North Atlantic would soon take place.

The background for such an incident had been carefully filled in by President Roosevelt. In August 1940 he had sent Admiral Robert L. Ghormley, Major General D. C. Emmons, and Major General George V. Strong to London for exploratory conversations concerning eventual "armed co-operation with the British Commonwealth." After some months of conversations with important officers in the British armed services, Admiral Ghormley, in October 1940, sent to Admiral Stark a full report on his mission. Stark, in turn, presented to Secretary Knox on November 12 a memorandum on national objectives. One of the most important items in this memorandum was "the prevention of the disruption of the British Empire." In order to achieve this objective, in January 1941 a series of secret staff conversations began in Washington. Two months later (March 27, 1941), the ABC-1 Staff Agreement was consummated which envisaged a "full-fledged war co-operation when and if Axis aggression forces the United States into the war."

One of the sections of this agreement was aimed at creating an incident that would "force the United States into the war." It contained the following explosive phraseology: "Owing to the threat to the sea communications of the United Kingdom, the principal task of the United States naval forces in the Atlantic will be the protection of shipping of the Associated Powers." In order to carry out this task the Royal Navy hastened to give the United States Navy the "benefit of its experience, and of the new devices and methods for fighting submarines that had already been evolved." The responsibility "now assumed by the United States Navy meant the organization of a force for escort-of-convoy." On February 1, 1941, this patrol force was given "the new and appropriate designation of Atlantic Fleet," and its commander, Rear Admiral Ernest J. King, was promoted to the rank of Admiral and designated Commander in Chief Atlantic Fleet. The first naval incident was almost at hand.

On April 10, 1941, the destroyer *Niblack* (Lieutenant Commander E. R. Durgin), in the waters off Iceland, picked up three boatloads of survivors from a torpedoed Netherlands freighter. As the last men were being pulled aboard, the sound operator made contact on a submarine. The division commander, D. L. Ryan, immediately assumed that the submarine was approaching for an attack so he ordered Mr. Durgin to drop some depth charges which caused the submarine to retire. This was the action between United States and German armed forces.

As the system of convoy escorts developed in accordance with Anglo-American plans, other incidents were bound to occur. On April 17, John O'Donnell, well-known newspaper commentator, published a statement that "battlecraft" of the American Navy and Coast Guard were "giving armed escort to munition-laden British merchantmen leaving American ports." The President, through his secretary, Mr. Early, replied that American naval forces were merely on "neutrality patrol" in the Atlantic. He then charged that Mr. O'Donnell was guilty of a "deliberate lie." On April 25, during a press conference, the President expressly denied that naval escorts were being provided for fleets carrying lend-lease goods, and he developed at great length the difference between patrolling and convoying. A month later (May 27), in a national broadcast, he insisted that the delivery of war matériel to Britain was "imperative" and then stated that he had extended "our patrol in north and south Atlantic waters."

It was evident to Senator Taft that the President's broadcast disclosed "an intention on his part to push further and further toward war without consulting the people. . . . His speech contains vague threats of aggressive, warlike action to be undertaken in his sole discretion." Two weeks later the *Washington Post* printed a story by two columnists, Alsop and Kintner, to the effect that more than a month earlier there had been an encounter between American and German vessels of war and this had been followed by offensive operations on the part of an American destroyer. The columnists were making a specific reference to the *Niblack* incident which had been kept very quiet by the authorities. Secretary Knox promptly denounced this story but failed to confirm or explicitly deny it. In further statements he was purposely vague.

While these exercises in double talk were being carried on, the President was taking active measures to see that Greenland did not fall into German hands. On January 9, 1941, the Department of State issued a release indicating that an American consulate had been established at Godthaab, and that provision had been made for the purchase in the United States of small arms for the Greenland police. These steps were followed by the signature (April 9, 1941) of an agreement authorizing the United States to occupy

Greenland for defensive purposes. Inasmuch as the Danish Minister in Washington (Henrik Kauffmann) had no authority to conclude such an agreement, he was recalled by the Nazi-controlled Danish Foreign Office. He preferred to remain in Washington and was recognized by Secretary Hull as the regularly accredited minister. Needless to say, from the viewpoint of international law, this whole transaction was legally indefensible.

In the meantime the Führer was showing a strong determination to adhere to his policy of keeping out of war with the United States. In May 1941 the German attitude was summed up at a meeting between Hitler and his naval advisers:

> Whereas up to now the situation confronting submarines and naval forces on operations was perfectly clear, naval warfare in the North Atlantic is becoming increasingly complicated as the result of the measures taken by the U.S.A. In order to help Britain, the American neutrality patrol, which was hitherto confined to the area within the American neutrality zone, has been reinforced and considerably extended toward the east to about 38° W., i.e. as far as the middle of the Atlantic. The true character of the American neutrality patrol is shown by the fact that vessels on patrol have also been instructed to report by radio any battleships encountered. . . .
>
> We have laid down the following rules for naval warfare in order to comply with German political aims with regard to the U.S.A.:
>
> No attack should be made on U. S. naval forces and merchant vessels.
>
> Prize regulations are not to be applied to U. S. merchant ships.
>
> Weapons are not to be used, even if American vessels conduct themselves in a definitely unneutral manner.
>
> Weapons are to be used *only if U. S. ships fire the first shot.*
>
> As a result of these instructions and of the constant endeavors on the part of Germany not to react to provocation, incidents with the U.S.A. have been avoided up to the present time.
>
> It is unmistakable that the U. S. Government is disappointed about this cautious attitude on the part of Germany, since one of the most important factors in preparing the American people for entry into the war is thus eliminated. The U. S. is therefore continuing its attempt to obliterate more and more the boundary line between neutrality and belligerency, and to stretch the "short of war" policy further by constantly introducing fresh measures contrary to international law.

The next naval incident involving German-American relations was the sinking of the American merchant ship (May 21, 1941) *Robin Moor,* New York to Cape Town, by a German submarine. There was no visit or search but the crew and passengers were allowed to take to open lifeboats. As the sinking occurred outside the blockade zone it is evident that the submarine commander disregarded orders concerning American ships. Admiral Raeder immediately issued orders to prevent further incidents of this nature, and Hitler, after confirming these instructions, remarked that he wished to "avoid any incident with the U.S.A." On June 20 the President sent a message to Congress in which he bitterly criticized Germany as an international outlaw.

He followed this message with another move in the direction of war. On July 7 he ordered American occupation of Iceland. Two days later Secretary Knox gave a statement to the press which implied that the American patrol force in the North Atlantic had the right to use its guns when the occasion arose.

This occasion arose on September 4, 1941, when the destroyer *Greer*, bound for Iceland, was informed by a British plane that a submerged U-boat lay athwart her course some ten miles ahead. The *Greer* at once laid a course for the reported submarine, and after having made sound contact with it, kept it on her bow for more than three hours. During this period a British plane dropped four depth charges in the vicinity of the submarine without effect. Finally, the submarine commander grew tired of this game of hide-and-seek and launched a torpedo which the *Greer* was able to dodge. When the *Greer* counterattacked with depth charges, the submarine launched another torpedo which was avoided. When sound contact with the submarine could not be re-established, the *Greer* resumed course for Iceland.

On September 11 the President gave a broadcast which presented a distorted version of the *Greer* incident. He conveniently forgot to tell that the initiative had been taken by the *Greer*: "She [the *Greer*] was flying the American flag. Her identity as an American ship was unmistakable. She was then and there attacked by a submarine. Germany admits that it was a German submarine. . . . We have sought no shooting war with Hitler. . . . The aggression is not ours. Ours is solely defense." American vessels would now shoot at sight.

In the face of this serious incident that clearly showed the aggressive character of American naval patrolling, Hitler maintained his policy of avoiding difficulties with the United States. On September 17 orders concerning American merchant vessels exempted them from attack, even when in convoy, in all zones except that immediately surrounding the British Isles. In the Pan-American safety belt "no warlike acts" were to be carried out on German initiative.

The American answer to these pacific gestures was to authorize escort duty for American destroyers. It was arranged that an American escort group, based on Argentia, should take over from a Royal Canadian Navy escort at a designated place off Newfoundland and hand over the convoy to a Royal Navy escort at an agreed mid-ocean meeting place. Convoying was now an established practice, and it should be kept in mind that Secretary Knox, during the lend-lease hearings, had frankly admitted that he regarded convoying as an "act of war."

This *de facto* war in the Atlantic soon produced another incident. On October 16 five American destroyers rushed from Reykjavik, Iceland, to the help of a convoy that was being attacked by submarines. On the following day, while in the midst of fighting, the destroyer *Kearny* was struck by a torpedo and slowly made its way back to Iceland. It had deliberately moved into the center of a pitched battle between German submarines and British and Canadian warships and had taken the consequences. It was not long before President Roosevelt gave to the American people a twisted account of the incident. On October 27 he recounted the happenings on October 16 and 17 and asserted that he had "wished to avoid shooting." America had "been attacked. The U.S.S. *Kearny* is not just a Navy ship. She belongs to every man, woman, and child in this Nation. . . . Hitler's torpedo was directed at every American." In order to give additional overtones of villainy to his description of Nazi wickedness he then stated that he had a secret map made in Germany which disclosed Hitler's plan to put all the continent of South America under his domination. But that was not all. He had in his possession another document made in Germany that revealed Hitler's intention, if he was victorious, to "abolish all existing religions." It should be evident that the "forward march of Hitlerism" should be stopped. . . . "We are pledged to pull our own oar in the destruction of Hitlerism." The American Navy had been given orders to "shoot on sight." The Nazi "rattlesnakes of the sea" would have to be destroyed.

This declaration of war was confirmed by the *Reuben James* incident. On October 31, while the *Reuben James* was escorting a convoy to Iceland, some German submarines were encountered about 600 miles west of that island. The American destroyer was struck by a torpedo and rapidly sank. Only 45, out of a crew of about 160, were saved. When the news of the sinking of the *Reuben James* reached Germany, Hitler remarked: "President Roosevelt has ordered his ships to shoot the moment they sight German ships. I have ordered German ships not to shoot when they sight American vessels but to defend themselves when attacked." On November 13, 1941, the directives for conduct of German warships when encountering American naval vessels remained pacific: "Engagements with American naval or air forces are not to be sought deliberately; they are to be avoided as far as possible. . . . If it is observed before a convoy is attacked that it is being escorted by American forces, the attack is not to be carried out."

Germany was trying desperately to stay out of war with the United States. America's attitude was clearly stated by Sumner Welles at Arlington on November 11: "Beyond the Atlantic a sinister and pitiless conqueror has reduced more than half of Europe to abject serfdom. It is his boast that his system shall prevail even unto the ends of the earth. . . . The American people after full debate . . . have determined upon their policy. They are pledged . . . to spare no effort and no sacrifice in bringing to pass the final defeat of Hitlerism and all that which that evil term implies. . . . We cannot know, we cannot yet foresee, how long and how hard the road may be which leads to that new day when another armistice will be signed."

To the mind of Welles and to others in the White House group it was obvious that America was really in the war. But the American people did not realize that momentous fact, nor did they know that they were pledged "to spare no effort and no sacrifice in bringing to pass the final defeat of Hitlerism." It was easy for Mr. Welles to speak glibly of sacrifice. He had long enjoyed wealth and high social position. The word "sacrifice" had always been excluded from his dictionary. As the spokesman for the President he was suddenly breaking to the American people the dread news that they had become involved in a war they had ardently wished to avoid. The war hawks of 1941 were never tired of sneering at the majority of Americans as benighted isolationists who had tried to build a Chinese wall around the United States and thus cut it off from all foreign contacts. They knew their sneers were patent lies. America had never been isolated from the social, economic, religious, and cultural forces that shaped the modern world. Thanks to its geographical position it had escaped the recurring tides of conflict that had crumbled the walls of ancient civilizations and washed away the heritage men had earned through dauntless courage and high endeavor. Americans had been isolationists only against war and its evident evils, and their country had grown prosperous beyond the dreams of the founding fathers. But in 1915, President Wilson began to nurse the thought of sharing America's ideals and wealth with the rest of the world, and two years later he led us into a foreign war that he hoped would make the world safe for democracy. But this theme song turned sour in American ears when it led to the great parade of 1917 which ended for many men in the vast cemeteries in France. It gained new popularity after 1933, and with Roosevelt as maestro, the old macabre accents began to haunt every home. In 1941 his orchestra of death was anxiously waiting for the signal to begin the new symphony. He had hoped for a German motif but Hitler had refused to assist with a few opening martial notes. Perhaps some Japanese statesman would prove more accommodating! At any rate, after the *Reuben James* incident had fallen flat he turned his eyes towards the Orient and sought new inspiration from the inscrutable East. He found it at Pearl Harbor when Japanese planes sounded the first awesome notes in a chorus of war that is still vibrating throughout the world.

&ᔆ ᔓ&

THE *twenty-second admendment to the U. S. Constitution guaranteed the uniqueness of Franklin D. Roosevelt. No future President will have more than two terms unless he inherits the Presidency during the declining two years of a Presidential term. The men who implemented the amendment fulfilled an ancient hope of Thomas Jefferson, but they also responded to the extraordinary fact that there dwelled in the White House between 1933 and 1945 a man who had four times appealed to the American electorate and four times gained their heavy endorsement. "That man" as his enemies labeled him had cast a formidable shadow, one that neither they nor the generation touched by the fire of his eloquence could ever escape.*

But a curious aspect of the historical treatment of Roosevelt's career is that little has been done on it beyond the New Deal years. The splendid drama of the struggle to turn about the depression reached its apogee in the overwhelming victory of 1936 and within a year it struck its nadir as Congress turned aside his plea to "pack the Court." By 1938, a conservative

Republican-Southern Democrat coalition arose to turn back further legislative experimentation for almost a quarter of a century. The New Deal, in the words of the poet, ended not with a bang but a whimper. Yet, even as the New Deal stumbled to its close, the events of a world at war crowded in to undermine the façade of isolation behind which Americans had retreated in 1919. Whether Americans wanted it or not, World War II forced the United States to accept its role as a world power. The very vastness of the war enterprises, their continuing impact, their still undefined consequences, have left historians groping to put together a coherent portrait of Roosevelt's awesome third term.

In his final campaign speech of 1940, Roosevelt declared: "This generation of Americans is living in a tremendous moment of history." Between the moment when these words were spoken and nearly five years later when Japan signatured its capitulation in Tokyo Bay, Americans learned how tremendous a moment it was. By that time Roosevelt had died, even as the winds of April 1945 proclaimed victory in Europe. When his death, foretold in every 1944 campaign photo, came, Americans found it hard to believe. The long familiar gestures, the arch inflection of his voice, the jaunty sally when things were black, had given a tone and style to a nation. Something more, too, was gone: a man to the manor born, who, in some mysterious way, had restored hope when all reason said it should have long since fled. It also brought the generation that had followed his lead face to face with the grimmest of human reminders, that all flesh must perish, and with it a lesson which teaches that no generation worth its salt should need an indispensable man.

James MacGregor Burns (1918-) has captured in kaleidoscopic fashion those final tumultuous years. By profession a political scientist, Burns successfully fused the techniques of his profession with that of the historian to give us one of the more brilliant studies of Roosevelt the politician. It emphasized the four-time President's awareness of detail and circumstance that permitted him to meet the needs of his time. It also reminds Americans bred to view the politician with suspicion that in the consummate specimens of that breed of animal we place our trust.

ROOSEVELT: THE LION AND THE FOX

by James MacGregor Burns

The bombs that shattered the fleet in Pearl Harbor shattered as well the stalemate in Roosevelt's war policy. In the first hours of turmoil after news of the attack there were some who could think only of the fleet's lack of readiness. Connally turned savagely on Knox with a barrage of questions. Others thought the President should issue a long review of his policy toward Japan in his war message.

But the President would have none of it. To him the only important fact was the fact of war itself. "We are in it," he kept saying to his advisers. When he appeared before a joint session next day and somberly asked Congress to declare the existence of a state of war, the two most important words in his short speech were "Hostilities exist." The crucial act had occurred for which the President could find no substitute in speech or deed. "Hostilities exist"—a few climactic hours had taught the lessons that Roosevelt had never quite been able to teach.

"I think the Boss really feels more relief than he has had for weeks," one cabinet member said to another as they left his study. When Germany and Italy declared war on the United States four days after Pearl Harbor, world battle lines had formed.

From the President's behavior during the following weeks one might have thought that all that had gone before had been merely preparation for this hour—as perhaps it was. Roosevelt, said Sumner Welles, a close observer at the time, "demonstrated the ultimate capacity to dominate and control a supreme emergency, which is the rarest and most valuable characteristic of any statesman." It was like 1933 all over again, but projected onto an infinitely larger stage. Roosevelt was businesslike, serene, cheerful, grave, tireless, confident.

Backed now by a united people, he could exploit his superb flair for bringing warring parties together behind a common goal. Labor-management unity was a brilliant case in point. During the year before Pearl Harbor coal miners, shipbuilders, airplane-engine workers, and tens of thousands of others had gone on strike. The President had had to seize several defense plants. The central issue was "union security"—an issue so divisive that it had caused the collapse of the nation's chief mediation agency. Ten days after Pearl Harbor a "warm, confident, buoyant, serious" President summoned labor and employer delegates to the White House, told them it would be a "thrilling thing" if they could agree soon on basic problems, and proceeded to set up a board to work out a compromise on union security that was to prove one of the most creative and enduring achievements of the war administration.

All the President's command and confidence were needed during the early months of 1942, as the nation suffered staggering reversals along the vast Pacific front. Japanese forces swallowed Guam, Wake, the Philippines. Malaya, Burma, the Dutch East Indies fell. Everywhere the Axis maintained its relentless advance: in North Africa the Germans drove the British back into Egypt; they seemed to have the Russians on the point of collapse; they still exacted a heavy toll in the Atlantic. The Japanese landed in the Aleutians, reached the borders of India, threatened Australia.

Not only did Roosevelt have to maintain an air of resolution and confidence during the long, dreary days of defeat, he had to stick to the central strategic decisions—to make the main effort first against Germany while holding off Japan—in the face of the "Japan-firsters" who looked on that nation as America's only real enemy. Roosevelt worked amid a thousand pressures. He had to mediate among his own rival services, among theater commands, between war front and home front, between the desperate needs of Russians and British. As usual the more exacting problems moved relentlessly along the lines of command into his office; as usual the President tackled them cheerfully, turning quickly from crucial questions of strategy, to administrative minutiae, to galling problems of personnel: as usual he operated tirelessly among the never-ending babble of politicians, admirals, legislators, generals, diplomats, bureaucrats.

The President understood, too, that his soldiers' slow, grudging retreat was buying time for the economy to shift into high gear. Having turned from one expedient to another in the months before Pearl Harbor, he established in January 1942 a relatively centralized mobilization direction in the War Production Board. Exploitation of the nation's enormous resources was the main job of 1942 and one that called for a tenacious fight against inflation as war spending neared one hundred million dollars a day. Here again, Roosevelt seemed to have been superbly trained for the job. No longer did he face the need to decide between the agonizing alternatives—between spending and budget balancing—for which he had never been educated. That decision had been made for him. Now his job was to stave off the inflationary pressures of businessmen, labor, farmers. The notions that had run through his economic thinking for years—notions of a balanced economy, of a central harmony of interests, of mutual sacrifice for mutual gain—supplied an indispensable background for his efforts toward stabilization.

Roosevelt's utter concentration on the task at hand—winning military victory—raised difficult problems, just as his absorption with winning elections at whatever cost had created difficulties during the peace years. It was all very well for Hopkins, reflecting his chief's attitude, to apply to every policy the simple test "Will it help to win the war?" but such a test was likely to ignore broader strategic aspects of winning the war—and the relation between winning the war and defending democracy. Two examples illuminate the dilemma:

Early in 1942 Roosevelt authorized the military to uproot thousands of Japanese-Americans on the West Coast and relocate them in concentration camps in the interior. To the military this seemed a wise precaution, but in the long run it was a compromise with the ideas the nation was supposed to be fighting. Again, in September 1942, exasperated by the failure of Congress to pass a bill to stabilize the cost of living, including the prices of farm commodities, Roosevelt in effect ordered Congress to act in three weeks and warned that if the legislators failed to act he would. Congress sullenly complied. Here was an astonishing usurpation of power in a nation fighting for democratic ideas and processes.

Roosevelt would have made the same defense of his drastic actions as had another war president eighty years before. "Was it possible," Lincoln asked, "to lose the nation and yet preserve the Constitution? A limb may be amputated to save a life, but a life is never wisely given to save a limb." Yet a democratic people always faces the ultimate question, Which is life and which is limb?

During 1943, the tide turned. In May, Allied forces drove the enemy out of Tunisia. Two months later they invaded Sicily: two months after that, Italy: and on September 3, 1943, Italy surrendered. Elsewhere the massive counterattack slowly gained momentum. American troops mopped up the Japanese in Guadalcanal and Buna, launched amphibious assaults in the Solomons, New Georgia, New Guinea, Tarawa. The American and British navies were winning the Battle of the Atlantic. Most decisive of all, the Russians drove the Germans back from Stalingrad early in the year after an epic siege.

By the end of 1943 victory for the Allies was no longer seriously in doubt. The question now was less whether they would win than whether they could win in such a way as to make a lasting peace more likely.

This year was also a year of the great international conferences, where questions of war strategy and postwar peace policy were taken up. Roosevelt and Churchill met at Casablanca, Washington, and Quebec: Roosevelt, Churchill, and Stalin met at Teheran. At this last conference the thorny problem of the second front was finally settled, and soon afterward General Dwight D. Eisenhower was made its supreme commander.

Teheran brought together three towering personalities and a "concentration of physical power and political authority unique in the whole history of mankind." Roosevelt beforehand was keenly confident of his capacity to establish a workable and mutually beneficial personal relationship with Stalin. So he did—as long as negotiations involved immediate problems of beating the Nazis. But on the long-run strategic questions involving the pattern of power in Europe after the war the President's preoccupation with military victory put him at a disadvantage to both Churchill and Stalin. Yet Roosevelt probably believed that the crowning need both for winning the war and securing the peace was the visible fact of Allied co-operation.

"I may say that I 'got along fine' with Marshal Stalin," he told the people in his Christmas Eve 1943 fireside chat, ". . . and I believe that we are going to get along very well with him and the Russian people—very well indeed." And he told Miss Perkins gleefully how he had broken the ice with Stalin by deliberately baiting Churchill about his Britishness, his cigars, and his habits.

If Roosevelt had to deal with Stalin in the posture of alliance, he had to deal with Hitler in the posture of war. It was a battle not only of armies and navies but of ideas and symbols as well. The Fuehrer, a master of propaganda, interpreted the war to his people as a struggle of the masses against the plutocratic nations of the world. The President, now the Allies' chief propagandist with a constituency of three-quarters of the world, affirmed Freedom as the supreme symbol of the cause for which the Allies fought. As Hitler sought to divest this symbol of any meaning except liberty to exploit the masses, Roosevelt sought to strengthen the idea of Freedom as a positive idea—as freedom to gain peace and security after the war. Roosevelt, in short, was compelled as a means of winning victory itself to fashion means of attaining postwar goals: one result was that during 1943 a series of "united nations" conferences began to plan postwar social and economic arrangements.

During all this time the home front was never free of storm and controversy. A "little cabinet" of Byrnes, Rosenman, Hopkins, and the President's personal chief of staff, Admiral William D. Leahy, struggled to clear bottlenecks and settle interagency feuds, but the war management reflected the familiar administrative habits of the commander in chief. Some "second-level" decisions he refused to delegate, and he continued to play officials and agencies off against one another. As in the past, the results were not altogether happy. Feeling between Hull and Welles was so sharp that the latter resigned as under secretary of state, and Wallace and Jones warred against each other so openly over international economic policy that the President removed both of them from their posts in this field. Still, the crucial goal at home—mobilization without severe inflation—was achieved.

It was in the party and legislative arena that the domestic political hostilities were sharpest. Right after Pearl Harbor Roosevelt had, quite characteristically, demanded an end to "partisan domestic politics" for the duration. He had even suggested that the two national party organizations be converted to civilian defense. But partisan politics would not die so easily. Under the inexorable calendar of American elections the regular off-year congressional contests were fought in 1942. Roosevelt carefully avoided Wilson's mistake of asking for a Democratic Congress; still, his party almost lost control of Congress. The Democratic margin in the House fell from 91 to 14, and 8 seats were lost in the Senate.

The inexorable political calendar brought also the presidential election of 1944. With the anti-third-term tradition broken, Roosevelt could eschew his devious preconvention tactics of 1940. So a week before the Democratic convention in mid-July 1944 Roosevelt wrote the national chairman a simple, direct letter stating that he would serve again if "the Commander in Chief of us all"—the people of the United States—should order him to do so in November.

"All that is within me cries out to go back to my home on the Hudson River," Roosevelt wrote, but "we of this generation chance to live in a day and hour when our Nation has been attacked, and when its future existence and the future existence of our chosen method of government are at stake."

When it came to the vice-presidency, though, it was the same old Roosevelt. He made half-promises to more than one aspirant, refused to tell Vice-President Wallace frankly that he could not back his nomination if it divided the convention, and yet wrote Wallace a letter stating that he was his "personal" choice. Harry Truman was surprised to find that he was the President's official choice; he would run, the Missouri Senator told Roosevelt's men, "but why the hell didn't he tell me in the first place?"

On one matter the political wheel came full circle. In June 1944 Roosevelt talked with Rosenman about the subject he had toyed with again and again in his four decades of political activity: party realignment. "We ought to have two real parties—one liberal and the other conservative," he told Rosenman. The Democratic party must get rid of its reactionary elements in the South and attract to it the Republican liberals. He asked Rosenman to take the question up with Willkie, who had just been shouldered out of the Republican running by the G.O.P. regulars. At a secret meeting with Rosenman in New York early in July, Willkie expressed enthusiastic support for the idea of party realignment, and he agreed to work plans out jointly with the President. But on one thing Willkie was insistent. He could not meet with Roosevelt until after the election. At a time when he was still trying to keep some leverage in the Republican party he feared that co-operation with the President would be misinterpreted as a "sellout" on his part to the Democrats.

Roosevelt, however, wanted to pursue the matter before election, and it was here that his reputation for cunning and indirectness tripped him up. The more the President pressed for an early meeting the more Willkie was convinced that he was engaged in an electing tactic rather than in a long-term strategic effort. A series of leaks to the press about the indirect communication between Roosevelt and Willkie served only to heighten the latter's suspicion. In any case, it was too late; for Willkie, who had always spent his energies recklessly, died of a coronary thrombosis in October. Thus was lost perhaps the supreme opportunity in a generation for party realignment.

The President now faced his fourth campaign for office—this time against the vigorous, youthful Dewey, who in 1942 had won the governorship of New York over the divided Democrats in that state. Roosevelt's tactics followed the classic pattern: long inspection trips, patient "nonpartisanship" while Dewey lambasted the "tired old men," and then a series of swift thrusts in the last few weeks of the campaign. The first of these thrusts was the most devastating—the Teamsters Union speech that answered Republican libels against "my little dog, Fala." From then on, a Democrat commented, the race was between "Roosevelt's dog and Dewey's goat."

Roosevelt's victory over Dewey by a margin of 333 electoral and about 3,600,000 popular votes was one more testament of his masterly campaigning. It was also a tribute to his supreme direction of military operations. In June, Allied armies had surged into Normandy; in midsummer American troops drove the Japanese out of Saipan and Guam; in October they landed in the Philippines. As the war fast reached its climax, issues of peace became ever more urgent.

The great tasks of peace lay ahead—but now, as the year of victory neared, Roosevelt was desperately tired. The ceaseless toil and tension of the war years were leaving their mark. Like the great actor he was, he could shake himself out of his weariness and take his old role before the people. Fighting off campaign rumors about his condition, he had handled the exacting "Fala" speech—which so easily could have flopped—with exquisite skill; he had driven gaily for hours through New York streets in a cold, driving rain. But at other times he seemed quite different. His face went slack; he slumped in his chair; his hands trembled more than ever.

Yet so swiftly did he shift from dullness to buoyancy that even while his friends were whispering to one another about their concern there would be fresh reports that the President was showing his old form.

Roosevelt was desolately lonely, too, lonely in the midst of the White House crowd. Just as he had always stayed partly in the world symbolized by Hyde Park, so had he kept around him people who had represented that world. But they were slipping away. Sara Roosevelt died in 1941, and the President remarked to Eleanor that perhaps she had departed this world at the right time, for she might not like the postwar world. Endicott Peabody died late in 1944, and Roosevelt wrote his widow that the "whole tone of things is going to be a bit different from now on, for I have leaned on the Rector in all these many years far more than most people know. . . ." McIntyre died in 1943, Missy LeHand the following year. Eleanor Roosevelt was often away on long war tours; all four Roosevelt sons were in uniform.

On January 20, 1945, Roosevelt took the oath of office for the fourth time; to save money and energy the inaugural was held in front of the White House rather than at the Capitol. He spoke for only a few minutes. "In the days and the years that are to come, we shall work for a just and honorable peace, a durable peace, as today we work and fight for total victory in war. . . ." As the President spoke, Allied troops in Europe stood on the threshold of victory. Hitler's armies, except for a precarious hold in Hungary and northern Italy, had been forced back onto German soil. In the Pacific, American forces were preparing heavy assaults on islands barely a thousand miles from Tokyo.

"We can gain no lasting peace if we approach it with suspicion and mistrust—or with fear," the President said in his inaugural; and in this spirit he met with Churchill and Stalin two weeks later at Yalta. Roosevelt faced resolutely this supreme test of Big Three co-operation. He was tired; he was frail; Churchill noticed that his face had "a transparency, an air of purification, and often there was a far-away look in his eyes." But even at Yalta, he could be as gay, charming, and buoyant as ever. His mind moved as quickly and as acutely as ever over the great range of problems that the conference considered.

Out of the hard bargaining at Yalta issued a series of compromises. No nation had its own way. Stalin made concessions on German reparations, on voting arrangements in the projected world organization, on the question of a French zone of occupation in Germany, and on several other matters. Moreover, the date of Russia's entrance into the war against Japan was fixed. Yet Stalin also gained some large demands. While the conference did not "give" him Poland, which was already occupied by Red troops, the terms of the agreement may have facilitated ensuing Soviet control of that country. And in the Far East Stalin was granted the Kurile Islands, the southern part of Sakhalin, and extensive spheres of influence in North China.

Had Roosevelt, the man who boasted of his prowess as a "hosstrader," finally been outbargained? Many would later cry that he had. Yet a verdict must take account of the different operating methods of the two men. Roosevelt, as always, was acting pragmatically, opportunistically, tactically. As usual, he was almost wholly concerned about the immediate job ahead—winning the war. Japan had yet to be overcome, and the military advised that the invasion and conquest of the homeland would be long and fanatically resisted. The first test of the atomic bomb was long in the future. His generals and admirals insisted—and the President agreed—that a Russian attack on Japan was essential.

Stalin, on the other hand, was thinking already of political arrangements in the postwar world. This granite-hard son of serfs, schooled in blood and violence, had always thought and acted several moves ahead of his adversaries—this was one reason he had defeated them. He had, moreover, few illusions about the postwar world; his revolutionary and Marxist background had taught him that, however friendly the Roosevelts and Churchills might be now, the inexorable laws of history would produce new tensions among nations, and Russia would have to be strong. Churchill, too, was aware of the political implications of victory; he, too, whatever his romantic Edwardian temperament, could see the storms ahead—had he not written bluntly that "the story of the human race is War"? But Churchill, unlike Stalin, did not have the continental land power to give strength to his strategy.

Roosevelt, a match for these men in the military direction of a war, was handicapped, when it came to the considerations of peace, by the belief that better days must lie ahead. Poignantly, in his inaugural address just before Yalta, he had quoted his old schoolmaster Peabody as saying that in life there would always be peaks and valleys, but that the "great fact to remember is that the trend of civilization itself is forever upward; that a line drawn through the middle of the peaks and the valleys of the centuries always has an upward trend." But Marx and Lenin seemed to have taught Stalin better than Peabody taught Roosevelt.

Such, at least, was the verdict of some of those who looked back from the years of bitterness and disillusion that followed the war. The verdict of still later years might be different. For beyond the military and political considerations of Yalta was the supreme accomplishment that Roosevelt wished to present to the world—the fact of Three Power co-operation. It was quite characteristic of him that in the existence of this accomplishment as interpreted by him to a world hungering for leadership, he should see the best chance of a lasting peace. Again and again, in his report to Congress on the Yalta Conference, his words came back to the supreme fact of the unity of the three great powers. Later generations, looking back from more tranquil years, might see this as the crowning achievement of Yalta—one that dwarfed even the most far-reaching maneuvers of the Machiavellians.

Even so, Roosevelt made one colossal—though understandable—miscalculation. His plans assumed that he, as President of the United States for another four years, would be around to keep the fact of one world alive, to symbolize it for peoples everywhere, to mediate between Stalin and Churchill. But time was fast running out.

Roosevelt's voice was strangely thick and blurred as he told Congress about Yalta. He stumbled and halted; he ad-libbed irrelevancies. At times his face and words flamed with the old eloquence, then it seemed to ebb away. Thus it was constantly in the final weeks. His body seemed to sag heavily in his chair or in the arms of his porters; his hands trembled so that the act of fixing his pincenez or lighting his cigarette took all his powers of concentration; his gray-blue eyes clouded, his face went slack, his head hunched over. Then, suddenly, miraculously, the old gayness and vitality would return. At his last press conference in Washington the repartee raced from Canadian relations to the new peace organization to New York City politics to Yalta to night baseball; the President was as quick, humorous, and deft as ever.

At the end of March Roosevelt left for Warm Springs. The usual crowd was waiting when the train pulled into the little Georgia town. There was the usual bustle of activity at the end of the rear car. But something was different. Roosevelt's big frame, slumped in the wheel chair, seemed to joggle slightly as he was rolled along the platform. His face, once so strong and well fleshed, seemed wasted; the jaw, once so firm, quivered perceptibly. A murmur swept through the crowd.

But as usual, after a few days of rest, the gray pailor faded, some of the old vitality returned. Doctors sent reassuring reports to Eleanor Roosevelt in Washington. Sitting in his cottage, watching the fresh green countryside under the the warm sun, the President was able to relax, to look over new stamps, to play with Fala, to think about the past and about the future.

It was early April, and the culmination of the war was at hand. Reports arriving daily told of victories on all battlefronts. In Europe, American and Allied troops were sweeping into the heart of Germany. In the Pacific naval forces were fighting off the heaviest Japanese air attacks of the war and clamping their grip on Okinawa. It was the culmination for Roosevelt too. He knew that war in Europe would be over in a few weeks. He knew now that Japan could not fight long against the power that would be massed against her after Germany's defeat. He knew that delegates from the united nations would meet soon in San Francisco to set up the permanent peace organization, and he knew that the United States would join it.

It was a time for rest—a time when the President could think about the long vacation that he would take in the summer and about a trip to Britain, a time when he could even toy with the idea of quitting the presidency as soon as the big jobs were done. He could think about the house at Hyde Park that was awaiting him, about the library with its mass of papers and mementos.

It was time too—though no one knew it at the moment—for a last look at the living man.

Those who knew Roosevelt best could agree fully on only one point—that he was a man infinitely complex and almost incomprehensible. "I cannot come to grips with him!" Ickes cried more than once, and the words were echoed by a host of congressmen, politicos, diplomats, and bureaucrats who dealt with the canny politician in the White House. His character was not only complex, Robert Sherwood observed, it was contradictory to a bewildering degree.

The contradictions continually bemused or galled Roosevelt's lieutenants. He was almost unvaryingly kind and gracious, yet a thin streak of cruelty ran through some of his behavior. He remained unruffled and at ease under the most intense pressures; yet when pricked in certain ways he struck out at his enemies in sharp, querulous words. He found ways to evade bores and know-it-alls, yet he patiently listened to Ickes' complaints and demands hour after hour, week after week, year after year. He juggled huge figures with an almost casual air, yet he could work long minutes over a knot to save the string and over a telegram to cut it down to ten words. He liked new ideas, people, and projects, but he wanted an element of fixity in his surroundings. He shifted nimbly from one set of policies to another—from economy to spending, from central planning to trust busting, from intervention abroad to neutrality, from party action to national action.

In many little ways inconsistency ruled: in the way he thanked some subordinates for their efforts and said nothing to others, intervened in some administrative matters and ignored others, had four men doing a single job in some instances (as Flynn once complained) and one man doing four jobs in others, was unaccountably frivolous about some matters and grave about others.

And there was the most baffling quality of all—his sheer, superb courage in facing some challenges, and his caution and indirection in facing others. He acted instantly, electrically, on certain decisions, and unaccountably postponed others for months. It was not strange that he should follow Machiavelli's advice that a leader must be as brave as the lion and as shrewd as the fox, for this had long been the first lesson for politicians. But his metamorphoses from lion to fox and back to lion again mystified even his intimates.

Roosevelt's complexities stemmed in part from the demands of political life. Gladstone once remarked that he had known and studied politicians for sixty years and they still remained to him a mysterious breed. Democratic politics is a highly competitive profession, and the successful politician must know how to conceal his hand and present different faces to different groups. Too, Roosevelt took a particular delight in mystifying people by keeping something up his sleeve. But the source of his complexity lay deeper than this.

Roosevelt was a complex man mainly because he was a deeply divided man. More than almost any other political leader of his time, he experienced a lingering between two worlds.

He had been born and raised in a class and in a tradition that formed the closest American approximation to an aristocracy. At home, at Groton, at Harvard, at the right houses of Boston and New York, he had absorbed a core of beliefs and a sense of security and assurance he would never lose.

His background always brought the needle of his compass, no matter how it might waver for a time, back to true north. The major premises on which this society operated might be inarticulate, or at least fuzzy, but they had meaning. These premises were: that men can live together only on the basis of certain simple, traditional ethical rules; that men are essentially good and those who are not can be improved by example and precept; that despite ups and downs the world is getting better; that the wellborn must never compromise with evil; that the gentleman must enter government to help the less fortunate, that he must enter politics to purify it. And the turn-of-the century world seemed to validate these ideas: it was stable, secure, peaceful, expansive.

Roosevelt was projected out of this world into bizarre and unanticipated phases of the twentieth century—a decade of muckraking, a decade of Wilsonian reform at home and Wilsonian idealism abroad; a decade of postwar cynicism and reaction; then the climactic years of depression, the New Deal, abroad the rise of brutish men to power, and the coming of a new war.

Some nineteenth-century men could not effectively make the shift to the new century; insecure and frightened, they clung not only to the old moralities, as did Roosevelt, but also to the old methods, the old ways of business, the old distrust for government; they huddled within their class barriers. Roosevelt, however, made the jump with ease. He did so for several reasons: because he had not met absolute success socially at Groton or Harvard—for example, in his failure to make the best club in Cambridge— and thus was not absolutely committed to the old ways and institutions; because of the influence of Eleanor and Theodore Roosevelt; because he was drawn into the variegated political life of New York State; because he was vital and curious and ambitious.

Still other men of his generation, rejecting the past completely, found some kind of fixed mooring somewhere in this strange new world—but, again, not Roosevelt. He made no final commitment to any part of that world—not to Wilsonian idealism, nor to business money-making, nor to radicalism, nor to internationalism. Partly because of quick adaptability, partly becauses of the diverse make-up of his intimates, partly because he had little need for personal introspection, partly because of his tremendous self-assurance, he was able to shift back and forth among segments of this world and to make himself at home in all of them.

Success fed on success; as Roosevelt found that he could carry off brilliantly a variety of roles—as party leader, as man of affairs, as bureaucrat, as Hyde Park squire, as governor, as campaigner, as a heroic battler against polio—he played the roles more and more to the hilt. This was one reason why he presided so joyously in the White House, for today the great President must be a man of many roles. Roosevelt was a superb actor in the literal sense—in the way his face, his gestures, the tilt of his head communicated feeling, in the perfect modulation of voice and the timing with which he read his speeches, in his sense of the dramatic. He was a superb actor in the far more significant sense that he was responding in each of his roles not merely to an assigned script but to something within himself.

The result was a man of no fixed convictions about methods and policies, flexible as a broker because he had to mediate among conflicting worlds and experiences. To some, like Hoover, he seemed a "chameleon on plaid" because of this enormous flexibility. Indeed, even to some of his friends he seemed almost in a state of anomie, lacking any guideposts at all, because he rejected so many doctrines and dogmas. Quite naturally, because the mask often was almost impenetrable, they could not see the inner compass of certainty and rightness.

Caught between two worlds, Roosevelt compartmentalized his life. The results sometimes were ludicrous, as when he tried to force opposites to work together and could not understand why they failed. The results were at times unfortunate, for Roosevelt's pseudointegration of his roles weakened his capacity to supply strong leadership and to make long-term strategic decisions or commitments when these were needed. It allowed the warring ideas and forces in American society not only to beat against him from outside but, because he incorporated as well as reflected these forces, to divide him from within.

Yet Roosevelt's flexibility and opportunism had tremendous advantages too. In a time of whirling social change he could move fast to head off crisis at home and abroad. In a time when experimentation was vital, he could try one method, quickly drop it, and turn to another. In a time when Americans had to be educated in the meaning of events, he could act as an interpreter all the more effectively because he spoke so many languages of social experience. Leading a people of sublime diversity, presiding over a nation of nations, he could say with Walt Whitman:

> Do I contradict myself?
> Very well, then, I contradict myself,
> (I am large, I contain multitudes.)

Lincoln Steffens once remarked that Theodore Roosevelt thought with his hips. Franklin Roosevelt's thinking was perhaps no more cerebral, but he thought with all five senses, perhaps with a sixth too. He had a radar set that could point in all directions, acute, sensitive, recording everything indiscriminately, and restoring the image in the responsive instrument that was Roosevelt's mind.

Was there then no hard center, no core personality, no final commitment in this man? Watching his quicksilver mind run from idea to idea, visitors could hardly believe that stone or steel lay under the bright, smooth flow of talk. But something did. The more that mask and costume are stripped away from Roosevelt, the more the turn-of-century man of Hyde Park, Groton, and Harvard stands out.

Roosevelt, for all his deviousness, was basically a moral man in the sense that he felt so intensely the need to do right that he had to think he did right. He believed in doing good, in showing other people how to do good, and he assumed that ultimately people would do good. By "good" he meant the Ten Commandments and the Golden Rule, as interpreted by Endicott Peabody. He meant the "simple rules of human conduct to which we always go back," as he said in 1932. He meant "old-fashioned standards of rectitude," as he said in signing the truth-in-securities bill in 1933. Significantly, Roosevelt always looked back into the past for his moralities; he did not try to fashion them anew.

These rules were not very precise, and Roosevelt did not want them to be precise. It was enough that they were there. Once when Eleanor Roosevelt raised with him the question of their children's religious upbringing, he said simply that they should go to church and learn what he had learned. "But are you sure that you believe in everything you learned?" his wife persisted. "I really never thought about it," he said with a quizzical look. "I think it is just as well not to think about things like that." But he expected others to understand his simple rules of conduct, and to understand his own allegiance to them. When Richard Whitney's financial irresponsibilities were disclosed, Roosevelt's wealthy friends wrote to compliment him on not using the unhappy incident as part of a political attack on Wall Street. The President was amazed at the letters. "I wonder what sort of man they think I am," he said.

Vague though it was, this set of moral rules embraced one idea in particular that was of cardinal importance to Roosevelt and to his country. This was the idea of man's responsibility for the well-being of his fellow man. It was simply an extension of Sara Roosevelt's notions of noblesse oblige, but it found enormous meaning in the new conditions of the twentieth century. For it underlay Roosevelt's most important single idea— the idea that government had a positive responsibility for the general welfare. Not that government itself must do everything, but that everything practicable must be done. Whether government does it, or private enterprise, is an operating decision dependent on many factors—but government must insure that something is done.

Such was the essence of Roosevelt's morality; such was the core of beliefs far below the surface.

Some politicians preach morality because it is safe to do so, because they prove thereby that they are on the right side between Good and Evil, because they reach the largest common denominator among their audience, not because they take their own preachments too seriously. Not so Roosevelt. Probably no American politician has given so many speeches that were essentially sermons rather than statements of policy. Like a preacher, he wanted and expected his sermons to serve as practical moral guides to his people. Roosevelt was so theatrical that his moral preachments were often dismissed with a smile. Actually he was deadly serious.

Only a man deadly serious and supremely confident could have spent the time Roosevelt did trying to educate and elevate not only his own people but foreign leaders who seemed to others to be beyond redemption. There was something pathetic and yet almost sublime in the way that Roosevelt sent message after message to Hitler and other dictators. Partly, of course, it was for the record; but even more it was an expression of Roosevelt's faith in the ultimate goodness and reasonableness of all men. His eternal desire to talk directly with his enemies, whether congressmen or dictators, reflected his confidence in his own persuasiveness and, even more, in the essential ethical rightness of his own position.

To Theodore Roosevelt the presidency was a "bully pulpit." To Franklin Roosevelt it was the same—"pre-eminently a place of moral leadership. . . ."

How explain, then, the "other side" of Roosevelt—his shiftiness, his compromises, his manipulations? Why did he so often act like a fox?

Roosevelt was not an absolute moralist about means because, whatever his hopes or illusions about man's possible redemption and ultimate goodness and reasonableness, he had few illusions about man's nature. He knew that some men were selfish, irrational, vengeful, and mean. The practical statesman or man of affairs encounters ambitions and passions in his daily experience that put man in a strong, harsh light. Roosevelt got his education at the hands of tough labor leaders like Lewis, city bosses like Murphy and Hague, agrarian demagogues like Long, and—on the level of pure evil—Hitler and his camp followers. He learned the uses of power.

Roosevelt overcame these men because he liked and wanted power and, even more, because he wanted to defend the position of strength from which he could lead and teach the people. To seize and hold power, to defend that position, he got down into the dusty arena and grappled with rival leaders on their own terms. So sure was he of the rightness of his aims that he was willing to use Machiavellian means; and his moral certainties made him all the more effective in the struggle. To the idealists who cautioned him he responded again and again that gaining power—winning elections—was the first, indispensable task. He would use the tricks of the fox to serve the purposes of the lion.

During the war years Roosevelt became interested in Kierkegaard, and this was not surprising. The Danish theologian, with his emphasis on man's natural sinfulness, helped explain to him, Roosevelt said, why the Nazis "are human, yet they believe like demons." From Peabody's homilies to Kierkegaard's realities, from the world of Hyde Park to the world of Hitler, the way was long and tortuous; the fact that Roosevelt could traverse that road so surely, with so little impairment to his loftiest ideals, and with such courage and good humor, was the final and sure test of the man.

Holmes had been right—a second-rate intellect but a first-rate temperament. To examine closely single aspects of Roosevelt's character—as thinker, as organizer, as manipulator, as strategist—is to see failings and deficiencies closely interwoven with the huge capacities. But to stand back and look at the man as a whole, against the backdrop of his people and his times, is to see the lineaments of greatness—courage, joyousness, responsiveness, vitality, faith, and, above all, concern for his fellow man. A democrat in manner and conviction, he was yet a member of that small aristocracy once described by E. M. Forster—sensitive but not weak, considerate but not fussy, plucky in his power to endure, capable of laughing and of taking a joke. He was the true happy warrior.

Warm Springs on Thursday, April 12, was sunny and pleasant. Roosevelt sat in his cottage looking over his stamps. He had put on a dark blue suit and a Harvard-red tie for a painter who was doing his portrait. Sitting in his brown leather chair near the fireplace, he seemed unusually chipper and gay. For some reason he took his draft card out of his wallet and tossed it into a basket nearby. Then he looked at some reports with intense concentration.

Suddenly the President groaned. He pressed and rubbed his temple hard—then the great head fell back inert. Carried to his bed, he lived, breathing heavily but unconscious, for about four hours. He died at 4:35 P.M.; it was fourscore years almost to the day since Lincoln's death.

The news sped to Eleanor Roosevelt in Washington, to Harry Truman, summoned suddenly to the White House from Capitol Hill, to Winston Churchill, who felt as if he had been struck a physical blow, to soldiers, sailors, and marines on far-off battle fronts. To four of these fighting men went a message from their mother: "He did his job to the end as he would want you to do." At the Capitol building a young congressman, groping for words, spoke for his generation: "He was the only person I ever knew—anywhere—who was never afraid. God, how he could take it for us all." Everywhere men and women wept, openly and without shame.

"All that is within me cries out to go back to my home on the Hudson River," Roosevelt had said nine months before, and now at last he would return. Through the dark Southern night the funeral train moved slowly back to Washington. Marines and infantrymen escorted the black, flag-draped caisson through the streets of Washington, while a huge crowd stood silent and unmoving. There was a brief, simple service in the East Room of the White House; then the body was placed again on the funeral train, and Roosevelt for the last time traveled the old, familiar route along the Pennsylvania Railroad's main line through Philadelphia and into Manhattan, then across Hell Gate bridge and up along the Hudson.

At the siding on the riverbank below the home, the coffin was moved from the train to a caisson drawn by six brown horses. There followed a lone horse, hooded, stirrups reversed and a sword hanging from the left stirrup—symbolic of a lost warrior. Marching in rigid columns of three at slow funeral cadence, the guard escorted the body up the steep winding road, through the dark woods, to the little plateau above. Behind the house, framed by the rose garden, were assembled the family and friends, old servants and retainers, and files of soldiers and sailors standing at rigid attention on the expanse of green grass.

A river breeze off the Hudson ruffled the trees above. A military band sounded the sad notes of its dirge. Muffled drums beat slowly and a bugler played the haunting notes of Taps as the coffin was slowly lowered into the grave. The warrior was home.

JAPAN *did more than sink the Pacific fleet at Pearl Harbor on December 7, 1941; it put an end to the American illusion of isolation. For a brief moment, it brought the United States face to face with military defeat at the hands of a foreign enemy. When four days later, Germany and Italy declared war on the United States, the country was obliged to fight a global war. To achieve this end, a maximum force of 12,466,000 was mobilized; the economy was geared to produce equipment which not only guaranteed the American fighting man all his requirements but also assured our allies of adequate supplies for their own forces; and American forces carried out campaigns throughout the Pacific, in Northern Africa, Italy, and in western Europe. When the war ended, the United States was undoubtedly the most powerful nation in the world.*

But the conduct of the war posed complex questions of strategy. After long discussions and with a large dissent from General Douglas MacArthur, the major focus of the war's strategy was made Europe. The unconditional surrender of Hitler's Germany signified the Allied determination to destroy Nazism root and all. The systematic bombardment from the air of Germany accelerated as the war continued until most German cities were either partially or totally in ruins. The invasion of North Africa in November 1942 and the subsequent invasion and surrender of Italy in the summer and autumn of 1943 drew the noose tighter around the Third Reich. When on June 6, 1944, a combined British-Canadian-American army invaded Normandy, Germany found itself fighting a three-front war against Russia in the East, the western Allies in the West, and Allied armies in Italy and Yugoslav partisans in the Balkan mountains.

German forces fought desperately. The monstrosity called Nazism had compromised German integrity almost beyond redemption. And a vengeful Europe, ravished as she had not been since Attila the Hun had swept across her land, waited to wreak her revenge. A fearful Germany held off her conquerors as long as she could but in the spring of 1945 the end came. In the battered ruin of Berlin, a demented Hitler ended his fantasy with a bullet shortly before the city's fall to the Russians. The revolting dimensions of Hitlerian savagery were revealed as Dachau, Buchenwald, Auschwitz, and numberless other concentration camps released their surviving victims and revealed their awesome toll of innocent dead. The Germans who came to negotiate peace at Reims on May 8, 1945, went on to Nuremberg to be tried for crimes against humanity. And the United States remained behind to stand guard on the Rhine.

Kenneth S. Davis (1912-) is, like many of the more recent historians, a trained journalist. He combines a sense of the human detail with the felicitous phrase. His study of the war in Europe is less a thoroughgoing history of that conflict and more a sequence of illuminating vignettes. The immediacy of the events and their overwhelming and continuing impact makes it unlikely that any historian in our time will be able to give that struggle its definitive treatment.

EXPERIENCE OF WAR

by Kenneth S. Davis

In Third Army Headquarters near Hersfeld, Germany, news of the President's death comes to George S. Patton in his trailer-truck via a midnight BBC broadcast. Eisenhower and Bradley, visiting Patton this day, have gone to bed in a small house nearby. Patton promptly goes to them with the news and the three generals sit together in Eisenhower's bedroom until two o'clock Friday morning trying to comprehend the meaning of this event, trying to determine its probable consequences. For all three of them the news climaxes a most memorable day. They have visited a salt mine at the village of Merkers where troops of the 90th Division, three days ago, discovered a huge cache of Nazi loot—some $250,000,000 in gold (most of it in gold bars) and hundreds upon hundreds of stolen art objects. They have visited, too, the first concentration camp that any of them has ever seen, at Ohrdruf, overrun by the Third Army two days ago.

Ohrdruf is not one of the really big important institutions like Buchenwald, Belsen, Dachau, Erlau, soon to be exposed to the world by the swift advance of Allied arms; it is not a major extermination camp set up for the "final solution" of the "Jewish problem," like Auschwitz with its four huge gas chambers with adjacent crematoriums. Ohrdruf is but a run-of-the-mill example of Nazi German *Kultur*. Nevertheless the sight and the smell of it, and the heard description of its practices, have sufficed to sicken the three generals. (Patton, at one point, stumbled over to a corner and vomited.) The stink of death was thick in their nostrils even before they reached the stockade. It rose from more than three thousand corpses flung into shallow graves and from hundreds of others lying stacked in sheds or scattered along the streets—emaciated, mutilated, putrefying bodies, covered over with maggots and blowflies. A guide shows the visitors a gallows from which prisoners attempting escape were hanged as the German generals who attempted Hitler's assassination were hanged, their necks in a noose of piano wire, their toes just touching the ground. From five to fifteen minutes of delicious spectacle were provided by each hanging for fun-loving Germans. Also seen is the whipping table where a naked man can be made to stand with his feet in stocks while two guards bend him over and a third fun-loving German beats him to a bloody pulp with a thick stick or heavy cowhide whip. It becomes possible to believe what will later be revealed to be true —that the Germans have deliberately, methodically, as a matter of high Government policy, murdered more than six million human beings—men, women, and children—in camps especially constructed for that purpose. Auschwitz in Poland, the largest and most efficient of these camps, killed no fewer than six thousand a day during its period of peak performance.

Eisenhower is determined that what he has seen that day shall be seen, through broadcast and eyewitness report and photographs, by all the world. He is determined to prevent any future dismissal of these horrible realities as "just war propaganda." Accordingly he has sent messages to both London and Washington—he did so as soon as he returned to Patton's headquarters —urging the two Governments "to send instantly to Germany a random group of newspaper editors and representative groups from the national legislatures" to view the obscenity which lies at the heart of Nazi-Fascism and then make uncensored report of it to the public at large.

The ruin at the heart of Berlin that night is compounded by another RAF bombing raid. At midnight, fire rages through the smashed Chancellery while the incredible monster who has loosed upon the world the greatest horrors of all history huddles in his deep bunker beneath the Wilhelmplatz, a rat in a hole. Adolf Hitler, though not yet fifty-six years old (he will be next week, on April 20), has now the appearance and many of the traits of a senile man. His face is gray and slack, his eyes dull, save when insane rage (and insane rage is frequent) distorts his features and transforms his gaze into a baleful glare. Sometimes his head wobbles uncontrollably, often his hands tremble, and his left arm, the one injured by the July bomb, hangs loose and apparently useless. He has lost all contact with reality. He con-tinuously issues orders that cannot possibly be obeyed and raves about "treason" and "betrayal" when they are not obeyed. He turns for slender comfort to astrology, striving desperately to believe that a "miracle" is fore-cast by the stars to occur in the latter half of April—a supernatural inter-vention that will save him and his Germany. Meanwhile he does his best to make sure that all Germany will go down with him into the final darkness, for he can no longer really hope. Certainly he can see no basis for hope in the news that has come to him all day from the battlefields. The U. S. First Army has driven into Leipzig. The U. S. Ninth Army has cut north of the Harz Mountains where five German divisions will soon be encircled. The Americans are on the Elbe, have flung a bridgehead across it to match the bridgehead the Russians have thrown across the Oder in the east. Both to the east and to the west the enemy stands in overwhelming strength just thirty miles or so from Berlin. Soon, inevitably, the capital will be in enemy hands.

And yet, will it?

Sometime after midnight comes a ring on Hitler's private phone and he picks up the receiver to hear Goebbels' excited, exultant voice saying: "My Fuehrer, I congratulate you! Roosevelt is dead! It is written in the stars that the second half of April will be the turning point for us. This is Friday, April the thirteenth. It is the turning point!" Goebbels toasts this death in the best champagne, and others are similarly overjoyed—the Minister of Fi-nance in Berlin, for instance, who feels "wings flutter through the room" when he hears the news, the wings of the "Angel of History" marking the "turn of fortune" for Germany. And Hitler's own crushed spirits are briefly raised.

But only briefly . . .

For there now fell upon the writhing, bleeding body of Nazi Germany the final flesh-shredding lashes of the war. In the north, the British struck through Bremen and on across the Elbe to Hamburg and Lübeck. The Americans, having reached the Elbe, struck southeastward into Czechoslovakia and Austria and to the German border of Switzerland. In Italy, the Anglo-American armies and the Poles struck northward into the Po Valley, Polish troops taking Bologna on April 21 (they there destroyed the famed First German Parachute Division); three days later the Allies were across the Po on a broad front. Simultaneously, the Russians opened their attack across the Oder and drove again westward on a front of more than two hundred miles, scoring great successes everywhere against the hardest resistance the Germans could still make. On April 25, at Torgau on the Elbe, some seventy-five miles south of Berlin, units of the 69th Division of the U. S. V Corps greeted with loud cheers units of the Russian 58th Guards Division, and the slender portion of Germany yet unoccupied was split in two. Next day there was riotous celebration at Torgau, Russians and Americans fraternizing with many spontaneous demonstrations of mutual admiration. Bradley issued a special order of the day in which he praised Marshal Konev's First Ukrainian Army, of which the 58th Guards was an element. "These armies have come down from the ruins of Stalingrad and Sevastopol, across the scorched cities of the Ukraine," Bradley said. "In two years they have smashed fourteen hundred miles through the German Army to drive the enemy from Russia and pursue him to the Elbe. . . ."

On the same day as the meeting on the Elbe came the signal for a general uprising of Italian Partisans in northern Italy. They seized control of Milan, Venice, and many other cities. Mussolini, now a haggard old man, fled northward with a German convoy, accompanied by his young mistress, Clara Petacci. Though he wore a German helmet and greatcoat he was recognized and, on April 28, while ensconced in a farmhouse on Lake Como, was seized by a Partisan band. He and his mistress were stood against a wall and shot. Their bodies were then taken to the Piazza Loretto in Milan and dumped there with the bodies of a dozen other Fascists at or near the spot where fifteen Partisans had been executed by the Nazi-Fascists months before. In the last view the world was to have of him he was hanging by his heels from a meat hook, his mistress beside him, being kicked and stoned and reviled by a huge crowd of the people (very different in temperament and outlook from the Germans) whom he had tricked and cajoled into disaster. Much photographed, thoroughly described in print by eyewitnesses, the scene was gruesome and shocking (Churchill was outraged by it) but perhaps beneficent in its long-term impress upon the popular mind, and upon history. For in the future, whenever power-lustful young egotists animated by childish dreams of "glory" saw pictures of the great Mussolini on his balcony—strutting, arrogant, contemptuously looking down upon a sea of upturned faces—they could not but see also in their mind's eye this final picture of a gaunt old man, his jaw smashed by an angry boot, hung up like butcher's meat before a huge mob that cursed and spat upon him.

Equally sordid—indeed, nastier somehow, and more obscene—was the end of the Nazi Fuehrer.

On April 28, Adolf Hitler learned via a BBC broadcast that Heinrich Himmler, whom he had always deemed the most loyal of his subordinates, had been engaged in secret negotiations with Count Bernadotte, head of the Swedish Red Cross, aimed toward a surrender of all German forces in the West to Eisenhower. (Even in this final hour, Himmler hoped to arrange a peace in the West which would enable German armies to concentrate against the Russians, perhaps with active Anglo-American support.) He raved, frothed at the mouth, turned purple with congested blood, then collapsed into a stupor. After that he was drained, it seemed, of all emotion save a dull, embittered despair. He began to make preparations for suicide and the destruction of his body. Very early in the morning of April 29 he went through the formality of marriage with his mistress of many years, a vapid, bovine young woman named Eva Braun who was determined to die at his side. He then dictated his last will and "Political Testament," repeating in the latter the ugly falsehoods by which he had lived. That afternoon, as the Russians, who had broken into the city on April 23, fought only a block away from the shattered Chancellery, news came to him of Mussolini's death. Everything was finished. . . .

Next day, Monday, April 30, shortly before 3:30 in the afternoon, Adolf Hitler killed himself with a pistol shot through the roof of his mouth, his bride dying beside him of self-administered poison. Their bodies, carried up into the Chancellery garden during a brief lull in the Russian shelling, were soaked with gasoline and burned.

His "Thousand-Year" Reich died with him. All German and Italian Fascist troops in northern Italy and western Austria were surrendered unconditionally to the Allies on May 2, the instrument of surrender being signed in the palace of the Bourbon kings at Caserta, twenty miles from Naples. Next day British forces took Hamburg and on the day after that arrangements between Montgomery and German Admiral Doenitz (whom Hitler had named as his successor) were concluded for the unconditional surrender of all German forces in Holland, northwest Germany, and Denmark. The terms were signed on May 5. On the same morning the First and Nineteenth German armies surrendered to the Allied 6th Army Group in the south. Only shattered remnants of the German Seventh Army now remained in opposition to Eisenhower's forces.

On the afternoon of the following day, a German delegation arrived at Eisenhower's headquarters to arrange the unconditional surrender of *all* German forces, those on the Eastern as well as Western Fronts insofar as the two yet remained separate. The headquarters was in a trade school building in Rheims, France—a dreary, red-brick structure. The delegation was composed of Colonel General Alfred Jodl, recently appointed Chief of Staff of the disintegrating German Army; General Admiral Hans Georg von Friedeburg, commander of the impotent German Navy; and Jodl's aide, Major General Wilhelm Oxenius. Beetle Smith, SHAEF Chief of Staff, acting for Eisenhower, served as chairman of the surrender conference, which was also attended by General François Savez of the French Army and General Ivan Susloparoff of the Red Army. Hours were required to arrange the technical details of surrender but finally, at 2:25 in the morning of May 7, the discussions were completed. Correspondents were assembled in the map-walled war room and here, without ceremony, Jodl, Smith, Savez, and Susloparoff signed the Instrument of Unconditional Surrender. It was 2:41 when the last signature was completed.

Nearly two days later, or at half an hour before midnight of Tuesday, May 8, 1945, this Instrument of Unconditional Surrender was ratified in Berlin in a ceremony designed to express and stress the unity of the Western Allies with the Soviet Union. Here Field Marshal Wilhelm Keitel signed for the German Army, Admiral Georg von Friedeburg for the German Navy, and Colonel General Hans von Stumpf for the German Air Force. Air Chief Marshal Sir Arthur Tedder signed as Eisenhower's deputy, General Carl A. Spaatz of the U. S. Air Force signed for the United States, Lieutenant General Jean de Lattre de Tassigny signed for France, and Marshal Georgi Zhukov signed for the Soviet Union.

After five years, eight months, and seven days of war, a ruined Europe entered upon an uneasy and dubious peace. . . .

Germany lying prostrate in the dust that summer, naked and bleeding from such a scourging of war as no other major power had received since ancient Carthage, presented a spectacle that appalled mankind. Pity was evoked by it in humane breasts. How could it fail to be by the sight of women and children and old men scrabbling for food in garbage heaps among the ruins of scores of towns, dozens of once-great cities? By the sight of child prostitutes soliciting with words obscene and gestures obscene along rubble-heaped streets of night? By the sight of people without arms, without legs, without eyes, their bodies twisted and their faces scarred by explosive fire and steel? By the evidences everywhere abundant, everywhere reflected in grief-darkened eyes and terror-frozen faces, of what had been suffered by all these people, the physically uninjured along with the wounded, during the long fury that had crushed their nation? Pity was overtly asked for. Jodl had asked for it at the surrender table in Rheims. Granted permission to speak, after having signed the instrument of surrender, he had stood up very stiff and straight and, staring straight ahead, had said in a voice hoarse with emotion: "With this signature the German people and the German forces are, for better or worse, delivered into the victors' hands. In this war, which has lasted more than five years, both have achieved and suffered more than perhaps any other people in the world. I can only express the hope that the victors will treat them with generosity."

But pity was not the only emotion evoked. There was horror and disgust also as, days passing into weeks, more and more was revealed of what these poor suffering Germans had actually "achieved" during the last five and a half years.

Many square miles of countryside had been drenched with the stink of death day after day as crematorium chimneys poured forth white acrid smoke from the burning bodies of human beings killed, not one by one (that might have given their deaths some individual dignity), but in batches of a dozen to two hundred at a time. Doctors of medicine by the score had performed horrible "medical experiments" on living men and women and children and had made reports of them to meetings of medical societies, reports of no scientific value whatever that were nevertheless seriously discussed by the most eminent of the nation's medical practitioners, and with no evidence of personal revulsion. Farmers and industrialists had worked thousands of slave laborers literally to death in mines and fields and factories; bankers had stuffed their vaults with dental gold extracted from the teeth of murdered Jews. Hundreds of bleached human skulls, and of handbags and gloves and lampshades made of the skin of concentration camp victims, were displayed as souvenirs in Nazi German homes. And all these horrors, actively perpetrated by thousands and thousands of these poor suffering Germans, had been passively permitted—without protest, often with approval—by millions upon millions of others.

Such knowledge, falling heavily down upon the Western mind, plunging deep into the individual self, was like a sharp-edged stone dropped into a still pool. Ripples spread out from it in wider and ever-wider circles. "This is what *Nazis* are capable of!" one began by saying, with loathing and with scorn. Later one said, with equal loathing but less certain scorn: "This is what *Germans* are capable of!" One said at last, with loathing still but with a drastic reduction in scorn, since there was now drastically reduced that sense of otherness on which scorn depends: "This is what *men* are capable of!" And as these ripples spread horizontally the stone itself sank down and down until it struck against the very bottom of the soul, its sharp edge cutting deep, and forced upward a cry of anguish that was also a question filled with terror: "This is what *I* am capable of?"

Thus there was an inner as well as an outer necessity, a psychological as well as an objectively historical need, to round up Nazi war criminals following the unconditional surrender of Germany and to arrange for their public trial and stern punishment.

Fat Hermann Goering, long the Number Two Nazi, originator of the concentration camp and commander of the Luftwaffe, surrendered to American troops in Austria a few hours after the Berlin ratification of the instrument of Germany's surrender. By then or shortly thereafter the Allies held captive, among others, Rudolf Hess, the Number Three Nazi, long Hitler's deputy; Alfred Rosenberg, the "philosopher" of the Nazi Party; Joachim von Ribbentrop, the ruthless, overbearing Nazi Foreign Minister; Julius Streicher, notorious sadist and pornographer, editor of *Der Sturmer;* Ernst Kaltenbrunner, one of those with the highest responsibility for the mass extermination of Jews; and Robert Ley, leader of the German Labor Front, under whose administration slave laborers had suffered and died by the thousand. Heinrich Himmler, chief of the Gestapo, the greatest (under Hitler) mass murderer of all time, was captured by British troops near Hamburg on May 20 but promptly committed suicide by biting into a vial of poison concealed in his mouth. Goebbels, having murdered his six children with injections of poison, had had himself and his wife shot to death by an SS orderly on the day following Hitler's suicide. Ley was soon a suicide in his cell.

The others would be among those who sat in the prisoners' dock at Nuremberg with the camera eyes of the world focused on them while their enormous crimes were spread upon the public record in frequently nauseating detail. Sitting there day after day, week after week, month after month (the trial would run from November 20, 1945, to October 1, 1946), they would be denied the possibility of future investment with such glamor of wickedness as invests, say, the mythical Mephistopheles or the historic Borgias. They would become, after a while, boring in a peculiarly horrible way, being so monotonously vicious, so gross and repetitious and unimaginative in their murderous cruelties. They would shrink then in the eyes of the world to their true dimensions as banal, shabby, nasty, craven creatures whose proper fate was to be hustled out of life as quickly as possible and shoveled into holes, like so much stinking garbage.

Nor was all this mere vengefulness: it was also exorcism. There was in it, certainly, the spirit of the Old Testament, a sense of justice as punishment and retribution, but at the same time there was not wholly absent from it the spirit of the New. For in a deep psychological sense, and in a way that might be deemed a bridge between Old and New, the Golden Rule applied insofar as those who sat in judgment did indeed do unto others as they would have others do unto them should they ever be guilty of the least of such crimes as these. The judgment at Nuremberg, in other words—the condemnation of these sordid creatures of hate—was in part a protection of self from self on the part of those who judged. It raised another wall against the possibility that a similar evil might break out of the inner recesses of their own beings into the light and air of the actual world. . . .

The same motive was operative at the San Francisco Conference of the United Nations between April 25 and June 25, 1945. But it operated in a different way. Here too was a clear realization of the dangers of depending too exclusively upon pure self-restraint for the prevention of evil in the world, whether that restraint be exercised by individuals or by sovereign States, but here the emphasis was not upon punitive sanctions but upon the institutionalized implementation of good will, the organized reduction of the incentives and opportunities for national aggression and war. It was an emphasis sadly flawed by continuing and even growing dissension between Russia and the West.

More evident every day of that spring and early summer was the probability that Roosevelt had been correct in his assessment of his personal standing with Stalin, and of his consequent ability to exert an ameliorative influence upon the relations between Stalin and Churchill, and between Molotov and the foreign offices of London and Washington. With his death was lost a medium of fair exchange between East and West. Lost also was a perspective whereby differences that flatly contradicted one another when viewed close up were revealed to be complementary aspects of a larger whole—a perspective that suggested and even imposed a synthesis, a fusion into coherent organism, of what were initially warring oppositions. His successor was determined to follow his policies; no one could have sought with greater humility or sincerity to do so at the outset. But in the face of novelty (and there was certainly for him an abundance of novelty in those days of swift transition), Harry Truman was hard put to find what these policies were. Did they or had they ever in fact existed as clear and definite designs? Roosevelt, it would appear, had approached the problems of war and peace as he had formerly approached the problems of economic depression, not with a set of consistent ideas (an ideology) but with a set of attitudes, of ways of feeling and responding to stimuli. And these, being rooted in the complexities of his character and shaped through his many-leveled ambiguities, could not be transmitted to another. Nor precisely imitated. Gone, then—and mourned by none more than the Russians—was that unique and highly flexible compound of patience and firmness, that "ear" (he had "played it by ear") so sensitively attuned to slight variations of tone and rhythm, that steadily glowing good will, which had done so much to facilitate the work of Yalta and had promised so much for San Francisco.

Truman was a very different kind of man. His was a simpler intelligence, his a much more combative disposition, even game-cocky beneath the temporary humility. He saw the world in primary colors; his spectrum contained few of the subtler shadings. Impulsive and emphatic, he envisaged himself as a man of quick decision, a man who "got things done" with a minimum of palaver and waste motion. Hence his inability, despite his striving, to continue the mixture as before of patience and firmness in his dealings with Soviet fears and suspicions and with the acts rooted in these. Inevitably the proportions were altered. There was less of patience, more of firmness, the latter hardening as the former waned—and of course such personal rapport as there had been between the White House and Stalin was now wholly lost.

Expressive of a part of Truman's character was an episode of his fourth week in office. On the day Germany's surrender was announced, Leo T. Crowley, the Foreign Economic Administrator, and Joseph C. Grew, Acting Secretary of State (Stettinius was then in San Francisco), came to the Oval Study, bringing with them an order drastically and abruptly reducing the flow of Lend-Lease aid to our European allies. They gave reasons. A compelling one for Truman at that time was conveyed through their statement that Roosevelt had "approved" the order but not signed it, the implication being that he certainly *would* have signed it had he continued to occupy the chair in which Truman now sat. It was necessary to do so in order to keep faith with the Congress, whose original intention had been to extend Lend-Lease only to those nations at war with Nazi-Fascism; the European war having ended, European Lend-Lease must be at once curtailed and soon terminated. Perhaps unstated that day but certainly in the minds of Grew and Crowley (it later rankled Truman that these two had arrogated to themselves a policy-making function properly belonging to him) was a conviction that the United States would be foolish to continue aiding a Soviet Union bent on pursuing her own aims in Europe regardless of the wishes and interests of others. To do so, they might have indicated, would be to implement with our resources a policy inimical to ours. At any rate, the reasons actually given "made good sense" to Harry Truman. "I reached for my pen," he later said, "and, without reading the document, I signed it." He promptly regretted having done so. The abrupt slash was palpably unfair to Allies who, after all, had spent a larger proportion of their available blood and treasure in the common cause than the United States had done. It certainly militated against that early entry of Russia into the war against Japan which the Joint Chiefs of Staff continued to deem imperative. And three days after it was issued, while Moscow's prompt and peeved protest to Washington reverberated harshly in San Francisco, threatening to abort the United Nations organization, the order was rescinded. But by then grave damage had been done. Stalin, despite or because of his own penchant for coercive tactics, resented what seemed to him an effort to force Soviet compliance with American wishes regarding the Government of Poland, and regarding the voting procedure in the Security Council of the United Nations—the latter an issue soon to deadlock the San Francisco Conference.

It was in part to undo the harm done by the Lend-Lease order that, two weeks later, Harry Hopkins went to Moscow to confer with Stalin as the President's personal emissary. This was to be the last mission of his life. He had come out of the hospital in Rochester against the strong advice of his doctors in order to attend Roosevelt's funeral. He had remained in Washington in order to give Truman the benefit of his uniquely intimate knowledge of what Roosevelt had felt, had hoped and feared and intended, for the future. He was obviously terribly ill. To Robert Sherwood he "looked like death, the skin of his face a dreadful cold white with apparently no flesh left under it." But his spirit, Sherwood also noted, flamed bright as ever through his frail, emaciated body, and when he talked of the necessity to finish the great unfinished work on which Roosevelt had been engaged, ". . . fire was shooting out of his sharp eyes in their sunken sockets." Truman also took note of the physical illness, the spiritual fire. Was the former too great to permit the latter to be used to thaw the ice forming around Soviet attitudes toward the West? Truman wanted to know. Hopkins was at first dubious; he would have to consult his doctors, he said. But he knew (as others did) that there was no one else in the world who could undertake such a mission to Moscow with equal prospect of success, knew too that the situation was urgent to the point of desperation (the San Francisco Conference was in serious trouble by the third week of May). Accordingly he flew from Washington on May 23, was joined by Ambassador Harriman in Paris, and landed in Moscow on the evening of May 25.

He was Truman's personal emissary—but he was also in a real sense Roosevelt's. He came as a yet-glowing vital element of the dead President; he could speak with Roosevelt's voice as well as his own, his own being that of a man who had proved under great pressure his personal courage, frankness, trustworthiness, and commitment to Soviet-American friendship. This, joined to the authority Truman gave him, constituted his unique qualification for face-to-face negotiations with Stalin. They were fruitful negotiations. A frank and full discussion of the differences between the two Great Powers laid a foundation for limited but substantial agreements. Stalin set the date of August 8 for the Russian invasion of Manchuria, provided the Chinese Government agreed to the proposals made at Yalta. (The Chinese, as has been said, did promptly agree.) He agreed to meet with the President and Churchill in the Berlin area in mid-July. He reaffirmed the Yalta agreement to join Britain and the United States in insuring that the reconstituted Polish Government held free elections and protected individual rights and liberty, though as regards this last there were qualifications whose practical application would soon be regarded by the West as violations of the agreement. There was no clear understanding between Hopkins and Stalin as to the extent to which the "principles of democracy" (which Stalin said were "well known and would find no objection on the part of the Soviet Government") could or would be actually operative in Poland. "He said . . . that in regard to the specific freedoms mentioned by Mr. Hopkins [freedom of speech, assembly, press, and religious worship], they could only be applied in full in peacetime, and even then with certain limitations," says the official record of Stalin's remarks on this point. "He said for example the fascist party, whose intention it was to overthrow the democratic governments, could not be permitted to enjoy to the full extent these freedoms. He said also there were limitations imposed by war. All States when they were threatened by war on their frontiers were not secure and had found it necessary to introduce certain restrictions." More definite, though far from meeting the wishes of Britain and the United States, was Stalin's agreement to honor his Yalta pledge to the extent of including in the reorganized Polish Government certain Polish leaders not of the Lublin-Warsaw group; a list of the names of those to be invited in was made up and approved.

The most resounding immediate success of Hopkins' six long conversations with Stalin was the settlement of the issue of voting procedure in the United Nations Security Council. At Yalta, it will be remembered, the Russians had agreed to a U. S. voting formula whereby a distinction was made between (a) decisions to consider and discuss a dispute between nations (this was deemed a "procedural" matter in that it consisted of deciding upon an agenda) and (b) decisions to investigate and make recommendations for the pacific settlement of disputes or, this failing, to impose sanctions. The former were to require seven affirmative votes (in a Council of eleven) for adoption, not necessarily including all five votes of the permanent Council members, whereas the latter were to require seven votes *including* all permanent members. In other words, the Big Power veto would not apply to "procedural matters" but *would* apply to "all other matters." At San Francisco, however, the Russians retreated from this position. The chief Soviet delegate, Andrei Gromyko (Molotov had by then returned to Moscow and was taking part in the talks with Hopkins) announced that before he could approve the statement incorporating this arrangement in the UN Charter he would have to consult Moscow, and the whole Conference waited on tenterhooks while he did so. If Russia remained adamant, the Conference would surely fail. No Charter could be adopted. There would be no United Nations organization, no machinery whatever for effectively ameliorating the Punic War situation which already seemed in danger of developing between Russia and the United States.

Hence the joy in Washington and San Francisco when, following a conversation in Moscow on June 6, during which it appeared that the opposition to the American position was primarily Molotov's and that Stalin had concurred in it only because he hadn't grasped the question, Hopkins cabled the President that "Marshal Stalin agrees to accept the United States position regarding voting procedure in the Council." According to Robert Sherwood's account, "This was the real news that the San Francisco Conference had been saved."

By June 25 the work was done: on that day, the Charter was unanimously adopted. President Truman addressed the Conference's closing session. "The Charter of the United Nations which you have just signed is a solid structure upon which we can build a better world . . ." he said. "Between the victory in Europe and the final victory in Japan, in this most destructive of all wars, you have won a victory against war itself."

As for Harry Hopkins, having returned from his long journey seemingly none the worse for it physically, he breakfasted with the President in the White House on June 13. Truman was fulsome in his expression of personal gratitude. He urged Hopkins to accompany him to Potsdam where (it had been decided) the Big Three were to meet in mid-July, but Hopkins wisely pointed out that his presence at that meeting would be unfair to James F. Byrnes, whom Truman had chosen to replace Stettinius as Secretary of State as soon as decently possible after the San Francisco sessions ended. If Hopkins were at Potsdam, Churchill and Stalin out of habit and long familiarity would inevitably address to him questions properly addressed to Byrnes, undercutting the new Secretary's prestige and authority. It was a point whose validity Truman could not deny.

So when Hopkins left the White House that morning it was in the knowledge that he was leaving public life, probably forever—and he could congratulate himself on leaving it at a moment of popular triumph such as he, in all his years of dedicated Government service, had never known before. In early July he formally resigned his numerous Government posts. He had by then only a little more than six months of fretful and pain-ridden life remaining to him. He died on January 29, 1946.

❦

If the experience of mankind in the twentieth century were to prove little else, it has proven that man's capacity to destroy man has grown geometrically. During the Walpurgis Night of World War II, horror succeeded horror. The concentration camp with its apparatus for the systematic ex-

termination of humans reduced genocide to a ledger book of cost and profit. The bombing of cities not only leveled them but eliminated the distinctions between soldier and civilian, for by war's end, it was no longer certain whether the front lines or the rear areas were safer. The firestorms that consumed 135,000 lives in Dresden, Germany, on the night of February 13-14, 1945, and 83,793 Tokyo residents on the night of March 9-10, 1945, fulfilled the wildest expectations of those who had preached that inflicting terror from the skies upon the enemy would assure victory. But this was as nothing compared to what was to come. In a single moment of August 6, 1945, the explosion of an atomic bomb over Hiroshima, Japan, released a force equivalent to 16,000 tons of TNT, wiping out the lives of 71,379 residents. Three days later, a second atom bomb exploded over Nagasaki killing more than 30,000 men, women, and children. Six days later, the Emperor of Japan decreed surrender and with it World War II had ended.

But the callous inhumanity of man to man revealed during the war posed ethical and moral questions of the most fundamental nature. Not the least of these has been whether the use of the atomic bomb was necessary to force Japan to its knees. The man who ordered its use, Harry S. Truman, believed it necessary, and he remains convinced that his order saved lives. Others such as our former ambassador to Tokyo, Joseph Grew, wondered whether a "categorical" guarantee of the Emperor system would have eliminated the need to use the weapon. Others wonder whether a demonstration of the weapon in some remote, uninhabited or cleared spot would have proven sufficient to convince the Japanese leaders of the futility of continued resistance.

To answer these questions, Herbert Feis (1893-   ), long an economic adviser to the State Department, has examined Japan's decision to surrender. He possesses unimpeachable credentials since his previous diplomatic histories of World War II have explored The China Tangle *(1953),* The Road to Pearl Harbor *(1950), and the complex relations among the Grand Alliance of Russia, Great Britain, and the United States during World War II. They are basic sources to which all future historians will have to turn when treating of the subjects. The same methodical exploration of available evidence which informed his earlier works along with the balanced judgments he draws are evident in his investigation of Japan's decision to surrender. From the web of evidence, he draws the uncertain conclusion that there was probably little else the American government could have done to avoid use of the atomic bomb.*

Since Hiroshima, the destructive capacities of modern weaponry has continued to escalate; their use might well lead to the extinction of mankind. But no amount of historical analysis can answer whether mankind will choose to use them. It can, however, state precisely the issue facing mankind. In the course of telling his story, Feis explains how Hiroshima was chosen to substitute for the original target of Kyoto originally favored by American military leaders. It seems that "one evening during the early spring of 1945, a young man in uniform, son of an old friend, who was a devoted student of Oriental history came to dinner with the Stimsons

[Henry Stimson was the Secretary of War]. The young man fell to talking about the past glories of Kyoto, and of the loveliness of the old imperial residences. . . . Stimson was moved to consult a history which told of the time when Kyoto was the capital and to look through a collection of photographs of scenes and sites in the city. Thereupon he decided that this one Japanese city should be preserved from the holocaust." Feis concludes with a question: "To what anonymous young man may each of the rest of us owe our lives?" As we live under the shadow of thermonuclear self-destruction, may we not even wonder whether there will be another anonymous young man to plead for us?

JAPAN SUBDUED

by Herbert Feis

May 1945. The war in Europe was over. The members of the coalition were about to enter upon joint occupation and control of Germany. The Charter of the United Nations was being conceived at San Francisco. Truman, Churchill, and Stalin had agreed to confer about the many unsettled European situations.

Japan, all alone, was fighting on. The United States was assembling ever larger forces—army, navy, and air—for the next great actions in the Pacific. The Soviet government was transporting divisions to the Far East for deployment along the Manchurian frontier. The British Commonwealth was planning the expulsion of the Japanese from the south Pacific and southeast Asia. The Chinese were getting ready to start a march toward the coast in the Canton-Hong Kong area, to be their first offensive since their country was invaded.

The structure of Japanese life and production was being smashed and burned. The Japanese Navy and Air Force were but remnants of what they had been. But the spirit of defiance was still alive in the armed services and among the people—unwavering in their acceptance of suffering and the sad stroke of death. In Okinawa over one hundred thousand Japanese, hunted with mortar and fire, shelled from the sea and bombed from the air, were refusing to give up. Japanese suicide planes were flinging themselves in exalted desperation against the off-shore American fleet—with frightening effect. These grim experiences were taken as proof that the ordeal still ahead might be long and agonizing.

How could it be ended surely and quickly? The American managers of the war were giving thought to three sets of measures, all of which were being shaped for use.

The obvious and perhaps most certain way was to beat down the Japanese until they could no longer fight on—by enlarging the assaults on Japan and Japanese armed forces wherever they could be reached, by air and sea and on land, culminating in the invasion of the Japanese home islands.

Another was by inducement. The Japanese might agree to submit before they were utterly crushed if the coalition (including perhaps the Soviet Union, not yet at war with Japan) informed them how they would be regarded in defeat. Might not even this hardy nation, if assured of tolerable treatment after surrender, be brought to give up before it was reduced to the last extreme of misery? Might not the elements who knew the war was lost prevail, if a promise was given the Japanese people that after their means of making war were broken, they would be allowed to re-engage in peaceful pursuits, determine their own political forms and future, and that their fighting men would not be kept in long captivity?

The third, most secret, was by shock. The Japanese might be awed into surrender when they found out that a refusal could lead only to utter destruction—because their enemies had an irresistible new weapon and the Soviet Union was joining them.

Each of these routes could lead to the end of the war; or two or three of them could do so, in combination or in succession. Within the American government each had its own group of activators who nursed their plans and evolved their policies more or less separately from the others. The three were conjoined only in fitful and irregular consultation between the men in the small circle of ultimate decision-makers, and with the President.

The ideas of the heads of the military organization—the Joint Chiefs of Staff and top commanders of our forces—were centered on strategic plans for the advancement of the assaults by sea, land, and air on going lines, and in preparations for the next greater operations. Although not opposed to trying, they thought it unlikely that promises of leniency could induce surrender until the Japanese armed forces were thoroughly subdued. Some officials in the State Department had long been advocating an appeal to the preservative sense of the Japanese people before the struggle reached its portended climax. Secretary of War Stimson joined them in June. However, he conceived the exposition of our intentions as an accompaniment to an ultimate warning of destruction, fused by the atomic bomb. He was Chairman of the small group (known as the Interim Committee) who knew most about the progress and potentialities of this emergent secret weapon, and hoped that its burst would bring the war to an almost instant end.

*   *   *   *   *

The prime incentive of the effort to make an atomic bomb had been to assure and hasten the defeat of Germany. But as the great dimensions of the task became apparent and hard new problems were met, the President and his scientific advisers in 1944 had been compelled to face the fact that the war against Germany might be over before the bomb was achieved. Yet they decided that it was imperative to carry on with unlessened intensity because of the wish to have the bomb to use against Japan and the prospect that rival countries would turn to the same task.

All this time the group who knew most about the progress in the making of the atomic bomb nursed the thought that this weapon, climaxing other destructive assaults, might do what they did not think a promise of fair treatment would do—cause the Japanese to surrender even before the expeditionary force set out for the invasion of Japan.

As early as September 1944, Vannevar Bush and James B. Conant, the two scientists who headed the governmental research effort, had foretold in a letter to the Secretary of War that atomic weapons would be of great importance by the summer of 1945. They predicted that the advantage which the United States had was temporary and might well disappear or even be reversed because essential knowledge in the field was so widespread.

On December 30, 1944, the Commanding General, Manhattan District Project, Leslie R. Groves, in a report to Marshall had repeated his prediction of the success of the enormous secret effort to make an explosive weapon which would use the energy of fissured atoms. The first paragraph read:

"It is now reasonably certain that our operation plans should be based on the *gun type bomb*, which, it is estimated, will produce the equivalent of a ten thousand ton TNT explosion. The first bomb, with our previous full scale test which we do not believe will be necessary, *should be ready about 1 August 1945*. The second one should be ready by the end of the year and succeeding ones at . . . intervals thereafter."

Groves had then gone on to state that "Our previous hopes that an implosion (compression) type of bomb might be developed *in the late spring* have now been dissipated by scientific difficulties which we have not as yet been able to solve. The present effects of these difficulties are that more material will be required and that the material will be less efficiently used." But he believed that *"We should have sufficient material for the first implosion type bomb sometime in the latter part of July"* and more during the rest of 1945. He anticipated that the explosive force of the first specimen of this implosion type would be equivalent to about 500 tons of TNT, and that the effectiveness of those to follow should increase toward 1000 tons and, if some problems were solved, to as much as 2500 tons. In this great underestimate he had at the time the company of many of the engaged scientists.

Groves had also reported that while the current plan of operations was based on the (presumed) more certain and more powerful gun type bomb it also provided for the use of the implosion type bombs when they became available. A special air group had been organized which was assisting in essential tests and being trained to use these bombs. Therefore he asked Marshall whether the time had not come to acquaint various senior officers of the Army, Air Force, and Navy of the project so that they might proceed with necessary preparatory plans.

President Roosevelt had approved this measure about a month before he left for Yalta. The work had gone apace; and on March 15th Stimson had told the President when it was likely that specimens of the new weapon would be in hand, and had stressed the need to prepare for the event. And on March 23rd Sir James Chadwick, the British technical adviser to the Combined (U. S.-British) Policy Committee on Atomic Affairs which had been formed in Washington, had been impressed enough by what the Americans told him to inform Sir John Anderson, the Cabinet Minister in charge of the British part in the project, that it was "as certain as such things can be that the weapon would be ready in the later summer."

Stimson had continued to follow each advance intently, noting in his Diary after a visit to the works in Tennessee in early April that although "success is ninety-nine percent assured, yet only by the first actual war trial of the weapon can the actual certainty be fixed." About this time reports that the Germans had an active establishment for making atomic weapons in an area located in the zone of occupation to be assigned to France caused a tremor of alarm to run through the American government. But this news turned out to be false.

During the last month before his death, Roosevelt had ruminated over this impending development, trying to discern how it might be made to serve the cause of enduring peace and international cooperation. But he had come to no positive conclusions.

Within an hour of Truman's induction into office (on April 12th), Stimson had lingered after the first Cabinet meeting to tell him briefly of the immense undertaking under way. Byrnes, who had been Director of War Mobilization, soon thereafter had advised him in quiet tones which did not entirely disguise the note of awe, that the explosive being perfected was powerful enough to destroy the whole world. Vannevar Bush, Director of the Office of Scientific Research and Development (known as OSRD), had presented a special technical account of the operation for his information.

On April 23rd Groves, in a report prepared for the President, had confirmed his forecast that the weapon would be ready "within four months, that is by the end of August at the latest." Thereupon, Stimson determined that the new President ought to be thinking ahead far harder than he seemed to be about the use and control of the weapon. Truman asked him to come to the White House Executive Office at noon on the 25th. The budget of news that morning was exciting. The Conference at San Francisco was about to open. The American and Russian troops were shaking hands on the Elbe. The Americans had at last broken the impasse in the struggle for Okinawa. And before him was a message from Stalin about the quarrel over Poland ". . . which showed plainly that Churchill and I were going to have persistent, calculated resistance from Stalin in our dealings with the Russians."

Stimson, making use of Groves' report, wrote a memo which he showed to Marshall. He agreed with its facts and analysis. To escape possible notice by the watchful reporters, Stimson came into the Executive Office by the front door and Groves by the side door. Together they persuaded the President to persist in his perusal of the memo from the first paragraph to the last. At the end Truman seemed to his visitors impressed but not astounded. The first paragraph affirmed that "Within four months we shall in all probability have completed the most terrible weapon ever known in human history, one bomb of which could destroy a whole city."

The question of whether or not this foreknowledge might assist us in our diplomatic relations with other countries, particularly the Soviet Union, he left to the consideration of the President and the State Department. But

Stimson and his military associates felt main responsibility under the President for the decision, whether, when and how the new weapon should be used in the war against Japan, and in connection with what strategy.

And beyond these urgent questions loomed a cluster of still greater ones. What would the command of controlled atomic force mean in the future to mankind, to the nature of international society and the question of war and peace? "The world," Stimson predicted, ". . . would be eventually at the mercy of such a weapon. . . ." Its control "will undoubtedly be a matter of the greatest difficulty and would involve such thoroughgoing rights of inspection and internal controls as we have never heretofore contemplated. Furthermore, in the light of our present position with reference to this weapon, the question of sharing it with other nations and, if so shared, upon what terms, becomes a primary question of our foreign relations. Also our leadership in the war and in the development of this weapon has placed a certain moral responsibility upon us which we cannot shirk without very serious responsibility for any disaster to civilization which it would further. On the other hand, if the problem of the proper use of this weapon can be solved, we would have the opportunity to bring the world into a pattern in which the peace of the world and our civilization can be saved."

After these solemn observations about the profound significance for human affairs of this new force, Stimson had sought the President's approval for the formation of a committee to consider the whole range of questions —political, military and scientific—which would arise in connection with the eventual disclosure of the project, and the question of the use of the weapon. The Secretary of War conceived that this group would make recommendations to the Executive and Legislative branches of our government.

The Committee, which became known as the Interim Committee, was constituted at once. The President and Stimson decided, in order to assure and indicate that all aspects of the development would be considered, that this group should be entirely civilian; for this reason not even General Groves was included. Stimson was the Chairman. Byrnes was chosen by the President to represent him. The other members were the Under Secretary of the Navy, Ralph A. Bard, Assistant Secretary of State, William L. Clayton, a specialist in international trade who, however, took a vocative part in the work of the Committee, and three scientists who were doing significant work in the direction of the project, Vannevar Bush, the Director of OSRD, James B. Conant, Chairman of the National Defense Research Committee, and Karl T. Compton, Chief of the Office of Field Service in the OSRD. George Harrison, appropriately or ironically as the impression may be, President of the New York Life Insurance Company, was selected as Secretary and acted as Chairman when Stimson was absent. Subsequently, an Advisory Panel of scientists was also formed. They were J. Robert Oppenheimer, Director of the Los Alamos Laboratory, Arthur H. Compton, Director of what was called the Metallurgical Laboratory of Chicago, Ernest O. Lawrence, Director of the Berkeley Radiation Laboratory, and Enrico Fermi, who had been in charge of the first controlled chain reaction experiment, all physicists who had made and were making great theoretical contributions to the conception and production of the new weapon. Stimson, in daily consultation with his able Assistant Secretary of War McCloy, and General Marshall, tended to direct the work of the Committee although he was not present in person at all of their meetings.

It had met informally for the first time on May 9th. During the following weeks, while its members were sorting out their thoughts, the scientists engaged in the design of the bomb strove harder than ever to make sure that it would be in hand by summer. As recalled by Robert Oppenheimer, "The deadline never changed. It was as soon as possible"; and "After the collapse of Germany, we [the scientists] understood that it was important to get this ready for the war in Japan. We were told that it would be very important to know the state of affairs before the meeting at Potsdam at which the future conduct of the war in the Far East would be discussed." Haste was deemed more important than perfection. Again as remembered by Oppenheimer, ". . . I did suggest to General Groves some changes in bomb design which would make more efficient use of the material. . . . He turned them down as jeopardizing the promptness of the availability of bombs."

Concurrently Stimson was keeping the British well informed. On April 30th Field Marshal Sir H. M. Wilson, Head of the British Joint Staff Mission in Washington and a member of the Combined Policy Committee on the Atomic Bomb, let Anderson know that "the Americans propose to drop a bomb sometime in August." Wilson then went on to raise two connected questions: "Do we agree that the weapon should be used against the Japanese? If for any reason we did not, the matter would presumably have to be raised by the Prime Minister with the President. If we do agree, various points still arise on which it would be desirable to have consultation with the Americans. . . . Whether any warning should be given to the Japanese."

On May 14th Stimson reviewed for Anthony Eden, the Secretary of State for Foreign Affairs, who was in Washington, what had been achieved and told him of the then current time-table for production and testing of the bomb. But Churchill loitered in his response and instruction to Field Marshal Wilson. Was it only because of the crush of business following the German surrender? Or was he skeptical about the scientists' predictions? Or was he merely puzzled over the decisions that would leap up around the flame and smoke as soon as the weapon was proven? Whatever the reason, Churchill, who was communicating with the President every day about the unsettled situation in Europe, did not enter into direct personal discussion with him about this great impending occurrence until they met in Potsdam.

Meanwhile the Interim Committee was formulating its answers to various crucial questions which were recorded in conclusive language after the meeting held on May 31–June 1. By then, it will be remembered, the Joint Chiefs of Staff had determined on their plans of invasion and the President had decided to defer any extensive exposition of our intentions toward Japan until he met with Churchill and Stalin in mid-July.

No complete or consecutive record of the discussion at this or other sessions of the Interim Committee was kept, only some summary notes and brief statements of conclusions. I have tried to supplement these by talk or correspondence with several of the members. But, nursed as they were on truth, time has attenuated their memories. What one man recalls clearly another has forgotten; what one emphasizes as a focus of discussion, another hardly remembers as having been considered; what one believes to have been an accepted view, another doubts.

The discussion started in the morning of the 31st, the Scientific Panel being present, and continued at lunch; then that Panel retired for an hour or two while the members of the Committee talked among themselves, after which it rejoined the Committee. On the next day the Interim Committee met with the other Advisory Panel, four industrialists whose companies had carried out important work in the engineering and operation of the great plants at Oak Ridge and Hanford (W. S. Carpenter, Jr., of Dupont, George H. Bucher of Westinghouse, James White of Tennessee Eastman, and James Rafferty of Union Carbide). When they left, the Committee agreed on several main conclusions.

Before outlining the area within which the group was being asked for its judgment, Stimson summarized his ideas about the nature and meaning of the great joint achievement. He was bent on making the scientists understand that he and Marshall did not regard it merely as a new weapon but as a revolutionary change in the relation of man to the universe, with more effect on human affairs than the theory of Copernicus and the law of gravity. So he stressed his realization that success in utilizing the energy of the atom would mean either the doom or perfection of civilization; it might turn out to be a Frankenstein's monster that would devour all or a blessing that would make the world secure. How, under ruling conditions of state and society, could it best be developed, used, and controlled? Marshall spoke to the same effect.

In the first phase of the ensuing discussion to which A. H. Compton, Fermi, Conant, and Oppenheimer contributed, three stages in the development of the bomb were differentiated. The first was the production of enough U-235 for the type of bomb already mastered; this type, it was reckoned, would have an explosive force equivalent to anywhere between 2000 and 20,000 tons of TNT. The second was the production of enriched materials from which plutonium or new kinds of uranium could be obtained; a bomb containing these materials, it was reckoned, would develop an explosive force of between 50,000 and 100,000 tons of TNT. In the third, and more remote stage, in which the product of the second would be used as a detonator of heavy water, it was considered possible that the resulting weapon might produce an explosive force equal to 10 million up to even 100 million tons of TNT. It is not to be wondered that the reflections of those whom history had placed within the chamber of responsibility for the employment and control of these weapons were somber.

After these explanatory presentations the Committee and the Advisory

Panel of Scientists were consulted about a wide range of problems posed by the prospect of possession of the bomb. Of these, two in particular have a place in this narrative:

1) How was the new source of explosive power and energy to be controlled internationally; and in that connection how much should be revealed to the world, especially to the Russians, about the nature and method of production of the new weapon?

2) How was the bomb to be used in the war against Japan? The recommendations sponsored by the Committee confirmed the ideas favored by the few officials who had the actual power and ultimate responsibility for decision: Truman, Stimson, Marshall, Byrnes.

About the first of these questions, as Stimson had told Roosevelt in their last talk, there were two views, ". . . one of them being the secret close-in attempted control of the project by those who control it now, and the other being the international control based upon freedom both of science and of access."

Proponents of the first course were supposing that if the Russians were compelled to duplicate our achievement by themselves it would take them a long time to do so, while proponents of the other course believed that they would be able to do so in a few years. At an earlier meeting of the Interim Committee there had been great differences in the individual surmises about this question. The wish to have other expert opinion was one of the reasons why the Interim Committee had invited the Scientific Panel to meet with it on May 31–June 1, and the chief reason for the presence of the other Advisory Panel of four industrialists.

But the forecasts again scattered widely. Those ventured by the industrialists ranged from five to ten years if the Soviet Union had to rely on its own talent and resources; quicker if it was aided by German scientists, engineers, and production experts. General Groves, deeply impressed by the difficulties that had to be overcome in the manufacture of the weapon and perhaps poorly informed of Soviet capacity for industrial achievement, seems to have made the longest estimate. The surmises of the members of the Scientific Panel scattered cautiously over a shorter period. Byrnes has subsequently recalled the general impression which he derived from this phase of the discussion. "Because it was a vital point in any decision on a system of control, I asked both groups how long it might take other governments to produce atomic bombs. The question, of course, was not only one of physics, but one of materials, of engineering skills, of technical know-how and many other factors. From all the information we received, I concluded that any other government would need from seven to ten years, at least, to produce a bomb."

Bearing on the problems of control and international collaboration, the question of what could be expected of the Soviet government again brought forth a diversity of opinions. Oppenheimer suggested that we ought not to prejudge the Soviet attitude, and that we might start tentative and general discussions with them, while not disclosing details of our productive effort. Marshall also seemed hopeful that the Russians might be cooperative. In regard to the direction of policy in the atomic weapons field, he was inclined to favor the formation of a combination among like-minded powers, bringing Russia into line by force of this coalition. And he raised the question whether it might be advisable to invite two prominent Russian scientists to witness the anticipated test. But Byrnes remarked that he was afraid that if any information were given the Russians, even in general terms, they would ask to be brought into partnership with us and the British.

The talk was then directed to the other great question Stimson had in mind. The morning before the Committee met, Stimson had once again talked over with Marshall, Groves, Harrison, and Bundy ". . . how we should use this implement in respect of Japan." *How* not *whether*, the reader will note; and it was about how and not whether that the Committee and the Scientific Panel were consulted in the discussions that began the next day. As related by one of the members of the Scientific Panel: "Throughout the morning's discussions it seemed a foregone conclusion that the bomb would be used."

That had been the impelling purpose from the start. Stimson was counting on the new weapon to bring the war to an end "before the locking of arms came and much bloodshed." To all engaged in its development that was a conclusive justification for its use—to cause Japan to surrender as quickly as possible, and so end the agony and loss of lives, American and Japanese.

No one challenged the use of the bomb against an unwarned and vulnerable target in Japan if that was the only way to achieve this commanding purpose. But thought was given to possible ways of effecting it in some more sparing fashion. Two of those discussed were: to give an informative advance notice of the nature and destructive power of the new weapon; and/or give a demonstrative detonation of it in some uninhabited area. Regrettably the available records and reminiscences do not enable the historian to determine for himself whether these and other possibilities were "carefully considered" as Stimson thought, or to tell with assurance the reasons why all were discarded. . . .

At the end of this afternoon session (on May 31), after the discussion of various targets and the effects to be produced, Secretary Stimson expressed the conclusion, on which there was general agreement, that we could not give the Japanese any warning; that we could not concentrate on a civilian area; but that we should seek to make a profound psychological impression on as many of the Japanese as possible.

The members of the Interim Committee (on June 1, at the end of the two-day consultation with the two panels) deemed their examination thorough enough to state conclusive opinions. After Byrnes so proposed, they unanimously adopted three recommendations:

(1) The bomb should be used against Japan as soon as possible.

The Committee by this time knew the order in which, and the schedule on which, the two different types of bomb were being completed. It had in mind the arrangements for shipping the components of one type—the type that was used at Hiroshima—to the Pacific while preparations were being made to test the other type at Alamogordo.

The wish to cast the bomb into the scale of war as quickly as could be was stimulated by the hope of suspending the transfer of American youth to the Pacific and by the wish to dispel the vision of an embattled landing in small boats on the shores of Japan. Whether it was also animated by a desire to end the war before the Soviet armies had swarmed over Manchuria, remains a matter of conjecture. Maybe so, although the American government was counting on Soviet entry into the war to supplement the impact of the atomic bomb—together to compel recognition that instant surrender was the only way to avert extinction.

(2) The bomb should be used on a dual target—that is, on a military installation or war plant surrounded by or adjacent to houses and other buildings most susceptible to damage.

It was thought that the experienced effect of the bomb on such a target would make the maximum impression on the military and civilian members of the Japanese government who would decide whether to yield to our demand for unconditional surrender. Any other course was deemed by Stimson and his associates on the Interim Committee to involve a ". . . serious danger to the major objective of obtaining a prompt surrender from the Japanese."

(3) It should be used without explicit prior warning of the nature of the weapon by which we meant to enforce the call to surrender.

The reason later given by Stimson for this conclusion was that "Even the New Mexico test would not give final proof that any given bomb was certain to explode when dropped from an airplane. Quite apart from the generally unfamiliar nature of atomic explosives, there was the whole problem of exploding a bomb at a predetermined height in the air by a complicated mechanism which could not be tested in the static test of New Mexico."

This uncertainty remained although even by this time varied tests had been made in flight with a simulated bomb casing and components, and the proximity fuse. The detonation mechanism of the atomic explosion in one of the two kinds of bomb—the gun type—had been so often tried and had so proven itself that there could be very little doubt of its effectiveness under circumstances of use. But the more complicated and delicate mechanism in the other kind—the implosion type—could not be adequately tested under ordinary flight conditions until several weeks later.

The responsible group was also influenced by the opinion, to which I shall revert, that prior divulgence of the nature of the new weapon would hinder rather than serve our wish to end the war at once. For it was deemed unlikely that this would cause the Japanese to surrender, and that it might lessen the effect of the bomb when it was dropped; unexplained, it would be the more fearsome.

Byrnes at once acquainted the President with the recommendations of the Committee. He explained them against the background of the plans sponsored by the Joint Chiefs of Staff, which contemplated the invasion and its many, many casualties. At the end of this talk the President ". . . expressed the opinion that, regrettable as it might be, so far as he could see, the only reasonable conclusion was to use the bomb."

On June 6th Stimson gave the President a more systematic account of the conclusions arrived at by the Interim Committee. The ensuing talk focused on two connected sets of questions. One was what should be told the Soviet government, and whether, by offering the Soviet Union partnership in the development of this great new force, we might cause it to be more amenable in some current troubling issues, such as Poland. The other was how it might be controlled in the future. In that regard, Stimson reported that the Committee had been able to make only one suggestion. The American government should take the lead in securing an accord between the nations whereunder each and all would be obligated to make public any work done in the atomic field, and in the formation of an international committee with power to conduct adequate and continuous inspection in all countries. He said he favored such an effort, but foresaw that Russia might not be willing to submit to a satisfactory system of control. Until that was established, however, he thought that the American government should not reveal how the weapon was made and should proceed to accumulate enough fissionable material and weapons "as insurance against being caught helpless."

Soon thereafter, a number of scientists in Chicago who had contributed to the conception of the bomb, having learned of the recommendations of the Interim Committee, revolted against the way the result of their work was to be used. After days of agitated talk the Chicago scientists' committee (known as the Franck Committee) sponsored a memo which was hurried to Washington. Since Stimson was out of town it was left with Harrison. Its import can be conveyed from a few extracts.

"It could be suggested that the danger of destruction by nuclear weapons can be avoided—at least as far as this country is concerned—either by keeping our discoveries secret for an indefinite time, or else by developing our nuclear armaments at such a pace that no other nations would think of attacking us from fear of overwhelming retaliation.

"The answer to the first suggestion is that . . . the fundamental facts of nuclear power are a subject of common knowledge. . . . In Russia, too, the basic facts and implications of nuclear power were well understood in 1940, and the experience of Russian scientists in nuclear research is entirely sufficient to enable them to retrace our steps within a few years, even if we should make every attempt to conceal them. . . .

". . . [as for] the second of the two suggestions. . . . The answer is that all that these advantages can give us is the accumulation of a larger number of bigger and better atomic bombs.

"However, such a quantitative advantage in reserves of bottled destructive power will not make us safe from sudden attack. . . . In no other type of warfare does the advantage lie so heavily with the aggressor. . . .

"One possible way to introduce nuclear weapons to the world—which may particularly appeal to those who consider nuclear bombs primarily as a secret weapon developed to help with the present war—is to use them without warning on appropriately selected objects in Japan. . . .

"Russia, and even allied countries which bear less mistrust of our ways and intentions, as well as neutral countries may be deeply shocked by this step. . . . It is not at all certain that American public opinion, if it could be enlightened as to the effect of atomic explosives, would approve of our own country being the first to introduce such an indiscriminate method of wholesale destruction of civilian life.

"Thus, from the 'optimistic' point of view—looking forward to an international agreement on the prevention of nuclear warfare—the military advantages and the saving of American lives achieved by the sudden use of atomic bombs against Japan may be outweighed by the ensuing loss of confidence and by a wave of horror and repulsion sweeping over the rest of the world and perhaps even dividing public opinion at home.

"From this point of view, a demonstration of the new weapon might best be made, before the eyes of representatives of all the United Nations, on the desert or a barren island.

"After such a demonstration the weapon might perhaps be used against Japan if the sanction of the United Nations (and of public opinion at home) were obtained, perhaps after a preliminary ultimatum to Japan to surrender or at least to evacuate certain regions as an alternative to their total destruction. . . .

"It must be stressed that if one takes the pessimistic point of view and discounts the possibility of an effective international control over nuclear weapons at the present time, then the advisability of an early use of nuclear bombs against Japan becomes even more doubtful—quite independently of any humanitarian considerations. If an international agreement is not concluded immediately after the first demonstration, this will mean a flying start toward an unlimited armaments race. . . .

"(In summary) We believe that these considerations make the use of nuclear bombs for an early unannounced attack against Japan inadvisable. . . .

"If the government should decide in favor of an early demonstration of nuclear weapons, it will then have the possibility of taking into account the public opinion of this country and of the other nations before deciding whether these weapons should be used against Japan. In this way, other nations may assume a share of responsibility for such a fateful decision."

The views expounded in this memorandum were considered by the Scientific Panel of the Interim Committee in a special meeting at Los Alamos. In the responsive formal report which the Panel submitted to Stimson on June 16th they stated, albeit with some regret or misgiving:

"Introductory: You have asked us to comment on the initial use of the new weapon. This use, in our opinion, should be such as to promote a satisfactory adjustment of our international relations. At the same time, we recognize our obligations to our nation to use the weapons to help save American lives in the Japanese War.

"To accomplish these ends we recommend that before the weapons are used not only Britain, but also Russia, France and China be advised that we would welcome suggestions as to how we can cooperate in making this development contribute to improved international relations.

"The opinions of our scientific colleagues on the initial use of these weapons are not unanimous; they range from the proposal of a purely technical demonstration to that of military application best designed to induce surrender. Those who advocate a purely technical demonstration would wish to outlaw the use of atomic weapons, and have feared that if we use the weapons now our position in future negotiations will be prejudiced. Others emphasize the opportunity of saving American lives by immediate military use, and believe that such use will improve the international prospects, in that they are more concerned with the prevention of war than with the elimination of this special weapon.

"We find ourselves closer to these latter views; we can propose no technical demonstration likely to bring an end to the war; we can see no acceptable alternative to direct military use."

Here we may pause in our narrative to comment on the nature of some of the issues raised by the Franck Committee and of some of the comments related to these issues in the report of the Scientific Panel.

Some of the matters reviewed in the Franck memo were within the professional knowledge of its sponsors; notably how long it might take other countries, particularly the Soviet Union, to produce the bomb; and what would be the effect, if measured in comparison to the effect of tons of TNT, of the detonation of the bomb (20,000 tons, it was forecast). They turned out to be roughly correct, remarkably so, in fact, since the group were not involved in the industrial effort which had gone into the production of the components of the bomb. The members of the Scientific Panel, while not endorsing these judgments of probabilities, did not dissent from them.

The recommendations in the Franck memo were also in part derived from or supported by opinions concerning some matters about which its authors could at best venture only bold guesses. Such for example was the degree of risk of failure of a demonstration of the bomb mechanism when dropped from a moving airplane under hazard of weather and enemy interference. Another was how great and impressive the effect of the bomb would be if used in a demonstration on a barren island, or desert, or at sea.

But the supporting exposition in the Franck memo roamed far beyond the realm of scientific knowledge, and the advice proffered was supported by surmises concerning human behavior about which neither the Franck group nor the Scientific Panel were especially informed or qualified. They ranged over the whole political and military landscape and beyond the visible horizon. That the Chicago group was aware of this is indicated by the fact that they called themselves "A committee on Social and Political Implications."

Would a demonstration have enough impact on the Japanese ruling group to cause them to submit to our demand for unconditional surrender? Would it be impressive enough to dispose other nations to enter into an agreement which would avert a competitive race in the production of atomic weapons, and confine this new force by a reliable international accord? Would it convince nations that in order to survive they would genuinely have to renounce war? Or to achieve any or all of these imperative purposes was it necessary to give undeniable proof, in the brutal ledger of life and death, of the tremendous destructive power that men could now command and use against each other?

Such interrelated elements of the problem of decision were not in the scientific realm. What the Scientific Panel had to say about them could only have been personal impressions, influenced to an unknown degree by pertinent but not conclusive views about physical components of the problem. That the members of the Scientific Panel were aware that this was so is evidenced in another section of the report they submitted:

"With regard to these general aspects of the use of atomic energy it is clear that we, as scientific men, have no proprietary rights. . . . We have . . . no claim to special competence in solving the political, social and military problems which are presented by the advent of atomic power."

Oppenheimer, the chief drafter of the Report of the Panel, reminiscently testified, "We didn't know beans about the military situation in Japan. We didn't know whether they could be caused to surrender by other means or whether the invasion was really inevitable. But in back of our minds was the notion that the invasion was inevitable because we had been told that. . . . We thought the two overriding considerations were the saving of lives in the war and the effect of our actions on the stability, on the strength and the stability, of the postwar world. We did say that we did not think exploding one of these things as a firecracker over a desert was likely to be very impressive. This was before we had actually done that. The destruction on the desert is zero. . . ."

It would be a mistake to attribute the decision to use the bomb against a genuine target primarily to the advice of the Scientific Panel. Stimson and other members of the Interim Committee had reached this conclusion previously, and the opinion of the Scientific Panel was just confirmatory. For, as tersely recalled by Stimson, "The conclusions of the Committee were similar to my own, although I reached mine independently. I felt that to extract a genuine surrender from the Emperor and his military advisers, they must be administered a tremendous shock which would carry convincing proof of our power to destroy the Empire. Such an effective shock would save many times the number of lives, both American and Japanese, that it would cost."

During the following weeks Stimson and Groves strove their utmost to hurry the completion of the arrangements for the test of the bomb in New Mexico and for its use against Japan. When, during the meeting at the White House on June 18th, Stimson was called on to comment on the proposed invasion plan, he said that he accepted it as the best thing to do "but he still hoped for some fruitful accomplishment through other means." On that same day, after protracted delay in dealing with the subject, Churchill instructed Field Marshal Wilson to find out from Stimson and Marshall whether and by what route they intended to consult the British government in regard to the use of the new weapon. Wilson learned that they intended soon to approach the British "as to the best means of recording concurrence by His Majesty's Government to the operational employment of an [atomic weapon]." For unexplained reasons it was agreed that "the most satisfactory procedure" would be to record the decision in a Minute of the Combined Policy Committee, whose next meeting was due to be held on July 4th, rather than through the Combined Chiefs of Staff.

On July 2nd—during which interval Stimson had again reviewed the plans for testing the bomb in New Mexico and for its use against Japan with Wilson and Makins of the British Embassy—the British Embassy in Washington received a message from Anderson reading, "Prime Minister has approved my proposal that agreement to decision to use Weapon should be recorded at next meeting of [the Combined Policy] Committee. Prime Minister mentioned that he would naturally wish to discuss this matter with President at 'TERMINAL' [the Potsdam Conference] and that it would be as well that Committee should take note of this."

Whatever the nature of Churchill's reserved thought, the British and Canadian representatives on the Combined Policy Committee recorded their concurrence on July 4th. Present at this meeting besides the members of the Committee: Stimson, Field Marshal Wilson, Hon. C. D. Howe (Canadian Minister of Munitions) and Dr. Vannevar Bush, there were the Earl of Halifax (British Ambassador to the United States), Sir James Chadwick, General Groves and George Harrison, and the Joint Secretaries, Harvey Bundy and Roger Makins. Field Marshal Wilson stated that the British government concurred in the use of the T.A. weapon against Japan. He added that the Prime Minister might wish to discuss this matter with the President at the forthcoming meeting in Berlin. The Minutes record that:

"The Committee: Took note that the Governments of the United Kingdom and the United States had agreed that T.A. [for the code designation Tube Alloy] weapons should be used by the United States against Japan. . . ."

British acquiescence in American plans thus seems to have been almost a matter of course. For this the official British historian, who presumably has seen many if not all of the British records of discussions within the British government and with the Americans, has offered several explanations: (1) that the United States had played the main part in the conduct of the war in the Pacific and had made the greatest contribution; (2) that the decision as to the use of the bomb against Japan was deemed by the British authorities to be in the field of military operations against that country, and as such, primarily one for the U. S. Joint Chiefs to decide; and (3) that the British share in the partnership which led to the production of the bomb was limited. As summed up in this account: "The balance of power, both in the atomic project and in the Pacific, lay too heavily with the United States for the British to be able, or to wish, to participate in this decision. They therefore preferred to acquiesce in it without more ado, relying on talks between the President and the Prime Minister at Potsdam to learn the reasons for it and to influence if need be, the manner of its execution."

It is likely, moreover, that Churchill and at least some of his advisers, civil and military, were swayed by the thought that the same bomb which upset the Japanese rulers would also impress the Soviet authorities.

The American group, headed by Truman and Byrnes, was scheduled to leave two days later by ship for the Conference at Potsdam. Just before their departure Stimson told Byrnes that the President had agreed that he should fly over to join them. For by then it was known with virtual certainty that the crucial first test of the bomb would be made just as they were due to arrive at the conference site in Germany.

The Chiefs of Staff were the mentors of military plans to compel surrender by combined assault. The Secretary of State was custodian of the text of the Proclamation to be addressed to the Japanese people, telling them how they would fare if they surrendered, and warning them that they would be destroyed if they refused to heed the warning. The Secretary of War was the guardian of the hope that if the Japanese government disregarded this summons to surrender, we would be able to smite Japan so astounding a blow that it would have to yield at once. Never was a group so triply armed.

*   *   *   *   *

Beneath the relaxed formalities on board the U.S.S. *Augusta* there was the vibrant secret that an air group at Tinian was under orders to drop an atomic bomb on Japan on the first day in August that the weather permitted visual bombing. This event was awaited with subdued impatience.

The group at Tinian who were in readiness to drop the bomb had been compelled to wait out unfavorable weather over all of Japan during the first days of August. But reconnaissance planes which flew over the target area on the night of the 5th reported back that the prospect for the next day was better. The order was given to the planes to set forth on the historic mission.

At 2:45 on the morning of the 6th by the watches of the crew of the plane, the *Enola Gay*, which was carrying the bomb, started on the long flight from Tinian. It was followed closely by two observation planes which carried cameras, scientific instruments, and trained witnesses. The take-off was dangerous because the bomb load was heavy, and it took skillful piloting to gain the necessary upward lift even from the lengthened runways. Three other B-29's of other air groups had crashed in practice not long before.

The trip to Japan was smooth. Dawn over Japan was sultry but somewhat clear. About 7:00 o'clock (Hiroshima time) the Japanese early-warning radar net detected a small number of aircraft headed toward southern Japan, and a preliminary alert was sounded throughout the Hiroshima area. Soon afterwards an American weather plane circled over the city, but withdrew without bombing. So an "all clear" signal was sounded. The people began their daily activities thinking that the danger was passed.

At 8:00 Japanese watchers spotted two B-29's heading toward Hiroshima. The radio stations broadcast a warning advising the people to take shelter if these appeared over the city, adding, however, that the mission seemed to be one of reconnaissance rather than bombing. Most factory and office workers were already at their places of employment and those who were en route continued on their way. Many school children and some industrial workers were engaged in building firebreaks and evacuating valuables to the country. The two planes were seen in the skies over the urban area at high altitude. But since many of those below who watched their flight thought the intruders had come merely to reconnoiter, they did not heed the advice to seek protective shelter.

Aboard the *Enola Gay*, the assembly of the bomb had been completed, making it a "final bomb." Colonel Paul W. Tibbets, the pilot, received word from the weather plane near Hiroshima indicating that the chance of placing the bomb on the target was good. "This," to quote the Air Force official history, "sealed the city's doom." The *Enola Gay* swung into its purposeful run-in at 8:11. The bombardier, navigator, and radar operator took charge; the altitude was over 31,600 feet. The bomb was released. It was of the type different from that tested in New Mexico. It was known by its makers and attendants as the Lean Boy or Thin Boy. It contained uranium 235 as its fissionable material enclosed at the opposite ends of a gun barrel. The two sections of material were brought together in the critical mass and exploded by a proximity fuse when a gun mechanism at one end of the barrel shot the smaller of the two parts into the other.

The detonation had been timed to go off before the bomb hit the ground to increase the radius of the blast. There was a terrible explosion over the central section of the city. A white flash of blinding intensity was all that many saw before they were blown to bits or struck down by flying fragments, or burned by the wave of searing heat that flashed out from the explosion. A heavy cloud of smoke and dust spread, cloaking the city in a pall of darkness. Hundreds of fires breaking out everywhere soon transformed it into a blazing inferno and, as the fires kept on, into a waste of ashes and smoldering ruins. Those who had escaped with their lives, many of them burned, in agony and confusion sought refuge elsewhere.

The members of the crew of the *Enola Gay*, on their return to Tinian, had a far-away look in their eyes at the memory of what they had seen and when they tried to talk about it the words fell over one another.

On board the *Augusta*, while the President was at lunch with the crew in the mess hall, a rushed message was handed to him. "Big bomb dropped on Hiroshima August 5 at 7:15 P.M. Washington time. First reports indicate complete success which was even more conspicuous than earlier test." A few minutes later a corroborating report with more details came in. After reading these messages to Byrnes, he signaled to the men that he wanted them to listen to news he had just received. Leaving them clapping and cheering, he went to the wardroom to tell the naval officers of the great exploit. "I could not," he has recalled, "keep back my expectation that the Pacific War might now be brought to a speedy end."

In Washington, August 6th was rainy. As soon as Marshall got word the bomb had gone off, he telephoned Stimson who was at his home on Long Island. The President and the Secretary of War authorized the issuance to the press of the prepared statements. The tenor of these had been made more ominous after receipt of the reports of the New Mexico test. Presumably the involved British officials, possibly Churchill himself, were consulted about the final changes, since during the whole process of composition they had been given ample opportunity to comment and propose amendments.

The one over Truman's name made known that an atomic bomb had been dropped on the city of Hiroshima, an important Army base; and that it had more explosive power than twenty thousand tons of TNT. "It is an atomic bomb. It is a harnessing of the basic power of the universe. The force from which the sun draws its power has been loosed against those who brought war to the Far East."

Astounded and awed, the world read on to the closing lines: "It was to spare the Japanese people from utter destruction that the ultimatum of July 26 was issued at Potsdam. Their leaders promptly rejected that ultimatum. If they do not now accept our terms, they may expect a rain of ruin from the air, the like of which has never been seen on this earth. Behind this air attack will follow sea and land forces in such numbers and power as they have not yet seen, and with the fighting skill of which they are already well aware."

The President also used this most dramatic circumstance to tell the world how the American government proposed to deal with the new force which had been broken out of the atom, saying in part:

"It has never been the habit of the scientists of this country or the policy of this Government to withhold from the world scientific knowledge. Normally, therefore, everything about the work with atomic energy would be made public.

"But under present circumstances it is not intended to divulge the terminal process of production or all the military applications, pending further examination of possible methods of protecting us and the rest of the world from the danger of sudden destruction.

"I shall recommend that the Congress of the United States consider promptly the establishment of an appropriate commission to control the production and use of atomic power within the United States. I shall give further consideration and make further recommendations to the Congress as to how atomic power can become a powerful and forceful influence toward the maintenance of world peace."

◄§ §►

THE *fate that America managed to sidestep in 1919 overtook her after 1945. Whether she preferred it or not, she had the role of the dominant world power. Upon her military might depended the preservation of capitalism and self-government throughout a good part of the world. Though the guns fell silent with Japan's surrender on September 2, 1945, in the decades that have followed, the world has lived betwixt war and peace, a state popularly labeled the "cold war." In Europe, a Germany divided for administrative purposes at the Potsdam Conference of July-August 1945 has, for all practical purposes, been partitioned, as neither the United States and its client allies nor Russia have been able to find a basis for reuniting the Germans. To forestall the final collapse of western Europe, the United States under-*

wrote its territorial integrity, subsidized its economic recovery, fostered its union, while protecting it with the umbrella of American power. The ideological challenge of Communism persuaded the United States to develop a policy of "containment" designed to halt its expansion. Wherever Communism raised its head, American power moved to close its path.

In Asia, when war ended, China seemed firmly under the control of Chiang Kai-shek, but that control soon proved illusory. The long, often overlooked struggle between Chiang and his Chinese Communist adversaries, now that Japan's efforts to conquer China were ended, burst into view. Despite massive military aid, by December 1949, the nationalist government of Chiang had retreated to Formosa, surrendering control of the Chinese land mass to their Communist foes. State Department white papers traced Chiang's fall to corruption within his government, while at home, Congress aired charges that subversive elements in the State Department had aided the Communists to attain their victory. The Truman administration responded to the ominous extension of Communist power by extending "containment" to Asia.

The containment policy was put to the test in Berlin when the Russians blockaded the city between June 1948 and May 1949 but Allied air power provided the western zone with needed supplies. Unable to prevail, the Russians pulled back. Again on June 25, 1950, when armed elements of the North Korean Communist regime invaded South Korea, President Truman ordered the commitment of American forces under the United Nations to repulse the aggression. Near victory eluded the Americans when a massive Chinese intervention produced a stalemate. When the Korean armistice was finally signed on July 27, 1953, some 54,246 Americans had died in the struggle. But the division of Korea was restored to about what it was when the invasion opened. The willingness to accept a draw instead of victory indicated that Americans were generally prepared to accept a confined Communist power as a permanent world resident.

As American military power maintained its precarious dominance, the vast industrial complex that had lain dormant during the long years of the Great Depression and come alive only to provide the instruments of victory in World War II faced the task of proving it could provide a society of plenty. American technology had an enormous advantage: alone of the great world powers, the United States had emerged unscathed, its physical plant intact; its towns, cities and farmlands unscarred by the visitations of war. Also for a brief moment the United States alone possessed mastery of the atom. With these advantages, the country set to work building a new prosperity for itself while providing war-ravaged economies with the means to rehabilitate their plants. The sheer volume of American productivity revealed to the world's gaze the maturation of America as a world power.

But as those who in previous centuries have wielded power have learned, the possession of power carries with it the complementary obligation to use it wisely. Lord Acton, the British historian, once warned that power corrupts and that absolute power corrupts absolutely. America, as the most powerful nation in history, if Acton were to prove correct, was in mortal danger of losing, as Walt Whitman once warned, its soul. There existed a check on such a happening in the American preoccupation with defining the national purpose, of making more perfect their still-imperfect society and of assuring the world and themselves that where others have failed they will succeed. Elsewhere a man might be known by his works, but in a still-predominantly Protestant America, as John Calvin had long ago preached: "Works without faith is no works." Americans, living on the verge of a near material paradise, protected by the power to destroy possible enemies, even the world, absolutely, have struggled since the war to define their identity and purpose, even as the obligations of their power send them into the far reaches of the earth, on missions which are only vaguely understood. We also reach out with the Russians to conquer space, race to set foot on the moon first, but without anyone quite knowing why.

The pace of change has made some Americans fearful that perhaps we move too fast into tomorrow losing along the way the older virtues. It has made us susceptible to accepting charges of treason or at least failure in high places. As the unnatural power balance left in the wake of World War II began to rectify itself, and as the Russians joined us in the thermonuclear club, the change was equated by some Americans as treason. It was a sentiment that Senator Joseph McCarthy of Wisconsin fed upon, but fortunately the extremity of his charges proved his undoing. The strength of American institutions prevailed. But a bitter memory lingered. Even as Americans turned in 1952 to the comforting figure of Eisenhower as their President, the Supreme Court prepared to hear and find on Brown v. Topeka. Its decision in 1954 sent crashing into ruin the long-held doctrine of separate but equal facilities as adequate to secure the rights of black Americans. Within a nation that subscribes to the proposition that "all men are created equal," it has long been painfully obvious that if a man's skin is black, the proposition is non-applicable. Since 1954, the black American has made his exploitation grimly apparent to his long-blind white fellow American with street demonstrations, sit-ins, riots and the thousand other devices of protest. What white America would not give freely, black America has extracted as the price of social peace. Perhaps only a vigorous assertion of black manhood could dissuade whites of their long-held belief of black contentment or shake whites from their placid ignorance of their black countrymen. No matter, the old order is changing and both whites and blacks know it.

As one bulwark after another falls, as one taboo after another fades, a new America dimly casts its shadow. It received inspired description in the words of a young President who saw "a new frontier" and for one thousand and thirty-six days drew the rules for both American and world politics. Then in a single moment in Dallas, two bullets ended his crisp and articulate intelligence. A stunned nation paid homage to its murdered first Roman Catholic President. The life of the Republic briefly paused and then throbbed on.

In the life of men, death is an ending; in the life of nations, death is a beginning. By an assassin's decree, the voters of 1960 had chosen two Presidents, one who, in a singular act of political abnegation, had surrendered his masterdom of Congress to accept the largely empty honor of the Vice-Presidency. The accession to the Presidency of Lyndon B. Johnson marked *the first time in American history that the American equivalent of Prime Minister had become Chief Executive. Within days of his inaugural, a regular flood of legislation covering civil rights, social welfare and national planning poured forth from Congress, ending the long stalemate in constructive legislation that had begun in 1938. Even as the nation turned to the unfinished business of building a more perfect union, the long agonizing Vietnam war cast its shadow upon the life of another generation of American men. Thus in 1966 America again lived in a world of mixed hope and fear.*

For the historian the point in time had been reached where life edges into and overtakes history. The why of the ongoing American experiment is still explored in search of meaningful answers. In the selection that follows, Henry Steele Commager (1902-   ), Professor of History at Amherst College, poses some of the many questions that still agitate American life. It is in search of answers to such questions that the living generation will make history. And the historian unborn will have prepared for him his legacy, the job of unraveling what made our time tick.

THE AMERICAN MIND

by Henry Steele Commager

Changes in the habits, practices, and morals of the twentieth-century American were, on the whole, consistent with those in the realm of ideas. With the growing emphasis on conformity, eccentricity was no longer so amiably indulged; the passion for creating "characters" which the more popular novelists showed was itself evidence of a felt need. It would be misleading to insist that Americans were less self-reliant than formerly, but certainly society as a whole was far more interdependent, and with interdependence went some impatience with independence. The nineteenth-century farmer and craftsman had not needed to rationalize his enterprise into a philosophy, but the practical disappearance of any enterprise really private brought, as so often, a nostalgic rationalization. Americans had always been gregarious, and even with the inevitable associations of urban life and the growth of self-confidence, the habit did not abate. If lodges and clubs attracted them less, business and professional associations claimed them more insistently, and they could scarcely read a book or listen to music or take a walk except in groups. Life became increasingly regimented. Regimentation was not, as political critics would have it, a product of government regulation or of a Communist conspiracy but of a technological economy, and it was, perhaps, inevitable. The necessity of living in the same kind of houses, doing the same kind of work, using the same machinery, reading the same newspapers, was paralleled by the desire to use the same soap, eat the same breakfast food, laugh at the same radio jokes, admire the same movie stars, and digest the same magazine articles as did everybody else.

Technology and abundance freed men and women from much of the hard physical work that had absorbed the energies of their grandparents. Americans still worked harder than most other peoples, but the work week declined from sixty to forty hours, vacations stretched from one week to a month or more, children were kept out of the labor market until they were eighteen or twenty years old, insurance companies implored men to retire at fifty, and small families, small flats, and labor-saving machinery relieved women from most of the drudgery of housework. For the first time in history leisure became a major problem. Americans, who had all but discovered time, now had so much of it on their hands that they scarcely knew what to do with it, yet they lived energetically rather than leisurely, getting and spending and laying waste their powers. Veblen had discovered in conspicuous leisure the hallmark of class, but where leisure was commonplace it ceased to be conspicuous, and for the professional and the intellectual man it became almost fashionable to work long hours. For the others, the automobile, the movies, and the radio did much to ameliorate the situation; unnecessary travel became necessary to the economy; books rescued some from boredom, and magazines designed to be looked at rather than read multiplied by the hundred. With the passing of the necessity for hard work, the old Puritan idea that work was a virtue and idleness a vice went glimmering, while prosperity, the easy speculative profits of the twenties and the forties, government responsibility for security, high income and inheritance taxes, the vicissitudes of economy and fluctuations in the value of money, all combined to make other Puritan virtues like frugality and thrift seem outmoded. Yet generalization here, as the Lynds discovered in their study of *Middletown*, is dangerous. If work ceased to be a moral virtue it persisted as a habit, and businessmen who could well afford to retire clung tenaciously to their jobs, while rural and small-town Americans still subscribed to the "gospel of hard work." And though thrift was no longer cultivated for moral reasons, insurance and banking statistics showed that Americans continued to provide, as best they could, for the future. If there was a change here from the nineteenth to the twentieth century, it was in the future that was envisioned: where an earlier generation had saved in order to leave an estate, the new generation was inclined to save for more immediate and personal purposes —an automobile, vacations, education, or retirement.

Prosperity and machinery made possible a degree of self-indulgence unknown in a more exacting age, and it was the opinion of many foreign observers that not only the women and children but the men as well were pampered. Certainly there was no asceticism in American life and little self-denial. The second World War imposed but few restrictions and no austerity upon the American people, yet Americans did not, on the whole, react well to such restrictions as were required, and the rationing of such commodities as meat and gasoline was widely evaded. Americans were generous, but a test such as the admission of a few hundred thousand displaced persons—who might possibly compete in the labor market or demand houses or spread alien doctrines—found them inhospitable and grudging. Children took parental support for granted well into their twenties, and it was far more common for young couples to be supported by their parents or even for young men to be supported by their wives than it had been half a century earlier. Most Americans took for granted, too, comforts unknown to all but the rich in other countries. They overheated their houses, insisted upon a car and a radio, consumed incredible quantities of soft drinks, ice cream, candy, and cigarettes, and spent enough annually on liquor and cosmetics to have supported the whole population of less fortunate countries. Luxury and self-indulgence should, perhaps, have led to debility, and those who still subscribed to the Puritan virtues were constantly recalling the latter days of the Roman Empire, but no one familiar with the conduct of American soldiers in the second World War would argue that American youth was soft or effeminate or that America was suffering from a failure of nerve.

Twentieth-century America, even more than nineteenth-, seemed to be a woman's country. The supremacy of woman could be read in the statistics of property ownership, insurance, education, or literature, or in the advertisements of any popular magazine. Women ran the schools and the churches, they determined what would appear in the magazines and the movies and what would be heard over the radio. As many girls as boys attended college, and women made their way successfully into almost every profession. There were a hundred magazines designed especially for their entertainment or edification, and among them some with the largest circulation, while most metropolitan newspapers had a page for women and every radio station a series of programs directed exclusively to their supposed needs. As women spent most of the money, the overwhelming body of advertisements was addressed to them, and advertisers found it advisable to introduce the feminine motive even, or especially, where they hoped to attract men. Traditionally women had ruled the home, but only in America did they design it, build it, furnish it, direct its activities, and fix its standards. Most American children knew more of their mothers' than of their fathers' families, and it was the opinion of many observers of World War II that the silver cord bound American youth more firmly than the youth of any other land. It was appropriate enough that an American, Lester Ward, should have propounded the theory of the natural superiority of the female sex which he called gynecocracy, and American experience appeared to validate the theory.

There was a change, almost imperceptible, in the standards of sportsmanship. The professional spirit largely supplanted the amateur, college athletics were invaded by professionalism, football and basketball became big business. Professional sports themselves were marred by one scandal after another, while evasions of the amateur requirements by those who contended for amateur titles became so commonplace as to cease to be a scandal. As the commercial element entered sports, earning power became more important than the game itself, and the game became primarily a spectacle. Colleges and universities hired coaches who were paid as much as their presidents, spent millions on stadia, bought or seduced players, and retained them, as often as not, without any reference to academic qualifications.

President Eliot of Harvard had objected to intercollegiate football because he discovered that the attack was directed against the weakest point in the opposition line: the objection was creditable, and was not voiced by his successors. Where English spectators applauded the play, Americans cheered the team, and where English applause was spontaneous, American cheering was organized, and the "cheer leader" was unique to America. Standards of sportsmanship took on something of a class tinge, vindicating the interpretation which Veblen had advanced in his *Theory of the Leisure Class*. Polo, sailing, riding, skiing, and even hunting and fishing were associated with the upper classes and governed by formal rules, and those who indulged in them were expected to observe both a ritual and a ceremonial habit, while baseball, which became the national pastime, ceased to be a major college sport. Yet the habit of fair play was deeply ingrained, and standards of sportsmanship remained high. The phrase "good sport"—all but untranslatable into other languages—still held connotations flattering to the American character. The tendency to regard both politics and business as a game persisted, and if this suggested immaturity, it implied, too, a wholesome willingness to abide by the rules of the game, acquiesce in decisions, and accept defeat cheerfully.

More significant, perhaps, than modifications of formal ideas or informal habits, were changes in moral attitudes and practices. The problem of popular morals is infinitely complex, for nothing lends itself less readily to reliable statistical analysis, and in no other realm are judgments so likely to be empirical and subjective. It seems fair to say that while the moral standards of the nineteenth century persisted almost unchanged into the twentieth, moral practices changed sharply, and that though the standards persisted the institutions that had sustained them and the sanctions that had enforced them lost influence and authority. It was this conflict between tradition and practice, this collapse of older sanctions before the creation of new, that accounted in considerable part for the increase in nervous breakdowns and other psychological and moral disorders in the generation after the first World War.

The most striking change was in the realm of religion. Americans were still formally Christian, and increasing numbers of them saw fit to maintain a nominal connection with some church, but few admitted any categorical connection between religion, church, and morals. "It was largely because of the continued strength of religion that the code of morals in most American communities remained extremely rigid," Allan Nevins could write of mid-nineteenth-century America. The churches of that time, he pointed out,

> scrutinized behavior sharply. They counselled the drinker, rebuked the swearer, admonished all vice, and expelled any persistent wrongdoer. Employers who were church-members usually imposed their moral standards upon subordinates. Most Protestant bodies showed a strong hostility to habitual tippling, and several sternly reprobated the sale and use of liquor in any quantity. They all maintained an unbending code in matters of sex-relationship.

A century later the church, no longer able to satisfy the spiritual needs of the community, had largely forfeited its moral function and assumed, instead, a secular one—that of serving as a social organization. The public school, too, was less concerned with the training of character than with preparation for a job or for college, while private schools and denominational colleges that clung to the old responsibility were rarely sufficiently isolated to fulfill it. And an urbanized America was no longer exposed to the discipline imposed by Nature and by large families. The moral instructors of the new generation were the movies, the radio, and the press, and while they recognized their responsibility—negatively in the form of censorship and positively by precept, advice, and example—their values were meretricious and their standards shabby.

The waning influence of religion could be traced even in literature. The new generation was not familiar with the Bible, as its forebears had been. Religious books poured from the presses, but only theologians appeared to read them, while the layman was familiar neither with theology nor with religious history: when he sought spiritual consolation he was inclined to find it in such a book as Joshua Liebman's *Peace of Mind*. Lloyd Douglas' *The Robe* was in the tradition of *Ben Hur*, but no popular novelist addressed himself to the problem of religion in modern life as had Harold Frederic and Margaret Deland and Winston Churchill a half-century earlier. And in the two decades between the wars only four religious books—all of them dealing with the life and times of Christ—were listed among the "best sellers," while no less than forty books of mystery and detection joined what Frank Luther Mott called the Golden Multitude.

The most obvious and the least reliable index to morality was the record of the police courts. Statistically lawlessness was on the increase, but the frowning statistics which, after all, reflected new categories of legal offenses, more effective law enforcement, and improved statistical techniques as much as the state of public morals could be discounted. If the record did indicate that the twentieth-century American was no more law-abiding than the nineteenth-, it suggested that he was less given to violence, lynching, and rioting, or to sharpness and chicanery. Yet modern lawlessness, though less violent than that of the nineteenth century, had perhaps more serious consequences: thus, though assault and murder were less common in 1940 than in 1840, the automobile inflicted annually as many casualties as any war in which Americans had ever engaged. Lawlessness, here, seemed rather a matter of self-indulgence and recklessness than of criminality, but the consequences for its victims were no less painful. So, too, with other manifestations of impatience with the restraints of the law or of regulations. There were interesting philosophical reasons why Prohibition was vulnerable, but the reasons why millions of Americans flouted the Volstead Act were not philosophical but hedonistic. Logic and patriotism alike required conformity to the rationing system of World War II, but nonconformity was common and the black market somewhat blacker in America than in Britain. And while the standards of commercial and business honesty had undoubtedly improved over the years, the record of some ten thousand bank failures during the decade of the twenties and the panic years contrasted unhappily with the record of Canadian and British banks during the same period.

No less serious was the persistence of what might be called, paradoxically, official lawlessness. The example was set by federal and state legislators who violated their oaths of office by stubbornly refusing to honor the plain requirements of the Fourteenth and Fifteenth Amendments to the Constitution, who were responsible for the wave of red-baiting laws and for the alien deportations that disgraced the decade of the twenties, and who again and again grossly abused their powers of examination and investigation. There was an open conspiracy, local, state, and national, to reduce Negroes and Orientals to the status of second-class citizens, and violations of the constitutional rights of Negroes in the South were so much the normal thing that when a Negro in that section actually exercised some of the rights guaranteed him by his Constitution it was news. Police officers, particularly in the cities, were all too often guilty of brutality or of grave violations of the rights of prisoners, and the very term "third degree" achieved unpleasant notoriety as an Americanism.

Yet no one familiar with nineteenth-century American politics could doubt that political morality had improved. Not since Reconstruction, to be sure, had Americans witnessed corruption in high places as shocking as that which dishonored the Harding administration. Yet war presents at once the greatest temptations and the widest opportunities to private greed and chicanery, and neither the first nor, as far as the record is available, the second World War was attended by that venality which stained the pages of the history of the Civil War. That *Shame of the Cities* which Lincoln Steffens described had faded, and Lord Bryce's conclusion that municipal government was the one conspicuous failure of American democracy was not insisted upon by his twentieth-century successors. Nor could any fair historian of the American Senate, after the enactment of the Seventeenth Amendment, charge that body with treason, as David Graham Phillips had done at the beginning of the century. If a corrupt alliance between business and politics persisted, it was no longer ostentatious but concealed and apologetic. Civil service reform had gone steadily forward, the great majority of public offices were now removed from the patronage, and the spoils system was no longer the chief lubricant of party politics.

The most conspicuous and probably the most profound change in popular morals was in the realm of family and sex relationships. Marriage came to seem more tentative, virtue more relative, and parental control less authoritative than had been assumed even a generation earlier, and the Seventh Commandment, long the most rigorously enforced, came to be regarded almost as irreverently as the Third and the Fourth. Statistics illuminate but do not explain the change. They show a decline in the birth rate from more than thirty-five per thousand in 1890 to less than twenty in 1945 and a change in the size of the average family from over five to less than four; they reveal a sevenfold increase in the divorce rate for the country as a whole and, in the Lynds' *Middletown*, approximately one divorce for every two marriages; they confess a sobering upturn in juvenile delinquency, and especially in the number of juveniles guilty of sex offenses.

No single explanation accounts for the change in family relationships, for the declining size of the family, or the increase in divorces and in juvenile delinquency. A wider knowledge of contraceptives, the emancipation of women, late marriages, an aging population, and the shift from country to city, all contributed, but even combined they leave much unexplained. Birth control is, after all, an effect, not a primary cause; late marriages were accompanied by such improvements in medicine as enabled women to bear children later in life; and anyone familiar with the teeming population of city slums knew that the birth rate was not necessarily dependent upon a rural environment. It is equally difficult to account for the startling increase in divorce. There is no evidence of a comparable increase in cruelty or non-support or even marital unfaithfulness, the traditional grounds for divorce, and it is probable that the upswing in the divorce rate was to be explained rather by the greater ease in obtaining divorces, higher standards of marital happiness, and self-indulgence, rather than by any general deterioration of marriage relations.

Nor could the historian confidently draw moral conclusions from his study of vital statistics. Moralists might regard a shrinking birth rate as a shirking of responsibility, but it was by no means clear that society profited from a high birth rate, and a comparison of Denmark and India suggested that there was no necessary correlation between civilization and population. Even some moralists, outside the Catholic church, were ready to agree that divorce was often better than unhappy marriage. And clearly juvenile delinquency was to be explained rather by the impact of depression and of war than by any peculiar depravity in the youth of the new generation.

Sex was still regarded by a large segment of the population as Sin, and the very vocabulary of morality testified to its importance, for such words as virtue, purity, and even morality and immorality carried sexual connotations. Yet both the old taboos and the old integrities were dissolving. Puritanism gave way to hedonism, inhibitions to experiments, and repression to self-expression. Advertisers pandered shamelessly to the erotic instinct, the moving pictures appealed to it, and novelists exploited it, and all used a franker vocabulary than had been customary. The Kinsey report on sex habits made clear that by the mid-twentieth century neither chastity nor continence nor marital fidelity could be taken for granted, and no one familiar with the statistics of the divorce court or the Army Medical Corps or juvenile delinquency could doubt that looseness in sexual morality had serious social consequences.

At the same time neither the new attitude toward sex nor the new code of conduct were necessarily unwholesome. The double standard of morals, never as strong in America as on the European Continent, was relaxed in favor of the single; and, if the single standard meant that women were not expected to be more moral than men rather than that men were expected to be as moral as women, the new realism was preferable to the old hypocrisy. Those antisocial diseases which had so long and so idiotically been called social were now publicly discussed and effectively treated, and medical science held out hope that they might be eliminated in a generation. Morally, immodesty was no worse than false modesty; and censorship boards to the contrary notwithstanding, there was no evidence that the literary treatment of sex impaired the morals of even the most susceptible. Sex education was accepted as a duty of parents and made its way even into some of the more progressive schools and into popular magazines and books, and if much of the romance that had long surrounded sex was dissipated, so too was much of the mystery, and with it the fear and frustration and suffering.

It cannot be said that the second World War tested the American character as it did, in different ways, the British, the French, and the German, but it did dramatize that character and, as it were, recapitulate it. Certainly no evaluation of the American character could ignore the fact that the greatest crisis of modern history found American public opinion sensitive to the moral issues involved, that this war united Americans as had no previous war, that it was fought for what seemed unselfish ends, and that Americans generally supported a just peace and a postwar program of unparalleled generosity.

How profoundly five years of war affected American economy and society was clear even during those years; how they affected the American mind and character has yet to be determined. The American was sure of his own superiority and of his invulnerability; did Pearl Harbor and the Battle of the Atlantic give him pause? He had a high sense of fair play, even in war; did his experience with German and Japanese methods of warfare undermine this? He was optimistic about his world and his future; did contact with pessimism and frustration, and the disappointment of high hopes after the war, moderate this optimism? He was adolescent in some of his interests and many of his pleasures; did the grim experience of war mature him? He believed neither in evil nor in the Devil; did Buchenwald and Dachau corrupt him? He was an amateur, distrusting the expert and the specialist; did Manhattan Project convert him? He had been careless of authority and hostile to discipline; did military service persuade him to mend his ways? He had never acknowledged a military caste and rarely rewarded military service with social prestige; did the war make for the creation of a military elite? He had celebrated the virtues of individualism, especially in the economic realm; did the spectacle of what could be achieved by great impersonal organizations, military and economic and administrative, abate his individualism? He had been, on the whole, moral, generous, kindly, and romantic; did exposure to different standards of morality and to opportunities for self-indulgence impair his moral standards? He had known only his own country and was content with its character, its institutions, and its standards; did familiarity with the civilizations of Britain, France, and Italy disturb his satisfaction or suggest other standards and practices?

It is possible to answer these questions tentatively. On the whole the war would seem to have confirmed those traits which we have distinguished as peculiarly American rather than to have changed them. It confirmed Americans in their optimism, their self-confidence, and their sense of superiority, for it ended, after all, in the greatest of victories and one for which they could claim a major part of the credit. They had bet on material power, on machinery and science, on organization and the assembly line, on a citizen army and a democratic system of government—and they had won. They had been sure that America was the best and the happiest of nations, and what they had seen overseas had strengthened this conviction. They were opportunistic and found that their inspired opportunism somehow paid dividends, and few of them realized how much planning and farsightedness went into the conduct of the war. Their army was the most democratic of major armies and it had fought well. They were used to material comforts, and their government supplied them with such comforts as no other armies knew; they took the envy of less fortunate peoples and soldiers as a proper tribute and gave generously of their surplus. They were, most of them, honorable, brave, and idealistic; the war did not force them to abandon honor for treachery, soldiers fought as bravely at Bataan or Okinawa or Bastogne as their forefathers had at Bunker Hill or Gettysburg or the Argonne, and idealism remained not only an individual characteristic but an official policy.

To the extent that all this is true, the war merely deepened certain traits in the American character. Did it change any or introduce new departures? In some respects the American outlook and character may have been affected. Probably Americans overseas were broadened by their experience with other peoples and civilizations, and some assuredly learned that superiority in plumbing did not necessarily mean superiority in all the amenities of life or in moral qualities. Cultural isolationism dissolved, along with economic, political, and military, and the average American of 1950 probably knew more about European society, literature, and politics than had his father or his grandfather. Certainly Americans emerged from the war less self-centered and more conscious of the economic interdependence of all nations and of their responsibilities for the maintenance of sound international economy. The military came to occupy a larger place in the American scene than ever before and to exercise an unprecedented influence on the formulation of political policy, though General Eisenhower's refusal to enter the presidential race of 1948 undoubtedly checked a growing inclination to reward military success with political office. The war dramatized changes in moral standards and conduct. No previous American war had discovered such a breakdown of personal integrity, such looting and destructiveness, such sexual promiscuity. It at once exacerbated race relations and advanced racial equality: the total effect was to bring the whole issue of race out into the open, to expose the gap between the pretense of equality and the reality of inequality, and to force the government to take some action toward bridging that gap. Finally the achievements and responsibilities of the war seemed to have brought, along with a sense of power, bewilderment and confusion. Americans knew that theirs had become the most powerful nation on the globe, but they were, for the most part, embarrassed rather than exalted by their position and their power.

The decade of the twenties had been one of prosperity, materialism, and cynicism, and it was perhaps cynicism that made the strongest—though not the most permanent—impression on the American mind. Disillusionment, to be sure, was by no means unique to Americans: what was remarkable was that it should have embraced not only the Old World, whose failings had inspired it, but America too—the American past, American culture, American society and economy. The depression, as we have noted, made much of this disillusionment seem unreal or merely literary and made clear that both repudiation and flight were luxuries in which only those indifferent to the fate of the nation could indulge.

Even more emphatic was the impact of war and chaos in the thirties. If the depression tempered impatience with alleged imperfections, the rise of totalitarianism abroad encouraged gratification with undeniable blessings. By contrast with the barbarism that so speedily overwhelmed many ancient nations, American failings came to seem superficial, her sins almost innocent. Theodore Dreiser could write of *Tragic America* and Archibald MacLeish that "America was Promises," but Americans knew instinctively that it was Europe that was really tragic, and that—the depression notwithstanding—American promises had been as largely fulfilled as any others that had been held out to sanguine men.

Thus, economic convulsions at home and political, social, and moral convulsions abroad brought a reconsideration of the significance of America, a search for what was valid in the American past, sound in the American present, encouraging in the American future. In a world where familiar ideas such as democracy, liberty, equality, the dignity of man, and the rule of law, were callously repudiated, it was no longer possible to take them for granted, and there came, in America, a more scrupulous examination of their meaning and a more exacting test of their efficacy. As had happened in the days of transcendental reform just a century earlier, old institutions and faiths and practices were called before the bar of reason and required to justify themselves.

The search for the meaning of American civilization, given such urgency by the breakdown of European, was stimulated, too, by official policy. Franklin Roosevelt, as richly informed in the history and traditions of his own country as any president since Jefferson, was no less concerned to save the spiritual than the material heritage of the nation, and for the first time in American history artists and writers found themselves beneficiaries of large-scale governmental support along with bankers and industrialists, workingmen and farmers. The Federal Arts Project, to whose manifold activities an enlightened government appropriated altogether some fifty million dollars, was an expression of the principle that literature and art, music and drama, were as essential to the happiness and prosperity of the nation as any merely economic activities and that those who engaged in them were legitimate objects of the patronage of the state. Under its auspices painters depicted the American scene on thousands of canvases and re-created the

American past on the walls of countless post offices, courthouses, and libraries scattered over the land. Constance Rourke, biographer of those unmistakably American artists, Audubon and Charles Sheeler, and sympathetic student of many aspects of the American past, directed the great "Index of American Design," a collection which for the first time made known the richness of American folk art—furniture, woodcarving, textiles, embroideries, hardware, and decorations. Archives long moldering in obscurity were dusted off, catalogued, and indexed, and moribund local historical and genealogical societies took a new lease on life. The Federal Writers' Authority prepared that magnificent series of state and local guidebooks which eventually provided Americans with better Baedekers than any other country possessed. And the Library of Congress collection of American prints and photographs of old houses revealed what most Americans had forgotten, the existence of an authentically American tradition in architecture.

Inspired, then, by the depression and by the spectacle of catastrophe abroad and stimulated by governmental patronage, the rediscovery of America took varied and vigorous form. It was in part that what was imperiled seemed doubly dear, that—as Stephen Vincent Benét wrote—

> There are certain words,
> Our own and others', we're used to—words we've used,
> Heard, had to recite, forgotten, . . .
> Liberty, equality, fraternity.
> To none will we sell, refuse or deny, right or justice.
> We hold these truths to be self-evident.
>
> I am merely saying—what if these words pass?
> What if they pass and are gone and are no more,
> Eviscerated, blotted out of the world? . . .
>
> They were bought with belief and passion, at great cost.
> They were bought with the bitter and anonymous blood
> Of farmers, teachers, shoemakers and fools
> Who broke the old rule, and the pride of kings . . .
>
> It took a long time to buy these words.
> It took a long time to buy them, and much pain.

It was in part, too, that many things heretofore neglected or ignored took on new significance. A new regional literature, more authentic and less sentimental than that of the 1880's, celebrated every section of the country. Rachel Field and Dorothy Canfield were less concerned with recording the fate of New England spinsters or uncovering evidence of decadence than Alice Brown and Mary Wilkins Freeman had been and more concerned with suggesting that New England had not yet exhausted her vitality. T. S. Stribling and Marjorie Rawlings, Allan Tate and Eudora Welty—to say nothing of Caldwell and Faulkner—wrote less sentimentally about the New South than James Lane Allen and Thomas Nelson Page had written about the Old. Louis Bromfield explained Ohio, and Ruth Suckow, Iowa, and

Marie Sandoz, Nebraska, and Frank Dobie, Texas, while Vardis Fisher and John Steinbeck made clear that the West was no longer primitive—and not very romantic. No section or state, scarcely a city or county, was so poor as to lack its literary chronicler, and if most of this new outpouring of local color was negligible as literature, it was significant as sociology or psychology. Historical novels, which had declined in popularity since the days of Winston Churchill and Mary Johnston and S. Weir Mitchell, once more found an audience avid to learn history the easy way and conscious of their debt to the past; and competent craftsmen like Kenneth Roberts, Walter Edmonds, Esther Forbes, and Margaret Mitchell exploited this new interest. Those who found reading too difficult or too time-consuming were able to absorb their history through the films, and *Gone With the Wind*, in book and moving-picture form, gave millions of Americans a sense of the grandeur and misery of the Civil War.

Poetry, too, caught the infection; the *Spoon River Anthology* gave way to *The People, Yes* and *The Waste Land* to the *Western Star*. Carl Sandburg, who had immersed himself in Lincoln, prophesied that

> Across the bitter years and the howling winters
> The deathless dream will be the stronger
> The dream of equity will win.

Paul Engle told his countrymen that

> it is time
> To leave this wandering always on the earth
> And take from the hawk his flying wisdom, soar
> On the keen edge of the world's wind, veer and hover
> Until you take the very stars for your eyes.

And Stephen Vincent Benét, who had already written the epic of the Civil War, *John Brown's Body*, and who had "fallen in love with American names," turned at the end of his tragically short life to a poetic re-creation of the migration of those people who followed the Western Star, to celebrate, with almost religious exaltation,

> this dream
> This land unsatisfied by little ways,
> Open to every man who brought good will,
> This peaceless vision, groping for the stars,
> Not as a huge devouring machine
> Rolling and clanking with remorseless force
> Over submitted bodies and the dead
> But as live earth where anything could grow . . .

Historians, geographers, sociologists, philologists, and many other scholars marched with the novelists and the poets. History abandoned the debunking so popular in the twenties, and returned to the task of understanding the national character set it by Adams and Turner and Parrington. Scholars like Douglas Freeman, Samuel Eliot Morison, Allan Nevins, and Marquis James re-created the American past, critically, but sympathetically and even affectionately. Historians like Walter Webb, economists like Rupert Vance, sociologists like Howard Odum used the tools of their special technique to illuminate the nature of sectionalism and to integrate sections and the nation. There was an outpouring of books celebrating the American land: the *Rivers of America* series, which traced the advance of white civilization up a hundred river valleys, inaugurated by Constance Lindsay Skinner, herself novelist, historian, and poet; a regional series, a mountain series, a lakes series, and scores of books content with mere pictorial illustration. Even more important were projects to make available the rich material of the American past. Americans had long and gratefully acknowledged their paternity but had known in fact relatively little about the Father of their country: now the writings of Washington were properly edited and published by the government itself, and Douglas Freeman undertook to write a definitive biography. Jefferson had long been acknowledged a veritable arsenal of democratic thought, but not until the Princeton University Press and the *New York Times* combined to publish a definitive edition of his writings under the editorship of Julian Boyd was his full stature appreciated. And when, in 1947, the last restrictions were removed from access to the Lincoln papers, scholars prepared to rescue the Great Emancipator from the realm of legend and present him as he actually was through his own writings and those of his contemporaries.

As early as the twenties, Vernon Parrington had pointed the way to a livelier appreciation of what was American in American literature, and in the next two decades younger critics like Francis Matthiessen and Alfred Kazin repudiated alike the precious isolation of the humanists and the bitter estrangement of the Marxists and interpreted the American past as something to be understood rather than to be fought. Van Wyck Brooks, most distinguished of the rebellious critics of the early years of the century, no longer insisted upon the dichotomy between Edwards and Franklin, between high-brow and low-brow in American culture, but in a series of volumes of exquisite artistry recaptured the flavor of the past and found it both palatable and exciting. Emily Dickinson and Herman Melville and Thoreau had already been restored to their proper places in the gallery of great Americans, and the 1940's saw Henry James rescued from that expatriation which he had imposed upon himself and recaptured for American literature. H. L. Mencken's masterly study of the American language suggested that the English language had had a new birth of freedom in the New World, while the energetic collection of American folklore, folk songs and ballads, and of native American humor all testified to an interest in the American past not only discerning but confident.

Artists, too, turned away from the Beaux Arts tradition to rediscover an American one. That art should have its roots in native soil and should reflect the homely concerns of the common people had been a concept familiar enough in the past, but persistent colonialism, rich but artistically illiterate patronage, the prestige of Düsseldorf, Munich, Barbizon, and the Left Bank, had long obscured the principle in America. Yet from the days of Copley and Peale—to say nothing of Audubon and Wilson—there had been a vigorous native art; and in the early years of the new century, under the inspiration of Eakins and the leadership of such painters as Sloane, Bellows, Luks, Myers, and Pendergast, it attained distinction. It remained for the decades of the thirties and forties to rediscover the genre painting of Eastman and Mount and Bingham, to appreciate the drawings of Russell and Jackson and Remington, to celebrate the great tradition of American cartoons, and to produce a flourishing school of painters whose subject matter and technique were native and who enjoyed both prestige and patronage. Thomas Hart Benton was as authentically American as his distinguished ancestor; John Steuart Curry was equally at home in the plains of Kansas or the cotton fields of the deep South; Grant Wood bathed the rolling hills of Iowa in color and sentiment, and with Dale Nichols and Doris Lee revived something of the Currier and Ives technique; Charles Sheeler found beauty in the farmhouses and barns of the Pennsylvania Germans and the Shakers; Dorset, New Hope, and Taos developed schools dedicated to interpreting the varied beauties of Vermont, the Delaware Valley, and New Mexico. If architects discovered little that had not been implicit in the writings of Horatio Greenough in the mid-nineteenth century and explicit in the teaching of Louis Sullivan and Frank Lloyd Wright at the beginning of the twentieth century, it was interesting that the decades of the thirties and the forties witnessed the belated appreciation of these pioneers in the creation of an American tradition, the masterly studies of American architecture and technology by Lewis Mumford, and the restoration of colonial Williamsburg and of parts of old Salem and Deerfield.

"If there is one test of national genius universally accepted," wrote Ralph Waldo Emerson of England in 1847, "it is success." A test invoked by Emerson cannot be ignored nor a material one submitted by a Transcendentalist disparaged. Passionately American as he was, Emerson was constrained to admit that by this test mid-nineteenth-century England was the best of all countries, the one with the greatest store of national genius.

If that test were indeed valid there could be no doubt, a century later, which country in the world possessed the richest resources of national genius. That Americans had been largely successful in what they undertook was undeniable. They had—at least in large measure—formed a more perfect union, established justice, insured domestic tranquility, provided for the common defense, promoted the general welfare, and secured the blessings of liberty for themselves and, it was to be hoped, for their posterity. They had lifted the burdens from the shoulders of men, given to immigrants from the Old World a second chance, cherished the principles and promoted the practices of freedom, advanced social equality, promoted material well-being, furnished a climate favorable for the nourishment of talent, championed the cause of peace, undertaken and largely fulfilled their responsibilities in the community of nations.

It was, in every way, a spectacular achievement and one with few parallels in history. It was not wonderful, perhaps, that America should have achieved mere material success, for no other nation had been more bounteously endowed with natural resources or more fortunate in its inheritance of human. But there seemed no compelling reason why she should have achieved success in the realm of mind and spirit as well. A young nation, with tasks to perform chiefly material, without traditions of church or aristocracy, without learned or even leisure classes, isolated from the main currents of European thought, reverting on every frontier to primitive conditions, her original stock exposed to continuous dilution, her society fluid and her economy unsettled, she seemed condemned from the beginning to that cultural mediocrity of which so many visitors, from Tocqueville to Arnold, complained. That she should have produced a Carnegie, a Rockefeller, a Vanderbilt, a Ford, an Edison, an Eads, a Roebling, a Mahan, or an Eisenhower was natural enough. That she should have produced in half a century a Henry Adams, a William James, a Louis Sullivan, a Thomas Eakins, a John Dewey, an Edwin Arlington Robinson, an Oliver Wendell Holmes, a Vernon Louis Parrington, a Thorstein Veblen, a Willard Gibbs, was more surprising. That within a century and a half of the founding of the Republic she should have taken indisputable lead in science, medicine, law, education, and the social sciences and made contributions of lasting merit to art, architecture, literature, and philosophy was unexpected by all but those who knew best the deep roots of the American character and the fertile soil in which it flourished.

All this was cause for gratification but not for complacency, and the American of the mid-twentieth century was inclined to complacency. Along with spectacular triumphs, physical and intellectual, went frustrations and failures. Americans had failed to preserve and enhance the natural resources with which a benevolent Providence had endowed them. They had failed to realize fully the promise of freedom and equality held out first to immigrants and then to Negroes. They had failed properly to maintain that sanctity of law and inviolability of justice to whose maintenance they were pledged. They had failed to provide adequate education for all children able to profit from it or medical aid for all those who needed it or full security for the weak and the infirm and the perishing classes of society. Although in most respects their civilization was as high as any on the globe, they had failed as yet to create ideal conditions in which a spacious civilization might flourish.

Only a perfectionist would submit these failures as an indictment or hold that a people who had left undone some of those things which it should have done had forfeited its claim to virtue or to greatness. Judged by the standards of the Old World, the American failures were venial; it was something of a tribute to America that in judging her performance new standards were necessarily invoked. And both standards and judgment were, also of necessity, tentative. For it was clear that the American character, notwithstanding its relative maturity, was still in process of development, that the course which that development would take was still open, and that the future promised to be no less interesting than the past. For it was still true, a century and three quarters after Turgot's famous letter to Dr. Price, that this people was the hope of the human race; it was still true, a century after Longfellow had penned the lines, that

> Humanity with all its fears
> With all its hopes of future years
> Is hanging breathless on thy fate.

If laws of history were ever to be formulated, Henry Adams had predicted at the beginning of the nineties, they must of necessity be based in large measure on American experience. After the lapse of sixty years whose crowding wars and disasters gave some support to Adams' theory of the collapse of civilization itself, American experience was even more relevant to the formulation of those laws than Adams himself had realized. Both the peoples of the Old World and of the New acknowledged that America would direct, if it did not indeed control, the course of world history in the second half of the twentieth century, and outside Russia and her satellite countries few looked upon this prospect with misgivings. If a future directed by America was not wholly clear, neither was it a blank, and those who knew that nation best were satisfied that it meant intensely and meant good. For the America that would shape the unknown future was an America whose character had been formed in the known past, and if the lineaments of that character had not yet hardened into fixed patterns, they were at least recognizable and familiar. The future was precarious, but it was not an enigma. It presented, perhaps at best, a series of questions, but the very phrasing of those questions, their grammar and vocabulary and frame of reference, was dictated by the American past and the American character and confessed confidence in reasonable answers.

Out of an amalgam of inheritance, environment, and historical experience, Americans had fashioned a distinctive character; could they preserve and develop that character in a changed environment and under the impact of a new set of historical experiences? Adventure, experimentation, and mobility had marked their character; with the frontier gone, immigration dammed up, and resources running low, could they retain their enthusiasm for fresh experience and novel ways, their ingenuity and adventurousness? They were wonderfully inventive in the physical and technological realm; would they prove equally resourceful in the realms of social institutions and of morals? They had achieved the highest standard of living known to history; how would they live? Their society had changed from rural to urban; would they learn to master the city as their forefathers had mastered the country? Immigration had all but ceased; what would be the final product of the interracial melting pot? Fifteen million Negroes confronted one hundred and thirty million whites; would racial conflicts continue to frustrate democracy, or would they find a solution to the racial problem through ultimate amalgamation or through the establishment of such economic and social security as would permit mutual tolerance?

They had created an economy of abundance; could they fashion a political mechanism to assure the equitable distribution of that abundance? They had become the richest people on the globe; would they use their wealth to prosper society or to display power? They were democratic in law; would they be democratic in fact? They were equalitarian by conviction; would they be equalitarian in conduct? They had developed technology to its highest point; would they learn to make technology their servant rather than their master? They were using up their natural resources more rapidly than they were replacing them; would science reverse the process, or would they be forced to a lower standard of living or to economic imperialism? Agreement upon fundamentals had enabled them to maintain a two-party system; would the clashing ideologies of a new age destroy that agreement and fragmentize their politics? They had solved the ancient problem of liberty and order; would they succeed in maintaining order in a war-troubled world without such suppression of liberty as would change the character of their state? They had become increasingly like the peoples of the Old World; could they avoid the clash of doctrine and opinion, the conflict of church and state, of class and party, of race and section, that had for so long rent Europe with dissension and war?

They had inherited a system of law fashioned for the needs of a small, rural society and designed to safeguard the rights of property rather than of persons; could they adapt that law to an urbanized and democratic society which placed human above property rights? Their society had been almost wholly classless; would inequalities of wealth create and divide classes? Their culture had been derivative; could they create a culture of their own? They had the largest educational system in the world; for what would it educate? They enjoyed more leisure than any other western people; how would they use it? They had all but banished God from their affairs; who or what would they put in His place? They had never faced the problem of evil; would the palpable evil of the modern world persuade them to reconsider their idealism? They had begun to question the validity of traditional moral codes; could they formulate new ones as effective as those they were preparing to abandon?

They had relaxed their moral standards and habits; would they preserve themselves from corruption and decadence? They were idealistic; could they make their ideals work? They were pragmatic; could they preserve their pragmatism from vulgarization? They were generous; would their generosity extend to the moral sphere? They were good natured; would their good nature grow to magnanimity? They were intelligent; would their intelligence solve the problems of the future? They cherished a faith in reason but yielded to a philosophy of determinism; would they succeed in reconciling rationalism and determinism as their fathers had reconciled science and religion?

They had made the atomic bomb; would they use it for purposes of civilization or of destruction? They had achieved such power as no other modern nation had ever known; would that passion for peace which Henry Adams had named the chief trait in their character triumph over the temptation to establish a Pax Americana by force? They had fulfilled the responsibilities imposed upon them by the past; would they meet the challenge of the future?

The whole world had an interest in the answers which history would make to these questions.

Index

Note: The names of historians who have contributed articles to this work are listed in **BOLDFACE TYPE.**